The Ancient World

HARPER'S HISTORICAL SERIES

Under the Editorship of Guy Stanton Fora

The Ancient World

Volume One

Empires and City-States of the Ancient Orient
and Greece Before 334 B.C.

by
JOSEPH WARD SWAIN

PROFESSOR OF HISTORY UNIVERSITY OF ILLINOIS

HARPER & ROW PUBLISHERS
NEW YORK and EVANSTON

To My Kinsman

JAMES ARNOLD BLAISDELL

Professor of Biblical Literature, Beloit College, 1903–1910
President of Claremont Colleges, 1910–1936

My First and Best Teacher of Ancient History

Contents

Editor's Foreword   xiii

Preface   xvii

Introduction: **The Dawn of History**

     I.   The Coming of Man   3

     II.   The Neolithic Revolution   25

Part One: **The Ancient Orient**

     III.   Mesopotamian Cities   59

     IV.   Early Egyptian Dynasties   96

     V.   The First Great Empires   130

     VI.   Assyrians and Persians   165

     VII.   The Hebrews   202

Part Two: **The Greek City-States**

     VIII.   Homeric Greece   247

     IX.   Social and Political Revolutions in Greece   281

     X.   The Greek Renaissance   320

     XI.   The Age of the Persian Wars   357

     XII.   The Athenian Empire   391

     XIII.   Periclean Athens   429

     XIV.   Fourth Century Greece   475

     XV.   Panhellenism and Philip of Macedon   514

Epilogue

The Legacy of Greece   547

Bibliography   553

Index   569

Maps

A Few Neolithic Sites in the Near East   30

Mesopotamian Cities   66

Egypt and Her Neighbors   101

Egyptian and Hittite Empires   136

Assyrian Empire   173

Persian Empire   189

Palestine and Her Neighbors   204

Minoan and Mycenaean Greece   252

Greek Colonies in the East   284

The West in the Sixth Century   291

Greece in the Sixth Century   302

Attica   306

The Persian Wars   377

The Athenian Empire, 450 B.C.   409

The Peloponnesian War   417

Empire of Dionysius I of Syracuse   525

Plates

		Facing page
1	Paleolithic Art: Bison, Sorcerer, Willendorf Venus	20
2	Tell Judaidah	42
3	Model of a Ziggurat, Babylonian Writing	74
4	Hammurabi's Code, Babylonian Cylinder Seal	75
5	Khafre, The Sheik el Beled	102
6	The Pyramids at Gizeh	103
7	Scenes from the Tomb of Ti	126
8	Egyptian Statuettes	127
9	Kings and Queens of the Eighteenth Dynasty	154
10	Amenhotep, Akhnaton and Nofretete	155
11	House at Amarna	160
12	Rameses III, Hunting	161
13	Assyrian Winged Bull, Lion	182
14	Babylon Under Nebuchadrezzar	183
15	The Apadana Stairway	194
16	Triumphal Monument of Darius the Great	195
17	Cnossus: Stairway, Throne Room	254
18	Cnossus: Ladies of the Court, Athletic Scenes	255
19	Lion Gate at Mycenae	264
20	Frescos from Tiryns	265
21	Demeter and Persephone with Triptolemus	332
22	Boy Playing Lyre, Wrestlers	333
23	Styles of Greek Vase Painting	348

Plates

24	Archaic Greek Statues (Sixth Century)	349
25	Pericles	402
26	Parthenon, Erechtheum	440
27	Wounded Niobid, Discobolus	441
28	Theater at Epidaurus	444
29	Sophocles, Euripides	445
30	Herodotus, Thucydides	462
31	Socrates, Plato, Aristotle	508
32	Demosthenes	536

Editor's Foreword

THE EDITOR OF A HISTORICAL SERIES AS WELL AND FAVORABLY known as the one in which this volume takes its place always has one uncertainty. The uncertainty is not about the merits of the volume or the competence of the author. The choice of the latter and the approval of the manuscript eliminate that from his mind. The uncertainty comes when he asks himself: Who reads an editor's foreword? To whom should it be addressed? To the teacher who will find the text an aid but not a substitute for scholarship and good teaching? Or to the student for whom it is also an aid but not a substitute for studentship and wider reading and his own thinking about man's rough road from cave to cathedral?

I choose to write, as has the author, for the student, though my chances of being read are less than his. I do it because I envy the student who will review in this volume the pageant of history tracing man through times measured by geologic ages down through periods reckoned by the rise and fall of the empires he built. The ancient history I studied as an undergraduate was a mere fraction of this vast evolution, with the very idea of evolution ignored. Almost my first realization of the civilizations in the Fertile Crescent, in the Aegean, and in the Egypt that lay behind Greece and Rome came by happy chance years later when, as a graduate student in the University of Berlin, I made the acquaintance of a striking-looking young American scholar who had been asked to help German scholars decipher and edit the inscriptions found in the valley of the Nile. Once a pharmacist in Rockford, Illinois, he had deserted drugs to become a world authority on a civilization whose mind as well as its material achievements he lived to record in vivid English. On page 128 you will find a sketch of him, and I hope you will supplement it by reading his biography by his son.

The point that impressed me about the manuscript of the present volume was that it uses, as has no other text, all the scholarship since Breasted's day to enrich and broaden the story of the civilizations to which the Greeks, and ultimately our own world, fell heir. The story of that heritage is not a closed book. Archaeologists have still more excavations to make. Even manuscripts may turn up unexpectedly. Just a few weeks ago I heard one of the four greatest authorities on the history of the ancient Near East affirm without reservation the authenticity of a manuscript of the book of Isaiah discovered by two Bedouin goatherds in 1947 in a cave in the wild hills south of Jericho. It antedates by a thousand years any similar Hebrew text. Perhaps this volume may make some user a life-long student of worlds as yet but half revealed. What is revealed may at points challenge old half-truths and complacencies. But that should not trouble the thoughtful, for a college education that disturbs no one is not an education worth the four most precious years in any student's life.

For most of us the stream of history becomes navigable with Greece and Rome. If we no longer read their languages, the language we speak, the books we read, the buildings we erect, the art, philosophy, and law we emulate are voices that speak insistingly to even the most present-minded. The revolution that in the past century has brought the city to dominance in our own life follows a pattern the student can trace in their history. The physical divisions that complicated the efforts of ancient Greece to federate or unite are still factors in the Greece of our day. The Italy of the Renaissance with its city rivalries and great families with their retainers would be easy for Cicero to understand, and the shades of Caesar have been invoked in our day to bolster a sawdust imitation. The political institutions and thought of Greece and Rome were familiar to the scholars in the group who hammered out our constitution. The writings of the thinkers, poets, orators, dramatists, and historians of Greece and Rome were the backbone of higher education from the Renaissance well into the nineteenth century. Some part of their values is recovered for this student generation when in this volume the author summarizes their major contributions. Do not let the narrative of deeds done through the ages divert you from trying to rethink the best they thought.

Finally, as a fellow student with you in these days of recurrent crises and anxieties, I should want to know whether this long perspective of history increases or diminishes one's faith that men may rise on stepping stones of their dead selves to higher things. You will have seen civilizations rise and fall and even be forgotten. What faith died with them, what challenge of their day did they fail to meet? What have we for a foundation that they did not have? What price must we pay to retain it? Can security be bought only by forfeiting individual liberty? Perhaps we should not press history too hard for answers to the problems we must solve in our own day and our own way. At least her hand when we take it is cool and reassuring. That much faith I have in history and in the youth who study it and derive from it breadth and depth for the decisions they must make as world citizens.

GUY STANTON FORD

Preface

More than thirty years ago, when I was first embarking upon the serious study of ancient history, I was somewhat annoyed by the enthusiastic remark of a polite lady. I had just been presented to her as a graduate student in the university, and she had inquired what I was studying. "History," I replied. Her face lit up as she exclaimed, "History! How fascinating! History certainly is being made just now!"—this was in 1916, during the Battle of Verdun—and she went on to ask what field of history engaged my attention. When I said that I was studying ancient history the kind lady's face fell, but she managed to remark, "It must be very nice to know all about those old times." Then we had to find some other topic for conversation.

I was annoyed by this lady's remark for two reasons. In the first place, I resented her tacit assumption that the way to "make history" is to rush out and kill a few million people. I did not share this view, even then. Perhaps I already had a vague inkling of the fundamental truth, which years of further study have impressed upon me more deeply, that "history" is not "made" by the alleged heroes whose bloody deeds it records, sometimes to the exclusion of virtually everything else, but by the historians who study it and write it.

In the second place, I was dismayed by my new acquaintance's further assumption that it is impossible to "make" ancient history at all: you merely commit it to memory. As a matter of fact, history is constantly being made and remade by the historians, and since the moment of this historic conversation (historic at least to me) they have been making ancient history very rapidly. In some fields of history a good survey written half a century ago would today require rather slight revision. Such a book on Greece and Rome, however, would need countless alterations, and one on the ancient Orient would now be of little value. In no other field has so much history been made in so short a time. The present volumes attempt to sketch this new history of the Ancient World in language that can be understood by the beginning student and other nonspecialists.

This new history of the Ancient World is due in large part, of course, to the discoveries of the archeologists, papyrologists, epigraphers, and philologists that have come in such numbers during the present century. The older writers were often far from the truth in such fundamental matters as chronology, and they were completely ignorant of many things which we now consider essential to an understanding of antiquity. But all this is only half the story. An equally important reason why our ancient history differs so widely from that of fifty years ago is the fact that today we regard the Ancient World from a different point of view and therefore we arrange its history differently.

In the old days ancient history was considered valuable chiefly as supplying background for the study of the Greek and Latin classics. It therefore was customary in American colleges to cover the field in two distinct but more or less parallel courses dealing respectively with Greece and Rome in the periods when their literature was especially flourishing. Today it no longer seems so desirable to divide the Ancient World into two parts according to the language spoken by the leading men of the period—or even into three parts by prefixing an introductory chapter or two on the ancient Orient. We now regard ancient history merely as that section of world history that began with the earliest civilizations of the Near East and ended with the great changes that accompanied the collapse of the Roman Empire.

The diversity within this unity is very great, however, and it is not always practicable, or even possible, to adhere strictly to chronological sequence in telling its history. The old threefold division into Orient, Greece, and Rome therefore crops up again in a new and different form. Oriental civilization appeared first, to be sure, but it did not die with the Persians, or even with Alexander the Great. In 600 A.D. it was a more powerful force in the world than it had been in 400 B.C., yet the older historians said little or nothing of its important developments during that long period. I have endeavored to tell something of this story. Likewise Greece did not die with Alexander or with the Roman conquest of the empires set up by his immediate successors. On the contrary, Greek influence in the Ancient World was growing steadily during the opening centuries of the Christian Era, and the Graeco-Oriental empire of Byzantium remained powerful for a full thousand years after the collapse of the Roman Empire in the West. Moreover, we no longer see Rome through the eyes of chauvinistic Roman historians or disgruntled Greeks. The Romans did not go out and subjugate the world with violence and brutality out of sheer lust for conquest. They were dragged into world politics much against their will, but they eventually united the world and maintained the longest period of peace that the West has ever known. In doing so they succeeded where many before them had failed, and their success was due in large measure to the great degree of liberty they left to conquered peoples and to the fact that they were much less brutal than their predecessors had been.

It is when studied from this point of view that the Ancient World has the most to teach us, both as a guide and as a warning. Nevertheless its achievements in literature and art, in philosophy and religion, still rank among the most brilliant in the world. All these things deserve our careful attention. The first volume of the present work therefore discussses the beginnings of civilization and the civilizations of the city-states and empires of the ancient Orient and Greece. The second volume, beginning with the campaigns of Alexander the Great, centers around the world's long struggle for political and cultural unity, its temporary success, and its ultimate failure.

The idea that historians "make history" by writing histories is not confined to the Preface of this book. To understand a nation it is necessary to know not only its true history but also the history which its people believed. I therefore devote more space than is usual to the historical conceptions of the various peoples whom I discuss, and to their historians. The great historians living in antiquity are treated at length, and an attempt is made to show the relation of their work to the activities of their contemporaries. And since the modern epic of ancient history is the creation of scholars, I direct attention to a few of the great historians of the past two centuries who have shared conspicuously in its creation. At the end of several chapters a Note discusses one or more writers who have contributed in distinguished fashion to our knowledge of the matters dealt with in that chapter. Of course only a few historians out of many could be mentioned, and, as it seemed desirable to mention men of as many different sorts as possible, some scholars were necessarily left out whose contributions to our view of ancient history may have surpassed those of others included in the list. It is hoped that even these brief notices may help the reader to understand more clearly the nature and character of all historical writing.

The bibliography at the end of each volume gives only the more important recent books in each field. The works here listed can be read by persons with no technical training, and usually they give references to more specialized monographs. After some hesitation I have decided to include the more important books in French and German. Several genealogical tables are given, especially in the second volume, for at Rome the connections of the great senatorial families were so important that Roman history of the Republican period cannot be understood without them: in general these tables are based on those of Münzer in the Pauly-Wissowa *Real-encyclo-pädie*. The maps have been drawn especially for this book, and it is hoped that they, like the illustrations, will simplify the text. Thanks are due to the various museums whose treasures are here pictured, but especially to the staffs of the Oriental Institute Museum in Chicago, and the Museum of Fine Arts in Boston for aid in finding photographs. Biblical quotations are from Smith & Goodspeed, *The Complete Bible: An American Translation,* by permission of the University of Chicago Press.

JOSEPH WARD SWAIN

March, 1950

Introduction: The Dawn of History

I The Coming of Man

Historians formerly concerned themselves solely with that relatively recent past which was known to them from written records. Histories of classic Greece and Rome might begin with summaries of oriental or Greek mythology about the creation of the world and early man, but only in the nineteenth century did it become possible to prefix brief accounts of what was being accomplished in Egypt and Mesopotamia from five to three thousand years ago. Today even these advanced civilizations of the ancient Orient no longer provide adequate foundations for a history of the classic world. Before them stretch long ages about which much is known to scholars, and the modern historian of antiquity must base his studies upon a knowledge of this more ancient past. If "historic times," which began with the invention of writing, cover the last five thousand years of human history, the "prehistoric times" that preceded them cover at least half a million more.

Since historic and prehistoric times gradually shade off into one another, and since the men of early historic times owed much to their prehistoric ancestors, the later period can be described only after a preliminary survey of the earlier. It is equally difficult to write of prehistoric man without going back to the very origins of humanity. No clear line separates early man from his animal forebears, and we are thus gradually drawn back through the whole history of life upon our planet. And finally, this study of living things presupposes a knowledge of the history of the earth upon which they lived. We then discover the important truth that the history of mankind is but a part of universal history—the history of the earth

3

and what has happened upon it. If the historian, in the narrower sense of the term, is one who studies "historic" times only, his work must be supplemented by the archeologist who attempts to reconstruct prehistoric civilizations from their material debris, by the anthropologist who studies human races in their physical aspects, by the paleontologist who seeks to learn the history of life upon the planet from its fossil remains, by the geologist who studies earth history from the rocks, and even by the physicist and astronomer who investigate the origins of the planet itself. A century of collaboration by these scholars and scientists has now produced the outlines of a story that is marvelous and majestic beyond all the dreams of poets and theologians in previous ages. Man occupies only a line or two in this mighty epic, but in a sense the whole long story is merely the story of human origins.

Earth History

Scientists now assign to the earth an existence covering at least four billion years—perhaps more. The staggering immensity of this period impresses upon us the brevity of human history when compared to the whole span of earth history. Let us use a simple comparison and assume that these four billion years of the earth's history were compressed into one year's time. One hundred and twenty-five years would then go by as one second. According to this timetable, mankind first appeared on earth something over an hour ago; the pyramids of Egypt were built forty seconds ago; the Trojan War was fought less than half a minute ago; Caesar was murdered some sixteen seconds ago; Columbus discovered America less than four seconds ago; and by this same schedule the American Republic has existed less than a second and a half in the long year of earth history!

The earth itself has gone through an elaborate history. Four billion years ago it already had a solid crust, parts of which were covered with large bodies of water, and it was surrounded by an atmosphere. Its temperature was moderate. Already forces were at work which have continued to operate upon it from that day to this. Repeatedly in the ages that followed, mountain chains and lofty plateaus have been forced up by pressure from within and leveled out once more by erosion. Rivers carried with them vast quantities of silt washed from the rocks over which they flowed. This silt they deposited in the seas where it slowly built up new sedimentary rocks. Mountain ranges were thus worn down in the course of time, plateaus were cut up into hills, and whole emergences were reduced to low level plains. New mountains were then thrown up, only to be eroded once more, and the whole cycle was repeated again and again. The oldest mountain ranges that now wrinkle the face of the earth are the Urals and the Appalachians. Two hundred million years ago the Appalachians rose to heights of twenty thousand feet or more. Gradually they were worn down to plateaus. Later they were elevated another two thousand feet before erosion carved out the mountains which now rarely rise more than five thousand feet above sea level. All this took place during the last 10 per cent of geologic time. Such were the forces working upon the rocks and such the time during which they operated.

In the course of geologic history the earth's climate has fluctuated greatly. Coal deposits at Spitzbergen (80° North latitude) and in Antarctica within three hundred miles of the South Pole, and coral reefs off Greenland well within the Arctic Circle, show that these areas once enjoyed subtropical climate. On the other hand, glaciation—peculiar marks left by glaciers upon rocks—shows that the temperate zones have been covered repeatedly with thick sheets of ice. In general, however, the earth's climate has been somewhat warmer and more evenly distributed in the past than it is in the temperate zones today. It has been shown, moreover, that the cold periods came during or soon after the periods of great mountain eruption. Climate thus evolves in cycles synchronizing with those through which the surface of the earth has passed.

These cycles enable geologists to divide the history of the earth into five great Eras, each of which lasted many millions of years and was terminated by a great upheaval. Eras in turn are subdivided into shorter cycles known as Periods, which began and ended with lesser risings of the land and fallings of the temperature. Our concern here is with the last three Periods only—the Pliocene, which began about seven million years ago and lasted for over six million years; the Pleistocene or Glacial, which lasted more than half a million years and ended about twenty thousand years ago; and the Recent, which fills in the last twenty millenniums. During the Pliocene period the Cascade and Himalaya mountain ranges were thrown up; the first traces of men appear during the Pleistocene; but only in the Recent period have there been true civilizations.

The Glacial Period

During much of the Pleistocene period the American continent north of the Ohio and Missouri rivers was covered with ice sheets descending from three points in Canada. In Europe most of the British Isles, Holland, northern Germany, much of Poland, the Baltic states, and Russia north and west of Moscow were similarly covered with ice expanding southward from Scandinavia. Simultaneously, lesser glaciers descended from the Alps, the Caucasus, and the Himalaya mountains, and still other glaciers appeared in the Southern Hemisphere. These glaciers were solid masses of ice, sometimes a mile or more in thickness, comparable to those now found in Greenland and Antarctica. At their greatest extent they covered about eight million square miles, or nearly one seventh of the present land surface of the earth.

These ice sheets advanced and receded repeatedly during the Pleistocene period. There were four great periods of glacial advance, each going through two or more phases of secondary advance and retreat. They were separated by three interglacial pauses, each of which lasted many tens of thousands of years. In the opinion of many authorities, we may today be living in what is merely another interglacial pause. The fourth and most recent glacial advance began over one hundred thousand years ago, and the ice began to recede about twenty thousand years ago. The retreat was irregular, broken by several temporary advances, but about 5000 B.C. the European glacial front was established approximately at the point in northern Sweden where it has since remained.

During these glacial periods the climate was, of course, arctic in the vicinity of the ice sheets, but in France, Spain, and Italy it was merely rainy and cool in summer and very cold in winter. During the interglacial pauses, on the other hand, the climate was usually somewhat warmer than it is in the same localities today, and Europe was covered with forests which died down again when cool and arid weather heralded a new glacial advance.

Attempts have sometimes been made to learn more definitely the recent evolution of the earth's climate. There undoubtedly have been variations at different times, but efforts to trace their course do not inspire high confidence. The change of a few degrees in mean annual temperature and humidity would certainly exercise a marked influence upon human efficiency and conduct, and reliable tables showing the changes in the climate of different localities since the passing of the glaciers, if only they could be drawn up, would undoubtedly illuminate many a dark page in human history.

Our Early Ancestors

Men are mammals belonging to the order known as Primates. The lowest extant members of this order are the tarsiers, small nocturnal animals that live in the trees of the East Indies. Next in the scale are the lemurs of Madagascar, after which follow the monkeys and anthropoid (manlike) apes, and finally comes man. The earliest known species of the primatal order, a small insectivorous animal about the size of a cat, with a sharp muzzle and a long tail, lived in the Eocene period some sixty million years ago, but the earliest known fossil of an apelike creature, found in Egypt, dates from only about twenty million years ago. Later fossils of other genera of ape occur in Europe, and more frequently in India, where the remains of no less than eight genera and twenty-two species of ape, dating from Pliocene times, have been found in the Siwalik Hills.

These Primates all lived in the trees. At first they were so small that they could run along the branches like squirrels, but the apes were forced by their larger size and weight to swing by their arms from branch to branch. This mode of locomotion, technically known as "brachiation," played an important part in their evolution. First of all, it straightened them out and gave them an erect posture. Holding branches developed their thumbs, which enabled them to pick things up and hold them; and as the tree-dwelling Primates tended to squat on their hind legs when resting, their forelegs or arms were left free for handling things and "monkeying" with them. Life in the trees also gave added importance to the sense of sight, which was greatly sharpened in the higher Primates, while the sense of smell, upon which many mammals rely so much, tended to atrophy. Above all, however, brachiation developed the brain. It is easy enough to walk along level ground, but when an ape swings from branch to branch, often jumping fifteen or twenty feet through the air, his progress is irregular: he must calculate quickly the distance and strength of the bough he intends to grasp, for a mistake means injury or sudden death. Only the more intelligent apes survived. Thus in his back, his hand, his eyes, and above all in his brain, man to this day carries a precious heritage from his simian ancestors who lived in the trees.

The essential anatomical differences which distinguish men from apes spring largely from the fact that men, unlike apes, have descended from the trees and walk erect upon the ground. It is not possible to say definitely when or where or why this descent took place. A plausible theory (which is none the less only a theory) holds that it happened in northern India late in the Pliocene period. During this period the rising of the Himalaya Mountains gradually diverted the moisture-laden winds and substituted a temperate for a tropical climate. The dense forests north of the new mountains therefore died away and were succeeded first by parks and grasslands, later by deserts. Fossil remains show that these forests had been thickly inhabited by apes, among them many of the genus known as *Dryopithecus,* the most manlike of the Pliocene apes, which some authorities consider the ancestor of man as well as of modern chimpanzees and gorillas. The theory further suggests that the apes living south of the new mountains remained much as they had been structurally, but were forced to migrate southward. Some of them reached the East Indies and others Africa where, after undergoing certain structural changes, they became ancestors of the modern anthropoids. Those living north of the new mountains, on the other hand, saw their forests gradually disappear beneath them a million or so years ago, and were consequently forced to seek a new mode of life on the ground. They became the ancestors of man. Other investigators believe that the great change from ape to man occurred in east central Africa, where some very old human teeth and bones have recently been found. What caused the change in this case is not clear, but certainly it was not automatic. Either version allows humanity a history of a little over half a million years.

It is further surmised that when our early ancestors descended from the trees, they found their food by preying upon the herbivorous animals occupying the new grasslands that were then replacing the old forests. Various carnivores followed these cattle, likewise preying upon them and thus becoming rivals of the first "men." Though these primitive men were ill-equipped by nature with offensive and defensive weapons, they surpassed their rivals because their long arboreal existence had endowed them with such great advantages in hand and brain. Biologists now classify them as a separate family within the order of Primates, and they are called Hominidae to distinguish them from the modern apes (Simiidae). As their subsequent development followed different lines in different places, the hominids broke up into several genera, and these in turn into various species. All men now living upon earth belong to one species, *Homo sapiens,* but fossil skeletons prove that in the past there were other species of the genus *Homo,* and other genera of hominids. All members of the genus *Homo* may be called men, but anthropologists usually refer to members of other genera as hominids or, if they call them "men," they put the word in quotation marks.

The Ape Men

The earliest known hominid fossils are the top of a skull, part of the lower jaw, three teeth, and the left thighbone of a "man" belonging to the genus called *Pithecanthropus* (ape man) discovered in Java in 1891; parts of three skulls belonging to similar "men," one a child and one an adult of gigantic stature, were found in the same general locality between 1937 and 1940. Other important remains found near Peking, China, between 1927 and 1936, belonged to "men" of the genus now called *Sinanthropus*.

These bones are enough to prove that their owners were nearer to modern men than to apes and that they walked erect. Their craniums show that in size their brains were about halfway between those of the chimpanzee and those of modern man. Their brains were developed in the areas associated with speech, indicating that the possessors probably could talk a little, or at least communicate a few simple ideas by sounds. Fossils of other animals, found in the same strata as the Javanese hominid bones, show that the finds date from the middle Pleistocene period, probably from the second interglacial pause. Perhaps *Pithecanthropus* was somewhat earlier than *Sinanthropus*, but the two genera were roughly contemporary.

These early hominid fossils were found in Asia, presumably the original home of mankind, but they do not greatly antedate the earliest similar bones found in Europe. The lower jaw and teeth of an ancient "man" were found in a gravel pit near Heidelberg, Germany, in 1907. The jaw is large and powerful, but it has no chin and the teeth protrude like those of apes. Though the discoverer believed that this "Heidelberg man" lived during the first interglacial epoch, the best opinion now dates him in the second. The owner of the jaw belonged to a type of man that presumably came to Europe from Asia and was descended from ancestors roughly resembling *Pithecanthropus* and *Sinanthropus*, but he resembled modern man much more closely than the others. Anthropologists therefore classify him as *Homo heidelbergensis*. As he is thus recognized as a member of the genus *Homo*, he may properly be spoken of as a man.

Skulls of a decidedly different type have been found at various sites in recent years. The crania are larger and the foreheads higher than those of the Java and Peking men. Such are the Galley Hill skull, found in England in 1888 but long regarded as of doubtful date, and the far less questionable Swanscombe skull discovered there in 1936. Somewhat similar remains have recently been unearthed in Rhodesia in Africa. While there has been much dispute about these skeletons, scholars now tend to date them from the second interglacial epoch and therefore to regard them as roughly contemporary with the other early skulls. The differences between them and the others are so great, however, that they are classified as a separate genus, *Eoanthropus*.

Neanderthal Man

During the third interglacial and fourth glacial epochs Europe was inhabited by a species known as *Homo neanderthalensis*, or Neanderthal man. More than sixty skeletons of this species are extant, some of them virtually complete. When the first known Neanderthal skull was discovered at Gibraltar (1848), it attracted scant attention. The typical skeleton, from which the species derives its name, was found at Neanderthal, near Düsseldorf in Germany (1856). Other skeletal remains have since been found in Belgium, at several places in France, in Spain, in central Germany, in Yugoslavia, and more recently, in the Crimea, in Palestine, and in Italy near Rome.

As reconstructed by modern anthropologists, the Neanderthal men were short, males rarely exceeding five feet three inches in height and females being somewhat shorter. Their posture was slouching, their necks short and immensely muscular, their faces and heads were thrust forward, and they were heavily muscled. They must have been powerful brutes. Though they had no chins, their teeth protruded less than those of the Heidelberg jaw; and like apes, they had heavy ridges over their eyes. Their foreheads were low and receding, and their mental development was slight though their brain capacity equaled, or was even slightly superior to, that of the average European of today. The skeletons found in Germany and eastern Europe date from the third interglacial epoch, those of western Europe and Palestine all are from the fourth glacial epoch. It therefore seems probable that these men came out of Asia during the third interglacial epoch (or perhaps earlier, with the Heidelberg man as their ancestor or advance guard) and were later driven west or south by the advancing fourth glacier. Western Europe certainly was inhabited before the Neanderthal men arrived, though no earlier skeletal remains have yet been found. The Neanderthal men sur-

vived the rigors of glacial climate in southern France, but became
extinct toward the close of the fourth glacial epoch.

Homo sapiens

   Even before the end of the Glacial period, men of an entirely different species appeared in western Europe. These newcomers closely
resembled modern man. They had well-developed chins, their faces
were vertical, their foreheads high, their craniums large. Anthropologists classify them and their descendants as members of the species *Homo sapiens*—the supposedly intelligent species in the human
family—to which all men on earth today belong. Some authorities
believe that the newcomers mingled with the Neanderthals, but if
the two groups really belonged to different species of the genus
Homo, as now seems incontrovertible, their progeny would have
been sterile hybrids. We may therefore assume that the Neanderthals were exterminated. Possibly many were killed, but others
starved after being worsted in the struggle for the limited supplies
of food: their heavy bodies put them at a disadvantage when com-
peting with the more lithe newcomers, who also enjoyed the further
advantages of greater adaptability and higher intelligence.
   Darkness still surrounds the origin of *Homo sapiens.* The species
may have been quite ancient when it first appeared in Europe at the
end of the Pleistocene period. Mankind apparently divided into several genera soon after descending from the trees, and further sub-
division into species may have come soon after. The species *Homo
sapiens* may therefore be as ancient as *Homo heidelbergensis* or
other species of the genus *Homo.* In that case its members presumably lived for countless millenniums in some out-of-the-way place,
perhaps in central or southwestern Asia, where their fossil remains,
if any, are still awaiting discovery. Both the Galley Hill and the
Swanscombe men may belong to an early form of this species and
indicate stray raids into western Europe made in the second interglacial epoch. At any rate, *Homo sapiens* rapidly spread over the entire earth toward the end of the fourth glacial epoch. He supplanted
all other species of man but, even before the great dispersion, the
species had subdivided into the different races now composing hu-

manity. To distinguish the various races of man belonging to the species *Homo sapiens* from all other hominids and from other members of the genus *Homo,* the newcomers are called "neanthropic."

Early Paleolithic Civilization

Our knowledge of prehistoric man is not derived wholly, or even largely, from his skeletal remains. While fossilized bones may teach us something of man's early distribution and racial groups, we learn little from them about his manner of living and gaining a livelihood, his ways of acting and thinking, or the extent to which he had mastered nature. Yet these are the very things which historians most want to know, and fortunately evidence regarding them can be found elsewhere.

From the very infancy of the race, man has made things. At first he presumably made them of wood, bone, and other soft and pliable materials which were rather perishable and of which few traces remain. Next he learned to fashion flint by chipping off the edges, and these flints, once fashioned, have remained in the form he gave them. At still later times men learned to make things of other enduring materials. These products of human skill and workmanship are called *artifacts.* From hundreds of sites in every part of the world the diligence of archeologists has collected millions of these artifacts, which teach us much about the character and life of the men who made them. Since so much of our knowledge of prehistoric times comes from the study of stone artifacts, archeologists once called all prehistoric times the "Stone Age." Further researches have led them to divide the period into the Old and New Stone Ages, which are ordinarily called Paleolithic and Neolithic respectively.[1]

Nearly all early artifacts are tools. From the first, men were not only manufacturers but also tool users and, above all, tool makers.

---

[1] The word Paleolithic is derived from two Greek words, *palaios,* "old," and *lithos,* "stone"; Neolithic comes from *neos,* "new," and *lithos.* When the science of archeology was young, scholars distinguished the two ages by the methods used to sharpen stone tools: paleolithic men sharpened their flint knives by chipping small bits from their edges, neolithic men by grinding them. This distinction is no longer considered very important, but the two periods were none the less characterized by two different and successive types of culture. The essential differences between them will be developed in the next chapter.

The first two abilities they shared with other animals. Birds build
nests and beavers build dams, and it might even be said that apes
use tools when throwing stones at enemies or when beating them
with clubs. But only man has the ability to fashion tools to be used
for something else. When men had learned to give an edge to a piece
of flint, they had a tool that could be used for many purposes, and
from that day to this they have been inventing new and more serviceable tools to help them in their various enterprises.

Man's earliest tools were very simple. The first presumably were
clubs and other weapons—the skill and efficiency with which men
can liquidate large numbers of their fellow men may still be taken as
an index to their "progress" in "civilization"—but men soon invented
tools having more peaceful purposes. Among the first of these tools
of peace was the "fist-hatchet," a pear-shaped stone with one end
rounded to fit the hand and the other end chipped to an edge or
point. Men also learned to make flint pounders, scrapers, and cut-
ters. Wooden handles were attached to fist-hatchets to make rude
axes. In later times men developed a surprising variety of specialized tools, sometimes displaying great skill and artistic ability in
their manufacture.

Other archeological finds give further clues to life in Paleolithic
times. Layers of ashes found at various places in connection with
stone artifacts (and even with the bones of *Sinanthropus*) indicate
that these early men could make fire or, more probably, that they
knew how to preserve for their own use a fire started by lightning or
other natural causes. Though fires may sometimes have been used
by men simply for warming themselves, a more important use was
for cooking meat, even if, in the absence of metal spits or pottery
bowls, such roasting must have been rather crude. It is not improbable, moreover, that even in this early day a blazing fire aroused religious sentiments in the human breast, just as it has among so many
fire-worshipers of later times.

Archeologists have found the bones of animals killed and eaten by
these early men. Many are the bones of horses and cattle or similar
animals, yet, strange to say, they often include those of such gigantic
beasts as the hippopotamus, the rhinoceros, and the elephant. Since

individuals, or even small bands of men, could not successfully have attacked such powerful prey, the hunt must have been a co-opera-tive enterprise in which large packs of hunters participated. More-over, as small flint weapons could not have been very effective against such thick-skinned animals, it seems probable that men had by this time learned to build snares and traps.

As there are no natural supplies of flint near many of the sites where flint artifacts have been found, there must have been trade of some sort from early times. Trade implies a high intellectual devel-opment and the use of language. Likewise, the perpetuation of in-formation about making tools would have been virtually impossible without some use of language. And finally, it is interesting to note that the leg bone of our *Pithecanthropus* has marks indicating that its owner had been severely wounded but had recovered from his in-juries: he must have been incapacitated for a time, during which his fellows must have fed and cared for him, thus betraying something akin to humanitarian sentiment.

What a "Culture" Is

Men did not come naturally by their technical knowledge of how to do and make things, or by their social institutions and patterns of action. They learned both from long and arduous experimentation and labor, and they passed on this knowledge to their descendants. Taken collectively, the knowledge and institutions which are trans-mitted from one generation to another constitute what we call *cul-ture.* Different peoples have done things in different ways, and we therefore say that they have different cultures. We may contrast the culture of modern Europe and America with that of China or medi-eval Europe, and we speak of "primitive culture." As a matter of fact, early men created many primitive cultures which can be distin-guished by their material remains. Archeologists ordinarily call these cultures by conventional names derived either from a charac-teristic feature or, more commonly, from the locality where they were first studied.

Archeologists formerly believed that each invention was made once, and once only, and that artifacts of the new styles were carried about by wanderers and traders, or imitated by neighboring peoples, until they reached all parts of the world. Though such diffusion of culture has undoubtedly taken place throughout the long course of history, more recent studies have made this "diffusionist" theory seem highly improbable, at least in its extreme form. The human race had scattered widely before the first important inventions were made, and the same inventions were made over and over again by different peoples in different parts of the world. Whatever similarities appear between cultures in widely separated localities and at widely different times are to be considered coincidental and the result of similarities of the problems different men have had to solve and the materials with which they have had to work. The next few pages will sketch the development of culture in western Europe, mostly France, where it has been studied with especial care, but it must be borne in mind that cultural evolution took a somewhat different course in other places.

Early Cultures in Europe

The beginnings of archeological history are beclouded by a controversy in which much ink and gall have been expended. This dispute concerns certain flints found at various places in Europe and north Africa. They are known as eoliths or "dawn stones" (from the Greek words *eos,* "dawn," and *lithos,* "stone") and they *may* have been shaped somewhat by man. While some archeologists maintain that these eoliths are true artifacts, others insist that they were shaped only by natural forces. It is not improbable that the first flints used by man were shaped naturally and that men gradually learned to improve upon nature, but it is now difficult, if not impossible, for an archeologist to determine which stones were shaped wholly by nature and which were slightly touched up by man. Enthusiasts have found eoliths dating from the first interglacial epoch, but their claims are so doubtful that it would be unwise to argue the presence of "man" at so early a date from this slight evidence alone.

We have much better archeological evidence for human culture in Europe during the second interglacial epoch. There were no artifacts in the gravel pit at Heidelberg, but a number of interesting ob-

jects were found near the famous skull at Piltdown. Flint artifacts
from the second interglacial epoch have also been found at other
places in England, and many places in France and Belgium, and in
Spain. Even better artifacts come from Egypt, whose quite distinct
culture seems to have been more highly developed than any other in
the world at that time: here well-made fist-hatchets have been found
which date from the second interglacial epoch.

The third interglacial epoch is much better known. Early in that
period a culture called Chellean prevailed in western Europe. The
characteristic tools of this time were fist-hatchets which were much
better than those appearing previously in Egypt. These Chellean
tools were independent inventions, not mere imitations of those
made more than a hundred thousand years before in Egypt, as the
"diffusionists" would have us believe. Then in the latter part of the
third interglacial epoch a new culture, called Achulean, appeared in
western Europe, producing a wide variety of new flint tools. There
were scrapers for cleaning the inside of animal skins, large sharpened tools eight inches to a foot long which were probably used as
picks, small pointed stones sharpened on both sides which seem to
have been spearheads, and smaller ones which archeologists call
borers. What shelters these men had must have been mere huts or
wigwams built of sticks and skins, but the large number of scrapers
and borers found in Achulean sites seems to indicate that they had
learned to make fur clothing, sewing skins together with tendons
through holes punched by borers. The men who made these things
were primarily hunters who lived in the open, and as their flints are
usually found in terraces along rivers, they are called "river drift
men." Unfortunately no skeletons have been found to suggest their
appearance and racial affinities.

Mousterian Culture of the Neanderthals

While Chellean and Achulean cultures were flourishing in France,
a much inferior type of culture, known as pre-Mousterian, prevailed
in central and eastern Europe. Several thousand flint instruments
have been unearthed in this area, yet they include none of the fist-
hatchets so characteristic of the Chellean and Achulean cultures.

These pre-Mousterian artifacts are often found in connection with skeletons of the Neanderthal men who inhabited central Europe during the third interglacial epoch, and are undoubtedly the work of men of this race.

The fourth glacial advance drove Neanderthal men from central Europe into France, where they developed the culture now called Mousterian. As the climate of France was cold and moist in those days, men sought shelter in caves. Here their remains were much better preserved than in the open, and we consequently know much more about the Mousterian "cave men" of Neanderthal race than we do about their "river drift" predecessors. Though they learned to make fist-hatchets, they did not make many or good ones, and their knives were not so good as those made in Achulean times. Their scrapers and borers, on the other hand, were better, perhaps because these tools were so essential to making the fur clothing rendered necessary by the glacial climate.

In two or three sites archeologists have found human skeletons which seem to have been laid out carefully, as if in formal burial. Possibly the Mousterian implements found nearby were intended for use by the deceased in the next world, which would indicate the benign influence of religion and a belief in some sort of immortality. At other Mousterian sites human bones have been found broken open, as though to extract the marrow, and human heads split as though to lay bare the brains—which suggests the more horrid rites of cannibalism.

The Mousterian age in France was one of cultural decline. The rigors of the climate made life difficult, food was scanty, the caves were unhealthy, and physical degeneration began. The cultural decline may also have resulted in part from the fact that Neanderthal men did not have the creative ability of their predecessors. They were better fighters, but that is the best that can be said for them. Had more favorable climatic conditions prevailed, Neanderthal men might have made greater progress, but their slowness in learning what little they knew indicates that they had gone about as far as their brains could carry them. Had they remained supreme, Europe today might be populated only by men at the cultural level of modern Australian aborigines. At any rate, the Neanderthals were unable to compete successfully with the new and aggressive races that presently appeared, and toward the close of the Glacial period they were supplanted by neanthropic men (*Homo sapiens*), after having dominated western Europe for at least one hundred thousand years.

Upper Paleolithic Civilization

Neanthropic peoples first appeared in Europe at about the time when the glaciers were beginning their final retreat, approximately twenty thousand years ago. The newcomers belonged to various races (or subdivisions of the species *Homo sapiens*) and, arriving at different times from different directions, they brought several new cultures with them. Though the famous Cro-Magnons were not the first of these neanthropic invaders, they were the most gifted. After migrating from southwestern Asia through northern Africa, they entered western Europe and dominated it for several thousand years. Meantime men of a very different race, called the Brünn men, had entered central Europe through the Balkans. Advancing westward, they drove the Cro-Magnons beyond the Pyrenees into Spain, but after a stay of several centuries they disappeared. The Cro-Magnons reoccupied their former territory and even spread into central Europe. The first Cro-Magnons brought with them a culture called Aurignacian, which was presently superseded in France by the Solutrean culture of the Brünn men. When the Cro-Magnons resumed their cultural supremacy, about 10,000 B.C., they developed a new culture, called Magdalenian, which was the finest produced in paleolithic times.

The Cro-Magnons were hunters, especially fond of pursuing the wild horse and the reindeer: near one site is a refuse heap of horse bones which, it has been estimated, contains the bones of one hundred thousand animals. As the climate of western Europe was still cold, men usually lived in caves, though they had learned to build huts or houses. They showed greatly improved technique in chipping flint, and they made tools of bone or reindeer horn. At this time, moreover, the bow and arrow first appeared. Several cave-paintings of Magdalenian date show hunters using these weapons, one broken

Aurignacian carving seems to show a man in the act of drawing a bow, and small Aurignacian flints have been found that might well have been arrowheads. The rapid victory of neanthropic man over

● **Paleolithic Men Hunting Reindeer.** This drawing, found in a cave at Alpera, Spain, shows Cro-Magnon men hunting reindeer with bows and arrows. Presumably it was believed to possess magic powers to aid the hunters. Note the three arrows in one of the deer. (*Courtesy, American Museum of Natural History, New York.*)

the Neanderthals may have been due in large part to this superior weapon.

After the Solutrean interlude, which was a period of cultural decline, Magdalenian culture spread throughout western Europe. The wide variety of tools then in use, and the skill shown in their manufacture, indicate a high degree of specialization among the men who

● **Note for Plate 1.** These three pictures illustrate paleolithic art of the Magdalenian period. The picture of the bison was found, with several others, in a cave near Altamira in northern Spain. The second painting is called "The Sorcerer" because it shows a man inside the skin of a stag. Presumably he was a magician who hoped to attract game or otherwise aid the hunt by thus disguising himself. The painting was found in the Cavern of Les Trois Frères in Dordogne, southern France. The statuette is sometimes called the "Willendorf Venus," after the village near which it was found. Presumably it was believed to possess magic properties, perhaps to bring fertility to women who addressed it with the correct incantations. (*Photos, American Museum of Natural History, New York.*)

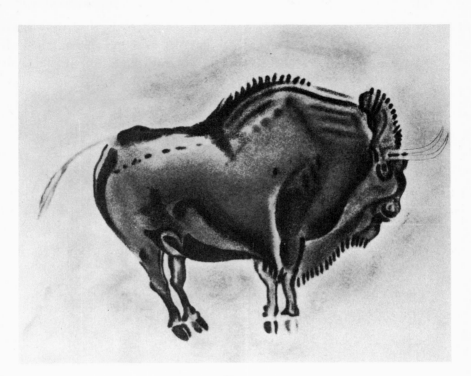

Bison

The Sorcerer

Willendorf Venus

Plate 1

made them. The tool makers, artisans, and artists of this time must have devoted their lives to improving their specialties. In Magdalenian graves we find ornaments made of shells coming from considerable distances, which would imply extensive trade or barter. The tribe was no longer a mere hunting pack: within it there was considerable division of labor and a specialization in different crafts. There must therefore have been an elaborate organization along economic, social, and political lines, though unfortunately we know nothing as to the exact nature of these institutions.

The crowning glory of Magdalenian culture was its art. Whereas Neanderthal man apparently had had little artistic feeling, the early neanthropic races everywhere showed high talents in this direction. Personal adornment was profuse: necklaces were made of shells or teeth, elaborate headdress was worn, and bodies were painted. Even in Aurignacian times men decorated the walls of their caves with drawings and made small statues of men and animals. Such artistic achievements do not appear during the Solutrean interlude, but in Magdalenian times early art reached its perfection. The realistic paintings of horses, deer, bison, reindeer, bear, and fish, which have been found in caves in northern Spain and southern France are now world-famous (see Plate 1). The walls of caves were also decorated with bas-reliefs, and statues were carved of men and animals. The skill shown by these Cro-Magnon artists is amazing. Their art presently went into decline, however, and before the end of Magdalenian times it had become so conventionalized and abstract as to be incomprehensible. The artistic tradition was lost, and thousands of years elapsed before the appearance elsewhere of art of comparable distinction.

Magic and Religion

We naturally ask why these works of art were made. Some of them perhaps possessed only esthetic value, others probably were connected with magic. The statuettes may have been fetishes, believed to possess magic powers, and the paintings may supposedly have helped in hunting the animals depicted. The paintings are usually found in the darkest recesses of caves, where their esthetic qualities could hardly be appreciated but where magic ceremonies could have taken place before or during the hunt. The cave paintings never depict animals not useful for food, nor plants, nor any inanimate things except houses. Sometimes the animals are depicted with spears or arrows in their sides. Perhaps men believed that repeating prayers and incantations before such pictures would enable them to shoot the animals more easily. The houses shown near, or even on, the animals might have been intended to draw these animals toward the camp by magic powers. The statues of women often exaggerated the parts associated with sex: possibly it was believed that appropriate incantations addressed to such statues would bring children to the votary.

The Cro-Magnons also had religious beliefs of a sort. Like all neanthropic men, they interred their dead in an elaborate and formal manner. The bodies were covered with red ochre, and weapons and useful tools were buried with them. Such practices indicate belief in a future life. Perhaps some of the statuettes were idols rather than fetishes (or "lucky" stones), and some of the cave paintings depict dances or rituals which may have had religious significance. Moreover, the existence of magic seems to imply the previous existence of religion: the idea of spirits and supernatural powers is fundamentally religious and is born of religious experience. The magician merely turned to powers of whose existence he had learned from religion, and used charms and incantations to constrain these forces to provide him or his clients with such material blessings as children or plentiful game.[2]

Presently life became more difficult for the Cro-Magnons, and their marvelous abilities went into decline. The climate of western Europe was growing warmer, and the moisture-laden winds, once deflected southward until they watered and fertilized the Sahara, began to blow across Europe. The broad European grasslands were overgrown with forests, first of pine and later of oak, and the great herds of reindeer and bison that had once roamed over the European tundra gradually disappeared. The men who had lived by hunting

---

[2] See note on Primitive Religion, p. 23.

these animals were forced to supplement their meat diet with shell-fish. The places of their habitation are today marked by "middens" —hillocks composed of thousands of cubic yards of discarded shells, among which have been found a few stone artifacts as well as the bones of animals and men. As these enormous middens are the refuse of centuries, the population of Europe must have been meager in those days, and the degenerate Cro-Magnons must have led miserable, half-starved existences.

Europe thus fell back into darkness after the brilliant achievements of the Cro-Magnons. Paleolithic man simply did not have the ability to find adequate food in the conditions then prevailing throughout Europe. But during these millenniums of European darkness, known as the Mesolithic or Middle Stone period, new and fundamental discoveries were being made in the Near East that eventually freed man from dependence upon the chance finding of food. These discoveries brought about what has aptly been termed the "Neolithic Revolution."

Note

Primitive Religion

We need not enter into the various theories put forward in recent years by anthropologists and sociologists to explain how religion first arose among men. Toward the end of the nineteenth century scholars began turning their attention to the religions of the "primitive" peoples alive today—especially to those of the Australian aborigines and the North American Indians—in the hope of finding among them earlier forms of the religions of the ancient world. These scholars assumed that the surviving primitive religions were virtually identical with those of Europeans in the Stone Age and that a clear and simple line of evolution could be traced from one form to the other. Such assumptions were quite unfounded and indefensible. The ancestors of the various races inhabiting paleolithic Europe separated from those of the Australians and American Indians hundreds of thousands of years ago. It may well be doubted whether their remote common ancestors had anything that could justly be called a religion. Even if they were religious, their earliest religions developed along very different lines in different parts of the world, and the Indians and Australians are very far from original man. The numerous attempts made in the nineteenth and early twentieth centuries to explain the religions of Egypt and Mesopotamia, or of Greece and Rome, by the phenomena of modern "primitive" religions have failed utterly.

Nevertheless, theorists have written interesting and stimulating books about these "primitive" religions. Sir James G. Frazer (1854–1941) collected an enormous amount of material on religious cults and folklore in a work entitled *The Golden Bough* (1st ed., 2 vols., 1890; 3rd ed., in 12 vols., 1907–15; abbreviated ed., in 1 vol., 1922). In this book he argued that religion sprang originally from magic—which is exactly the reverse of the view expressed in the text above. Frazer believed that the magician was a primitive but mistaken scientist who had learned from observation something of the uniformity of nature, and of cause and effect, and who vainly attempted to constrain natural forces by his charms and spells. The French sociologist Émile Durkheim (1858–1917) published an important work, *Les formes élémentaires de la vie religieuse* (1912; Eng. tr. by J. W. Swain, 1915), in which he criticized Frazer severely and built up an elaborate theory of his own about the origin of religion. Durkheim laid great emphasis upon the social origins and importance of religion and suggested that men's ideas of gods and supernatural powers first sprang from the ecstasy produced by the wild camp-meeting-like rituals of primitive peoples. Other writers, among them the disciples of the American anthropologist Franz Boas (1858–1942), have devised other explanations of the origin of religion.

Though no one of these theories has received universal, or even wide, acceptance, their authors are at least to be given credit for raising problems that demand explanation. Moreover, these writers have made valuable analyses of social institutions (including religion), and it is safe to say that no one who reads their books will ever again regard such institutions in the old naïve way. Every student of ancient history should familiarize himself with the writings of the anthropologists, reading them carefully but critically, and learning what he can from them. But he will be well-advised to quote them sparingly and to beware of trying to fit history into any ready-made pattern of progress.

II The Neolithic Revolution

Paleolithic men were merely food-finders. Dependent for their subsistence wholly upon hunting and finding, they inhabited only the more favored parts of the earth, and they never were numerous. Their small and frequently changing groups had no need to develop complicated social institutions. The pursuit of game led them from place to place, which made it difficult for them to accumulate property or to learn how to make more than a few small and simple tools. Their whole existence was brutish and precarious. Neolithic men, on the other hand, were *food-producers* as well, and they no longer needed to rely so completely as their predecessors upon the free gifts of nature.

Neolithic culture first arose in the Near East, the region surrounding the eastern end of the Mediterranean Sea and extending eastward into modern Iran. Here agriculture and the domestication of animals were first developed. New and more dependable sources of food led to a great increase in population. Men abandoned their wandering existence to settle in villages. They accumulated material possessions with greater ease and began making things that could not easily be carried about. Houses were built, pottery was invented, looms were made for weaving cloth. More persons could devote their attention to activities other than the immediate securing of food, and a greater division of labor became possible. Men could be supported from the surplus food while constructing public works—storehouses, temples, irrigation canals—or while clearing forests or draining swamps. Such public works of a productive sort marked the beginning of capitalist economy. Social institutions became more

25

complicated, and political and religious organization expanded. A larger number of persons could devote themselves to artistic creation or to religious, moral, and scientific speculation. In brief, the change from paleolithic to neolithic culture touched virtually every phase of human activity. Though it came gradually through many centuries, it is well named the "Neolithic Revolution."

The Fertile Crescent

The scene of this Neolithic Revolution was the Near East, and more specifically the region known as the "Fertile Crescent." This region is a semicircular belt of arable land enclosed on all sides by deserts, mountains, or the sea. At one end lies the fabulously fertile valley of the Nile, and at the other are the equally rich plains of Mesopotamia, watered by the Tigris and Euphrates rivers. Between these two highly fertile regions the arch of the crescent is formed by the less fertile but none the less habitable Palestine and Syria, running northward along the eastern end of the Mediterranean, and the hilly district south of the Kurdistan Mountains which connects Syria with Mesopotamia. South and east of the arch, the Arabian Desert separates Palestine from Mesopotamia, and east of the Tigris the Zagros Mountains separate the Fertile Crescent from Persia.

Egypt is divided by nature into two parts, Upper and Lower, which are southern and northern Egypt respectively,[1] and the line dividing them lies in the vicinity of the ancient Memphis or the modern Cairo. Lower or northern Egypt, which is the Delta of the Nile, was a swamp and probably uninhabitable until four or five thousand years before Christ, but Upper Egypt was inhabited from very early times. This Upper Egypt is a narrow valley cut more than one hundred feet deep into the plateau that is now desert; its width varies between twenty and thirty miles, and its length from Cairo south to the First Cataract of the Nile is more than five hundred

---

[1] The modern practice of putting the north at the top of a map is very apt to cause confusion in this case. As the Nile flows from south to north, Upper Egypt is below Lower Egypt on the map.

miles. It was well fitted by nature to be the home of an agricultural neolithic civilization. Every summer the Nile overflowed its banks, watering the fields and leaving upon them a thin layer of fresh soil brought from the jungles of central Africa. This irrigated land now forms a strip from two to ten miles wide which, being constantly renewed, is of inexhaustible fertility; but on both its sides the high-water level of the river marks the beginning of sandy desert. Ten thousand years ago this region differed greatly from what it is today. The valley bottom was largely marsh, game was more plentiful than now, vegetation spread far beyond its present limits, and groves of trees stood where today there is only sand. Moreover, this rich Nile valley, guarded on the east and west by deserts that were well-nigh impenetrable, was accessible only from the north and south. The early Egyptians suffered relatively little from marauding invaders, yet they were not so remote as to escape all vitalizing influences from abroad. Thus an equable climate, a fertile soil, habitual peace, and occasional stirrings from without, united to make ancient Egypt a fruitful home of higher civilization.

At the opposite end of the Fertile Crescent lie the broad alluvial plains of Mesopotamia, which are the gift of the Tigris and Euphrates rivers just as Egypt is the gift of the Nile. The northern or upper half of Mesopotamia is commonly called Assyria, the southern or lower half, Babylonia. Assyria rests upon solid rock foundations but Babylonia, like the Delta of Egypt, is built on silt brought down by the rivers and was an uninhabitable swamp until barely six thousand years ago. When the first civilization began in Babylonia, about 4000 B.C., the head of the Persian Gulf, into which the rivers empty, was seventy-five or one hundred miles north of its present location. The silt brought down by the rivers has filled in the Gulf at the rate of about a mile and a half a century (or an average of seventy-five feet a year), and has raised the level of the plain so much that neolithic artifacts are now found many feet below the surface. Like Upper Egypt, Upper Mesopotamia was well-adapted to agricultural life in early times, and neolithic civilization appeared there almost as soon as it did in Egypt. Palestine and Syria, being hilly, are less well adapted to agriculture than the plains of Egypt and Mesopotamia, and the evidence now available indicates that neolithic culture did not reach them until a thousand years after its appearance elsewhere.

Its Early Inhabitants

Paleolithic artifacts have been found at many places in the Fertile Crescent, but especially in Egypt. Fist-hatchets somewhat resembling those of Chellean France have been found in terraces dating from the Egyptian equivalent of the second interglacial epoch, and the country has probably been inhabited continuously from that day to this. The absence of skeletal remains renders it impossible to determine the races then inhabiting Egypt, but a dozen skeletons of Neanderthal type have been found in nearby Palestine, dating from the equivalent of the fourth glacial epoch. Contemporary with the Magdalenian culture of Europe (roughly 10,000 B.C.) was the Sebilian culture of Egypt. Artifacts show that their makers were skillful in fashioning stone, but their artistic powers did not equal those of the Cro-Magnons. Though we have no bones of these men, it is safe to assume that they were neanthropic. Sebilian culture was presently destroyed by invaders coming from the Sahara.

During the fourth glacial epoch, the moderating and moisture-laden winds, blowing from the Atlantic, which now water western Europe, were deflected to the south by the advancing ice. They thus brought to northern Africa a period of heavy rains and moderate temperature which made most of the Sahara, known to us today as a desert, into a well-watered grassland fit for human habitation. This region was inhabited by neanthropic men early in their dispersion (perhaps 20,000 B.C.), and it became the homeland of what we call the Mediterranean race. When the glaciers in Europe receded, the winds began to follow a more northerly course and the Sahara gradually became drier until it reached its present desert state. Soon after 10,000 B.C., desiccation had advanced so far that its inhabitants had to seek new homes. As much water was still frozen in the glaciers, sea level was considerably lower then than now and the straits separating Africa from Europe were much narrower. Mediterranean

men driven from the Sahara therefore found little difficulty in crossing to Europe by way of Gibraltar or Sicily. Here they encountered,
conquered, and absorbed, but did not exterminate, the decadent Cro-
Magnons. Today the descendants of these Mediterranean invaders
form the bulk of the population of Spain, southern Italy, and southern France, and a notable part of that of the rest of France, southern
Germany, and the British Isles. Other Mediterranean peoples entered Egypt and Libya, and are now called Hamites. Still others
crossed from Africa to Arabia by the Straits of Bab-el-Mandeb at the
southern end of the Red Sea. They became the ancestors of the
Arabs and other Semites of historical times. From the Arabian Desert
they filtered into various parts of the Fertile Crescent. Other Mediterranean peoples advanced along the coast to Syria and Asia Minor
and some even found their way to Crete.

Meantime other peoples, of quite different racial stock, were migrating from their home in central Asia (perhaps Turkestan) for
much the same reason. Their homelands too were drying up. These
peoples are often called members of the Alpine race. Some of them
reached Europe at an early date. Perhaps the Brünn men represent
an early wave of these Alpine migrations. Beginning about 7000 B.C.,
these invaders reached Europe in greater numbers, apparently entering through southern Russia. Their descendants form a large part
of the populations of central and eastern Europe today. Other Asiatics turned south and occupied the mountainous country north of
the Fertile Crescent and others advanced along the Zagros Mountains. From these points they spread out into Mesopotamia, Syria,
and Asia Minor. Those who settled in the Kurdistan and Persian
highlands found predecessors with whom they mingled to form the
sub-race usually called Elamites. Those who reached Syria and Asia
Minor intermarried with the Mediterraneans whom they found in
possession of the land to form the Armenoid subrace. Men of the
latter group developed and passed on to their descendants distinctive
physical characteristics, notably a large aquiline nose and thick lips,
which many amateur anthropologists consider Jewish traits—though
they really are Asiatic, not Semitic, and are often shared by members
of the Alpine race in Europe.

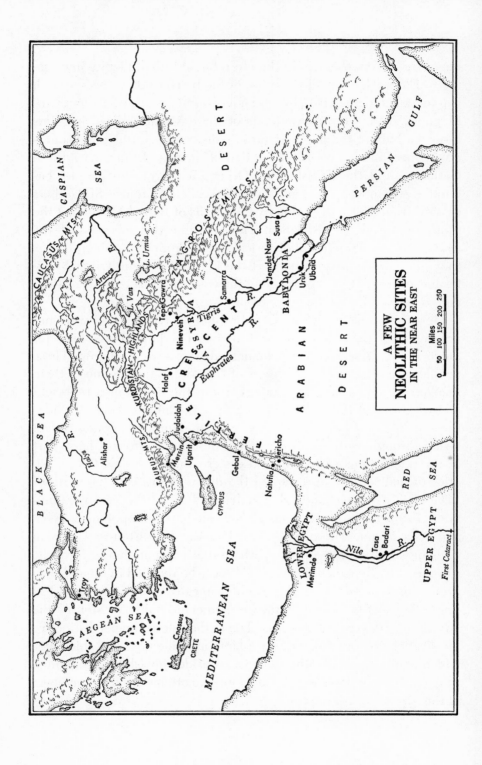

A FEW
NEOLITHIC SITES
IN THE NEAR EAST

Miles
0 50 100 150 200 250

BLACK SEA

CAUCASUS MTS.

CASPIAN SEA

Araxes R.

L. Urmia

Van

TAURUS MTS.

KURDISTAN HIGHLAND

ZAGROS MTS.

DESERT

PERSIAN GULF

Alishar

Habs R.

Troy

AEGEAN SEA

Cnossus

CRETE

MEDITERRANEAN SEA

CYPRUS

Mersin

Ugarit

Judaidah

Gebal

Natufia

Jericho

Tepe Gawra

Nineveh

Halaf

ASSYRIA

Tigris R.

CRESCENT

FERTILE

Euphrates

Samarra

Jemdet Nasr

Susa

Uruk

Ubaid

BABYLONIA

ARABIAN DESERT

RED SEA

LOWER EGYPT

Merimde

Nile

Tasa

Badari

UPPER EGYPT

First Cataract

R.

The Neolithic Near East

Very little is known of the culture of the Mediterraneans or the Alpines before their great migrations began. In Europe they showed a sorry decline from Magdalenian standards. Men at this time lived largely on fish, uncultivated vegetables, and berries, and they must have led dreary and desolate lives. At some of the later sites traces of crude pottery have been found, and the bones of dogs that may have been domesticated. But not until about 3000 B.C. did any marked changes in their manner of life appear.

The Mediterraneans who advanced eastward into Egypt and Asia made more rapid progress. The earliest traces of them come from Palestine. About fifty skeletons of Mediterranean type were discovered in an ancient cemetery some twenty miles from Jerusalem. These "Natufian" men lived in caves and were primarily hunters, but rude flint sickles suggest that they had a slight knowledge of agriculture. There is no evidence allowing us to date this isolated culture accurately, but it was neither widespread nor long-enduring. Probably, however, it was before 5000 B.C.

A second very ancient site has been discovered at Mersin, in the Cilician plain just around the corner of the Mediterranean from northern Syria. The evidence indicates that this site too was occupied as early as 5000 B.C., but not much can be said of the civilization of its first inhabitants. It is not even possible to say whether these men were Mediterraneans or Alpines or something else, though it seems probable that they belonged to the former race.

Neolithic Culture in Egypt

The neolithic civilization of Egypt began long before the first Pharaohs, in what are ordinarily called "predynastic" times.[2] The

---

[2] An Egyptian priest named Manetho, who wrote a Greek history of Egypt about 275 B.C., arranged the kings whom he knew in thirty groups called dynasties. This arrangement has been retained by historians down to our own day. The first king of the 1st dynasty, whom Manetho called Menes, lived about 3000 B.C. while the 30th dynasty ruled in the fourth century before Christ. The three millenniums which these dynasties cover constitute the "dynastic" period of Egyptian history; when archeologists discovered earlier civilizations in Egypt, they called them "predynastic." The chronology of predynastic Egypt cannot be given accurately in years, but archeologists have traced its cultural development with great care. The pottery from several

earliest example of this culture yet found is the Tasian, which flourished in middle Egypt perhaps as early as 4500 B.C. Men were still nomadic and lived largely by hunting and fishing, but they had discovered the art of making crude pottery to hold liquids and grain. They gathered and ate cereals, and probably cultivated them as well. Perhaps they made a kind of linen cloth, but their textile arts were not highly developed. At any rate, the Tasians had reached a stage of civilization far beyond anything known to their contemporaries in mesolithic Europe. The few available skeletal remains from this period indicate a mixture of Mediterraneans with some other people, presumably the descendants of the Sebilian inhabitants of Egypt.

A more advanced neolithic culture has been found at Badari, not far from Tasa in middle Egypt. The early Badarians lived in villages, understood agriculture, and kept domestic animals which they pastured in what is now desert country. They also fished and hunted the game which then abounded. They wore clothing made of skins or coarse linen, and adorned themselves with necklaces, bracelets, and anklets made from shells, ivory, or stone beads, or occasionally from beads of copper. They advanced far in the manufacture of pottery, and they made curious statues of female figures. These Badarians must have been an eminently peaceful people, for we find no warlike weapons in their graves, there are no examples of broken bones or injuries, and a considerable proportion of those buried in their cemeteries had reached old age. Skeletal remains show that they were of the Mediterranean race, but occasionally they show noticeable traces of Negroid blood. Persons of the same physical type are found in neighboring parts of Egypt today.

The sites near Badari were occupied for a few centuries, but toward the end of the fifth millennium (4000 B.C.) they were deserted.

---

hundred graves has been arranged chronologically according to its style, in fifty groups; to each group is assigned a number between 30 and 80, which is called its "sequence date" (S.D.); other earlier Egyptian civilizations have been discovered since this system was established, and their pottery is classified in S.D. 21–29; twenty numbers thus remain available should still earlier civilizations be discovered. The periods of time designated by these numbers vary considerably according to the rapidity with which pottery styles changed, but the accurate classification of artifacts, graves, and villages which this system has made possible provides a chronological background for the general progress of early Egyptian civilization.

Elsewhere in Egypt life continued much the same for several centuries, though during this period there was a heavy infiltration of Hamites from Libya on the west. The newcomers learned much from the Badarians, but they also imported ideas of their own and established the Amratian culture. Nearly half a millennium later, somewhat before 3500 B.C., came a fourth predynastic culture, called Gerzean, which differed notably from its predecessors. The new elements apparently were brought by Semites from Asia, who filtered in by way of Suez. Eventually these newcomers became so numerous as to leave a strong Semitic mark upon the Hamitic Egyptian language. The invaders first established themselves in the Delta, whence their culture gradually penetrated into Upper Egypt. After two or three centuries came a renewed infiltration of Asiatics, some of whom were distinctly broad-headed, which suggests an Alpine race. They established a new type of culture called Semainean, and their intermittent invasions lasted until after the establishment of the First Dynasty and the beginning of historic times shortly before 3000 B.C.

Libyan invaders of Amratian times (4000–3500) introduced the ass into Egypt and developed the cultivation of the olive. The Gerzean invaders from Asia brought new grains and the vine which they apparently had learned to cultivate in Palestine or Syria. This period also saw the first great irrigation canals, which carried the fertilizing waters of the Nile over a wider area, and the first artificial drainage of the swamps in the valley bottom and the Delta. As such public works were possible only through the combined labor of hundreds of persons, they prepared the way for closer political union and for such monuments of co-operative endeavor as the enormous pyramids and temples of later date.

In dynastic times Egypt was divided, for administrative purposes, into districts which were later called "nomes," of which Upper Egypt had twenty-two and the Delta twenty. It seems probable that these nomes were once independent principalities. We know that some of them existed in Amratian times, and nearly all of them can be identified shortly thereafter. Each nome took its name from some species of bird or animal, which was pictured on its flags and elsewhere as a sort of coat of arms. Thus one nome was named after the jackal, another after the cat, another the hawk, and so on. Possibly the animal in question served the people of its nome as a sort of god, comparable to the totems of primitive peoples today. These nomes were the first political units larger than the village, and while they probably originated through conquest by some powerful local chieftain, they became the basis for co-operation in building irrigation canals and other engineering works.

Objects found in the early graves bear witness to the antiquity of trade in Egypt. Shells from the Red Sea are found in Tasian burials, and it is believed that some of the lumber found in Badarian graves came from Syria. Boats made of papyrus reeds and propelled by oars were used by the Amratians; sails were added by the Gerzeans. In these boats men sailed up and down the Nile. Larger and stronger boats were presently constructed in which Egyptian sailors navigated the Red Sea to Punt (modern Somaliland, or perhaps Aden in Arabia) and the Mediterranean to Syria. Egyptian objects found in Crete show that these hardy mariners even headed across from the western Delta to that island, a journey which took them outside the sight of land for three or four days.

The first traces of writing appear in Amratian graves, where archeologists have found vases decorated with drawings and peculiar line markings. Since all the vases of a single grave are usually marked in the same manner, the lines are interpreted as proprietary marks, showing the beginning of writing as well as the progress of the idea of private property. Other marks, dating from late Gerzean times, resemble characters of the later Egyptian hieroglyphics.

Tombs of the predynastic era show an interesting architectural evolution which indicates a corresponding development of ideas about life after death. The early Badarian graves were oval holes in which the body, wrapped in cloth or fur, was placed in a contracted position, accompanied by a few vases or other possessions. Later the graves became rectangular, wooden coffins were used, and eventually underground tombs were built whose brick walls were plastered and decorated with scenes from daily life. The tombs were thus made into elaborate homes for the dead, and articles of value were placed in or near the coffins, presumably for the use of the deceased in the next world. Flights of steps led down to the doors of the tombs, and in late predynastic times superstructures resembling houses were built above ground. A few centuries later these superstructures developed into mighty pyramids. Thus even in predynastic times the Egyptian was haunted by a fear of annihilation, took consolation in picturing a life beyond the tomb, and went to great trouble and expense to make his future life a pleasant one.

Neolithic Culture in Mesopotamia

While the neolithic cultures of Egypt were the creation of men of Mediterranean race, those of Mesopotamia were created largely by Alpines. A few centuries after 5000 B.C., Elamite mountaineers began descending from their highland homes into the Assyrian plain, where they presently established neolithic civilization. Archeologists have studied several neolithic villages in the vicinity of Nineveh on the upper Tigris, at Samarra about halfway down that river, and at Halaf which is further west, about halfway to the Mediterranean. This earliest neolithic civilization is sometimes called Halaf culture, from the latter site. The men who created it were familiar with agriculture, but they continued to hunt, using arrows, slings, and maces to kill their prey. They had polished stone axes, some with perforated holes for handles and some with double edges. They also made remarkable pottery upon which they painted curious geometrical designs, and they had clay figurines which may have been idols. The earlier houses were circular in shape and built of sun-dried mud brick resting on stone foundations. Toward the end of the neolithic period, villages had cobbled streets, storehouses filled with grain, and rectangular houses.

While these Assyrian villages were in their prime, the lower reaches of Mesopotamia, like the Delta of the Nile, were still uninhabitable swamps. The alluvium gradually rose, however, and settlers entered Babylonia, perhaps advancing from the firm land to the north or perhaps coming down from the hills to the east. During the course of the fourth millennium (4000–3000 B.C.), several neolithic civilizations arose in lower Mesopotamia. The earliest, called Ubaid culture because it has been studied especially at Tell al-Ubaid, began about 3750 B.C. and lasted for several centuries. The second, called Uruk culture, lasted from about 3300 to about 3000. This was succeeded by the Jemdet Nasr period, which lasted for some two centuries, until about 2800. Then came historic times and the beginning of what is called the "Early Dynastic" period in the history of Babylonia.

The early Ubaid culture at first showed little change from the Halaf culture found further north, but before the period was over men had learned to make boats and to spin and weave, and their pottery was so fine that some authorities believe it must have been made on a potter's wheel. Before long these inventions had spread as far as the Indus River to the east and the Caucasus Mountains to the north. Uruk culture was the work of invaders who brought a few new ideas and presently developed many others. Their pottery was a red or grey ware, unpainted but sometimes decorated with simple incised patterns. The newcomers were also great builders. At Uruk they built a temple on an artificial mound over thirty-five feet high, using as foundation limestone blocks which must have been brought from considerable distances. Sometimes the village streets were laid out along the lines of the compass, and these people knew how to build a true arch. Marks found on clay tablets show that the first steps toward writing were taken during the Uruk period. In the Jemdet Nasr period painted pottery again appears, and is called "polychrome" because both red and black paint were used. The decorations include very realistic drawings of animals and men in place of the schematic designs of earlier times. Wheeled carts were invented, as shown by the clay model of one which closely resembles the "covered wagon" of pioneering days in America. Pictographic writing was expanded with signs that could be used to spell new words and thus express abstract ideas. And toward the end, copper objects appeared in profusion, showing that Mesopotamia was emerging from the Neolithic into the Age of Metals.

While it seems fairly well established that the Ubaid culture was primarily the creation of Elamites from the north or east, the subsequent racial history of Mesopotamia is still a matter of controversy. At the beginning of historic times, about 2750 B.C., this region also contained men belonging to two non-Elamite races—Semites who were Mediterraneans coming indirectly from Arabia, and Sumerians whose earlier history and racial affinities are unknown. The Uruk culture, with its red unpainted pottery, seems to trace back to northern Syria, which suggests that its authors were Semites. This would also indicate that the Jemdet Nasr culture, with its polychrome pottery, was the work of the Sumerians. People of this latter race may have begun to enter Babylonia during the Uruk period; during the Jemdet Nasr period they ruled the land; and it was under them that historic times began in Mesopotamia.

Neolithic Europe

It thus came about that, during the fourth millennium before Christ, the Fertile Crescent was dotted with villages whose inhabitants practiced agriculture and the other neolithic arts, while other peoples in this general area were wandering from place to place, caring for their flocks and herds. It was only at the very end of the millennium—when trade, metallurgy, and writing heralded the dawn of a new age in the Fertile Crescent—that neolithic culture first appeared in Europe. Probably the Europeans invented much for themselves, but there can be no doubt that part of the new culture was brought to them from the Near East, both by the invasions of new peoples and by cultural borrowing—the adoption by a people of the ideas and manner of life of their neighbors.

The first group of invaders who brought neolithic culture to Europe were Armenoids from Asia Minor. Members of this race had occupied Crete, some of the Aegean Islands, and parts of Greece, in the second half of the fourth millennium. Others, crossing the Bosporus or the Hellespont, advanced through the Balkans to the Danube Valley. Mingling with the earlier inhabitants of this region, they presently formed the Dinaric sub-race, which resembles the Armenoid in many ways and to which most Balkan peoples of today belong. The cultural status of these peoples before they began their great migrations is not well known, for Asia Minor has not yet been carefully explored archeologically. An early village at Troy, near the Hellespont, was founded before 3000 by men with a neolithic culture. Similar cultures have been found at a few other points along the Aegean coast and at Alishar in the central plateau. After the invaders had established themselves in Europe, between about 2800 and 2600, their culture spread through the Danube Valley. Grains and domestic animals appeared, undoubtedly brought from the Near East. Men made excellent unpainted pottery, learned to spin and weave, and began to live in well-built villages. Their manner of life was eminently pacific, and almost no weapons have been found among their remains. This central European neolithic culture is called Danubian.

While neolithic culture was thus entering central Europe from the southeast, other peoples were carrying it to southern and south-western Europe by another route. Mediterranean peoples were migrating westward across northern Africa and presently established themselves and their culture in southern Italy, Sicily, Malta, Sardinia, and especially in southern Spain. As these peoples made much of their journey by water, they cannot have been numerous, but their culture was adopted to some extent by the natives already inhabiting these various lands. This western neolithic culture has been best studied in the vicinity of Almeria, a seaport in southern Spain. Here the native inhabitants scarcely emerged from the mesolithic stage of civilization, but they acquired a few domestic animals and learned a little about agriculture. Their pottery was primitive and their tools show only a slight improvement on mesolithic technique. Much the same may be said of the early neolithic cultures of southern Italy, the islands, and north Africa.

Neolithic culture was brought to the west by traders from the Near East in search of copper. The older centers were by now far advanced in the Copper Age, and the great demand for this metal sent Egyptian and Cretan traders scouring the Mediterranean. As soon as they learned of the Spanish deposits of copper, traders, prospectors, and miners arrived, bringing neolithic and copper implements and introducing a little agriculture for their own use. But these copper hunters were never numerous enough to be called invaders, and at first the native population was not much affected by them. The local inhabitants acquired animals from the traders and learned something about agriculture, but the copper objects found in Spain dating from this period were not the work of native hands. Usually they were just flashy gewgaws such as sophisticated traders might palm off on ignorant savages. Nevertheless, neolithic culture spread from Spain to France and England. Eventually it came in contact with the other neolithic civilization that had come up the Danube from the East, and in Belgium, western Germany, and Switzerland the two cultures mingled to a certain extent.

Perhaps the best known examples of the resulting European neolithic culture are to be seen in the celebrated Swiss lake-villages which flourished about 2500 B.C. Sometimes houses were built on logs laid on the mud along the shores of the lake; sometimes they were built on piles driven into the mud; and sometimes they were built on rafts held in place by piles at the corners. Rows of such lake-houses were built to form quadrangles along the shore or over the open water. In the latter case, the houses were connected with each other by bridges, and the village could be entered only by a narrow causeway. The inhabitants of these lake-villages were descended in large part from the mesolithic people of central Europe, but they derived much of their neolithic culture from the outside. The earliest lake-villages were in western Switzerland, and their new culture apparently came from Spain; the villages in eastern Switzerland, on the other hand, show a cultural affinity with the Danubian civilization. As Swiss neolithic culture reached its full development, elements from the two sources were commingled. When remains of these villages were first discovered in the middle of the nineteenth century, they aroused much romantic enthusiasm, and the life of their inhabitants was depicted in idyllic colors. Subsequent discoveries have shown that this culture did not differ radically from European neolithic culture elsewhere.

The "Nordics"

At just the time when neolithic culture reached its height in central Europe, men of another sort began invading central Europe from southern Russia. These men are now known as the "Nordics." They were simple nomads, principally caring for their bands of sheep, their herds of cattle, and their horses. Only rarely did they turn to agriculture. Their habitations were tents or huts of wattle and mud. They apparently learned the potter's art from the Danubians, and their inferior pottery is called "corded ware" because it was decorated with marks made by pressing cords into the wet clay. In strong contrast to the peaceful peasants of central Europe, these Nordics were great fighters, and their most characteristic contribution to Europe was the two-edged battle-axe. Even these battle-axes they did not invent, but copied them from a type used in Mesopotamia. They also used wagons very similar to those used centuries earlier in Mesopotamia. In southern Russia the Nordics buried their dead in mounds, now called "kurgans," but they presently adopted the practice of cremation, which is now considered one of their distinguishing characteristics.

Shortly before 2500 these Nordics first came in contact with the European peasant farmers of Romania and Transylvania. A little later they carried their battle-axe culture into Denmark and Sweden, and then (about 2300) into Bohemia and Hungary, in each case invading from the east. The Nordic invaders usually did not kill or drive out the peasants whom they conquered, but allowed them to continue cultivating their fields as before, while the conquerors set themselves up as a ruling aristocracy. They imposed their language upon the conquered peoples but, as has happened on many another occasion in world history, the conquerors presently learned the arts of civilization from their victims. A considerable mixture of blood took place. The blending of these various races and cultures in central Europe created a new people, with a fairly high civilization and great ability in war, who early in the second millennium began to take an important part in world history.

Neolithic Culture

Neolithic culture was not the same everywhere, of course, and the villages of the Near East differed much from those of central Europe. In general, however, the characteristic features of the new civilization derived from the two fundamental innovations—agriculture and the domestication of animals. Apparently dogs were the first animals to be domesticated. They probably had long been following the hunters' camps as scavengers, devouring food that had been thrown away. When men found them useful as watchdogs, they fed them and thus domesticated them. Many early breeds of dog resemble the jackals still found in the Near East, which suggests that they were domesticated in that region. Others resemble the European wolf and may have been used, even in neolithic times, to pull sleds like their descendants, the modern Huskies. The domestication of cattle, sheep, goats, and swine came somewhat later. Such domestication was more than mere taming, for it included learning to breed new animals. The original long-horned cattle ranged over much of Europe and Asia, and might have been domesticated anywhere; but our sheep, goats, and swine seem to be descended from species that were indigenous to the Near East. We cannot say with certainty how they were captured or tamed: perhaps men and animals alike were driven to the oases by the advancing desiccation, and there men learned the advantages of saving some animals rather than killing all immediately.

As the possession of these animals assured a supply of meat, many peoples abandoned hunting and devoted themselves to driving their herds from one pasture to another, just as the pastoral peoples of the Near East do today. Men presently discovered that their animals might do more than provide meat. On learning the value of milk, butter, and cheese, they began dairying. They also domesticated beasts of burden, notably the ass in Libya or Egypt and the camel in southwestern Asia. The horse was tamed much later, either in central Asia or in southern Russia. Geese were domesticated rather early, perhaps in neolithic times, but the other barnyard fowl do not appear until a few centuries before Christ.

The art of agriculture has been discovered many times. The culture of maize was discovered by the Indians of Central America, that of millet and rice by the Chinese, and that of millet, barley, and wheat by the peoples of the Near East. Although millet was perhaps the earliest grain cultivated in the latter region, wheat was from early times the most important crop there and in Europe. Several different species of wheat appear in neolithic graves, and their distribution provides supplementary evidence of the migrations sketched above. A form of wheat called "emmer" grew wild in Abyssinia and was cultivated in Egypt from Badarian times onward; thence it spread to Crete and across northern Africa to Spain, France, and Britain; and it appears in some of the western Swiss lake-dwellings. Thus it followed the Egyptian neolithic culture of the Mediterraneans. Common wheat was domesticated in Afghanistan and taken to Mesopotamia, Syria, Asia Minor, the Danube Valley, central Europe, and some eastern Swiss villages. Around these primary crops developed the cultivation of many others: in Egypt and north Africa oats and flax as well as peas and other vegetables were grown; in the Afghanistan-Mesopotamian area, beans, peas, lentils, and carrots. The date palm is native to Arabia and Mesopotamia, the olive to northern Africa, the fig to Afghanistan, and the vine to Syria. The other fruit trees apparently were brought from the East in later times, and only the crab apple is native to Europe.

• Note for Plate 2.   The picture on the opposite page shows the "step trench" up the side of Tell Judaidah, a site in northern Syria which has been excavated by the Oriental Institute of the University of Chicago. The "tell" (or hill) is entirely artificial, being the accumulation of thousands of years of human occupation. The different levels shown in the picture may be dated by objects found in them: typical finds at each level are pictured in the column at the right. Thus the top level contained the ruins of a Christian church, built between 300 and 600 A.D. Level II, dating from 64 B.C. to 300 A.D., had Roman objects, symbolized here by a lamp. Level III, 500–64 B.C., had Greek and Persian objects, symbolized by a coin of Alexander the Great. Level IV, dating from the Syro-Hittite period (about 750 B.C.), contained inscriptions in Hittite hieroglyphics. Level V, about 1300–1000 B.C., had pottery from the Aegean area. Level VI, about 1400 B.C., contained pottery imported from several places, showing extensive trade. Level VII, about 1800–1600, showed cultural connections with the Mesopotamia of Hammurabi's day. Level VIII, about 1800, showed the influence of Egypt and the Hyksos. Levels IX and X showed trade with northern Mesopotamia. Level XI contained a cylinder seal from Ur of the First Dynasty (about 2500 B.C.). In Level XII, about 3000 B.C., were found six copper statuettes, three male and three female, and there were traces of the fabric in which they were wrapped; these statues of gods and goddesses of fertility are the oldest known representations of the human figure in metal. Level XIII had excellent pottery. Level XIV, perhaps as early as 4000 B.C., was a neolithic Syrian village. (Photo, Oriental Institute.)

Plate 2. Tell Judaidah

Farming methods were at first very primitive. Holes were poked in the ground with sticks, and seeds were dropped in. A great advance came when sharpened flints were fastened to long handles and thus made into hoes, which enabled men to cultivate garden plots more efficiently. The plow, by which whole fields could be cultivated, was not invented until the beginning of the Age of Metals. Sickles for harvesting the grain were made by fastening flints to curved sticks. Threshing was done by laying the ears of grain on a threshing floor and driving cattle over them to trample out the kernels; the flail was not invented until about a thousand years before Christ. Grain was ground into meal in mortars, and millstones found in Syria date from the beginning of the Bronze Age. Artificial irrigation was used in Egypt and Mesopotamia from neolithic times. The river floods, of course, provided natural irrigation, but even in these early times men learned to increase the area flooded by running water through ditches they had dug.

Settled Life Encourages Inventions

Agriculture produced fundamental and far-reaching changes in the character and mode of life of the peoples who practiced it. When wandering hunters settled down to become sedentary farmers they began to build houses. At first they made walls of rushes daubed with mud, and roofs thatched with palm leaves or straw; later they built stone foundations to keep out rain water, and made side walls of sun-dried brick. They built their houses close together in villages for the sake of protection, and they walked back and forth to their fields every day, taking their tools and animals with them. The villages usually were located on the tops of hills, or *tells,* which were more easily defended and healthier than the valley bottoms (see Plate 2). Farming thus led to the village community by which rural life is still characterized in the Old World.

Settled life encouraged the accumulation of tangible property, which would have been a hindrance to wandering hunters, and encouraged inventions of primary importance in human history. For example, men now learned how to make pottery. This art, like that of agriculture, was probably invented several times: it is native to

America, it was discovered in China, possibly it originated independently in Europe and central Africa, but it received its highest early development in the Near East. Even in paleolithic times men had made baskets from reeds or switches; sometimes they daubed these baskets inside and out with mud and used them to hold grain or even liquids. When they discovered that the reed framework was unnecessary, they began making clay pots shaped like baskets or else resembling the leather bags or gourds which they had formerly used as water containers. The earliest pottery was sun-dried, but men soon learned to bake it, first in an open fire and later in an oven, and they developed the art of painting it. The potter's wheel, which enabled them to make thin round pots, was invented in the Near East in the late neolithic times.

The ancient art of basket-making also developed into the textile industry. Plaited wickerwork readily suggested mats of woven reeds or grass, but true cloth could not be made until thread had been invented. In Badarian times flax was spun with the aid of small clay spindles, or "whorls," which were whirled rapidly by hand and whose momentum twisted an even thread. These early whorls, hundreds of which have been found in ancient sites, were virtually identical with those used the world over until the close of the Middle Ages in western Europe. The first important improvements upon them came in the fourteenth century after Christ, and the spinning-wheel was not invented until after Columbus had discovered America. At first the threads probably were woven by hand, but before long looms were invented. A few small bits of neolithic cloth have been preserved by unusual chemical action, and there are bits of pottery showing the marks of cloth pressed upon them before they were baked.

A characteristic tool of neolithic times was the celt, a stone axe or adze with a polished edge. These tools were used to cut down trees and work up lumber, and they indicate an advancing knowledge of carpentry. Since good lumber was scarce and expensive throughout the Near East, it was used sparingly, usually for furniture and other small objects, but in the heavily forested parts of Europe it was used for large buildings. At some period in the fourth millennium carpenters invented the wheel and built wagons, and before the end of that period they had also learned to build large boats, capable of navigating the Mediterranean and Red seas. At first the boats were propelled by oars, but later sails were invented.

At this time, too, a knowledge of metallurgy began to appear in the Near East. Hammered copper and gold were used for ornaments and were left in tombs as early as the beginning of the fourth millennium; before the millennium ended, numerous objects were cast in copper. By this time men had learned to recognize copper ores, knew how to smelt them, and could cast the metal. This smelting and casting certainly required the use of some sort of blast furnace, for the melting point of copper (1085° C.) is higher than could be reached by a simple wood fire. Other metals, such as silver and lead, whose melting point is considerably lower than that of copper, were also used to some extent, but the melting of iron was still impossible. These various types of workmanship, and especially ceramics and metallurgy, required a great amount of technical knowledge and artistic skill. Such knowledge and skill were not acquired easily, nor were they shared by everyone. We may therefore assume that even in neolithic times there were craft guilds of limited membership which possessed an inherited lore regarding various trades.

Communal Social Institutions

These developments in the manner of life wrought profound changes in social institutions. The early pastoral peoples, especially the Semites, used a form of social organization which we call the "patriarchate." An old man, roughly corresponding to the Biblical Abraham or a modern Arab sheik, ruled over his wives and children, and also over his servants and retainers and their children. As they had discovered that men as well as animals can be domesticated, they also had slaves. The members of this group resembled an enormous family as they wandered about with their flocks and herds. In a sense the patriarch might be called the father of the tribe. While men undoubtedly owned small portable possessions individually, the important property, namely the flocks and herds, was held in common. The patriarch might say that the animals were his, but in reality they belonged to the whole group, which cared for them, defended them, and derived its sustenance from them. This expanded family was therefore a social, economic, and political unit.

Early agricultural societies developed a parallel form of social organization called the "matriarchate." Though the matriarchate passed away in the Near East long before the beginning of historic times, it left traces sufficient to prove that it had once been powerful there. The distinguishing characteristic of this system lies in the fact that under it men trace descent, not through the father, but through the mother. The ruler of the group was a husband or son of the "queen." These early agricultural societies also developed a simple form of communism somewhat resembling that of the patriarchal herdsmen. Individuals might acquire private property in movables and perhaps in houses, but not in agricultural land. The fields were held in common by the group. All the peasants worked side by side when sowing and reaping, and the crop was stored for the whole village in common storehouses.

At a later period, but long before the end of neolithic times, the matriarchate was replaced by a revised patriarchate, perhaps because of conquest by pastoral nomads. Under the new patriarchal system the peasants continued to do the agricultural work as before, but were forced to give a part of the crop to their new rulers. The conquerors, on the other hand, gave various services to the community, notably protection against other raiders. They also made possible much of the further economic advance of the community by encouraging the potters and other craftsmen to improve their wares, since they alone had the wealth to pay for better things. It was these patriarchs also who collected the surplus produce which was subsequently invested in irrigation canals and other public works. They were the "capitalists" of the community.

Society thus took on a much more elaborate organization than before. Soldiers and capitalists, artisans, peasants, and slaves brought a division of labor which made necessary a greater social solidarity. Sometimes this solidarity was obtained by force, but in the long run force can never be a satisfactory basis for social relationships. Most men must be persuaded to accept their station in life and to obey their rulers voluntarily. Often this persuasion was the work of priests, who made up one of the oldest specialized professions. Priests were supposed to possess magic or divine powers, and in those days they actually did possess superior wealth, education, and intelligence. We shall see in subsequent chapters that while Egyptian priests supported and advised the kings, those of Mesopotamia often took the rule into their own hands.

Languages in Neolithic Times

Neolithic times also provide us with our first evidence, direct and indirect, of what the languages spoken by men were like. It is useless to speculate upon the character of paleolithic communication. The increasing knowledge and the growing complexity of life that characterized neolithic times led, of course, to a great development of language; and the invention of writing, which came at the end of this period, has preserved for us a record of its spoken forms. Modern linguistic science has also been able, by the comparative method, to learn much about languages that were never committed to writing or of which we have only scanty written records.

No connection can be established between the different languages spoken by the major divisions of mankind: perhaps members of the species *Homo sapiens* had not yet developed anything that could properly be called a language at the time of their dispersion. However, most of the languages spoken in Europe and the Near East throughout historic times can be divided into three great families associated respectively with the Mediterraneans who came from Africa, the Elamites and Armenoids of Near Eastern Asia, and the Nordics of Europe.

The languages of Mediterranean origin fall into several groups, two of which contain languages that are still spoken. They are called "Hamitic" and "Semitic" after the two Mediterranean subraces that spoke them in neolithic times. The Hamitic languages include ancient Egyptian and its successors of Christian times, Demotic and Coptic; the Libyan and Berber languages spoken today in parts of north Africa; and several groups of languages in central Africa and Somaliland. The Semitic languages were spoken by the peoples who came out of Arabia. They include Akkadian (Babylonian) and Assyrian, Phoenician, Aramaic, and Hebrew, and the modern Arabic which Moslem conquerors of the seventh and eighth centuries of the Christian Era carried to Egypt and north Africa as well as over the whole former Semitic field. The languages originally spoken by the Mediterraneans of southern and western Europe presumably were akin to Hamitic and Semitic, but unfortunately we know nothing about them.[3]

The languages spoken by the peoples of Asiatic origin are less familiar. Of those spoken by the early Alpines of central Europe we know nothing. The languages once spoken by the ancient Armenoids of Asia Minor and Crete are preserved in inscriptions and writings which so far have resisted all efforts at decipherment, but the kindred language of the Elamites was deciphered in the nineteenth century. Some writers use the word "Asianic" to designate this whole family of languages, but others call them "Japhetic," to contrast them with the Hamitic and Semitic groups which include most of the other known languages spoken in the Near East in ancient times. These names are of course derived from Ham, Shem, and Japheth, the three sons of Noah in the Biblical legend of the flood.

The third great language group, ordinarily called "Indo-European" or "Aryan," is associated with the Nordics. It includes all the tongues spoken in Europe today except Basque (spoken in the Pyrenees), Turkish, the Finnish languages, and Magyar spoken in Hungary. In neolithic and later times, Nordic warriors advanced over Europe and parts of Asia, imposing their languages upon the peoples whom they subjugated. The conquered peoples never learned them well, however, soon forcing them into new forms and eventually developing dialects into new languages.

The Indo-European languages can be divided into two groups, Eastern and Western. The Eastern division includes, among others, Sanskrit, which was taken into India before 1500 B.C. and survives

---

[3] A few resemblances to Hamitic forms appearing in the Indo-European (Nordic) Welsh have sometimes been explained as survivals from the time when Mediterraneans were the dominant race in Britain. Rather unsuccessful attempts have been made to find Hamitic or Semitic parallels for old geographic place names in western Europe: for instance, the first syllables of Iberia, Hispania, and Hibernia may be variants of the definite article of the original Mediterranean language, which becomes *he* in some Hamitic languages and *i* in modern Berber.

in various dialects as well as serving as a sacred language for Hindus; Persian, which was introduced into that country a few centuries later by a kindred people; the various Slavic tongues, ancient and modern (Old Slavic, Russian, Polish, Czech, Serb, Bulgar, etc.); and modern Armenian. Sanskrit was forced upon a Dravidian (Indian) people, the others upon broad-heads of Asiatic origin, and Nordic blood is virtually non-existent among most of the peoples now speaking these eastern Aryan tongues. The Western group, too, is made up of several subdivisions: Hittite, which was spoken in parts of Asia Minor in the second millennium before Christ; Greek, including ancient and modern dialects; Latin, including the various ancient Italian dialects as well as its descendants, the modern Romance languages, Italian, French, Spanish, Portuguese, and Romanian; Celtic, spoken in western Europe and the British Isles for many centuries after the political decline of the Mediterraneans there, but now limited to Irish, Welsh, and Breton; and lastly the Germanic languages, including various ancient tongues such as Gothic and Anglo-Saxon, and the modern German, Scandinavian, Dutch, and English.

These three great families of languages were firmly established in neolithic times, and their subsequent developments furnish us with an invaluable guide to the later cultural history of the Western World. Before the time of Christ the languages of the ancient Asianic or Japhetic group had been virtually squeezed out by the dominant Semitic and Aryan languages.

Folklore and Religion

Neolithic times also saw a great quickening of the intellectual life. Settled life led to the accumulation not only of material things but also of ideas. When groups of men lived for many generations in a small locality, they learned to know its characteristics and history in a way that would have been impossible for hunters ever moving onward in the pursuit of game. Hills and rocks and giant trees became associated with stories and legends that were passed on from generation to generation, and languages had now developed to a point where elaborate stories could be told. These legends then became integral parts of the life of the community.

If we may judge these early legends by the vestiges that remained into literary times, they contained lore of all sorts—theories as to the origin of the world and man, the history of man and his cultural progress, and stories of the inspiring deeds performed by heroes of old. They played the part in neolithic society that popular science and history play in modern times. Of course the legends were not true, yet the men who told them and heard them believed them and based their conduct upon them as much as we base our actions upon our beliefs and folklore. The village whose inhabitants all shared legends of this sort was bound together not merely by economic and political ties: it was an intellectual community as well. In the long run, the creation of such communities, built upon a heritage of common ideas, was as important as the creation of economic and political groups.

Finally, the neolithic period witnessed great religious development. We have already seen that paleolithic men sometimes believed in supernatural powers and human immortality, and that they went through various ritual practices in conformity with these beliefs. Their views regarding supernatural powers were greatly elaborated by the neolithic peasants. Familiar spots were associated with spirits, while sacred places and oracles became famed far and wide. Altars and "gilgals" (sacred circles of stone) were erected where, at stated seasons, great religious festivals were attended by people from the whole countryside. These celebrations usually coincided with the important seasons of the agricultural year—planting, the first fruits, and the harvest—and from very ancient times men regarded the reappearance of vegetation in the spring as symbolic of human immortality, which they celebrated with appropriate springtime rites at our Easter season.

During this period there developed an elaborate priesthood whose duty it was to see that religious ceremonies were correctly performed and to keep spirits and gods propitious. When sacrifices and offerings were made to the gods, it was the priests who actually received them and subsequently looked after the property of the gods. The priests thus became a wealthy caste. As their duties also included the explanation of the world to men, they became theologians, scholars, and even scientists after a fashion. They were the first intellectual class. Their wealth and knowledge gave them power, and usually the priests were the most influential group in the community. More than anyone else it was they who bound communities together by intellectual bonds as well as economic and political ones.

Elaborate theologies and mythologies were constructed to explain the various religious ceremonies and to set forth the attributes of the supernatural powers. Many gods were worshiped and, as was fitting to an agricultural people, the greatest of all the gods was usually some form of Mother Earth, the giver of life to her children. The worship of this Great Mother spread over the whole Near East in neolithic times. Statuettes representing her are often found by archeologists, and occasionally these neolithic figurines represent Mother and Child—a theme widely used in later religious art.

The pastoral peoples, on the other hand, ordinarily pictured supernatural powers somewhat differently. Nomads were less inclined to think of their gods as inhabiting definite places, and were therefore less likely to build altars and temples for them, to construct elaborate mythologies about them, or to make statues of them. Though they often carried sacred stones and fetishes about, in general they tended to associate the supernatural powers with the sky, the heavenly bodies, and other phenomena which were always with them in their wanderings. The stars, the planets (especially Ishtar, our Venus), the sun (Shamash), and the moon (Sin, whence Mount Sinai, the "moon mountain"), played a prominent part in the religion of early Semitic nomads. The early Nordics, on the other hand, had a sky god who was called *Dyuas pitar* in Sanskrit, *Zeus pater* in Greek, *Jupiter* in Latin, and *Tiu* in old German: under the latter name he is still honored on the third day of our week. Thus while agricultural and matriarchal peasants were addressing their supplications to Mother Earth, the pastoral and patriarchal nomads worshiped the Sky Father. The fundamental religious ideas of the Mediterranean world of classical times can be traced back to the worship and mythology which grew out of the commingling of these neolithic types of deity.

The White Races

In this chapter we have used the word *race* many times and we have
repeatedly referred to such racial groups as Mediterraneans, Alpines,
Dinarics, Armenoids, and Nordics. These men were the mesolithic
and neolithic invaders of the Near East and Europe. Many migrations have since occurred within that area, but invasions from without have been few and, racially speaking, unimportant. The men
discussed in this chapter were the ancestors of the modern European
or "white" race. As recent years have heard much loose and indiscriminate talk upon this subject of race, it will be well to get straight
in our minds once and for all what "race" really is, and more especially what it is not.

Race is purely a biological matter. A race is a large, and perhaps
widely scattered, group of persons whose common descent is shown
by hereditary physical characteristics that are transmitted from generation to generation. Among the characteristics which anthropologists regard as especially important indications of race are the shape
of the head (whether relatively long or broad when viewed from
above); the texture of the hair (woolly, wavy, or straight); the color
of the skin, hair, and eyes; the shape of the nose; and stature. Using
color as such a criterion, humanity can be divided into three great
groups: Whites, Negroes, and Mongols. But each of these groups is
composed of a wide variety of distinct races which have had little or
no connection with each other since the original dispersion of *Homo
sapiens*. These lesser races of the same color are therefore no more
closely related to one another than they are to groups of a different
color.

Modern writers often divide the white races of Europe into three
great groups which they call respectively the Mediterranean, the
Alpine, and the Nordic. The Mediterraneans are the short, slight,
dark-skinned, black-haired, black-eyed, long-headed men who came
up out of the Sahara as that region dried up. They are especially
numerous in southern Europe, but many entered France, western
Germany, and the British Isles. The Alpines too are rather short, but
with a tendency to corpulence; they are broad-headed, their hair

and eyes are brown, and their skin is lighter than that of the Mediterraneans. They apparently came from central Asia. Their greatest concentration at present is in a belt stretching east and west across central Europe, from the Atlantic to Russia. The Dinarics of the Balkans and the Armenoids of Asia Minor are of somewhat similar origin, but much Mediterranean blood flows in their veins. They are usually taller than the European Alpines, their aquiline noses are prominent, and (especially among the Armenoids) their round heads seem almost pointed. The Nordics are tall, long-headed, blond, blue-eyed, and have a pinkish white skin. From an early home in Russia they spread out to Germany, Scandinavia, and Great Britain, where they formed aristocracies; in later times they and their mongrel followers occupied most of Europe, again as aristocracies.

This picture of racial conditions in Europe is highly schematic and only vaguely resembles the confused actuality. The "typical" Mediterraneans, Alpines, and Nordics described above are purely ideal types toward which individuals tend, but there probably is no one in the world today who shows all the qualities of one group and no others. Throughout human history small groups of men have been wandering about, interbreeding with other groups whom they met. When the Cro-Magnons and later peoples were conquered by new invaders, some were killed or driven away by the conquerors, to be sure, but others were enslaved or married and, in the course of time, assimilated. This process was repeated whenever a tribe conquered its neighbors and occupied their territories. Even in early times, moreover, slave traders carried individuals away from their kinsmen; artisans and traders migrated freely to foreign parts; and marauding chieftains seldom measured the skulls of adventurous young warriors seeking to join their bands. There has been a great mingling of races throughout all history. Men of "pure" race do not exist anywhere on earth today, and in fact there never have been men of that sort. Talk of "pure" race is utter nonsense.

Race and Culture

Race, being a biological matter, has no inherent relation to culture. A man's race is determined before his birth, his culture afterward. A child kidnapped at birth, for example, would retain the racial characteristics of his parents, but would acquire the culture of the people among whom he was raised. It is true, nevertheless, that in early times the members of a race tended to share the same culture. Sudden and extensive changes in the culture of a locality, therefore, usually indicate invasion by a new race. This superficial parallelism of race and culture comes from the fact that individuals acquire their culture by education, ordinarily from their parents or other members of that cultural group. Even in early times, moreover, one type of culture was often shared by members of different races, and much of the present volume will be devoted to the story of how cultures have spread beyond racial frontiers, of how one people has absorbed, modified, and developed the culture of another.

Nineteenth-century writers often laid great emphasis upon the languages spoken by various peoples as indications of race. Since language is merely one element of culture, it cannot be used for such a purpose. The Negroes in the United States, for example, speak English as their mother tongue. Enthusiastic philologists who deduced racial history from linguistic history thus fell into many grave errors. Nevertheless, it is true that once the general outlines of racial and cultural prehistory have been established by the sounder methods of anthropology and archeology, philology can profitably be used to supply further details regarding the life and culture of a prehistoric people.

Race likewise has nothing to do with nationality. Only in ancient Greece or in rather recent times have men dreamed of uniting by the spiritual bonds of nationality all the inhabitants of a large geographic area. A glance at the map will show that the nations of modern Europe cut squarely across racial frontiers. North Germans are largely Nordic, south Germans Alpine; north Italians are largely Alpine, south Italians Mediterranean. Many modern Frenchmen are Alpine, and therefore related to south Germans, north Italians, and Slavs; but in northern France there are many Nordics whose racial affiliations are with north Germany and England, and in southern France there are Mediterraneans more closely related by blood to south Italians and Spaniards, and even to Algerians, than they are to

most Frenchmen of central and northern France. There is no such
thing as a French or German, or Greek or Latin, or Jewish race; and,
of course, members of almost every race under heaven share American nationality.

Alleged Racial Qualities

Much has been written in recent years about the merits and shortcomings of different races. It is quite possible, of course, that the talents and abilities of whole peoples may vary somewhat as do those
of individuals. It is true that certain races—notably those in central
Africa, Australia, and Polynesia—have not built up high civilizations
of their own, but who can say whether this backwardness is due to
incapacity or to environment? Most races have shown great creative
powers. The accomplishments of the Mayas, Aztecs, and Incas in
pre-Columbian America were amazing. The Chinese developed a
culture as high as any known in Europe until a century and a half
ago. The achievements of the Dravidians in India astonished Alexander the Great and the British of the eighteenth century. Our own
American civilization is the joint creation of Mediterraneans, Alpines, and Nordics, Negroes and Mongols. In the course of this book
it will appear that high civilizations have arisen most frequently in
regions where there has been much cross-fertilization of race and
culture.

Great quantities of ink have been sacrificed to a discussion of the
psychological and spiritual qualities of races, and especially those of
the European races. Most of what has been written is pure moon-
shine. In general, persons who think of themselves as belonging to a
certain race claim for that race a monopoly upon physical beauty,
spiritual idealism, creative ability, and true civilization, while they
accuse the members of all other races of ugliness, materialism, lazi-
ness, and barbarism. Nordic champions have been conspicuously vo-
cal of late years, growing lyrical about their universal genius and
their superiority over all rivals. Unfortunately, however, other writers have been so unkind as to picture this magnificent race as composed largely of wandering fighters and drunkards who have taken
from others whatever civilization they possess. It may be true that

the Nordics and Mediterraneans have been more bellicose than the Alpines; they have also produced more great builders and explorers. But it is also worth noting that while Alpines may sometimes show a willingness to accept their lot as sedentary peasants, many of them have been distinguished as philosophers, poets, musicians, and artists. An exceptional number of the great religious leaders revered by the Western World have been men of Mediterranean race. No race has a monopoly on barbarism or culture.

Part One: The Ancient Orient

III Mesopotamian Cities

WHEN CITIES FIRST BEGAN TO OVERSHADOW THE NEOLITHIC villages of the Near East, shortly before 3000 B.C., a new period in history was born. These early cities were not just villages that had grown larger. The villages were inhabited by peasants who worked in their fields every day, but the inhabitants of the city were craftsmen, merchants, and government officials. As the city dwellers differed radically from the peasants in their whole manner of life, their domination brought with it a new spirit and a new type of civilization. Villages and agriculture continued to exist, of course, and throughout antiquity most people were peasants. Their manner of life changed markedly as the centuries went by, but the cities contributed most of the new ideas that characterized the new day. Ancient civilization was always fundamentally a city civilization, and it began with this urban revolution.

The rise of cities would of course have been impossible without a greatly increased food supply, and it necessarily was preceded or accompanied by various inventions which increased the yield of the soil. The most important of these inventions was the plow. Heretofore, farmers had broken the soil with hoes that were merely sticks with sharpened flints fastened to their ends. With such tools a man could scarcely cultivate more than a garden plot or raise much more food than his own family would consume. With a plow and an ox, however, he could cultivate a larger field and produce more food. Men also learned to extend the acreage under cultivation with large irrigation works. The extra food thus produced went to feed the cities.

At about the same time the use of metal became more prevalent. Probably the first metal to attract attention was gold, from which it was easy to make simple ornaments. Copper beads were widely used for the same purpose in early times, and virtually all the early sites in the Near East contain metal objects of one sort or another. Therefore archeologists often call the Near Eastern Neolithic period Chalcolithic ("copper-stone"). Pure copper, however, is too soft for tools, and toward the end of the fourth millennium men began hardening it with alloys and making serviceable metal weapons and tools. The early and middle centuries of the third millennium are therefore called the Copper or Early Bronze Age. Not until late in the millennium did men discover the classic formula for bronze—90 per cent copper and 10 per cent tin—and thereby inaugurate the true Bronze Age.

As the smelting and casting of copper required great skill and long training, a specialized class of artisans arose who spent their lives working with metal. Simultaneously, improvements in other trades such as pottery-making—the potter's wheel had only recently been invented—gave further stimulus to specialized craftsmanship and brought a further division of labor. Artisans then congregated in the cities. Industrial development also brought into being a merchant class. Supplies of metal could be procured only in a few favored places, and the widespread demand for raw copper stimulated trade. Artisans living in the cities also needed the food which merchants brought them from the surrounding countryside. And finally, the merchants distributed manufactured products far and wide to their ultimate consumers. Cities thus became the centers of far-flung industrial and trading enterprises.

The rise of specialized industry and urban life also presupposed the existence of considerable amounts of capital. This capital consisted of improvements upon the land, houses, buildings, and irrigation works, boats and beasts of burden, supplies of raw material, finished products awaiting sale, and supplies of food to sustain artisans and traders during the manufacture and sale of commodities. In a sense this capital was the creation of the whole community, but control of it inevitably fell into the hands of a few individuals who were skillful at using it to augment economic production still further.

These economic developments were greatly facilitated by still another of the great inventions of the period—the invention of writing. The complexities of the new urban economic life were so great that accurate records became a vital necessity. Most early writing recorded business transactions, but it was not long before writing was used for other purposes as well. It is by no means fortuitous that the transition from prehistoric to historic times coincided with the rise of capitalism and cities.

The rise of industry and cities also forced the creation of strong governments. The wealth of the cities excited the covetousness of neighboring peoples and made strong defenses necessary. The extensive division of labor brought disputes which governments undertook to settle. And above all, the new economic organization led to a class conflict between peasants and city people. The former produced the food which the latter had to receive regularly. Sometimes the food was bought, or obtained by barter, but not enough could be acquired thus because the cities did not produce enough goods which the peasants wanted to pay for the food they needed. Governments had to exact further deliveries of food, which a modern accountant would probably charge to rent, interest, taxes, payment for protection, gifts to the gods, and the like. The food thus acquired was sent to the cities. Force was often required to make the system function smoothly, and this force was provided by the men who also defended the city from its foreign enemies and raiders.

The Babylonian City-States

The southern or lower half of Mesopotamia, known to us as Babylonia, was a region admirably adapted to the new urban life. Its broad alluvial plains, watered by the Tigris and Euphrates rivers and by a complicated system of irrigation canals, produced amazingly large crops and an abundant supply of food. The two rivers provided highways for boats, while caravans could easily travel overland from one city to another. Many of the new inventions first

appeared in this part of the world, and it happened that the raw materials necessary for the new manufacturing were available nearby.
Above all in importance, however, was the economic prosperity of
the late neolithic period in the Near East which permitted the accumulation of the necessary capital.

As we shall see in the next chapter, equally favorable conditions
prevailed in Egypt, where urban life appeared at about the same
time. Cities sprang up in western Asia Minor and in Crete during the
second millennium, but there were none in southern Europe until
after 1000 B.C., and few north of the Alps before the Christian Era.
Although the great inventions—the plow, metallurgy, and trade—
reached these remote regions in the third millennium, they were not
followed by cities until many centuries later. Europe lagged behind
the Near East because her relatively poor soil, even when cultivated
by the plow, could not produce the surplus food required to feed
large city populations. There were few natural highways comparable
to the great rivers of the Near East, by which supplies of food could
easily be carried to central spots. And above all, the poverty of Europe prevented the accumulation of capital on a large enough scale
for city life.

A Capitalistic Priesthood

From these early times a distinctive feature of Babylonian city
civilization was the form taken by her capitalistic organization. It
was euphemistically said in Babylonia that capital belonged to the
gods; but in practice the control of it fell to the priests. The resulting
economic system may well be called "theocratic capitalism"—capitalism controlled by the gods through their priests. The priests had
obtained enormous wealth, much of which they turned into productive capital, and consequently they were able to dominate the economic life of their day. In fact, the whole history of the ancient Near
East is colored by these priestly capitalists, and only rarely in history
have the clergy gained power equal to that of their early Babylonian
confreres.

The story of how the priests achieved this high position is long
and complicated. From a very early period, perhaps even from pa-

leolithic times, priests had formed a professional caste to look after relations with the gods. They enjoyed the leisure necessary to acquire special skills, to speculate upon the gods and nature, and to build up a lore which they passed on to their successors through education. In neolithic times it came to be widely believed that good crops were given to men by the gods as a favor, and that this favor might best be obtained through the intervention of priests. It was also believed, both by the priests and by the community as a whole, that men should begin by seeking divine aid with sacrifices offered to the gods, and afterward show their gratitude for an abundant harvest with thank offerings. Part of the offering was consumed at the time of the sacrifice; another part was saved by the priests for future consumption; and still another part was stored up as wealth belonging to the god but entrusted to the care of his priests. The priesthoods thus became wealthy, with cattle and large stores of grain as well as supplies of the precious metals and other gifts presented to the gods.

Sometimes the priests lent cattle to peasants, retaining ownership not only of the animals themselves but also of their offspring. Speculative modern writers have even suggested, with high plausibility, that the calf was probably taken back by the lender soon after birth, thus becoming the first form of interest. Grain might be lent as seed and taken back with interest after the harvest. When inanimate things were lent, an equivalent return was demanded year by year. On other occasions the wealth accumulated by the priests was used to dig irrigation ditches, thus bringing new land under cultivation. These fields were claimed for the god; others came to him as gifts or were taken in payment of debts which the unhappy borrower could meet in no other way. As what once entered priestly hands rarely left them again, the priests gradually came to control the whole agricultural life of the community, and because of their superior education and wide experience they could direct it more intelligently than could the individual peasants.

Another share of the priestly wealth was devoted to the construction of magnificent temples which, in the course of time, became great community centers. Traders found good markets in the vicin-

ity of such temples, and priests were often of help in business negotiations. Contracts were confirmed by oaths taken before the god
and in the presence of a priest. Valuables might be stored more
safely in the sanctuary of a temple or its yard. The education of the
priests enabled them to make written records of business transactions. Having learned the principles of investment and interest from
their agricultural operations, the priests sometimes made loans to
traders and manufacturers, charging interest for their services. The
priests were then able to influence the economic development of the
country by granting or withholding loans for various purposes, and
often they went into business on their own account—or on the god's.
The temples had large staffs of officials who busied themselves with
all manner of things in fulfilling their duty of caring for the god's
property. At the top of the hierarchy was the *patesi,* who not only
looked after the god's estate but governed the city as well. The
priests actually became the government, and the state became a theocracy—a state governed by its gods through their priests.

Nature of the City-State

Early in the third millennium, Babylonia was divided into a large
number of autonomous city-states. At the center of a rather small
area was the city itself, and around it for several miles in every direction lay the fields where food for its citizens was raised. The peasants
lived in villages scattered over the countryside. At first they may
have enjoyed great liberty, but a large proportion of them were reduced eventually to the status of serfs of the god, whom they served
as paid laborers or sharecroppers under the direction of the priests
or their agents.

The city itself centered around the temple of the god. Nearby
were a market place, workshops of many sorts, the gorgeous residence of the priestly rulers, and the more modest residences of rich
merchants and lesser officials. The whole city was surrounded and
protected by a wall of sun-dried brick, outside which were the hovels that served as homes for the poor. Many cities contained several
thousand inhabitants, large numbers of whom were employed by

the god in one capacity or another. Such city-states were regulated and governed by priests, some of whom were concerned largely with political administration, others with economic activity, others with religious rites and ceremonies, and still others with scholarship, science, theological and philosophical speculation, and other intellectual activities. For many centuries these priest-ruled cities remained the cultural centers of civilized life.

Of course different city-states quarreled with each other from time to time, and sometimes they went to war. Occasionally a powerful city or ruler would conquer and annex its neighbors, or unite them into some sort of domain ruled by a *lugal,* or "king." Local affairs probably remained largely in the hands of the old priestly *patesi,* yet conquest altered the old theocratic government. The kings relied especially upon military force and set up military aristocracies. They were always careful to concoct and broadcast deeply religious justifications for whatever they did, usually announcing that they were merely acting as agents for the gods whose will they carried out. The military powers thus came into rivalry with the priesthood, and the kings eventually transferred many of the functions of government to secular officials. Naturally the earlier kingdoms were neither large nor firmly established, and many kings ruled simultaneously in different parts of the country. Babylonian records tell how one "dynasty" after another held sway over larger or smaller areas, but not until after the middle of the third millennium did a single *lugal* successfully rule the greater part of Babylonia.

Sumer and Akkad

The alluvial plains which we call Babylonia—as distinct from Assyria farther north—were then known as "the land of Sumer and Akkad." Sumer was the southern part of the Babylonian plain, while the northern part was called Akkad. The distinction between Sumer and Akkad was not merely geographic, however, for two quite different peoples inhabited the two districts—or, to be more exact, men of different racial types predominated in the mixed populations of the two parts of lower Mesopotamia. The Akkadians were Semites

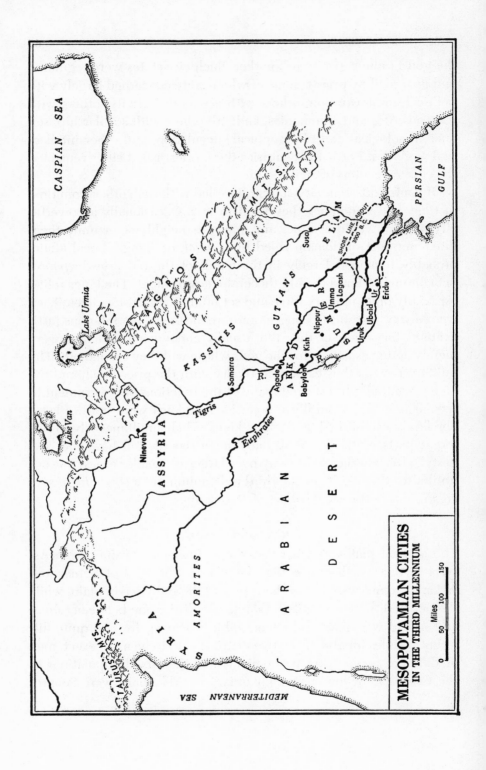

MESOPOTAMIAN CITIES
IN THE THIRD MILLENNIUM

who had filtered in from Syria and Arabia; but in spite of long research and discussion, the origin of the Sumerian remains problematic.

Sumerians began dominating Babylonia culturally in the Jemdet Nasr period (about 3000 B.C.) though they had lived there even in the Uruk period. Some authorities hold that the Sumerians invaded Babylonia at the beginning of the Uruk period (about 3300), while other recent investigators prefer to believe that they were the aboriginal population who occupied the region as soon as it was reclaimed from the marshes and the Persian Gulf. No one knows positively whence the Sumerians came or what other peoples, if any, were kindred to them. They were broad-headed, short, and thickset, and originally they were doubtless of Alpine race. Their language shows no connection with any other known tongue: presumably it belonged to the Japhetic or Asianic group, though even this presumption cannot be proved. Whatever their origin and racial affinities, these Sumerians were a highly gifted people. They dominated Mesopotamia politically for several centuries in historic times, and their culture continued to dominate the area long after the Sumerians themselves had been overwhelmed by Semitic immigrants. Sumerian cultural supremacy covered almost a thousand years, whose confusing political history may be summarized around four periods: the First Dynasty of Ur (about 2500); Semitic rule under Sargon of Agade (after 2300); a Sumerian revival under the Third Dynasty of Ur (about 2100); and a second Semitic rule under Hammurabi of Babylon (1728–1686).

The First Dynasty of Ur

Late Sumerian king lists begin with two dynasties which they call the First Dynasties of Kish and Uruk respectively. These lists are absurd as they stand, for they assign to the twenty-three kings of Kish a total rule of more than twenty-five thousand years, and twenty-three hundred to the twelve kings of Uruk. Nevertheless, archeology supports the claim that each of these cities enjoyed a day of glory in the first half of the third millennium. The city of Nippur likewise had an ancient past, though its name does not appear in the king lists. It was a city of high importance in the religious history of Sumer, but apparently its rulers never made serious efforts to dominate all Babylonia politically. Archeologists have also discovered advanced civilization at several other Sumerian sites, notably at Lagash. This period of Babylonian history, from about 3000 to 2500, is called Early Dynastic.

The king lists become more credible when they speak of the First Dynasty of Ur, whose first king, Mes-anne-pada, began to rule shortly before 2500.[1] This city is known to Bible readers as the reputed birthplace of Abraham, and its First Dynasty is said to have reigned for 177 years. From this period date the Royal Tombs of Ur, whose discovery was one of the spectacular achievements of Near Eastern archeology in its golden age of the 1920's. The tombs display great artistic skill and fine workmanship as well as wealth in gold and gems. Carvings found here and in contemporary buildings elsewhere give delightful and informative pictures of the life of the time.

There can be no doubt that the Royal Tombs date from the period of the First Dynasty of Ur. A seal bearing the name of Mes-anne-pada's wife was found in their ruins, and there is a written record, made much later, of a temple built by that king. A temple at nearby Ubaid, built in the same general style as the tombs, bears the inscription: "A-anne-pada, king of Ur, son of Mes-anne-pada, king of Ur, has built a temple for the goddess Nin-khursag." In one inscription Mes-anne-pada calls himself "*lugal* of Kish," a city more than one hundred miles away. Probably he means no more than that he had

---

[1] All reckonings of Sumerian and Akkadian chronology are based on Hammurabi of Babylon, the last important king of the early period. Dates ranging over a period of five hundred years have been suggested for this king. The evidence for them is of three sorts: archeological, which gives sequences but no exact years; king lists, which seem to enable a scholar to compute a date by dead reckoning but which are deceptive because they often list contemporary dynasties as ruling one after another; and astronomical, especially eclipses and risings of the planet Venus, which were recorded in Hammurabi's time. Recent evidence favors a date at the end of the eighteenth century B.C. for Hammurabi, which is much later than those previously suggested. Sidney Smith has lately proved (*Alalakh and Chronology*, 1940) that Hammurabi ruled over Syria after the withdrawal of the Egyptian kings of the 12th dynasty, which occurred shortly after 1800. Astronomical evidence has enabled other scholars to fix his date, with what seems high certainty, at 1728–1686. Other dates are computed from these by using the king lists.

forced the king of that ancient city to acknowledge some sort of subserviency for a moment. Another inscription tells us that A-anne-
pada restored a building at Nippur, a city almost as far from Ur. The
dynasty of Mes-anne-pada must therefore have controlled a rather
wide territory though it did not rule all Babylonia.

Lugal-zaggisi of Uruk and Sargon of Agade

Cities and dynasties thus engaged in countless wars against each
other for hegemony, until a certain Lugal-zaggisi (about 2289–64),
once *patesi* of Umma and later *lugal* of Uruk, made himself master
of the greater part of Babylonia. He conquered many cities, and apparently he destroyed Lagash completely. A lament for the city written at the time has survived, as has a tablet which invokes a goddess
and implores her to "cause Lugal-zaggisi to bear this wickedness on
his shoulders." At the same time the king was heralding his benefactions to other cities, notably Ur, Uruk, and Nippur. His grandilo-
quent inscriptions declare that he had been invested by the great
god Enlil with "dominion of the world . . . from the rising to the
setting sun," and he boasted of conquests from "the Lower Sea [the
Persian Gulf] across the Tigris and Euphrates to the Upper Sea [the
Mediterranean]." We may doubt whether he actually ruled this vast
territory, but it is not improbable that his raids reached out in many
directions. We know that at this time Sumerian culture was spreading far beyond the confines of Sumer and Akkad, its influence appearing strongly at Nineveh to the north, and apparently Sumerian
traders even reached Syria and Asia Minor. The king's raids undoubtedly followed the routes known to these early traders, but we
must remain in doubt as to his ultimate purposes. Was he acting as
the chief capitalist of Babylonia, fighting for new trade routes and
defending old ones, or was he a military adventurer—perhaps merely
a freebooter? His own answer, which he piously passed down to pos-
terity, claimed that he acted simply as the servant of the god Enlil.

Nevertheless, Enlil seems to have been dissatisfied with these
spectacular services, for he presently transferred his favor to the
Semite, Sargon of Agade (2277–21), who defeated and captured

Lugal-zaggisi about 2264. Semites had long been filtering into Babylonia. As they came in small groups they readily absorbed Sumerian culture, and there apparently was little racial antipathy between the two peoples. Sargon was therefore able to champion both Semites and Sumerians against the ruthless militarism of Lugal-zaggisi.

Myths and legends soon clustered about this remarkable man, many of them doubtless arising in his own lifetime—for it seems safe to assume that if men are ever going to tell legends about a hero they will begin doing so before his death. The stories told how Sargon, the son of an obscure mother and an unknown father, was floated down the river by his mother in a basket of reeds (like Moses, Cyrus, and several other famous Orientals) and was rescued by a gardener. It was said that he later became cupbearer to the king of Kish. Whatever his origin may have been, Sargon became king about 2277 and ruled at Agade, a city which he built and where he founded a dynasty. All Akkad took its name from this city. Sargon apparently started his career as a champion of gods and men against the aggression of Lugal-zaggisi, but he soon surpassed his enemy in all directions. In the course of a reign of fifty-six years, he subjugated all Mesopotamia, led raids against Elam to the east, and advanced to Syria and possibly even to Cyprus in the west. In his last days he too was faced by revolts at home, and it seems that he was murdered by his own troops.

Sargon was succeeded by his two sons, and later by his grandson, Naram-Sin (about 2197–60), who momentarily restored to Babylonia the unity and glory achieved by Sargon. His conquests covered more territory than his grandfather's, and he proudly called himself "king of the four quarters of the earth." But eventually he too was overthrown, and the ensuing anarchy caused one ancient chronicler to exclaim, "Who was king? Who was not king?" Constant wars so weakened Babylonia that barbarians from the northeast, called Gutians, were able to swarm over the land. For ninety years their tyranny and misgovernment prevailed until at last, about 2060, a king of Uruk drove them out. His triumph did not long endure, however, and with the defeat of Uruk, rule passed to the Third Dynasty of Ur.

The Third Dynasty of Ur and Hammurabi of Babylon

The establishment of the Third Dynasty of Ur (now dated from about 2053 to 1944) ushered in a revival which brought Sumerian culture to its highest development. After a duration of slightly more than a century, however, this regime was superseded by two mutually hostile dynasties, followed by a Semitic dynasty whose sixth king was the famous Hammurabi (1728–1686). Regarding this great man we are exceptionally well-informed. In his day most of Babylonia was again united under one king, whose power reached far beyond the frontiers established by Sargon and Naram-Sin. All Syria fell under Babylonian rule. Since the collapse of the Third Dynasty of Ur, this region had been held by the Egyptian kings, but Hammurabi restored Babylonian political and cultural hegemony, and the Syrians, who of course were Semites distantly related to those of Babylonia, now adopted much Babylonian culture, including cuneiform writing, mythology, and law. This cultural influence continued for many centuries after the passing of Babylonian political power in Syria.

Babylonia reached her highest glory in the days of Hammurabi, but with him her day of glory came to an end. His successor ruled for thirty-seven troubled years. In 1677 Babylonia was invaded by the Kassites, a warlike race of mountaineers from the east, and three years later they effected a permanent division of Hammurabi's empire. The Kassites took the eastern part; the kings of Babylon retained the western and central parts; and the southern part went to a new dynasty sometimes called the Second Dynasty of Babylon or the "Sea-Land" dynasty. These three dynasties ruled in their respective spheres for almost a century and a half, until the Hittites raided Babylon from Asia Minor about 1595. The raiders withdrew after punishing the city for aiding one of their enemies in Syria, but Babylon was so weakened that she and the Sea-Land kingdom both fell before renewed Kassite attacks. The Kassites then ruled all Babylonia for upward of four centuries. Their rule was a period of almost utter darkness.

	A	B	C	D	E
	Original pictograph	Pictograph in position of later cuneiform	Early Babylonian	Assyrian	Original or derived meaning
1					bird
2					fish
3					donkey
4					ox
5					sun day
6					grain
7					orchard
8					to plow to till
9					boomerang to throw to throw down
10					to stand to go

● Diagram showing pictorial origin of ten cuneiform signs. (From *J. H. Breasted, Ancient Times.*)

Cuneiform Writing

The Sumerians invented the form of writing that we call "cunei-form." Like all primitive writing, it was at first pictographic: men tried to represent things or ideas by means of pictures. Sometimes the pictures were carved on wood or stone, but usually the Sume-rians drew them on soft clay which was later dried or baked. Soon they learned to make marks with the three-cornered end of a reed stylus which, when pressed lightly into soft clay as shown in Plate 3, left wedge-shaped marks—"wedge" in Latin is *cuneus*, whence our "cuneiform." At first scribes outlined pictures as best they could with the straight lines of these wedges, but later the figures became so schematic and standardized that they retained only slight resem-blance to the things pictured. Each symbol, or "ideogram," repre-sented one word. With such marks the scribes easily suggested nouns naming concrete things, but they found it more difficult to represent verbs, and it was impossible under this system to picture abstract nouns or proper names.

The next step in the history of writing came when men began as-sociating ideograms with sounds rather than with the things they pictured. By putting together symbols representing different sounds, it was possible to represent the word for an abstract idea or to build up a complicated proper name. Certain ideograms then lost their original pictographic meanings and stood only for sounds. The Sume-rian language contained many one-syllable words for things that could easily be drawn, which greatly aided the scribes in writing complicated words. By Early Dynastic times they had learned to write every word in the language with combinations of about four hundred ideograms (word symbols) and about one hundred purely syllabic signs (sound symbols).

In due time the Semites began to write their Akkadian language with the same Sumerian characters. Disregarding the original picto-graphic meaning of the ideogram, they simplified the symbol beyond all recognition as a picture and reduced the number of characters. Nevertheless, a certain number of symbols were retained with their original ideographic meaning. Other peoples later adapted these same characters to fit their own languages, simplifying them and reducing their number still further, until in the sixth century B.C. the Persians learned to write their Indo-European language with only forty-one cuneiform characters.[2]

Although the clay tablets on which the Sumerians wrote were nearly always rectangular in shape, they varied in size: small ones were perhaps two by three inches, others were six by eight inches, and some were even larger. The writing ran in lines from left to right, as in our books. Legal documents, contracts, and the like were written on these clay tablets, often being authenticated by a seal stamped at the bottom while the clay was still wet. Sometimes a simple stamp was pressed into the clay, but more commonly a cylinder seal was used. Such a seal consisted of a cylindrical piece of stone an inch or more in length and about half an inch in diameter. Its sides were elaborately carved with a scene from mythology or social life. When the cylinder was rolled across the soft clay, it left an impression of this scene on the tablet, thus serving as a sort of signature (see Plate 4). Often a layer of moist clay was wrapped about the tablet and sealed, thus forming an envelope that could easily be broken off but could not be replaced without the seal.

Clay tablets were eminently satisfactory for short documents— contracts, orders, receipts, brief records, charms, curses, and the like —but not much could be written on one tablet. In case more space were required, prisms of clay were sometimes used. These prisms might be a foot or more in height and eight or ten inches in diam-

---

[2] See note on the Decipherment of Cuneiform, p. 94.

• Note for Plate 3.   Lofty towers, such as the one reconstructed in the upper picture, were very common in Babylonia from ancient times. At the top of this ziggurat was a temple to Marduk, the chief god of Babylon. Structures such as this presumably suggested the Biblical story of the "Tower of Babel" (Genesis 11:1–9), by which men hoped to climb into heaven. Perhaps the long flight of steps by which the priests ascended to the temple suggested the story of Jacob's dream (Genesis 28:10–15) in which he saw steps going up to heaven with angels ascending and descending on them.

The lower photograph shows an ancient cuneiform tablet and stylus, held in the correct position for writing. (*Photos, Oriental Institute.*)

Model of a Ziggurat

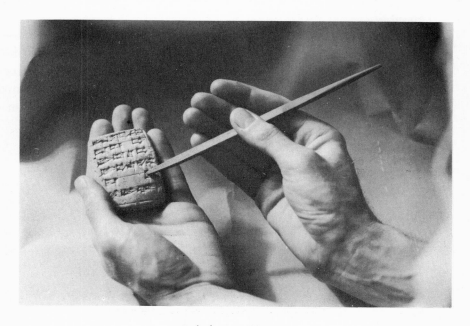

Babylonian Writing

Plate 3

Hammurabi's Code

Babylonian Cylinder Seal

Plate 4

eter, thus providing six or eight large spaces for writing. While such prisms were more satisfactory than a number of separate tablets, they were expensive and apt to break, and all their surfaces could contain no more than is printed on five or six small pages in a modern book.

Sumerian Numbers and Measures

The Sumerians invented a peculiar numerical system whose influence may be observed throughout antiquity and even today. At first they counted on their fingers, like all primitive peoples, and therefore they made ten the basis of their numerical system. Unlike other peoples, however, they did not continue the decimal system by making one hundred their next fundamental unit and one thousand the next after that. Instead they multiplied ten by six, making sixty the next unit. Sixty was then multiplied by ten, giving six hundred as the third unit; this was multiplied by six, making thirty-six hundred the fourth; and so on with alternating multiplications by six and ten.

Although the Sumerian method of writing numbers was complicated, addition and subtraction caused them no great difficulty. The multiplication table for small numbers could be committed to memory, as with us, but for the multiplication of large numbers and for division, they depended on written tables. They also knew how to write and how to deal with certain sorts of fractions. The Sumerians

---

• Note for Plate 4.   The upper photograph shows the carving at the top of the famous stone on which the Law Code of Hammurabi was inscribed. Here we see Hammurabi receiving the Code from the hands of the sun god Shamash. The scene is reminiscent of the Biblical story of how Moses received the Ten Commandments from the hands of Yahweh on Mount Sinai (Exodus 31:18). This carving was made about 1700 B.C., at least three centuries before the earliest date assigned to Moses.

Cylinder seals are small cylinders of stone, about an inch long and half an inch in diameter, with the sides carved to leave an impression when rolled over soft clay. The lower photograph shows such an impression, a picture of a Babylonian plow and drill. Note that the writing on each side is identical, showing that the seal has been rolled through one complete revolution. (*Photos, Oriental Institute.*)

were much interested in solving numerical problems, and they invented an elementary form of algebra, though they made little progress in geometry. The Semites had once used a straight decimal system in counting, even as we do today, but when they took over Sumerian writing they also adopted the Sumerian numbers and retained the sexagesimal system for academic and scientific matters. In fact, to this day we use it for our sixty minutes and sixty seconds.

The Sumerians followed a lunar calendar, starting a new month with each new moon. For short periods, months could be counted as of thirty days each, but twelve lunar months, amounting to twelve complete lunations (cycles of the moon), filled only 354 days. To make this lunar year coincide with the solar year of about 365 days, an extra month was added every three or four years. The month was subdivided into four weeks, with each day named after one of the heavenly bodies (the same ones we use today), but since the weeks were regulated by the phases of the moon, they occasionally contained eight days rather than seven. Day and night were divided into six periods apiece, each equal to two hours of our time. Standard weights and measures, with numerous units of length, area, and capacity, were also invented by the Sumerians. The standard *mina*, made up of sixty *shekels*, was slightly more than our pound, and sixty *minas* made one *talent*.

Sumerian Religion

The most conspicuous physical feature of a Sumerian city was its ziggurat—a steep pyramidal mound, artificially built of bricks and earth, upon which rested a temple reached by a long flight of steps (see Plate 4). The temple was considered the residence of the god, with whose portraits and statues it was decorated, and whose altar it contained. It has been suggested that the Sumerians built their temples on such lofty bases because, before entering the flat plain of Babylonia, they had dwelt in a mountainous country where they grew accustomed to worshiping their gods on mountain tops. At any rate, the Biblical writer undoubtedly had such a ziggurat in mind when he wrote about the Tower of Babel, which men built in the hope of climbing into heaven; and to the same source we may trace the story of Jacob's dream of a ladder (or steps) reaching to heaven with "angels of God ascending and descending on it."

The temple was a civic center as well as a residence for the god. We have already seen something of the part played by its priests in the economic and political life of the city, and on important festivals the temple was the scene of ceremonies and rituals which were as much patriotic as they were religious. Fortunately we are able to form some idea of what these ceremonies were like. Ancient sculptures show processions; the words of prayers and hymns have been preserved on clay tablets; and the importance of music in the ritual is shown by the large number of musicians and singers mentioned in lists of the temple staff. The elaborate ceremonies were primarily of a religious nature, to be sure, but it is not easy to separate religion and patriotism in a theocratic state, and the rituals often commemorated military victories or other secular events. They must have been very impressive, and the cult of the gods undoubtedly raised the morale of the citizens and stimulated civic patriotism.

The gods worshiped in these temples were at first purely local spirits whose appearance and character were believed to resemble those of idealized men. They were as independent of one another as were the cities which worshiped them. Even if two cities happened to use the same name for their god, the two deities were quite distinct entities with different attributes, powers, rituals, and myths. When the cities came into closer contact with each other, men began to speculate about the relationships of their respective deities. Sometimes they claimed to recognize the same deity in different forms, but more often they preferred to work out alleged relationships between the various gods. The gods were assigned places in a large pantheon, and an elaborate mythology was constructed to explain their relationships to each other. Thus Anu, a sky god worshiped especially at Uruk, came to be recognized as the greatest of the gods. His close rival for supremacy was Enlil of Nippur, often associated with storms. In later times, during the rule of the Babylonian dynasty, the Babylonian god Marduk achieved the highest place. A fourth of the great gods, Enki of Eridu, was considered a son of the sky god Anu, and was associated with water. The gods all had their wives and children, their divine friends and foes, and their followers with whose aid they ruled heaven and earth. No definitive and universally accepted arrangement of the pantheon could be made, however, for the prestige and power of the various deities rose and fell with the fortunes of the cities that worshiped them. Nonetheless, the major outlines of a system appeared in which the social organization of the gods vaguely reflected that of their worshipers upon earth.

Ishtar and Tammuz

These major gods—the patron deities of the great cities—were supplemented by others of less political importance who were perhaps closer to the lives and hearts of their worshipers. Many of these lesser deities were forms of the old Earth Mother who had long been worshiped under different names at different places. Perhaps the most famous of the ancient fertility goddesses was Innini, whose cult at Uruk dated back to very early times. The Semites later identified Innini with one of their goddesses named Ishtar, whose fame and worship spread throughout Syria and Palestine. The Syrians knew her as Astarte, the Old Testament writers called her Ashtaroth, and centuries later the Jews still preserved her name in the form Esther. Ishtar's importance throughout Babylonia made her the principal rival of Antu, the wife of Anu, king of the gods. Her character as a fertility goddess was shown by her ability to grant her worshipers crops or lambs or children; but from early times the Babylonians made a distinction, later perpetuated by Plato, between the earthly and the heavenly Ishtar. The earthly Ishtar looked after reproduction and sex, especially in its cruder manifestations, and sometimes her temples were simply brothels. The other Ishtar was heavenly, both literally and figuratively. She was identified with the brightest of the planets (our Venus) and she was worshiped as the idealized mother. She was often pictured with a babe in her arms, and she came to be regarded as a sort of mother to the whole human race, listening willingly to men's troubles and sorrows and alleviating them as best she could. One careful student of the prayers and hymns addressed to her, many of which have been preserved, called this heavenly Ishtar the *mater dolorosa* of the Babylonians.

Closely associated with the cult of Ishtar was that of Tammuz. While this deity was variously reported to be the son, the brother, or the lover of Innini or Ishtar, his name (from the old Sumerian form, *damu-zi*, "faithful son") indicates that at first he was considered the son of Mother Earth. Tammuz was associated with grain and flowers, perhaps with vegetation generally, and the hymns have much to say about his benefactions to man and beast. He has been called the Sumerian "Good Shepherd." The myth tells of his death and descent into the nether world, where the sorrowing Ishtar found him after a long search and whence she finally rescued him. In some versions of the myth, Ishtar makes the hazardous journey in search of Tammuz because of her love for humanity, which was perishing because of his absence and the consequent failure of vegetation; other versions explain her grief merely by the loss of a lover.

This myth of a dying and rising savior god became the basis of an elaborate cult. In this part of the world vegetation dies down from summer heat, not from winter cold, and everywhere the midsummer month, when the ceremonies took place, was named Tammuz. Worshipers mourned then for the dead Tammuz, accompanying their wailings with fasting and other ascetic practices. A few days later their sorrow was turned to joy as they celebrated his resurrection, which had saved humanity. This cult was a simple and early form of the observance of Passion Week followed by Easter Sunday.

The worship of such gods and goddesses apparently had spread throughout the Near East in neolithic times. Though our earliest evidence comes from Sumeria, we also know that at a very early date Tammuz and Astarte were worshiped in Syria, notably at Gebal (Byblus), and many centuries later, about 600 B.C., the prophet Ezekiel was scandalized to see women at the north gate of the temple in Jerusalem "weeping for Tammuz." Similar rites reached Egypt in equally ancient times as the worship of Isis and Osiris. In Greece they were performed at Eleusis and explained by the myth of Demeter and Persephone, which closely paralleled that of Ishtar and Tammuz. At a still later date the myth and cult of Tammuz was to reach Greece again under another name. It was customary for the Sumerians and their successors to address the god as "My Lord Tammuz," which in Semitic languages became *Adoni Tammuz*. The Greeks of historic times learned of this cult, probably through Byblus and Cyprus. Mistaking the title for a name, they called the god "Adonis." Since Astarte had by this time been identified with Aphrodite, and later with Venus, the old myth underwent a metamorphosis and has reached us through Ovid and Shakespeare as the story of Venus and Adonis.

Many Sumerians believed that Tammuz was more than the god who brought back life and vegetation to a dying earth: he also conferred immortality upon the men and women who worshiped him. Belief in immortality had an ancient origin in Babylonia, for the builders of the Royal Tombs of the First Dynasty at Ur certainly looked forward to a future life. Cattle, servants, and even wives were murdered and placed in the tomb with the dead man in order that he might enjoy himself properly in the next world. Such ideas and practices go back to paleolithic times. The cult of Ishtar and Tammuz strengthened this belief in immortality and did much to refine it. Throughout the Near East, wherever the old neolithic cult of Mother Earth was found, men saw an analogy between the seed which dies, is buried, and rises from the dead, and the fate of men who die and are buried, presumably to rise again. The resurrection of Tammuz was therefore taken as foreshadowing the immortality which he conferred upon his worshipers. It must be added, however, that this hope of immortality was shared by only a small fraction of the population. About all that most people looked forward to, or hoped for, were health and prosperity, sons, and a long life here on earth.

Astral Deities and Familiar Spirits

Other aspects of the Babylonian religion originated in the worship of the heavenly bodies. Among the great gods were two named Sin and Shamash, whose names are the Semitic words for "moon" and "sun." Just as the old Sumerian gods later received Semitic names, so these astral deities were given Sumerian as well as Semitic names. Even so, however, they never achieved a high place in the Sumerian pantheon. This neglect suggests that in general the great gods—patrons of cities—and the agricultural gods were of Sumerian origin, while the astral deities had been brought by the Semites from the desert. Presently the Sumerian and Semitic pantheons were amalgamated to a considerable extent, and the old Sumerian deities came to be identified with planets, stars, or constellations. Thus Ishtar was identified with the planet we call Venus, and Tammuz with the bright star Sirius. Perhaps this last identification may be explained by the fact that Sirius, after two months of invisibility, rose at dawn just at the time of year when Tammuz was supposed to rise from the dead.

Religious veneration of the heavenly bodies led to careful observations of the stars and their movements. Temples contained observatories of a sort, where information about the heavenly bodies was carefully collected and recorded. By the time of Hammurabi, planets were clearly distinguished from stars, the major planets and more prominent stars had been named, and many constellations had been traced. In many cases the names then given to the constellations were those which they still bear today. Star-worship thus made the Babylonians the world's first astronomers.

In addition to these great gods there were countless minor deities, good and bad—some of them the spirits of heroes of olden time, others demons. One order, called *igigi,* were heavenly spirits under the rule of Anu. Others, known as the *anunnaki,* were earth spirits ruled by Enlil. Their number was almost infinite, though the round number 3600 was sometimes given, just as it was sometimes said that there were sixty of the great gods. The ordinary man in Babylonia felt himself much closer to these spirits than to the great and powerful gods of his city. Every man had his familiar spirit who looked after his interests and who was, in a manner of speaking, his patron saint. This guardian spirit was the object of his private devotions. He worshiped it, talked to it, even wrote letters to it. Like other people of simple mentality, he used all his arts of persuasion upon this familiar spirit—wheedling it, coaxing it, threatening it, bargaining with it, bribing it. In return for these attentions, the spirit might do him minor favors and help him in his daily enterprises. Or, if the favor required were too great for the spirit to accomplish by his sole power, he might intercede for his friend with one of the great gods who, under ordinary circumstances, could hardly be expected to give much of a hearing to a mere mortal, especially if he were one of humble station in life.

Omens and Magic

Since the gods ruled the world and, more specifically, the cities of Babylonia, it was necessary for them to have some means of communicating their desires and plans to their lieutenants upon earth. This they did through signs of one sort or another. The Babylonians devoted great care to observing and interpreting these omens, of which they kept full records. Men recognized many ways in which the gods might communicate their will or indicate the future. When the *patesi* of a city wished to learn the divine orders, he might sleep in the temple: his dreams there, properly interpreted, would give him the desired information. Professional dream-interpreters studied the subject carefully and compiled books on the meanings of dreams. Another favorite method of determining the will of the gods was by observation of the liver of a sacrificed sheep. Anything unusual in its appearance was considered ominous. Clay models of livers have been found with lines dividing the surface into about fifty sections and with marks indicating what might be expected if an abnormality appeared in any particular section.

Their astral religion led the Babylonians to see special significance in the stars. The foundations of astrology, as we understand it today, were not laid until a century or two before Christ, but even in Sumerian times men thought they saw connections between the course of the heavenly bodies and that of human events. The moon was considered especially significant. They believed that its eclipses portended great happenings and, like some people today, they regarded certain of its phases as more propitious than others for various undertakings.

There were also inspired persons who spoke words supposedly

put into their mouths by the gods. Presumably here, as is usual in modern cases of glossolalia or "speaking with tongues," the prophet uttered only incomprehensible syllables believed to be the words of the god speaking through him. Someone else then interpreted the strange sounds, prefacing his interpretation with the words, "Thus saith the god." This manner of "prophesying" continued common in the Orient throughout antiquity.

Lastly, a few words must be said about the Babylonian conception and practice of magic, for these remained potent throughout ancient times. The magician, it must be borne in mind, was really an elementary sort of technician who was trying to harness the forces of nature for the benefit of himself or his clients. Usually he accepted the prevailing view of the universe and its forces, and in Babylonia this view was of religious origin. The magician sought out new ways of mastering spiritual forces of whose efficacy he had learned from the priests. Thus it was universally believed that sickness, or at any rate many kinds of sickness, could be caused by evil spirits or demons. The magician tried to cure the disease by casting out the demons, his favorite methods being imprecation and conjuring. The tablets have preserved hundreds of charms and incantations that were used against such demons. Matters of everyday life—such as plowing, planting, building a house, or casting metal—were accompanied by elaborate rigmaroles of which we can only say that they did no harm. While all primitive peoples behaved in this way, the Babylonians reduced their magic to a system more thoroughly than did most other peoples. Their system then won great fame far beyond the borders of Babylonia, and it remained in repute for many millenniums after the fall of Sumer and Akkad. Even in the days of the Roman Empire, magicians and astrologers of every sort were known as "Babylonians" or "Chaldeans."

Sumerian Literature

Cuneiform tablets have preserved to us a few samples of the literary works of the Sumerians, but they are samples only. As writing was a monopoly of the priests, the literature committed to writing was mainly of religious interest. There are indications, however, that the

Sumerians also had a secular literature which included songs, ballads, and stories. Moreover, the Babylonian practice of writing on clay tablets made it difficult to record long compositions. While we have a few poems that cover several large tablets, most of those that have been preserved fill only one tablet, and rarely does a Sumerian poem contain as much as one hundred short lines. It seems quite probable that Sumerians recited from memory longer epics, now lost because they were never written down. The majority of the famous poems have been preserved only in Semitic translations which go back at least to the time of Hammurabi. The translators edited, revised, and expanded the texts before them so frequently that it is now difficult or even impossible to decide which parts of a poem are Sumerian and which are Semitic interpolations. Scholars are usually of the opinion, however, that the greater part of the famous Babylonian stories and poems goes back to Sumerian originals.

The type of literature most copiously represented in our samples consists of prayers and hymns, composed in meters familiar to students of the Book of Psalms. Each line is broken into halves, the second paralleling or amplifying the thought of the first. The Sumerian hymns also remind us of the Psalter by their turns of expression and occasionally by their underlying ideas as well; sometimes they praise the gods, and sometimes they resemble the imprecatory or penitential psalms of the Old Testament. They are our principal source of information in tracing the progress of Sumerian religious and ethical ideas. Such poems as "The Descent of Ishtar into Hades" tell us much about Sumerian mythology, and some of the hymns contain passages of high poetic power and beauty.

Stories of Creation

When modern scholars first began to read the cuneiform tablets, somewhat after the middle of the nineteenth century, they were struck by the resemblance of Babylonian myths to the stories told in the first chapters of Genesis and to certain fables of Greek mythology. Particular attention should be given to the various Babylonian accounts of Creation, of which at least half a dozen have been preserved. They do not harmonize very well with one another, and there obviously was no standard story, universally accepted in all details. Yet a few general principles seem to underly them all. Creation is always pictured as the work of the gods, though only rarely is an indication given as to the exact way in which the gods created the world. It was not a veritable creation out of nothing, for the Sumerians seem never to have conceived of a time when nothing at all existed. Creation for the Sumerians was the establishment of order in chaos.

One version of the Creation story, coming from Eridu at what was then the head of the Persian Gulf, tells how everything was at first covered with water and how dry land presently rose above this water—just what the citizens of Eridu could see happening before their eyes in the Gulf. The gods then created plants and animals and men. Sometimes they created men first and other living things afterward, as in the second chapter of Genesis; sometimes the creation of man was their crowning achievement, as in the first chapter of Genesis. Usually it is said that the god made men out of clay—like pottery perhaps—which reminds us of the Biblical statement that Adam was formed "of the dust of the ground." Nearly all the stories attribute the creation of man to the gods' need for someone to worship them, to offer sacrifices to them, and to do the necessary work in their fields. From such stories as these, theologians easily deduced implications regarding the chief end of man that would explain and justify the actual lot of the peasants in the theocratic city-states of Babylonia. Sometimes the poems go on to tell how the gods—not men—built great irrigation systems, founded cities, and created the other works of civilization.

The most famous of these Creation stories is not primarily a story of creation at all but a hymn in praise of the mighty deeds of Marduk, the patron god of Babylon. It was sung or recited at a festival in his honor on the fourth day of the new year. This poem is almost a thousand lines in length and has been preserved on seven tablets, some of which are badly damaged. It opens with a statement that long before heaven and earth were "named," Tiamat and her husband Apsu—apparently old water-deities—brought forth the other gods. When some of these gods rose up and slew Apsu, Tiamat undertook to punish her rebellious progeny. The children, led by Ea, were helpless until Marduk championed their cause, killed Tiamat in battle, and cut her body in two. One half of it he made into heaven and the other half into earth. Marduk then fixed the stars and constellations in heaven, created men upon earth, and finally founded Babylon. The Greeks had a very similar myth about Cronus and Zeus.

The Creation passages come on the fifth tablet, most of which is so badly damaged as to be illegible, but the first and last parts of the story show a close parallelism with the first chapter of Genesis. The creation of the firmament and of the heavenly bodies at the beginning of the story and of man near its end, with a period of celebration and rest afterward, suggests that the other living creatures were created in the interim as in the Hebrew version. Very likely their origin was described in the broken middle section of the tablet. The Hebrew version declares that God made the light on the first day of creation, though the sun and moon were not created until the fourth day. Sunday School scholars have sometimes been puzzled about the source of this early light, and even about the meaning of "day" and "night" during the first three "days" of creation, before the sun and moon existed. The Babylonian version resolves the difficulty by pointing out that in this early period light emanated from the gods themselves, who were luminous—a rational enough explanation in an astral religion.

The poem as it now stands dates approximately from the time of Hammurabi, but parts of it are clearly of more ancient origin. The description of Marduk's great battle with Tiamat, for example, sounds as if originally written for the storm god Enlil. The poem remained popular for many centuries. About 250 B.C. a Babylonian priest named Berosus wrote a history of his country in Greek which contained parts of this epic; and a Greek philosopher named Damascius, who lived at Damascus about 500 A.D., summarized its genealogy of the gods. There can be little doubt that the Hebrews were familiar with this story early in the first millennium before Christ, and that their thinking was influenced by it.

Another literary work from Babylonia, preserved in four separate versions, is the story of Adapa, a priest of Eridu. Adapa had committed an offense for which he was called to account before the gods. In the course of his trial, it came out that Ea had already revealed the secrets of heaven to Adapa, and the gods were therefore persuaded to grant him immortality. When the bread and water of life were offered to him, Adapa feared poison, and by refusing them he lost this priceless boon. This story is slightly reminiscent of the Biblical story of the first man, Adam. The Babylonian story reminds us of Adam's offense, of Jehovah's concern because "the man is become as one of us, to know good and evil," and of Adam's failure (though not from fear of poison) to eat the fruit of the "tree of life." The story of Adapa is of interest for another reason as well. One of our four copies of the story is a tablet found in a collection unearthed at Tell el-Amarna in Egypt, with interlinear translations in ink which show that it had been used as a textbook by Egyptian students of the Akkadian language. The other tablets in this collection were letters sent to Egyptian kings from Palestine about 1400 B.C. The Adapa tablet thus shows how widely the Babylonian language and literature were studied for many centuries after Babylon ceased to be a political power of importance.

The Gilgamesh Epic

The longest of the Babylonian epics is that recounting the deeds of Gilgamesh, a mythical king of Uruk. It was written on twelve large tablets found at Nineveh, and it contained some three thousand lines, of which about half are still legible. Like other great epics such as the *Odyssey* and the *Aeneid*, this poem opens with an introduction telling the reader briefly of the vast range of its hero's wanderings and the magnitude of his struggles. Gilgamesh himself was said to be "two-thirds god, one-third man" (exactly how this strange proportion was achieved remains unexplained) and he had as his companion a wild man from the forest named Engidu. After various adventures, the wanderers met the goddess Ishtar, who fell in love with Gilgamesh. He reproached her with the misfortunes that had befallen her earlier lovers—including Tammuz—and repulsed her advances. She therefore sent a bull to gore him, but Engidu was killed instead.

Gilgamesh was thus brought face to face with death and immortality, and the remainder of the poem (the last four tablets) deals with his quest for eternal life. Hearing that one of his ancestors, Utnaphishtim, had escaped death, Gilgamesh hunted out the old man, who eventually told him of a marvelous plant growing at the bottom of the sea which would confer immortality upon anyone who ate of it. Gilgamesh dived into the sea and obtained the plant, with which he hoped to gain immortality for himself and his people at Uruk. Unfortunately it was stolen from him by a serpent. The last tablet of the twelve tells how the hero visited the lower world, found Engidu, and tried in vain to bring his friend back to the world of the living. As in similar visits made to the underworld by the heroes of the *Odyssey* and the *Aeneid,* Gilgamesh learned something of the fate of man after death, but the future he saw seemed rather dark and dismal. The author of this great poem obviously did not share the views of Ishtar's worshipers about blessedness hereafter.

The interest of scholars in the Gilgamesh epic was first aroused by the eleventh tablet, in which old Ut-naphishtim tells his descendant of a great flood he survived in his youth. The story so closely resembles that of the Biblical flood that Ut-naphishtim has sometimes been called "the Babylonian Noah." According to the story as he told it to Gilgamesh, the great gods decided to destroy mankind by means of a flood, but Ea warned Ut-naphishtim in time, ordering him to prepare the ship in which he saved his family, mechanics of every sort, and the birds and beasts of the field. After the storm was over, the hero sent out birds, as in the Biblical account. When they did not return, he knew that the waters had subsided and that he might safely open the doors of his ark. Like Noah in the later account, he then sacrificed to the gods, who in gratitude resolved never again to let loose such destruction upon the earth.

Several other accounts of the flood, some preserved on tablets dating from about 2000 B.C. and another told by Berosus, show the popularity of this legend in ancient Babylonia. Of the influence of the

Babylonian story upon the Hebrews there can be little doubt. In a hilly country like Palestine such a legend seems out of place; but the broad flat plains of Babylonia, which are covered with water every spring, form a natural basis for the story of a flood that supposedly covered the whole earth. In recent years a few archeologists have claimed to find evidence of a great flood in the ruins of various Babylonian cities and have argued that such a great flood—universal from the Babylonian point of view—actually took place. Unfortunately the levels which various archeologists mark as "diluvian" differ in age by many centuries. It seems best, therefore, to assume that Utnaphishtim's flood was merely an imaginative exaggeration of what occurred in Babylonia every year.

One other aspect of the flood story deserves brief mention. The Sumerians, like the Hebrews, believed that conditions before the flood were so idyllic that men then lived to amazing ages. The Biblical Methuselah, who is said to have lived for 969 years, has excited the youthful wonder and skepticism of many. Yet even Methuselah seems quite ephemeral when compared with the kings who ruled before the Sumerian flood. Their reigns lasted from 18,600 to 43,200 years, and the eight antediluvian kings together are supposed to have ruled a total of 241,200 years! After the flood, however, the figures taper off rapidly, as in the Old Testament, until they show Sumerians ruling no longer on the average than modern kings.

Sumerian King Lists

These various writings are of course mythological rather than historical, but in the time of the Third Dynasty of Ur (the twenty-first century) a serious historical work appeared. Perhaps the recent expulsion of the Gutians had aroused a new patriotic enthusiasm for all things Sumerian. At any rate, shortly thereafter someone conceived the idea of compiling a list of all the Sumerian kings from antediluvian times to his own day. After collecting materials from many cities, the chronicler arranged the kings in sequence according to his idea of how it should have been. Judging from conditions in his own day, or perhaps projecting his own patriotic aspirations into the past, this author believed that each king on his list had ruled all

Babylonia. This idea was of course erroneous, but it dominated his work. The historian arranged his kings in "dynasties," or groups from one city, which ruled one after another until the last member was conquered by a foreign city. A new dynasty then took over the rule of all Babylonia. The list of kings in a given city, who really ruled continuously, was therefore broken into several dynasties separated by long periods when a foreign dynasty supposedly was ruling the whole land. In this way the author managed to put the flood about 32,500 years before his own time. If we omit the fantastic reigns of the kings immediately after the flood (or even if we assign to them average reigns of twenty-five or thirty years), we find that the list still covers almost two thousand years. If, on the other hand, we recognize the fact that several dynasties ruled simultaneously, we find that the records are amazingly accurate for the five centuries before the author's own time. The unknown compiler of this king list was the first historian to undertake a large piece of historical research and reconstruction. His figures, properly criticized, form the basis of our present knowledge of Sumerian chronology.

The Code of Hammurabi

French archeologists working at Susa in the ancient Elam (part of modern Iran) discovered in 1901 a large black stone covered with cuneiform writing. Study soon showed that the stone had once been set up in Sippar, whence it presumably had been removed by an Elamite conqueror. Its inscription is the longest yet found in cuneiform—about eight thousand words—and it records a code of laws drawn up and published by the Babylonian king Hammurabi. As similar laws had prevailed in Babylonia for many centuries it seems probable that Hammurabi's work was chiefly codification. Even the idea of codification was not new, however, for a simpler code, of which twenty-five laws remain, had been drawn up under the Third Dynasty of Ur. Hammurabi and his lawyers did their work so well that his code superseded all others and more than a thousand years later men still studied "The Judgments of Righteousness which Hammurabi, the great King, set up." Though the king actually issued this code of laws, it theoretically was of divine origin, like the Mosaic

Law of the Hebrews and most other early law codes. A bas-relief at the head of the stone shows Hammurabi standing in a suppliant attitude before the god Shamash, who is seated on a mountain handing to Hammurabi the stone inscribed with the laws (see Plate 4). This scene reminds us strongly of the Hebrew story of Moses receiving the Ten Commandments on two tables of stone from the hands of God on Mount Sinai. Moreover, many of the laws in Hammurabi's code closely resemble parts of the Mosaic Law as recorded in the Old Testament.

From other sources we know something of Sumerian law in earlier times. We have brief texts of a few laws issued by earlier kings; we have judicial decisions that came to have the force of law; and we have countless contracts and other official documents drawn up in accordance with the law. These various bits of information show us that while the Code of Hammurabi was fundamentally Sumerian in origin, it also contained much that was not to be found in Sumerian law. Some innovations may have been due to Semitic influence, but the majority came in consequence of centuries of social and political development. The old Sumerian theocracy had been weakened and the state had gradually been secularized. The king's officials now exercised more power than the temple officials, and they performed many of the duties formerly assigned to priests. But the long prologue and conclusion, as well as the bas-relief decorating the stone, show how earnestly Hammurabi invoked divine sanctions, and how he desired to have his subjects regard him as an agent of the gods. He boasted at length of his own conquests and of his benefactions to humanity, but he sought to make it clear that he had been chosen specifically by the gods to perform all these services.

The Code of Hammurabi shows Babylonian society divided into three distinct classes: an aristocracy called the *amelu;* a middle class called the *mushkinu;* and the slaves. In earlier times, only the first and last had been mentioned, and it is not at all clear how the middle class came into being. Certainly this class was not a racial group, for men with Sumerian and Semitic names are found in all three classes. Probably it was not military or the result of the rise of the kings. The suggestion that its members were descended from emancipated slaves is only a theory. Nevertheless it is clear that the *mush-kinu* held a subordinate position in Babylonian society. The word used to designate them was taken into Arabic and thence into French, where it has become *mesquin,* "mean" or "paltry."

The *amelu* filled the high offices of church and state and commanded the army. Some of them held large tracts of land from the king or the priests, working these estates with slaves or hired labor, while others engaged in business on a large or small scale. The *mush-kinu* were mostly shopkeepers, small merchants, artisans, or laborers. Slaves made up a considerable part of the population. Most of them had been captured in war, though many had been bought from foreign slave-traders, and of course others were born in slavery. While the slave was the property of his owner, the law alleviated his unfortunate position in several ways. He could own property, engage in business, or borrow money in his own name. Under certain circumstances he might protest being sold; and a slave of either sex might marry a free person and become the parent of free children. Finally, slaves might even buy their freedom, for which purpose the priests often lent them money.

In early times the administration of justice had rested in the hands of the *patesi* and the temple officials, but a generation or two before Hammurabi, new courts appeared that were presided over by king's judges. Thereafter there were two sets of higher courts, in addition to the minor local courts for trivial matters. Appeal was allowed from the lower to the higher courts and ultimately to the king himself. Trial by ordeal was permitted in certain cases, such as sorcery, but usually the case was settled by a judge or arbitrator after he had heard witnesses and arguments from each side.

As we read the Code of Hammurabi today we are impressed by the severity of the sentences imposed, and comparison with earlier practice indicates that punishments under the Code were more severe than those formerly inflicted. A wide range of crimes carried the death penalty: murder, brigandage, stealing (especially from a temple), several sex offenses, gross neglect of duty, and false accusation of a capital crime are among those mentioned. In the case of lesser crimes, Babylonian law often followed the principle of "an eye for an eye, a tooth for a tooth." Other offenders were punished by mutilations or flogging, and in many cases fines were imposed. It is worth noting that the punishment for injuring an aristocrat was higher than that for injuring one of the *mushkinu*, but that a guilty aristocrat was sometimes punished more severely than a common man who had done the same thing.

The greater part of the Code is devoted to civil law. Long passages deal with family matters. Every legal marriage in Babylonia was based on a definite contract drawn up beforehand. In most cases the bridegroom gave the bride's father a gift (a relic of the ancient practice of bride purchase) and the father gave his daughter a dowry which remained her own property and eventually passed to her children, or to her father's heirs if she died childless. A woman might be divorced, especially if she were barren, or she might give her husband a concubine—as Sarah did to Abraham in the Old Testament—but a woman who broke her marriage vow might be punished by drowning. There were elaborate laws regarding the ownership of land, sharecropping, leases, and mortgages. Other laws regulated wages, either for labor or for professional services—notably those of a physician. All important business contracts had to be recorded in writing, and the Code dealt at length with breach of contract and business malpractice. The laws show that business was conducted on the basis of barter, and that wages and rents were paid in kind. There was a growing tendency to regard grain as a universal medium of exchange. For large transactions, stipulated weights of the precious metals were used, though money was not invented until many centuries later.

The Sumerian Legacy

Babylonian civilization ranks as one of the world's first high civilizations, and it endured for almost a thousand years. Its creators made discoveries that have since been imitated or adopted by all civilized peoples. Some of their fundamental creations were of a simple material sort, such as weapons or tools; others were techniques in agriculture, commerce, or building; still others were scientific or theological ideas. The early Sumerians worked out a political system whereby large populations lived under a theocracy. This system was perpetuated among the Hebrews and other oriental peoples, and it has been the indirect model of countless experiments in the course of European history. Sumerian religious speculations sometimes reached lofty heights, and parts of their mythology, as preserved by the Hebrews, were accepted as sober history by most educated Christians until a century or two ago. Their sense of justice was embodied in a famous and influential code of laws. Even after their original creative impulse had spent itself, and they had been conquered by the barbarian Kassites, their civilization continued to dominate southwestern Asia. It was carried from Babylonia to Syria and Asia Minor. It reached Palestine and was known in Egypt, and traces of its influence have been found far to the East in the recently discovered ancient civilization of the Indus Valley. Even the ancient Greeks cannot be understood without constant reference to the Sumerians and their heirs. In the whole ancient and modern history of Europe there is no great people that is not indebted for something to these early Sumerians.

Note

The Decipherment of Cuneiform

Cuneiform writing was used in the Near East for almost three thousand years before knowledge of it passed away, shortly before the birth of Christ. The decipherment of these forgotten languages was one of the spectacular achievements of nineteenth-century scholarship. The English soldier, diplomat, and scholar, Sir Henry Rawlinson (1810–1895), rightly takes first place among the great decipherers, but the work was advanced by many persons. The first step was taken when the German-Danish traveler, Karsten Niebuhr, published copies of inscriptions he had seen at Persepolis in 1765. Scholars turned their attention to the matter and easily saw that the inscriptions were in three separate languages, later identified as Old Persian, Elamite, and Assyrian. A German high-school teacher of the classics, Georg Grotefend (1775–1853), guessed at the opening formula, recognized three proper names, and identified several letters in one of the Persian inscriptions (1802); but he knew nothing of oriental languages and could proceed no further. Young Rawlinson went to India in 1827 and six years later was sent to Persia to reorganize the Shah's army. After learning modern Persian thoroughly, he became interested in cuneiform inscriptions, and in 1845 he copied the famous Behistun inscription set up by Darius I about 518 B.C. (see Plate 16). This, too, was a trilingual inscription in the three languages mentioned above. Rawlinson was by this time familiar with the work of other scholars, largely through correspondence, and he succeeded in making a translation of the whole Persian inscription, which he published in 1846.

Meantime others had been attempting the same task, especially a brilliant Irishman named Edward Hincks (1792–1866)—a clergyman of the Anglican church in Ireland—who, being a better philologist than Rawlinson, was able to perfect his translations. The second column of the Behistun inscription, in Elamite, caused less trouble and was translated by Edward Norris from Rawlinson's copy in 1852. Meantime the third column, in Assyrian, had been translated and published by Rawlinson in 1851. These achievements attracted wide attention among scholars, but they also aroused skepticism until the decipherers were put to a test. A newly discovered Assyrian inscription was lithographed in 1854 and copies were sent to various scholars with requests for translations. Rawlinson, Hincks, and others accepted the challenge, and their translations turned out to be so similar that there could be no reasonable doubt of their essential accuracy. Later, other ancient languages written in cuneiform were deciphered, the series being completed in 1916 when the Czech scholar Hrozny learned to read a Hittite language written in cuneiform characters. The decipherment of Sumerian caused more controversy than any other, but the matter was virtually settled before the end of the nineteenth century. Even today, however, Sumerian cannot be read with the same certainty as Assyrian, and occasional texts still cause trouble. An interesting account of the labors of nineteenth-century explorers, excavators, and decipherers in the Near East may be read in R. W. Rogers, *A History of Babylonia and Assyria* (vol. I, 1900); see also Seton Lloyd, *Foundations in the Dust, a Story of Mesopotamian Exploration* (1947).

IV Early Egyptian Dynasties

NEOLITHIC CIVILIZATION BEGAN IN EGYPT A LITTLE EARLIER than in Mesopotamia, and it developed there along rather different lines. The reasons for these divergencies were partly geographic. The first Mesopotamian villages were located in Assyria, where the soil was not fertile enough to support a large population or a high civilization. Not until many centuries later, after the Babylonian swamps had become fertile plains, could city civilization arise in Mesopotamia. The rich valley and Delta of the Nile, on the other hand, were ready for intensive cultivation at a much earlier date. Civilization thus got an earlier start in Egypt than in Babylonia.

At the same time nature provided the Egyptians bountifully with much that was denied to the Babylonians. Stone, plentiful in Egypt, was absent in Babylonia. Neither country produced good lumber, though the Egyptians were better situated than the Babylonians to import it from the Syrian Lebanons. Copper was available to Egyptians in the nearby Sinai Peninsula; and the papyrus plants that flourished in the Nile provided a writing material far superior to the clay tablets of Babylonia. However, these very blessings tended to make Egypt self-centered. Foreign trade was less necessary and less important, and cities were neither so large nor so independent as in Babylonia. Egyptian civilization was therefore less varied than Mesopotamian.

Moreover, Egypt was better prepared than Babylonia by geography for political unity. The broad Babylonian plains, at first broken by swamps, were conducive to the rise of many cities, which constantly made war upon one another. Only after centuries of conflict was a precarious unity achieved. On the other hand, the Nile bound Egypt together. Its narrow valley provided little space to maneuver armies, and whoever controlled the river could easily dominate its banks. Egypt therefore was ruled by a single government almost a thousand years earlier than Babylonia. Furthermore, the uninhabitable deserts on each side of Egypt kept off invaders, while Babylonia suffered grievously from Elamites and other enemies. Throughout much of the early third millennium, Egypt enjoyed the blessings of unity and peace, while Babylonia was suffering from civil wars and foreign invasions.

Secular Spirit in Egypt

The early unification of Egypt was an important factor in turning the subsequent history of the country in directions different from those taken in Babylonia. While in each case unity was achieved by military men, these conquerors arrived late in Babylonia and never gained a complete supremacy. At first the Babylonian cities were ruled by priests whose activities touched every aspect of life in the city-state, and Babylonian kings were never able to throw off this theocratic heritage. The Egyptian kings suffered no such handicap. Even before the unification of Egypt, these kings had begun performing most of the secular functions performed by the priests in Babylonia. They became the great capitalists; they owned the land; they constructed and maintained the irrigation systems; and they or their agents discovered and operated foreign mines and conducted foreign trade. It was to them rather than to the priests that men turned for aid and relief in times of distress. In Egypt it was the kings who dispensed justice. They built up great bureaucracies (comparable to the priesthoods of Babylonia) with whose aid they governed the country, and even the priests who presided over Egyptian temples might be considered members of this bureaucracy.

The Egyptian king was also head of the religious organization of the country. Even in predynastic times he proclaimed himself a god, and religion became a state affair, managed for the advantage of the government. As individuals and as a people, the Egyptians were as religious as other nations, and they developed elaborate systems of ritual and mythology; yet in early times their priests exercised no great political power. Egyptian religion was therefore very different from Babylonian. Many of the differences sprang from the fact that the people believed the Egyptian kings to be gods, while Babylonian kings, except in one or two instances, claimed to be merely the favorite servants of the gods. Egypt was essentially a secular state from the first, but Babylonia remained largely a theocracy throughout its history.

The secular spirit of the Egyptians reached far beyond matters of government. The triumphs of architecture in Babylonia were temples; those of early Egypt were royal tombs and pyramids. The scholars and scientists of Babylonia were priests while those of Egypt were servants of the king. Babylonian law theoretically came from the gods and was administered by their agents; that of Egypt came from the king and was administered by his officials. Babylonian ethical thought was largely religious and supposedly of divine inspiration; Egyptian ethics was secular, and ethical writings were popularly attributed to the kings of Egypt or their ministers. While the Babylonians never ceased speculating in theological terms, the Egyptian mind was always secular and worldly. Such fundamental differences as these came in large part from early divergencies in the governments of the two countries. Ultimately they may be traced to geographical conditions that encouraged different classes of society in the two states.

Prehistoric Union of Egypt

Early in the fourth millennium Egypt was divided into provinces or "nomes," and we have already seen how these nomes were gradually united into two kingdoms known as Upper and Lower Egypt. There were twenty-two such nomes in Upper Egypt and twenty in Lower Egypt. Upper Egypt, or the Nile Valley, had its capital at Ombos, while that of Lower Egypt was at Behdet in the western part of the Nile Delta. The dividing line between the two states ran a little south of ancient Memphis or modern Cairo. This division rested upon fundamental geographical differences, and the distinction between Upper and Lower Egypt has remained powerful throughout history. Lower Egypt—the Delta—reached an advanced stage of civilization earlier than the South, but we know less about it, principally because its ancient sites are buried under many feet of mud while those in the Nile Valley farther south are easily accessible.

About 3300 B.C. a temporary union of all Egypt was effected. There is no written record of so early a union—the Egyptians had forgotten it before they began writing history—but secondary evidence has convinced scholars that for a time the kings of Lower Egypt ruled the whole country from a new capital at the head of the Delta, a city called Heliopolis ("City of the Sun") by the Greeks and known as On in the Old Testament. Some of the evidence for this first union is archeological and a little vague, based on the expansion of northern (Gerzean) culture into Upper Egypt. Further proof is seen in ancient myths describing a mighty struggle between Set, the god of Ombos in Upper Egypt, and Horus, once the god of Behdet and later worshiped throughout Lower Egypt. The victory of Horus seems to reflect a conquest by the kings of Lower Egypt. We also know that there was much colonization of Upper Egypt from the North at this time, and it seems probable that the new cities—often bearing northern names and worshiping northern gods, especially Horus—were military posts set up by the kings of Heliopolis to hold their new provinces in order.

The new rulers did much to improve the country by building great irrigation systems, introducing new crops, and undertaking other civilizing works. Nevertheless their united kingdom soon collapsed. Egypt again fell into two parts, with a new capital of Upper Egypt at Hieraconpolis, far north of Ombos, while that of Lower Egypt was withdrawn to Buto in the northern part of the Delta. Perhaps lesser kingdoms lay between these two large ones for a while. It is important to note, however, that the kings of both parts of Egypt now identified themselves with the god Horus, and that the name of the new capital of Upper Egypt (Hieraconpolis) means "Falcon-burg," the falcon being a symbol of Horus. These facts suggest that the new rulers of Upper Egypt had come from the North as a military aristocracy during the Heliopolitan period. The collapse of the union was presumably accompanied by much fighting, for Lower Egypt was so weakened that new invaders forced their way into the Delta from Asia. The fall of the united kingdom, about 3200, coincided with the end of Gerzean culture and the rise of Semainean.

The Old Kingdom

Several generations passed before political unity could be restored to Egypt. Much of this time was spent in wars, in which Upper Egypt usually had the advantage, and of which archeologists have discovered a few records. Thus the "Narmer palette," a carved piece of slate bearing that king's name, was found at Hieraconpolis and dates from the late predynastic period. This carving shows a king, wearing the white crown of Upper Egypt, who holds and clubs a defeated enemy; Horus's falcon holds a rope running through the nose of a man near whom is a sign for the Delta; and at the bottom of the palette two men are shown running for their lives. On the other side of the slate, Narmer, now wearing the red crown of Lower Egypt, inspects a battlefield covered with dead Northerners. These carvings obviously record a victory of Narmer over the men of Lower Egypt. Further evidence of his victories is to be seen in a mace head, once owned by Narmer, whose carving boasts of the enormous booty he took from his enemies.

A second union of all Egypt was effected about 3100 B.C.[1] Its author was Aha-meni, whom the Greeks called Menes and whom they listed as the first king of the First Dynasty. Menes was a native of Upper Egypt, where his tomb, together with those of his successors from the first two dynasties, has been found at Abydos. After uniting Egypt, Menes built the city of Memphis, which lies a little north of the frontier separating Upper from Lower Egypt and only about twenty miles from Heliopolis, and he made this new city the capital of his united Egypt.

---

[1] Dates in Egyptian history before 2000 B.C. can only be tentative round numbers; those for the Middle Kingdom and Empire are established within a decade; and not until 663 B.C. is absolute accuracy possible. In general this book follows the Borchardt-Edgerton chronology (1935–37), as given in George Steindorff and Keith C. Seele, *When Egypt Ruled the East* (1942). It puts the Old Kingdom slightly later than do Breasted and Meyer, but thereafter it differs very little from these earlier chronologies.

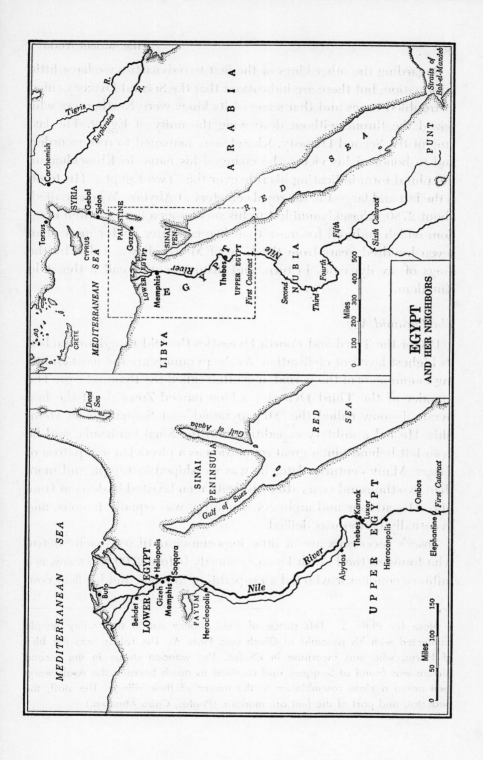

EGYPT
AND HER NEIGHBORS

Regarding the other kings of the first two dynasties we have little information, but there are indications that the Second Dynasty ruled in troubled times and that some of its kings were Northerners who seized the throne without destroying the unity of Egypt. The last king of the Second Dynasty, Khasekhem, managed to restore order, and in honor of his victory he changed his name to Khasekhemui, the plural form indicating his rule over the "Two Egypts." His tomb is the last and largest in the royal cemetery at Abydos. When he died, about 2780, Khasekhemui left to his successors a firmly united kingdom which endured for more than five centuries, or for more than seven hundred years from the time of Menes. It was ruled by the kings of six dynasties in turn, and historians now call it the "Old Kingdom."

The Pyramid Age

Under the Third and Fourth Dynasties the Old Kingdom reached its highest levels of civilization. As the pyramids are the most enduring monuments of the period, it is often called the Pyramid Age. The founder of the Third Dynasty, a king named Zoser, built the first pyramid—now called the "step pyramid"—at Saqqara near Memphis. He led a military expedition into the Sinai Peninsula, and he even left behind him a great reputation as a physician and patron of letters. Many centuries later he was worshiped in Egypt, and more than two thousand years after his death men boasted of descent from him. His advisor and architect, Imhotep, was equally famous, and eventually he too was deified.

Zoser's successors are of little importance until we reach Snefru, who founded the Fourth Dynasty shortly before 2700. He too was a military conqueror who led an expedition to Sinai, and his fleet con-

---

• Note for Plate 5. This statue of Khafre once sat in the valley temple connected with his pyramid at Gizeh (see Plate 6). The falcon was the bird of Horus, who was incarnate in Khafre. The wooden statue in the second picture was found at Saqqara and received its name because the Arab workmen noted a close resemblance to the mayor of their village. The staff, the pedestal, and part of the feet are modern. (*Photos, Cairo Museum.*)

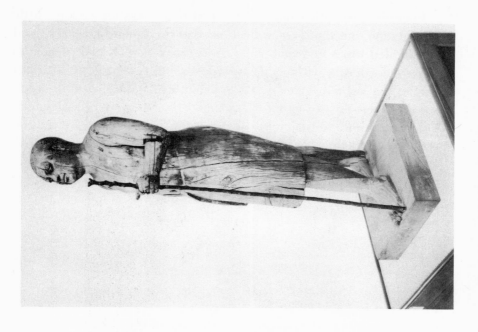

Khafre

The Sheik el Beled

Plate 5

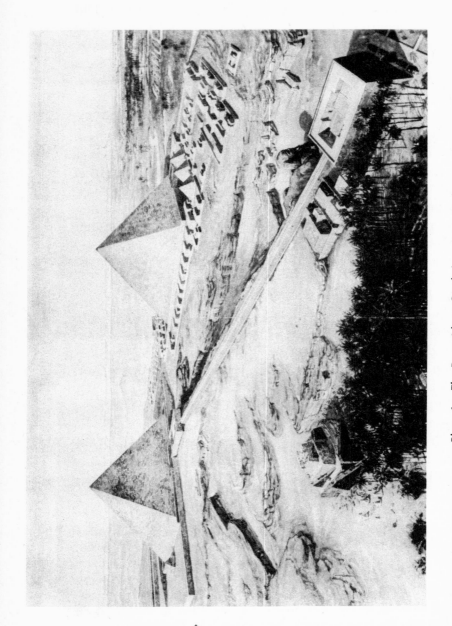

Plate 6.   The Pyramids at Gizeh (reconstruction)

tained several vessels over 170 feet long. He built a large pyramid at Medum near Saqqara. The most famous of all the rulers of the Old Kingdom were Snefru's son and grandson, Khufu and Khafre, who built the two large pyramids at Gizeh, north of Memphis (the ones usually visited today by tourists: see Plate 6). The last of the great pyramid-builders was Menkaure, probably a brother of Khafre, who ruled a little after 2600. His pyramid, the third of the group at Gizeh, is only about half the size of the others.

The pyramids were primarily tombs for the kings, designed to preserve their bodies throughout eternity. Modern writers suggest that building these enormous monuments served political purposes as well. During the four months in the year when the Nile was in flood, Egyptian peasants could not work in their fields. As they had nothing to do and presumably were always short of rations, they probably grumbled, and they might eventually become a menace to the peace of the land. Building the pyramids may thus have been a form of unemployment relief—the most colossal piece of boondoggling known to history. All this, however, is only conjecture. From the religious point of view the pyramids were failures, for they did not protect the bodies of the kings. From the political point of view they were no more successful in the long run, for they bankrupted the kingdom and caused their builders' names to be reviled in Egypt many centuries later. Yet the pyramids have stood through the ages as evidence of Egypt's vast wealth and of the administrative skill shown in organizing workmen and providing materials.

About 450 B.C., more than two thousand years after the building of the pyramids, the Greek historian Herodotus visited Egypt and was told about them by priests whom he met. He records, among other

---

• Note for Plate 6. The pyramid to the left is that of Khafre, with its valley temple in the lower right hand corner of the picture and the sphinx nearby. The pyramid was connected with the temple by a long causeway, up which the blocks of stone were dragged from rafts in the river when the pyramid was under construction. The second pyramid is that of Khufu, with three small pyramids for members of the royal family and mastabas, or tombs, for his nobles surrounding the large pyramid. (*Reconstruction by Hoelscher.*)

things, that Khufu and Khafre (whom he calls Cheops and Chefren) were impious and wicked kings who oppressed the people and insulted heaven by closing the temples, but that the next king brought back justice to men and gods. This priestly legend contained an element of truth. The unpopularity of Khufu after his death is evidenced by the fact that he is the only king of the period none of whose statues has been preserved. They presumably were destroyed in an effort to wipe out the very memory of a hated king. Moreover, the Fourth Dynasty was soon overthrown by a revolution in which religion played a conspicuous part. The kings of the first four dynasties had usually been worshipers of Horus, though a few professed loyalty to Re: thus Khufu's sons were named Khaf-re and Menkau-re. The kings of the Fifth Dynasty, on the other hand, addressed their worship exclusively to this new god. Nearly all were named after him; each officially proclaimed himself a "Son of Re"; and this epithet remained part of the Egyptian royal style thereafter. We have records of lavish donations by these kings to their god, and for the first time in Egyptian history, priests began to benefit from the attentions of the government. It is no wonder, therefore, that their remote successors informed Herodotus that the new dynasty had "restored justice."

In most ways life under the Fifth Dynasty went on much as before. Egypt apparently was no longer quite so prosperous, but her creative powers and her artistic skill were not impaired. The Fifth Dynasty ruled for almost a century and a half, until about 2400, when it was succeeded by the Sixth Dynasty, which lasted for another hundred and fifty years. Conditions improved slightly under the new dynasty, and some of its kings were able and energetic men; but the great days were over, and with the fall of the Sixth Dynasty, about 2250, the Old Kingdom came to an end.

The Egyptian State

At the head of the Kingdom of Upper and Lower Egypt, which thus endured for upward of seven centuries, stood the divine king. The progress of his status, and much of Egypt's early political history, may be learned from the development of the royal title. At the end of the Old Kingdom the king officially bore five titles, after each of which came a special name that he assumed upon entering office. First came the Horus name, doubtless dating from the first union of Egypt, which indicated that the ruler was Horus Incarnate. Second came a name identifying him with the two goddesses of Hieraconpolis and Buto, and presumably dating from the days of the divided kingdom. Next came the "Golden Horus" name, perhaps in commemoration of the military victories leading up to the second union. The fourth title proclaimed its owner "King of Upper and Lower Egypt," the former being represented in the hieroglyphics by sedge or marshgrass, the latter by a bee. Lastly, the king was styled "Son of Re." Several other royal epithets were added by subsequent kings, but these five titles remained standard. The king was thus constantly reminded that he was the ruler of a dual monarchy and that he must never slight either half of his kingdom. In the earliest times he wore the white crown of the South and the red crown of the North alternately, but later the two were united into one crown which retained the distinctive features of each. The royal palace had two doors, one for each kingdom, and the name most commonly used for the king was the fourth listed above, which emphasized the dual nature of the kingdom.

In the early period the king exercised personal leadership, both in the field with the army and at home in the direction of all sorts of civil activities. In later times, especially under the Fifth and Sixth Dynasties, the work of government was done largely by others. The king was surrounded by an elaborate court, filled with nobles enjoying sinecure posts, and he became difficult of access. The palace, and later the court, were called the *Per-'o*, or "Great House." About 1400 B.C. this term began to be used for the king himself, being roughly equivalent to "His Majesty"; and five hundred years later it became a royal title, prefixed to the name of the king. In this latter sense it has come down to us, through the Bible, in the form "Pharaoh."

The king always had many assistants, the chief of whom was called his vizier or prime minister. Under the later dynasties of the Old Kingdom, the vizier became more powerful than the king himself. We have seen the importance of Imhotep, the famous and to some extent legendary vizier of Zoser. Ptahhotep, who served several kings of the Fifth Dynasty, was equally famous and important. These viziers and their assistants lived with the king in the "Great House" at Memphis.

Other high officials, called "nomarchs," were sent out to govern the nomes. Some were put in charge of offices which survived from the days when Upper and Lower Egypt were separate kingdoms, while others looked after the local government of the nomes. The nomarchs, who were appointed by the king or his vizier, policed their districts, collected the taxes, dispensed justice, kept up the irrigation systems, and served as high priests for the local gods. They were chosen from the aristocracy of Egypt, and often were relatives of the king. Eventually they became so powerful that the rise and fall of kings and dynasties meant little to them. Thus we have the record of one nobleman who was born under Menkaure, married a daughter of the last king of the Fourth Dynasty, and served and was honored by the first three kings of the Fifth Dynasty. As there was always danger that ambitious nobles might rebel against the king, the central government encouraged its officials to spy upon one another, and presumably it was to distract the nobles from ambitious dreams that the kings (*i.e.*, the governments) of the Fifth and Sixth Dynasties gave them sinecures and entertained them lavishly at court. The "Sons of the Sun" found themselves in much the same predicament as Louis XIV, the "Sun King" of France, who likewise gathered his nobles about him at Versailles in order to keep their minds off politics and rebellion.

The lower ranks of the bureaucracy were filled with the "scribes." Every ambitious and intelligent boy who could afford it wished to become a scribe, which was the sure route to wealth and power. The Egyptian bureaucracy, like so many others, eventually became so huge that it was unmanageable and oppressive, and it was a severe drain upon the treasury of Egypt. The bankruptcy which was the principal cause of the decline of the Old Kingdom is sometimes attributed to the conspicuous waste of building the pyramids. More likely the wealth of Egypt was dissipated by the idle nobility and especially by the ubiquitous army of scribes.

The kingdom of Menes stretched from the First Cataract of the Nile north to the Mediterranean. South of the Cataract lay Nubia, whence invaders sometimes launched minor raids into Egypt. The early kings therefore sought to protect their frontiers by occupying territories further south, but there were no attempts at extensive conquest. The Sinai Peninsula attracted the attention of Egyptian kings by its copper and precious stones. Kings of the First and Second Dynasties left inscriptions there recording their achievements, and under the Fourth Dynasty the peninsula became virtually a colony of Egypt. The Fourth Dynasty sent trading expeditions, which were royal enterprises, down the Red Sea to Eritrea and Somaliland, then called Punt. From early times, perhaps even from the days of the Second Dynasty, Egyptian traders had sailed the Mediterranean to Syria and occasionally to Crete. Under the Fourth Dynasty, large quantities of lumber were imported from Syria. Egyptian armies sometimes invaded Palestine, and one record seems to indicate that in the early days of the Sixth Dynasty an expeditionary force crossed the Mediterranean and landed north of Mount Carmel in Phoenicia. Egyptian culture was thus carried far beyond the valley of the Nile, but only in Sinai did the Egyptians of the Old Kingdom attempt permanent settlement or conquest.

The Middle Kingdom

The fall of the Sixth Dynasty, about 2250, was followed by two centuries of whose history little is known. Its collapse brought a sweeping social revolution, traces of which still remain. The tombs of the old kings were violated and robbed, their statues were broken and overthrown, their temples were destroyed. The revolution was directed primarily against the corrupt and oppressive bureaucrats employed by the central authority, as is shown by an inscription set up by one of the new rulers who boasted, "I rescued my city from the terrors of the royal house."

The revolts brought great suffering to Egypt, and especially to the nobles and scribes who had prospered under the old regime. These men expressed their grievances in a literature of which several fragments remain. An author named Ipuwer, whose sympathies were obviously with the old upper classes, describes the lawlessness of the times, and then complains that craftsmen no longer work and that traders no longer bring back the products of distant lands. "The land turns round as does a potter's wheel," laments Ipuwer, which is his way of saying that the old aristocracy has been overthrown and their place taken by worthless or criminal upstarts. "He who had no yoke of oxen is now possessor of a herd. . . . He who could never build a boat for himself is now an owner of ships, while he who once owned them now merely looks upon them, for they are no longer his. . . . He who was once a robber is now a wealthy lord. . . . Laughter has perished and is no longer made; it is now mourning which pervades the land, mingled with wailing."

Other writers drew equally distressing pictures of the times, and some also dreamed of better days to come. Following the secularist tradition of Egypt, these prophets looked forward to a good king (not to a god) who would lift them out of their present misfortunes. We have several descriptions of what a good king would be like, and of how he would re-establish justice throughout the land; and there are prophecies of his coming. Literary fragments sometimes show a spirit that is truly messianic, their authors sharing the view expressed by the Hebrew prophet, many centuries later, who exclaimed, "Zion shall be redeemed by justice."

In spite of these bitter complaints and soaring expectations, we must not assume that all Egypt had fallen into barbarism. There still were oases of culture where knowledge of the old times was preserved, where art was appreciated and literature and learning were cultivated, and where something of the old spirit survived. In fact, these very laments and expectations show that the old Egypt had not been utterly forgotten and that men confidently expected its return.

Thebes Under the Twelfth Dynasty

Thebes, which eventually became the capital of Egypt, was only a minor place in the days of the Old Kingdom; and its god Amon, later the most powerful god in the Egyptian pantheon, was then an unimportant deity. After the fall of the Sixth Dynasty, Nubian tribesmen overran the whole Theban area, and they seem to have left descendants in high places, for the statues of later kings sometimes show Negroid features. While the Seventh and Eighth Dynasties were ruling Lower Egypt from Memphis, and the Ninth and Tenth Dynasties were dominating Middle Egypt from Heracleopolis, the rulers at Thebes gradually built up their power in the South and started their city on its way to glory. Seven Theban kings are listed as the Eleventh Dynasty, which ruled from about 2150 to 2000. The first of them took Abydos from the king at Heracleopolis; half a century later another led his armies into Lower Egypt; and still others made expeditions overland to the Red Sea and south into Nubia. During this period, however, local nomarchs accorded only slight recognition to the kings at Thebes, under whom they supposedly held office, and Egypt was not a strongly united country.

When the last king of the dynasty died, his vizier Amenemhet seized the throne and founded the Twelfth Dynasty. An able and vigorous leader, Amenemhet presented himself to the public as a man likely to realize the messianic dreams of the prophets. He completed the reuniting of Egypt, and his dynasty presided over a second brilliant period in that country's history, now known as the Middle Kingdom (2000–1780). Nevertheless, the nomarchs retained great freedom, for which reason writers sometimes call this period the Feudal Age.

As the new kings presently found that their capital must have a more central location than Thebes, they established their residence in the neighborhood of Memphis. Here they built pyramids for themselves, but their continued interest in Thebes is shown by their constructions at nearby Luxor and Karnak. These kings also devoted great attention to developing the district, now known as the Fayum, surrounding a lake which empties into the Nile from the west about fifty miles above Memphis. Important irrigation works were built there, and thousands of acres were brought under cultivation. Unity and reform brought economic prosperity to Egypt, whose leaders now revived and developed the cultural traditions of their ancestors, but this period of glory quickly passed. After the fall of the dynasty, Upper and Lower Egypt again fell apart, with the Thirteenth Dynasty ruling in the South and the Fourteenth in the Delta. Some fifty years later new invaders, called the Hyksos, swept over Egypt from Asia and brought a period of darkness comparable to that brought to Babylonia by the Kassites.

The kings of the Twelfth Dynasty had resumed the expansionist policies of the later dynasties of the Old Kingdom. Amenemhet carried on extensive campaigns against Nubia, and about a century later that region was conquered and fortified as far south as the Second Cataract of the Nile, which is approximately at the frontier between modern Egypt and the Sudan. The copper mines of the Sinai Peninsula, which had been idle since the Sixth Dynasty, were again put in operation. Egyptian ships again visited Crete. And, above all, the Egyptians developed close connections with Syria and Palestine. Recent findings by archeologists show that the political and cultural influence of Egypt reached far beyond the coastal cities into the interior. From about 2000 to 1800 Gebal and other Syrian cities were Egyptian dependencies. This empire had collapsed before the end of the Twelfth Dynasty, however, and we have already seen that Syria then fell to Hammurabi of Babylon.

Egyptian Writing

Like all other early scripts, Egyptian writing[2] began as picture writing, but unlike Sumerian and Babylonian, it retained its pictographic features to the end. In predynastic times, long before true writing was discovered, pictures with meaning were carved on stone. Writing was greatly amplified under the first two dynasties, and before the time of the Fourth Dynasty the standard Egyptian manner of writing was established. The language continued to develop, however, reaching its classic form in the days of the Middle Kingdom, and it became a dead language a few centuries before the birth of Christ. Until that time an educated Egyptian could have read inscriptions dating from the days of the Fourth Dynasty without much trouble, though the style of carving—the handwriting, so to speak—and many turns of expression would doubtless have seemed as queer and old-fashioned to him as Chaucer's English does to us. He would

---

[2] See note on Champollion and Egyptian Hieroglyphics, p. 128.

probably have found earlier inscriptions as difficult as we find Anglo-Saxon.

The earliest Egyptian writing was carved on stone, but in early dynastic times men discovered a new and cheap writing material. In the shallow water along the banks of the Nile grew the papyrus plants—familiar to Bible readers as the bulrushes among which the infant Moses was hidden—and from their stalks a kind of paper could be made. Our word "paper" is derived from the Greek word for papyrus. As these plants grew only in Egypt, that country retained a monopoly upon the manufacture of paper throughout antiquity. In damp climates this papyrus-paper disintegrated after a few years or decades, but in dry Egypt it endured longer, and if buried in dry sand it would last indefinitely. In our own day thousands of pieces of papyrus with writing on them have been rescued from the sands of Egypt. The great majority of our papyri date from the Greek and Roman periods of Egyptian history (about three centuries before and after Christ), but many go back to the Eighteenth Dynasty, others to the Middle Kingdom, and a few to the Old Kingdom.

Though all the characters used in formal Egyptian writing were carefully drawn pictures of objects, they fell into two classes, some of which indicated the meaning of the word, others its pronunciation. Each word was therefore written twice. The earlier forms, now called "determinatives," were pictures of what the word indicated. If this could not be drawn, a sort of charade was made up to give the reader an idea of the word, and Egyptian scribes showed amazing skill at thinking up picture-word combinations. Such writing was not adequate, however, and a supplementary system of writing had to be invented. Scribes arbitrarily selected the signs for short words beginning with various sounds and used them to represent that sound only, thus creating a sort of alphabet. Other signs stood for sounds which we represent with two or even three letters. All these signs represented only consonantal sounds, serving as a sort of shorthand to remind the reader of the pronunciation of a word, and they were written before the determinatives. Since vowels were never written in Egyptian, we cannot know exactly how words were pronounced, though sometimes it is possible to guess at the pronunciation from

Coptic (a late form of Egyptian, written in Greek characters in the early centuries of the Christian era) or from ancient transliterations into Greek or Assyrian characters.[3] A modern font of Egyptian type must include characters for twenty-four simple letters (plus variant forms of several), dozens of compound letters, and hundreds or even thousands of determinatives.

This formal style of writing is called *hieroglyphic*, from two Greek words meaning "sacred" and "carvings." In Greek times it was used mostly for inscriptions, though it was also used on papyrus for religious and other especially formal texts. Other writing on papyrus was done, even in early times, in a simplified script known as *hieratic* ("priestly"), in which the old drawings were so hurriedly copied as to be scarcely recognizable. In Greek times a third and even simpler script, known as *demotic* ("popular"), was used for the popular dialect of the day.

The Egyptian method of writing numbers was much simpler than the Babylonian. As their numerical system was purely decimal, they escaped many of the difficulties that beset the Babylonians with their sexagesimal system. A separate mark was invented for each power of ten, up to one million, and this mark was repeated as often as necessary: the system therefore resembled our Roman numerals, except for the Roman intermediate figures V, L, and D. In each system a single straight mark indicated one, but the higher figures were far more complicated in Egyptian than in Roman. Like the Babylonians—and all the other peoples of antiquity too, for that matter—the Egyptians had great trouble with fractions, and especially with those whose numerator was greater than one. Before the Fourth Dynasty they had learned to perform simple operations of arithmetic

---

[3] In scholarly books today no vowels are indicated in transliterations from the Egyptian, but in more popular works, words are made pronounceable by the arbitrary insertion of *e*'s. Because of our ignorance of Egyptian vowels, I follow the practice of most modern writers in calling Egyptian cities by the Greek names given them after the conquest of Alexander the Great (332 B.C.). No such names were ever used by the ancient Egyptians, of course, but it is easier to say and remember Memphis than *Mn-nfr*, Heliopolis than *'Iwn.w*, Hieraconpolis than *Nhn*. The names of men and gods cause greater trouble. Scholars usually follow or Anglicize the Greek transliterations (especially those of Manetho, who wrote about 275 B.C.) if such are available and fairly close to the Egyptian consonants; otherwise they arbitrarily make up pronunciations, though these modern writers are not always consistent with each other or even with themselves.

and to compute various areas and volumes; but they never went beyond this point. The building of the pyramids must have raised many mathematical problems, but the Egyptians managed to solve them by methods which seem very cumbersome to us.

Science and Literature

The Egyptians invented a calendar that was far superior to the lunar one used in Babylonia. Early in the Pyramid Age, they began using a year of 365 days, which they divided into three seasons, known respectively as "Flood," "Seedtime," and "Harvest." Each season was subdivided into four months of thirty days each, making a total of 360 days, and five extra days were added at the end of the year. This Egyptian year was based primarily upon the floods of the Nile which fertilized Egypt annually and upon which her life depended. Of course the Nile does not begin rising, or reach its flood, on exactly the same day each year. As it happens, however, the star Sirius—the brightest of the fixed stars, called Sothis by the Egyptians—is visible on the eastern horizon for a few moments before dawn toward the middle of July, just when the Nile begins to rise. The Egyptians noticed this fact and associated the beginning of the new year both with the rising of the Nile and with the "heliacal" rising of Sirius. By studying records of the risings of Sirius, they arrived at a year of 365 days. This is called a "Sothic" year. Of course this calendar was not quite accurate for a year really is about eleven minutes short of 365¼ days. Modern calendars therefore make a correction by inserting leap years.

The Egyptians used no leap years, which caused their New Year's Day to slip back one day every four years, until it presently showed no connection with Sirius or the rising of the Nile. During a period of a little less than 1460 years (365×4), a whole year would be lost and New Year's Day would momentarily return to its correct position in the actual year. This period of 1460 years is called a "Sothic cycle." Since we have evidence that the Sothic New Year's Day coincided with the rising of the star in 139 A.D., modern writers can compute the error in the Sothic calendar at any given date. The ancient Egyptians occasionally recorded the day on which the heliacal rising of

Sirius actually took place in a certain year of a certain king's reign: from this information it is possible to calculate the years of the reign in question according to the Christian Era. Much of our Egyptian chronology for the period of the Middle Kingdom and after is based on such calculations, and since our detailed chronology of the whole Near East in the second and third millenniums was calculated from this Egyptian chronology, it all rests ultimately upon these Sothic dates.[4]

In medicine, too, the Egyptians made greater progress than the Babylonians. In each country medicine started as magic, but while it never really emerged from that stage in Babylonia, the Egyptians made a start toward scientific medicine. Their superiority was doubtless the result in part of the practice of mummification. The Babylonians considered it sacrilegious to dissect a corpse, and therefore had only the vaguest ideas regarding the internal organs. The Egyptians, on the other hand, made careful studies of anatomy, even noting the general similarity of the organs of men and beasts. Several lengthy medical papyri, dating from the Middle Kingdom or later, include large sections of what is probably a medical treatise written under the Old Kingdom. Some passages in these books give directions for treating wounds and fractures, others give prescriptions for curing diseases. Modern physicians say that some of the drugs prescribed may have been helpful, but that others were worthless or perhaps even harmful. Interspersed with these more or less scientific

---

[4] The German historian Eduard Meyer (see note, p. 473) counted back three Sothic cycles and declared that this calendar must have been introduced on July 19, 4241 B.C. (according to the Julian or "Old Style" calendar). He proudly labeled this "the earliest fixed date in history." Meyer also argued that even at this early time the Egyptians must also have created a more accurate calendar of 365¼ days. Many scholars were not convinced by Meyer's reasoning, but his prestige was so high that no one cared to contradict him openly—though some writers quietly corrected minor errors in his astronomy and arithmetic. Recent criticism has been more open. In 1938 a German exile living in the United States, O. Neugebaur, published an important article, "Die Bedeutungslosigkeit der 'Sothisperiode' für die älteste ägyptische Chronologie," in the *Acta Orientalia*, XVII (1938), pp. 169–195. Here he proved to the satisfaction of most authorities that much of Meyer's reasoning was false, and suggested that the Egyptian calendar of 365 days was based primarily on observations of the Nile, not of the stars, and that only later did it become associated with Sirius. A calendar of 365¼ days was unknown until after Alexander the Great. Moreover, it was shown that Meyer introduced one whole Sothic cycle too many into his computations. The suggestion that the Egyptian calendar was invented about 2780 (in the days of Zoser) is much more plausible than Meyer's fantastic date 4241 B.C.

passages, however, we find countless formulas and spells which are pure magic. Such charms may sometimes have been a part of the physician's "bedside manner," used to inspire the patient's confidence, but there can be no doubt that he believed in their efficacy himself. The doctor was still essentially a magician, though experience had given him a little scientific knowledge.

Classical Egyptian Literature

Much of the literature of the Old and Middle Kingdoms was of a religious character, but their secular mentality and their possession of papyrus-paper enabled Egyptians to produce a more elaborate profane literature than the Babylonians; or at least, more extensive fragments of such literature have been preserved to us. Our fragments show that literature of a high order appeared under the Old Kingdom, and that the period between the Old and Middle Kingdoms was even more fruitful in literary works. The literature dating from the Middle Kingdom became classic in Egypt, and was imitated and made the subject of classroom instruction throughout the remainder of Egyptian history. Indeed, its influence reached far beyond the borders of Egypt and continued long after the last Pharaoh had passed from the scene.

The Babylonians undoubtedly told each other stories but, so far as we know, they never committed such trivialities to writing. Several Egyptian stories from an early period have been preserved, however, and as we read them we are struck by their resemblance to those in the *Arabian Nights*, compiled in Egypt more than three thousand years later. Thus the "Story of the Shipwrecked Sailor," dating from the Middle Kingdom, is highly reminiscent of "Sindbad the Sailor," not only in the marvelous adventures of its hero but even in details of its literary style. The "Story of Sinuhe," likewise dating from the Twelfth Dynasty, gives the adventures of an Egyptian in Palestine and Syria. Just as the authors of the *Arabian Nights* were fond of dating their tales in the reign of Harun al-Rashid, so the author of this romance dates it in the days of Amenemhet. A Middle Kingdom tale about magicians is located at the court of Khufu, and includes a prophecy of the coming of the Fifth Dynasty.

The Egyptians also collected books of proverbial wisdom. Fragments of several such collections have been preserved—partly perhaps because they were often used as copybooks in schools. Just as the Hebrews later attributed all their proverbial wisdom to their great king, Solomon, so the Egyptians assigned theirs to various kings or viziers. The most famous of these collections passed as the work of Ptahhotep, vizier to a king of the Fifth Dynasty. Another bears the name of Amenemhet. The advice given in these proverbs is of a very practical sort, addressed primarily to young men of the scribal class and telling them how to get ahead in the world. It is not very different from the admonitions contained in the Biblical "Proverbs." We have already seen that the dark period after the fall of the Old Kingdom produced pessimistic literature, such as the "Song of the Harper," whose burden was, "Eat, drink, and be merry, for tomorrow you shall die," and the "Dialogue of a Misanthrope with his Soul" on the desirability of death. There was also a literature of social criticism and utopian dreaming, notably the "Admonitions of Ipuwer."

Our inability to pronounce Egyptian words correctly makes it hard for us to appreciate Egyptian poetry, though its meters and parallelism of thought resemble those of Babylonian and Hebrew poetry. Egyptians apparently had no great epics comparable to the Gilgemish epic, but our fragments of their poetry include examples of the songs of workers, drinking songs, and especially love songs. Some of the latter remind us strongly of passages in the great love song of the Old Testament that is known as the "Song of Songs."

Egyptian Religion

The Greek historian Herodotus sarcastically remarked that the Egyptians were "the most religious of peoples," and proceeded to show that in his day their religion amounted to little more than the scrupulous observance of inane or ridiculous ceremonies and taboos. He made no effort to hide his contempt for the Egyptian gods and their worship. Herodotus, of course, knew Egypt only at a time when its old religion had given way to mere sacerdotalism and religiosity. In earlier times Egyptian religion would not have merited his sarcasm. Religious thought and expression in Egypt developed during the centuries from forms resembling those of the most primitive religions to others that compare favorably with the best that ancient paganism produced. We shall even have occasion to remark more than once upon the contributions of Egypt to Judaism and Christianity.

In predynastic times each Egyptian city had a special god as its patron and protector. These gods usually were pictured in the form of animals or other living beings. Thus Horus, the god of Behdet, took the form of a falcon; Anubis appeared as a jackal; and the god of Buto was a snake. In time these gods were brought into more human forms, and we find Anubis depicted as a man with a jackal's head or Horus as a man with the head of a falcon. If such combinations were not feasible, the god was pictured as accompanied by the animal or as wearing its symbol. The gods were likewise endowed with various other human qualities and characteristics, good and bad.

The god was often taken as a symbol of his city, and his power was in a sense the power of the city. If one city conquered another, for instance, its god was regarded as victorious over that of the defeated city. Thus for a while Set was supreme in Upper Egypt and Horus in the Delta. After the First Union of Egypt, Horus was everywhere regarded as the supreme god. The conquered gods did not cease to exist, however, any more than their cities did: they merely accepted the suzerainty of Horus and continued to look after local affairs. In addition to these city gods there were countless other spirits and supernatural beings, somewhat resembling the jinn and afreets in the *Arabian Nights,* who might be invoked, appeased, and cajoled, but who played no important part in the religion of Egypt.

Re and Osiris

The great god Re was a deity of quite a different sort. While his origin is unknown, it is clear that, unlike Horus, he had never been the local god of any Egyptian city. He first appeared in the Delta, and it seems not improbable that he was brought to Egypt by invaders from Asia, perhaps in the period after the collapse of the First

Union. His name became an Egyptian word for the sun, and his symbol was the obelisk, pointing to the sun. Since Re had no special connection with any single city, worshipers could easily present him as a universal god—or at least as a god of all Egypt, which in those days amounted to much the same thing for most Egyptians. There was a famous temple to Re at Heliopolis, with a large staff of priests, long before such institutions became common elsewhere. From this focal point the worship of Re was propagated to all Egypt.

In early dynastic times theologians, or mythographers, identified Re with Horus and Aton (the local god of Heliopolis), later with Amon of Thebes, and with various other gods of universal pretensions. Some of the gods with whom he was identified were city gods, others were personifications of nature. Mythologies were then elaborated to arrange the various gods in their places, with different systems handling the problem in different ways. One version pictured Geb (Earth) and his wife Nut (Sky) as the parents of Re (Sun), thus establishing a triad or trinity which remained popular throughout Egyptian history.

Mythographers at Heliopolis concocted a more ambitious theology about their god. Re was declared to be the first god, who brought forth—in a manner sometimes described as a sneeze—two gods named Shu and Tefnet (Air and Moisture). These two in turn gave birth to Geb and Nut, and finally Geb and Nut bore Osiris with his wife Isis, and Set with his wife Nephthys. The old trinity was thus replaced by an "ennead" or ninefold divinity. Other theologians, worshipers of the craftsman-god Ptah of Memphis, were dissatisfied with this glorification of Re and constructed still another myth in which they attributed everything to special creation by Ptah. For many centuries Egyptian thinkers continued to exercise their intellects upon this fundamental problem of whether the gods and the universe were begotten or made. When the kings of the Fifth Dynasty set themselves up as "Sons of Re" they inaugurated the practice of giving him lavish gifts, and established a state-supported priesthood to serve him. The Heliopolitan theology became official and the begotten gods prevailed throughout Egypt.

Osiris was a god of a different type. Myths told how he was murdered by his enemy Set, who cut his body to pieces and threw them into the Nile, and how Osiris's wife Isis, and their son Horus, hunted for the pieces until they found them all and brought the god back to life. Accordingly Isis came to be recognized as the perfect wife and mother, Horus as the dutiful son, and the three gods together as the ideal happy family. While these confused myths contain elements drawn from various city religions, Osiris himself was not a city god. He was one of the dying and rising gods, comparable to Tammuz in Syria and Babylonia, and like them he was associated primarily with vegetation.

Although Osiris seems to have come from Asia, and was worshiped in the Delta earlier than in the South, there were temples to him in all parts of Egypt in historic times (mythology related how a temple was built wherever Isis or Horus found a piece of Osiris's body) and the principal center of his cult was at Abydos. Such being the character of Osiris, it is not surprising that in historic times he was worshiped especially by the peasants of Egypt. Like Tammuz, he rewarded his worshipers with good crops in this world and with a vague and shadowy life in the nether world hereafter. At first there was marked rivalry between Osiris and Re, but as time went on Osiris managed to improve his position and to force his way into the official theology. He was recognized as the father of the powerful Horus; he and Isis were admitted to the ennead of Heliopolis; and the Pharaoh proclaimed himself the incarnation of Osiris as well as of Horus and Re.

In later times (Twelfth Dynasty) Osiris became a powerful force in democratizing Egyptian religion and Egyptian conceptions of the hereafter, and Abydos became a holy city visited by pilgrims from all over Egypt. Long after such official gods as Re and Amon had been overthrown and forgotten, Osiris was still worshiped. A few years before the birth of Christ, the famous Cleopatra officially masqueraded as Isis; and late in the first century after Christ, the Greek Plutarch wrote a sympathetic account of Isis and Osiris.

Egyptian Views on Immortality

From the earliest times the Egyptians had devoted great care to assuring the comfort of their kings and nobles in the next world—though we must avoid the error of those writers who assume that the Egyptians, really a merry and light-hearted people, were constantly haunted by the fear of death and annihilation. Before 4000 B.C., the Badarians gave formal burial to their distinguished dead, placing in their graves food and whatever else they might need. The large underground tombs of late predynastic times were sumptuously furnished, and in early dynastic times mastabas—house-like superstructures erected over the tomb—received equal attention. It will be recalled that Zoser, first king of the Third Dynasty, erected the famous step-pyramid at Saqqara, and that the great pyramids at Gizeh served as tombs for the kings of the Fourth Dynasty. These elaborate monuments were built in the hope of protecting the king's body and thus assuring his continued happiness.

As a further safeguard against annihilation, the Egyptians of the Pyramid Age invented the art of mummification. The viscera and brains of the corpse were removed and preserved in jars; the remainder of the body was treated with special oils; the cavities were filled with linen and spices; and the whole was wrapped tightly in linen. Hundreds of these mummies have been preserved to our own day. Kings and rich men also set aside endowments to buy bread, "beer that would not grow stale," and other necessities to be placed in their tombs, and to hire men to look after them. These caretakers—called "ka-priests"—were probably the first professional priests in Egypt, and their salaries were so generous that we read of one such priest who saved enough to endow his own tomb lavishly. In spite of these precautions, however, robbers often broke into the tombs, stole part or all of the rich furnishings, and carried off or destroyed the corpses.

Mere preservation of the body, together with provision of adequate food and drink, was not considered enough to insure the king's eternal felicity. On the walls of the pyramids of the late Fifth and Sixth Dynasties are many inscriptions giving further instructions as to what should be done. These "Pyramid Texts" are our earliest long theological documents. Some of the texts are magical charms pure and simple, or incantations designed to speed the king on his way; others are hymns in his praise. All shed light upon the religious conceptions popular in ancient Egypt. These texts are to be associated with the religion of Re rather than that of Osiris, and many of the statements and ideas expressed in them are much older than the inscriptions. They tell us that the king was not only the son of Re, but also his incarnation. Various suggestions are given as to how the god became incarnate in a man, and one striking passage graphically describes how the king ate the body of the god and thus became divine. Other texts describe the journey of the king to the next world, where he joined the gods in the sky. After reaching the celestial sphere, the king eternally enjoys that bliss which flows from association with Re.

Morality and Immortality

Magical charms and incantations were not enough to get the kings and nobles into this heavenly home, however, and several of the Pyramid Texts clearly express the belief that admittance depended upon conduct during life. There were moral requirements for admission to this Egyptian heaven. Kings and nobles therefore set up inscriptions on the doors of their tombs in which they listed their good deeds at length and solemnly averred that they had avoided the sins specifically mentioned: "I gave bread to the hungry, clothing to the naked, I ferried him who had no boat. . . . I never oppressed anyone. . . . Never did I take the property of any man by violence; I was the doer of that which pleased all men." The offenses of which many declared themselves innocent included such misdemeanors as blasphemy, reviling the king, gossiping, giving vent to anger, and even loquacity, as well as the more heinous sins of murder, stealing, cheating, lying, adultery, and temple-robbing.

Skeptics may question the historical accuracy of these public professions of virtue, which seem intolerably boastful to us—apparently no case has yet been found of a man who confesses that he is a miserable sinner or who claims that he is suffering from a broken and a contrite heart—but the inscriptions are of historical value none the less. The rhetoricians who composed the royal epitaphs were describing what they considered the ideal king, and their words show how high was the Egyptian conception of social justice. Pharaohs did many things without scruple which we would consider most reprehensible, even in a monarch; yet modern rulers occasionally fall short of Egyptian standards of justice. The sentiments expressed in these inscriptions were further idealized in the troubled times that followed the collapse of the Old Kingdom when, as we have seen, prophets foretold the coming of a king who would redeem Egypt with justice.[5]

In the Pyramid Age celestial bliss had been regarded as the special privilege of the king and of great nobles who were permitted to build tombs near his. Lesser persons might look forward only to a dark and joyless existence in the subterranean realm of Osiris. The Pyramid Texts show, however, that Osiris was already making his influence felt in the official solar theology. The social upheavals that followed the collapse of the Old Kingdom greatly advanced his prestige. New upper classes appeared whose members had but recently risen from obscurity and probably had once been worshipers of Osiris. Though they may have adopted the official state religion in consequence of their rise to social distinction, they presumably retained many of their ancestral beliefs and religious sympathies. At any rate, under the Middle Kingdom the religions of Re and Osiris became inextricably commingled. Celestial immortality was thrown open to everyone. Moral conduct according to the standards of Re remained the way to achieve it, but Osiris became the judge who determined whether or not an individual might proceed to the celestial regions. Those whom he refused to let pass apparently stayed in the old nether world, a place full of serpents, crocodiles, and fire. Eventually these ideas developed into our popular view of a "heaven" of bliss for the righteous in the sky and a "hell" of torture for the wicked under the ground.

While serious people believed that only high moral conduct would insure celestial immortality, others preferred magic to morality— doubtless because it was easier and cheaper. Formulas, spells, incantations, and passwords, very similar to those found in the Pyramid Texts, were written inside the lids of coffins, where the dead man might study them at his leisure and, having learned them by heart, repeat them to Osiris. These are called the "Coffin Texts." At a some-

---

[5] See note on James Henry Breasted, p. 128.

what later period (Eighteenth Dynasty) these spells were written on papyrus and placed in the coffin with the mummy: over two hundred such incantations—some several pages long—have been collected and are now known as the "Book of the Dead." Even under the Twelfth Dynasty the priests of Re sold books of formulas that were guaranteed to get their possessors into heaven. At a slightly later date priests sold blank forms, with spaces where the purchaser's name might later be written in, declaring that the holder was a righteous man. One manufacturer of such blank forms even had the effrontery to threaten Re with deposal if he failed to honor this passport to heaven that was sold by his priests!

Egyptian Art

In no field did the Egyptians show their superiority over the Sumerians more brilliantly than in the arts, and especially in architecture and sculpture. The Sumerians had their art, of course, and the tombs of the early kings at Ur are impressive, though perhaps rather gaudy. But this first burst of higher art was not maintained and archeologists have found few pieces of art in Babylonia that have more than historic interest. Even the best temples were built of sun-dried brick and, like lesser edifices, they have now disintegrated so completely that it is not easy to form a just idea of their original appearance. While Sumerian architects found solutions to difficult problems in brickwork, and erected elaborate buildings, they never equaled their Egyptian contemporaries. Sumerian artists carved statues in stone, but as each block had to be transported long distances, stone was too rare and expensive to permit much experimentation. Sumerian statues are stiff and unnatural, and the clay figurines seem more like caricatures than portraits. Even in the lesser arts the Sumerians rarely did superior work.

The early Egyptians, like the Mesopotamians, built their houses of wattle and mud, and before long they learned to build with sun-dried brick. Trees apparently were somewhat more plentiful in Egypt then than in dynastic times and the larger houses, such as the early royal residences, were built of lumber as well as brick. Egyptian residences had flat roofs, surrounded by parapets, and several houses were built around a central court, where the inhabitants did their cooking and lived most of their lives. We would know little about these houses, even the best of them, were it not for a peculiarity of the Egyptian people. They wished their royal tombs to look like houses and when they began building these tombs with stone, they reproduced even insignificant details. Thus they carved stone pillars in the shape of the bundles of papyrus stalks used to hold up the roofs of houses, with fluting to separate the stalks and with capital and base simulating the leather straps that once held the bundle of reeds together. Many centuries later the Greeks took over this form and adapted it to make the Doric column.

Pyramids and Temples

Our earliest examples of great Egyptian architecture are to be seen at Saqqara, a suburb of Memphis. Saqqara is famous as the site of the pyramid of Zoser, the first king of the Third Dynasty. It is also famous for the tombs of the nobles of the Fifth Dynasty, and recent excavations have disclosed a royal cemetery dating from the First Dynasty. Among the tombs is one of Menes which apparently was built later than the one at Abydos. Only a few years ago important discoveries were made in the immediate vicinity of the pyramid at Saqqara, for when archeologists cleared away the sand from its base, they found the ruins of elaborate structures which probably reproduced in stone the main features of the royal palace at Memphis, with its courts, colonnades, and temples. It is said that the architect who planned this vast edifice was Imhotep, the king's vizier. If so, he proved himself to be one of the world's great architects.

Other kings of the Third Dynasty experimented with the pyramid form until the supreme examples of this type of architecture were built at Gizeh, another suburb of Memphis, by three kings of the Fourth Dynasty, Khufu, Khafre, and Menkaure. Even the statistics of these enormous structures are interesting. The pyramid of Khufu, the most imposing of the three, is slightly larger than that of Khafre, and its dimensions are about twice those of the third pyramid in the group. Its base measured 756 feet on a side—it therefore covered about thirteen acres—and its height was 481 feet, or about one-half the height of the Empire State Building. Its volume was some 3,277,000 cubic yards, and it was built of about 2,300,000 separate blocks of stone whose average weight was approximately two and one-half tons each. The interior stones were limestone; the casing, now gone except for a few remnants at the top of Khafre's pyramid, was of a far superior white limestone. The burial chamber was lined with polished granite.

The stones were floated down the Nile on rafts from quarries several miles upstream and were dragged up a causeway built of earth to the site of the pyramid. Tiers of stone were then laid down, one above another, and after each tier was completed the causeway was built higher. After the pyramid was finished, this road was removed. The builders used no power but man power; they had levers and ropes, but no pullies; and they apparently used balls of granite about a foot thick as rollers upon which they dragged the stones up the causeway. Though the workmen had no tools made of stronger material than stone and rather soft copper, they shaped the stones skillfully and carefully. In show places, such as the coffin chamber, the joinings of the stones are so close as to excite the marvel of modern visitors.

In front of the pyramid, to the east, stood a mortuary temple. Part of the old causeway was retained, and upon it was built a covered corridor leading from this temple to another more than a quarter of a mile away. This second temple stood at the high-water bank of the Nile and is called the Valley Temple. Near the large pyramids were several small ones, in all probability for members of the kings's family; and near Khafre's Valley Temple is the Sphinx, the statue of a strange creature with the head of a man and the body of a lion, which was carved from a natural protrusion of rock (Plate 6).

Egyptian temples under the Old and Middle Kingdoms were largely temples to the kings—who, of course, were believed to be gods. In predynastic times there were small edifices, dedicated to other gods, which were called "shelters of the gods." At Heliopolis there apparently was a large temple to Re, centering around a small obelisk; others were built after he was officially recognized by the kings of the Fifth Dynasty. Osiris too had temples, the most famous of which was at Abydos. Unfortunately the ruins of these temples are so scanty that it is now impossible to form an idea of their architecture. We are more fortunate with the temples to the kings. Architecturally speaking at least, the king was the great god of Egypt, and near the tomb of every king stood one or more magnificent temples dedicated to him. The most magnificent of these was the "Valley Temple" attached to Khafre's pyramid, whose ruins have enabled modern architects to form an excellent idea of what the original building was like.

Carving and Sculpture

In sculpture Egyptian achievements were even more remarkable than in architecture. Formal writing in Egypt was a form of sculpture, and it seems not improbable that the Egyptians' love for such carving, and their skill at it, were in large part responsible for the fact that they continued to use the primitive and cumbersome hieroglyphics for some three thousand years. Writing of this sort very likely developed out of sculpture, for in predynastic times, before the invention of writing, stone palettes were decorated with carved pictures of the sort that later became hieroglyphics. The famous Narmer palette, made just before the beginning of the First Dynasty, has such carving and also the hieroglyphic signs to indicate his name. In later times, walls were covered with reliefs marvelously depicting scenes from daily life. The Fifth Dynasty mastaba of the noble Ti at Saqqara was especially famous for its carvings (see Plate 7).

From predynastic times Egyptian artists also experimented with sculpture in the round, using both wood and stone as materials. Under the Fourth Dynasty they attained high skill. Thus the wooden statue known as the "Sheik-el-Beled" (Sheik of the Village) is so

---

• Plate 7. Ti was a noble of the Fifth Dynasty, who built a tomb at Saqqara. The first scene shows shipbuilders at work; the second scenes are from agricultural life—plowing, milking, driving goats, hoeing.

Plate 7.   Scenes from the Tomb of Ti

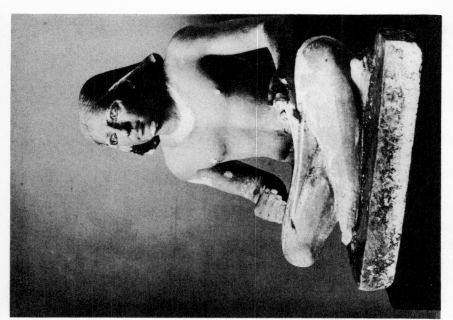

Seated Scribe

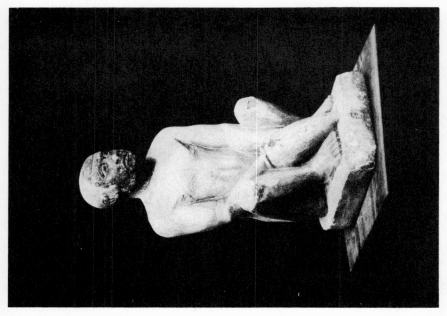

Potter

Plate 8. Egyptian Statuettes (*Photos, Cairo Museum*)

called because the Arab workmen who dug it up were struck by its lifelike resemblance to the mayor of their village. The statue of Khafre, also dating from the Fourth Dynasty, which was dug up near the Valley Temple in which it once stood, is one of the world's great pieces of sculpture (Plate 5).

Fewer examples of early Egyptian painting have been preserved, although we know that Egyptian sculptors often painted their reliefs and statues, and that pictures were painted on stucco walls. Tombs have been found whose walls were decorated with paintings of birds and animals or of scenes from daily life (Plate 7). The tombs of the kings and nobles once contained great quantities of jewelry as well as table services and other articles made of the precious metals. As such objects could easily be carried away by robbers, only a few examples of the work of Egyptian goldsmiths of this period remain, but what we have shows that these men were not less gifted than their fellow craftsmen working in other art media. Reliefs and paintings often show harpists and other musicians, but we know virtually nothing about Egyptian music.

Egyptian artists scored great triumphs under the Fourth Dynasty. Good work was done in later times—we have excellent portrait busts from the Fifth and even from the Sixth Dynasty—yet the new pieces lack the force and character of those dating from the great age. Artists became imitators rather than creators, and they tended to cut corners whenever possible. While kings went on building pyramids until the close of the Middle Kingdom (more than sixty were built in all), the later pyramids cannot be compared with those at Gizeh, either in size or in construction. Usually they were mere casings of stone, filled with small stones, rubble, and sand. Often the casings have caved in, and it is sometimes difficult to recognize a pyramid in the hillock which is all that now remains. The other arts met the same fate, and even the political revival under the Twelfth Dynasty failed to restore the old spirit. Before the decline set in, however, Egyptian artists had created one of the great periods of art in all history. Egyptian artists, like Egyptian theologians, thus attained an immortality surpassing that of the mighty kings who sought it with such lavish expenditures of the labor and wealth of their subjects.

Notes

Champollion and Egyptian Hieroglyphics

Through a fortunate accident scholars found Egyptian easier to decipher than Babylonian. Napoleon's soldiers happened to find a stone bearing a trilingual inscription near the Rosetta mouth of the Nile in 1799. The British subsequently took it to London, where it may now be seen in the British Museum. This "Rosetta Stone" had been set up in 196 B.C. by the Greek king Ptolemy V Epiphanes, with an inscription in three languages: the ancient hieroglyphics, Demotic (the native Egyptian of the time), and Greek. Scholars easily read the third version and tried to fit its known meaning to the first two inscriptions. By noting the position of proper names in the Greek text, they soon discovered and analyzed into their constituent characters the name of Ptolemy and one or two other words, but the complexities of the determinative system baffled them for many years. The riddle was finally solved by a young Frenchman named Jean François Champollion (1790–1832). He announced his first success in 1822, and before his death he was able to read simple Egyptian texts. He wrote an Egyptian grammar and compiled an elementary dictionary. The difficulties of the language rendered progress slow at first, but scholars eventually mastered Egyptian. Adolf Erman (1854–1937), unquestionably the leading Egyptologist of his day, published a truly scientific grammar in 1880, and in 1897 he obtained the financial support of various German learned societies for an Egyptian dictionary to include every word found in an inscription or on a papyrus. Almost a million cards were prepared and, after thirty years of labor by the Egyptologists of many countries in Europe and America, the *Wörterbuch der ägyptischen Sprache* was published by Erman and Grapow in five volumes (1926–31). A. H. Gardiner published a large and thorough *Egyptian Grammar* in 1927.

James Henry Breasted

James Henry Breasted (1865–1935) was the foremost American Egyptologist of his day. Born in a small Illinois town and educated in a small denominational college, he worked for a while in a drug store before entering a Congregational theological seminary in Chicago. Doubts regarding the inerrancy of the Scriptures convinced the idealistic young man that he could not conscientiously become a clergyman, but his studies of Hebrew opened to him the fascination of the Orient. He therefore went to Berlin to become a pupil of the great Egyptologist, Adolf Erman, and there he took his doctor's degree in 1894. Throughout the remainder of his life he was Professor of Egyptology at the University of Chicago.

After ten years spent in collecting and translating the principal literary sources for Egyptian history, Breasted published his *Ancient Records of Egypt* (4 vols. and index) in 1906–07. This monumental collection of source materials remains indispensable to every serious student of the subject. The *History of Egypt* (1905) is a literary history based on these researches. Much new material has come to light since this book was written, especially for the early period, but after more than forty years the greater part of the work stands as solid as ever. Breasted never lost his early religious idealism of a left-wing Protestant sort, and his interest in religion often guided the course of his studies. His doctor's thesis was a study of Akhnaton's famous "Hymn to the Sun" (see p. 157), and he was the first scholar to recognize the character and importance of the Pyramid Texts and messianic fragments. In 1912 he published his *Development of Religion and Thought in Ancient Egypt*, which was primarily a study of these texts and of the demands for social justice that found expression in messianic dreams. Twenty years later he went over the same material again in *The Dawn of Conscience* (1933).

Breasted's interests reached far beyond ancient Egypt, and in his *Ancient Times* (1916; 2nd ed., entirely rewritten, 1936) he published the first brief but scholarly account in English of the whole development of antiquity from the Stone Age to Charlemagne, properly emphasizing the importance of the ancient Orient for Greece and Rome. For many years this book, in various editions and abridgments, was the standard high-school text on ancient history. Meantime Breasted had visited Egypt with several different epigraphic and archeological expeditions, and after World War I he persuaded Mr. John D. Rockefeller, Jr., to make large grants for the systematic study of the ancient Near East. Breasted was the founder and first director of the Oriental Institute at the University of Chicago, where he gathered about him many of the leading Orientalists of America and Europe. Under his leadership the Institute became the world's principal center for the study of the Ancient Orient. See Charles Breasted, *Pioneer to the Past: the Story of James Henry Breasted, Archeologist* (1943).

V The First Great Empires

KNOWLEDGE OF THE INVENTIONS AND DISCOVERIES MADE in Babylonia and Egypt during the third millennium soon spread far and wide. Other civilizations sprang up in nearby parts of the world, to which the products and ideas of the older centers were carried by traders and soldiers. Crete became the seat of a new civilization in the days of the Old Kingdom in Egypt, and Troy (in northwestern Asia Minor near the Hellespont) was not far behind. Cretan mariners, who were more adventurous than the Egyptians, visited the most remote parts of the Mediterranean. Trojan traders likewise traveled from Egypt in the south to the Danube valley in the north. Both Cretans and Trojans knew Egypt well, and each acquired a knowledge of Babylonian civilization through Syria.

Repercussions from the great achievements of the Near East spread more slowly to central and western Europe. The inhabitants of these parts of Europe were just entering the neolithic stage of civilization as the kings of the First Dynasty united Upper and Lower Egypt, and Europe did not advance beyond that stage until a thousand years later. Traders seeking gold or precious stones sometimes visited the western Mediterranean lands, sold the natives a few trinkets and gewgaws, and perhaps told them something of what was being done in the Near East. It is not improbable that an occasional European may have visited the Near East with these traders, perhaps as a prisoner or a slave, and later returned to his own people with stories of what he had seen. But not much oriental influence can be seen in the various European cultures of the third millennium. Europe was developing along its own lines.

Archeologists find traces of several new inventions in western Europe toward the end of the third millennium. In the first place, tombs and monuments built of enormous stones began to appear in Malta and Sardinia, in Spain and southern France, and along the Atlantic seaboard from Portugal to England and Sweden. The tombs are called "dolmens," and show a vague resemblance to Egyptian mastabas. In other places, rows of flat stone slabs were set up, as in a modern cemetery; presumably they too were grave markers. Sometimes temples were built of huge stones. The most famous of the latter is the great Stonehenge in England, which apparently dates from the end of the period, about 1700 B.C. The men who built these huge monuments are now called the megalith builders ("megalith" means "big stone"). As the megaliths usually are within a few miles of the sea, it is assumed that their builders were primarily sailors and traders who traveled up and down the Atlantic coast and even entered the Mediterranean. Imaginative writers have seen Egyptian influences at work upon the megalith builders, but more probably the Europeans developed the style themselves. Similar megaliths are to be found in many other parts of the world—including ancient America and various Pacific islands—where Egyptian influence is out of the question.

A little later pottery of a new and distinctive type began to appear in western and central Europe. It is called "bell beaker" pottery because the jars are shaped like inverted bells. The people who made this pottery apparently wandered about in small bands, somewhat like gypsies, taking their potters and coppersmiths with them, trading and fighting as occasion offered. Both megaliths and bell beakers bear witness to the growing importance of commerce. Thus at about the time of the Third Dynasty of Ur, or of the Middle Kingdom in Egypt, western Europe began to emerge from the neolithic stage of civilization and to develop trade.

At about this time, too, came the invention of bronze. There has been much discussion as to where this epoch-making invention first appeared. The most probable answer is that it did not appear suddenly at any one place and that it may have been invented independently on several occasions. Smiths had long been experimenting with various methods of hardening copper with alloys, and toward the end of the third millennium they began mixing it with tin in the ratio of ten to one, thus producing true bronze. Such bronze appeared shortly before the end of the millennium (perhaps about 2200 b.c.) at Troy and in the Aegean area, and before long it was also being manufactured in central Europe. Here it caused a new demand for raw materials not found everywhere, thus giving a great impetus to trade, and it made possible the manufacture of new weapons superior to any heretofore available. Bronze daggers began to supplement the metal battle-axes that had long been in use, but swords were not possible until several centuries later.

The Great Migrations

Confusion was increased early in the second millennium by a series of great migrations which started in central Europe. It will be recalled that the neolithic peoples of central Europe were a mixture of Alpine peasants with Nordic warriors, and that the Nordic aristocrats had imposed their Indo-European languages upon the farmers. As soon as this population became larger than could be supported comfortably by the agriculture of the day, men needed more room. Ambitious leaders set out upon great careers of conquest. They did not advance with large conquering armies but in small groups, wandering about much as the bell-beaker folk had done before them, accompanied by their families as well as by their potters and smiths, looting here and there, and sometimes settling down to become local aristocrats ruling over the native peasants of the vicinity.

Thus some groups forced their way into northern Greece and others into northern Italy, where they became the first to speak languages akin to Greek and Latin. Others migrated westward from southern Germany and Alsace into northeastern France and Belgium, taking Celtic dialects with them. At about the same time still others crossed the Hellespont into Asia Minor. Members of this last group are now known as Hittites. They began entering Asia in small groups about 1900; during the next two hundred years they spread over most of central Asia Minor, and in the seventeenth century before Christ they built up a strong kingdom there which eventually played a major part in the international politics of the Near East.

Meantime other migratory warriors were invading the countries lying to the east of Mesopotamia. The fact that these peoples spoke Indo-European languages indicates that some at least were of Nordic descent. At the same time differences between their languages and those of Europe show that their separation from the western group must have occurred long before. While the European Nordics were forcing their rule upon the Alpine peasants, their cousins were advancing eastward; and after absorbing various peoples whom they found wandering about the steppes of southern Russia, they settled in the district east of the Caspian Sea. These peoples were herdsmen rather than farmers; they were very fond of horses; and they used light battle-chariots which eventually revolutionized military tactics. At about the time when the Europeans started on their great advances southward, these eastern "Aryans" began a series of similar migrations. Some of them entered the valley of the upper Indus from the northwest. These men spoke Sanskrit, the ancestor of several modern Indian languages, and their descendants composed the Vedas, which are still regarded as sacred literature by Hindus. Other groups went farther west and entered Persia, where they found a variety of primitive peoples over whom they gradually gained an ascendancy. These Iranians were the first Persians to speak an Indo-European language. They worshiped several of the gods mentioned in the Vedas, and apparently they retained a few contacts with their Indian kinsmen.

Smaller groups of adventurers advanced still farther west, passed through northern Persia, and made themselves leaders of warlike bands that preyed upon the rich Babylonian cities. Although the Kassites who conquered Babylonia after the death of Hammurabi certainly were not Aryans, they often were led by Aryan adventurers. We find a few Aryan names among the Kassites, who occasionally worshiped Aryan gods. It was they who introduced the horse and war chariot into Babylonia. Other invaders of the same general sort passed north of Assyria, organized bands of natives in these regions, and created kingdoms for themselves. Before 1700, one group of these Aryans had made themselves the aristocratic rulers of a large kingdom known as Mitanni, on the upper Tigris and Euphrates. Their capital seems to have been at the ancient site of Halaf. Others led their conglomerate hordes into Syria, perhaps even reaching the Mediterranean. These groups of adventurers were not numerous, however, and they never succeeded in imposing Aryan languages upon their followers and subjects.

Other invaders of other races were adding to the confusion of the Near East. Semitic peoples were on the move in northern Syria, especially in the district between the great bend of the Euphrates and the Mediterranean, which centers around Carchemish, Aleppo, and Haran. A group of Semites pushed down the Euphrates from this general region before 1800 and established the Babylonian dynasty of which Hammurabi (1728–1686) was the sixth member. At about this time, other Semites moved south to Moab and Ammon, in modern Transjordania, and still others reached Palestine. This great migration is reflected in the Biblical stories of Abraham, who is said to have started from Haran. Still other Semites from this general region expelled the Egyptians from the Syrian coast cities which they had held for almost two centuries under the kings of the Twelfth Dynasty. A century later their kinsman Hammurabi extended his power over this Syrian region, and perhaps over Palestine as well, but soon after his death the whole country was overrun by new invaders from the north.

The third racial group to invade the Fertile Crescent early in the second millennium were the Hurrians, probably to be identified with the Biblical Horites. They were men of Armenoid race, distantly related to the builders of the first neolithic villages in northern Assyria, and their homeland was the mountainous country around Lake Van in eastern Asia Minor. They made great progress in the art of war, but in general they were barbarians. Before the time of Hammurabi, Aryan leaders had begun recruiting among them, as among their Kassite kinsmen, and presently Syria was invaded. Sometimes Aryan leaders led these raids, and sometimes the Hurrians made forays on their own account. After they had entered Syria, the leaders enlisted enterprising Semites in their bands. Syria fell into a number of petty states, and the invaders, growing bolder, swept south over Palestine.

In the last quarter of the eighteenth century they entered Egypt in large numbers. Here they were called Hyksos. They occupied much of the Delta and eventually their leaders became the kings of the Fifteenth Dynasty, ruling Lower Egypt from about 1675 to 1567. As the equally barbaric Kassites were then ruling Babylonia, civilization everywhere reached a low ebb. Confusion reigned throughout the Near East until order was at last restored by the rulers of the great Hittite and Egyptian empires.

The Hittites in Anatolia

The earliest settlers in Anatolia (the peninsula between the Black Sea and the Mediterranean, often called Asia Minor) were a few Mediterraneans who presumably had come from Africa by way of Syria. Most of Anatolia was later occupied by farmers of Armenoid race, distant kinsmen of the Hurrians who occupied the highlands further east. Though Anatolia has since been invaded repeatedly, its indigenous population still consists largely of the descendants of these early Armenoids. Their neolithic village civilization is scarcely known, however, for it has been studied at only two or three sites in the vicinity of Troy in the extreme northwest, and at Alishar in east-central Asia Minor.

During the third millennium traders began to cross the Anatolian Peninsula from east to west, proceeding from Babylonia to the Aegean Sea at Troy. A neolithic village, known to modern archeologists as Troy I, existed at this site as early as 3000. Some five centuries later there grew up the city called Troy II, whose importance as a trading and bronze-manufacturing center has already been mentioned. This city prospered for several centuries. Babylonian traders reached out in that direction as early as the days of Lugal-zaggisi and Sargon (2300–2200) and they apparently knew routes across Anatolia. This trade was still important in the days of the Third Dynasty of Ur. Cuneiform tablets found in Cappadocia bear witness to important trading centers there about 1950. The tablets show that Cappadocia—and probably Asia Minor generally—was still in the stage of village economy and was ruled over by minor princelets, a few of whom are mentioned by name. The inhabitants of the whole area, who are called Hatti, presumably were descendants of the original Armenoid settlers.

Founding the Hittite Empire

Such was the situation about 1900 when the Hittites first began their migrations from Europe. The route that they followed is not

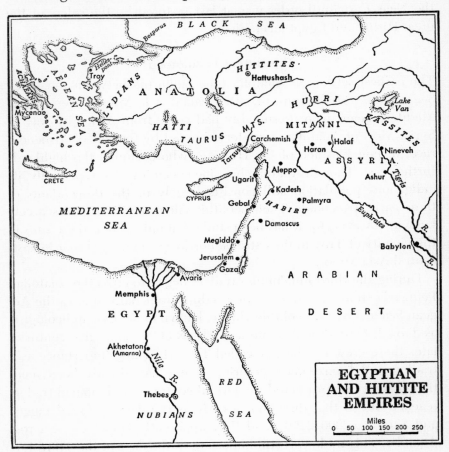

EGYPTIAN AND HITTITE EMPIRES

certain, but they presently occupied much of central Asia Minor, becoming most numerous in the valley of the Halys River. At first they contented themselves with subjugating the native populations and setting themselves up as local aristocracies. Ambitious leaders then united most of central Anatolia under their rule, and established their capital at Hattushash, about one hundred miles due east of the modern Turkish capital, Ankara. In the seventeenth century they fought with the Hurrians on the eastern frontier and made occasional raids into Syria, where they captured Aleppo. In 1595 they made a great raid against Babylon, to punish her for aiding her Syrian allies against them, and they overthrew the last king of the dynasty of Hammurabi. They made no effort to hold the Babylonian territory thus occupied, but they again devastated the Hurrian country on their return.

The two centuries that followed the sack of Babylon are a dark period in Hittite history. Our annals picture each king of the sixteenth century as a usurper who drove out his predecessor; and for the fifteenth century the annals are blank. Nevertheless, there are reasons to believe that the wars with the Hurrians continued throughout the century, and that the Hurrians won important successes.

A new dynasty seized power at Hattushash in the fifteenth century. These kings were quite different from those ruling formerly, and they spoke a somewhat different language. The old kings had used a language known as "Nasili," which scholars usually call "cuneiform Hittite" because it was written in Babylonian characters. The new kings continued to keep their official records in that language, but they spoke and used in their numerous inscriptions a new language now known as "hieroglyphic Hittite." Though scholars have now read cuneiform Hittite for upwards of thirty years, they have only recently achieved their first successes in deciphering Hittite hieroglyphics. Some authorities believe that the new language was influenced by Aryan leaders of Hurrian bands during the dark period beginning a little after 1600. At any rate, Hurrian influences appear strongly in the culture of Anatolia at about the time that the hieroglyphic inscriptions begin.[1]

The Hittite Monarchy

The Hittite monarchy differed fundamentally from the Egyptian or Babylonian in that the king was neither a god as in Egypt nor a

---

[1] See note on the Rediscovery of the Hittites, p. 163.

priest as in early Babylonia. At first he was primarily a warrior, the leader of the host in battle, and he was surrounded by chieftains who formed a council, called the *pankush,* to give him aid and advice. The Hittite archives contain treaties between the kings and their nobility, showing the great power of the latter. Writers have sometimes compared the *pankush* to the council of Greek chieftains in Homeric times or to the Roman senate. The treaties have been praised as early Magna Chartas, establishing limited monarchy in a constitutional and peculiarly "Nordic" manner, but it is wise not to press analogies too hard. No doubt the Hittites brought various ideas about government with them from central Europe, as did their Greek and Roman cousins, but the nature of the Hittite government can best be explained by local conditions in Anatolia.

The Hittite invaders, who were relatively small groups of foreign conquerors divided into countless bands with no political unity, came to rule over a large native population. Their precarious position forced a certain unity upon the Hittites, yet local chieftains could not, and need not, be forced to surrender all liberty to a central government. In this way a loose confederation under king and council gradually grew up. After the disturbances of the middle period of Hittite history, a stronger central government was organized, and oriental ideas of absolutism appeared. Perhaps these ideas were brought from the East by the new dynasty which then rose to power; but it is equally possible that this new absolutism was a native development, designed to prevent a recurrence of civil war and invasion. As the earlier kingdom was a union of lesser states, it naturally took on feudal traits, with the successors of the former local princes serving as vassals of the king. The new dynasty retained this general system, increasing its power over the vassals and adding new vassals with further conquests. The chief care of the kings of each dynasty was to raise large armies and maintain their loyalty; and as the economic life of their empire was largely agricultural, the rulers found it easiest to give estates to vassals in return for military service.

It is not possible to describe accurately the extent of the Hittite Empire. Only a few cuneiform Hittite tablets or inscriptions have been found outside Hattushash, although Hittite hieroglyphics have been reported from many places in central and eastern Asia Minor and in Syria. The early kings apparently ruled the valley of the Halys from the Black Sea south to the Taurus Mountains, but their power did not reach far west of the river. The later dynasty probably held the eastern two-thirds of Anatolia, from the Black Sea to the Mediterranean, and much of Syria.

Hittite Civilization

The fact that the early Hittites adopted cuneiform writing is typical of much of their cultural history. When they entered Asia, they were fighters, at a low cultural level, but they were quite ready to learn what they could from others. Babylonian merchants were still to be found at several places in Anatolia, and from them the Hittites learned to write with cuneiform characters. They took over the Sumerian syllabic signs used in writing the Semitic Akkadian and fitted them as best they could to their own Indo-European language. Their models were the cuneiform characters as written in the days of the Third Dynasty of Ur (about 2000), which indicates that the Hittites must have begun writing soon after entering Asia. The origin of the Hittite hieroglyphics, on the other hand, is quite obscure. While the system of determinatives resembles that used in Egyptian, it is impossible to see a resemblance between the pictures used by Egyptians and those used by Hittites.

The library at Hattushash contained dictionaries listing equivalent words in Hittite, Akkadian, and Sumerian in parallel columns; and there were a few literary works from Babylonia, including fragments of the Gilgamesh epic, translated into Hittite and into Hurrian. While the Hittites did not create a great literature of their own, their annals show marked originality, being fuller and more literary than the bald chronicles of Babylonia. The tablets also tell us much about Hittite law. Although no comprehensive code, comparable to that of Hammurabi, has survived, numerous fragments of laws show that the Hittite kings had different, and possibly more humane, conceptions of justice than he. For example, offenders were never sentenced to mutilation or similar punishments.

The willingness of the Hittites to adopt the ideas of other peoples makes it difficult to know much about their religion, though the records mention many gods worshiped in their domain. The great majority are Hattic deities, who antedate the Hittites, or else Hurrian gods who were brought in during the last centuries of the Empire. The Hittites undoubtedly brought gods of their own from Europe, but of them we know little. Among the old Hattic gods were vegetation deities of the ordinary neolithic sort, including a mother goddess who eventually achieved the title of "Great Mother of the Gods." As such she was taken to Rome a thousand years after the fall of the Hittite Empire, and there she was worshiped for many centuries. With her was a male deity sometimes called Attis, who was equated with the Babylonian Tammuz: his very name betrays his Hattic origin.

The temples of the Hatti were protected by the new rulers. Their priests, who often enjoyed theocratic powers resembling those of their Sumerian confreres, were allowed to continue governing their temple-states, holding them as fiefs under the king. These temple-states of Anatolia became so important that many of them survived one political system after another. Persians, Greeks, and Romans granted the priests the same right to rule that the Hittites had accorded to their predecessors long before.

The Eighteenth Dynasty in Egypt

The Hyksos, who invaded Egypt in waves after about 1750, were marauders of Hurrian and Semitic ancestry. Their leaders ruled the Delta of Egypt from about 1675 to 1567 as the kings of the Fifteenth Dynasty. They owed their victories not only to their fighting abilities and to their superior bronze swords, horses, and war chariots, but also to the weakness of Egypt after the passing of the Twelfth Dynasty. The Hyksos established their capital at Avaris, a city in the northeastern part of the Delta, whence they ruled the whole Delta and collected tribute from all parts of Egypt. As more than a hundred kings are mentioned as ruling during the century of Hyksos domination, Upper Egypt must have been divided into many petty principalities, each tributary to the Asiatic invaders. The Hyksos could not bring back prosperity to Egypt, however, nor even establish a strong government.

Meantime, the Theban kings of the Thirteenth Dynasty continued to rule a small district in the south until about 1675, when they were succeeded by the Sixteenth Dynasty, and some thirty years later by the Seventeenth. Other Egyptian cities, gradually regaining their strength and learning to fight in the Hyksos manner, followed Theban leadership in rising against the invaders. Shortly after 1600 the Hyksos king decided that he must eliminate this menace to his authority. His first step, if we are to believe a legend current in Egypt some four centuries later, was to complain that his royal slumbers were disturbed by the incessant bellowings of the hippopotamuses in a pool at Thebes—five hundred miles away!—after which he marched his army against the offending city. We have the mummy of the Theban king, with its head horribly bashed in, showing that he was killed in the battle; but since the king's body was not lost, his army must have retained possession of the field. The war was continued by his son, who reunited Upper Egypt and probably captured Memphis. Within a few years this king was succeeded (1570) by Ahmose I—probably his half-brother—who took Avaris after a siege of three years and drove the last Hyksos from Egypt.

The New Kingdom, or Empire

Ahmose is listed as the first king of the Eighteenth Dynasty, and the glorious period in Egyptian history which he inaugurated is known as the New Kingdom, or the Empire. The new ruler and his associates thought they were restoring the old Egypt of the Twelfth Dynasty, as in a sense they were. Egypt was again ruled by Egyptians; the reconstructed bureaucracy governed much as before, though it ruled from the new capital at Thebes; and attempts were made to continue the literary and artistic traditions of the old days. Nevertheless there were many differences between the new Egypt and the old. The feudal nobility, which had been so important under the Middle Kingdom, had been largely eliminated by the Hyksos, and the comparative speed of reconquest had prevented the rise of new local aristocracies. Ahmose had conquered Egypt and it was his. He rewarded his friends for their aid, but at the same time he kept them from becoming strong enough to question his authority. The central government became more powerful than it had been since the Pyramid Age a thousand years before. A second difference lay in the greatly increased importance of the priests of Amon. This Theban deity had been identified with Re under the Twelfth Dynasty, but neither he nor his priests played an important part in politics. Now Amon became the first god of the kingdom, in whose honor enormous temples were built and to whose priests great tracts of land were given. Sometimes these priests became so powerful that they could, and did, defy the king with success. Eventually, under the Twenty-first Dynasty (1085–945), they became kings themselves.

The New Kingdom was highly militaristic. Ahmose and his associates were military men who had learned all that the Hyksos could teach about military science, and after the long Hyksos oppression it was easy to convince most Egyptians that safety lay only in strong military power. Much of the history of Egypt during the next century can be interpreted as flowing from a "fear psychosis" engendered by the Hyksos invasion. Heretofore the Egyptians had been a highly peaceful people, rarely turning their thoughts beyond the Nile Valley. During the next hundred years, their armies won the greatest empire that the world had yet seen. Her sufferings under the Hyksos made Egypt an imperialistic and predatory state.

Though Ahmose had other wars to fight after the expulsion of the Hyksos—notably a campaign to drive back the Nubians to the south—his energies during the remainder of his reign were directed chiefly to organizing his kingdom. The major part of this task he accomplished before his death (1546), and his two successors set out on a policy of foreign conquest. Amenhotep I (1546–25) and his son-in-law, Thutmose I (1525–08), each conducted extensive campaigns in three directions. They pushed the frontiers south to the Fourth Cataract of the Nile (the Twelfth Dynasty had ruled only to the Second) and set up a special government for this Nubian province. They drove the Libyans away from the western frontier of the

Delta. And finally, their raids into Syria reached the Euphrates near Carchemish. Booty from Syria not only financed the wars and the government at home, but also made possible great building programs and enabled the kings to bestow lavish gifts upon Amon and his priests. This imported wealth restored prosperity after the long poverty of the Hyksos period. The bureaucracy and trade expanded rapidly, and Egypt was reconstructed, economically and physically. Egyptians had every right to be enthusiastic over their new prospects.

Hatshepsut and Thutmose III

Thutmose's insignificant successor, Thutmose II, was soon pushed aside by the famous Hatshepsut, who became the first great queen known to history. She was the daughter of Thutmose I by his principal wife, and the half-sister of Thutmose II, to whom she was married and by whom she had two daughters. Her chief rival was Thutmose III, son of Thutmose II by a concubine. As a boy, this third Thutmose had been a priest of Amon, and shortly before his father's death his fellow priests staged a *coup* in order to make him king. On a formal and public occasion the statue of Amon bowed before the young man to indicate divine favor. Thutmose II was so impressed by this miracle that he proclaimed the young priest his heir and married him to Nefrure, his daughter by Hatshepsut. Within a short time Thutmose II died and Hatshepsut became the principal wife of her son-in-law, the boy Thutmose III.

During the next twenty-two years Hatshepsut ruled Egypt (1504–1482). Even before her first husband's death, Hatshepsut and her faction had been causing the government great annoyance, which may have been the reason why Thutmose II (who seems to have been an invalid) so carefully designated his successor. Factions at court then forced Thutmose III and Hatshepsut to follow opposing policies. Through her mother, Hatshepsut was descended from the great Ahmose, the founder of the Eighteenth Dynasty who had driven the Hyksos from Egypt, but she and her party were now eager to enjoy peace and the fruits of their victory. She therefore opposed further military adventures and wished to devote her energy and revenue to promoting trade and prosperity. Thutmose III, on the other hand, favored his grandfather's imperialistic policies, as did his father's officials and the priests of Amon, who had profited so richly from the spoils of Syria.

When the friends of Thutmose III told all Egypt of the miracle wrought in his behalf by Amon, and dwelt upon the undesirability of having a woman as ruler, Hatshepsut topped his miracle with a greater one. She had inscribed upon the walls of her temple a story of how Amon himself had appeared to her mother, the Princess Ahmose, in the form of Thutmose I, and became her father. Such stories of miraculous births had already cropped up repeatedly in Egypt, usually being put forward by usurpers. The political implications of the present miracle are especially interesting. It established the purity of Hatshepsut's divine status beyond cavil, for it added the divinity of her father Amon to that which she inherited from her maternal great-grandfather, Ahmose I. At the same time Thutmose III, whose mother had been a mere concubine, was left in a most humiliating and human position, with scarcely any divinity to him.

As Hatshepsut was then in middle age, at the height of her physical and mental powers, and had the support of a strong faction, she was able to dominate her young husband. A few inscriptions hailed him as king; but he was soon forced into the background, and Hatshepsut ruled in her own name. In her inscriptions she called herself "king," even inventing a feminine form for this masculine word. During her reign there were no foreign wars, though the so-called trading expeditions she sent to Punt probably were little more than piratical forays. She boasted of her building operations, including the restoration of temples destroyed by the Hyksos—a highly significant boast. Her most famous construction, however, was her temple and tomb at Deir el-Bahri, built against the cliffs opposite Thebes. During her reign Egypt apparently was prosperous and happy, but as soon as she died (about 1482) her husband gave vent to the accumulated hatred of twenty years. He attempted to obliterate all memory of his wife by ordering that her name be effaced from all her monuments or that the inscriptions be covered over with masonry. Thutmose also reversed her political policies and devoted himself to imperialistic aggression.

Thutmose's Military Conquests

Thutmose had emerged only second best from his controversies with the divine lady who was at once his aunt, his mother-in-law,

EGYPTIAN KINGS OF THE EIGHTEENTH DYNASTY

Ahmose I (1570–1546)
|
Amenhotep I (1546–1525)
|
(Mutofret) = Princess Ahmose = Thutmose I (1525–1508)
|
Isis (concubine) — Thutmose II = Hatshepsut = Thutmose III
(1508–1504) (1504–1482) (1504–1450)
|
(Meretre) = Thutmose III = Nefrure
(1504–1450)
|
Amenhotep II (1450–1425)
|
Thutmose IV (1425–1412) = (Mutemuya)
|
Amenhotep III (1412–1375) = Tiy   Eye (?)
|
Amenhotep IV Akhnaton (1387–1366) = Nofretete
|
daughter = Smenkhkare   Tutankhamen = daughter = Eye
(1372–1368?)   (1366–1357)   (1357–1353)

and his wife, yet he became one of the world's great military conquerors. He has aptly been called "the Egyptian Napoleon." The inscriptions telling of his achievements are so detailed that we can follow the progress of his campaigns and even work out the maneuvers in some of his great battles. Leaving Egypt in April, 1482, with an army of perhaps 20,000 men, Thutmose quickly marched north along the coast of Palestine and crossed Mount Carmel to Megiddo, where he won his most famous victory and captured the city after a siege. He also took three lesser cities, occupied much of central Syria, built a fortress to secure his conquests, and early in December returned to

Thebes, laden with an immense booty. During the next several years he made at least fifteen other expeditions to Syria, sometimes by land and sometimes by sea. He occupied the whole of Palestine and Syria, and pushed his frontiers north to the Euphrates at Carchemish. Finally, in his last campaign (1462), he succeeded in capturing Kadesh, the strongest city in Syria.

While these military campaigns were conducted during the summer months, the king was equally busy during the winter. Every year he made a tour of inspection of Egypt, personally looking after the details of many public enterprises. Part of the gold and slaves brought from Syria went to the priests of Amon; another part was used in great building programs (including an enormous temple at Karnak); and another part was given to his assistants. Trade continued to flourish, and Thebes became a large, beautiful, and wealthy city, fit to be the capital of a great empire.

Thutmose appointed an official called "the governor of the north countries" to receive the tribute from conquered states, and he stationed troops there to prevent insurrection, but he allowed the conquered kings and princes to continue ruling their former territories as long as they paid their tribute regularly and aroused no suspicions of intended revolt. The kings were required to send their sons as hostages to Egypt, where the boys received an Egyptian education, and where no pains were spared in impressing upon them the irresistible might of Egypt, the folly of rebellion, and the benefits that would flow from co-operation with her. When the old king in Syria died, his son would be sent back to rule in his place, perhaps accompanied by an Egyptian wife and her retinue. In most cases, therefore, the Egyptians could count on the loyalty of the new king. Moreover, the Egyptians brought Syria peace such as she had never known before; the province prospered under the new regime; and the annual tribute probably was not excessive in view of the services Egypt rendered.

Weakness of the Egyptian Empire

Not much need be said of Thutmose's immediate successors. They were not men of importance, but for a while the Empire remained prosperous because tribute continued to pour in. The Empire reached the pinnacle of its glory under Amenhotep III (1412–1375). Nevertheless, the forces that were to destroy it were already visible, as we have learned from several fortunate discoveries in recent years. The first of these discoveries came in 1888, when a cache of about 350 clay tablets, covered with cuneiform writing, was unearthed at a spot in Middle Egypt called Amarna. Amarna had been the site of a new capital built by Amenhotep IV (1387–66), and the tablets were letters sent by various rulers in Asia to this king or to his father, Amenhotep III. They contribute so much to our knowledge of the first half of the fourteenth century that the period is now usually called the "Amarna Age." Amarna itself has since been excavated with especial care. Secondly, the Hittite archives, unearthed at Boghazköy (Hattushash) about twenty years later, add to our knowledge of international affairs at this time. In 1929, finally, French archeologists stumbled upon a most important site at Ras Shamra, a village in northern Syria on the Mediterranean coast about thirty miles south of the mouth of the Orontes River, the ancient Ugarit, where other aspects of Egyptian imperialism may be studied.

The Amarna letters give us a vivid picture of Egypt's foreign affairs in the days of Amenhotep III. In the first place, the fact that the letters were written in the Babylonian language is highly significant. Egypt had conquered Palestine and Syria, but the Babylonian tradition there, going back at least to Hammurabi, was so strong that Egyptian officials had to learn Babylonian cuneiform in order to read letters from their Syrian subjects. The letters also show that while the prestige of Egypt was still high throughout the Near East, her position was by no means a happy one. There are letters from the Kassite king at Babylon, from the king of Mitanni, and from several lesser kings, all begging for gifts of Egyptian gold. The Egyptian kings apparently made it a practice to subsidize the rulers of foreign states with whom they wished to maintain friendly relations. As we would expect, the Asiatic kinglets often received their doles in a highly contumelious spirit, expressing their gratitude with pointed references to the inexhaustible wealth of Egypt (where gold was said to be "as common as dust") and with whining requests for more. Other letters show that these kings sometimes sent their daughters to marry the king of Egypt. Some of the letters contain professions of loyalty from Egyptian vassals in Syria; others report disloyalty; and still others warn of foreign enemies. Taken as a whole, the Amarna letters show that power politics was conducted in the Near East by means of treaties, diplomatic alliances, subsidies, royal marriages, and war. Though the Egyptians still held the upper hand, their position was constantly threatened by newcomers, and they were often exploited and blackmailed by their alleged friends and satellites. The whole situation sounds quite modern.

The discoveries at Ras Shamra are equally informative. This site had been occupied since the Stone Age, and Babylonian influence was felt there even in the Jemdet Nasr period, about 3000 B.C. An important city called Ugarit arose on this site, and under the Twelfth Dynasty it had connections with Egypt. At the next level above were found seals and other evidence of the renewed Babylonian influence in Syria under Hammurabi. Ugarit apparently controlled a wide area from the Mediterranean Sea to the Syrian Desert. After the time of Thutmose III, Ugarit again was under Egyptian control, though ruled by native Semitic kings. In the period of its golden age—which coincided with the Amarna Age in Egypt—the port of Ugarit was the busiest in northern Syria, with a conglomerate population drawn from far and near which spoke at least half a dozen languages. The fundamental population was Semitic, speaking a language closely resembling Phoenician, but there were also Hurrians and Mitannians as well as men from Cyprus and Crete and even from faraway Mycenae in Greece. Among other things the excavators found a factory for manufacturing the purple dye that later made the Phoenicians famous. Ugarit was a prosperous city, with its government and commercial classes loyal to Egypt. Archeology supports the statement in one of the Amarna letters that the city was destroyed about 1360 by an earthquake and overwhelmed by a tidal wave. Though rebuilt in part, Ugarit never regained its former importance.

Marauders in Syria

The Amarna letters give us a different picture of conditions elsewhere in Syria. About fifty miles south of Ugarit was a district called

Amurru, inhabited by Amorites. Although the king of Amurru and his son professed the deepest loyalty to their Egyptian overlord in various letters found at Amarna, they really were engaged in creating a central Syrian kingdom for themselves. The father wrote obsequious letters to Amenhotep, referring to himself as the king's "slave, the dog of his house," and deploring the fact that his enemies had seen fit to lie so outrageously about him and his intentions. But we have more than fifty letters in which the king of neighboring Gebal complains of Amorite aggressions and begs for aid—always in vain. Gebal, like Ugarit, was a great trading center and really loyal to Egypt, as the rich commercial cities of Syria usually were. The rural districts, on the other hand, were seething with discontent, and ambitious leaders were taking advantage of the situation to make themselves independent kings. Amenhotep III did little or nothing to aid his friends, and Egyptian power declined rapidly in Syria.

The authors of the Amarna letters also complain that Egyptian territories in Syria are being attacked from every side, a charge which is substantiated by records from the Hittite archives. The Hittite Empire was now firmly established under an aggressive king, Shuppiluliumash. The king of Mitanni had entered into an alliance with Egypt against the Hittites, though it apparently did him little good, for a few years later the Hittites inflicted a shattering defeat upon Mitanni and reduced the country to tributary status. Egypt thus lost a major ally and was effectively separated from Babylon. During these years the Hittites also encouraged and aided the Amorites, and eventually they took over the kingdom, ruling northern Syria almost to Damascus. Though Ugarit was not occupied, it lost most of its territories and was forced to supply mercenaries to the Hittite army.

Meantime, other marauders from the West were preying upon Hittites and Syrians alike. A people known as the Achaeans—the Greeks of the Trojan War—had by this time established a powerful kingdom at Mycenae in Greece. After destroying the principal city of Crete, about 1400, their pirates swept the Aegean and ventured along the southern coast of Asia Minor. Hittite records complain of the ravages of the "Ahhiyava"—who undoubtedly were Achaeans —and Egyptian records show that the raiders attacked not only

Syria but even the Egyptian Delta itself. In the new Ugarit that was built after the pro-Egyptian city had been destroyed by the earthquake about 1360, Mycenaeans were so numerous that modern excavators speak of the place as a Mycenaean colony.

Still other marauders were attacking Egypt's Syrian possessions from the East. These enemies were Bedouin out of the Arabian Desert, who forced their way into the fertile territory in large numbers. The authors of the Amarna letters frequently complain of the depredations caused by these invaders, among whom they mention a people they called Habiru, recognized by scholars as the ancestors of the Hebrews.

Egypt Neglects Her Empire

The letters from loyal vassals contain frequent appeals for aid against rebels and invaders, but they also make it quite clear that such aid was rarely granted. Though we have no direct evidence as to why the Egyptian kings thus let their empire go to pieces, a review of the general situation suggests several reasons for this neglect. Conditions in Syria became bad only toward the end of Amenhotep III's long reign of thirty-six years. For many years he had managed to maintain the Empire intact by clever diplomacy and subsidies, and now that he and his advisers were old men, they could not convince themselves that stronger action was necessary. Nevertheless, rebellion in Syria halted the tribute, funds were no longer available for lavish subsidies, and their whole diplomatic edifice came tumbling down. The military leaders, who had prospered under Thutmose III and his two successors, had gradually lost their influence at court under Amenhotep, their power going to civilian bureaucrats instead. Papyri bear strong witness to the antagonisms that arose between scribes and soldiers. Amenhotep's government, like that of Hatshepsut a hundred years before, was interested in Egypt rather than in the Empire, and leaders of the dominant faction showed little desire to spend money on foreign diplomacy and wars likely to augment the prestige of their military rivals. And lastly, a part of the blame for this imperial inertia must be laid upon the queen.

Early in his reign Amenhotep III had married a commoner named Tiy, the daughter of a minor priest and priestess, for whose low birth he was forced to apologize, even in the official announcements of the wedding. Tiy was a woman of forceful character, though intellectually she seems to have been quite incapable of taking a large view of a situation or of rising above personalities. The Amarna letters credit her with exercising great influence in the government, and she was the first Egyptian queen whose name is given beside that of the king in official inscriptions.

Tiy gave her support to the faction at court that was neglecting the Empire. No doubt the various Asiatic princesses whom her husband took as secondary wives found frequent occasion to remind her painfully of her own humble origins. It is quite possible that when the daughter of the king of Mitanni arrived in Egypt with an enormous number of gifts and a retinue of no less than 317 ladies of the court, Tiy regarded her as a rival and was not pleased. Amenhotep had also married two Babylonian princesses, the sister and the daughter of the reigning king; yet when that king repeatedly asked to receive an Egyptian princess (a daughter of Tiy) in exchange, he was told bluntly that Egyptian princesses just did not do such things. The good man was eventually reduced to begging for the hand of a lesser Egyptian lady, frankly admitting that he hoped to pass her off as the royal article in Babylon. In another letter the same king complains of the unaccountable disappearance of his sister, apparently suspecting foul play. Amenhotep's reply is not reassuring, and harems then were much what they were later. While it would no doubt be fanciful to see the finger of Tiy in each of these unpleasant happenings, we may take it for granted that she rarely used her powerful influence to promote the interests of her various co-wives' fathers.

After the death of Amenhotep, when Tiy's young son was just beginning his rule, the king of Mitanni tried to win her favor with gifts. Soon, however, he was complaining bitterly that his subsidies were not what they had been under the old king and even that his ambassadors were being arrested in Egypt. A few years later, Egypt stood idly by while Hittite armies destroyed the power of Mitanni, which was the greatest single misfortune that befell Egyptian rule in Asia.

Akhnaton's Reformation

In 1375 Amenhotep III died and was succeeded by his son Amenhotep IV, who had already been co-regent with his father for twelve years. The new king is better known by the name Akhnaton, which he assumed a few years later, and in our own day has been the most discussed man in Egyptian history. Discussion centers especially on his religious reforms. Our information concerning him and his reforms comes largely from inscriptions and carvings in the tombs of his nobles at Amarna, where lofty views are expressed in impressive language. How many of these ideas were truly the king's, how much he owed to his advisers, and how much was the result of the general evolution of Egyptian religion, we cannot say. Some modern scholars hail Akhnaton as one of the great religious geniuses of history; others insist that he personally had little to do with the religious movement that bears his name. There is similar disagreement as to his motives and his aims, though clues for the interpretation of his policies may be suggested by a brief survey of political and religious conditions in Egypt at the time of his accession.

Egypt had by now been a predatory state for a full century. Nubia provided gold, but the money which Amenhotep III spent so lavishly had come largely from Syrian tribute. Before the old king's death, revolts in Asia had seriously curtailed this income; and, as usual in the Orient, the appearance of a new sovereign was a signal for further revolts. The Empire suffered great losses in the early years of Akhnaton's rule. Conditions in Egypt were also highly unsatisfactory. The debility of Amenhotep in his last years is shown not only by his passive foreign policy, but even by his portraits, which picture him as fat, flabby, and decrepit (see Plate 10). His final sickness seems to have been a long affair, for news of it reached the king of faraway Assyria, who had time to send a wonder-working statue of Ishtar to Thebes in a vain attempt to save his royal paymaster's life. Such conditions were fraught with danger in a country where much depended upon the personality of the ruler, and the Amarna letters indicate that the court was highly demoralized in Amenhotep's last days.

The new king had to reform all this, and in his reforms he was much influenced by his mother Tiy. She in turn was inspired largely by hatred of the old court and its policies, and she brought in a large new personnel. Moreover, some of the new king's associates were not public servants of the highest type. These new officials had to be rewarded generously, and therefore new sources of revenue had to be found at once. It would have been strange indeed if covetous eyes had not been cast upon the vast riches of Amon.

This was also a time of changing theological views. The kings no longer viewed their divinity as under the Old Kingdom. They retained their old titles, to be sure, and still called themselves gods, but their theories regarding the way in which they had become gods incarnate were somewhat more sophisticated. Both Hatshepsut and Amenhotep III published intimate details about their miraculous births as the children of Amon with no earthly fathers. On the other hand, we have a statue of Amenhotep II kneeling as he offers gifts to the gods: heretofore Egyptian kings had always associated with other gods as equals. The priests of Amon, who had been of little political importance under the Old and Middle Kingdoms, began in the time of Thutmose III to form a rich and powerful caste. Their wealth was drawn from the proceeds of Empire, and naturally they favored the aggressive imperialism from which they profited so largely. Amon became the great god of the Empire, the physical father of the king perhaps, and the patron deity of a politically powerful priesthood.

Other deities than Amon continued to exist, however, and among them was Re of Heliopolis, who had once been a favorite of the Egyptian kings. Re had a priesthood in many parts of Egypt, and his theology was far more elaborate and civilized than was that of his upstart rival Amon. For example, Re was never accused of going around in human form begetting children. From ancient times Re had sometimes been called Aton, which was a word for the physical sun, and under the Empire he was often addressed by this name.

Aton had an important temple near Thebes, and it happened that the high priest of this temple was a brother of Tiy. Akhnaton resided there as a boy, and there he was crowned king. It seems very likely, therefore, that Tiy deliberately raised her son in the faith of Aton in order to oppose this god to Amon and the imperialistic system which she detested.

Akhnaton's Early Years

When Akhnaton's mummy was discovered early in the present century, competent anatomists declared that it was the body of a man only twenty-five or twenty-six years old. A few Egyptologists insisted that the mummy could not be his, but the great majority of them now accept it as authentic. Akhnaton ruled in his own name for nine years, so even if the age assigned to the mummy be stretched a little, he must have come to the throne when less than twenty years of age. Moreover, though Amenhotep III and Tiy had several daughters in the earlier years of their wedded life, they had been married for almost a quarter of a century before their son and heir was born. He therefore grew up during the years when the court of his debilitated father was falling into decline. The mummy also bears out what was already suspected from portraits of Akhnaton, namely, that he was an invalid and slightly deformed, with spindly legs and an unduly large head. The poor boy's physical misfortunes no doubt intensified his distaste for the rough and aggressive military caste whom his mother hated so cordially. Under the circumstances, it seems unwise to attribute the religious revolution entirely to Akhnaton; but it would be an even graver mistake to leave his personality entirely out of the story.

It is obvious that, if Akhnaton was only in his teens when he became king, he had little personal influence over the government during his early years. Some writers even speak of a regency by Tiy, and the principal minister was a man named Eye, who had long been closely associated with her. He later built an elaborate tomb for himself at Amarna, on the walls of which he tells of his services to Akhnaton and of his lavish rewards (see Plate 10). Equally important was Akhnaton's beautiful wife Nofretete (see Plate 9). Al-

Thutmose III, from Karnak
(Cairo Museum)

Queen Tiy, from Medinet Gurob
(Berlin Museum)

Akhnaton, from Amarna (Louvre Museum)

Nofretete, from Amarna
(Berlin Museum)

Plate 9.   Kings and Queens of the Eighteenth Dynasty

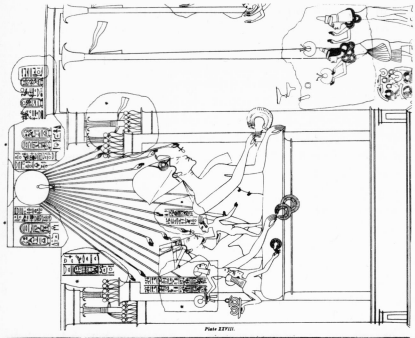

Plate XXVIII.

Akhnaton and Nofretete

Amenhotep

Plate 10

though her origin has been much discussed, there really is no firm evidence upon which to base theories: she almost certainly was an Egyptian, and she seems to have worked closely with Eye. An inscription in Eye's tomb speaks of him as the "father of the god," which is often interpreted as meaning "father-in-law of the king." Perhaps he was Nofretete's father. Another passage refers to Eye's wife as "nurse of the queen." Nofretete is frequently pictured with her husband, and inscriptions indicate that she, like Tiy, took an active part in government. She bore Akhnaton six daughters but no son.

During the early years of Akhnaton's reign the official worship of Amon went on much as usual, with the young king himself participating. Even in those early years, however, he built (or at least started) a temple to Aton in the midst of the temples to Amon at Thebes. In the fourth year of his reign (1372), orders were issued for the construction of a new city at the site now known as Amarna, about halfway between Thebes and Memphis. Within two years this city, called Akhetaton ("Horizon of Aton"), was ready, and Akhnaton made it his capital. At this time, too, the king changed his name from Amenhotep ("Amon is satisfied") to Akhnaton ("Spirit of Aton"). By these moves he inaugurated a great struggle with the priests of Amon and their god which filled the remainder of his reign. Unfortunately we cannot trace the course of this conflict chronologically, but it does not seem likely that the program was planned as a unit beforehand. More probably, one measure was piled upon another as the struggle increased in bitterness.

Akhnaton's most important step was closing the temples of Amon and confiscating their vast properties. No doubt this measure was dictated as much by financial necessity as by theological zeal. Build-

---

• Note for Plate 10.   Carving showing Amenhotep III as an old man, with Queen Tiy at his side. (Photo, British Museum.)

In the second picture Akhnaton stands at a window, throwing down gifts to Eye and his wife. Behind the king are his queen and three small children. Note the Aton disk, with rays and hands, two of which hold the ankh, or sign of life. From the tomb of Eye at Amarna. (Davies, The Rock Tombs of Amarna, VI, pl. 29. Egypt Exploration Society.)

ing and decorating the new capital had required great outlays from the already depleted treasury, and the Syrian tribute had by this time dwindled to a mere trickle. Another measure against Amon was the deliberate chiseling out of his name from inscriptions wherever it occurred. As Akhnaton thus defaced even the name of Amenhotep, Tiy seems to have inspired her son with a hatred of his father comparable to that which Thutmose III felt for his wife. The attack was carried to other deities as well, until the very word "gods" (in the plural) was deleted from inscriptions. Even then the unhappy king was not satisfied. At last he ordered the hostile gods deprived not only of their property, their honors, and their inscriptions, but even of their existence. He thus reached a theological monotheism which left Aton the sole god in the universe.

The New Theology

Financial and personal considerations had driven Akhnaton to religious reform, but it would be a grave mistake to assume that they were the sole cause of what he did. Such an explanation would be as silly as is the statement, occasionally heard even today, that England became Protestant merely in order that Henry VIII might marry new wives and seize the monastery lands—though in his case, as in Akhnaton's, financial and personal motives certainly played their part. The whole religious development of the Near East during the second millennium tended in the direction of monotheism. As different peoples became better acquainted with each other, they amalgamated their gods until, eventually, one supreme god was made to include all others. Tablets from Ras Shamra give the local Semitic god El a clear superiority over all rivals; and once or twice in the Amarna letters Syrian chiefs use the plural form *ilanu* with a singular verb to indicate God in the abstract, just as the Hebrews later used the plural form *Elohim*. Imperialism promoted monotheism.

Tendencies toward monotheism appeared in Egypt from the time of Amenhotep III. A hymn of praise to Amon, dating from his reign, hails that deity as "sole lord." The priests of Aton were even more inclined to monotheism. Perhaps the fact that they were a minority and out of power enabled them to adopt new ideas more quickly, and to sympathize more readily with the new religious conceptions of the day. At any rate, it was their god Aton, rather than the powerful Amon, who came to be recognized as the universal god. As Aton was the sun, he could not be represented by a statue and there were no idols in his cult. He was worshiped out of doors, and in his great temple at Akhetaton the high altar stood in an open court. Unlike Amon, who stood for the aggressive and predatory imperialism of the day—the fierce noonday sun, so to speak—Aton represented the helpful and life-giving sun. The sculptors of the Amarna Age devised a curious way to express this idea. They drew the disc of the sun, with rays emanating in every direction, and at the end of each ray they drew a human hand to show that Aton touched and helped all the earth. Often one or more of these hands would hold out an *ankh*—which is the *crux ansata,* a cross with the upper end stretched and bent into a loop—the Egyptian symbol for life (see Plate 10).

Hymns to Aton were inscribed on the walls of several tombs at Amarna, the most famous coming from the tomb of Eye. In impressive language this hymn describes the beauty of the world that Aton created and his tender care for it and for all his creatures. Several passages so closely resemble verses in Psalm 104 that many scholars believe there must be some connection between the two poems, and parts of this splendid "Hymn to Aton" would not seem out of place in a Christian hymnal.[2]

Amarna Art

The Amarna Age was also a revolutionary period in Egyptian art, as we learn from the ruins of Akhetaton and from the famous tomb of Akhnaton's son-in-law, Tutankhamen. The architects of the earlier Eighteenth Dynasty invented little, and their buildings are very like those of the Twelfth Dynasty except that they are bigger. Great wealth and a great empire seemed to awaken an enthusiasm for

[2] It might even be said that, if this hymn is indeed the inspiration of Psalm 104, it *has* found its way into our hymnals, for that Psalm in its turn inspired Sir Robert Grant's well-known "O worship the King, all glorious above." The hymn to Aton has been published repeatedly in translation, notably in J. H. Breasted, *History of Egypt,* pp. 371 ff., where the corresponding parts of Psalm 104 are printed in parallel columns.

great size. Sculptors too became enamored of the enormous—witness the two colossal statues of Amenhotep III near Thebes, usually called "the singing colossi of Memnon" because they were reputed to hail the rising sun with song. But a magnificent head of Thutmose III shows that Egyptian sculptors were still capable of splendid work (Plate 9).

A new spirit appears in the sculptures, reliefs, and paintings at Amarna. Critics suggest that Akhnaton in his youth had made the acquaintance of a group of unorthodox artists to whom he gave a free hand in building and decorating his city. While Egyptian artists had always striven for realism, at Akhetaton their desire to be true to nature went to extremes. Carvings of the king emphasized and even exaggerated his ugliness, and efforts to escape the formal dignity of the old statues sometimes led to a laborious and strained "informality." We cannot help feeling that the revolutionary artists of the Amarna period sought novelty rather than truth. Nevertheless, they sometimes produced excellent results. Painters and sculptors show a real love of nature, as did the author of the "Hymn to Aton." The bust of Queen Nofretete, found at Amarna, is one of the most beautiful in the world—but it is in the older tradition.

The wealth and splendor displayed in the tomb of Akhnaton's son-in-law, Tutankhamen, rather took away the breath of the archeologists who opened it in 1922. At first they were ecstatic in their enthusiasm for the skill of the Amarna artists who had wrought its treasures; but on cooler second thought critics noticed that many of these works were flashy and bizarre, comparing badly with the solid achievements of the Old and Middle Kingdoms. Egyptian art was already decadent in the Amarna period, and thereafter it never produced great works again.

Akhnaton's Failure

Though the theological and artistic ideals of the Amarna Age were not wholly new, it seems certain that Akhnaton was personally responsible for forcing their development. The king was a fanatic whose illness perhaps contributed as much as his family background or the opposition of the priests of Amon to making him relentless toward critics. Earlier rulers of his dynasty had rather humanized themselves in their relations to gods and men, but Akhnaton exaggerated his unique position. He put himself forward as the son of Aton, the sole god of the universe, and demanded obeisance such as earlier kings of Egypt had never received. Tomb reliefs at Amarna show courtiers and soldiers cringing and bowing low before him in a manner unknown before or later. The young king doubtless stored up much ill will for himself by such demands.

While the discontinuance of formal Amon worship may not have been a matter of great consequence to the common people of Egypt, the closing of countless minor temples certainly disturbed the superstitious populace. Moreover, the powerful families, many of whom had prospered as richly as the priests under the old regime, were not prepared to give up now without a struggle. Though Akhnaton apparently never faced armed rebellion, it soon became clear to his close associates that he was fighting a hopeless battle. His mother was dead, and his wife Nofretete presently deserted him, or was exiled to the northern quarter of Akhetaton. She took with her the young Tutankhamen, her protégé and son-in-law, and apparently Eye accompanied the queen. Akhnaton's eldest daughter had been married to a man named Smenkhkare, who now became co-regent with his father-in-law. We have no indication of his age—he may well have been older than Akhnaton, though his wife must have been only ten or twelve years old at the time of her marriage—and he died about four years after becoming co-regent. Shortly thereafter Akhnaton himself died (1366).

Akhnaton was succeeded by his second son-in-law, Tutankhamen. The new king was only a boy, and he owed his position to his wife and to the patronage of Nofretete and Eye. Their dispute with Akhnaton had probably been precipitated by the king's extreme measures against the old religion, and their protégé, who had once been named Tutankhaton, now showed his break with the new by adopting the name ending with "Amen" in place of "Aton." As king he made his peace with the priests of Amon and returned the capital to Thebes. The city of Akhetaton was abandoned; its houses of sun-dried brick soon collapsed; and the place became the desert which it has remained to the present day. After an otherwise unimportant reign of nine years, Tutankhamen died (1357) and was given a gorgeous burial by the priests of Amon.

Then came an amazing event which shows that Akhnaton's revolution had not been entirely religious. A few years ago a cuneiform Hittite tablet from Hattushash was found which told how Shuppiluliumash, the powerful Hittite king, at this time received a letter from Tutankhamen's widow, asking him to send one of his sons to become her consort and co-regent of Egypt! She was the sole surviving member of Akhnaton's family, and though the worship of Aton had already been abandoned, she was willing to take this step to prevent the government from falling to the rival party. Shuppiluliumash apparently was as much surprised as we, for he sent a messenger to verify this strange request. The messenger returned with a favorable report, and the king sent his son. The young man was murdered, however, on reaching Egypt. Probably the king had dallied too long, and the situation in Egypt was so desperate that the widow had taken other measures. She married her father's old counsellor, Eye, and he became king as her consort. If Eye really was the father of Nofretete, the young queen thus entered into a formal marriage with her own grandfather!

Though Eye's abandoned tomb was still decorated with the glorious "Hymn to Aton," he was now a worshiper of Amon and for a few years he ruled Egypt from Thebes. When he died, about 1353, a soldier who had been stationed in Palestine in the days of Akhnaton, and who had never withdrawn his loyalty from Amon, established a military dictatorship in Egypt. He claimed to be the legitimate heir of Amenhotep III, and he ruled for thirty-four years. The last vestiges of Akhnaton's revolution were stamped out. Statues of the king were mutilated or thrown down, his name was chiseled out from inscriptions, and whenever it became necessary to mention him in official records he was called simply "the criminal of Akhetaton."

• Note for Plate 11. This picture on the opposite page shows the reconstruction of a house of an Egyptian noble of the Amarna period. (*Photo, Cairo Museum.*)

Plate 11. House at Amarna (reconstruction)

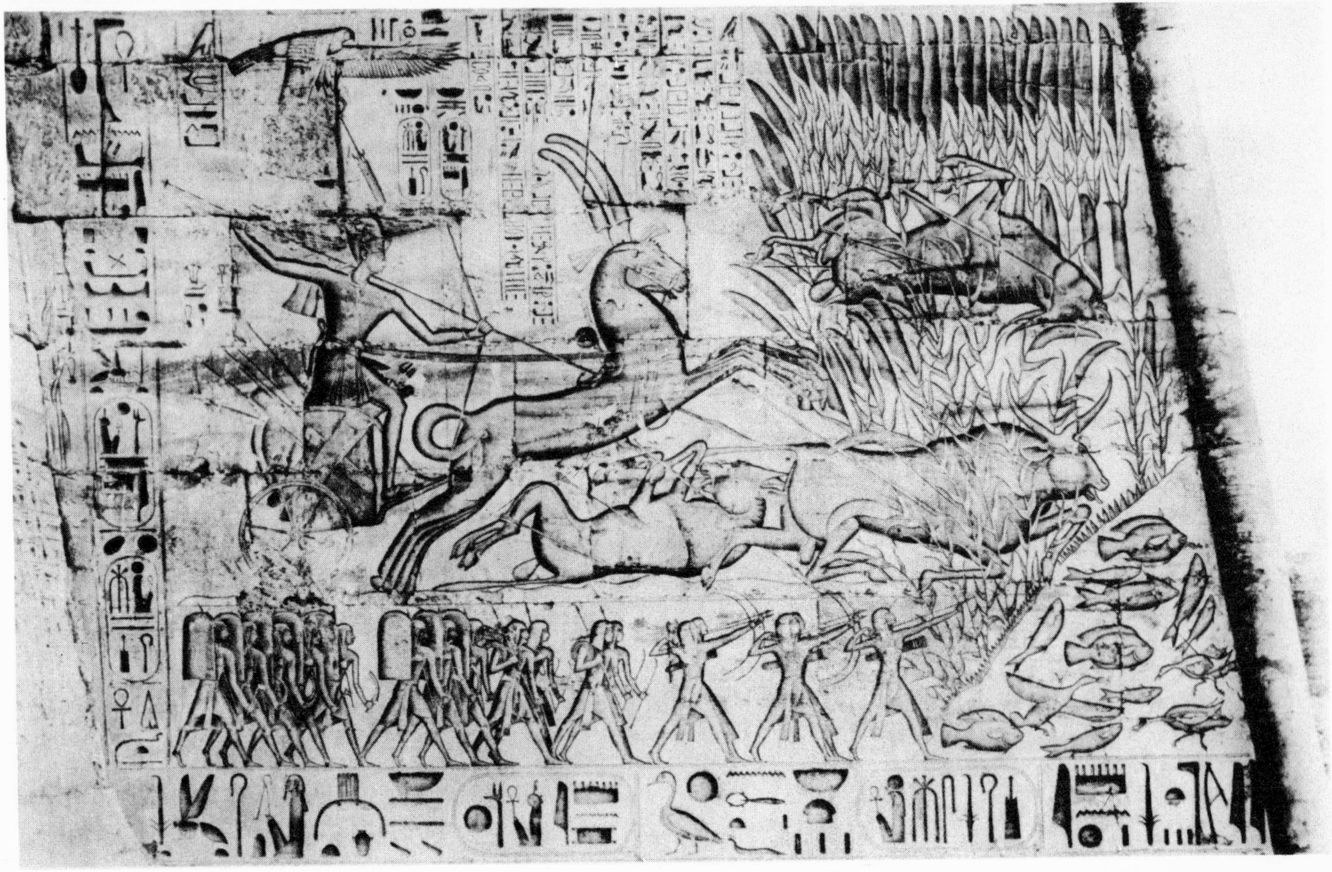

Plate 12.   Rameses III, Hunting

The Decline of Imperial Glory

The military autocracy, which pulled Egypt together again after the ruin wrought by a quarter of a century of revolutionary confusion, made the country so strong that there was hope of regaining the Empire that had been lost. Then came Rameses I, who ruled for barely a year but who founded the Nineteenth Dynasty, which remained in power for over a century (1319–1200). Its two great kings were Seti I (1318–1299) and Rameses II, whose long reign lasted from 1299 to 1232. These kings carried the war into Syria with great success. Of the achievements of Seti we can speak only in general terms, but the boastful inscriptions set up by Rameses tell us all— and indeed considerably more than all—that he accomplished in his many wars.

The Hittites had prospered during the fourteenth century, and their great empire now included most of Anatolia, all northern Syria, and other states. In 1294 they gathered a great army to oppose Rameses, whom they ambushed near Kadesh. If we are to believe Rameses, the Hittites were decisively defeated. The Hittite king, on the other hand, claimed that he had pursued the defeated Egyptians as far as Damascus. The wars continued, with varying fortunes, for fifteen years until at last, in 1278, the kings of the two countries drew up a treaty, of which we still have copies both in Egyptian and in cuneiform Hittite. The kings swore an eternal peace, and they divided the contested lands, with northern Syria going to the Hittites and southern Syria, including modern Palestine, to Egypt. Rameses then married the Hittite king's daughter and passed the remaining forty-six years of his reign in peace.

Merneptah, the thirteenth son of Rameses II, succeeded him and

---

• Note for Plate 12.   This wall relief from the temple of Rameses III at Medinet Habu shows the king hunting wild bulls in a marsh. Two bulls are already dead, and the king urges on his horses in order to dispatch the third. Note the fine swing of the marching men in the lower level. Compare the elaboration of these carvings with the simplicity of those in the tomb of Ti (Plate 7) made almost fifteen hundred years earlier. (*Photo, Oriental Institute.*)

ruled for ten years (1232–22). His short reign was notable chiefly for attacks upon Egypt from the West. For almost two centuries raiders from the Aegean area had been growing bolder, attacking Crete, Asia Minor, and Syria. Latterly they had beset north Africa whence, with the aid of native Libyans, they now raided Egypt itself. Meantime, others attacked Egypt from the sea, among them men called Aqaiwasha, who may be identified with the Achaeans or Homeric Greeks. Merneptah drove the pirates off, and for a moment Egypt had peace. His successors were men of little strength; they were in constant quarrels over the succession; and other raiders attacked Egypt.

After several years of ups and downs, Rameses III (1198–67) became the second king of the Twentieth Dynasty. He was the last of the great kings of Egypt. He fought against various sea raiders, among others a group whose name the Egyptians wrote "P-l-s-t." They are to be identified with the Biblical Philistines. Some of them Rameses took into his service, sending them to guard the Palestinian cities along the Mediterranean coast. Conveniently forgetting their master, the mercenaries then made themselves the independent rulers of the southern coastal plain. From these Philistines the whole land eventually took the name Palestine. Rameses III was followed by nine other kings of the same name, none of them important, who ruled for seventy-five years. Egypt in their day was exhausted, her empire was gone, and her decay was far advanced.

During the Twenty-first Dynasty, which ruled from 1085 to 945, the successive high priests of Amon at Thebes ruled Egypt as kings. Then followed three dynasties of Libyan kings (945–712), and under the Twenty-fifth Dynasty of Nubian kings (712–663) Egypt was conquered by the Assyrians. During these long centuries kings occasionally arose who could galvanize Egypt into a semblance of life, build a few temples, and lead Egyptian armies into Asia. Foreigners sometimes still looked upon Egypt with respect, but the days of her glory were over.

The Hittites too had fallen upon evil days. In the thirteenth and twelfth centuries new migrations from Europe entered Asia Minor across the Hellespont. The Phrygians attacked the Hittites from the

West and about 1200 they overthrew the Hittite Empire in Asia Minor. Hittite kings continued to rule in northern Syria, however, and here they continued to set up inscriptions in hieroglyphic Hittite until they were conquered by the Assyrians in the eighth century. Their kingdom is called "Syro-Hittite," to distinguish it from the great empire of the second millennium. The Phoenician cities became independent and entered upon a prosperous period in which their ships scoured the Mediterranean and colonies were founded in north Africa and Spain, even beyond the Straits of Gibraltar. Palestine and Canaan were torn between the Philistines and the Hebrew invaders from the desert, with an occasional feeble attempt by an Egyptian king to reassert authority in the rebellious province. This chaotic twelfth century also saw the kings of Assyria start up the path to empire and glory.

Note

The Rediscovery of the Hittites

The story of the rediscovery of the Hittites is one of the romances of modern scholarship. On several occasions Old Testament writers mention the Hittites as a powerful people, yet the Greek and Latin writers knew nothing about them. It was sometimes held as a reproach against the Bible that it attributed such importance to an insignificant or perhaps even nonexistent people. But when scholars began to read Egyptian and Assyrian inscriptions they found references to a people called Kheta or Khatti who, they decided, might be the Biblical Hittites. Perhaps the Bible was more nearly right than had been supposed. Then travelers began reporting inscriptions in a new type of writing at several places in Syria and Asia Minor, and scholars surmised that this writing might be Hittite. An English orientalist, A. H. Sayce (1845–1933), who had long been urging the importance of the Hittites, wrote a small popular volume about this people under the title, *The Hittites: the Story of a Forgotten Empire* (1888). Much of what Sayce said was wrong, and it was concerned largely with the late "Syro-Hittites," but it was he who rescued the Hittites from oblivion. In that same year (1888), German archeologists began to dig at Zengirli, on the northwestern frontier of Syria toward Asia Minor, thinking that this was the Hittite capital. They found a number of interesting things, though not what they were looking for, and the Hittites again lost face.

Nevertheless, material regarding them continued to appear in Asia Minor and Syria, and even in Egypt, and in 1906 a German Assyriologist, Hugo Winckler, began to excavate the ruins at Boghazköy, a village in central Asia Minor. He found that this ancient site had once been the Hittite capital, Hattushash, and he had the good fortune to stumble upon a collection of about 10,000 clay tablets which proved to be the royal archives. Many of the tablets were written in Akkadian cuneiform and easily read. Winckler created something of a sensation among scholars when he published a treaty made by a Hittite king with the king of Mitanni, which was sworn to before Indra, Mithra, and other Aryan gods, for this was our first intimation that Indo-Europeans had entered the Near East at so early a date. The great majority of the tablets were marked with cuneiform characters in an unknown language. During World War I, a Czech scholar, F. Hrozny, managed to decipher them. He showed that their language was Indo-European, with many grammatical forms and root words rather similar to Latin, and that it was the official language of the Hittites, the ultimate Nordic ancestry of whose leaders was thus disclosed. But fundamental differences from the eastern Aryan languages, such as Sanskrit and Persian, showed that these Hittites were quite distinct from the Indra-worshiping rulers of Mitanni. Other tablets were written in still other languages—eight in all—including other Indo-European dialects, native Asiatic languages, and Hurrian, as well as Akkadian and even Sumerian.

The hieroglyphic inscriptions, which were the first to attract attention, still remain undeciphered. Scholars have worked at them for many years, and at last Hrozny, Gelb, and others seem to have solved the major difficulties in deciphering them (I. J. Gelb, *Hittite Hieroglyphics* I–III [1931–42]). It is to the cuneiform tablets, however, that we owe our present appreciation of the importance of the Hittites and most of our knowledge of Hittite history, law, literature, and religion. Sixty years ago the importance of the Hittites was only vaguely suspected. Since that time a rather small group of scholars has added a new empire to history and given us a wholly new picture of the Near East in the second millennium before Christ.

VI Assyrians and Persians

The SECOND MILLENNIUM BEFORE CHRIST HAD BEEN THE Bronze Age; the first millennium was to be the Age of Iron. Small pieces of this metal, probably of meteoritic origin, had long been used as jewelry, and during the last century of the Egyptian and Hittite empires iron began to appear in larger quantities. Probably the art of smelting iron was discovered in Anatolia, where the Taurus Mountains supplied easily accessible ore. At any rate, this was the earliest important center for its production. A letter from the Hittite wife of Rameses II vainly begs her brother for gifts of this precious metal. The use of iron spread rapidly thereafter and archeologists date the beginning of the Iron Age in the Near East from about 1200. Nevertheless, three or four centuries were to pass before the Assyrians, the first great military power of the Iron Age, were able to equip whole armies with iron weapons and thus to inaugurate a new period in the history of warfare. Although these centuries between the fall of Egypt and the rise of Assyria were politically chaotic, they were the great period of Phoenician trade and culture, and they witnessed the infiltration of Arameans through much of the Near East.

Phoenicians and Arameans

The Phoenician cities were the first to recover from the devastation wrought during the last century of Egyptian rule in Syria. Phoenicia extended along the Mediterranean coast from Mount Carmel on the south to the mouth of the Eleutherus River more than a hundred miles to the north. It was hemmed in on the east by the Lebanon Mountains, which are rarely as much as twenty miles from the sea and whose spurs often touch the water's edge. The country was thus divided naturally into small districts, each of which easily became a city-state. As harbors are plentiful along the narrow strip of coast, while fertile land is scarce, geography forced the Phoenicians to become traders, and for several centuries after the fall of Egypt their ships dominated the eastern Mediterranean.

Paleolithic and neolithic artifacts have been found at many Phoenician sites, and Phoenician cities were important trading centers even before the days of the Old Kingdom in Egypt. Perhaps the oldest of these cities was Gebal, but Tyre and Sidon were almost as ancient. The inhabitants of these cities were men of Semitic race who had come up out of Arabia through Palestine and along the Mediterranean coast, probably about 3000 B.C. The Egyptians called them Fenkhu, which meant "shipbuilders," and our "Phoenician" probably comes from this word through the Greek.

Gebal and Tyre had been loyal to Egypt in the Amarna Age, no doubt because their commercial prosperity depended upon it, but presently each city was captured by the Amurru. A century later both were in the hands of Rameses II, and like other Phoenician cities they suffered severely at the hands of sea raiders shortly after that king's death. The raids stopped in the twelfth century, perhaps because of disturbances in the Aegean region, whereupon the Phoenician cities were able to re-establish themselves as independent city-states. In later times these cities traced their history back to a founding, or more accurately to a refounding, in the twelfth or eleventh century before Christ. At first Sidon seems to have been the more important city, but Tyre was leader during the greater part of the period of Phoenician independence.

The Phoenicians soon began building a great commercial empire. South of them were the Philistine seaports of Ashdod, Ashkelon, and Gaza, competitors of Tyre and Sidon but never their serious rivals. By this time Canaan, inland to the east and north of Philistia, had been occupied by Hebrews, who were often at war with the Philistines, and in the tenth century Hiram, king of Tyre, entered into close friendship with the Hebrew king, Solomon. The two monarchs were brought together less by mutual hostility to the Philistines than by trade interests. They traded with each other and even co-operated in sending expeditions through the Gulf of Aqaba to the Red Sea and Africa, whence (according to the Scriptures) Solomon derived "gold, and silver, ivory, and apes, and peacocks." After the death of Solomon, Hiram seized much of the region in northern Palestine that is called Galilee, thereby securing the route to Damascus, the western terminus of caravan trade with Babylonia. Meantime Tyrian sailors were coasting north to Cyprus, where they established several colonies, and along the southern coast of Asia Minor from Tarsus as far as Rhodes. Before 900 they frequently visited Crete, the Aegean Islands, and Greece itself.

In the ninth century, Tyrian merchants, venturing still farther afield, founded colonies in the western Mediterranean. Before 800, they had established themselves in Malta, Sicily, and southern Sardinia; at several places in north Africa, the most important of which was Carthage; at Malaga in Spain; and even at Gades, outside Gibraltar. In Spain they obtained tin from mines in Britain, although it is doubtful whether Phoenician ships made the last stage of this long journey. While the Phoenicians were more famous as traders than as manufacturers, they were skillful at making cloth and other commodities and particularly famous for a purple (or crimson) dye which they had learned to manufacture and use.

The Phoenician cities reached the height of their power and prosperity in the eighth century, after which they declined before the rising might of Assyria. Even in the ninth century Tyre, Sidon, Gebal, and other cities had paid the Assyrians tribute, which they found cheaper than war; and, as time went by and Assyria's demands rose higher, refusal to pay was regarded as rebellion and punished as such. At last Sidon was destroyed in 677, and ten years later Tyre was reduced to a sort of vassalage. The city was not destroyed, however, and it remained the commercial center of the eastern Mediterranean until captured by Alexander the Great (332 B.C.).

Phoenician Culture

The ancient Greeks attributed the invention of the alphabet to the Phoenicians, and modern discoveries support their contention. We

SINAITIC	CANAANITE-PHOENICIAN	EARLY GREEK	LATER GREEK	LATIN	ENGLISH
ꓭ ᕒ	ꓘ ꓞ	A	A	A	A
☐ ☐ ⫏	9 9	ꙅ ꙅ	B	B	B
ˎ L ᄂᄂ	1	1	⎰	C G	C, G
ꓷ ꓂	△ ᴀ	△	△	D	D
ꓻ	㇕㇕	ꓶ	ꓮ	E	E
ᴏ	Ꙝ	Ꙝ	ꓵ	F V	F, U, V, W, Y
＝ (?)	ꙅ ꙅ	I	I		Z
ꓻ ꧁	ᄇ H	ꓭ	ꓭ	H	H
	⊗	⊗	⊗		(Th)
ꙮ ꙰	ꓜ	Ꙍ	Ꙍ	I	I, J
＋ ꙅ	ꓘ ꓴꙅ	ꓘ	ꓘ		K
9 6 ꙶ	ᄂᄂ	ꙶᅥᄀ	L ∧	L	L
ᄴ	ᄴ ᄴ	ꙏ	ꙏ	M	M
ꓱ	ꓴ ꓱ	ꓦ	N	N	N
⇦ ⇨	ꗇ ᄒꙅꙅ	ꓫ	ꓫ	X	(X)
ꙫ 0	0 0	○	○	O	O
ꙍ	ꙅꙅꙅ	ꙅ	ꓒ	P	P
8 ∞	ꓜᄂꓜ	ꓟ	M		(S)
ꙭ	ꙅꙅꙅ	Φ	ꙅ	Q	Q
ꙮ ꙫ Ꙭ	ꓞ	ꓞ	ꓑ	R	R
ꙍ	W	ꙅ	ꙅ	S	S
＋	✕	T	T	T	T

• Diagram showing development of the alphabet. (*From table prepared by Martin Sprengling; courtesy, Oriental Institute.*)

have already seen how Egyptians supplemented their ideographs with twenty-four characters representing simple consonantal sounds, though they never learned to write without the use of determinatives in addition to these letters. Explorers in the Sinai peninsula have found markings, dating from the days of the Twelfth Dynasty, which resemble Egyptian consonantal signs but which apparently spell Semitic words. Obviously some Semite, who could read and write Egyptian, had conceived the brilliant idea of writing his own language with these characters, disregarding the determinatives while doing so. Somewhat similar marks were found on a vessel, dating from about 1800, that was unearthed at Gebal, where Egyptian influence always was strong. These marks in time evolved into the twenty-two consonantal signs of the Phoenician alphabet. Hebrew and other Semitic languages were originally written with these same characters.

Tablets found at Ras Shamra show that in this area, where the Babylonian cultural tradition was still strong as late as 1400, men continued to write on clay tablets with cuneiform characters. They had learned the principles of alphabetic writing from their Phoenician neighbors, however, and they invented a cuneiform alphabet of their own. Still further north, inscriptions were written in Phoenician characters, whether the language used was Phoenician or Aramaic. Arameans then carried a modified Phoenician alphabet through Babylonia and Persia to India itself. Several centuries later the Phoenicians taught their alphabet to the Greeks, who improved it by adding signs for the vowels (using characters for Semitic consonantal sounds not found in Greek) and gave it to the Romans, who in turn passed it on to western Europe.

Although the Phoenicians invented this new and more efficient form of writing, they used it for little except business documents. We have no traces of a Phoenician literature, and our evidence for other writing is indirect. A certain Philo of Byblus, who wrote in Greek in the first century after Christ, tells us of a mythographer named Sanchoniathon, who lived at Byblus about 1000 B.C. and wrote on the creation and genealogies of the gods. Philo's brief summary of the work shows that its views followed the general pattern established by Egyptian and Sumerian writers on such matters.

Other evidence shows that a number of gods, called Baals, were worshiped up and down Syria, from Ras Shamra to Canaan. Many of these Baals were local deities, such as Melkart of Tyre or Eshmun of Sidon, the "lords" (*Baalim*) of their cities. Sometimes a city worshiped a "lady" (*Baalat*), such as the "Lady of Beirut" or the "Lady of Gebal," instead of a Baal. These Ladies were forms of the old Earth Mother, the "Lady of Gebal" being named Astarte—the "Ashtoreth" of the Old Testament. She had much in common with Ishtar; and her lover, called Adonis by the Greeks, was identified with the Babylonian Tammuz. Gebal was one of the principal centers in the Near East for the worship of this dying and rising god. As elsewhere in the Near East, the fertility cults often assumed a licentious character, and other religious practices were sometimes very cruel. Like several neighboring peoples (including the Hebrews), the Phoenicians occasionally offered their gods human sacrifices, and in Carthage they continued to do so at least until the fourth century.

A famous story in the Old Testament tells us that when Solomon wished to build his great temple at Jerusalem he found that there were no craftsmen among the Hebrews capable of such an undertaking. He therefore called upon his friend, Hiram of Tyre, to provide the materials and labor. The story may be true, yet the Phoenicians themselves show up badly as artists when compared with their contemporaries in Egypt and even in Babylonia. Modern archeologists have found many statues and other works of Phoenician art, though none is of superior or even mediocre merit, and all are patent imitations of Babylonian or Egyptian models. The Phoenicians were primarily business men, and their civilization was essentially commercial.

Aramaic Expansion

While the Phoenicians were thus pushing their maritime empire to the west, another Semitic people, the Arameans, were occupying the territory east of the Lebanon Mountains and laying the foundations of a great commercial empire there. Early in the second millennium these Arameans had lived in the northern part of the Syrian Desert, between Damascus and Babylon, whence they began pushing out in many directions as early as the Amarna Age. Among them were the Habiru, who forced their way into Palestine. Others helped found the kingdom of Amurru, while still others turned east, crossed the Euphrates, and occupied parts of Babylonia. Somewhat later, after the decline of Egyptian and Hittite power, other Arameans pushed into northern Syria and occupied the fertile fringe north of the desert. The early records picture them as raiders and freebooters —which they doubtless were. Before long, however, they learned that trade too had its profits, and their cities, such as Damascus and Palmyra, became great caravan centers.

The Arameans founded many tiny states in the territories they occupied but they never created a united Aramaic Empire. David and Solomon fought against them, and sometimes claimed fantastic conquests. Wars between the Arameans and the Assyrians began in the twelfth century in the vicinity of Palmyra and not until four hundred years later did they end with the Assyrian absorption of all Aramaic territory. The loss of political independence did not destroy the Arameans, however, for they continued trading in Syria and Babylonia. Their caravans followed the edge of the desert from the Red Sea north through Damascus to Syria, and they reached Assyria and Babylonia by going east from Aleppo through Haran or from Damascus through Palmyra. The fact that the Aramaic language was written alphabetically, and therefore was much easier to learn than cuneiform Assyrian writing, made it the language of trade, and Aramaic scribes served one military power after another. Aramaic became a *lingua franca,* spoken everywhere in the Near East, until the Mohammedan conquerors of the seventh century after Christ replaced it with the kindred Arabic.

Assyrian Conquests

While Phoenicians and Arameans were thus building up their great commercial empires, the Assyrians were slowly gaining military supremacy in the Near East. Assyria, in the northern half of Mesopotamia, had been much influenced by Babylonian culture in the great

days of the third millennium. It suffered less than its neighbor Babylon from Kassite invasions, partly, perhaps, because it was poorer
and therefore less attractive to the barbarians, and partly because it
was protected by surrounding hills. For several centuries the Assyrians led a precarious existence, however, and during this period of
confusion and violence they developed the military spirit which was
to characterize them ever after. In the fourteenth century, they had
a large share in the destruction of the kingdom of Mitanni, most
of whose territory they obtained. A hundred years later, when Rameses II was endeavoring to wrest northern Syria from the Hittites,
able and warlike Assyrian kings were pushing back raiders on every
side. They advanced their frontiers to the north, far into Hurri country, and they attacked and defeated the Hittites as well as the Kassites. After the elimination of Hittite and Egyptian power, the Assyrian kings commanded the strongest armies in the Near East. At
the end of the twelfth century, Tiglath-Pileser I (1115–02)[1] of Assyria ruled the broad territory between the Tigris and the northern
Euphrates at Carchemish, raided Syria, and entered into diplomatic
relations with Egypt. But his death was followed by another period
of darkness, and the first period of Assyrian power came to an end.

Tiglath-Pileser's successors lost much of what he had won. Assyrian territories were invaded by hill tribes from the north, or by
Arameans advancing from the south, and raiders cut the trade routes
that skirted the foothills from the upper Tigris to the Mediterranean.
Aramean traders also cut into the profits of their Assyrian competitors. During the tenth century the Assyrians greatly improved their
army, thanks to the new iron weapons; and two kings of the ninth
century made extensive conquests in the West. Their good fortune
did not long continue, however, for the Assyrians became entangled
in a series of difficult wars with Urartu, a kingdom in Armenia north
of Lake Van. Here their armies met with serious reverses. Although
they managed to keep the great trade route open, thus assuring the
life line of their empire, the Assyrians could not turn their attention
to the West again for almost a century.

---

[1] The chronology in this and the following chapter is usually that of Olmstead.

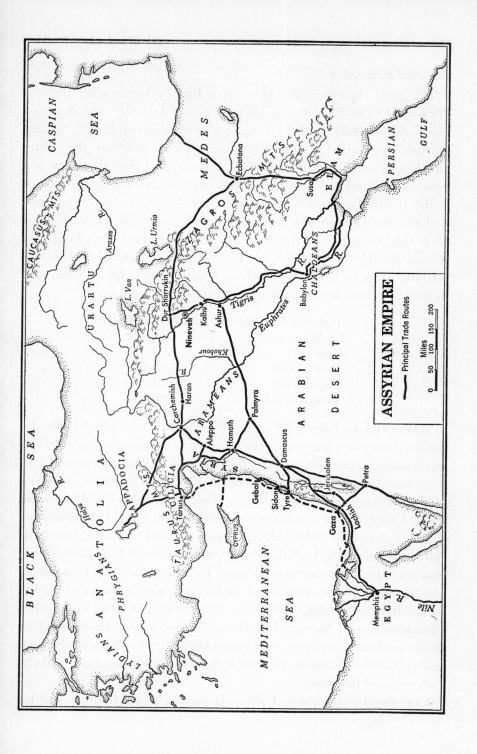

ASSYRIAN EMPIRE

— Principal Trade Routes

Miles
0 50 100 150 200

Imperial Expansion

The great expansion of the Assyrian Empire began with Tiglath-Pileser III (746–28); it was virtually complete before the death of Esarhaddon (669); and the Empire was overthrown in 612. Six important kings ruled over Assyria during this century of glory. The annals give us rather full accounts of their wars, but the story is a complicated and confusing one whose details are of little interest or profit. It will therefore be simpler to trace Assyrian expansion in one region after another not bothering to chronicle the campaigns of each king in order. As the Assyrian annalists fitted each king to a standardized pattern which left no place for individuality, it is impossible to give character sketches of these monarchs, and the best that can be done is to list their names for ready reference:

Tiglath-Pileser III	746–728
Shalmaneser V	728–722
Sargon II	722–705
Sennacherib	705–681
Esarhaddon	681–669
Ashurbanipal	669–626

When Tiglath-Pileser III seized the throne of Assyria in 746, the Kassite kings had long since been driven from Babylonia, and their weak native successors were unable to resist the Aramean and Chaldean invaders who swept over the country from the west and even planted colonies east of the Tigris. Thereafter for several centuries lower Mesopotamia was known as Chaldea after one Aramean tribe. As these Aramean and Chaldean invaders often attacked Assyria itself from the south, Tiglath-Pileser was forced to intervene in Babylonian affairs. He reduced the king of Babylon to a state of vassalage, but the disturbances continued, and in the very last year of his life he made himself king of Babylon. Within a short time, however, a Chaldean named Merodach-Baladan united several Aramean tribes under his leadership, entered into an alliance with Elam to the east, and proclaimed himself "King of Babylon" (721). Not until 710 did Sargon expel the usurper.

Continued confusion in Babylonia caused Sennacherib to lose his patience. He sacked the city of Babylon, scattered its population, turned its site into a swamp, and proclaimed himself King of Sumer and Akkad (689). His son and successor, Esarhaddon, had passed his youth at Babylon and now he romantically deplored the city's sad fate; with even greater sorrow he learned what a severe blow the destruction of this principal trading center had been to the imperial treasury. He therefore rebuilt and resettled Babylon, adopted a conciliatory policy toward its new inhabitants, and enjoyed peace in his time. Rebellion broke out anew under Ashurbanipal, who captured the city in 648 and proclaimed himself its king. He was no more successful than his predecessors in pacifying this restless province, however, and Babylonia remained a spear pointed at the heart of Assyria. In the end a Chaldean named Nabu-apal-usur, better known to us under his Greek name Nabopolassar, who was a descendant of Merodach-Baladan and also called himself "King of Babylon," took a leading part in the overthrow of the Assyrian Empire (612).

A second center of danger to the Assyrian Empire lay to the north in the kingdom of Urartu, whose inhabitants were descended from the Hurrians of old. Tiglath-Pileser invaded the country, besieged the king in his own capital, and punished him so severely that for many years he was incapable of further aggression. In 714 renewed attacks forced Sargon to invade Urartu again. A few years later a horde of barbarians, known as the Cimmerians, crossed the Caucaus Mountains from Europe and inflicted such defeats upon Urartu that that kingdom never recovered.

Syria and the West

After his pacifications of Babylonia and Urartu, Tiglath-Pileser III turned his attention to Syria and the West. It was not difficult for him to resume control of the territories that had broken away during the last century, and in 735 he was ready to advance against Damascus. After occupying the Philistine coast as far south as Gaza, he advanced through the territory of Israel, replacing its king with a subservient vassal, and captured Damascus in 732. The city was looted and destroyed, and large numbers of its inhabitants were deported to Assyria. At the time of his death (728) Tiglath-Pileser dominated all Syria and Palestine to the very gates of Egypt. His son Shalmaneser was faced with revolts in Tyre, Sidon, and other Phoenician cities, and in Israel. He reduced several of the rebel cities to submission, but Tyre successfully withstood a five-year siege. Samaria, the capital of Israel, was captured and destroyed in 722, and many inhabitants were carried away to Assyria by the next king, Sargon II.

Shalmaneser also made important conquests in Anatolia. It seems probable that the district we know as Cilicia had been conquered by Tiglath-Pileser III; Shalmaneser added Cappadocia, north of the mountains. Still farther west, the Phrygians ruled the old Hittite region of central Anatolia under a king known to the Assyrians as Mita, to the Greeks as Midas. He occasionally raided Assyrian territory in Cilicia and even forced his way into Syria. To prevent further raids of this sort, Shalmaneser occupied extensive territories and made allies in Cappadocia.

During the next several years both Midas and the king of Urartu instigated revolts among these northern allies of Assyria. Sargon therefore decided that he would thoroughly pacify the whole northern frontier. In 709 he ordered the governor of Cilicia to punish Midas. Assyrian arms were victorious as usual, and Midas was forced to pay tribute. Various kings in Cyprus likewise became tributary at this time. A few years later the Cimmerians, after defeating Urartu, advanced against the Phrygians, and so weakened them that they were presently destroyed by their neighbors to the west, the Lydians. Sargon, on the other hand, had fortified his new provinces so strongly that he was able to hold back the Cimmerian flood, though he lost his life in the fighting (705). Thereafter the Assyrians dominated the eastern half of Anatolia until almost the end of the next century.

During the greater part of this period of Assyrian advance, Egypt had been ruled by the Libyan kings of the Twenty-second Dynasty (945–731). Though these kings had neither the power nor the desire to intervene strongly in Syria, they frequently instigated minor rebellions there and supported a pro-Egyptian party against the pro-Assyrian party in each tiny state. The dynasty fell in 731 and, after almost twenty years of confusion, the Nubian Twenty-fifth Dynasty seized Egypt in 712. The new dynasty at once inaugurated a more active Syrian policy. Severe revolts were repressed by Sargon in 711 and Sennacherib decided upon strenuous measures to stamp out disaffection in his rebellious Syrian provinces once and for all.

The most famous episode in the new program came in 701, when Sennacherib attacked Hezekiah, king of Judah. He captured forty-six cities and villages—including Lachish, the second city in the king-dom—and boasted of taking 200,150 prisoners, only a small fraction of whom could have come from Judah if this odd figure is correct: perhaps he really took only 2150 prisoners. The campaign reached its climax in a siege of Jerusalem—the siege commemorated in Lord Byron's well-known lines beginning "The Assyrian came down like the wolf on the fold." Sennacherib failed to take Jerusalem. The Bible tells us that an Angel of the Lord smote the Assyrians, and Herodotus reports a story that rats ate their bowstrings. A modern scholar has attempted to harmonize the two legends by suggesting that perhaps the Angel of the Lord took the form of bubonic plague carried by the rats! Certainly it is true that in antiquity such plagues often made protracted sieges more deadly to the besiegers than to the besieged. Although Jerusalem was not taken, the Jewish kings learned their lesson. Hezekiah paid an enormous tribute and caused no more trou-ble, and his successors remained dutiful allies of Assyria.

Egyptian intrigues in the Phoenician cities were soon resumed, however, and in 677 Sidon was induced to revolt. After capturing and destroying the rebellious city, Esarhaddon decided that peace could be assured only by the subjugation of Egypt. He invaded that country in 675, occupied much of the Delta in 674, and took Mem-phis in 671. Upper Egypt soon surrendered. Esarhaddon then placed Assyrian governors over the whole country, but Egypt remained rest-less. Presently some of the governors fled or were driven from their posts. Esarhaddon was on his way to Egypt with a new army to re-store order when he died late in 669. The army continued its march and temporarily pacified Egypt. Assyria's Empire included all the lands dominated by ancient oriental civilization.

Ashurbanipal and the Fall of Assyria

When Ashurbanipal, the last and most famous of Assyrian kings, succeeded Esarhaddon in 669, Assyrian power had passed its zenith. The Empire was being attacked by enemies within and without. The reign of Ashurbanipal was in many ways a brilliant and splendid period, though he was constantly fighting to retain what he had inherited. Shortly before the death of Esarhaddon, the former Nubian king of Egypt began efforts to regain his throne. The Assyrians were able to defeat him, but, to prevent further disturbances, they decided to support native Egyptian governors against the Nubian pretender. In 663 they set up a certain Psammetichus as their vassal king. Within a few years this man was calling himself an independent sovereign, and later he was reckoned the founder of the Twenty-sixth Dynasty of Egypt (663–525).

Meantime Gyges, king of Lydia in Asia Minor, had overthrown the Phrygian kingdom and annexed its territory. He now became an ally of Psammetichus. Presumably he would have shown even greater hostility to Assyria had not the Cimmerians again become so troublesome that he was forced to eat humble pie and pay homage to Assyria in return for military aid against the barbarians. Ashurbanipal also had trouble on his northeastern frontier, where the Medes were beginning to attack Assyria. And above all, he had constant trouble with Babylon, where his brother allied himself with the Elamites to revolt against Ashurbanipal. The Assyrian king managed to defeat Elam; Babylon was captured after a long siege (648); and Elam was annexed a few years later (about 636). During these disturbances Psammetichus severed the last bonds uniting Egypt to Assyria (651).

We have no records of the last years of Ashurbanipal's reign, but we know that he died in 626. Except for Egypt, his father's Assyrian Empire was still intact. He had added Lydia as a tributary ally and had defeated the Cimmerians. His armies were still victorious in their wars, and his capital at Nineveh was the largest and most magnificent city in the world. A superficial observer might believe that the Assyrian Empire still stood in all its glory. In reality it was only a hollow shell. The fatal blow fell in 612 when an army of Medes and Chaldeans attacked Nineveh, and the Assyrian Empire collapsed like a house of cards.

Assyrian Civilization

If we are to appreciate the true place of the Assyrians in the history of culture, we must remember who the Assyrians were, for not everyone in the Assyrian Empire was an Assyrian. The true Assyrians lived in the plains watered by the upper Tigris River, where they built such famous cities as Ashur and Nineveh. This region had been inhabited by an Armenoid population in the fifth millennium. At an early date Semites began filtering in from the desert, and in historic times they formed the dominant part of a mixed population. Hurrians and other northerners entered Assyria during the second millennium, and Arameans during the first. Race mixture was further promoted by the imperial policy of moving large populations from one part of the Empire to another for disciplinary reasons. Assyrian culture was a mixed culture influenced by all these peoples.

Until the time of Hammurabi, Assyria had been largely a cultural colony of Babylon, and in general her culture was a continuation of the Babylonian. The Assyrian language was almost the same as Akkadian, and it was written in the same cuneiform characters. Assyrians read Babylonian literature, practiced Babylonian magic, and worshiped Babylonian gods. Nevertheless, there was much in the Assyrian culture of the seventh century that was not Babylonian. The Assyrians enriched the Sumerian and Babylonian cultural traditions with additions from many sources, but their own contributions were largely of a militaristic sort.

Assyrian militarism was based in part upon the growing use of iron weapons, but to an even greater extent it relied upon the discipline and military spirit which had been bred into the people during the difficult days of the second millennium. The military caste developed high technical skill, but it has remained notorious for the cruelty with which it waged war. It must be pointed out, however, that the Assyrians probably were not much worse than their less infamous rivals. All wars are cruel. The peculiarity of the Assyrians lay in the fact that they boasted of the atrocities they committed. We have countless in-scriptions and carvings recording how they impaled their prisoners, skinned them alive, and indulged in other refinements of torture. Other peoples did such things too, but the Assyrians published their cruelties far and wide in order to create terror among their enemies —and by this calculated frightfulness they won a reputation in his-tory which is perhaps more odious than they deserve.

Militarism made the Assyrian government autocratic and despotic. The Assyrian kings and generals could command, but they could not govern; and as frequently happens under such conditions, despotism led to assassination. An unusual number of the great kings of Assyria —including Tiglath-Pileser III, Sargon II, and Esarhaddon—came to power after the murder of their predecessors, and there were countless unsuccessful attempts upon the lives of sovereigns. The assassins may have justified their bloody deeds by referring to their victims' crimes and the eternal justice of the gods, but they were without exception men already high in the military caste who had not the slightest intention of reforming the old system: they merely wished to take it over and enjoy it themselves. Repeated assassina-tions or attempted assassinations made even kings cowardly, and they became more conscience-stricken, more panicky, more despotic, and more cruel as one regicide followed another.

Assyria had never been a city-state like those of Sumeria. Even in early times it was a tribal or national state. At first its principal city was Ashur, on the middle Tigris. A second capital was built farther north at Kalhu, which was beautified by Tiglath-Pileser III. Sargon II founded a new city still farther north, which he named Dur-Shar-rukin, or "Sargonsburg." He probably wished to have his headquar-ters closer to his enemies on the northern and northeastern frontiers. His successors were still dissatisfied, however, and Sennacherib moved the capital to nearby Nineveh, where it remained until the fall of the Empire. Nineveh was a large and magnificent city. An armed camp and a trading center, embellished with immense and gorgeous buildings, it was typical of Assyria at its worst and its best. Its imposing ruins were among the first to be excavated by modern archeologists.

Although Nineveh was the principal residence of the Assyrian king, and the seat of the central government, it contained less of a bureaucracy than Memphis or Thebes in their day, for the sprawling Assyrian Empire could not easily be governed from one central spot. The kings therefore divided their empire into numerous provinces, each of which was administered by an Assyrian general. These generals commanded the troops stationed in their provinces, collected the tribute, administered justice, repressed rebellion—and, it must be added, sometimes took advantage of their miltary power and their distance from the center of the Empire to plot rebellion on their own account. In general, the provincial organization worked out by the Assyrians was maintained by one conqueror after another until Roman times. The Assyrians brought peace to their empire, but the best that can be said for their rule is that its sole alternative, the anarchy of many tiny and constantly warring city-states, would doubtless have been much worse.

Protectors of Culture

In early times, the importance of Assyria lay principally in the fact that it was crossed by the major trade route of the Near East. Caravans traveling from Babylonia to Syria, Asia Minor, and Egypt found it most convenient to follow the east bank of the Tigris north to the foothills. Here they turned west, forded the river, and then skirted the hills north of the desert to Syria and the sea. The Assyrians commanded the fords of the Tigris and charged heavy tolls for their use —tolls which they proudly called "tribute." Since it was so much to their advantage to have trade prosperous, the Assyrians realized that they could not afford to allow marauders from the hills or the desert to rob or destroy passing caravans. They therefore undertook to keep the whole route open for those who would pay tribute, and the merchants who paid it clearly got their money's worth. The historian who wishes to be realistic must admit that the Assyrian Empire owed its existence not only to its superior army but also to the fact that its kings, like modern American gangsters, successfully sold "protection" to traders throughout the Near East.

The Assyrian kings also used other devices to promote the trade

upon which they depended. Even their practice of scattering rebellious populations in different parts of the Empire happened to work
out that way, for these displaced persons, torn from their former
occupations, often took up trade as a livelihood. They quickly found
that they had former friends or kinsmen in other cities with whom
they could enter into partnerships and thus do business in many parts
of the Empire. The traders who made up the majority of the population of the cities, even of Nineveh, were not Assyrians. They sprang
from the various peoples whom the Assyrians had conquered, and it
was for their benefit that the Assyrian armies were constantly waging
wars against barbarian freebooters. The Assyrian kings boasted of
their military prowess, and called themselves "Kings of the Universe"; yet as soon as the merchants made up their minds to do business under other governors, the militaristic Assyrian Empire came to
a sudden and inglorious end.

The Assyrian militarists added very little to other aspects of culture. They collected great libraries like that of Ashurbanipal at Nineveh, which they filled with copies of Babylonian and Sumerian
works, and to these collections we owe most of our knowledge of
those ancient literatures. The Assyrians produced little literature of
their own. Almost the only form of creative writing in which they
surpassed their predecessors was that of historical annals. Their
chronicles were a great improvement upon those of the Babylonians,
but they apparently learned the new style from the Hittites through
the Hurrians. In architecture, sculpture, and the other arts the Assyrians surpassed the Babylonians, although this excellence, too, was
due in large part to Hurrian influence. While the Assyrians con-

---

• Note for Plate 13. These mysterious creatures are the "cherubs" of the
Old Testament. This one once served as the side of a palace gateway at the
residence of Sargon II at Dur Sharrukin, now Khorsabad in Iraq. It is carved
in calcareous stone similar to alabaster, is sixteen feet high, and weighs forty
tons. It now stands in the museum of the Oriental Institute in Chicago. (Photo,
Oriental Institute.)

The relief of a lion in glazed brick comes from Babylon and dates from the
Chaldean period (612–539 B.C.).

Assyrian Winged Bull

Lion

Plate 13

Plate 14. Babylon Under Nebuchadrezzar (reconstruction)

tinued to worship the old Babylonian gods, they elevated their own god Ashur to a position far above all others. Conquered peoples were allowed to worship as they chose, but Ashur's military triumphs won him many voluntary worshipers among his victims. He thus became a supreme god. The Assyrians, however, were still far removed from the monotheism that was then arising in other parts of the Near East. The Assyrians defended the civilized world from the warlike barbarians who surrounded it on every side, but they added little to its civilization. They were preservers of culture rather than its creators.

The Chaldean Empire

The decline and fall of the Assyrian Empire was accompanied by far-reaching political changes throughout the Near East. Psammetichus had been strengthening Egypt throughout his long reign (663–609), and he left the country more prosperous than it had been at any time since the great days of the Empire. His successor Necho (609–595) hoped to re-establish the imperial glories of Egypt and actually occupied all Syria soon after the fall of Nineveh. Josiah, king of Judah, had begun to follow an independent course after the death of Ashurbanipal, conquering various neighboring peoples and dreaming of restoring the frontiers of David and Solomon, but he was killed in battle by Necho at Megiddo (608). Meantime an Assyrian nobleman was rallying the remnants of Assyrian power at Haran, where he assumed the title of "King of Assyria." Necho decided that a weak Assyria, ruled by such a man, might form a useful buffer state between the new Egyptian territories and the two great powers, Babylon and Media, that were then rising in the East. He therefore concluded an alliance with the Assyrian and sent troops to aid him. The allies were disastrously defeated at Carchemish in 605,

---

• Note for Plate 14. This painting, by M. Bardin, follows Unger's reconstruction of Babylon in the sixth century. In the foreground is the Ishtar Gate, adorned with bulls and "dragons" in brick relief. Through this gate ran a great avenue leading to the temple quarter of the city. In the center are the famous "Hanging Gardens of Babylon," and in the background rises the ziggurat. (Photo, Oriental Institute.)

however, and Babylon inherited the western provinces of Assyria.

The Chaldean, or Second Babylonian, Empire succeeded the Assyrian. Its culture and many of its people were descended from the Babylonians of old, but its ruling classes were Chaldeans whose Aramean ancestors had invaded Babylonia early in the first millennium. The first king of the new Empire was Nabopolassar, who had commanded the Babylonian armies during the siege of Nineveh. In 604 he was succeeded by his son Nabu-kudurri-usur, whom Biblical writers called Nebuchadrezzar. (In most modern Bibles the first *r* is incorrectly printed as *n*, "Nebuchadnezzar.") His long reign (604–562) coincided with the Golden Age of the Chaldean Empire.

Nebuchadrezzar had commanded the Chaldean army that defeated the last Assyrian resistance at Carchemish in 605. He followed up his victory by occupying all Syria and the cities of the Philistine coast, in spite of constant Egyptian encouragement to Judah and the Phoenician cities to resist. The Chaldean king occupied Jerusalem twice, in 597 and again in 586, deporting many Jews to Babylonia. On the first occasion, Nebuchadrezzar set up a puppet king of his own in Jerusalem, but after the second capture of the city he abolished the Jewish monarchy. Though less successful at Tyre, he received tribute from the island city after a siege that lasted thirteen years. Later he led a great expedition against Egypt and even reached Memphis, but he was unable to hold so advanced a position. When Nebuchadrezzar died a few years later, the Chaldean Empire included Babylonia, the southern part of Assyria, the trade route across to the Mediterranean, and all Syria and Palestine. Egypt was independent. The Medes, on the other hand, held Nineveh along with the northern half of the former Assyrian Empire. Nebuchadrezzar's wife, whom he had married at the time of his father's alliance against Assyria, was a Median princess, and throughout his reign the two powers preserved friendly relations with each other.

The Chaldeans had by this time been settled in Babylonia for several centuries and had absorbed much ancient Babylonian culture. There were also many descendants of the former populations, who retained the old culture of Sumer and Akkad. The priests no longer governed the country, of course, but Nabopolassar and his son were careful never to offend them. These priests continued their scientific studies of astronomy, keeping careful records, recognizing the uniformity of nature, and even learning to predict eclipses with tolerable accuracy. Nebuchadrezzar apparently took little personal interest in such scientific pursuits, but he was much interested in fortifying and beautifying Babylon. He disclosed high talents as a military engineer and architect, and it was he who made Babylon the huge and impressive city that Herodotus described a century and a half later (see Plate 14).

The Fall of Babylon

Nebuchadrezzar was succeeded on the Chaldean throne by his son, Amel-Marduk (Evil-Merodach in the Bible), who ruled for only two years (562–60). His reign introduced a troubled period of more than twenty years which brought the Empire to ruin. While perhaps racial feeling had something to do with the troubles of the time, greater weight must be attributed to controversies between the priests of Marduk and the military and business leaders. The struggle was between the friends and the foes of Nebuchadrezzar's imperialism, which the military men, the merchants, and the Arameans usually favored, while the priests and the old Babylonians opposed it. Nebuchadrezzar had placated the priests with lavish gifts, but Amel-Marduk threw himself into their hands. He was murdered and succeeded by his brother-in-law, who had been one of Nebuchadrezzar's generals. The usurper died four years later, and the tragedy was repeated: his son tried to rule for the benefit of the priests and was promptly assassinated by the imperialists.

The last king of Babylon was a man named Nabu-naid, or Nabonidus (556–39), an Aramean, son of a priest (or priestess) in the temple of the moon goddess Sin at Haran. During his first years, Nabonidus was a vigorous warrior, suppressing revolts in various provinces, leading a campaign into Arabia, and rebuilding the temple at Haran. Then he suddenly went into retirement, passing his time in scholarly studies and developing an interest in archeology. He appeared in public only to perform unimportant acts. The actual government fell to his son Bel-shar-usur—the notorious Belshazzar of the Biblical

Book of Daniel. The explanation of Nabonidus's retirement is not easy, but it seems most likely that the old king was held a prisoner by the priests. He undoubtedly had offended them by rebuilding the the temple of Sin at Haran; and if Belshazzar was Marduk's agent, we can readily understand why a Biblical writer should depict him as a monster of iniquity. It is also possible, however, that Belshazzar was an extreme militarist and nationalist, for whom his father was not aggressive enough. This, too, would have been enough to make him odious to his Jewish subjects.

These party quarrels played havoc with the imperial system. The government lost the confidence of a wide variety of important persons, who began to think that a fundamental change would advance their interests. At just this moment Cyrus the Persian was rising above the horizon, and many in the Chaldean Empire looked to him as the man who could bring such changes to pass. When Cyrus advanced into Babylonia, one city after another went over to him, and at last Babylon itself was taken without fighting (538). By this time Nabonidus was dead, and Belshazzar was killed a few days after the capture of the city. The Chaldean Empire collapsed more quickly than the Assyrian, though not so completely. Assyrians are unknown to history after the battle of Carchemish, but for many centuries Babylon remained an important city, pre-eminent for her merchants and scholars.

Medes and Persians

The capture of Babylon in 538 completed the founding of the Persian Empire. Unfortunately, we know little of the early history of these Persians, who were to dominate the Near East for the next two centuries and who played a prominent part in world history throughout the remainder of antiquity. Their native country, the modern Persia or Iran, is not attractive. Its backbone consists of two great mountain ranges spreading out from Armenia and the Caucasus: the first is the Zagros range, which runs south along the eastern frontier of Mesopotamia to the Persian Gulf, while the second, the Elburz range, runs eastward, south of the Caspian Sea, until it eventually reaches the Hindu Kush Mountains in Afghanistan at the frontier of

India. The central Iranian plateau, surrounded by these mountain ranges and the sea, is largely an uninhabitable salt desert.

This mountainous country was inhabited from early times by men of Armenoid race, speaking languages remotely akin to those of the Hurri, Hatti, and other early Asiatics: in fact, one of these languages, Elamite, appears in the Behistun inscription, which was the key with which Rawlinson deciphered cuneiform. Among the various tribes occupying the Zagros region the most important were the Elamites to the south and the Gutians and Kassites who dwelt farther north. Excavations at Susa, not far north of the Persian Gulf and west of the Zagros Mountains, show an Elamite civilization, as old as that of nearby Babylonia, which was much influenced by the latter yet is fundamentally different. The Susans were scarcely typical of the Elamites as a whole, however, and they were even less typical of the other mountaineers. While the mountaineers of the Zagros region had scarcely emerged from the neolithic stage of civilization at the middle of the second millennium, they were hardy warriors whose raids sometimes wrought great havoc in Mesopotamia. Archeologists have only scratched the Elburz region, but scattered finds of pottery indicate that it was inhabited by peoples of similar culture.

Such was the situation in Persia when invaders from the northeast appeared about 1800 B.C. These invaders spoke an Aryan language and are called Iranians. As we have seen (p. 133) they came in small bands and the earlier groups quickly crossed Persia to make themselves leaders among the Kassites, the Mitanni, and the Hurri. Not until several centuries later did large groups of Iranians again invade Persia. During the tenth and ninth centuries, migrations were renewed from the East Aryan homeland in Asia beyond the Caspian Sea. Some of the invaders advanced southward to occupy eastern Persia while others followed the Elburz Mountains westward to the region southwest of the Caspian.

The Empire of the Medes

We know little of the history of the eastern Iranians, but Assyrian records from about 835 mention "Medes" who had settled between the Caspian and Lake Urmia. While the Assyrians were busy fighting off the attacks of the mountaineers from the Zagros region, and occasionally making raids deep into their territory, Iranian tribes pushed southward from the Caspian, following the eastern fringe of the Zagros Mountains until they reached the Persian Gulf. The mountaineers were thus caught between two warlike enemies, Assyrians to the west and Iranians to the east, and eventually they were crushed. Iranians and Assyrians then stood face to face. Early in the seventh century a certain Khshathrita, whom the Greeks called Phraortes, ruled a large territory between the Zagros Mountains and the Caspian as king of the Medes; and further south, across the Zagros Mountains from Elam, Teispes, the son of Achaemenes (Hakhamanish), ruled provinces known as Parsumash and Parsa, from which our word "Persia" is derived.

Fortunately we have literary evidence showing something of the character of the Iranians who invaded Persia, for in the huge collection of Persian religious texts known as the Avesta, compiled many centuries later, there are poems dating from this early period. They picture a society such as the invaders must have formed. Men were divided into three classes: priests, warriors, and farmers, and the most important of the three were the warriors. The poets vividly describe their heroes' delight in war, and they tell us how, armed with arrows and lances, these warriors pursued their enemies in strong chariots drawn by swift horses. In time of peace they devoted themselves to raising horses and cattle, but they knew little about agriculture. Nevertheless, they were more or less settled, for we read of their large and beautiful houses, with doorposts and columns and windows, and of the many rich treasures they had accumulated. Not everyone in Persia was an Iranian, however, and when Darius I set up his Behistun inscription in three languages—Persian (Iranian), Elamite, and Babylonian—he gave evidence of the polyglot character of his country. The population and culture of historic Persia thus sprang from three separate sources, but it was the Iranian aristocrats who governed the men of other races. They took pride in just administration, and among all the peoples of antiquity only the Romans surpassed them in their idealization of good government as the chief end of man.

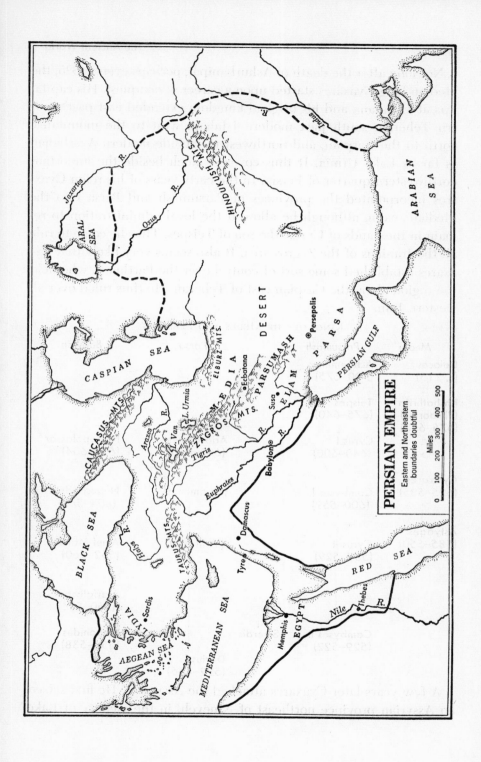

PERSIAN EMPIRE

Eastern and Northeastern
boundaries doubtful

Miles

0 100 200 300 400 500

Not long after the death of Ashurbanipal, perhaps even in 625, the Median king Cyaxares started upon a career of conquest. His capital was at Ecbatana and his original kingdom extended east past modern Teheran, south past modern Isfahan, west to the mountains, north to the Caspian, and northwest to include modern Azerbaijan as far as Lake Urmia. It thus covered much beside the important northwestern quarter of Persia. In the early years of his reign Cyaxares incorporated the provinces of Parsumash and Parsa into the Median realm, although he allowed the local administration to remain in the hands of Cyrus, the son of Teispes. Thus he came to rule all the Iranians of the Zagros area. It also seems very likely that Cyaxares established some sort of control over the Parthians, who held the region along the Caspian east of Teheran. He thus ruled over all western Iran.

KINGS OF THE MEDES AND PERSIANS

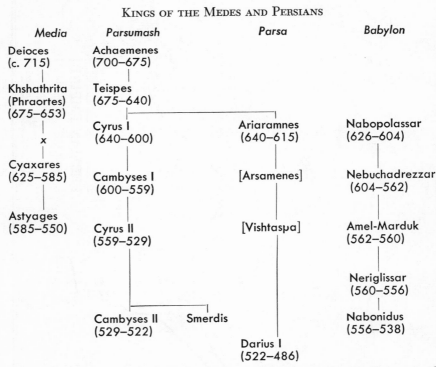

Media	Parsumash	Parsa	Babylon
Deioces (c. 715)	Achaemenes (700–675)		
Khshathrita (Phraortes) (675–653)	Teispes (675–640)		
x	Cyrus I (640–600)	Ariaramnes (640–615)	Nabopolassar (626–604)
Cyaxares (625–585)	Cambyses I (600–559)	[Arsamenes]	Nebuchadrezzar (604–562)
Astyages (585–550)	Cyrus II (559–529)	[Vishtaspa]	Amel-Marduk (562–560)
			Neriglissar (560–556)
	Cambyses II (529–522) Smerdis		Nabonidus (556–538)
		Darius I (522–486)	

A few years later Cyaxares attacked the Assyrians. He first seized an Assyrian province northeast of Nineveh, in the vicinity of Lake

Urmia, and in 612 he captured the Assyrian capital jointly with his Chaldean ally, Nabopolassar. The remainder of his long reign Cyaxares spent in occupying and pacifying the northern half of the former Assyrian Empire. By 590 he had reached the Halys River in Asia Minor, where he came in conflict with the king of Lydia. Five years later the two kings arranged a settlement by which the Halys remained their frontier. Cyaxares then died, after a reign of about forty years (585). He was succeeded by his son, Astyages, who had failed to inherit his father's genius. The new king quarreled with the Chaldeans, and he might eventually have attacked Babylon had he not been defeated and captured by Cyrus II (550). With his defeat the short-lived Median Empire came to an end.

Cyrus Founds the Persian Empire

While Phraortes was establishing the first Median kingdom, Achaemenes (famous as the founder of the Achaemenid Dynasty of Persian kings) and his son Teispes were spreading their rule in Parsumash and Parsa. Shortly before his death in 640, Teispes divided his kingdom between his two sons, Kurash (Cyrus) receiving Parsumash, while Parsa went to the younger son, Ariaramnes. For more than a century these two branches of the Achaemenid family continued in feud. When Cyaxares the Mede asserted his supremacy over the southern provinces, he allowed Cyrus and his son, Cambyses, to administer them both. They called themselves kings of Parsumash, but for almost a century the descendants of Ariaramnes remained kings without a throne. The first Cambyses died in 559 and was succeeded by his son, Cyrus II, who is often called Cyrus the Great.

In later times the marvelous birth and youth of this Cyrus were described in romantic stories (of which Herodotus gives us samples), but apparently he reached the throne through regular channels. He soon began plotting against his overlord, Astyages, however, and in 550 he raised the standard of rebellion. Astyages marched against him with a large army and won an indecisive battle; then in a second battle the defection of important Median nobles at a critical moment enabled Cyrus to take Astyages prisoner. After this victory Cyrus captured and looted Ecbatana, claimed to be Astyages' successor, and established the Persian Empire.

Cyrus occupied the former Median territories without difficulty, but presently he was attacked by Croesus, king of Lydia. In the course of his counterattack, Cyrus captured Sardis (546), and within a year or two he added most of the rest of western Asia Minor to his empire. He then returned to Persia, seized the former Elamite territories, and occupied the Babylonian provinces at the head of the Persian Gulf. After several cities in this region had voluntarily surrendered to him, Cyrus was ready to attack the capital itself, and in 538 one of his generals occupied Babylon. Nine years later Cyrus was killed in battle, fighting against an obscure tribe on the Armenian frontier. The empire left by Cyrus included all southwestern Asia, from eastern Persia to the Mediterranean and Aegean seas, from the Caucasus Mountains and the Caspian to the Persian Gulf.

Cyrus was succeeded by his incompetent son, Cambyses II (529–22), during whose reign Egypt was annexed (525). Cambyses was called back from Egypt by news of a revolt at home, and on the road to Persia he died, probably by suicide. Rebellious priests were trying to seize power in the name of Bardiya, or Smerdis, a younger son of Cyrus: this Smerdis actually was dead, and the boy whom they protected was the brother of a priest, but for seven months he was accepted as king.

This situation played into the hands of Darius, who was a descendant of Ariaramnes and therefore an Achaemenid through the minor branch of the family. He slew the false Smerdis, and for three years civil war tore the Empire asunder, but by the end of 519 Darius was in control everywhere. His own version of the revolt and its repression appears in the famous inscription at Behistun (Plate 16). Darius apparently sent a military expedition to India, of which only vague intimations now remain; he crossed the Bosporus to invade Europe about 513 or 512; he had trouble with his Ionian provinces in the years following 499; and in 490 came the campaign against the Greeks which culminated at Marathon—all of which will be discussed in a later chapter. These various campaigns were the result of his misfortunes rather than of his policy, however, for by nature Darius was not an aggressive warrior. He was primarily the organizer and administrator who set up a system of centralized rule, divided the Empire into satrapies (based largely upon the old Assyrian provinces), built a new and magnificent capital at Persepolis (Plate 15), and gave the Persian Empire the form it retained until it was overthrown by Alexander the Great (330 B.C).

Zoroaster and the Persian Religion

Darius accepted the religious teachings of the Persian prophet Zarathustra, whom the Greeks called Zoroaster. This religion was then rather new, but it later came to be one of the world's great religions. Our knowledge of Zoroaster, and of the religion of the Medes and Persians before his time, is derived largely from the earliest parts of the Avesta.[2] The kernel of this huge work consists of the Gathas— hymns reputedly written by Zoroaster himself and certainly emanating from the circle of his earliest disciples. They give us a picture of the pre-Zoroastrian religion of Persia as well as of Zoroaster's teachings, and the later writings in the Avesta show how the prophet's ideas were distorted by his followers. The religious history of early Persia thus went through four stages. First came the neolithic religion of the earliest known Persians, which resembled that of their neighbors and kinsmen further west in Mesopotamia. Next came the Iranian invaders with very different ideas. Then Zoroaster reformed their religion. And finally, we find the religion actually practiced by his followers, which was a commingling of elements from the three earlier sources. Concerning the earliest stage of religion in Persia we know little that is distinctive, and only with the coming of the Aryans does our knowledge of Persian religious history begin.

In early historic times the Iranian religion was dominated by a

---

[2] The Avesta and ancient commentaries upon it are published, in English translation with introduction and notes, in seven of the fifty volumes of the *Sacred Books of the East* (1879–1910), a famous collection edited by F. Max Müller which was one of the triumphs of British scholarship at the end of the last century. Another, and perhaps smoother, translation of the Gathas appears as an appendix to J. H. Moulton, *Early Zoroastrianism* (1913). The Avesta is not easy reading, and the excerpts in various recently published "Bibles of Humanity" usually consist of the "best" passages, as judged by twentieth-century Christian standards of excellence, rather than those most typical of the religion or those most highly regarded by its adherents.

caste of priests, known as the Magi. These Magi entered Persia with the Aryan invaders from central Asia, but they presently amalgamated the religions of the conquerors with those of the conquered and even added borrowings from the Semitic religions of Assyria and Babylonia. The early Persians, like migratory and pastoral peoples elsewhere, considered temples inappropriate to their deities and held their religious services on the tops of hills or mountains. A favorite ceremony centered around the sacrifice of cattle to the gods. An ox was slaughtered and cut to pieces while the Magi chanted hymns recounting the glorious deeds of gods and heroes. The meat was then left on the grass for a while, in order that the gods might have an opportunity to take their share, which consisted of its spiritual part. The sacrificer and the priest then divided the remainder for their own use. These early Persians, like their Sanskrit-speaking cousins in India, always had great reverence for fire. The Indians had a god named Agni (Latin *ignis*, "fire") whom the Persians called Atar (cognate with the Latin *atrium*, the room in the early Roman house which contained the hearth). Both Persians and Indians built fire-altars on which they carefully tended ever-burning flames, as did the Vestal Virgins at Rome. These early Persians looked forward to a future life but the details of their theology concerning it are unknown to us.

The Persian Aryans, again like their Indian cousins, spoke of gods of two sorts, the *ahura* and the *daeva*. It is interesting to note, however, that in the two countries the two types of deity developed in opposite directions. In Persia the *ahura* was regarded as a good god, with the name eventually reserved for the supreme deity, while in India he became an evil spirit; in Persia the *daeva* was a "devil," while his Sanskrit counterpart, the *deva*, became a good god like the cognate Latin *divus* or *deus*. The original difference between *ahuras* and *daevas* is not clear. They were not the gods of the conquerors and the conquered respectively, for old Aryan gods are found in each

---

• Note for Plate 15. This photograph shows the stairway leading up to Darius's palace at Persepolis. The soldiers in the reliefs are the king's guards, known as "The Immortals." (*Photo, Oriental Institute.*)

Plate 15. The Apadana Stairway

Plate 16.   Triumphal Monument of Darius the Great

group. More likely the *daevas* were the vegetation gods of peasants, while the *ahuras* were the more abstract gods of primitive herdsmen, yet even this cannot be the whole story. The most important of the *ahuras* was Ahura Mazda, the "Wise God," an old sky god who later became supreme. Mithra and other ancient *ahuras*, as well as Indra and other *daevas*, also retained prominent places in the Persian pantheon.

Zoroaster, the Prophet of Ancient Iran

Zoroaster appeared as a reformer of this primitive religion. Regarding the prophet's life not much is known, even his date and homeland having been the matter of hot dispute. Greek writers sometimes endowed him with a fantastic antiquity, reaching back four thousand or even six thousand years before Christ, while Persian tradition gave 660 and 583 as the dates of his birth and death. Many recent writers accept the Persian tradition as reasonably accurate, and believe that he lived in the eastern or northeastern part of Persia, where political and social conditions, religion, and even language were rather different from those prevailing among the early Medes and Persians.

Persian mythology tells us that Zoroaster's birth was accompanied by miracles of diverse sorts, even the *daevas* taking to momentary flight. At the age of twenty he withdrew to the desert, where he spent ten years reflecting upon the great problems of life and death. At the age of thirty he began to preach, but during the first ten years he won only one convert, his cousin. Success began about 618 with the conversion of an otherwise unknown king named Vishtaspa. Thereafter Zoroaster fared better, both religiously and socially. Con-

---

• Note for Plate 16. This view shows the famous Behistun Inscription, set up by the Persian king, Darius I (522–486 B.C.), at Behistun in modern Iran. It consists of four parts: the relief sculptures and inscriptions in three languages, ancient Persian, Babylonian, and Elamite. The inscriptions tell how Darius triumphed over all his enemies and became ruler of the Persian Empire. They were first copied by Henry Rawlinson in 1845 and were the key which unlocked cuneiform writing to modern scholars. (*Photo, George Cameron, Oriental Institute.*)

versions became more frequent, and he took the daughter of the king's counselor as his third wife. The last years of his life were troubled by religious wars during the course of which Zoroaster was killed, in the seventy-seventh year of his life and the forty-seventh of his religion.

Zoroaster resembled several of the Hebrew prophets, notably Amos, in that he was at once a religious and a social reformer. Whatever his own social origin may have been—we can only assume that he was an Iranian—Zoroaster set himself up as a champion of the peasant and herdsman. His language was bitter about the violence and disorder caused by the evil men who made up the military caste and their Magian allies; and he vividly pictured the dark side of a military society, showing how heroes turned gangster to rob and murder their friends and kinsmen if foreign enemies were not readily available. He prayed for a strong king to establish justice throughout the land. Perhaps he fell at times into the very human error of attributing every form of moral turpitude to his political and theological adversaries, but there can be no doubt that he was a man who saw the advantages of settled and peaceful life now that the period of invasions was over. Zoroaster's prime interest, however, was in theological matters, and he believed that if men would only follow the will of Ahura Mazda, all these abominations would cease.

This great sky god Mazda had been worshiped by the Iranians from time immemorial. Originally he had been identical with the Indian god, Varuna, whose name is preserved in the Greek word *ouranos*, "sky." Zoroaster raised him to a position high above all other gods, and associated him with truth, justice, and good order. The name Mazda associated him with wisdom, which was regarded as divine; and Zoroaster often compared him to light, in which we may perhaps see a legacy from the ancient fire-worship. Lesser divine beings were pictured as Ahura Mazda's ministers, six in number, and came to resemble angels, whereas the ancient *daevas*, whom Zoroaster ordinarily called "Liars" and compared to darkness, remained his implacable foes. Life was pictured as a constant struggle between the forces of justice and those of evil, and every good man was urged to proclaim himself a friend of Ahura Mazda and an enemy of the *daevas*. The present world was the scene of this mighty conflict, but there could be no doubt that, in the end, the forces of justice would triumph. Zoroaster even spoke of a "Kingdom" to come after a renovation of the present world and the eradication of evil; but in the meantime men must struggle constantly for justice, since on the last day each will be judged according to his works. Zoroaster's views on eschatology—"the doctrine of last things"—thus closely resembled those of popular Christianity today.

The Zoroastrian State

There is no evidence that the Median kings, or Cyrus, or Cambyses were followers of Zoroaster, or even that they were familiar with his teachings: apparently they accepted the conventional religion of their day as taught by the Magi. Darius, on the other hand, was sincerely attached to the new doctrine. His father's name was Vishtaspa, which suggests that he may have been named after the other Vishtaspa, the royal protector of Zoroaster. Presumably the younger Vishtaspa was born only a few years after the prophet's death, and it was no doubt easy for a king in exile to sympathize with the lofty principles embodied in Zoroaster's attacks upon current injustice and lies. Of his son Darius's religious nature and attachment to the new religion there can be no doubt. He came to the throne after the revolt of the Magi and the false Smerdis, which may have encouraged him to share Zoroaster's low opinion of the priestly caste. In his Behistun inscription Darius declared emphatically that the rebellion had been due to "the Lie" and he thankfully attributed his own victory to Ahura Mazda. As a good Zoroastrian, Darius must have disapproved of much that his royal predecessors had done, yet he was not prepared to let the Empire fall to pieces, for his religion enjoined good government. He therefore seized control and reorganized the government along better lines. After order had been restored, Darius abstained as far as possible from further warfare (the Scythian and Greek campaigns were forced upon him; see pp. 365 ff.) and he devoted himself to making Zoroastrian ideas of justice prevail.

Zoroaster had often expressed his wish for a strong king who would establish justice throughout the land by ending the minor banditries of local chieftains. Darius put himself forward as just such a man, doing away with the chieftains and sending out his satraps to govern in their places. He governed with self-conscious rectitude according to the precepts of Zoroaster and with the aid of Ahura Mazda. The religious views of his subjects made little difference to him, providing only that they did not inspire revolt, and he thus came to practice religious toleration toward his subjects. These ideas made Darius an ideal oriental despot: a man far removed from the populace, whom he governed with divine wisdom. The pomp and circumstance of court ritual were augmented enormously in order to impress upon the public mind the uniqueness and remoteness of the sovereign. Darius was a man of genius as well as a man of conscience, and during his reign things went well. Unfortunately, his successors did not possess equal ability, and the Persian Empire fell into decline. Perhaps the later kings were not as bad as their Greek enemies alleged, but only a few of them were either good kings or good Zoroastrians.

The Later History of Zoroastrianism

In spite of their numerous shortcomings, the later kings of Persia often invoked the name and ideas of Zoroaster, and their royal favor both helped and debauched the new religion. The Greek historian Herodotus visited the East some thirty or forty years after the death of Darius, and his history contains an interesting paragraph on Persian religion. What he describes is the old religion of the Magi, and there is no mention either of Zoroaster or of his distinctive doctrines, which probably were not yet accepted in the circles frequented by the Greek visitor. Early in the next century, however, the Greeks began talking about the prophet and his teachings. As the later kings were even less inclined to missionary zeal than Darius, this expansion of Zoroastrian ideas is to be attributed to the Magi. When the Zoroastrian king was firmly seated on his throne after the failure of their revolt in 522, these priests apparently decided to make another try for power by adopting and exploiting the royal religion that they could not conquer. At least they accepted Zoroastrianism and became powerful advisers to the kings. Nevertheless, their religious views differed widely from those of the prophet himself, for the Magi retained much of the old religion of which Zoroaster disapproved. They also added much learned from Chaldean priests and others.

The new Persian religion was a syncretism, or amalgamation, of ideas from all parts of the Empire, and it became a truly imperial religion. Old Aryan gods such as Mithra were again raised to prominence beside Ahura Mazda, and early in the fourth century a Persian king set up a statue of Anahita, an old fertility goddess sometimes identified with Ishtar. In the fourth century before our era, priests and kings hailed these three great gods—Ahura Mazda, Anahita, and Mithra—as a supreme trinity.

The Magi also developed elaborate rituals, quite out of keeping with the spirit of Zoroaster, in which they preserved much that was either Iranian or Semitic, and to which they added much that was new. They set forth their views in books which they attributed to Zoroaster, and they wrote elaborate commentaries upon his authentic teaching as preserved in the Gathas. We may cite but one example out of many. They taught that all history—past, present, and future—fell into millenniums, or periods of a thousand years each, through which it was possible to trace the progress of the struggle between Ormazd (as they called Ahura Mazda) and Ahriman, the leader of the *daevas*, not named in the Gathas. They then added that, after a certain number of millenniums, the victory of Ormazd would usher in a thousand years of bliss. This happy period they called "the millennium." On the basis of their studies they even tried to predict with priestly precision exactly when Ormazd would triumph and this ultimate "millennium" arrive. In spite of these intellectual activities, however, the popular mind associated the Magi primarily with dream interpreting and magic, ancient arts inherited from their earliest predecessors: our word "magic" can, of course, be traced back to their name.

The subsequent history of the Zoroastrian religion may be summarized in a brief paragraph. It is said that Alexander the Great destroyed many Zoroastrian books when he took Persepolis (331 B.C.) and that he persecuted the religion. At any rate, he robbed the religion of its former royal protection and prestige. In the course of the third century before Christ, the Iranian Parthians reconquered Persia, which they governed until the third century after Christ. We know little of the religion of the Parthian Empire; but under the Sassanians, who ruled from 226 A.D. until the Mohammedan conquest in 642, Zoroastrianism was the official religion of Persia. This was the great age of the Zoroastrian faith, when the Avesta took its present form. The Gathas were supplemented with various hymns and liturgies of later date, elaborate rules for purification, and other bits of priestly law as well as commentaries and elaborations written in Pahlavi, the language of Sassanian Persia. The resulting compilation is almost as large as the Old Testament. The Mohammedan conquerors suppressed the Zoroastrian religion with great vigor, but a group of devotees fled to India, where about one hundred thousand of them still exist and are called Parsees.

Zorastrian Influence in the West

Meantime many Zoroastrian ideas had spread to the West. Long before Alexander, Persian nobles had migrated to Asia Minor, taking their gods with them. Mithra was especially popular with these pioneers, and his cult was widely disseminated. The Mithra worshiped in Anatolia was primarily the pre-Zoroastrian deity of the Iranians. As time went on, however, many of the higher aspects of Zoroaster's teaching were grafted upon the original stalk, as were ideas taken from Semitic and Anatolian religions. The resulting Mithraism was very popular in the days of the Roman Empire, especially in the army, and in the third century of our era it was Christianity's chief rival. Had conditions then been just a little different, Mithra might have won, in which case we today might be worshiping a Persian rather than a Jewish god.

Zoroastrian ideas also entered the Roman Empire by other routes, brought by missionaries from Persia and by Europeans who had sought light in the East. Plato, writing early in the fourth century before Christ, expressed many Magian ideas and even named Zoroaster; and in the third century the Stoics borrowed heavily from him. In the first two or three centuries of our era there was a widely prevalent type of pagan religious thought known as Gnosticism. The "wisdom" of the Gnostics was a compound of Egyptian, Semitic, and Persian elements mixed with an attentuated Platonic philosophy.

Many thinkers of the early Christian Church were influenced by Zoroaster through Gnosticism and the Stoics. In the fourth century after Christ another, but rather perverted, form of Persian religious thought known as Manichaeism was equally influential with them: even St. Augustine called himself a Manichaean for a while. Traces of the religious contribution of Persia to the West may still be seen among us. We speak of the "powers of light" and the "powers of darkness," and of the "millennium" in good Persian style. Much of our folklore about angels and devils is of Persian origin. December 25 was first observed as the birthday of Mithra. Baptism was an ancient Persian rite. Many popular conceptions of the Last Judgment can be traced to Zoroastrian sources, and our word "paradise" is derived from the Persian word for "park." Along with these superficial symbols, much of the noblest thought of the ancient Orient found its way into our religion. As a leading American student of ancient Iran and the biographer of Zoroaster (A. V. W. Jackson) has well remarked, in commenting upon the Gospel story of the Three Magi at Bethlehem: "It is a fine thought to associate the two faiths in this adoration of the Magi—the worshipers of light itself bowing before the majesty of the newborn Light of the World."

VII   The Hebrews

A SPECIAL PLACE IN THE HISTORY OF THE ANCIENT ORIENT must always be reserved for the Hebrews. Writers in medieval and early modern times would have paid this tribute as a matter of course. In the nineteenth century, however, the discovery of the amazing cultural achievements of the great empires of the Near East seemed to reduce the significance of the Hebrews. Much of the originality formerly attributed to them disappeared, and even their religious ideas no longer seemed so unique as formerly. Extremists began to suggest that they mattered little in the cultural life of the ancient Near East. This minimizing of Hebrew importance went too far. It is true that the Hebrews absorbed much of the civilization of the Near East, for Palestine lay across the main highways from Egypt to Mesopotamia and was frequently crossed by traders and soldiers who disseminated the ideas as well as the material products of their various countries. However, the Hebrews always held themselves aloof from other peoples. They accepted much from their neighbors, but they were sharply critical of what these neighbors had to offer, and they always modified what they took to make it fit their own tastes and ideals. More than any other people, the Hebrews were the spiritual aristocrats of the ancient Orient, and what they passed on to the later world was a highly refined version of ancient oriental civilization. The importance of the Hebrews in history is, therefore, far greater than that of any of their contemporary neighbors, and the old writers were not far wrong when they made the legacy of the ancient world descend from three great cities— Jerusalem, Athens, and Rome.

The Scriptures speak of Palestine as "a land flowing with milk and

honey"—a phrase that could have occurred only to an inspired patriot or a wanderer straight from the desert. The modern tourist finds
the barren limestone hills of Palestine uninviting, though perhaps
they were more attractive before deforestation and erosion had
ruined the land. Nevertheless, even in antiquity the hill country of
Palestine was rarely suitable for more than grazing sheep, goats, and
cattle. In large areas, only a few acres here and there in the valley
bottoms could have been used profitably for agriculture, and much
was barren desert.

Palestine is not large, even if we include Philistia and Transjordan.
The distance from the Mediterranean to the Jordan River ranges between twenty-five and forty miles, and from the northern boundary
to the desert at the south (from Dan to Beersheba, in the Biblical
phrase) is a distance of about 140 miles. The arable part of Transjordan is smaller and poorer. The total area of the country is about
10,000 square miles, or approximately that of Vermont. Its population today is slightly over one and a half millions, but in antiquity it
probably never rose much beyond half that figure. Palestine may be
divided into four belts, running from north to south: first, as one ap-
proaches from the west, come the coastal plains, Philistia to the
south and the plain of Sharon farther north; next is the central hill
country, a southern extension of the Lebanon Mountains of Syria;
then comes the Jordan rift, a deep crack in the earth's surface, at the
southern end of which lies the Dead Sea, 1289 feet below the level
of the Mediterranean; and east of the Jordan the land tapers off into
desert. The central hill country, which was the part first occupied by
the Hebrews, may be subdivided into three sections. The southern
part, extending from a line a few miles north of Jerusalem southward
to Hebron and Beersheba, was known as Judah, or, in Roman times,
Judea. The middle part was called Israel, its principal city was Samaria, and along its northern edge lay the great plain of Esdraelon,
about twenty miles wide, extending from the Jordan to the Mediterranean. North of the plain the third section, Galilee, surrounded the
lake of that name which empties into the Jordan. During nearly all
the first millennium before Christ, however, Galilee was under foreign rule.

Archeologists have found the skeletons of several Neanderthal
men in Palestine, and here too are traces of the only truly mesolithic
culture yet discovered in the Near East. Early neolithic cultures, dating from before 3000, have been found in the Jordan Valley, at Jerusalem, and at other sites. During the third millennium, Semites

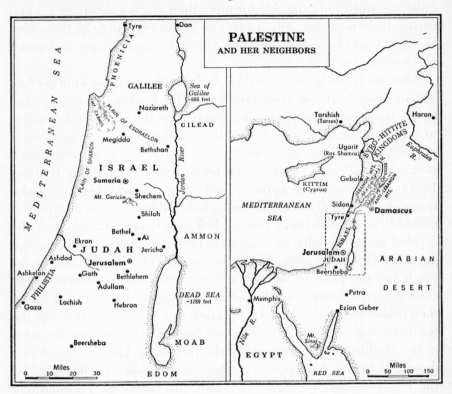

poured into Palestine from the deserts to the east and south, and
Armenoid peoples came down from the north. Evidences have been
noticed of Egyptian cultural influence dating from the Old and Middle Kingdoms, and Babylonian civilization made itself felt in the
days of Hammurabi. In the eighteenth century the Hyksos crossed
the country on their way to Egypt, and at almost every archeological
site excavated in Palestine a rich Hyksos level has been found. Egypt
ruled Palestine in the days of her empire and left important monuments, but few Egyptians settled there permanently.

The pre-Hebrew inhabitants of Palestine, whom the Hebrews called Canaanites, were a mixture of several Semitic and Armenoid elements, with the Semites predominating. Throughout Palestine, Phoenicia, and most of Syria, one language was spoken with only dialectic differences; the same gods were worshiped in about the same manner; and in general the same ideas were current. The Hebrews from the desert adopted the language and much of the culture of their Canaanite predecessors and thereby became heirs of almost the entire Near East. In fact, the prophet Ezekiel, writing early in the sixth century showed that he was not a bad historian of culture when he declared to the Hebrew people: "Your father was an Amorite, and your mother a Hittite."[1] His Amorites may be interpreted as Semites in general; and his Hittites were not the Aryan aristocrats of Anatolia but men of the Syro-Hittite kingdom who were for the most part Hurri of Armenoid ancestry.

The Coming of the Hebrews

The Amarna letters speak of peoples invading Palestine from the east, whom they call Habiru. This word is interpreted as meaning "strangers" or "robbers," but possibly it had already become a proper name, even in the Amarna Age. Cuneiform tablets dating from the time of Hammurabi use the word for Semitic tribesmen entering Babylonia from the desert. The Habiru of these earlier documents lived in the northern part of the Arabian Desert, around Haran, which lends color to the Biblical legend that Abraham, the mythical progenitor of the Hebrews, once lived in that city and later migrated south to Palestine. The Amarna letters picture the Habiru as entering Palestine from the east early in the fourteenth century, and mention cities which they captured. Archeology supports this general picture. It is therefore safe to assume that the earliest Hebrews were Semitic nomads who forced their way into Palestine from the east about 1400 B.C., after several centuries of wandering in the desert.

The problem of Hebrew origins is much complicated by the Old

---

[1] Throughout this book, quotations from the Bible usually follow J. M. P. Smith and E. J. Goodspeed, *The Complete Bible: an American Translation* (Chicago, 1939), by permission of the University of Chicago Press.

Testament stories telling how Joseph, the great-grandson of Abraham, went down into Egypt followed by his whole family and became prime minister of the country, how the Hebrews dwelt there for many years until they were enslaved by the Egyptians, and how they eventually were led forth by Moses. These stories raise so many difficulties that nineteenth-century writers often rejected them entirely. Scholars today are more cautious. An Egyptian inscription from the days of Rameses II (1299–32) says that " 'Apiru" labored in Egypt at that time. This certainly does not prove that every detail of the Biblical narrative is true history, but it does indicate that Hebrews were in Egypt. The dates of the going down into Egypt and of the Exodus are the subject of further controversy. The Jewish historian Josephus, writing about 90 A.D., declared that Joseph lived in the days of the Hyksos (about 1700) and that Rameses II was the Pharaoh of the oppression: it seems not improbable that a late editor of the Hebrew text of the Old Testament also held this view (see page 226, note 6), which is shared by several eminent scholars. A more plausible theory suggests, however, that a small band of Hebrews may have gone down to Egypt about 1400 as part of the general movement that took most of their kinsmen into Palestine. The Exodus probably occurred in the days of Rameses II and, as recorded in the Bible, the children of Israel probably wandered in the Sinai Peninsula and the desert for at least a generation before entering the land of Canaan.

Invasions of Palestine

Scholars have thus come to the conclusion that the Hebrew invasions of Palestine were a far more complicated procedure than is pictured in the Biblical narrative. Instead of one decisive conquest under Joshua, there apparently were two major invasions, each followed by a long and gradual absorption of Canaanite territory and population. While excavations at Jericho show that the city was carried by storm and destroyed about 1400, and while one of the Amarna letters mentions an Habiru named Joshua, we must not assume that he was the Biblical hero of that name. The Biblical narrative proceeds to describe the capture and destruction of nearby Ai. Recent excavations have shown, however, that at that time the site of Ai had already been deserted for several centuries; perhaps the chronicler confused Ai with Bethel, two miles away, which was destroyed at about the same time as Jericho. Both the Bible and the Amarna letters say that Shechem was taken by the Hebrews, and these statements are supported by archeology. Other discoveries substantiate in a very general way the narratives found in the Biblical books of Joshua and Judges.

It is not difficult for archeologists to distinguish Canaanite from Hebrew remains, for the Canaanites had a highly developed city civilization with well-built houses and other things to match, while the Hebrews were still nomads living in tents or huts and are recognizable especially by their inferior pottery. They held the hill country of central Palestine while the Canaanites held the valleys and the low country, especially the plain of Esdraelon: the very word Canaan means "low country." Ever since Hyksos times, the Canaanites had had war chariots, which they used to hold invaders at bay in the flat valleys but which were not serviceable in the rough hill country. The Hebrew invaders were not numerous, when compared to the total population of Palestine, and their infiltration was slow; but eventually they became settled in their new homes, intermarried with Canaanites, and adopted their language together with much of their culture.

The second Hebrew invasion came from Egypt at least a century and a half later. As we have no record of fighting between the newcomers and the older Hebrews, and as there is no reason to believe that they had maintained contact with their distant kinsmen which would have made them welcome immigrants, it seems probable that they settled in a different part of Palestine. They may have entered Canaan from the south, rather than from the east as had the earlier invaders, and occupied the territory later known as Judah. If this were the case, it would help explain many differences in the culture and religion of the two peoples as well as their later political dissensions. The Biblical narrative drops a few hints of such an invasion from the south, but the historical record is so inadequate that even for a brief sketch of what happened the historian must resort to much that is sheer conjecture.

Early in the twelfth century, not long after the second invasion of Palestine, a group of people known as the Philistines appeared in the neighboring coast cities. We have seen that these Philistines were mercenary troops, probably from western Asia Minor, whence they had been driven by advancing Phrygians or Lydians. They had raided Egypt in the days of Rameses III (1198–67) and were later hired to defend the coastal cities of Palestine. Before long, however, they forgot their employer and usurped rule for themselves. Their power centered in the three coast cities of Gaza, Ashkelon, and Ashdod, but they also held important inland cities such as Gath and Ekron. Once they had secured themselves in the coastal plain, the Philistines dreamed of conquering all Palestine. This ambition led to conflict with the Hebrews, who by now had subjugated the Canaanites of the hill country. The Philistines had the advantage of superior armor and iron weapons, and their adversaries, besides being menaced by Canaanite revolts, were divided and constantly quarreling amongst themselves. About 1080 the Philistines captured Shiloh, an Israelite sanctuary, and carried away the sacred Ark of the Covenant to Ashdod. These raids eventually forced a military and political union upon the Hebrews, and after the establishment of a central monarchy the Hebrew kings were able systematically to reduce their enemies to impotence. The Philistines passed from history and, except for their name (which eventually was applied to all Palestine) and their introduction of iron into the country, they left few traces of their sojourn save in the memories of the Hebrews.

The Hebrew Monarchy

In the early centuries of their life in Palestine, the Hebrew tribes were governed by magistrates whom the English translators of the Bible call "judges." The Hebrews themselves used the Canaanite-Phoenician word *shophet*, a word which we come across again many centuries later as the official title of the rulers of Carthage (Latin *suffetes*, often translated "consul"). This Canaanite title for Hebrew chiefs indicates the deep and abiding influence of the earlier inhabitants upon the newcomers and raises a suspicion that many early "judges" were in fact Canaanites. Each judge ruled a rather small district. In time of war he was leader of the host raised in his district, but there was no higher political union among the early Hebrews.

The Philistine menace made closer union essential, and about 1015 B.C. a certain Saul became "king" of all the Hebrews. As he was primarily a warrior, Saul fought successfully against the Philistines to the west and against various desert tribes to the east. A few miles north of Jerusalem, he built a rude fortress, whose ruins have recently been excavated, and here he established his capital. However, his authority did not extend far beyond central Palestine, even in time of war, and in time of peace it virtually disappeared. Though victorious at first, Saul was defeated at last by the Philistines, after which he fell upon his sword and died. His friends, wishing to perpetuate the monarchy in his family, tried to make Saul's son king in his place, but rule presently passed to his rival, David.

David and Solomon

Later generations of Hebrews honored David as one of their great legendary heroes. He was pictured as a shepherd boy who with his bare hands had killed a lion and a bear; he was the courageous stripling who slew the Philistine giant Goliath (another legend attributed this mighty deed to an otherwise unknown Elhanan: II Sam. 21:19); he was the sweet singer whose music calmed Saul during fits of insanity and to whom the whole Book of Psalms was later attributed; he was the bosom friend of Saul's son, Jonathan, yet hated by Saul; while still a boy, he was anointed king by the prophet Samuel after a long search which reminds us of the story of Cinderella. The most probable story of all reported that he had been a brigand chieftain, with headquarters in a cave at Adullam, who rented out his men to Saul or to the Philistines as occasion offered.

While David's youth thus became the subject of legend and romance, the story of his later years is preserved in an excellent historical narrative composed within a few years of his death (II Sam. 9–20). David like Saul, was primarily a warrior, but unlike Saul he was much besides. Perhaps his most important achievement was the conquest of Jerusalem, which he made the political and religious capital of his kingdom. His wars against the Philistines were so successful that this enemy caused little serious trouble thereafter. Much of Transjordan was added to his kingdom, whose frontiers were thus pushed to the neighborhood of Damascus.

Moreover, David succeeded where Saul had failed in making the wartime union of the Hebrew tribes permanent. He founded a dynasty which ruled at Jerusalem for upward of four centuries. Perhaps Saul's failure had been due in part to the fact that he belonged to the tribe of Benjamin, one of the weakest among the Hebrews, and therefore did not enjoy the undivided loyalty of any strong group. David was a member of the powerful tribe of Judah and a native of Bethlehem. He easily won the allegiance of the whole South, and minor rebels could not alienate the loyalty of the tribes of central and northern Palestine. While it is impossible to give the exact dates of his reign, we know that he began to rule at Hebron in southern Judah shortly after the year 1000, that he took over the remnants of Saul's kingdom some seven years later, and that his reign lasted from about 1000 to 960.

David was followed by his son Solomon. David had been the great fighter who built up an empire; Solomon was the administrator who gave that empire a stable organization. Legend made Solomon famous for his wisdom—even attributing the Biblical Book of Proverbs to him—and if wisdom is to be equated with administrative skill, this reputation is justified. The Hebrews now began to enjoy the fruits of their earlier struggles, and in later times they fondly recalled the days of Solomon as a time when every man dwelt safely under his own vine and fig tree.

Solomon was an oriental potentate, and he made his kingdom equal in splendor to the other small kingdoms in the vicinity. He married a daughter of Shishak, the founder of the Twenty-second Dynasty in Egypt, and to the best of his ability made his court resemble that at Thebes. He surrounded himself with his numerous wives and concubines, his eunuchs, his ministers, and his bureaucrats. The Egyptian alliance enabled him to conduct profitable trading expeditions in the Red Sea to Punt. Solomon was also a son-in-law of Hiram, king of Tyre, with whose permission and aid he sent trading fleets in the Mediterranean as far as Tarshish (Tarsus) in Asia Minor.

Perhaps the most famous of Solomon's works was the Temple which he had built at Jerusalem. As a matter of fact, this temple was at first little more than the chapel of his enormous palace. Nevertheless, it became the center of the official Jewish cult. Nothing now remains of either palace or temple, though an excellent example of Solomon's building projects has recently been unearthed at Megiddo. Here he had a large palace behind which were stables to accommodate four hundred horses and their chariots. At many other places he erected public buildings and temples to Hebrew and pagan gods. Tradition reported that Solomon ruled for forty years (a round figure signifying one generation), but it seems more likely that he died about 935, after a reign of approximately twenty-five years.

The Divided Kingdoms

Solomon's reign was a glorious period in Hebrew history, but its splendor cost the people many sacrifices. During the king's last years there was much dissatisfaction, especially in the central and northern parts of the kingdom. The Biblical narrative intimates that the unrest was caused by heavy taxation. It was magnified, however, by important economic differences between the North and the South. The North, being agricultural and relatively rich, paid the greater part of the taxes, while the court was located at Jerusalem in the South, which was pastoral and poor. These dissensions led to a revival of the old distinction between the tribes who had entered from the east about 1400 and those that entered later from the south. While the Philistine menace had brought the two groups together, the decline of their enemies enabled them to quarrel with each other again in safety. Finally a bad situation was made worse by the intrigues of the Egyptians, who hoped that a division of Palestine would promote their interests.

A few years before Solomon's death, an Israelite named Jeroboam attracted attention by his criticisms of the king. When Solomon ordered him executed, Jeroboam sought asylum in Egypt. A few years later, after Solomon had been succeeded by his son Rehoboam, the Israelites complained to the young king of their heavy taxation. Rehoboam refused to promise relief, whereupon Jeroboam returned from Egypt to lead a rebellion, and the Hebrew state was split asunder. The southern tribes remained loyal to Rehoboam, and kept the old capital at Jerusalem. The northern tribes made Jeroboam king and established their capital at Shechem—a city which had been a religious center in the days of the judges. The breach between Israel and Judah was never healed, and the rival kingdoms quarreled and fought with each other for two hundred years. During the confusion attendant upon the revolution, Hiram of Tyre seized a large part of Galilee, and a few years later Arameans took the rest. Not until 104 B.C. was "Galilee of the Gentiles" again under Hebrew rule.

The Kingdom of Israel

During the next two centuries the Northern Kingdom, or Israel, being larger and wealthier than Judah, played a more conspicuous part in Near Eastern history. But unfortunately here, as so often in history, revolution begat revolution, and seven dynasties were overthrown by violence during a brief period. Out of a score of Israelitish kings whose deeds are chronicled in the Old Testament, only four or five require special mention. Omri (885–74) seized control of the kingdom, moved the capital from Shechem to Samaria, and made himself so prominent that the Assyrians called the country Bit Humri ("House of Omri") thereafter. His son Ahab (874–52), though terribly maligned by the Old Testament writers, was the greatest of the kings of Israel. He engineered an alliance with the king of Tyre, whose daughter Jezebel he married. He sought to end the barren feud with Judah through an alliance and the marriage of his daughter Athaliah to the king's son. He conquered territory in Moab, east of the Dead Sea, and he waged victorious wars against Damascus. When a king of Assyria invaded Syria, Ahab contributed 10,000 infantry and 2000 chariots to the force that stopped him (854).

The prophets of Israel hated and defamed Ahab's wife Jezebel with a special venom because she worshiped foreign gods, and ten years after his death they inspired an adventurer named Jehu to overthrow the dynasty. Jezebel's death shows that she must have been a true aristocrat, while Jehu, though a friend of the prophets, was merely a bloodthirsty savage. After Jehu had murdered her son, Jezebel attired herself in all her finery and calmly awaited the inevitable. Jehu ordered her thrown from a window, trampled her to death under the feet of his horses, and had her body thrown to the dogs. After indulging in a drunken debauch, Jehu liquidated the old royal family with about seventy murders and followed this purge with a general massacre of his adversaries. He ruled for twenty-eight years (842–14). His two incompetent sons maintained the dynasty until 785, paying tribute to Assyria and allowing the king of Damascus to seize large sections of their kingdom.

Jeroboam II (785–45) redeemed the situation and regained the lost territories, but he was the last of Israel's important kings. His death was followed by a long-continued orgy of murder in which all the remaining kings save one met violent deaths. The Assyrians had by this time occupied Syria; they presently conquered Philistia; and after 734 Israel was a subject nation. When the last king, Hoshea, vainly attempted resistance, the kingdom was destroyed (722). Samaria became a province in the Assyrian Empire, and 27,290 Israelites were deported to Mesopotamia. These captives were from the upper classes and the leaders likely to cause trouble. Those allowed to remain in Palestine were the humble herdsmen and peasants whom the Assyrians had no reason to fear.

The Kingdom of Judah

The tiny kingdom of Judah had a less colorful political history. Only a few years after the revolt of the northern tribes, Jerusalem was occupied by Shishak of Egypt, who carried off the gold and silver ornaments of the Temple and left Judah a poverty-stricken and subservient state. Intermittent wars with Israel continued until the time of Ahab. Jehu tried in vain to seize Judah, actually killing the king and forty-two members of the royal family. However, Queen Athaliah, daughter of Jezebel and, according to the Biblical writers, herself a very wicked woman (an idolatress), managed to hide her infant son and thus to preserve the seed of David. She then ruled until her son came of age. More than a century later King Ahaz of Judah made an alliance with Assyria at the time of the attack upon Israel and Damascus (735), and Judah thus escaped destruction. Several years later Sennacherib made his famous attack upon Jerusalem (701), and thereafter Hezekiah and his son Manasseh (693–39) remained loyal vassals to the Assyrian king.

The death of Ashurbanipal (626) and the subsequent confusion in Assyria encouraged the Jews to hope for independence, and in 621 King Josiah launched a new policy that was both religious and political. Dreaming of nothing less than the re-establishment of the ancient kingdom of David and Solomon, he had actually made an important start toward realizing his ambitions when he was killed in battle with the Egyptians at Megiddo (608). For several years thereafter, the Jewish monarchy teetered between Egypt and Babylon, until Nebuchadrezzar decided to end the nuisance. His armies entered Jerusalem in 597, and again in 586, and on each occasion Jews were deported to Babylonia. In 586 the city was sacked and the Jewish monarchy was abolished.

Conflicting estimates of the number of Jews carried into exile are given in the Old Testament, but in any case the number was not large. One passage tells us that 10,000 were carried away into captivity in 597 while another gives the figure 3025, adding that 832 captives were taken in 586 B.C., and 745 five years later. If we assume that the second author counted only adult males while the first gave the actual number deported, we reach a figure of about 15,000 exiles all told, or perhaps 10 per cent of the population of Judah. About twice this number had been taken from Israel in 722. The exiles were soldiers and artisans, and we are told explicitly that the farmers were left undisturbed in their homes. Nebuchadrezzar was not illiberal in his treatment of the Jews who remained in Palestine. They were given a Jewish governor, and were allowed to retain their farms and their religion. In 581 the governor was assassinated by a member of the former royal family, which caused further deportations to Babylon. Thereafter the peasants of Judah led quiet and uneventful lives. Although a certain number of Arabs forced their way in from the desert, apparently there was no deliberate resettlement of the country, such as happened in Israel after 722.

Little is known of the history of the exiles in Babylon. The artisans presumably continued in their old trades while others turned to commerce, but it is doubtful whether many took up agriculture: the Jews in exile were city dwellers. Some of them eventually became wealthy in their new homes, and throughout the remainder of antiquity Babylon remained an important Jewish center. Nevertheless, many Jews longed to return to Palestine, and in the last days of the Chaldean kingdom they believed that a change of government might enable them to do so. Cyrus was hailed with joy by the Jews, even before his attack upon Babylon, and after his victory they were rewarded with a decree allowing those who wished to do so to return to Jerusalem.

We know only a few episodes in the political history of the Jews during the period of Persian supremacy (538–332). Soon after Cyrus issued his decree a handful of religious enthusiasts returned to Jerusalem and were quickly absorbed by their kinsmen who had never been in exile. Eighteen years later a more important group returned under the leadership of Zerubbabel, grandson of the Jewish king who had been carried into exile in 597. He was made governor of Judah, and his friend Joshua, son of a former high priest, became his high priest. With this company came the prophets Haggai and Zechariah. Goaded by the prophets, Zerubbabel rebuilt the Temple, which had been in a delapidated condition since 586, though apparently it was used for worship during the whole period.

After the completion of the new Temple at Jerusalem in 516, another period of darkness covered Judah until the coming of Nehemiah seventy-two years later. Nehemiah was one of the many Jews whose family had remained in Babylon after Cyrus's decree and, being a rich man, he had risen high in the favor of the Persian king. The king sent him to Jerusalem as governor in 444. In spite of strong opposition, Nehemiah rebuilt the walls of the city and ordered various religious and social reforms, especially in regard to the Sabbath and intermarriage with Gentiles. After twelve years he returned to Babylon. The last Jew of the Persian period of whom we have record

is Ezra, who came from Babylon in 397. He too had a large program
of reform, which he persuaded the Jews to accept. He made the Jewish state into a theocracy, governed by the high priests under remote
Persian supervision, and this type of government prevailed under
various foreign rulers for upward of two centuries.

The Samaritans

The political history of the Hebrews cannot be concluded without
a few words regarding the peoples of the Northern Kingdom after
722. Though Sargon placed the province under an Assyrian governor,
and then settled foreign peoples there, the great majority of the
population remained as it had been before—a mixture of Canaanites
and Hebrews. Many Israelites had worshiped the Jewish God before
their defeat and continued to do so afterward. Centuries later, the
Persians called the province Samaria and kept it distinct from Judea.
In the days of Nehemiah, the Samaritan governor apparently hoped
to have Jerusalem placed within his jurisdiction, for he was much
offended when Nehemiah rebuilt the walls of the city. The new
marriage laws also offended the Samaritans, whom Nehemiah, a
Babylonian Jew, did not regard as Jews at all. Ezra's activities deep-
ened the rift between the two peoples. While the Samaritans continued to worship the same God as the Jews, they worshiped him on
Mount Gerizim, near Shechem, not at Jerusalem. The Samaritans had
a Bible consisting of only the first six books of the Jewish Old Testament, and the texts of their books showed many variations from the
Hebrew. The schism really went back to differences dating from the
Hebrew conquest. They were perpetuated, after the brief union under David and Solomon, by the separation of the monarchies, and
continued until the destruction of Jerusalem by the Romans in 70 A.D.
Readers of the Gospels will recall how bitter was the feeling between
Jews and Samaritans in New Testament times. Even today a few
Samaritans worship on Mount Gerizim according to the old rules.

The Old Testament

The Hebrews produced the first large and imposing literature that
we have met in our survey of the ancient world. Earlier peoples had

their literatures, which historians value highly, but today these writings are read only by scholars. Hebrew literature, on the other hand, has been for centuries a source of pleasure and inspiration to persons of many persuasions and in many lands. We now print this literature in a single volume called the "Bible," from the Greek word *biblos*, "book," which in turn is derived from Byblus, as the Greeks called the Phoenician port of Gebal where in early times they obtained their supplies of papyrus-paper from Egypt. In this chapter, of course, we are concerned only with the Old Testament, which is the first part of the Christian Bible. This Old Testament was the work of many authors, some of whom were separated from others by many centuries, and it contains poetry and prose, history and fiction, philosophy and law. It therefore reflects a long development of Hebrew views on God and the world, on man and society, beginning with the beliefs and superstitions of primitive barbarians and rising to the lofty teachings of the great prophets. This Old Testament is our principal guide to the history of the Hebrews and to their religion.

As the Bible is a library, rather than a single book, there has always been a question as to exactly what writings it should contain. The list of books recognized as sacred is called the "canon." A reader who examines the various modern editions of the Bible used by Protestants, Catholics, and Jews will at once be struck by important differences in arrangement and content, for three different canons have been followed. In Protestant and Jewish Bibles the books are the same in number, titles, and content, though they are arranged in different sequence. The Catholic Bible contains several additional books and inserts additional sections in two of the books found in other canons.

The rise of these differences must be explained. The Jews did not finally decide upon their canon until about the time of Christ. For two or three centuries before this time, however, many Jews had been living outside Palestine in various parts of the Greek world. As they had forgotten their Hebrew, they were forced to read their sacred books in a Greek translation, or "version." This translation into Greek is known as the "Septuagint"—so called from the Latin word *septuaginta*, "seventy"—because of an old legend that the

translation was made by seventy scholars in the days of Ptolemy II
of Egypt (285–246 B.C.). Presently various new writings appeared,
either in translation or originally written in Greek, which had no
place in the Hebrew canon, though Greek-speaking Jews accepted
them as sacred none the less. As the early Christians used the Bible
in the Septuagint version, they accepted the entire Greek canon—as
does the Eastern or Greek Orthodox Church today.

Shortly before 400 A.D., a Latin version, known as the "Vulgate,"
was made by Jerome, who included all but one of the books listed in
the Greek canon. A standard edition of this version was issued under
the auspices of Pope Clement VIII (1592) from which the Catholic
translation into English, known as the "Douay Version," was made
in 1610 (revised 1750). When Luther made his famous translation
into German (1525), he returned to the Jewish canon, although he
kept the books in the new order to which he had become accustomed
in the Vulgate. Protestants call the non-canonical books the "Apocrypha" and occasionally include them in their Bibles between the
Old and New Testaments; today they more commonly omit the
Apocrypha entirely.[2]

For historical purposes the Jewish canon is the most useful because of the light it sheds upon the dates and character of the various
writings. In this canon the first five books are known as the "Torah,"
or "Law": Christians usually refer to them as the "Pentateuch"
(*pente* is the Greek word for "five," *teuchos* for "roll" or "book").
The second section of the Hebrew Bible, the "Prophets," is divided
into two parts, "Former" and "Latter"—the "Former Prophets" consisting of the historical books, the "Latter Prophets" of the writings
of the great prophets. The last section of the Hebrew Bible, the

[2] The famous English translation is the so-called "Authorized Version," published in
1611 at the command of James I, and therefore sometimes called the "King James
Version." This translation remained standard for more than two centuries and a half,
until the "Revised Version" appeared in 1884; an American revision appeared in 1901
and still another revision is promised shortly (the revised New Testament appeared in
1946). Two other recent English versions are those of James Moffatt (1924) and
The Complete Bible: an American Translation (1939), the latter including the
Apocrypha. A new English translation of the Vulgate by Ronald Knox has recently
been published.

"Writings," includes a wide variety of works.[3] The Torah was the part first recognized as sacred; the Prophets were added to the canon later; and in general the "Writings" were the last to be written, as well as the last to be admitted to the Jewish canon of the Holy Scriptures.

Biblical Criticism, Lower and Higher

A person wishing to use the Old Testament as evidence for matters of Hebrew history must of course subject it to critical study. As the criticism to be used is identical with that applied to all other historical documents, we shall explain here what this criticism is like and what critics are trying to do. Criticism is of two sorts, commonly called "lower" and "higher." Lower criticism is concerned with the text and asks the question, exactly what did the ancient writer say? The problem is more difficult than one might think. As every copy of an ancient book was written by hand, the probability of error was high, and no two copies of the same book were ever exactly alike. Words might be misspelled, misread, or misplaced, and whole lines might be misplaced, repeated, or dropped out. Later copyists, finding corrupt passages and attempting to rectify them, would often make matters worse.

Our oldest Hebrew manuscripts of the Old Testament date from the ninth century after Christ,[4] more than a thousand years after the

---

[3] The books of the Old Testament are arranged as follows in the Jewish canon:
Law: Genesis, Exodus, Leviticus, Numbers, Deuteronomy.
Former Prophets: Joshua, Judges, Samuel, Kings (each of the latter counted as one book, not two as in Christian Bibles).
Latter Prophets: Isaiah, Jeremiah, Ezekiel, the Book of the Twelve (the twelve minor prophets in Christian Bibles).
Writings: Psalms, Proverbs, Job, Song of Songs, Ruth, Lamentations, Ecclesiastes, Esther, Daniel, Ezra, Nehemiah, Chronicles.
It will be noted that the books of the Law are the same in all Bibles. Jews do not consider Ruth, or Chronicles-Ezra-Nehemiah, or Esther, as historical books, and they do not include Daniel among the Prophets. The "Song of Songs" is usually called the "Song of Solomon" in Protestant Bibles. Modern editions of the Apocryphal books contain: I and II Esdras, Tobit, Judith, additions to Esther, Wisdom of Solomon, Ecclesiasticus (Wisdom of Jesus ben Sirach), Baruch, additions to Daniel, I and II Maccabees. II Esdras is not printed in either Greek or Latin Bibles, nor I Esdras in the Latin.
[4] The oldest manuscript containing the entire Old Testament in Hebrew, now in

latest passages were written. The man who made this manuscript of course copied an older one, just as the man who made that one copied a still older one, and so on through at least a score of scribes, each of whom undoubtedly introduced changes of greater or less magnitude into the text before him. Fortunately, scholars have learned much about how such mistakes arise, and often they can correct the simpler errors after a careful comparison of old manuscripts with each other and with the early versions. Such study shows not merely scribal errors—a word or two or a line wrong here and there—but also long passages omitted or misplaced or inserted. Even yet, however, there are countless passages, obviously wrong, whose correct reading we have no means of knowing. For example, one passage (I Sam. 13:1) reports according to the present Hebrew text that Saul, the mighty man of war, "was a year old when he began to reign, and he reigned two years over Israel."

The "higher" critic has a more difficult and a more delicate task. He endeavors to answer such questions as these: who wrote the passage under consideration? when? why? what were his sources of information? how reliable were they? has the passage been tampered with since he wrote it? if so, by whom and in what way? In brief, the higher critic tries to assess the value of writings as historical evidence. His task is complicated by the fact that there were no copyright laws in antiquity. Men cared little about who wrote a book or passage. When an author sat down to write, he got material wherever he could find it, not hesitating to take and slightly modify long sections

---

Aleppo, dates from the second quarter of the tenth century (about 940 A.D.); the second oldest is dated 1009. There are older manuscripts, however, which give parts of the Old Testament. Thus a manuscript, made between 820 and 850 and now in the British Museum, contains the Pentateuch; another, made about 897 and now in Cairo, gives the Former and Latter Prophets; and a third, dated 916, has the Latter Prophets. A famous manuscript of the Samaritan Pentateuch (see p. 216) is said to date from 655 A.D., but this figure is probably much too low. On the other hand, we have several manuscripts of the Greek translation of the Old Testament that are several centuries older than any of these. The Vaticanus and the Sinaiticus date from the fourth century after Christ, while the Alexandrinus and the Freer manuscripts date from the fifth.

The world of Biblical scholarship was startled in 1947 by the announcement of the discovery in Palestine of several scrolls which were said to date from the first century before Christ. One of them contains the whole book of Isaiah in Hebrew, this manuscript being almost a thousand years older than the earliest extensive manuscript of the Hebrew Old Testament known heretofore. As scholars have not yet had time to study the new manuscript carefully, it is still too early to estimate its importance.

from other books. Later writers in turn copied and altered his book to suit their tastes.

In the whole of the Old Testament there is not a book that has not been revised repeatedly since it left the original author's hands. In fact, only a few of the briefer books (Ruth, Lamentations, and perhaps one or two of the minor prophets) can be regarded, even in the broadest and loosest way, as the work of individual authors. On the other hand, an author would frequently try to gain authority for his views by attributing them to some great man of the past. Thus it came about that the whole Torah eventually was attributed to Moses, the Psalms to David, and Wisdom literature to Solomon, though it cannot be shown that these heroes had any share at all in writing the books mentioned. Hebrew literature was not the work of twenty-five or thirty writers, as was once supposed, but rather of hundreds who wrote and rewrote it over a period of almost a thousand years. A few passages were written down in much their present form in the days of David and Solomon; others were composed only a century or two before the birth of Christ.

Documents Behind the Pentateuch

Perhaps the most interesting, though certainly not the most difficult, achievement of nineteenth-century higher criticism was the analysis of the Pentateuch into several separate documents. Heretofore, the traditional view had been that Moses wrote the Pentateuch and that it survived just as it had come from his hand. Careful study has shown, however, that the present text could not have been the work of one man, and that it contains much that is certainly post-Mosaic. Following a variety of clues, the critics analyzed the books into sections written by different authors at widely different times. One convenient clue was found in the word used for the Deity: in many passages he is called Yahweh (or Jehovah, translated "the LORD" in the King James Version), in others he is called Elohim (God). The passages using the Yahweh form make up a narrative of Hebrew history from the Garden of Eden to the days of the Divided Monarchy. Critics called this compilation the "J document," and believed that it was composed in Judah about 850 B.C. The passages using the name Elohim form a parallel account, often telling the same stories in slightly different forms. Critics called this document "E," and believed that it was composed in Israel at about the same time as "J." About 750 the two narratives supposedly were woven into one continuous narrative, now called "JE." Much of the Pentateuch still remained unaccounted for, however, and as the Book of Deuteronomy contained material written in a rather different spirit, it was referred to as the "D document," composed about 625. A fourth document, called "P" or the Priests' Code, was apparently put together after the Exile. Finally, the critics declared that the great documents, JE, D, and P, were woven together in the time of Ezra (about 400 B.C.) to form our Pentateuch—a theory now called the "Graf-Wellhausen theory" from two of its most brilliant proponents.

While in its main outlines this theory still stands, further study and the discoveries of archeologists have rectified many of its details. The process by which the Pentateuch reached its present form was far more complicated than these early critics suspected. They often spoke as though J, E, D, and P were individual authors, each of whom wrote a book. As a matter of fact, it is very doubtful whether J, E, D, or P ever existed as single and separate documents. In the ninth and eighth centuries before Christ, many writers composed stories in a style that we recognize in J and E. Seventh century thought and writing assumed the style of D; and after the Exile priests wrote in still another style, emphasizing new things and thinking in new patterns. Nor were primitive documents brought together on only one or two occasions. Such collecting and editing was going on throughout Hebrew history. On the other hand, archeology has made it certain that even the J and E writers were acquainted with legends and written records of earlier times that were far more accurate than the older critics were willing to admit. Nevertheless, the fundamental contention of the higher critics, namely, that the Pentateuch reached substantially its present form only at the end rather than at the beginning of ancient Hebrew history, is now denied by no competent scholar.[5]

---

[5] See note on the Higher Criticism, p. 241.

The Hebrew Historians

With the ground thus cleared, we may proceed to an examination of the historical narratives of the Pentateuch. The Book of Genesis, as its name suggests, gives a story of the origin of the world and of the human race and the early history of the Hebrews. The stories of creation, the patriarchs, and the flood are so similar to Sumerian accounts of the same things that no one can doubt the ultimate Sumerian origin of the Hebrew version. The only question is whether the Hebrews learned these stories from the Canaanites after entering Palestine or brought them from the desert, after having learned them from the Babylonians and preserved them during several centuries of wandering. Many scholars now prefer the latter view.

The remainder of Genesis tells of the exploits of Abraham, Isaac, and Jacob, the legendary ancestors of the Hebrew people, tracing their progress from Mesopotamia to Palestine and Egypt. The opening chapters of Exodus tell of the enslavement of the Hebrews in Egypt and of their escape from that land. These old legends were, of course, the creation of the Hebrews themselves, yet archeology has shown that often they retained local color remarkably well. In general, these stories had been preserved as ballads and epics, some of them perhaps dating from the days of the desert, while others may have arisen in Palestine in the days of the conquest and the judges.

The rest of the Pentateuch is given over to Hebrew civil and religious law, interspersed with brief stories of the wanderings of the Hebrews around Mount Sinai and in the desert. We have already seen that the older parts of the civil law go back to Babylonian precedents such as the Code of Hammurabi. As this law envisaged a settled agricultural and commercial life, and would therefore have been inappropriate to nomads in the desert, it is reasonable to assume that the Hebrews took it from the Canaanites, who in turn had acquired it from the Babylonians. Other parts of the law came from the desert, and still others evolved in Palestine. The laws of Deuteronomy closely resemble those enforced by Josiah at the time of his great reform (621), and in general they date from this period. The last great section of the law was the work of post-Exilic priests. These priestly legislators were antiquarians who revived ancient customs and invented new ones. Some of the former went back to primitive times, some of the latter were of a highly utopian character and probably no serious attempt was ever made to enforce them. Hebrew law thus went through an evolution closely parallel to that of early Hebrew historical writings, yet, in spite of obviously diverse origins, the whole law, like the early historical writing, was commonly attributed to Moses.

The four books of the Former Prophets continue Hebrew history from the conquest of Canaan to the Exile: Joshua and Judges tell of the conquest in variant forms, Samuel tells of Saul and David, Kings gives the history of Solomon and his successors. The earlier books are full of legends and hero stories about the conquest, most of them no doubt more or less contemporary in oral form with the events they narrate, but they were written down, with embellishments, in the days of the Monarchy. Their style is very similar to that of the J and E stories in Genesis. The last part of Samuel is a detailed and seemingly accurate account of David's reign which gives the impression of being the work of an eye-witness. It probably reached approximately its present form in the days of Solomon. The kings of Israel and Judah, like their more powerful colleagues elsewhere, kept official chronicles to which the compilers of Kings sometimes referred. A great part of the book, however, is devoted to the activities of the prophets, and long sections are taken from the lives of Elijah, Elisha, and Isaiah: panegyric in tone and abounding in miracles, these lives undoubtedly were written by disciples shortly after the times of their heroes. These four books of the Former Prophets probably reached their present form during the Exile or shortly thereafter.

Hebrew Methods in Chronology

A careful study of the chronology recorded in the Old Testament, taken at face value and with no attempt to determine its truth by comparison with other evidence, throws a strong light upon the methods used by Hebrew historians. It is best to approach the problem backwards, beginning with the kings of Israel and Judah and ending with Abraham. The length of the reign of each of the kings is given, with cross references showing in what year of the king of Judah each new king of Israel began to reign, and vice versa. It all seems very clear and simple until the reader checks by a few simple additions. It then appears that the reigns of the kings of Judah before the fall of Samaria total thirty-one years more than those of the kings of Israel during the same period, and that no cross reference after the first two reigns is correct. The figures presumably harmonized when the account was first written, and a few mistakes may be attributed to copyists, but the present chaos forces us to conclude that someone deliberately altered the lengths of reigns without bothering to change the cross references. This supposition is well borne out. If we add up the reigns of the kings of Judah, including the last years of Solomon at one end and the Exile at the other, we find the period from the First Temple to the Second was exactly 480 years, or twelve generations. Some editor must have stretched various reigns by about sixty years to make them fit a preconceived pattern. Moreover, the reigns of the kings of Israel from Jeroboam I to Hoshea are made to total exactly half this length of time, or 240 years. The man who rearranged this chronology obviously was obsessed with the idea of making it symmetrical.

Going a step further back in Hebrew history, we find that in I Kings 6:1 it is said that the period from the Exodus to the building of the First Temple was 480 years! If we add up the reigns of the individual judges, neglecting the years of foreign oppression, but add the forty years in the desert and also the reigns of Saul and David, this sum also is 480 years. Nor is this all. It is a noteworthy fact that in Exodus 12:40 the two oldest versions of the Old Testament (the Samaritan and the Greek) agree against the Hebrew in saying that the Hebrews were "in Egypt *and in Canaan*" for 430 years, in other words the period from Haran to the Exodus was 430 years. Abraham was 75 years old when he left Haran, after having lived there many years: if he left his native Ur at the age of twenty-five, the period from Ur to the Exodus was exactly 480 years! Thus we find that the four major events in the religious history of the Hebrews (Abraham leaving Ur, the Exodus and the Ten Commandments, the First Temple, and the Second Temple) followed each

other at intervals of exactly 480 years. These figures show how little
the Hebrew historians cared for chronological truth: what they
wanted was a cut and dried system.[6]

The Histories as Works of the Prophets

Other evidence reinforces our conclusion that Hebrew historians
were not inspired by the modern ideal of simply telling history "as it
really happened." Not only in chronology but in everything else, too,
they wished to make history fit a pattern, and in general their pattern
was a theological one. Thus the compiler of the Book of Judges made
his history follow one simple formula: the Hebrews worshiped Yahweh and were happy; they fell away, worshiped foreign gods, and
were punished with foreign oppressors; they repented, turned again

---

[6] It is even possible to trace the development of Hebrew chronological systems
through several stages, with one symmetrical system replacing another. (1) There can
be little doubt that contemporary records were saved, showing accurately the length
of each reign from David to the Exile. (2) The first revision of these figures stretched
the reigns to make all Hebrew history fall into three periods of 480 years each. Obviously this could not have been done until after the end of the last period (536), and
long enough afterward to permit the serious error regarding the date of the Second
Temple: this first artificial chronology was probably put together about the time of
Ezra. (3) A second revision came later when the words "and in Canaan," were
dropped from the Hebrew text, presumably by someone who wished to lengthen the
stay of the Hebrews in Egypt in order to make their entrance coincide with the
Hyksos invasions. He had probably learned of this invasion from Egyptian sources,
perhaps from Manetho, whose history was published about 275 B.C. At about the
same time, the Greek translators of the Septuagint greatly lengthened the already
venerable lives of the patriarchs, apparently in order to put them long before Manetho's First Dynasty. (4) Finally, more than a century later, some other editor
juggled the figures again for another purpose. The man who concocted this last chronology was something of a Zoroastrian, thinking in terms of millenniums, for he put the
Creation exactly four thousand years before Judas Maccabaeus, a great Jewish hero
who purified the Temple in 164 B.C. It is also interesting to note that the figures, as
they now stand in the Hebrew text, make the period from the Creation to the Exodus
amount to 2666 years, which is exactly two-thirds of the 4000 years from Adam to
Judas Maccabaeus. He apparently believed that the Second Temple was built in 538
(the year of the fall of Babylon and the Return from the Exile) and the First Temple
in 1018, that the Exodus was in 1498, and the Creation in 4164 B.C.

The dates printed in the margins of some modern Bibles were computed about
three hundred years ago by an Irishman, Archbishop Ussher. He selected the famous
date 4004 B.C. for the Creation of the world, not because the figures add up that way
(they don't), but because he, too, was a millennarian who wished to have Creation
exactly four millenniums before the birth of Christ. Anyone who takes the trouble to
add up the figures as they now stand in the Hebrew text will find that the good
Archbishop missed by 158 years. If the Second Temple was built in 536 (as Ussher
believed), then the Creation should have been put in 4162 B.C. Modern Jews, by a
different treatment of the figures, reach the date 3761 B.C. for the Creation.

to Yahweh, were forgiven, and prospered once more. This cycle was repeated a dozen times. Likewise, the compiler of Kings was interested primarily in moral judgments. Each of the kings of Israel, without exception, is said to have done "that which was evil in the sight of Yahweh," meaning that he worshiped foreign gods, and several of the kings of Judah were just as bad. In every case the people suffered terribly in consequence. The author usually is content to dismiss the king, after mentioning his sins (or his moral deeds, if a good king) with the formula, "And the rest of the deeds of X, and all that he did, are they not written in the Book of the Chronicles of the Kings of Judah?" These rather bald dynastic annals are then supplemented with much fuller accounts of the deeds of various prophets.

Hebrew historians were really interested in history only as it touched religion, and their neglect of its other aspects is well attested by archeology. Recent excavations have shown, for example, that Lachish was a rich and powerful city in southern Judah, second only to Jerusalem; but it had no religious significance, so the historians mention it only rarely and in the most perfunctory manner. The Hebrew historians were closely associated with the Hebrew prophets, and it is highly significant that in the Hebrew Bible their writings are called the "Former Prophets."

The Prophets and the Writings

The Hebrews recognized three major prophets, whose prophecies were collected in three separate books: Isaiah, who flourished from about 750 to 700; Jeremiah, who was active between 626 and 586; and Ezekiel, who was taken into exile in 597. In each case, however, the book contains more than the prophecies of the man after whom it was named. The first thirty-nine chapters of the Book of Isaiah center around his life and prophecies; but chapters 40 to 55 are the work of quite a different person, known as the Second Isaiah, who lived in Babylon about 540; and chapters 56 to 66 are from a different and still later man who lived in Palestine. As the Second Isaiah was fully as important as the First, it is not easy to understand why his writings should later have been attributed to the other man. The Book of Jeremiah was first put together by his secretary, a man named Baruch, who added his own memoirs of the prophet; but Baruch's work has been much altered. The Greek translation, made about 200 B.C., shows that even at that late date about one-fifth of the book differed markedly from modern versions. The Book of Ezekiel likewise has been subjected to drastic editing and many interpolations.

The Hebrews consider the writings of the twelve minor prophets as one book—"The Book of the Twelve." The individual books vary in length from one to eight closely printed pages, with the average about three pages. The books are not arranged in chronological order, but the earliest of the minor prophets, Amos, flourished about 760 while the latest, Jonah and Malachi, lived about 400 B.C. Substantial additions were later made to several of these books, and nearly all were touched up by subsequent editors. Taken as a whole, the books of the Prophets cannot have reached approximately their present form much before the second century before Christ, two or three centuries later than the books of the Law.

The last section of the Hebrew Old Testament, the Writings, contains books of many sorts, all later than those making up the Law and the Prophets. They are post-Exilic, and some date from the third and second centuries before Christ. The first of these books, the Psalms, was the hymnbook of the post-Exilic Temple. Some of the Psalms go back to the days of the Monarchy, others were written as late as 150 B.C., and all are anonymous. The Proverbs are likewise anonymous, and no date can be assigned to the book though several chapters closely follow an Egyptian collection of the same sort that dates from the ninth century before Christ. The early part of the Book of Job, with its bantering conversation between God and Satan, shows Persian influences, as does the Book of Esther. Of all the books in the Old Testament, Daniel is the easiest to date with relative certainty: it was written a year or so before the great events of 164 B.C. After this in the Hebrew canon come Ezra and Nehemiah, and last of all the Book of Chronicles, a recapitulation of Hebrew history from Adam to the decree of Cyrus authorizing the construction of the Second Temple. Though the author of Chronicles was largely dependent upon the earlier historical books for his material, he presents some seemingly reliable information not found elsewhere.

A comparison of Chronicles with Samuel and Kings is highly instructive. The earlier books were compiled by men who sympathized with the prophets, Chronicles by someone whose sympathies lay with the priests of the Second Temple. The latter writer omitted much that is found in the earlier books because it had no interest for him. He twisted some of it around and added material about the antiquities of worship, often projecting into the remote past institutions that really were of post-Exilic origin. Like his predecessors, he made Hebrew history revolve around sin and punishment, although the sins that interested him were those denounced by Nehemiah and Ezra rather than those to which the Hebrews had been disposed four or five centuries earlier. The chronicler thus exaggerated the qualities already noted in earlier historical books. He probably lived in the third century before Christ.

Hebrew Religion

Archeological research in the present century has done much to illuminate religious conditions in Palestine and Syria in the days just before the coming of the Hebrews. Ancient shrines have been excavated and statues of ancient gods and goddesses have been unearthed, and above all, the tablets found at Ras Shamra give myths and theologies and describe the rituals and priestly organizations that prevailed up and down the Mediterranean coast about 1400 B.C. We know something of the old fertility religions existing there from neolithic times. Traces of Babylonian religion from the days of the Third Dynasty of Ur and of Hammurabi have been found in southern Palestine. Egyptian temples were built there in the days of the Empire. And finally, archeologists have unearthed records of the gods, sacrifices, priests and holy men, and a mythology of the Canaanites. At the time of the Hebrew invasions, the gods and festivals of the Canaanites were largely agricultural. Their worshipers might expect rewards in the form of good crops and similar blessings. The gods had personal names, of course, but sometimes they were simply called Baals ("lords") or referred to by the old Semitic word *el*, which means "god." These gods were legion, but even in the fourteenth century there was a tendency to amalgamate them and to use the plural form of *el* as a singular noun indicating deity in general.

Yahweh Worship

Less information has come to light regarding the religion of the Hebrews while they were still in the desert. Almost nothing is known of the Habiru who entered from the east in the Amarna period, but the later invaders from the south are better known. They shared the views of other early Semites regarding spirits, the dead, magic, and the like, and they worshiped a god named Yahweh. There has been much discussion regarding the origin and name of this deity,[7] who was the tribal god of a people wandering in the desert south of Palestine. One of the Ras Shamra tablets mentions a deity named "Yw" who was worshiped there: he probably is to be identified with the Hebrew Yahweh.

The elaborate stories of Moses, the alleged founder of the Hebrew religion, are of course largely legend. It seems quite certain, however, that the Hebrew tribe of Judah, which led the southern invasion, had worshiped Yahweh while still in the desert. Perhaps this worship had been imposed upon neighboring tribes even before the invasion, perhaps only after the settlement in Palestine: in any case, all the southern tribes of Hebrews worshiped Yahweh at an early date. This Yahweh was worshiped with the sacrifices and festivals appropriate to a nomadic people. His most important festival was one which came in the spring at the time lambs were born. The ceremonies

---

[7] Even the correct pronunciation of his name is quite unknown. It is written with four consonants (יהוה) which are transliterated YHWH, but no one knows what vowels should be inserted or where. In post-Exilic times the name was considered so sacred that it was never pronounced. When reading the Scriptures aloud, a Jew would substitute *adonai* ("lord") for the divine name wherever it occurred, and men consequently forgot its vowels. Late in the Middle Ages a Christian scholar had the unhappy idea of transferring the vowels of *adonai* to the four consonants and thus coined the word "Jehovah," which, though utterly unjustified, is still in use. The King James Version of the Bible translates the divine name as "the LORD," the Revised Version prints "Jehovah." Ancient Greeks wrote the name *Iabé,* from which modern scholars coined the form "Yahweh." This artificial form is only a doubtful imitation of the ancient Hebrew pronunciation, but it offers a convenient way of distinguishing the tribal god of the ancient Hebrews from the very different Deity, Jehovah, whom we worship today.

centered around the sacrifice of a lamb, and presumably the worshipers expected that Yahweh would reward their piety with many lambs. These early Hebrews undoubtedly had other ceremonies as well, but it is difficult for us today to distinguish those that came out of the desert from those added later, for the Biblical account attributes them all to Moses.

The adoption of settled agricultural life in Palestine brought fundamental changes to the primitive religion of the Hebrews. The earlier invaders, who came from the east and settled in the north, apparently adopted much of the religion of the Canaanites, though they did not necessarily abandon their old gods in the process. The southern tribes, on the other hand, remained loyal to their desert god Yahweh and spread his religion to the north, even in the days of the judges. The Judean kings, David and Solomon, encouraged this religious imperialism, and after the division of the Monarchy many Israelites continued to worship Yahweh. Nevertheless Jeroboam made two golden calves, set them up in ancient sanctuaries at Bethel and Dan, and is reported to have issued the order: "Behold thy gods, O Israel." The Canaanites had worshiped bullock-gods before the invasions, and, as we saw above, each king of Israel thereafter "did that which was evil in the sight of Yahweh," that is, he worshiped other gods.

The situation was indeed difficult for the Hebrew immigrants. Yahweh had been a desert god, his worship was along lines adapted to a nomadic life, and in the popular mind its rewards were equally appropriate to the desert. The Baals, on the other hand, supervised agriculture and rewarded their worshipers with plentiful crops. It would therefore not be surprising if many a Hebrew came to the conclusion that, while Yahweh worship may have been satisfactory in the desert, it had now become necessary for him to re-examine and modernize his religious beliefs and practices. Three answers were given to this delicate problem. Many Hebrews simply went over to the Baals of the land and worshiped them. Others declared that it was impossible to remain faithful to Yahweh in Canaan and fled to the desert, where they organized ascetic groups of fanatics devoted to Yahweh. Still others took over the old Canaanitish ceremonies and dedicated them to Yahweh, confidently expecting that he would continue to look after them in their new homes. The great struggle raged for several centuries, and out of it came the early prophets.

The Early Prophets and Monolatry

The Canaanites had "holy men" whose activities much resembled those of the whirling dervishes in the Near East today or of the "holy rollers" in our own country. They danced and shouted until they had worked themselves into a frenzy, when they would utter unintelligible gibberish and do other strange things: this was called "prophesying." Men believed that such persons were possessed by a god who spoke through their mouths, and consequently regarded them highly. Moreover, even in sober moments, the prophets would speak for the god, serving as oracles predicting the future, giving advice, finding lost objects, and doing whatever else was expected of a man enjoying intimacy with the god. That the early Hebrews also had men of this sort is shown by a famous story of Saul: Saul once joined such a company of prophets, though they were ignorant men of low degree, and his neighbors exclaimed, "Is Saul also among the prophets?"

Before long the Hebrew prophets began speaking for Yahweh in much less primitive fashion. They were "men of God" who spoke in his name, it is true, but primarily they were champions of Yahweh against the Baals and their prophets. Most of them lived in the Northern Kingdom, where the Baals and temptation to worship them were strongest. Yahweh worship was much more firmly established in the South, where it was more ancient and where conditions more closely resembled those of the desert. There was therefore less need for prophets of the new type in Judah.

The most famous of the early prophets was Elijah, who lived in the days of Ahab (874–52). Long after he had been carried away to heaven in a chariot of fire, men continued to tell of his marvelous deeds, which even included bringing the dead to life, of how he denounced Ahab to his face, and above all of his attacks upon the worshipers of the Baals. The greatest of his triumphs came when he challenged the prophets of Baal to bring down fire from heaven and, after his spectacular victory, slew them to the number of four hundred and fifty. Like him, many other prophets of Yahweh wandered about the country, denouncing or ridiculing the Baals and their worshipers, and comforting the devoted servants of Yahweh. Others undertook to advise and admonish kings or inspired malcontents like Jehu to political rebellion. Still others collected and wrote up the old legends about Yahweh and their fathers which now constitute the "J" and "E" documents of the Pentateuch. They sometimes even united in organized groups known as the "sons of the prophets."

It is not easy to summarize the theological views of these early prophets, for there was no unanimity among them except in their championship of Yahweh. It is clear, however, that they were not monotheists. They worshiped Yahweh, and believed it sinful for Hebrews to worship other gods, but they never denied the existence of these other gods. In fact, they expected that other peoples would worship their own gods, just as Hebrews worshiped Yahweh. The Hebrew god was declared to be a "jealous god," yet surely he could not feel jealousy for gods that did not exist. Men like Elijah pictured the Baals as ridiculous and contemptible, but it never occurred to them to doubt their existence or even their power.

This principle of worshiping one god only, though admitting the existence of others, is called "monolatry," and is to be distinguished sharply from the monotheism which denies the existence of more than one God. The gradual evolution of the Hebrews from monolatry to monotheism is the most important, and also the most interesting, aspect of their history. The first steps were taken by the early prophets. They started with their tribal deity who was only one out of many gods, and in chauvinistic fashion they exalted him above all others. They proclaimed the Hebrews to be his chosen people and constructed a theory of history to show the marvelous things he had done in their behalf. Long ago, through their father Abraham, he had promised them the land of Canaan. He led them out of bondage in Egypt, and he helped them conquer Canaan. In return for these favors, he demanded that they worship him and him alone. On the many occasions when they forsook him and worshiped other gods, which was the greatest sin they could commit, he punished them

severely. If the Hebrews wished to prosper, they must worship Yahweh and Yahweh alone. This was the message of the early Hebrew
prophets.

Amos and Hosea

Toward the middle of the eighth century prophecy began to assume
a new form. The old "sons of the prophets" continued their customary
activities, but other prophets wrote the books now known by their
names. These authors continued to use the oracular form, composing
their messages in verse and prefixing to them the formula, "Thus saith
Yahweh," but their importance lay in what they said, not in how they
said it. The first of these writing prophets was Amos, a herdsman of
Judah, who flourished about 760. He migrated to Israel, then at the
height of its prosperity under Jeroboam II, and he was much distressed by what he saw there. He preached (or prophesied) at
Bethel, and his hearers forcibly suggested that if he did not like their
country he should by all means return at once to his own. Amos was
thus reduced to writing out his prophecies. He declared that the
luxury, dishonesty, oppression, and license which he had observed
in Israel were offenses against Yahweh as truly as was formal idol-
atry; in fact, the two forms of sin went together, for in Amos's opinion
a man could not worship Yahweh properly if at the same time he was
oppressing his neighbor. Amos thus began preaching what we today
call social justice.

Hosea, a prophet from the Northern Kingdom, came a few years
after Amos. His book opens with an account of his marriage and of
how his wife lost her love for him, bore children that were not his,
and, after finally leaving him, became a harlot in a pagan temple; but
Hosea still loved her and bought her back at the price of a slave.
Presumably this story is an allegorical romance, setting forth Hosea's
conception of the relations between Yahweh and Israel, though some
scholars insist that brooding upon this actual experience opened
Hosea's eyes to matters of wider import. Whether historically true
or not, the story dominates the book, which is filled with Hosea's
eloquent pleas for love and mutual obligations between Israel and
Yahweh, as in a perfect marriage.

The First Isaiah

The major prophets began with the First Isaiah. In a striking passage (chap. 6) he tells of a deep experience he underwent "in the year that King Uzziah died" (751), and he always thereafter believed that he was speaking for Yahweh. His early prophecies continued in the spirit of Amos and Hosea, foretelling punishment for apostacy, denouncing those who ground down the faces of the poor, and expressing Yahweh's disgust with those who substituted incense, the blood of bullocks, new moons, and sabbaths for justice and mercy. (The first two false forms of worship were Canaanitish, though now dedicated to Yahweh; and while the others may have been brought by the Hebrews from the desert, such celebrations did not come up to Isaiah's high conception of proper worship.) "Zion shall be redeemed by justice," he exclaimed, "and her converts by righteousness."

In the year 735 Rezin of Damascus and Pekah of Israel planned to force Ahaz of Judah into their alliance against Assyria. Isaiah went to Ahaz, and by predicting their speedy downfall persuaded him not to fear his opponents. He was firmly convinced that if Judah remained faithful to Yahweh, Yahweh would protect her; and, as a matter of fact, things came out just as Isaiah had foretold, and Judah was saved. The next thirty years were a troubled time, marked by the relentless advance of the Assyrians and the fall of Israel, but through it all Isaiah remained firm in his isolationist policy. Finally came the attack of Sennacherib and the siege of Jerusalem in 701. Isaiah again assured the people that all would be well, saying that the Assyrian armies marching against Jerusalem were led, not by the god Ashur, as was popularly supposed, but by Yahweh himself! Yahweh was merely using these armies to punish his sinful people, and he never would allow them to get out of hand and destroy that people utterly. "Shall the axe boast itself against him that heweth therewith?" Isaiah thus reached a position that was very near to monotheism. He did not state explicitly that no god except Yahweh existed, but when he affirmed that even the Assyrian armies were under Yahweh's command, he left nothing much for the other gods to do, and they might just as well not exist. Yahweh was indeed the only God whose power proved his existence.

Isaiah's isolationism may have saved Jerusalem, and his theology certainly marked a great step in the advance of Judaism, but the prophet did not at once persuade his fellow countrymen. They rejected his explanation of Assyrian success, preferring to attribute it to the might of Ashur, and during the next several years Yahweh lost much in prestige and worship. Hezekiah continued to rule over Judah for seven years after Sennacherib's attack and remained faithful to Yahweh. Then his son and successor, Manasseh (693–39), adopted a different policy. In politics Manasseh was a faithful vassal of Assyria, and in theology he was a subservient polytheist who thought it wise to placate all the gods. He therefore "reared up altars" to the Baals and planted groves where they might be worshiped. He worshiped "all the host of heaven" (Assyrian astral deities) and the "queen of heaven" (Ishtar, or perhaps Ashtoreth). He set up a statue, presumably of the the Assyrian king, in the Temple at Jerusalem. He "made his son pass through the fire" (the ordinary euphemism for human sacrifice, which was still practiced occasionally by the Hebrews and their neighbors); and he "shed innocent blood very much," doubtless by punishing the prophets who denounced his various doings. His son Amon (639–38) followed in his footsteps, as did his grandson Josiah (638–08) during the opening years of his reign. To these kings and many of their subjects it seemed that Yahweh had been defeated and that his cause was therefore lost.

The Deuteronomists and Jeremiah

During these years the "sons of the prophets," though persecuted, continued to champion Yahweh, and it was under these conditions that they developed the ideas set forth in the Book of Deuteronomy. More than ever they insisted that Yahweh alone should be worshiped: "Hear, O Israel, Yahweh is our God, and Yahweh alone." With an eye to present conditions, they made Moses say, "Though you say to yourselves, 'These nations are greater than I; how can I conquer them?' you must not be afraid of them, remembering rather what Yahweh your God did to Pharaoh and all Egypt." They even declared flatly that no other god than Yahweh existed, thus reaching complete monotheism. They also set forth the law of Yahweh at length. Although this law was attributed to Moses, they filled it with their own humanitarian ideals, and it is the Deuteronomic version of the law that is most frequently quoted with approval in the Gospels.

Presently the great Ashurbanipal died (626), and the Assyrian Empire was soon rushing to its fall. Then, in the eighteenth year of the reign of Josiah (621), the prophets discovered—or claimed to discover—an old book of the law in the Temple. The book was read to Josiah, who was deeply moved and immediately ordered various reforms it demanded. Scholars once believed that this book was our Deuteronomy. Such an identification raises many difficulties, but there can be no doubt that the book in question was written in much the same spirit as Deuteronomy. Josiah purified the Temple, cut down the groves, destroyed the altars, and slew the priests who had worshiped other gods. Inspired with enthusiasm for his new religion, he set out to reconquer the old domains of David and Solomon, carrying his religious reforms wherever he went; but, as we have seen, he was killed in battle at Megiddo in 608. Josiah's successors reversed his political and religious policies, and during the few remaining years of Judah's independence they preferred to follow Manasseh's example.

At this time arose the second of the great Hebrew prophets, Jeremiah. He has been much studied in recent years, and we know him better than any other man in Old Testament history. He began to prophesy in 626, five years before the reforms of Josiah, speaking in a Deuteronomic spirit. After the death of Josiah and the victory of Nebuchadrezzar at Carchemish three years later, Jeremiah's thoughts turned in new directions. Like his predecessor, the First Isaiah, Jeremiah was not only a prophet but also the most clear-sighted statesman of his day. Unfortunately, he found no Hezekiah to heed his advice. Jeremiah saw and declared that neither Egypt nor Babylon could be trusted as an ally, that efforts to play them off against each other were folly, and that resistance was out of the question. He therefore decided that it was best to trust in Yahweh alone. After the Exile of 597, he wrote a letter to the Jews in Babylon urging them to settle down and lead normal lives in their new homes, to make themselves good citizens of their new country, and to pray for the peace of Babylon. In the end Yahweh would reward them if they remained faithful to him. Jeremiah thus laid down the policy which most Jews have followed to the present day.

Jeremiah's new political policy required a revision of the basis of relations between Yahweh and Israel. Even the Deuteronomists had taught that Yahweh was the national god of the Hebrews and that they were his people, as determined by a formal covenant between them, first made in the days of Abraham and then solemnly ratified under Moses. The covenant was a national matter, binding the Hebrew people as a whole. Now, however, the Hebrews had ceased to exist as a separate nation or people. Jeremiah therefore began talking about a new covenant between Yahweh and individual Jews. This view of course opened the way for the conclusion, which Jeremiah seems never to have drawn although his disciples drew it, that even men who were not Jews by birth might enter into the new covenant with Yahweh and enjoy its benefits. Religion had been a national affair according to the earlier prophets. Jeremiah made it a strictly individual matter in which nationality and race have no part. He was the most modern of the Hebrew prophets, and the one most admired by Jesus.

Judaism and the Exile

The Jews who went into exile were faced with many grave religious problems. Those who formerly had been only lukewarm in their worship of Yahweh now abandoned him completely. Others made religion a symbol of nationality and became fanatical in their devotion to Yahweh. Still others found that for various reasons, some of them economic, it was desirable to maintain connections with Jews elsewhere and that the old religion was helpful in this regard. Finally, still others became acquainted with the religious thought of the Chaldeans, and later with that of the Persians, and incorporated foreign ideas into Judaism. There was not much of this syncretism, or blending of religions, during the half century of the Exile proper, but Babylon remained an important Jewish center for many centuries and eventually became the source of much that was new in later Judaism. Moreover, the Jews, torn away from their Temple, had to find new forms of worship in Babylon, and they developed a synagogue worship which differed much from the elaborate ritual of the Temple. They laid greater emphasis upon such distinctive practices as circumcision and Sabbath observance. They made strict rules forbidding intermarriage with Gentiles, and they revived antique customs that had long lain dormant. The Jews of the Exile laid the foundations of a new religion that is known as Judaism.

The Babylonian Exile also produced two of the great prophets, Ezekiel and the Second Isaiah. Ezekiel had been a priest at Jerusalem before he was taken to Babylon in 597. In his new home he longed for the old worship until he discovered that Yahweh could be worshiped anywhere, thus achieving a wider and more universal conception of God. Like the earlier prophets, he attributed the tribulations of the Jews to their sin of apostacy from Yahweh. In glowing language he predicted their eventual purification and pardon, and he dreamed of a liberated and theocratic Jewish state.

More important than Ezekiel was the anonymous prophet now known as the Second Isaiah. He published his prophecies about 540, when Cyrus was already high on the horizon. The new Isaiah therefore appeared as the bringer of good tidings, even naming Cyrus as the man by whom liberation would be accomplished. He had pondered long and deeply upon his people's fate and he had a larger and broader view of God than any of his predecessors. He was a complete monotheist, believing that Yahweh ruled all mankind—including Cyrus. He admitted that the Hebrews were God's chosen people, yet he believed that all mankind would eventually come to know him and worship him. In several dark and much debated passages, he speaks of the "suffering servant of Yahweh," whose unmerited afflictions would have a vicarious effect in redeeming the sins of others. He even suggests that the recent trials of the Jews might have a redemptive effect not only for the Jews themselves but for all mankind. These passages exercised a deep influence upon the thinking of Jesus and the early Christians.

The exiles who returned to Palestine from Babylon were largely fanatics, filled with the ideas of Ezekiel and the earlier prophets. Upon reaching Jerusalem they found many Jews who had never left the country and who did not share their fanaticism. A long struggle followed, in which the leaders of the exiles gradually won. It was their ambition to establish a state where everyone would voluntarily obey the Law of Yahweh. The Deuteronomists had once dreamed such a dream and had persuaded Josiah to follow their suggestions, but, during and after the Exile, Babylonian leaders of the Jews developed new ideas regarding the Law. They formulated a new code which Ezra brought to Jerusalem at the time of his famous visit in 397. He read it aloud to the people and they swore to obey it. The scene was in a way a fulfillment of Jeremiah's dream of a new covenant. We do not know exactly what Ezra read to the people, as it hardly seems likely that he read the whole Pentateuch. Nevertheless, the Torah was completed at about this time and was accepted thereafter as the definitive statement of the Law. The Jews of Palestine became a people governed by this Book of the Law, as interpreted by the priests, and theirs has ever since remained the classic example of a theocracy, or government by God.

Judaism Becomes a Universal Religion

This devotion to the Law, coupled with the rigid measures and racial exclusiveness of Nehemiah and Ezra, were no doubt what enabled the Jews to survive as a distinct group during the tumultuous centuries that followed, but they did scant justice to the broad universalism of Jeremiah and the Second Isaiah. The new leaders were strict monotheists, to be sure, insisting that Yahweh was the only God who existed or ever had existed, and that he was the God of all men. On the other hand, they were reluctant to draw the obvious conclusion that all men were his people. They stoutly maintained that the Jews were God's chosen people.

Nevertheless their racial exclusiveness did not pass without a challenge. The author of the charming little story of Ruth reminded his readers that the great David himself was descended from a Moabite woman. The story of Jonah sought to inculcate two important lessons: first, that it is impossible to escape from Yahweh, even in the remotest corners of the earth, and secondly, that God cared even for the people of Nineveh and would gladly have spared them had they been willing to listen to his prophet. At about the same time the prophet Malachi, who had been much influenced by Deuteronomy and the Second Isaiah, proclaimed that some day all men would worship Yahweh. Beginning with a phrase which the Persians had taken from the Sumerians to describe their empire, he declared, "From the rising of the sun even unto the going down of the same my name is great among the Gentiles; and in every place incense is offered unto my name, and a pure offering: for my name is great among the Gentiles, saith Yahweh of hosts." The exact meaning of this passage is much disputed, even the tense of the verbs being in doubt. Did Malachi mean to imply that already in every place pagans were unwittingly offering sacrifices to the one true God? Or did he mean that at some future time all men would embrace Judaism openly and worship Yahweh? In either case, he clearly believed that the unity and universality of God implies one and the same worship for all men. We thus find Hebrews surpassing even the Persians in proclaiming the unity both of God and of mankind. This was their greatest triumph and their greatest contribution to humanity.

Note

Higher Criticism and a few Higher Critics

The traditional view regarding the authorship of the Old Testament was that Moses wrote the whole Pentateuch before 1400 B.C., that David and Solomon composed the Psalms and Proverbs about 1000 B.C., and that the prophetical books were given their present form by the men whose names they bear. Those who still defend these theories are just as much higher critics as their opponents are, for they, too, are trying to answer the fundamental problems of higher criticism. The wide divergencies in the conclusions of the traditional and the modern schools of higher criticism spring from their use of different critical standards and methods. The traditional views were criticized, even in antiquity, by such pagan opponents of Christianity as Porphyry, in the Middle Ages by such keen thinkers as Abelard. Modern higher criticism began in the seventeenth century when the English philosopher Hobbes pointed out (in his *Leviathan*, 1651) many difficulties in the old views and hazarded several hypotheses, since borne out in general by modern research. Though various eighteenth-century writers noted the composite character of the Pentateuch, and the lateness of passages traditionally regarded as early, it was not until the nineteenth century that scholars emancipated themselves from the traditional views.

The first of the great higher critics was Wilhelm De Wette (1780–1849), whose liberal political views cost him his professorship at Berlin (1819) and exiled him for the rest of his life to the Swiss university in Basel. He was the first to notice that the Mosaic law was unknown to the Hebrews in the days of the judges and kings, and to show that the Book of Deuteronomy cannot be older than the seventh century before Christ. In the long run, the writings of Wilhelm Vatke (1806–82) proved more stimulating and influential, though his ideas and his book, *Biblische Theologie* (1835), were ignored for a full generation. He centered the Hebrew religion around the prophets, not Moses, declaring that the Law came after them rather than before, and thus he laid the foundation for a true account of the development of Hebrew history. The neglect accorded to his writings may be explained in part by their forbidding style, in part by the stiff Hegelian philosophy with which they are permeated, and in part by the growing ascendency of Ewald.

Heinrich Ewald (1803–75) was a brilliant scholar whose *Geschichte des Volkes Israel* (5 vols., 1843–59) enjoyed a wide popularity in the middle decades of the nineteenth century. He was a most learned man, with great literary skill, and he was also a public figure who suffered martyrdom for his liberal ideals. As early as 1837 he had been dismissed from his professorship at Göttingen for publicly urging liberal political reforms; after the Revolution of 1848 he was recalled to Göttingen and played an important part in reforming and liberalizing the Hanoverian Church; in 1866 he was again dismissed because of his protests against the Prussian annexation of Hanover. This misfortune did not silence the courageous old professor, however, and in 1874 Bismarck felt called upon to honor his 71-year-old critic by having him thrown in jail for three weeks. Liberal ideals also dominated Ewald's history and help explain his attitude toward the new higher criticism. He envisioned Hebrew history as a march toward liberty in religion. At its beginning was the strict Mosaic Law, then the liberal and humanitarian preaching of the prophets, then the freedom of the Gospels, and finally, at the very end, came ruin (with the destruction of Jerusalem in 70 A.D.) for those who resisted this new freedom. Ewald was thus led to criticize those who placed the Law after the Prophets, and in later times he was accused of having retarded higher criticism in Germany by a full generation.

Julius Wellhausen (1844–1918) was for a time Ewald's favorite pupil, but being an admirer of Prussia, he broke with his master in 1866. Their differences were more fundamental than politics. Though Wellhausen was the son of the pastor of a small Hanoverian town, his orthodoxy easily slipped away, and he insisted that the Bible must be studied exactly as the historian studies the historical texts of any other period. The old theological unction, of which Ewald retained much, was intolerable to his young pupil. For a few years Wellhausen taught Biblical theology at Greifswald, but such teaching was uncongenial and he resigned in 1882. Thereafter he held professorships in Semitic languages at Halle, Marburg, and (after 1892) at his alma mater, Göttingen. After his break with Ewald, Wellhausen had taken up the views of Vatke and his successors, which he developed and clarified. His *Prolegomena zur Geschichte Israels* (1878) gave them classic expression, and for almost half a century they dominated Old Testament criticism. They came to be known as the Graf-Wellhausen theory. (Karl Graf had expressed similar views a few years earlier.) Wellhausen's book was a youthful work of genius, completing the studies of many men and leaving little more to be said on the subject until new information came to light. Wellhausen, like his predecessors, neither knew nor cared for the new studies of Assyriology, archeology, and comparative religion, which have since added so much to our knowledge of the Hebrews. He therefore found that he had nothing more to say after publishing his *Prolegomena*. The *Israelitische und jüdische Geschichte*, published in 1894, was merely an expansion of an encyclopedia article dating from 1880. Wellhausen had had his fill of the Old Testament before reaching the age of forty, and he spent the next several years studying Mohammedanism and the Arabs. He was fascinated by the rapid expansion of the Mohammedan Empire and the Bismarckian methods sometimes used by the caliphs—in which, perhaps, he saw a parallel to his own times. In his last years Wellhausen returned to Biblical studies, but he devoted himself to the New Testament. (See Eduard Schwartz, "Julius Wellhausen," in *Gesammelte Schriften*, I [1938], 326–61).

The most brilliant of all the higher critics of the Old Testament was the Scot, W. Robertson Smith (1846–94). The son of a minister of the Scottish Free Church, Smith was educated at Aberdeen, and for a while he hesitated between natural science and theology. For two years he taught physics at the University of Edinburgh while studying in the theological seminary there. In the summers, he traveled and studied in Germany, where he made the acquaintance of Wellhausen and other higher critics. He became Professor of Oriental Languages in the Free Church seminary at Aberdeen in 1870. Six years later Smith created a sensation by the article "Bible" which he contributed to the ninth edition of the *Encyclopædia Britannica*. This was followed by two series of lectures, published under the titles, *The Old Testament in the Jewish Church* (1881) and *The Prophets of Israel* (1882). These books vie with Wellhausen's *Prolegomena* as classic statements of the Graf-Wellhausen theory. Heretofore this higher criticism had been virtually unknown in Scotland and England. (A South African bishop named Colenso had been accused of heresy in 1862 because he wrote a scholarly book questioning the Mosaic authorship of the Pentateuch; he had been led to question traditional views by an intelligent Zulu whom he tried to convert to Christianity.) Smith was tried for heresy by the Free Church and, though acquitted, he was deprived of his professorship (1881). He then accepted the editorship of the *Encyclopædia Britannica*, the ninth edition of which was then only about half finished: the wide extent of his knowledge fitted him admirably for this task, and he made this the most brilliant edition of the famous encyclopedia that was ever published. A few years later Smith became Professor of Arabic at Cambridge, which position he held until his death. Like his friend Wellhausen, Smith found that at the age of thirty-five he had little more to say about Biblical criticism. Through another friend, J. F. McLennan, he had become interested in the family systems and religions of primitive peoples, and his writings on these subjects deeply influenced the anthropologists of the next generation: both J. G. Frazer and Émile Durkheim (see p. 24) have expressed their indebtedness to him. The first fruit of his new studies was a volume entitled *Kinship and Marriage in Early Arabia* (1885), and he approached the Hebrew religion from the new point of view in his *Religion of the Semites* (1889). This last and most brilliant of all his books, which was epochmaking in its field, was delivered as lectures at Aberdeen. Unfortunately, only the first series of lectures was published, for sickness and his untimely death prevented Smith from preparing the other two series for the press. Nevertheless, this one volume shows that Smith was no longer a mere Biblical critic. He had become a founder of the modern scientific study of religious phenomena. See J. S. Black, *The Life of William Robertson Smith* (1912), and a sketch in James Bryce, *Studies in Contemporary Biography* (1904).

Part Two: The Greek City-States

VIII   Homeric Greece

THE GREEK PEOPLE FIRST BEGAN TO PLAY AN IMPORTANT part in world affairs in the last century of the Assyrian Empire. It is true that a rather high civilization had existed in the Aegean area almost a thousand years earlier, yet it was not until the eighth and seventh centuries before Christ that characteristic traces began to appear of the Greece that later ages revered so highly. This new Greece owed much to the empires of the ancient Orient, yet it differed from them fundamentally. It was Western, they were Oriental, and even in the sixth century the two showed contrasts that were as marked as are those between East and West today. For many centuries thereafter Europe and the Near East continued to influence each other profoundly, and to fight each other for supremacy, but in the sixth century the pendulum began swinging to the West. The remainder of ancient history is largely the story of Europe, and for three hundred years it is largely the story of the ancient Greeks and of their land, which they called Hellas.

This ancient Hellas was a small country. Comprising the Greek Peninsula, the Aegean Islands, and the Aegean coasts of Asia Minor, it covered less than 50,000 square miles—approximately the area of England or New York State and less than that of Illinois. About four-fifths of this territory was continental Greece, which fell into three parts of quite unequal importance. Northern Greece, consisting of Macedonia, Thessaly, and Epirus, made up about half of the peninsula. In classic times Macedonia was regarded as hardly a part of Greece; Thessaly, extending from Mount Olympus south to the Malian Gulf and from the Aegean west to the Pindus Mountains, con-

tained the largest plain and the best agricultural land in Greece but
it contributed very little to the political and intellectual life of the
Greek people; and west of these two districts was the mountainous
Epirus, sparsely populated and of little consequence. Central Greece
included the territory between these northern lands and the Gulf of
Corinth. Though it was a mountainous region, it contained such important places as Thebes and Delphi, the famous pass at Thermopylae, and Mount Parnassus, and at its eastern extremity lay Attica
with its principal city, Athens. South of the Gulf of Corinth was the
Peloponnesus, connected with the rest of Greece only by the twenty-
mile-wide Isthmus of Corinth. Immediately south of the Isthmus was
Argolis, the center of the first high civilization of Greece, and in the
heart of the Peloponnesus were Sparta and Olympia—the former famous for her military power, the latter for the Olympic Games.

Geographical Influences in Greek History

Geography always influences history, and the history of Greece
has been determined to a high degree by three geographical factors:
her mountains, the poverty of her soil, and her easy access to the sea.
Many mountain ranges divide Greece into countless tiny valleys, few
of which are more than ten or twelve miles long and six or eight
miles broad. As communication between neighboring valleys was always difficult, their inhabitants remained strangers to each other,
mutually suspicious and jealous, and often engaged in feuds. The inhabitants of the islands suffered from a similar parochialism. Each
Greek locality was fiercely loyal to its own liberty, and "Greece" consisted of countless sovereign and hostile states. The inability of these
petty states to effect a solid political union was the great tragedy of
Greek history. Attempts were often made to overcome this separa-
tism, and temporary leagues were sometimes organized. All such efforts failed, however, and Greece never became one state until an
imperfect unity was arbitrarily imposed upon it from without by
Macedonians, Romans, or Turks.

Geography also made Greece poor. Mountains and rocky hills rendered at least a third of her land uncultivable, and much of the remainder required back-breaking labor before it could be farmed.

Pastures were ordinarily fit only for sheep and goats, not for cattle and horses. The valley bottoms contained good land, to be sure, but their fertility was not to be compared with that of the broad rich valleys of the Nile and the Tigris. Greek rivers were short and swift; during the rainy season they turned into raging torrents, washing away soil from the hill sides; and in the dry season they lay stagnant, breeding mosquitoes. Greece has always been cursed with erosion and malaria. Stone walls built along the hill sides sometimes checked erosion, but the Greeks never found ways to control the floods or to combat malaria. When she became a thickly populated country, Greece could not provide enough food for her people; her standards of living fell pitifully low; and a Spartan king once remarked, "Poverty is our companion from childhood."

The Greeks found their salvation in the sea. Most of them lived within sight of the sea, and except in the heart of the Peloponnesus there were few places where one could not catch a glimpse of water from the top of a near-by hill. The irregular coastline afforded many harbors, and the islands of the Aegean were always visible, beckoning men eastward. These islands led the mariner by easy stages to Asia Minor and the East, while the Gulf of Corinth provided a gate and passageway to the West. It was only natural, therefore, that Greeks unable to wrest a living from their scanty and rocky farms should take to the sea. They acquired a horizon broader than any known to earlier peoples. Agricultural communities like Thebes and Sparta remained conservative and parochial, but the commercial centers such as Athens developed the sharp wits and versatility of merchants and mariners. Their eastward exposure brought them to the great centers of oriental civilization. The Greeks learned what they could from those with whom they came in contact, and at the same time they carried their own ideas with them wherever they went. Thus seafaring Greek traders cross-fertilized the whole Mediterranean basin.

The Greek Miracle

From a material point of view the Greeks must be numbered among the minor poverty-stricken peoples of the world, but their cultural achievements soared far above their meager environment. They were the most important people of antiquity—the most significant, that is to say, for the future civilization of Europe and of mankind. They were quarrelsome and arrogant, failures in the art of government, undistinguished as engineers or mechanics; yet in the realms of the mind they surpassed all peoples before and since. They laid the foundations of European literature and art, science and philosophy, and in each of these fields except natural science they equaled or surpassed the best of their successors. They created and lived in an atmosphere of intellectual liberty and free discussion, and they first among men freed themselves from the shackles of superstition. Their splendid achievements constitute the "Greek miracle" which humanists have praised with gratitude and eloquence from that day to this. Higher civilization, as we understand it, began with the ancient Greeks.

Minoan Backgrounds

In classic times the Greeks traced their history back to the Trojan War, which they sometimes dated about 1192–1183 B.C. The poet Homer's account of the war was taken as sober history, and around it clustered many legends, notably stories of the Argonauts who sailed the Black Sea in quest of the Golden Fleece and others dealing with a great war against Thebes. The periods before and immediately after the "Homeric Age" were known only from myths which the Greeks regarded as of doubtful historical value. The fifth-century Greek historians Herodotus and Thucydides each wrote a few sentences about the Cretan empire of a certain Minos, who lived before the Trojan War, but real knowledge of this early period first came from the excavations made by Heinrich Schliemann[1] at Troy and in Greece during the 1870's and 1880's. Digging at the site of ancient Troy, Schliemann unearthed nine cities, each built upon the ruins of its predecessor. The first of them was built almost two thousand years before the Trojan War. Schliemann and his successors thus opened up a whole new world and gave a new pattern to early Greek history.

---

[1] See the note on Heinrich Schliemann, p. 277.

Had Herodotus and Thucydides known as much as we now know about the early history of their country, they might have shown it going through phases closely paralleling those of European history as described by the standard writers of the late nineteenth century. They would have known about the "ancient history" of their country, which centered in the Cretan and Mycenaean civilizations to which they were deeply indebted and which they would have called "Homeric." After this came the Dorian invasions of the late twelfth and eleventh centuries, bringing a decline of culture and "Dark Ages" which might have been called "medieval." This period ended about 750 B.C. with a Renaissance corresponding to that in Europe in the fifteenth and sixteenth centuries after Christ. Finally, shortly after 500, began the Classic Age, which to Herodotus and his contemporaries would have been "modern times."

First Civilizations in the Aegean Area

Though no traces of paleolithic man have yet been discovered in Greece or the Aegean Islands, evidence of neolithic civilization has appeared at several sites in Thessaly and Crete. The earliest settlers in Greece apparently came from Asia Minor by way of Thrace during the great westward migrations late in the fourth millennium. The early Cretans, on the other hand, were men of Mediterranean stock who probably reached Crete by way of Caria (southwestern Asia Minor) many centuries earlier. Though the Cretans underwent a slight infusion of Alpine blood in later times, they remained predominantly Mediterranean in race until the collapse of their civilization about 1400 B.C. These first settlers in Crete and Greece were primarily pastoral peoples, though not ignorant of agriculture, and their pottery figurines show that, like so many neolithic inhabitants of the Near East, they worshiped the Earth Mother.

Somewhat after 3000 a copper civilization appeared in this Aegean area. It was first brought to Thessaly, apparently by invaders from the north, and it slowly spread at least as far south as the Gulf of Corinth. At about the same time a copper culture appeared in Crete. As there is no evidence of an important migration of new peoples into the island, it seems likely that the Cretans developed their cop-

MINOAN AND
MYCENAEAN
GREEK

per culture with a minimum of aid from the outside. At this time,
too, the earliest civilizations appeared in the smaller islands of the
Aegean, most of which seem to have been previously uninhabited.
The settlers who brought this culture to the islands probably came
from Crete, and large numbers of them also settled in southern
Greece. A homogeneous people, largely of Mediterranean race and
copper culture, thus occupied Caria, Crete, the Aegean Islands, and
southern Greece in the third millennium.

Simultaneously Asia Minor was becoming the home of still another
copper-bronze civilization, traces of which were found especially in
the second city of Troy. The ruins discovered there by Schliemann
were those of a fortress or citadel covering about an acre, around
which lay a rather large city. It was about three miles inland from
the mouth of the Hellespont—far enough from the sea to be safe

from pirates and minor raiders, yet close enough to dominate the straits. It was a prosperous trading center, whence merchants traveled south as far as Egypt and north beyond the Danube. In fact, Schliemann found in its ruins a stone which apparently had been brought from mountains at the frontier of China. The importance of Troy's trade, and the wealth of the city, are shown by the lavish construction of the citadel and by what he called "Priam's treasure"— a large chest filled with gold objects of great value. This second Troy was founded about 2500 and was destroyed by fire five or six centuries later, perhaps by Hittite invaders. Then followed a period of decline during which three distinct villages, now known as Troy III, IV, and V, were built one on top of another: none of them could be called important, for during Hittite supremacy in Anatolia the center of affairs was far to the east.

The Bronze Age in Crete

At the opposite end of the Aegean from Troy was the Cretan home of a civilization first laid bare by the excavations begun by the English archeologist Sir Arthur Evans in 1900. Evans called this civilization "Minoan," after the legendary King Minos, who is said to have once ruled Crete. He showed that, starting from remote neolithic origins, this Cretan civilization evolved through three clearly marked periods of copper-bronze culture which he called Early Minoan, Middle Minoan, and Late Minoan respectively. Pottery styles and articles from Egypt found at various levels in Crete, as well as characteristic Cretan objects found in datable sites in Egypt and Egyptian inscriptions referring to "Keftiu" (Cretans), enabled Evans to synchronize these three periods in Cretan history with the Old Kingdom, the Middle Kingdom, and the Empire in Egypt.[2] The contem-

---

[2] Evans subdivided each of these three periods into three parts, called Early Minoan I, Early Minoan II, etc. Traces of Egyptian influence in Early Minoan Crete date from predynastic times (before 3100) in Egypt, and this Early Minoan period lasted until about 2100; the Middle Minoan continued from 2100 to about 1600; and the Late Minoan from 1600 to 1100, with Late Minoan I, 1600–1500, Late Minoan II, 1500–1400, and Late Minoan III, 1400–1100. The Early and Middle Helladic periods on the mainland of Greece were perhaps a century or so later than the corresponding periods in Crete, and Late Helladic III, 1400–1100, is ordinarily called "Mycenaean."

poraneous civilization of the Greek mainland is called Helladic, that of the islands, Cycladic.

Not much is known about the copper civilization of Early Minoan Crete, though the Cretans made good pottery, used gold and silver well, and built rather large brick houses. Toward the end of the third millennium, bronze began to appear, thus inaugurating the Middle Minoan period. Cretan civilization reached its zenith a few centuries later. Crete's leading city in those days was Cnossus, located a few miles inland on the north coast opposite Greece, at a site that had been occupied since Neolithic times. A large palace was built there early in the Middle Minoan period, and about 1800 it was rebuilt on a much grander scale. Early in the Late Minoan period its rulers extended their sway over all Crete. The Golden Age of Minoan civilization then prevailed until the city was destroyed by raiders from beyond the sea about 1400. The ensuing period of decline lasted until about 1100, when new raiders from the Greek mainland destroyed all that was left of Minoan civilization.

The palace at Cnossus covered about five acres and consisted of a number of houses, some of them several stories high, which were built around a central court (Plates 17 and 18). The magnitude of the palace—it covered about four times the area of the citadel at Troy II—and the wealth to which it bears witness are no more impressive than are the engineering and artistic skill shown in its construction and decoration. On one side of the court a broad stairway led up to the throne room and a chapel; on the opposite side were a large hall and the king's private apartments. Other rooms served as offices for the king's assistants, and storerooms were filled with huge jars of grain, olive oil, and wine. The walls of the great rooms were decorated with two-edged battle-axes and with superb frescoes depicting scenes from Cretan life. This sumptuous building has been the marvel of the archeologists who have studied it.

The palace at Cnossus needed no stronghold save one small tower, for the kings had nothing to fear from other Cretans. The whole is-

---

• Note for Plate 17.   These two pictures give views of the palace at Cnossus, first a staircase, second the throne room with frescos restored in part.

Stairway

Throne Room

Plate 17

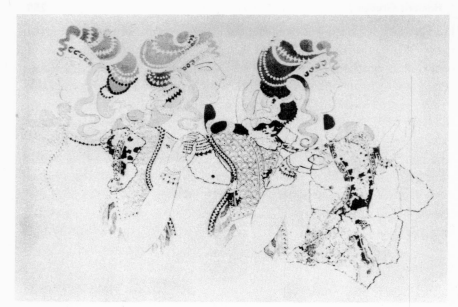

Ladies of the Court

Athletic Scenes

Plate 18

land was under their control, and their sole defense lay in a powerful navy. While the majority of the Cretans were peasants, there were other cities on the island, and at various places there were lesser palaces, dating from this same period, which presumably served as the residences of local lords who stood in some sort of feudal relation to the king at Cnossus. The wealth of the Cretans, and the importance of their commerce, are shown by great structures at many places. The road from Cnossus to Phaestus, forty miles away on the southern coast of the island, was paved with cobblestones and provided with bridges. At its northern terminus stood a caravanserai where the traveler might feed and water his animals, bathe, and then dine in a large hall beautifully decorated with frescoes of partridges. It has been estimated that Cnossus must have had a population of at least 100,000 persons.

Cretan Civilization

Archeologists often use superlative language when describing the beauties of life in ancient Crete. The excavations show that the Cretans, or at least the upper classes among them, had ample leisure for amusement and recreation. There were outdoor theaters probably used for religious or semi-religious processions and plays, and for various athletic events. The Cretans enjoyed boxing and gymnastic matches, as well as bullfights. Here the contestants did not try to kill the bull, as in Mediterranean lands today, but leaped or vaulted over him as he charged. Perhaps we should compare such events to rodeos rather than to bullfights (Plate 18). Not all amusements were so strenuous. The Cretans were devoted to music and the dance, and they played various wind and stringed instruments. The most impressive of all Cretan accomplishments, however, was their art, shown in murals and frescoes, pottery, jewelry, vases and cups of the precious metals, and in stone and clay figurines whose beauty, light-

---

• Note for Plate 18. The upper half of this plate, a fresco from Cnossus, shows ladies of the court; the lower half shows a cup (from Hagia Triada in Crete) decorated with scenes of boxing and bull-leaping.

ness, grace, and truth to nature have elicited the highest praise from modern critics.

Toward the end of the Early Minoan period, the Cretans invented a form of pictographic writing which they subsequently developed into a linear script written with ink on clay tablets. Though thousands of these tablets have been found, scholars have not yet deciphered the language. Most of the tablets seem to be inventories, or records of payments to the king; and as such, even undeciphered, they bear witness to the great bureaucracy that then governed Crete.

The religion of the Cretans was especially important for later times. Their principal deities were the Earth Mother and her son, whom the Greeks later called Rhea and Zeus. As elsewhere in the Near East, the Earth Mother was depicted in human form, accompanied by snakes, lions, or doves. Her son was often shown in pictures and carvings carrying a two-edged battle-axe, as did various Anatolian gods who eventually were identified with Zeus. Little is known about the other religious views of the Cretans. It seems likely, however, that they observed cults of the dead and of heroes; and we shall see that Greece preserved a strong substratum of Minoan beliefs about sin, punishment, purification, and immortality. It also seems probable that in Crete, as so often in the ancient Orient, the king served as high priest. The palaces and perhaps even private houses had altars and chapels, and the Cretans apparently saw symbols or habitations of their gods in trees and pillars. So far as we know, however, whole buildings were not set aside as temples.

The Greek historian Thucydides, writing about 400 B.C., remarked that "Minos was the first of whom tradition relates that he built a navy. He made himself master of a great part of what is now called the Hellenic [Aegean] Sea; he ruled the Cyclades; and he was the first to colonize most of them, driving away the Carians, and sending his own sons to rule them. He cleared pirates from the seas as much as possible in order that the revenues might more easily come to him." The historian's principal error here lies in attributing to one man—who was a legendary character at that—what was really the work of several centuries. The Cretans actually did command the seas, and modern writers often speak of the Cretan "thalassocracy" or command of the sea—from *thalassa,* a Greek word of Minoan origin meaning "sea." This thalassocracy was partly commercial and partly military and naval, with Cretans ruling over a kindred native population in the islands and on the mainland of Greece. Thucydides called these natives "Carians."

The Cretan commercial empire extended far beyond the Aegean area. Even in Early Minoan times Crete imported goods from Egypt; and countless articles from the Egypt of the Eighteenth Dynasty have been found at Cnossus. Cyprus and Syria were likewise visited by Cretan mariners, as were Italy and Sicily, and occasionally Cretan traders even reached Spain. The kings themselves probably participated financially in these far-flung commercial ventures; and, as Thucydides remarked, they maintained a navy to clear the seas of pirates and to fight off rivals.

The Minoan Legacy to Greece

The influence of Crete upon the Greeks of the Classic Age was profound, as the Greeks themselves were vaguely aware. Herodotus mentioned a few things they were supposed to have learned from the Cretans, and archeology and philology have enabled modern scholars greatly to augment this list of borrowings. The classic Greek language contained many words of Minoan origin, including place names which often end in *inthos* (Korinthos), in *ssos* (Halikarnassos, Knossos, Parnassos, in their Greek forms), or in *enai* (Mykenai, Athenai). Many words with these endings have come down to English through the Greek—labyrinth, hyacinth, and acanthus, or narcissus, cypress, and abyss. In Greek there are many more. Some are the names of plants and animals with which the Greek invaders from the north first became acquainted in their new homes; others show the deep cultural influence of the Minoans upon the Greeks. Among the latter may be mentioned the Greek words for various types of clothing, house decorations, gold work, and pottery (including the word from which our "ceramic" is derived), and the word for peace. Other Greek words of Minoan origin include those for sea, pilot, masthead, peddler, interpreter, road, bridge, and wagon. The list also includes several words for musical instruments and types of song, including "zither" and the words from which our "elegy" and "hymen" are derived; and there are a number of words connected with religion, including those for pure, prayer, and hymn. If we assume that, along with the word, the Greeks also adopted the thing or the idea from the Cretans, the wide extent of Minoan influence upon the Greeks is unmistakable.

There is an element of historical truth in what Greek mythology had to say about the Cretans. The legend that Zeus was born of Rhea in a cave on the Cretan Mount Ida may be regarded as symbolic of the Cretan origin of Greek civilization; and the legends about the fabulous King Minos contain in germ a sketch of Cretan history. It was said that Minos employed Daedalus—a famous craftsman, typical of Cretan skill in such matters—to build the "labyrinth" in which he kept a monster called the "minotaur." Seven Greek youths and seven maidens were sacrificed to this beast annually until the Greek hero Theseus slew it. As the Greek word *tauros* meant "bull," *minotaur* may be translated as "Minos's bull," and the legend may be associated with the frescoes showing bullfights. Moreover, the Carian (and presumably the Cretan) word for the two-edged battle-axe which decorated the palace at Cnossus was *labrys;* by the addition of the characteristic syllable *inthos,* this becomes *labyrinthos,* perhaps "the house of the battle-axes." It seems quite probable that the original labyrinth was the palace itself at Cnossus, whose size and complexity might suggest to primitive Greeks the idea of an unescapable maze. The legendary tribute of Greek youths and maidens may be connected with the practice, reported by Herodotus, of forcing men from Greece and the Cyclades to serve as rowers on Cretan ships.

The myths went on to tell how Daedalus and his son Icarus later escaped from Crete by making wings for themselves. When Icarus flew too high, and the sun melted the wax by which his wings were attached, he fell into the sea; but Daedalus safely reached Sicily and continued his marvelous works in his new home. Minos was murdered when he tried to bring Daedalus back, and his men founded the Sicilian town of Minoa. A second Cretan expedition went to Sicily to avenge the king's death, and during its absence Theseus returned to Crete and sacked Cnossus. At a still later date the Cretans were supposed to have aided the Greeks against Troy, which so enraged Minos—by this time among the gods—that he sent a famine which wiped out the entire population and made it necessary to repopulate the island with new invaders. These two disasters are perhaps confused recollections of the sack of Cnossus about 1400 and of the ultimate decline and fall of Minoan civilization about 1100, a century after the Trojan War. This decline actually was followed by invasions from Greece. Meantime, according to the myth, the gods had made Minos ruler of the lower world in recognition of his wisdom and justice. The mere persistence of such fables is an indication of the greatness of Minoan civilization and of its powerful influence upon the later development of Greece.

✓Achaeans and Dorians

While Greece and the islands were being exposed to the cultural influence of Crete, new invaders entered the peninsula from the north and eventually forced their rule upon it. We have already seen (page 38) that during the third millennium various Alpine and Nordic peoples occupied the valleys of the Danube and the Rhine from modern Hungary to Belgium. Here they gradually amalgamated with each other and with the earlier populations and built up a new culture, or rather, a series of new cultures. Large numbers of these peoples were broad-headed Alpines, though the Nordics dominated politically, and imposed their Indo-European languages upon the rest. Before long these central Europeans began expanding in many directions. Good bronze appeared at about this time, and one center of its manufacture was in Bohemia. The bronze weapons of the Europeans, as well as their horses, had much to do with their victorious advances. The Hittites, as we have seen, crossed from Europe to Asia Minor about 1900 and settled in the heart of that peninsula. At about that time, too, northern Italy was invaded from the Brenner Pass, the Celts began expanding from southern Germany into France and Belgium, and another group of central Europeans forced their way into Greece from Hungary through the Balkan Peninsula.

The newcomers into Greece were the Achaeans. Homer often

called his heroes *Achaioi,* and there is evidence from Hittite and Egyptian sources that the name was in common use long before his day. These Achaeans were the first to bring Nordic blood into Greece, and they spoke an Indo-European language which became the ancestor of classical and modern Greek. Not all the Achaeans belonged to one group, nor did they all come at one time. The first comers advanced slowly toward the south, with others following in their wake; and though they forced their way with violence and fighting, their coming proved to be less an invasion than an infiltration, one small group after another occupying valleys here and there. Two or three centuries may have passed before any considerable number of Achaeans reached the Peloponnesus.

There was little communication between these local groups. Men of each group intermarried with their predecessors, whose local culture they absorbed. Minor differences among the Achaeans were thus accentuated until three major groups could be distinguished by their different cultures and dialects. Those living in Thessaly and central Greece spoke Aeolic; those living in Boeotia and Attica, or on the neighboring island of Euboea, and perhaps some of those along the Gulf of Corinth, spoke Ionic; and the inhabitants of the Peloponnesus spoke Arcadian. All three dialects were well established in Greece toward the middle of the second millennium.

Mycenae

The principal Achaean center in Greece was at Mycenae in Argolis, a city standing about ten miles from the sea on a hill that dominated the whole Argive plain. The site had probably been occupied from neolithic times (it contains pottery fragments dating from the third millennium), but the earliest indications of an important city are six "shaft graves" which were cut vertically into the rock about 1600 B.C. These graves had not been disturbed until Schliemann opened them in 1876. Nineteen skeletons were found in the graves, all richly appareled, with gold masks over their faces; and the treasures buried with them included the largest amount of gold ever found by an archeologist.

About 1400 Mycenae was rebuilt on a magnificent scale, with

elaborate fortifications and a large palace which indicate that it had become a wealthy capital. Not far away, nearer the sea, lay the city of Tiryns, whose archeological history ran parallel to that of Mycenae. Perhaps Tiryns had once been the more important of the two cities, but in the great days it clearly was second to Mycenae. The Mycenaean culture of this period has been found at many other sites in Greece, even as far north as Thessaly and Epirus.

Achaean Raids and the Trojan War

The Achaeans began pushing overseas at about the time Mycenae was rebuilt. They were usually raiders rather than colonizers; they sought booty, not new homes; and they were drawn especially toward the rich cities of the Near East. Nevertheless, they traded to a certain extent, and sometimes they settled in the countries they raided. Cnossus was the first to suffer, for it was destroyed by Achaeans about 1400. The raiders also occupied several islands in the southern Aegean and sailed along the southern shores of Asia Minor until at last they reached Cyprus. Here some of them found new homes, and thereafter a part of the Cypriot population spoke the Arcadian dialect of Greek. Other Achaeans had already settled in Pamphylia, on the mainland northwest of Cyprus. Here too the Arcadian dialect was spoken in historic times.

A recently discovered Hittite text, dating from about 1335, speaks of "Ahhiyava" and its king "Antaravas." This Ahhiyava was undoubtedly Achaea, which in pre-Homeric Greek was called "Achaeva." Another tablet of about the same age speaks of a brother of the king of Ahhiyava as living in southern Asia Minor. Other Hittite tablets from the next century mention attacks upon Caria and Cyprus by men from Ahhiyava. The Achaeans also wandered still farther afield in their search for loot, as is shown by their attacks upon Syria and Egypt. A good many lived at Ras Shamra after 1350. Egyptian records complain of raids by various "peoples of the sea," though at first these raids were of no great consequence. At the end of the thirteenth century, after the death of Rameses II, Egypt fell into decline and the raids became more disastrous. Greek names appear in the lists of raiders. Thus one inscription tells how Merneptah about 1228 drove off various raiders, among them the "Aqaiwasha," who are generally identified as Achaeans. A generation later, in 1190, Rameses III defeated more raiders from the sea, among them the "Danauna," which may be the Egyptian spelling of "Danaoi" (Danaans), a name for the Achaeans often used by Homer. These Danauna had already been mentioned two centuries earlier in the Amarna letters.

Among the last of the great Achaean raids was the one immortalized as the "Trojan War." After the destruction of Troy II about 1900 B.C., the site was occupied by a succession of villages until at last the great Troy VI was founded, perhaps as early as 1600 and certainly before the middle of the millennium. Pottery and other finds indicate its close connections with the early Achaeans, with Crete, and with Mycenae in the days of her greatness. Nevertheless, Troy was fundamentally different. It was Asiatic, influenced even by the remote civilizations of Mesopotamia. Scholars formerly believed that Troy VI was the city captured by the Greeks about 1200. More recent excavations have shown, however, that this city was destroyed, probably by earthquake, about 1300, and rebuilt almost at once, partly from the debris. The new city (now called Troy VIIa) was presently sacked and burned. Its ruins contain little of intrinsic value, showing that it had been looted; but its pottery, of types common at Mycenae in her great days, indicates that Troy VIIa was destroyed about 1200. At first the sack of Troy did not have the unique character with which Homer eventually endowed it. The Greeks were attracted to Troy by its wealth, just as they were also attracted by the wealth of contemporary Egypt, and the famous raid on Troy was only one among many similar expeditions.

The Dorians and the Iron Age

The last two centuries of the second millennium witnessed new migrations of Europeans comparable to those which marked its opening. Just as the earlier dislocations followed the invention of bronze, so the later ones accompanied the beginning of the Iron Age in Europe. About the year 1200, new European tribes appeared in Thrace, and the Phrygians crossed to Asia Minor where they overthrew the declining Hittite Empire. At about the same time an iron culture—called "Villanovan" from a site near Bologna—appeared in Italy, and was carried throughout the peninsula by invaders from the north who spoke languages akin to Latin. Somewhat later the Celts developed an iron culture called "Hallstatt" from a site of that name in Austria. The forces causing these migrations also led to the Dorian invasion of Greece.

The Dorians were of the same general stock as the Achaeans, and probably entered the Balkan Peninsula at about the same time. For several centuries they lived in northwestern Greece, whence they were driven southward in the twelfth century by Illyrians and others from the northern Balkans or perhaps even from the Danubian plain. At an uncertain date, probably about 1100, they invaded northern Thessaly, pushing many of the Aeolians south into Boeotia and even into Attica, while they drove others across the sea to the islands as far as Lesbos off the coast of Asia Minor. Several centuries later these Aeolians occupied parts of that mainland, which became known as Aeolis. Simultaneously, a second group of Dorians crossed the Gulf of Corinth almost at its western end and occupied much of the Peloponnesus. After destroying Mycenae and other important cities, they subjugated all the old Achaean populations except those inhabiting the mountainous interior of Arcadia and a few who fled to Attica or to faraway Cyprus. While they did not actually invade Attica, the Dorians drove Ionians from Boeotia and elsewhere into that peninsula. Many of the older inhabitants of Attica, as well as many refugees, were then forced to seek new homes on the islands and along the middle shores of Asia Minor, a district which was thereafter called Ionia. Meantime, still other Dorians had crossed to Crete, where large numbers of them settled, imposing their rule and their dialect upon the native population. Dorians also occupied many islands in the southern Aegean, including Rhodes, and established themselves in Caria.

These folk migrations lasted until the end of the second millennium, after which the distribution of the Greek peoples, as shown by their dialects, was approximately what it remained throughout classic times. Aeolic was spoken in parts of Thessaly and on the northern Aegean Islands: somewhat later it was spoken in Aeolis as well. Ionic was spoken in Attica and Euboea, on the central islands, and in Ionia. Arcadian was spoken only in the central Peloponnesus, Pamphylia, and Cyprus. The rest of the Greek world spoke Doric dialects. The Dorians held Epirus and northwestern Greece, much of Thessaly and central Greece, the broad outer fringes of the Peloponnesus, the Isthmus of Corinth, Crete, the southern Aegean Islands, Rhodes, and parts of Caria as far as Pamphylia. These Dorians, never having felt the influence of Minoan culture, were far more barbarous than the Achaeans whom they supplanted. They destroyed Mycenaean civilization, and their invasion was followed by a darker period than any known in Greece since neolithic times.

Mycenaean Civilization

The Achaeans entered Greece as conquerors, owing their success to their superior bronze weapons and in part, perhaps, to their Nordic bellicosity. Nevertheless they did not exterminate the earlier inhabitants of the peninsula. They set themselves up as a small aristocracy to rule over the natives. Many, or perhaps most, of the older inhabitants were reduced to the status of laborers and peasants, but the Achaean overlords valued traders and craftsmen for their skills, and allowed them to continue in their professions. These men then brought Minoan civilization to Greece. At about the time of the early shaft graves at Mycenae, vines and olive trees were introduced into Greece from Crete; remarkable engineering skill (no doubt Cretan) was later shown in draining a large lake near Orchomenus; Mycenaean tombs and palaces were decorated by Cretan artists; pottery was made in imitation of Cretan styles. The conquerors were presently so dazzled by this strange new Minoan culture that they absorbed much of it themselves and their civilization became a blend of Achaean and Minoan elements.

Mycenae shows how widely the Northerners differed from the Mediterraneans, and how greatly life in Greece differed from that in

---

• Note for Plate 19.   The large lions shown in the picture on the opposite page stood over a gate in the walls at Mycenae.

Plate 19.   Lion Gate at Mycenae

Plate 20.   Frescos from Tiryns

Crete. The Cretans had been a peaceable people: they had weapons and armor, to be sure, as well as a navy; but their whole island was at peace and Cnossus could be left virtually undefended. The Mycenaean cities, on the other hand, were veritable citadels, built on hills and surrounded by high walls that rendered them almost impregnable. Within the walls were the royal palace, temples, and storehouses, as well as ample space in which the people of the countryside might take refuge in case of attack. Conditions on the Greek mainland evidently were far from peaceful.

The Achaeans retained certain fundamental types of architecture brought from the north. The Minoan palace at Cnossus consisted of a number of flat-roofed houses built at different times around a central court in true Mediterranean style. The principal buildings at Mycenae and Tiryns, on the other hand, were *megara* of the northern type. The *megaron* was an oblong building with a hearth in the center of the floor and with a gabled roof pierced by a hole to let out the smoke. In front was a porch with a roof supported by pillars, and before the porch was a court which in early times was probably surrounded by a fence. The *megaron* certainly originated in a country of snow and ice, with a climate much colder than that prevailing in Crete or even in Greece. The earliest *megara* resembled the log cabins of the American frontier, but after centuries of experimentation this type of architecture reached its finest expression in Greek temples such as the Parthenon.

These Achaean buildings also show northern influences in their decorations, even though they were decorated by Cretan artists. Many Mycenaean frescoes depict bullfights and traditional Cretan scenes, but some emphasize hunting and other northern sports (Plate 20). An Achaean patron apparently had told the Cretan artist what to paint. The massive gold in Mycenaean graves likewise betrays barbarian conceptions of splendor, and the Achaeans had a taste for building on a huge scale unknown in Crete. Thus a famous

---

• Note for Plate 20. These two frescos from Tiryns were undoubtedly the work of Cretan artists, but the subjects (spearmen and hunting the wild boar) were quite Achaean. (*Photos, National Museum, Athens.*)

tomb at Mycenae—the one which Schliemann imaginatively called the "treasury of Atreus"—has the largest dome built in pre-Christian times. In general, the Achaeans seized upon those aspects of the older civilization that were either gaudy or immediately practicable, but they never attained to Cretan levels of civilization.

Trade and Writing

While Achaean chieftains were indulging their tastes for war and glory, some of their subjects followed the humbler paths of trade. These Mycenaean traders, most of whom probably sprang from the older elements in the population, took over the trade routes of their Cretan kinsmen soon after Achaean raiders had destroyed Cnossus. Egyptian records rarely mention the Keftiu (Cretans) after 1400, yet Mycenaean pottery appears in the ruins of Akhetaton, the short-lived capital where Akhnaton ruled in the 1360's: Mycenaeans obviously supplanted Cretans in the Egyptian market almost at once. Mycenaean pottery has been found elsewhere in Egypt, and hundreds of Egyptian objects have been found in Greece, proving that trade relations continued for almost two hundred years. Discoveries in Palestine, Syria, and Cilicia tell the same story, and the Greek-speaking settlers in Cyprus and at Ras Shamra presumably were traders. The Mycenaeans also maintained trade connections with Troy in the fourteenth and thirteenth centuries. Pylos, on the western coast of the Peloponnesus, became an important city which owed much of its prosperity to trade with the West, and especially to the amber trade with central Europeans at the head of the Adriatic. There are also traces of Mycenaean pottery in southern Italy and Sicily, showing that even this corner of Crete's commercial empire did not escape the attention of her Mycenaean successors.

Recent discoveries have proved that writing was known in Mycenaean times and that Greek was then written in characters based on Cretan models. A few years ago (in 1939), American archeologists working at Pylos discovered a cache of several hundred clay tablets dating from about 1200 and marked with writing of the type known as Cretan Linear B. A few similar tablets have been found at Mycenae, and there are large numbers of them at Cnossus, all dating from the period 1400-1100. At first scholars suspected that this Linear B script, like the Cretan hieroglyphics and Linear A, was used to write some unknown Minoan language, but when the writing was deciphered (by M. Ventris in 1953) it was found that the language was an early form of Greek. The Achaean invaders, after conquering Crete about 1400, adopted the Cretan Linear A script but modified it extensively in fitting it to their Greek language. They then continued to use this Linear B script, both in Crete and in Greece, throughout the period of their supremacy.

The tablets now available are business records, inventories, and the like, but as yet no literary or religious texts have been found. They show us that Greek could then be written, but their relative scarcity makes it clear that such writing was rarely used. The Achaeans managed to do without much writing, even though the art was known to them—a fact highly significant in their cultural history. Moreover, even this meager knowledge of writing was lost during the Dark Ages inaugurated by the Dorian invasions. Centuries later, when the Greeks again felt the need of writing, they took over Phoenician characters and adapted them to form the classic Greek alphabet.

Social Organization

It is not easy to describe the social and political organization of the Achaeans and early Dorians. Mycenaean ruins give us a few hints, Homer gives others, and survivals into historic times enable us to conjecture further details about these early institutions. As similar organizations are found among the early Italians and other peoples distantly related to the Achaeans, they undoubtedly were of very ancient origin, dating back to the period before the great migrations. But the migrations gave them new forms and they developed rapidly after the Achaean conquest of Greece.

When the Achaeans and Dorians first invaded Greece, they were organized in strong patriarchal families, called *gene* (singular *genos*), which in turn were united in larger groups called "brotherhoods" (*phratrai*), and these in "tribes" (*phylai*). Each man belonged to a certain tribe and phratry by birth, but members of different tribes and phratries lived side by side in every community. In historic times there were three tribes in each Dorian community, and four among the Ionians, with the tribe in each case subdivided into three phratries. This organization was retained throughout Greek history. Members of each tribe and phratry believed that they were of common descent and even knew the common ancestor from whom the tribe or phratry took its name. This ancestor was of course mythical and the common descent doubtful, but for many centuries the members of these groups continued to eat sacred meals and to perform other religious acts together.

The *genos,* or family, was by far the most important of the three social groups. As the Achaean invaders gradually took over one Greek valley after another, the heads of various *gene* established themselves as local leaders. The leader's power rested ultimately upon his warriors, and as he and his descendants were virtually independent of all other rulers, the government of Greece fell to countless local chieftains. For larger enterprises, such as the Trojan War, several leaders might combine their forces, though each retained authority over his own men; and sometimes the more powerful warriors reduced their neighbors to a state of vassalage. Such conditions are pictured in Homer. The most important leader was called an *anax,* or "king." He was the commander in war, doing much of the fighting himself, but he had to lay important plans before the assembled army for approval, and he was surrounded by important chieftains who might be called his vassals. Though kingship was theoretically hereditary, Homer shows that it always was in danger of violent overthrow. The position of the kings rested upon military force, but it was strengthened by the supposed kinship of the kings with the gods, whose favor they might bring to their followers.

Several passages in Homer imply that Agamemnon was the supreme ruler of all Greece. This view is supported by one of the Hittite tablets mentioned above: a leader of the Achaeans in Asia Minor is spoken of as the brother (blood brother) of the king of Ahhiyava, who in turn is called "brother" by the Hittite king. This honorary title of "brother," which is also used for the kings of Egypt and Assyria, seems to have been reserved for important personages, and its use would imply that the king of Ahhiyava—presumably the king at Mycenae—enjoyed the prestige due only to the rulers of rather extensive domains. Nevertheless, we must not read too much into these diplomatic courtesies. The fortifications of Mycenaean towns prove that no one man could make good his authority and insure peace throughout Greece; and it is hard to see how a king at Mycenae could have ruled the whole peninsula effectively without at least as extensive a use of writing as was necessary in Crete for administering a much smaller and more compact state. While other Greek leaders may have shown deference before the king at Mycenae, even Homer indicates that there were several kingdoms in Greece whose rulers acted quite independently. At any rate, a principal consequence of the Dorian invasions was the destruction of whatever centralized power had been built up in Greece and a return to the rule of petty chieftains.

Mycenaean Mythology and Religion

The Greeks of classic times told countless tales of the great men who supposedly lived in the times before and during the Trojan War. These stories were passed down from generation to generation and, as might be expected, they took on new forms with successive tellings. There can be little doubt, however, that in their larger outlines they date from Mycenaean times. The various cities about which the legends clustered were important places in those days, and the importance of the legends seems to correspond with the Mycenaean importance of their settings. Thus the Oedipus stories centered about Thebes, the Theseus stories in Attica. More important even than these were the stories of Atreus and his family which centered in Mycenae. As the early Theseus stories reflected the relative unimportance of Athens in Mycenaean times, and failed to do justice to the subsequent greatness of that city, they were much expanded in later days. The stories centering about Mycenae, on the other hand, retained their primacy in spite of the political insignificance of this locality after the Dorian invasions. The Achaeans presumably brought stories and legends with them when they entered Greece, but these old stories, torn from their geographical settings, were

forgotten or thoroughly recast in Mycenaean times. The heroic age
of Greece was that of Mycenae, and the famous legends preserved
by later poets and mythographers reflect the life of that period as
accurately as the life of any time is reflected by its hero-tales.

The Achaeans brought with them a religion, traces of which may
be found in the religion of classic Greece, but Minoan religion remained equally powerful throughout Greek history. Among the
features of the classic religion that were clearly of Achaean, or northern, origin may be mentioned the sacred fire on the hearth, consecrated to Hestia (Latin, Vesta), which remained the center of family
worship and played an important part in public ceremonies. Such
sacred fires were to be found not only at Rome, consecrated to Vesta,
but also among the Nordic invaders of India, who worshiped a god
called Agni in Sanskrit (= Latin *ignis*, "fire"); and we have seen that
similar early practices may explain the fire-worship of the Persian
Magi. A Minoan origin may with equal certainty be ascribed to the
ceremonies which went back to the old cult of the grain goddess
Demeter, whose mother was the Cretan Earth Mother, Rhea. The
myth, which taught that life is immortal in spite of death and burial,
was acted out and explained to worshipers during ceremonies at
Eleusis, near Athens. This place had been a religious center long
before the coming of the Achaeans, and the ceremonies were of
Minoan or Carian origin. But usually the religious rites and beliefs
of the classic Greeks were of more complex origin and contained elements drawn from many different sources. Religious syncretism, or
the mingling of various religions, was far advanced even in Mycenaean times.

Purification and Sacrifice

The Minoans and Mycenaeans, like all primitive peoples, considered some things so sacred that they might be approached only
by persons who were ceremonially pure, and they had rites in which
only the pure might participate. Purity might be lost in many ways:
sometimes by acts which we would consider sins, such as murder
and sexual offenses, and again by acts to which we would attach no
moral significance, such as approaching a dead body or the victims of
certain diseases (*e.g.*, epilepsy, the "sacred illness") or eating certain

kinds of food. These acts brought defilement or, as the Greeks said, a *miasma* which had to be washed away. Rites of purification varied from simple washing—with fresh or preferably with salt water, in some cases with blood—to cleansing with fire and sulphur, fasting, sacrifices, and other elaborate penances. Even in classic times such purifications were a prelude to, or an important part of, the greater religious festivals. Thus during the Thargelia, held at Athens every year in May or June, the whole city was officially purified by ceremonially loading all its *miasmata* upon one man and driving him from the city. It has been conjectured that in earlier times this scapegoat was put to death as a human sacrifice, and that his sufferings were supposed to purify those who sacrificed him. We shall presently see that this matter of purity was as important in law and politics as it was in religion.

Homer had little to say of sin, defilement, and purification—he wrote as a minstrel to entertain people at joyful festivals where discussion of such somber matters would have been quite out of place—but he often spoke of sacrifices. Gifts were made to the gods on great occasions and small, in times of happiness and in time of anxiety. Sometimes the gift was a few drops of wine poured on the ground; sometimes it was a goat or kid, or even an ox; and on great occasions it might be a "hecatomb" (theoretically a hundred oxen but actually any large number). Mythology and later ritual practice lead us to suspect that in times of great calamity human sacrifice was not unknown: thus legend tells how Agamemnon sacrificed his daughter Iphigenia when the winds failed to carry the Greek fleet to Troy. Ordinarily, however, the sacrifice was a happy occasion, for it was followed by a banquet, shared by gods and men, at which the banqueters ate the food that had been sacrificed. As men believed that the gods enjoyed the sacrifices, they confidently anticipated that their gifts would be repaid. Often they uttered prayers during the ceremony to indicate what favors they expected in return.

Heroes and the Olympian Gods

From ancient times the Greeks had paid homage to famous heroes, such as Heracles, about whom they told countless stories and whom they honored with shrines. But what was the origin of these heroes?

Were they real men of earlier times whose exploits had been augmented by legend? or were they imaginary characters invented as the ancestors of families or the founders of cities from whom they took their names ("eponymous heroes" is the technical term for such persons)? or were they gods who had fallen from their high estate to become mere supermen—"faded gods," as scholars say? Whatever their origin, the heroes usually go back to Mycenaean times. Still more popular were the ancient cults of minor spirits, the *daimones* of field and forest, satyrs and sileni, nymphs and dryads, whose shrines and altars dotted the landscape and who were affectionately worshiped by farmers and shepherds throughout antiquity. In the end, they contributed much more to Christianity than the concept of the devil who, with his horns and his cloven hooves, was merely a modernized Pan.

Such lowly cults as these, going back to Mycenaean times, were more important in the living religion of classic Greece than was the worship of the mighty Olympian gods. The Olympians owe their fame to Homer, who pictured them as little more than glorified and immortal human beings, living together on Mount Olympus under the rule of Zeus, eating and drinking ambrosia and nectar, quarreling, intriguing, having love affairs with each other and with mortals, fighting and suffering, delighting in the sacrifices offered them by men, and constantly intervening in mundane affairs to help their favorites among mankind. Zeus was an old Nordic sky-god, who had absorbed many qualities and legends from the various Minoan deities with whom he was identified. Athena and Aphrodite were merely new manifestations of the old Earth Mother. Other gods had similar origins. It seems, however, that nearly all were well established in Mycenaean times, several centuries before Homer.

These great Greek gods, like those of all peoples, rather accurately reflected the characters and social organization of their worshipers, and it is possible to say that their hierarchy under Zeus was a heavenly replica of the loose feudalism that prevailed in Mycenaean Greece. This feudalism did not reappear on earth after the Dorian invasions, but it continued in heaven. However, the Greek gods, like Greek society in general, developed greatly during the troubled times that followed the invasions, and it is not safe to deduce very much about Mycenaean times from the Homeric heroes and their gods.

Homer

The Mycenaean Age cannot be studied apart from the Homeric *Iliad* and *Odyssey*. The former poem deals with the Trojan War, the latter with the wanderings of the Greek leader Odysseus on his way home. The *Iliad* does not give a complete history of the war but merely tells a few episodes in its ninth year. Agamemnon and Achilles quarrel over a girl who is part of the booty captured in a minor raid; Agamemnon seizes her by force, and Achilles, sulking in his tent, refuses to take further part in the fighting; the Trojans are therefore victorious for a while and their hero, Hector, kills Patroclus, who is Achilles' dearest friend; Achilles is thus roused to return to the battle, where he kills Hector; he gives magnificent funeral games for Patroclus and allows Priam, the aged king of Troy, to buy back the body of his son Hector, with whose funeral the poem closes. There are brief references to events earlier in the war, and everybody seems to know that Troy is doomed, but the poem centers around the wrath of Achilles and its dire consequences.

The main plot of the *Odyssey* deals with the events of a few days in the tenth year after the fall of Troy. The story opens on the island of Ithaca, home of Odysseus, where his wife Penelope has awaited his return for twenty years, refusing to make a choice among the many suitors who meantime are devouring his substance. The goddess Athena instigates Telemachus—the likable but weak-willed son of the great Odysseus, who has inherited his father's glory but is is being kicked around by the suitors and never amounts to much in his own right—to go to Sparta to seek news of his father. The scene then shifts to an island in the Mediterranean where Odysseus had been living for eight years as the prisoner and lover of a sea nymph named Calypso. On orders from Zeus, she allows Odysseus to build a raft and sail for home. After being shipwrecked off the coast of Phaeacia (a never-never land of pure romance), Odysseus tells the king of the Phaeacians about his adventures since the fall of Troy.

His narration includes such famous stories as those of the Trojan Horse, the Lotus Eaters, the Cyclops, Circe, Scylla and Charybdis, and even a descent into the Nether World where he met old friends and learned the future. The Phaeacians then convey Odysseus to Ithaca, where he kills the suitors and resumes his kingship.

The ancients had other epic poems dealing with aspects of the Trojan War, and with other heroic adventures in Mycenaean times. We know them today only by title or by brief excerpts or summaries of their contents. These lesser epics were contemporaneous with the Homeric poems, and treated of somewhat similar subjects, but no serious student ever thought of them as "Homeric," either in authorship or in quality. There are also thirty-three *Hymns,* in Homeric language, addressed to Demeter, Apollo, Hermes, Aphrodite, and other gods, which tell us something of mythology; and there is a parody of the *Iliad,* about three hundred lines in length, known as the *Batrachomyomachia,* or "The Battle of the Frogs and Mice." All these poems are of much later date than the two great Homeric poems.

The Homeric Question

The ancients believed quite firmly in the historic existence of a poet named Homer, who was the author of the *Iliad;* most of them believed that he also composed the *Odyssey;* but regarding his life and time they admittedly knew nothing. Legend usually reported Homer as having lived in one of the Ionian cities of Asia Minor. It was often said that he was blind. Herodotus thought that Homer lived "not before" 850, others placed him a century or two earlier, and no one suggested that he was contemporary with the events he described.

Modern scholarship attributes a much more complicated origin to the Homeric poems.[3] Even in Mycenaean times there apparently were professional bards who, on formal occasions, entertained the nobility, and perhaps the general public as well, by singing or reciting ballads about great heroes. These bards probably resembled those who composed the great German and Scandinavian epics of

---

[3] See note on F. A. Wolf and the Homeric Question, p. 279.

the European Middle Ages. They had learned much from their Minoan predecessors, both as to plots and as to epic techniques, and by borrowing freely from each other, poets slowly built up a mass of legend which was thereafter considered the matter appropriate for epic compositions. The poems were stored in the memory and passed from generation to generation without being written down. Though the old explanation that no one then knew how to write is no longer technically valid, markings on clay tablets could hardly record whole ballads, much less such elaborate works as the *Iliad* and *Odyssey*, which together fill almost a thousand printed pages. It was not impossible, on the other hand, for a bard to remember this much and even more.

During and after the Dorian invasions, many bards accompanied the refugees to Ionia and Aeolis, carrying in their heads their memorized poetic capital. But whereas the epic legend had formerly been a living body, constantly growing by the addition of poetic accounts of contemporary events, it now became a closed corpus dealing with the long-lost days of Achaean glory. The legends tended to cluster about the Trojan War, partly because this was the last, and therefore the most popular, of the great Achaean raids that preceded the coming of the Dorians, and in part perhaps because Aeolian and Ionian invaders liked to hear about the victories of Greeks over Asiatics.

Then arose a great poet whom we may call Homer. Thoroughly familiar with epic traditions and technique, he took what he wished from his predecessors, added his own poetic genius, and produced one of the world's great poems, the *Iliad*. This happened about the year 900 or shortly thereafter. The *Odyssey* was produced in much the same manner, by a second poet who lived a century or so later. As the poems presumably were not written down before 700, they doubtless underwent minor amplifications, and whole episodes may have been added—the "catalogue of ships" in the second book of the *Iliad* and the story of Odysseus's descent into Hades in the eleventh book of the *Odyssey* being two examples of such interpolation in the opinion of virtually all scholars. The Athenian tyrant Peisistratus (561–527) ordered an edition made of the two poems, and except for slight verbal changes such as all literary works underwent before the invention of printing, this edition was preserved in most subsequent copies of the Homeric poems.

Homer and History

Ever since the Dorian invasions and the Ionian migrations, the "Homeric" bards had realized that they were dealing with remote times when things had been very different—and very much better. They therefore tried to preserve the old spirit, and avoided mentioning things unknown in Mycenaean times. In this they were not always successful. They knew that the Achaeans wore bronze armor, and carefully preserved this tradition, but the Homeric poems made rather frequent references to iron, which was unknown in Troy VI and VIIa and of which only slight traces have been found in Mycenaean Greece. Likewise, Homeric geography is Mycenaean geography. Mycenaean remains have been found in all the famous places mentioned by Homer, and the rather surprising gaps in his geography mark places which seem to have been unknown to the Achaeans. Thus the Trojans are supposed to have found allies in the Troad (northwestern Asia Minor) and along the southern coast of the peninsula from Caria to Cilicia, which were regions often visited by Achaean raiders; but no allies came from the intervening Ionia, of which the Achaeans apparently knew little. One might think that the Ionian bards would have dragged in references to their own country, and their failure to do so indicates that they wished to keep the legends as they had received them.

The bards consistently pictured Troy as more oriental than Mycenae. Priam's harem of fifty wives is quite un-Greek, and the Homeric picture of Paris—who had caused the war but showed no zeal for fighting it—is an early example of the Greek view of oriental luxury and degeneracy. In most matters, however, the Trojans were good Greeks. Greeks and Trojans had no trouble talking to each other when they wished. Even the Trojan heroes have Greek names —all except Priam, whose Asiatic name, written "Perramos" in Aeolic, is the same as that of Pyramus, the hero of an Asiatic love story found in Greek mythology and preserved by Ovid and Shakespeare; it is probably the same name as that of Piram, a minor

Philistine king mentioned in the Bible. The dialect used by Homer is a mixture of Ionic and Aeolic, though even in Homer's day it apparently was a special language reserved for epic poetry. Philologists deny that it ever was spoken by anybody in everyday life.

The world pictured by Homer contained many historical elements but it really was a romantic and idealized world that never existed at all. Some parts of his picture date from the time of the Trojan War, others are older; many come from a period two or three centuries later, and many others are pure fancy. It is quite impossible now for literary criticism to separate the various strata, for they have been worked over countless times and fused into one coherent whole. If we equate "Homeric times" with the Mycenaean Age, we must admit the force of the remark of an American archeologist that "to put the matter epigrammatically, Homer knows very little about Homeric times."

Homer himself did not pretend to be a historian, and his importance is due, not to his skill at recording history, but to his power in making it. It is impossible to imagine Greece being what it was without Homer, for Homer created many essential aspects of Greece. He showed the Greeks the past from which they sprang. He provided them with the heroes whom they sought to emulate. His attitude toward the great problems of heaven and earth, of life and death, lay at the roots of their intellectual life. Even though Greeks occasionally criticized their poet, he always remained the prime factor in determining their attitude toward religion, art, literature, and everything else in which they excelled. We may accept Plato's statement that Homer was "the schoolmaster of the Greeks," and we may add that never in all history has a whole people enjoyed a comparable teacher.

Notes

Heinrich Schliemann

Heinrich Schliemann (1822–1890) is the most famous of archeologists. A son of the pastor of a small north German town, he received only a mediocre scholastic education and spent several years as a grocer's clerk. At the age of nineteen he embarked for South America, suffered shipwreck, and was washed ashore in Holland, where he lived for four years. In 1846 he went to Russia as the agent of a large importing and exporting company, and twenty years later he was a millionaire, able to retire from business. Meantime he had spent two years in California during the gold rush and, as he happened to be in Sacramento when California was annexed to the United States, he acquired American citizenship thereby. This citizenship he retained throughout his life, though in spirit he was a thorough cosmopolitan. During a second visit to America in 1868 he divorced his Russian wife and shortly thereafter went to Athens to marry a Greek girl of seventeen, whom he had selected from a number of candidates whose photographs were sent him, at his request, by the Archbishop of Athens. This second wife proved to be a most remarkable woman, who shared the difficult life at the "digs" and who was of incalculable aid to her husband in negotiations with local authorities.

Schliemann was an erratic genius, an enthusiast, a romantic, a man of boundless energy and infinite patience, quarrelsome and overbearing, a business man who knew how to get what he wanted though not always scrupulous as to how he got it. He had a mania for learning languages, of which he knew about twenty, including seven western European and three Scandinavian tongues, Russian and Polish, ancient and modern Greek, Latin, and even Turkish, Arabic, and Persian. He wrote books in four languages, and a high Turkish official once remarked that few Turks could write their mother tongue as well as he.

Schliemann was immensely vain and inordinately avid for fame. He was ambitious socially and showed great skill in acquiring and developing social contacts. When he first reached the United States as an unknown young man, less than thirty years old and knowing no one, he presented himself one evening at the White House, where President Fillmore received him and visited with him for an hour and a half. During his second visit to America, he discussed politics with President Johnson. He ingratiated himself with Gladstone and other political, intellectual, and social leaders in England and France, and last of all he developed social contacts in his own country. He built himself a house in Athens which rivaled the nearby palace of the king, who sometimes dropped in to visit him.

Schliemann's great enthusiasm was for ancient Greece. He tells us of his early chagrin at being taken from school before he could study Greek as his cousins had, and of his childish amazement and joy at hearing a drunken vagabond recite a hundred lines of Homer in the original Greek. At last, while in Russia, he was able to learn Greek. His infatuation with the subject was such that he tried to make himself into an ancient Greek, invoked Pallas Athena in his private devotions, corresponded with his second wife in Homeric Greek, and named her children Andromache and Agamemnon. He knew all Greek literature well, but he was entranced by Homer, and after retiring from business he devoted his wealth and his enormous energy to excavating sites mentioned in the Homeric poems. After preliminary surveys in 1868, he spent the summers of 1871, 1872, and 1873 digging at Hissarlik in Asia Minor, which he recognized—contrary to the general opinion at the time—as the site of ancient Troy. In 1876 he discovered the royal tombs at Mycenae, the home of Agamemnon; in 1879 and 1882 he was back at Troy; in 1880 he dug at Orchomenus; and in 1884 and 1885 he unearthed a huge palace at Tiryns.

These discoveries proved beyond doubt that a high civilization, hitherto unknown to scholars, had existed in the Aegean areas in the second millennium before Christ. But archeology was then a young science whose methods were not yet well established, and Schliemann was always an amateur and a dilettante whose romantic enthusiasm rushed him into all sorts of errors. In 1882, however, he enlisted the aid of a professional archeologist, Wilhelm Dörpfeld (1853–1940), who did much to raise the scientific value of his work. Schliemann rashly called a box of jewelry found at Troy "Priam's treasure," and identified a corpse found at Mycenae as Agamemnon's. Subsequent study has shown that each preceded the hero in question by several centuries. He believed that the Homeric Troy was the second city from the bottom at Hissarlik. After his death, Dörpfeld decided that it was the sixth; but excavations made between 1932 and 1938 by the American archeologist C. W. Blegen seem to show that the lower part of the seventh layer contains the ruins of the city destroyed by the Greeks about 1200. Having little interest in post-Homeric times at Troy, Schliemann dug through and destroyed much of what he was looking for. Schliemann, like Columbus, was one of those few and fortunate individuals who are permitted to discover a new world —even though in his case, as in that of Columbus, this new world eventually proved to be something quite different from what he thought it was. The biography by Emil Ludwig, *Schliemann, the Story of a Gold-seeker* (1931), though superficial, is rather interesting.

The Homeric Question

The problem of the origin of the Homeric poems constitutes the "Homeric question." Modern discussion dates from F. A. Wolf (1759–1824), though others had anticipated most of his views. Wolf was a quarrelsome professor at Halle, Germany, who invented the phrase "classical philology" (by which he meant the scientific study of the Greek and Roman worlds in all their aspects) and published his famous *Prolegomena ad Homerum* in 1795. (For his life see Mark Pattison, "Frederick Augustus

Wolf," in *Essays* [1889]). Wolf attacked the unity of the Homeric poems and, while he admitted the existence of a poet named Homer, he insisted that the *Iliad* was a patchwork in which the work of Homer was buried beneath a mass of later accretions. This view was very acceptable to the intellectual leaders of Germany in the early nineteenth century, for they took it as proving that the Homeric poems were splendid examples of the "folk poetry" then being praised by Herder and others under the influence of Rousseau. Countless German scholars endeavored to separate the poems into their component parts, and many of them eliminated "Homer" completely. The story of this phase of Homeric study is a saddening one, for only in New Testament criticism is it possible to find an equal amount of learned nonsense spun out of nothing.

For almost a generation Schliemann's discoveries made no serious impression on the philologists, but early in the twentieth century a new spirit began to appear in Homeric criticism. Eminent scholars defended the old view that the Homeric poems were essentially the work of one man. If some of these "unitarians" went too far, at least they overthrew the pretensions of the Wolfian school. Today the differences between unitarians and separatists are largely a matter of degree, for the former admit that Homer used earlier materials and the latter concede that the poems were put into substantially their present form by a poet of genius, not by some obscure Wolfian editor gifted only with a paste-pot and shears. In either case, the folk poetry came first (in Mycenaean times) and Homer afterward, which is exactly the opposite of what Wolf and his disciples taught. Among representatives of the separatist school may be mentioned U. von Wilamowitz-Moellendorff, *Die Ilias und Homer* (1916) and *Die Heimkehr des Odysseus* (1927), and Ed. Schwartz, *Die Odyssee* (1924); among the unitarians are Andrew Lang, *Homer and his Age* (1906), Walter Leaf, *Homer and History* (1915), and J. A. Scott, *The Unity of Homer* (1921); a more recent book, setting forth an intermediate position, is the brilliant work of M. P. Nilsson, *Homer and Mycenae* (1933), to which I am much indebted.

IX Social and Political Revolutions in Greece

THE DARK AGES USHERED IN BY THE DORIAN INVASIONS continued for more than three hundred years, and it was during these centuries that the Greece known to history took form. Whatever unity Mycenean civilization had given Greece was destroyed by the Dorians, who left each tiny village once more isolated from its neighbors. Within each community, however, the peoples of various origins became so thoroughly mingled that Greeks of historic times could no longer distinguish individuals of different racial stocks. The Greek people thus came into existence.

The social organization of the Greeks at this time was very simple. The population fell into two classes: the landowning aristocrats, and the peasants who tilled their fields and followed them in war. Though a few artisans were necessary, trade had virtually disappeared. The land was divided among the patriarchal families (*gene*), with the lower classes and the conquered peoples receiving fields and protection from great lords in return for loyalty and service. The head of the *genos* governed his district and recognized higher authority only vaguely, if at all. A social system resembling the feudal regime of medieval Europe thus prevailed during the Greek Middle Ages.

Toward the end of the ninth century before Christ, various forces began to undermine this simple organization of society. Natural increase raised the population to a point where there was no longer land enough for everybody. At the same time, Phoenician traders began to touch Greek shores bringing luxuries and novelties which stimulated covetousness in many breasts. Rivalry and ambition then goaded the aristocrats to seize and hold larger tracts of land for themselves in order to raise their prestige and their standard of living. Following this aristocratic example, the stronger and abler peasants grabbed additional fields for their younger sons, while the holdings of their average and inferior neighbors necessarily diminished. A bad season or a crop failure threw countless poor peasants into debt. Other peasants, after losing their land, became day laborers called *thetes*. The pressures of "progress" and increasing population thus caused many unfortunates to be exploited grievously by the wealthy. Since the old family system no longer protected its members, or even provided them with an adequate living, ambitious and energetic persons severed their connection with the *genos* and sought new means of livelihood elsewhere.

Hesiod's Picture of Peasant Life

The hard life of the peasant at the close of the Greek Middle Ages is vividly depicted in Hesiod's poem, *Works and Days*. A Boeotian farmer living about 800, Hesiod looked at the world through the eyes of a peasant, and his poem is a moral essay of some eight hundred lines on the peasant virtues of labor and thrift. He was primarily interested in the more successful sort of peasant—the man who had a farm, "a house, a woman, and an ox," who had a slave or two, and who perhaps had made his mark locally. Yet the poet lamented the unremitting labor to which such a man was doomed, his poverty, and the injustices which he must suffer from the nobles. Hesiod knew of other men even more unfortunate than such peasants: they were the *thetes* who had no land of their own, who were employed by others, and who were turned out of doors as soon as the working season was over. The poet sometimes gives the farmer hints about how to get the most work possible out of such wretches, but at the same time he warns how easy it is for any man to fall to this low estate. The magnitude of Hesiod's pessimism is shown in a famous passage describing the history of the world in five great ages, each worse than the one before: first came the golden age, then the silver and bronze ages, which were followed by the age of the heroes. Last of all came the age of iron in which the poet lived: might then made right, every man's hand was turned against his neighbor, and sorrow and endless toil were the lot of all.

In one passage, Hesiod suggested that if a farmer could not wring a living from his land he might supplement his scanty income by brief trading expeditions during the summer. There can be little doubt that in those difficult times many Greeks, nobles as well as peasants, followed his advice and took to the sea. Ever since the tenth century, Phoenician merchants had been visiting Aegean shores in increasing numbers, and from them the Greeks learned many of the tricks of trade. Piracy had always been an honored calling among the Greek nobility, who now began to find it more profitable to refine their rude profession and conform to milder rules. Early Greek traders were also explorers and adventurers, and the *Odyssey* shows that before 750 they knew most of the shores once visited by the Minoans of old. Mariners brought back tales of the many lands they had seen, and soon it occurred to the farmers of overcrowded Ionia and Greece that they might find homes in these strange new lands. The ensuing emigration and colonial expansion gave a new direction to the whole course of Greek history.

Greek Colonies in the East

Greek colonists were primarily land-hungry peasants in search of new fields. They settled in regions whose climate and soil were not very different from those of Greece and whose native inhabitants were so few in number or so backward in culture as to cause no serious trouble. Although commercial considerations had little to do with the original founding of colonies, Greek traders often visited them, and trade between the colonies and Greece soon became an important matter. Certain Greek cities made a business of transporting emigrants overseas because they alone had the necessary ships and the knowledge of places where colonies might profitably be founded. Such a city became the colony's *metropolis*, or "mother city." The metropolis retained no political power over the colony, but mother and daughter were often bound together by ties of

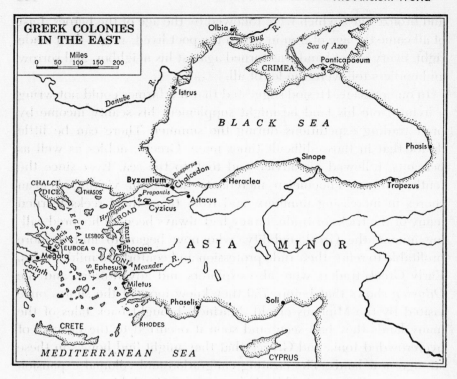

GREEK COLONIES
IN THE EAST

sentiment and blood, of language and religion, and the ties of commerce bound them still more tightly.

The actual planning of a colony was the work of an organizer, called an "oikist," who selected a site for the proposed colony, enrolled settlers, drew up laws for their government, and took them to their new homes. There he distributed lands among the colonists, established and regulated their religious cults, governed them, and sometimes was honored by them as a hero after his death. Often the oikist was an aristocrat, or the younger son of an aristocrat, who hoped to raise his status still higher, but sometimes he was a man of humble birth who had left home to become a sailor or merchant and then returned to lead a colony to some distant land that he had visited.

The earliest Greek colonies appeared in the eighth century, when men from Eretria and Chalcis, on the island of Euboea, settled Chalcidice. This three-pronged peninsula, reaching into the northern waters of the Aegean, took its name from the latter metropolis, which is said to have established thirty-two colonies before 600. Early in the seventh century, the Aeolians of Lesbos occupied the Troad and founded colonies on both sides of the Hellespont. Colonists from the Ionian city of Miletus presently dominated the southern shores of the Propontis, their earliest colony being Cyzicus (675). Meantime, settlers from Megara in Greece had likewise established themselves on the Propontis, first at Astacus (710), then at Chalcedon (685) at the mouth of the Bosporus on the Asiatic side, and lastly (about 660) at Byzantium on the European shore.

From early times sailors from Miletus in Ionia had brought home tunny fish from the Black Sea, but they hesitated to venture far upon its stormy waters—even though they sought to placate its evil spirit by calling it the Euxine, "Friendly to Strangers." The region was presently made still more inhospitable by savage invaders from Russia or Asia, known as Cimmerians, who overran northern Anatolia shortly after 700 (see page 175). By the middle of the century this danger was over, and colonists from Miletus began settling along the shores of the Black Sea. Sinope and Trapezus (modern Trebizond), on its southern shore, were founded or refounded about 630, but the great plains north of the Black Sea proved more attractive to colonists and toward the end of the century Greek colonies were established in the Crimean Peninsula. Meantime other Greeks had established themselves on the African coast opposite Crete, perhaps as early as the eighth century, and here Dorians founded Cyrene about 630.

The greater part of this eastern phase of Greek colonizing was thus the work of Ionians, and especially of the citizens of Miletus, who are said to have sent out ninety colonies. Ionia became the richest and most progressive part of the Greek world, and Miletus was its leading city. Her advantageous location at the mouth of the Meander River made her the natural commercial outlet for central Asia Minor, and her colonial empire added to her wealth and power.

The West in the Eighth Century

Colonial expansion into the western Mediterranean area was equally important for the Greeks, but before describing the foundation of these colonies, we must attempt a rapid survey of that part of the world as it was in the eighth century. The western Mediterranean area is more sharply separated by nature from Greece and the Orient than a hasty glance at the map would suggest. The western half of the Mediterranean is really a large lake almost completely surrounded by mountains. These mountains cause Italy to face west; they shut off the southern part of France (now called Provence) from the rest of Europe; they divide eastern and southern Spain from the central plateau; and in Africa they separate modern Morocco, Algeria, and Tunis from the Sahara Desert. This isolated region can be entered only through the Straits of Messana, two miles wide, separating Italy from Sicily, or through the gap between Sicily and Africa, or else through a few passes in the northern mountains. Only rarely is the strip of fertile land between the mountains and the sea more than a hundred miles wide, and often it is much narrower.

The early neolithic inhabitants of this whole region were men of Mediterranean race who had come north from the Sahara region. Some remained in North Africa, some crossed to Europe at Gibraltar, and others entered Italy by way of Sicily. Not all came at one time, however, and various groups showed wide differences. Those living in northern Africa in historic times were called Libyans and Numidians; those who crossed to Sicily were known as Sicels; and those who entered Europe by way of Gibraltar became Iberians in Spain or Ligurians in southern France and northern Italy. Except in Italy, these early inhabitants were virtually undisturbed by foreign invaders until the arrival of colonists from the Orient and Greece in the ninth and eighth centuries, and to the present day their descendants form the great majority of the population of the whole western Mediterranean area.

During the second millennium, Italy was often invaded from the north by peoples kindred to those then invading Greece. The first invaders crossed the Brenner Pass from central Europe into northern Italy shortly after 1900 B.C., just as the first Achaeans were forcing their way into Greece and the Hittites began entering Asia Minor. These invaders apparently were related, culturally at least, to the Swiss lake-dwellers, for they too built villages on piles over water for protection: their villages are called "palafitte" from the Italian word for "piles." The newcomers brought bronze tools and weapons and presumably they spoke an Indo-European language distantly related to Latin. Two or three centuries later other invaders, with a more ad-vanced bronze culture, entered the peninsula by the same route, per-haps from Austria or even from the Hungarian plain. They are called the "Terramare" peoples. There is no good evidence that these North-erners crossed the Apennines into central Italy, even though the na-tives of the latter region presently began using bronze tools. While the natives probably learned something from the Terramare peoples, archeologists believe that they learned more from Minoans and Mycenaeans who were active traders at this time.

Toward the end of the millennium, still other groups of Europeans made their way into Italy, probably in consequence of the general upheavals that produced the Dorian invasions of Greece. These new invaders are called "Villanovans"—from an Italian site near Bo-logna—and, like the Dorians, they had an iron culture. Before the end of the millennium they had crossed the Apennines and estab-lished themselves in central Italy as far south as the Tiber River and Latium. Others presently occupied the hill country throughout cen-tral Italy, and eventually they imposed their culture and their "Italic" dialects—closely akin to Latin—upon the whole peninsula.

Phoenician Colonies

Though Minoan mariners had penetrated to the western Mediter-ranean during the second millennium, the first oriental colonists in the West came from the Phoenician cities, and especially from Tyre. With the decline of the Egyptian Empire and the overthrow of Mycenae, these Phoenicians inherited dominion over the Mediter-ranean. Perhaps as early as 900 B.C. they sailed past Gibraltar to found a famous colony at Gades (modern Cadiz) on the Atlantic coast of Spain. During the next century they established posts at Gibraltar and at Tangier on the African coast opposite, at Utica in north Africa, on the islands of Sicily, Sardinia, and Malta; and about 800 they founded Carthage. By this time, Assyrian kings had already claimed tribute from the Phoenician cities on several occasions, and in the eighth century began the bitter struggle for independence which was to last for two hundred years. Sidon was destroyed by Esarhaddon in 677, and though Tyre's location on an island saved her from a similar fate, she was so distracted and weakened by fighting that her colonies were left to shift for themselves.

The earlier Phoenician colonies were little more than trading posts, occupying only enough land to provide defense and food for their garrisons. Carthage was a more ambitious settlement, with a considerable Punic (*i.e.,* Phoenician, as pronounced by Latins) population ruling over the native Libyans. She was therefore able to assume leadership of the Phoenicians in the West, and before 600 she had built up an empire which included all the old Phoenician colonies and several new ones. Carthaginian vessels, famed for their size and speed, sailed the whole Mediterranean, and Carthaginian merchants maintained close connections with their kinsmen in Phoenicia. They carried finished goods, especially cloth and articles of luxury, from the East to the West; and on return voyages they carried slaves, grain, precious stones, and raw materials, especially silver and copper from Spain as well as lead and tin which others had brought to Spain from Brittany and England.

Carthage was not noted for her literature or art, or for other higher aspects of civilization, and her religion was a barbarous worship of such Semitic gods as Tanit (Astarte) and Melkart. Nevertheless, Carthaginian merchants promoted the economic development of the West. Their powerful empire became Rome's chief rival, and though they eventually were defeated, they so firmly impressed their civilization upon the peoples of north Africa that the Romans could never assimilate them completely and, as soon as Rome's rule began to weaken, these peoples reverted to the Semitic civilization which they still retain.

The Etruscans

Meantime other colonists were invading the part of north-central Italy that lies between the Tiber River and the Apennines. This district is now known as Etruria or Tuscany, and the invaders are called Etruscans. There has been much speculation as to their origin, but modern archeology supports the ancient view that they came from a non-Greek part of western Anatolia. The first Etruscans in Italy were traders who came in search of iron, perhaps in the ninth century. A hundred years later, settlers began arriving in considerable numbers and established themselves as an aristocracy ruling over the Italian peasantry of Etruria. Some Etruscans then crossed the Apennines into the Po Valley while others migrated south to found Capua and other cities in the Campanian region of south-central Italy inland from Naples. To unite these Campanian settlements with Etruria, they also occupied the intervening Latium, and archeology supports old traditions that Etruscan kings once ruled Rome itself. In the days of their greatest power, toward the middle of the sixth century, the Etruscans dominated the major part of central Italy; their traders competed with the Carthaginians; and their ships sometimes reached the Mediterranean coast of Spain in spite of all that Carthage could do to prevent it.

Trade brought wealth and enabled the Etruscans to build such famous and beautiful cities as Caere and Veii, Clusium and Perusia. Each of these Etruscan cities, of which Roman writers sometimes listed twelve leaders, was an independent political unit, governed by a king or an oligarchy. The resulting lack of political unity so weakened the Etruscans that they could not successfully resist the formidable attacks that presently came from the outside, and about 500 B.C. their decline began. During the next two centuries Etruria was overrun repeatedly by Gallic raiders from the Po Valley, and shortly after 300 B.C. the whole country was conquered by Rome. But Rome itself, which had been ruled by Etruscan kings in the sixth century, did not play an important part, even in Italian affairs, until almost the end of the fourth century before Christ.

The Greeks in the West

Such was the Western world which the Greeks began to enter early in the eighth century. Many passages describing the West are found in the *Odyssey*, some of them perhaps only vague memories preserved from Mycenaean times while others undoubtedly reflect a new interest in the West that appeared in Greece after 800. Similar passages in Hesiod bear further witness to this interest. And above all, fragments of Greek pottery of the period 800–750, found at some thirty sites in Italy and Sicily, prove that Greeks traded with these regions in the first half of the eighth century. Here, as in the East, trade prepared the way for colonization, and in the second half of the century Greeks began founding permanent colonies in the West.

The first Greek colonies, in the West as in the East, were founded by Euboeans from Eretria and Chalcis. Toward the middle of the eighth century Eretrian colonists settled on the island of Corcyra, off the west coast of Epirus. Using this station as a base, others sailed farther west and founded Cumae just outside the Bay of Naples about 735. Soon other colonies were established in the vicinity, and eventually the whole shore of the bay was dotted with Greek settlements. Because of the Etruscans, Cumae remained the northernmost of the Greek settlements in Italy, but Poseidonia, about sixty miles to the south, was founded toward 600, and Elea, twenty-five miles farther along the coast, dates from about 535. Meantime, about 735, Chalcidian colonists had settled at Naxus on the east coast of Sicily near Mount Etna. Settlers from Naxus in turn founded colonies in eastern and northern Sicily, while pirates from Cumae are said to have founded Messana about 690 and Rhegium on the opposite Italian shore a few years later.

These colonists were Ionians, but about the same time Dorians from Corinth began making settlements in the West. They captured Corcyra about 735 and shortly thereafter founded Syracuse in Sicily, which for many centuries remained the most important Greek city in the West. Other Dorians settled elsewhere in Sicily and along the lower side of Italy. This first great burst of colonizing activity, which lasted about fifty years, was followed by a lull in the West until, at

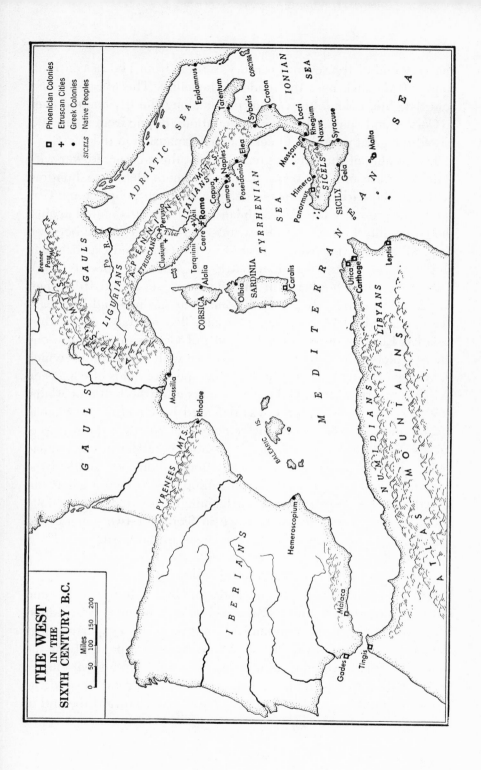

THE WEST
IN THE
SIXTH CENTURY B.C.

Miles
0   50   100 150 200

Phoenician Colonies
Etruscan Cities
Greek Colonies
Native Peoples
SICELS

GAULS

LIGURIANS

GAULS

PYRENEES MTS.

IBERIANS

Massilia

Rhodae

Hemeroscopium

Malaca

Gades

Tingis

BALEARIC Is.

MEDITERRANEAN

SEA

CORSICA

Olbia

SARDINIA

Alalia

Caralis

Coralis

NUMIDIANS

LIBYANS

ATLAS MOUNTAINS

Utica
Carthage

Leptis

ADRIATIC SEA

Brenner Pass

Po R.

APENNINES

ETRUSCANS

Clusium

Perusia

Tiber R.

Tarquinii

Veii

Caere

Rome

ITALIANS

Capua

Cumae

Naples

Poseidonia

Elea

Epidamnus

Tarentum

Sybaris

Croton

CORCYRA

IONIAN SEA

Locri

Rhegium

Naxus

Syracuse

Messana

Himera

Panormus

SICELS

SICILY

Gela

Malta

TYRRHENIAN SEA

the very end of the seventh century, settlers from Phocaea in Ionia founded Massilia, near the modern Marseilles. The Massilots then sent daughter colonies to various points along the Riviera and even to Corsica and Spain. These new foundations, dating from about 600, closed the great period of Greek colonial expansion in the West.

The coming of the Greeks precipitated a three-cornered war with Carthaginians and Etruscans that lasted more than two hundred years. In the earlier phases of the struggle each people fought by itself, but presently the Carthaginians and Etruscans united against the Greek interlopers. The Phocaeans then drove a wedge between these allies until they were defeated by the combined Carthaginian and Etruscan fleets in a great battle off Alalia in Corsica (535). Thereafter, the Phocaeans in Massilia were separated from their Greek kinsmen in Sicily by Carthaginians in Sardinia and Etruscans in Corsica. The Greek settlers at Alalia fled to Italy, where they founded Elea about eighty miles south of Cumae, and before long the Massilots were forced to sign a treaty with Carthage by which the two parties agreed to delimit their respective fields of expansion in Spain at Artemisium. Only eleven years after the battle of Alalia, however, the Etruscan navy was defeated by Greeks from Cumae (524), and fifty years later the remnants of Etruscan power were smashed by a Syracusan fleet in a second great battle off Cumae (474). These defeats, and the loss of Rome about 509, marked the beginning of Etruscan decline. Meantime, the Syracusans had inflicted a severe defeat upon a Carthaginian army at Himera (480) and thereby stopped Punic advance in Sicily for two generations. The Greeks thus became the leading power in the West.

Phrygia and Lydia

The economic revolution which came over Greece in the seventh and sixth centuries was further encouraged by conditions in Asia Minor. The Hittites of central Anatolia had long since been superseded by the Phrygians, who invaded Asia Minor from Europe at about the time the Dorians were invading Greece and built up a great empire there. At times their influence and power extended far beyond the Taurus Mountains in Cilicia and even into Syria. Toward the end of the eighth century, Phrygia was devastated by the Cimmerian invaders from the north, and the Phrygian Empire came to an end about 680 with the death of King Midas—the man famous in Greek legend for turning all that he touched into gold.

Power in Asia Minor then passed westward to the racially kindred Lydian kings who ruled from Sardis. After conquering the Phrygians and subjugating all the Greek cities of Ionia except Miletus, they ruled all Asia Minor west of the Halys River. High economic prosperity prevailed in Lydia, thanks in part to the gold washed down by the Pactolus River, but especially because of the skill of Lydian artisans and traders and because the great trade route from Assyria to the Aegean Sea crossed her territory. Lydia was a rich and powerful kingdom until her last king, the famous Croesus, was defeated and Sardis was captured by the Persians in 546.

The Ionian Greeks at first were friendly with the Lydians because of their common hostility to Phrygia, and after the Lydian conquest the Greeks were not destroyed or their culture ruined. Lydian and Greek each learned much from the other, and each profited by the other's prosperity. Moreover, the Assyrians (who had been allies of the Lydians against the Phrygians) often granted favors to the Greeks, who were rivals of the rebellious Phoenicians. Being free to trade at whatever Mediterranean ports were in Assyrian hands, Greeks settled in Cyprus, where they fought against the Phoenicians, and at Soli near Tarsus; but when they tried to occupy still more of Cilicia, the Assyrians drove them out. Greek traders visited Syria and Palestine frequently, as is shown by Greek pottery found there and by references to "Javan" (i.e., Ionia, which originally was "Ivonia") in various books of the Old Testament. However, the Greeks made no attempt to found permanent settlements in that part of the world. Egypt had long been known to the Greeks, and when Psammetichus revolted against Assurbanipal in 663, Greeks flocked thither, first as mercenary soldiers and later as traders. Toward the middle of the century, Greeks from Miletus founded Naucratis, a trading post near the Canopic mouth of the Nile, which soon became one of the most prosperous cities in Egypt—and all Egypt was prosperous under the Twenty-sixth Dynasty founded by Psammetichus.

The Greek Alphabet

Contact with the East gave the Greeks new ideas which led to inventions that were of prime importance in their economic and intellectual development. One of the first of these inventions was the alphabet. Perhaps as early as 800, Greeks began writing with an alphabet based on that used by Phoenician traders who visited the Aegean area. Presumably this writing was first used by business men to keep records; later it became known to rulers, and finally to literary men. The Greeks soon improved upon the Phoenician alphabet. The Phoenicians, like other Semites, could write their language comprehensibly with the use of consonants only, but Greeks felt the need of characters for vowels. They therefore adapted characters used for Phoenician consonants with no equivalent in Greek, and they added others for consonantal sounds not found in Phoenician (see chart on p. 168). After first following the Semitic practice of writing from right to left, the Greeks used the "boustrophedon" form (turning back and forth like an ox plowing a field), in which successive lines ran in opposite directions. Only in the fifth century did it become the universal practice in Greece to write from left to right, as all Europeans do today.

Greek merchants also used various oriental weights and measures, often preserving their Semitic names—as in siglos (*sheqel* in Phoenician) and mina (*manah*)—and retaining the relative values of different units according to the reckoning by sixties that the Sumerians had introduced: in early times sixty sigloi made one mina (about one pound) and sixty minas made one talent. The talent had been used even in Homeric times, but perhaps it too came originally from the Orient. This system of weights and measures was standardized, about 670, by a certain Pheidon, ruler of Argos and the neighboring island of Aegina: his "Aeginetic" standards, though later modified at Athens and elsewhere, continued in use throughout the Peleponnesus.

Greek Coins

It was from the Lydians that the Greeks learned to cast coins. Like other primitive pastoral peoples, the Greeks had once counted wealth in terms of cattle, taking the ox as a unit. In Homeric times, the value of an ox was equal to an amount of gold or copper called a "talent"—about 135 grains of gold (*i.e.*, a piece about one-third heavier than an American quarter and now worth nearly six dollars) or about sixty pounds of copper. However, nothing that could be called a coin was used in Homeric times. In the Orient, men had begun to use nuggets and bars of the precious metals as currency, valuing them according to their weight, whatever that happened to be, and weighing each piece whenever it changed hands. In the eighth century, Assyrian merchants, and later their kings, began to mark such bars to indicate their purity but not their weight. Lydian merchants imitated the practice, and a Lydian king stamped characteristic devices on small pieces of electrum (a natural alloy of gold and silver found plentifully in Lydia) to indicate both purity and weight. These were the first coins. Gold and silver coins were also cast, and the ratio between gold, electrum, and silver was set at 13⅓:10:1.

Within a short time Ionian Greeks too were casting coins, the Chalcidians presently followed suit, and about 670 Pheidon of Argos established a mint at Aegina. Since the Greeks had little gold and no electrum, they made their coins of silver, with copper pieces for smaller values. The Lydian gold coin was called a "statter"—a name derived from the Assyrian goddess Ishtar, or Astarte, whose image was often stamped on bars of metal. The Greeks used various standards for their silver coins, the commonest being the drachma, twenty of which equaled one statter. The drachma was worth six copper obols. Double drachmas and tetradrachms (4-drachma pieces) were also cast in silver, as well as fractions of the obol in copper. For larger transactions, value was computed in terms of minas ($= 100$ drachmae) and talents ($= 60$ minas), but no coins of such high value were cast.[1]

---

[1] As standards were changed from time to time, and as purchasing power fluctuated greatly, it is impossible to give satisfactory equivalents for these units in American money. Writers sometimes estimate the value of a drachma as about 18 cents, comparing the amount of silver in an Athenian drachma of the fifth century with that in an American dollar (which of course is "fiat" currency worth considerably more than its value as bullion). Such estimates are quite misleading. The purchasing power of a

The Economic Revolution in Greece

This colonial and commercial expansion effected a fundamental revolution in the economic life of Greece. While the Greek colonies were primarily agricultural, the commercial genius of the Greek people soon found ways to make them useful in developing trade. The colonists continued to live in Greek style and therefore desired many commodities not produced in their new homes. They were able to afford luxuries from Greece and made excellent markets for wine and olive oil, pottery, cloth, and other Greek wares. In exchange they sent grain, wool, dried and salt fish, and slaves to Greece. When colonists began to trade with neighboring tribes, Greek goods found their way to the interior of Italy and France. Traders penetrated central Europe by way of the Black Sea and the Danube while others reached the rich markets of Syria and Egypt. Trade became as important as agriculture in the Greek economy, and the Greek commercial empire extended from the Black Sea to Cyrene, from Syria to Sicily and southern France.

This great expansion of trade provided Greek manufacturers with growing markets and led to a rapid development of industry. While Greece had always had her artisans, they were not numerous in the Dark Ages. Now new inventions and technical devices, many of them borrowed from the East, and a more elaborate system of distribution, led to a great increase in industrial output. In earlier times the artisan had manufactured only on order from the ultimate consumer, or at most he might have a few pieces of his handiwork ready for customers. Now there appeared a class of middlemen who bought manufactured goods in quantity and found markets for them overseas. The artisan no longer knew the ultimate consumer, and mass production was introduced. When workshops were established in which proprietors employed a dozen or more men, a greater division of labor was made possible, and standardized products were turned out. Thousands of workers found employment, and industry vied

---

drachma about 500 was such that two obols (or "six cents") was considered a good day's wage for unskilled labor.

with commerce and agriculture as an economic foundation of the new Greece.

At first the most important industries were textiles and ceramics. Cloth had formerly been made by women at home, but world markets encouraged enterprising persons to buy wool, to employ others to spin, weave, and dye it, and to sell the finished product to traders. Pottery, too, was in great demand, either as containers for wine and olive oil, as tableware, or as works of art. Makers of cheap pottery quickly developed standard shapes and decorations, partly because the manufacture of such pieces required less skill, and partly to enable foreign purchasers to recognize their favorite wines and oils from their containers. True artists, on the other hand, found patrons willing and able to pay high prices for their masterpieces.

Industrial workers at this time were usually free men. There had been little slavery in Greece in the Dark Ages, and though it increased in the seventh century, the slaves then available were not fitted for highly skilled labor. Unless the free worker possessed exceptional skill, however, his lot was not a happy one. His hours were long and his pay meager. The managers of the workshops were themselves successful artisans, but prosperity encouraged them to unite with wealthy merchants to form a separate class in rivalry with the old landed aristocracy.

These changes in trade and industry, of course, brought varied repercussions upon agriculture in Greece. Agriculture, too, became capitalistic. Sometimes aristocrats acquired the capital for new types of farming by piracy or war; sometimes they married the daughters of rich merchants; and often they absorbed the prevailing capitalist mentality with no more capital than their ancestral estates. Capitalistic enterprise encouraged them to take up new forms of agriculture. When olive oil and wine were exported in quantity, progressive landowners found it profitable to set out orchards and vineyards. The resulting decline in grain production necessitated the importation of foodstuffs from the colonies. The new agriculture thus became profitable to both traders and landowners, but to the peasants it was disastrous. Though thousands of peasants flocked to the cities and colonies, the orchards and vineyards did not provide enough work for those who remained at home. Farmers sometimes tried to grub out new fields from the forests, burning or cutting down trees and thus ignorantly inviting the erosion from which Greece has suffered so much. Others borrowed money at ruinous interest and lost everything when they could not repay it. Sometimes they and their families were sold into slavery, or, more commonly, they became the serfs of wealthy landowners, with their wretchedness providing the somber background for a brilliant period of economic progress.

The Greek Polis

These economic developments were responsible for the rise of the Greek city-state. In classic times the Greeks knew that their country had formerly been dotted with peasant villages, called *komai,* and they believed that a city, or *polis,* was created by the union of several villages. While such unions undoubtedly occurred, a Greek *polis* always was more than a big village. It was a commercial center, and it had a very different political life. In early times, the *polis* was a citadel, built at the top of a hill (the "acropolis") and surrounded by walls within which stood the royal palace, temples, and other public buildings. The inhabitants of the city might take refuge there for a few days in case of raids, but their homes lay at the foot of the hill in what was called the *asty.* In the sixth century the city walls often were extended to include these houses as well as the acropolis. The word *asty* then came to be used for the city in its material aspect —a collection of houses—while the word *polis* referred to the abstraction of which a man was a citizen and to which he was patriotically loyal. The acropolis became the religious center, reserved for temples to the gods, and the center of secular life was established elsewhere. This significant change shows that the *polis* had ceased being a mere fortification and was idealized as the object of a religious and patriotic enthusiasm.[2]

The political and business life of the city centered in the "agora." This agora was an open square large enough to hold an assembly of all the citizens. Around it stood various public buildings whose num-

---

[2] See note on Fustel de Coulanges, p. 318.

ber and importance reflected the size and wealth of the city and the nature of its government. The most important building was the *prytaneum,* or "city hall." It usually was consecrated to Hestia, and on its hearth a sacred fire symbolized it as the hearth or home of the *polis.* The building served as the official residence of the chief ruler, and in it high officials and other especially honored persons occasionally ate sacred meals at public expense. Nearby would stand another building called the *bouleuterium,* used for meetings of the *Boule,* or Council. There would also probably be temples fronting on the agora. These buildings made the agora the center of the political life of the city; others made it the market place and the center of economic life. Porches or columned arcades, called *stoai,* were built to provide protection from the sun; in them, peddlars and merchants set up booths in which to display their wares, and here business was conducted. And finally, the agora and its arcades served as a social center where citizens congregated to converse about the news of the day, to debate political questions formally or informally, and to discuss other matters of greater or less import. Greek public opinion was formed in the agora.

The citizens of the *polis* made up the *demos*—the Greek word forming the first half of our "democracy," which means "rule by the people." In the sixth century, this word was used for the citizen body as a whole, with no distinction between upper and lower classes; in later times, it was applied to the populace as opposed to the aristocracy and to the "mob." Eventually, in the Attic comedy, "Demos" was made into a symbolic character much like the little fellow who sometimes represents the "common people" in American political cartoons. Citizenship was inherited, and Greek cities were most reluctant to extend its privileges to immigrants. Every important city therefore contained a large population of *metics* (resident foreigners, either Greek or barbarian) and slaves who did not belong to the *demos* and who had no share in the government.

As each Greek city jealously guarded its independence from all others, the *polis* was really a "city-state." Its territory extended beyond the walls far enough to include several villages and the fields from which the city drew its food, but in most cases this area was very small. In the fifth century Sparta ruled a territory of about 3250 square miles (two-thirds the area of Connecticut) and Athens ruled about 1000 square miles (about equal to Rhode Island), but they were the largest city-states. Argos had about 500 square miles, Thebes about 400, and Corinth about 350. The twelve city-states of Boeotia outside Thebes averaged less than 70 each, and the 600 square miles of Phocis were divided among twenty-two sovereign states. Not many city-states had a population of more than a few thousand persons, and in the majority a man might know nearly all his fellow citizens by sight. This political organization resulted from, and accentuated, the parochialism to which Greeks were foreordained by geography.

Military Power

While the Greek *polis* resulted from the commercial revolution of the eighth and seventh centuries, its fortunes were much influenced by new developments in military tactics which transferred power from the old rural aristocracy to the citizens of the new cities. Previously, Greek aristocrats had fought from chariots much like the Homeric heroes of old from whom they claimed descent, with individual champions challenging one another while their followers were an ill-trained rabble of no great military value. These old-style warriors were now replaced by "hoplites," who formed a well-drilled, heavy-armed infantry. Drawn up in a long line, called the phalanx, they advanced to battle in close formation, several ranks deep, and they fought at close range with spear and sword. They easily drove the old rabble armies from the field. Our first mention of hoplites occurs in accounts of a war fought about 700 between Eretria and Chalcis. The new type of warfare then spread rapidly through Greece, and before the end of the seventh century the Spartans had made the phalanx the most formidable fighting machine yet known to the world. Sometimes the hoplites were well-to-do citizens who bought their own armor; more commonly they were mercenaries. In either case, they served the new commercial city-states, and they tolled the knell of the old aristocracy as a military power.

Somewhat later, the introduction of the trireme wrought an

equally important change in naval warfare. Heretofore, Greek mariners had sailed in long boats propelled by oars and carrying a small sail. The largest of these boats, called "penteconters" because they had fifty oars, were slightly over one hundred feet long, which was the maximum length then possible. Greater power could be obtained only by finding new places for the rowers, and this was accomplished in the triremes which began to appear in Greece about 550. The seating arrangement of the rowers in triremes has been much discussed. Some authorities believe that the ships were so high that the rowers sat in three tiers, one above another. It is more probable that three men sat side by side on a slanting bench; to prevent their oars from interfering with each other, the rowers nearer the center of the boat sat slightly above and in front of those next the ship's side. The longer oars of the inner rowers emerged from slightly higher portholes in order to maintain their balance. The Greeks probably learned this arrangement from the Phoenicians, for ships of this type are shown in Assyrian carvings dating from as early as 700. A trireme carried a crew of two hundred men (170 rowers, 20 sailors, 10 soldiers), and for short spurts it could attain a speed of eight or nine knots per hour. Triremes were strictly war vessels, not used in trade since they had no cargo space, but they protected the larger and slower merchant vessels from pirates and enemies, and they drove competitors out of Greek waters.

The Rise of Tyranny

Closely associated with the progress of the *polis* was that type of government which the Greeks called "tyranny." The word did not then carry the evil connotation that it acquired in later Greece and that it bears today. The first "tyrants" were men who overthrew governments that were selfishly and inefficiently conducted by the landed aristocracy, replacing them with stronger governments that favored the commercial and industrial classes. Ordinarily the tyrants were no more cruel and oppressive than their predecessors had been, and it cannot be said that the essence of tyranny lay in its lawlessness or even in its violent seizure of power. Tyrannies were sometimes established peaceably, whereas the old aristocrats often used vio-

GREECE
IN THE
SIXTH CENTURY B.C.

lence to obtain power and governed quite arbitrarily afterward. The essence of early tyranny lay in the fact that it derived support from the new classes of society, in whose interests it governed. In nearly every case, the tyrant was a man who had acquired great wealth from industry or trade, and who used this wealth to gain friends and followers, or to hire mercenary hoplites who would establish him in power. Having once obtained power, whether lawfully or not, the tyrant fortified his position by rewarding his supporters and by endeavoring to destroy the political power of his opponents. By constantly appealing to the "people" against the aristocracy, the tyrants ultimately encouraged democracy in Greece.

The reforms of the early tyrants were usually desirable, even though the tyrant who effected them may have been inspired solely by personal ambition. The chief opponents of tyranny being the old aristocrats whose political power rested upon the *genos*, the tyrants did what they could to hasten the collapse of that moribund institution. Moreover, the old ancestral law no longer fitted the new social conditions prevailing in Greece, and the tyrants drew up new codes of law that were more appropriate to the new day. These new laws were written down, not merely confided to aristocratic memories. In thus consciously creating new laws, the tyrants followed precedents set by the oikists who drew up codes and constitutions for their colonies. At the same time, the administration of justice was taken away from the old aristocrats (of whose venality Hesiod had complained bitterly) and entrusted to new officials. The tyrants also interested themselves actively in the promotion of trade and industry. Under them the cities prospered mightily, and money was spent lavishly on public works such as agoras, aqueducts, sewers, roads, and public buildings. By these reforms the tyrants gained the solid support of the industrial and trading classes, while the populace was won over by steady employment and by elaborate spectacles, donations, and the arts of the demagogue.

The word "tyrant" is believed to be of Lydian origin, and certainly the earliest ruler to whom the Greeks applied the term was Gyges of Lydia (about 685–652). Herodotus tells an amusing but improbable story of how Gyges murdered his predecessor Candaules, whose wife and kingdom he then took over; other Greeks had other explanations of what happened, all of them rather unconvincing. A more recent theory connects Gyges' rise to power with the invention of coinage: it is said that he was a wealthy man who began casting coins while still a private individual and used them to hire mercenary followers with whose aid he seized power. Finally, in order to prevent possible rivals from repeating his exploit, he made the casting of coins thereafter a state monopoly. This version, too, seems rather "Herodotean," but behind it lie the indubitable facts that coins were first cast by private individuals and that the royal coinage of Lydia dates from the time of Gyges. At any rate, Gyges and his successors were tyrants in the good sense of the term, and the Greeks long continued to regard Croesus, the last of Gyges' dynasty, as a classic exemplar of tyranny.

Early Tyrants in Greece

The earliest tyrant of European Greece, Pheidon of Argos, is almost as elusive to the historian as Gyges. Even his dates are uncertain, though scholars usually say that he flourished in the second quarter of the seventh century (675–650) and was therefore a younger contemporary of Gyges. Argolis had been the center of Mycenaean civilization, and our scanty evidence seems to indicate that a Dorian kingdom there maintained high prestige through the Dark Ages. Presently this kingdom disintegrated, and Pheidon inherited only a meager portion of what his ancestors had once held. He made it his aim in life to regain his ancestral heritage, and at the time of his death he held the ancient kingdom and much besides.

After conquering the whole of Argolis and the neighboring island of Aegina, Pheidon instituted various "tyrannical" reforms (including coinage and standard weights and measures), and launched a great campaign of further conquest. He apparently hoped to acquire the whole Peloponnesus, which was the reputed heritage of his remote ancestor, Heracles. Pheidon actually obtained the eastern coast of the peninsula, forced the Eleans to let him preside at Olympic games, aided the Megarians in colonizing the Propontis, and inflicted a severe military defeat upon Athens. His military successes were due in large part to his use of hoplites. The cost of these expensive warriors forced him to make terms with the wealthy merchants of Aegina, where he set up his mint, and in later years his policies were often dictated by his commercially-minded allies. At least, this seems to be what Aristotle meant when he remarked that Pheidon began as a king and ended as a tyrant. But though Pheidon took the essential step toward tyranny, his sons failed to follow in his footsteps and continued to rule simply as kings until the fifth century. Perhaps they abandoned tyranny because there was no powerful trading class in their kingdom except at Aegina, which by their time had regained her independence.

Better illustrations of early tyranny may be seen in the neighboring cities of Sicyon and Corinth. Throughout the seventh century, both were wealthy manufacturing cities, notable for their pottery.

The founder of tyranny in Sicyon was a man named Orthagoras, who started life as a butcher or cook, and seized the government shortly before 650. He was succeeded by his brother Myron, who had been a victor in the Olympic games in 648, and his dynasty is exceptional among Greek tyrannies because it endured more than a century. The tyrants of Sicyon were famous for their mild rule and for their encouragement of the fine arts.

Tyranny was established at Corinth about 657 by a certain Cypselus, who had been a potter. His tyranny was contemporary with the great export of Corinthian pottery to the West, and he cast the first Corinthian coins. His son and successor, Periander (about 625–585), was the most famous of Greek tyrants and made Corinth the largest, most powerful, and most glorious city in Greece. More ruthless than his father, Periander exiled or exterminated the last of the old Corinthian aristocracy. By founding colonies in Epirus and Chalcidice he obtained the two ends of the land route across northern Greece and the rich silver mines of that region. The walls he built around Corinth were nine miles in length.

Details about most of those who made the period from 650 to 500 the "Age of Tyrants" are hardly worth recording. Other tyrants ruled Miletus, Samos, several Aegean islands, and various cities near Corinth, notably Megara and Epidaurus. The Greek cities of Sicily and the West also fell under the sway of tyrants, some of whom were more bloodthirsty than any that arose in Greece. Nor was tyranny confined to the Greeks at this time. Psammetichus and his successors of the Twenty-sixth Dynasty in Egypt resembled Greek tyrants in many ways, as did the Tarquins then governing Rome. Special attention must be given to the tyranny at Athens, however, not only because we have fuller information about it than about any other, but also because of its exceptional importance in the history of Athens and all Greece.

Tyranny at Athens

The early economic and political development of Attica—the district around Athens—was slower than that of many parts of the Greek world, and it followed a rather different course because such inven-

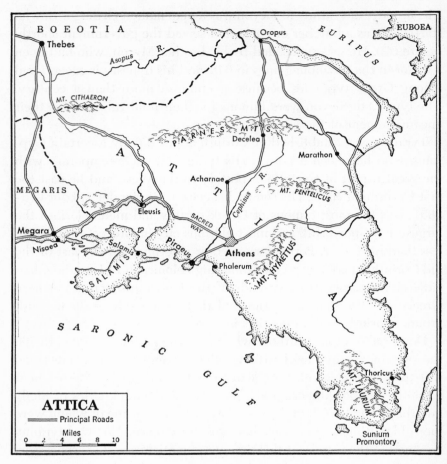

tions as coinage appeared there at a time when conditions were
much more primitive than those prevailing at Miletus or Aegina.
Attica is a peninsula, separated from the rest of Greece by a range
of mountains. It contains neolithic and Mycenaean remains, but apparently the Dorian invaders left it untouched. In historic times, the
inhabitants of the peninsula spoke a dialect of Ionic Greek, though
the greater part of them probably were descended from Minoan or
neolithic settlers. As was universal in Greece during the Dark Ages,
Attica was divided among many autonomous villages which were
gradually united into larger confederations until Athens ruled all

Attica. While force was sometimes used, the union usually was entered into voluntarily, and in any event the citizens of all communities received full Athenian citizenship. The unification of Attica was completed in the eighth century by the conquest and annexation of Eleusis.

At first Athens was governed by a king (*basileus*) who was aided by a council of nobles known as the Areopagus. Here as elsewhere, however, the aristocrats—ordinarily called eupatrids, "sons of good fathers"—gradually got the upper hand and deprived the king of most of his power. Early in the seventh century the king came to be chosen annually from the aristocracy, and his duties were limited almost entirely to acts of a religious nature. Beside him stood two other annually chosen officials, the *polemarch* who led the army, and the *archon* who looked after the civil administration. There were also six officials who recorded the laws and judicial decisions. After these reforms the Areopagus was made up of former archons. Only eupatrids were eligible to these high offices, and officials apparently were chosen by the Areopagus. Government was thus limited to the small eupatrid class, below whom stood three lesser ranks of citizens, classified according to their wealth: *hippeis* ("knights," or men rich enough to own a horse), *zeugitae* (men owning a "yoke" of oxen), and the *thetes,* who were the poor.

The tardiness of Attica's development was the result in large measure of her poverty. Her soil was rocky and poor except in the plain north of Athens, and not until grain was imported in quantity could Attica support a large population. Agricultural poverty was compensated to a certain extent by riches of other sorts, notably the silver mines of Mount Laurium at the tip of the peninsula, the clay beds along the Cephisus River from which excellent pottery could be made, and the famous marble of Mount Pentelicus. Even in the ninth and eighth centuries, Athenian potters produced a type of pottery called "Dipÿlon ware," and in later times ceramics became a major industry at Athens, where a large quarter of the city was called the "Ceramicus." The silver mines, on the other hand, apparently were not worked much until about 600. The Athenians took to the sea at a rather early date, but their harbor at Phalerum was constantly menaced by pirates from Salamis until this island was taken from Megara about 600. Athens had no part in the early colonial expansion, and she did not even cast her own coins until a few years before 600.

Cylon and Draco

In spite of her economic backwardness, Athens could not escape the political repercussions of the economic and social revolution in other Greek states. In Attica, as elsewhere, peasants were falling deeply into debt, and the *thetes* were ready to follow anyone who promised relief. The phalanx and hoplites appeared in Attica, and men financially able to provide their followers with heavy armor were in a position to seize the government whether they were eupatrids or not. Thus it came about that many years before a strong commercial class arose in Attica, ambitious persons coveted the glory that shone upon tyrants elsewhere and made premature attempts to establish tyranny at Athens.

The first recorded attempt of this sort was made by Cylon in 632. This young man, an Athenian eupatrid, was the son-in-law of the tyrant of nearby Megara. With the aid of hoplites provided by his father-in-law, Cylon seized the Acropolis at Athens, but the aristocrats drove him out and his followers were butchered by order of the archon Megacles. Before long, a plague broke out in Athens, which enabled Cylon's friends to charge that Megacles had violated the sanctuary of an altar while murdering his victims. Megacles and his family were banished, and the city was purified by a professional purifier from Crete. The story did not end there, however, for Megacles belonged to the powerful family of the Alcmeonidae. Robbed of their estates by exile, the Alcmeonids set out to redeem their fortunes by trade; they established a firm friendship with the kings of Lydia, and presently they became enormously wealthy. They then returned to Athens as embittered opponents of their former friends among the eupatrids. They suffered exile on more than one occasion, but they always returned. They became the most eminent family in the city and rarely was there a time in the next two centuries when an Alcmeonid was not prominent in Athenian politics (see genealogical chart, p. 400).

A few years after Cylon's fiasco, Draco was elected archon (621). Nothing is known of this man except that while in office he established a famous code of laws in harmony with the new spirit of the age. As Draco's laws were presently superseded by still other codes, we know little about them except that later they were regarded as unduly severe—an implication still carried by our word "Draconian." His law regarding homicide, which has been preserved, illustrates the general tendency of the whole code. Heretofore, the punishment of murder had been left to the kinsmen of the murdered man. Draco's law provided that a man accused of willful murder should be tried before the Areopagus, and if found guilty, executed. The prosecution was conducted by the family of the murdered man, not by a state official, and the state stepped in merely to make sure that the accused man really was guilty. Draco's law was designed to prevent the indiscriminate slaughter that sometimes accompanied a blood feud. Moreover, the new law protected the public interest before the gods by making sure of the proper purifications afterward. Draco thus reconciled the interests of family and religion with those of the general public, and in doing so he greatly limited the authority of the *genos*.

Solon

A more important Athenian reformer was Solon. In later times he was hailed as one of Greece's Seven Sages, and his fame was embellished by legends which ancient historians sometimes accepted as facts. We still have about three hundred lines from poems Solon wrote to set forth his purposes and achievements. Though a eupatrid by birth, Solon accumulated a fortune by trade, and he was of a conservative and judicious nature, anxious to avoid extremes. Admirers later said that his favorite motto was "Nothing in excess." His first political activity seems to have been agitation for the conquest of Salamis, and he commanded the expedition which conquered that island. He was rewarded with the archonship in 594, and during his term in office he effected many reforms that were both social and constitutional. The former centered around what he called "freeing the earth and man." Poor citizens had often been compelled to mortgage their families or even their own persons to secure loans, and many had been sold into slavery when they could not pay. Solon ordered the emancipation of all such persons and forbade such mortgages in the future. He also declared null the mortgages on the land itself, thus giving the poor a new start; but he refused the redistribution of all land demanded by more radical reformers. These measures he called the "shaking off of burdens."

A second group of Solon's laws reformed the calendar, the standard weights and measures, and the coinage. Heretofore, Athenian coins had been cast on the standard of Aegina, but Solon adopted that of Euboea, whose drachma was almost one-third lighter (70 Aegina = 100 Euboea). This measure had the double advantage of reducing the merchants' debts by one third and of enabling them to trade more easily with other states on the Euboeic standard—which was now much more widely used than that of Aegina. In such matters as inheritance, Solon granted the individual greater liberty from the shackles of family, thereby weakening the *genos* as a political power. He enacted laws against idleness and encouraged foreign artisans (known as "metics") to settle in Athens. And finally, he proclaimed an amnesty by which the Alcmeonidae—but not the friends of Cylon—were allowed to return to Athens.

While Solon improved the position of merchants and peasants at the expense of the eupatrids, his constitutional reforms were based on a statesmanlike realization that a stable government must receive the support of all classes. He left the actual direction of the government to the wealthy classes, to be sure, but he assured other citizens of a share in it. The old classification of citizens by wealth was revised, with a fourth class added for the very rich: the men of the richest class were called "500-bushel men" because they produced at least that amount of grain (really 750 bushels, for the Attic *medimnos* equaled one and a half bushels); the *hippeis* produced at least 300 *medimnoi* and the *zeugitae* at least 200; the rest of the citizens were *thetes*. Merchants reckoned their status according to their income, counting one drachma as equal to one *medimnos* of grain. In the final analysis, this organization was as much military as it was political, for it reflected the share which each citizen took in national defense. Members of the two highest classes were assigned to the cavalry; the *zeugitae*, serving as hoplites, formed the backbone of the new army; and the *thetes* were light-armed troops or rowers in the navy. Members of all four classes were allowed to attend meetings of the Assembly (called the *Ekklesia*), where they voted for magistrates and decided questions that were laid before them. They also sat as jurors in a new popular court, called the *Heliaea*, to which men convicted in the older aristocratic courts might appeal. Every citizen thus had a small voice in the government, though the important offices were still monopolized by the rich.

A new *Boule*, or Council of Four Hundred, was chosen from the three upper classes with one hundred from each tribe. It debated and prepared the measures that were later laid before the Assembly for ratification. It also took over many of the duties formerly performed by the Areopagus, but the latter body—still made up of ex-archons—continued to function as the court to try crimes against religion and the state, and before it any magistrate might be impeached. The number of archons was raised to nine by the addition of the six officials who had formerly been clerks entrusted with preserving copies of the laws and judicial decisions. The nine archons were chosen annually by a curious method: the Assembly chose forty names (ten from each tribe) from which nine were drawn by lot. Only men of the two upper classes might hold the archonship, but at least Solon's reform opened it to wealthy men who were not eupatrids.

Though many people expected Solon to set himself up as a tyrant, he refused to do so. Later he boasted that his refusal would be the chief foundation of his fame. At the expiration of his term as archon, he withdrew from the city, after asking the Athenians to keep his laws unchanged for ten years. On his return several years later, he took little part in politics though he lived until 558.

Peisistratus

Solon had scarcely left Athens when troubles broke out anew, for his reforms had created two bitterly rival parties in the state. Leaders of both factions sprang from the old eupatrid families, some of whom were willing to accept the new system while others were not. The reactionary aristocratic faction was called the "Plain" because the estates of the eupatrids lay in the plain north of Athens; their opponents, called the "Shore," consisted of those whom Solon had aided, and they were now led by an Alcmeonid, Megacles, grandson of the Megacles who had destroyed Cylon. Quarrels between the Plain and the Shore became so bitter that no archons could be elected in 590 or 585—years which are marked in the archon lists by the word *anarchia*. In 582, the archonship fell to a eupatrid who held it illegally for two years and two months, and who apparently planned to found a tyranny. Eventually he was driven out. The Megarians seized the opportunity to recapture Salamis, and this humiliation gave a new turn to Athenian politics.

Industry and trade throve at Athens during the thirty years that followed Solon's archonship, and a strong merchant class had grown up. At first, these men co-operated politically with the Shore, but presently they became restless in their alliance. The loss of Salamis was a great blow to them, and it made the political fortune of their leader, Peisistratus.

Peisistratus belonged to a eupatrid family. He was related on his mother's side to Solon, and in his youth he adhered to the party of the Shore. His great wealth he owed to silver mines at Laurium. Taking a leaf from Solon's book, Peisistratus led the expedition that recaptured Salamis about 570. He then organized a third political party, called the "Hill," which was dominated by the commercial interests. Peisistratus also attracted a great following among the urban populace, partly by his war reputation and partly because he freely distributed coins cast from the silver produced by his mines. When he claimed that he had been attacked and wounded by political opponents, he was granted a bodyguard, and with the aid of these men he seized the Acropolis (561). Though soon driven from

Athens, he presently entered into an alliance with Megacles, whose daughter he married, and again he took over the city (560). After a few years he quarreled with his father-in-law and once more was driven out (556). This time he fled to Thrace, where he acquired the silver mines of Mount Pangaeus. The silver thus obtained enabled him to hire mercenaries, with whose aid he returned to Athens and founded his third and last tyranny in 546. He ruled Athens thereafter until his death in 527.

Peisistratus carefully refrained from altering Solon's constitution. Archons and other officials were elected by lot as before. The assemblies and courts continued to meet. Peisistratus apparently held no official position, yet his popularity with the people enabled him to manage elections and to obtain the laws he wanted. After he had exiled his leading opponents (including the Alcmeonidae), he filled the Areopagus with men of his own faction. His opponents were disarmed, but he retained a large troop of mercenaries who lived with him in a fortified palace on the Acropolis.

Though the power of Peisistratus rested primarily upon the populace and mercenaries, his policies were usually designed to promote the interests of the commercial and industrial classes. He brought a prosperity to all Athens which caused men later to compare his reign with the mythical Golden Age. He created a large class of small landowners by distributing the confiscated estates of his opponents. He made many public improvements and beautified the city, building a new agora, an aqueduct, and several temples, thereby adding to his renown and giving employment to his followers. Though he levied a 5 per cent tax on agriculture, this burden was not great, and most of his lavish expenditures were met with silver from his own mines.

Peisistratus remained at peace with his Greek neighbors, but he actively promoted colonial expansion. A man who had helped him win his third tyranny was allowed to rule the island of Naxos. An aristocrat who might perhaps have become a formidable rival was sent to the Thracian Chersonesus where he was set up as tyrant. A few years later, about 535, Peisistratus conquered Sigeum on the opposite shore of the Hellespont, and placed it under one of his illegitimate sons. Another son was made ruler of the nearby island of Lesbos, where a considerable Athenian population was settled. These conquests paved the way for the importation of Crimean wheat to Athens, and Peisistratus thus laid down the main line of Athenian expansion. He was the Father of the Athenian Empire.

When Peisistratus died in 527 he was succeeded by his two sons, Hippias and Hipparchus. The former attended to politics while the latter looked after public improvements and the arts. For several years all went well and there was a general reconciliation. Trouble began again in 514, when Hipparchus was murdered. Thereafter Hippias's fright made him cruel and suspicious. A far more serious blow fell a little later when the Persians captured Thrace, including the Pangaean silver mines from which Hippias and his father had derived so much of their revenue. The Alcmeonidae, again in exile after 514, ingratiated themselves with the Delphic oracle by building a beautiful and expensive temple, and thereafter the oracle answered all inquiries with the refrain, "Athens must first be set free." Athenian aristocrats, likewise hoping for an end to tyranny, invited Spartan intervention. A Spartan army marched on Athens in 510; Hippias fled to Sigeum, and later joined the Persians; and the Athenian tyranny collapsed.

Sparta and the Greek Aristocracy

Tyranny in Greece arose in consequence of the economic and social revolutions that accompanied colonial expansion and the rise of trade, but not all Greece was disturbed by such developments. Thessaly and northern Greece remained agricultural and backward; there was little change in much of central Greece; and in the Peloponnesus, Sparta made herself the leader of agrarian interests and the old aristocracies everywhere by bracing herself to resist the new spirit.

Sparta, the principal city of the Peloponnesus, was located in Laconia, the valley of the Eurotas River and the heart of the best agricultural land of Greece. Laconia had been important in Mycenaean times (Sparta was the home of Menalaus and his wife, the famous Helen of Troy), but about the year 1000 it was overrun by

Dorian invaders. Recent excavations have shown, however, that civilization was not completely destroyed and that Sparta was in fact somewhat less barbarous than most of her neighbors in the Dark Ages. When economic conditions deteriorated in the eighth century, and other states began their colonial and commercial expansion, the Spartans preferred to seek relief by conquering their neighbors. About 740 they attacked Messenia, their neighbor to the west, and before the end of the century they had conquered the whole southern half of the Peloponnesus—thereafter called Lacedaemonia. They drove out many of the former inhabitants and reduced the rest to serfdom. Sparta thereby committed herself definitely to a militaristic and agrarian economy.

In later ages, the Spartans traced their peculiar social and political institutions to a law-giver named Lycurgus, who was supposed to have lived in the ninth century. But even the Spartans knew that he was largely mythical, and modern scholars usually deny his existence. The institutions attributed to him were the result of a long evolution which took place primarily during the seventh and sixth centuries, when other Greek states were in the hands of tyrants. This Spartan evolution began when a Messenian revolt, toward the middle of the seventh century, so frightened the Spartan overlords that fear of rebellion dominated their policy thereafter. Spartan leaders made it their principal aim to augment their military power. At the beginning of this century, Sparta had been a leader in Greek civilization, attracting artists and literary men from other parts of Greece. All cultural pursuits were now rigorously repressed as enervating; Spartans were forbidden to engage in trade; and the only lawful money was in the form of heavy iron bars. Sparta turned her back squarely upon the new life then dawning in other parts of Greece.

Under the new regime the population of Lacedaemonia was divided into three classes: the Spartans, the *perioikoi,* and the helots. The first class was made up of professional soldiers whose sole task was to defend the Spartan state against foreign and domestic foes. They were granted the best lands and helots to work them. The *perioikoi*—or "dwellers around"—were second-class citizens living in villages, owning their own fields, and enjoying considerable liberty in local matters. In time of war they fought as light-armed troops, and they were allowed to carry on whatever trade and industry were deemed necessary. The helots, who were descendants of the conquered peoples, were serfs belonging to the state. They worked on the farms of the aristocrats and both Spartans and *perioikoi* had every incentive to keep them in a permanent position of subserviency. It has been estimated that at the end of the sixth century there were about 25,000 Spartans, about 100,000 *perioikoi,* and about 250,000 helots, including the women and children in each case.

Lacedaemonia was governed by the Spartan "peers," or first-class citizens, all of whom were theoretically equal though in practice the great majority had little voice in political matters. Sparta had two lines of hereditary kings, belonging to rival families, who ruled simultaneously and who nominally governed the state and commanded the army. After the seventh century, however, these kings rarely exercised much power in time of peace. All Spartan peers over thirty years of age were members of the Assembly, which approved policies and elected magistrates, somewhat like the Athenian *Ekklesia,* but voting in Sparta was done simply by shouting, and the magistrates decided which faction had shouted the louder. The Assembly therefore had little real power. The "Senate" was composed of thirty members: the two kings and twenty-eight others, all above the age of sixty, who were elected for life by the Assembly. These men framed the general policies of state. Most important of all, however, were the five "ephors," elected annually by the Assembly, who were the magistrates charged with administering the state. They gradually took over most of the royal powers, dominating both Assembly and Senate; and the primitive method of voting in the Assembly made them virtually a self-perpetuating body.

Spartan Education

The whole education of Spartan youths was designed with their future duties constantly in view. As Spartan peers were a relatively small group supported by the labor of helots on state lands, the state might demand all their services and direct their entire education. Boys were trained to be good soldiers, girls to be the mothers of good soldiers. State supervision began at birth, for only those infants were permitted to live who passed the scrutiny of an examining board. Boys who survived this first test passed their childhood with their mothers. At seven years of age they were taken by the state for training until they reached the age of twenty. During these years they were subjected to a severe discipline designed to increase their physical strength and endurance, though mental training was almost wholly eliminated. When this rigorous drill was completed, the young Spartans entered the army as hoplites. They were permitted to marry, but they spent the greater part of their lives with the troops. Until the age of sixty, they were required to eat at least one meal a day with their companies at the barracks. This lifelong discipline made the Spartans formidable soldiers and inspired them with the spirit of obedience and respect for the law, but we shall see that totalitarian Sparta paid an appalling price for the power thus gained.

So successful were these reforms in the early days that Sparta became the strongest military power in Greece and was much admired by aristocrats everywhere. In later times, the "Lycurgan" system was praised as the last word in moral and political wisdom, and "Spartan virtue" was extolled as the natural product of this rigorous training. Praise became so extravagant that it is now impossible to describe the Spartan system in detail. We know it chiefly through the writings of Athenian aristocrats, and we cannot tell how much of their panegyric is accurate description and how much is sheer utopianizing. A recent student of these idealizations, writing under the significant title, *Le mirage spartiate,* has shown how greatly the sordid reality differed from the utopias pictured by bemused admirers.

The Spartan system may have produced armies that could win victories, but it could not produce leaders with the intelligence to make good use of their victories. Though more than once Sparta's armies put her in a position to dominate Greece, she failed to do so each time because of the intellectual and moral weakness of her

leaders. In the long run, the Spartan peers were the ones who suffered most under this system: brutalized by constant military drill,
their lives regimented in every particular, they could not hold their
own mentally or spiritually, or even physically, against their rivals.
Eventually they were almost exterminated. In the sixth century,
however, these catastrophies were as yet unforeseen, and everywhere Greek aristocrats who feared and hated tyranny looked with
favor upon the rising might of Sparta.

Note

Fustel de Coulanges

Among the first to recognize the true character of the ancient *polis*, and
the all-pervading influence of religion in its life was the French scholar,
N. D. Fustel de Coulanges (1830–1889). After studies at Paris and in
Greece, Fustel became professor of history at the University of Stras-
bourg in 1860, where he published his famous book, *La cité antique*, four
years later. In this book he emphasized the influence of religion in the ancient city, examined the religious nature of ancient patriotism, and attributed the decline of the city-state system to the various forces (first philosophy, later Christianity) which undermined this patriotic religion. The
book is a masterpiece, written in a brilliant and persuasive literary style,
and its fundamental ideas are usually sound—though individual statements often require extensive modification. The war of 1870 greatly disturbed Fustel, who entered into a pamphlet controversy with the famous
German historian of Rome, Theodor Mommsen (see biographical note in
Vol. II), regarding the justification of the war and the question of Alsace-
Lorraine. It is difficult to read these pamphlets today without conceding
that the brilliant Frenchman got decidedly the better of his Teutonic adversary.

Fustel had become professor at the École Normale Supérieure in Paris
in 1870, just before the outbreak of the war. His writing thereafter was
devoted largely to the period from the fourth to the ninth centuries after
Christ, when the Ancient World was passing into the Middle Ages. In a
large work, published in part posthumously, *Histoire des institutions politiques de l'ancienne France* (6 vols., 1888–1892), he strongly attacked
the then current theory that the German invaders into the western Roman
Empire destroyed nearly everything and rebuilt after their own tastes,
making Europe into an expanded Germany. He strongly defended the
Roman origin of most of the institutions of medieval France. The great

mass of material he collected is invaluable to scholars, but his extreme interpretations of it must be criticized carefully before they are accepted.

More important than Fustel's histories were his pupils. During his twenty years at the École Normale, he trained a generation of scholars in history and kindred subjects who, though not blind to his faults, gladly bore witness to his powerful influence upon their thinking. He helped make the period between 1890 and 1914 one of the most brilliant in the whole long history of French scholarship. Fustel was perhaps the most eloquent exponent of the theory, widely held toward the end of the nineteenth century, that history is an exact science, comparable to physics or chemistry, and he firmly believed that his own writings represented the same impersonal truth that characterized those of the natural scientists. No one questions his high sincerity, but the extreme views he set forth in his later writings show how difficult—if not impossible—it is to approach such an ideal. His views on the all-importance of religion were later taken up by leaders of French clericalism—which would have distressed Fustel greatly, had he foreseen it, for he was an *incroyant* who had no sympathy whatsoever with the political party that thus exploited his reputation and his ideas. See Paul Guiraud, *Fustel de Coulanges* (1896) and J. M. Tourneur-Aumont, *Fustel de Coulanges* (1931).

X The Greek Renaissance

URING THIS FERTILE SIXTH CENTURY THE INTELLECTUAL
and cultural life of Greece developed hand in hand with her economic, social, and political life, and every aspect of Greek civilization took on new forms. Strangely enough, scholars sometimes call this the "archaic" period in Greek history, presumably because its culture seems antique and primitive to persons whose principal interest lies in the more highly developed fifth century. Others refer to it as the "orientalizing" period because Greek artists and thinkers were then learning much from their oriental contemporaries. Neither of these names is very satisfactory, however, for the men of the sixth century were creating something that was then distinctly new and distinctly Greek. They learned much from their predecessors and from their oriental neighbors, it is true, but they were not "archaizing" or "orientalizing." On the contrary, their intellectual creations were clearly a consequence of the social and political revolutions of Greece in their day. These men of the sixth century, living under radically new conditions, found that their traditional guides to life were no longer adequate. They therefore created new ones, thereby instigating the great burst of activity that brought the stagnant Dark Ages to an end. At the same time, economic prosperity inspired an enthusiasm that enabled them to express the fundamental ideas of their age in brilliant fashion. A new Greece came into being, and this period of renewed creative activity can best be called "the Greek Renaissance."

In countless ways this new Greece resembled the Italy of the fourteenth and fifteenth centuries after Christ. The Greek tyrants were the Medici of their day, and the poets, artists, and thinkers who glorified their courts gave the age a place in the cultural history of Greece comparable to that of the Italian Renaissance in the history of western Europe. In each case, economic and political revolutions, characterized by commercial and colonial expansion, city-states, and tyranny, preceded and accompanied the intellectual rebirth, and the altered life of the new age engendered new ideas of many sorts. In fashioning these ideas, the ancient Greeks, like the Italians of the later period, could not escape the heritage of their past. They remained under the spell of Homer, just as the men of the Italian Renaissance continued to bear the marks of the Christian Middle Ages, and in each case old ideas reappeared in new forms after a long period of dormancy. The Italian humanists made a great fuss over their revival of pagan antiquity, and artists intentionally copied ancient models. There was a parallel, though quite unintended, resurgence of Minoan and Mycenaean ideas during the Greek Renaissance, especially in matters of religion. Nevertheless, in Greece as in Italy, the persistence of old traditions and the revival of still more ancient ones did not prevent the period from being essentially one of new ideals and a new spirit.

Homer had looked at the world through the eyes of the Greek nobility. He pictured his heroes as possessing to an eminent degree such aristocratic virtues as courage, honor, and a desire to excel, pride, magnificence, and hospitality to strangers. Hesiod, on the other hand, praised the more prosaic peasant virtues of hard work, attention to detail, and thrift, pushing the latter almost to the point of closefistedness. Subsequent literature, most of which was of aristocratic origin, shows that throughout their history the Greek nobility continued to hold Homer's views of excellence; and no doubt many peasants retained the Hesiodic virtues, though in later times they found no new spokesman comparable to him. But members of the new social classes that rose to prominence in the seventh and sixth centuries judged men by other standards than those extolled by Homer and Hesiod. They no longer admired the predatory qualities of the Homeric heroes, and to them justice seemed preferable to military glory. The virtue dearest to the hearts of the new moralists was moderation as shown in Solon's motto, "Nothing to excess," whereas the old heroes had been insatiable in their desires for many things beside honor and glory. The vice now denounced most eloquently was insolence, which embraced many qualities once highly esteemed in the heroes of the *Iliad*. A new way of life had given men a wholly different conception of moral excellence.

In sixth century Greece, as in sixteenth century Europe, a deep religious reformation accompanied the social revolution. Homer and the old aristocracy, and even Hesiod, had thought of the gods on Olympus as ruling the world much as the Greek nobles of that day would have liked to rule in their own mundane spheres. The gods had their long genealogies and all the other aristocratic trappings of the Greek nobility; they partook of the same virtues and vices as their aristocratic worshipers; they expected the same subserviency from their inferiors; and they showed the same high irresponsibility. Changing political ideals inevitably brought a decline of respect for such gods as these. In fact, the beginning of this disrespect is clearly visible in Homer himself, for it is difficult to believe that the poet really adored the deities of whom he told such scandalous tales. Moreover, the worship of the Olympians had long been supplemented by countless cults of far more ancient origin which were especially popular among the lower classes. These cults took on new importance when economic prosperity gave those who cultivated them a higher station in society. At the same time, the great migrations to the cities and colonies were tearing men away from their old shrines and old forms of worship, and introducing them to new and less localized cults. In the colonies, for example, men from many places united in the worship of gods selected by the oikist, and we shall see that new cults, such as that of Dionysus, swept over Greece in the sixth century without any official support.

At this time, too, Greek thinkers suddenly acquired much new information about the physical world and began developing new theories about it. Much of their factual information came from the Orient, where priests and scholars had long been accumulating scientific knowledge that had not come to the attention of the Greeks. But after the Greeks had once started studying these matters, their insatiable curiosity encouraged them to make further re-searches for themselves and they quickly overtook their eastern predecessors. More important than the new information, however, were the new theories based upon it. Here, too, the Greeks learned something from the Orient, but in general their theories were their own creation, bearing the unmistakable stamp of Greek origin. This speculation regarding the nature of the physical world was something new, and it was closely connected with the economic and political revolutions of the day.

In earlier times the Greeks had not thought deeply upon the origin of the universe. Hesiod vaguely attributed the creation of all things to the gods, whose genealogies he developed at great length, packing much homely wisdom into his account, but all this was only mythology and poetry about which he admittedly was not very sure. Regarding the origin of the world he could only say, as was appropriate in an agricultural society, that it grew out of something else, perhaps an egg or seed of some sort. But the sixth century was a time of active material construction: manufacturing was on a larger scale; houses and temples, aqueducts and roads, city walls and ships, were being built as never before; and Greek engineers were then achieving their greatest triumphs. All this creative activity fostered new mental patterns, and men asked more insistently than before how and out of what the world had been created. They began to think in the terms of engineering rather than those of agriculture. It is highly significant that the most active centers of sixth century speculation were the Ionian cities, especially Miletus, where the new industrial and engineering activities were most highly developed. Here intellectual pioneers cast the Homeric mythology aside and made valiant attempts to understand and explain the world in the light of the new knowledge, the new thought patterns, and the new social ideals.

Civic Religion

One of the more striking features of this Renaissance period was the rise of a civic religion centering around patriotism to the city-state. This new development was encouraged by the tyrants, but it merely exaggerated certain traits of the older Greek religion. The ancient Greeks never shared the modern ideal of a complete separation of Church and State. Magistrates were also priests, laws and institutions were supposedly of divine origin, public festivals assumed a religious character, and citizens had various religious duties which the state forced them to perform. A man usually might think or say what he pleased about the gods, but the state compelled him to worship them. Citizenship established a formal relationship between a man and his city's gods, and the political community was identical in membership with the religious community. The government of one could not be separated from that of the other.

In early times religious ceremonies were presided over by the aristocratic leaders of the community, though they usually received the aid and advice of professional priests. These aristocrats decided when and how the ceremonies should be performed, they interpreted religious law, and they offered the sacrifices. When the political power of the nobility declined and authority fell to elected magistrates, the new officials took over the control of religion. In this, as in so many matters, the new spirit first showed itself in the colonies, where men more easily broke away from old traditions and where the oikists decided what cults should be set up. Before long, however, the elected magistrates of Greece were making radical innovations in religion. All the great lawgivers issued sacred as well as civil laws. Nevertheless, the old intimacy of the aristocracy with heaven was still recognized to the extent of permitting only eupatrids to hold the specifically religious magistracies, and officials were selected by lot, which supposedly left the final choice to the gods themselves. Under their political leadership, worship of the gods inevitably became much secularized for it was aimed not only at securing the favor of the gods but also at stimulating the patriotic fervor of the worshipers.

At the same time the gods themselves took on a political coloring as the guardian deities of the particular city-state in which each happened to be worshiped. It had long been the custom in Greece for various social groups—towns, villages, tribes, or families—to worship minor deities and the heroes from whom their members believed themselves descended. The greater gods owed their grandeur in large part to the fact that they were worshiped by larger groups of worshipers. The tyrants of the seventh and sixth centuries encouraged the worship of the guardian deities of their cities, hoping that the prestige of their gods would rise with the splendor of their cult, and that this in turn would raise the prestige of the city and the patriotism of its citizens. Peisistratus in particular was much interested in guiding the religious enthusiasm of his subjects into patriotic channels. He expanded the myth and cult of Theseus, the alleged founder of the city; he showered favors upon many lesser cults; and above all he glorified the patron goddess of his city, Pallas Athena.

Athena was an old Minoan goddess, the protectress of citadels and cities, and at an early date she was identified with a rather similar Achaean goddess named Pallas. Her worship under one or both names was widespread in Mycenaean Greece, and in Homer she is pictured as a warrior in armor who befriended the Greeks. She had always been worshiped at Athens, which owed her its name, but her supreme position there dates from the days of Peisistratus. Herodotus tells a story of how the tyrant made use of the goddess. When about to return after his first exile he spread a report that Athena herself would bring him back to her city. He then dressed a tall, good-looking girl named Phye in armor to resemble statues of the goddess and made his triumphal entry into the city with her standing beside him in his chariot. Perhaps he hoped to deceive the populace with this masquerade—the Greeks were quite willing to believe that the gods often appeared on earth in human form—but more probably he intended it as an impressive pageant with a religious tinge. In either case, he was consciously exploiting Athena to promote his own political ends.

After firmly establishing himself in power, Peisistratus continued his attentions to his patron goddess. He put her picture and that of her owl on the coins he cast, where they retained the place of honor throughout Athenian history. On the Acropolis he built the Virgin Goddess a large temple, called the Parthenon (*parthenos* means "virgin"), and a century later this temple was replaced by the even more magnificent structure whose ruins still stand. Peisistratus also inaugurated the great festival known as the Panathenaea, which was celebrated every fourth year with athletic games, dramatic contests, and feasting. One of the principal features of this festival was the great procession depicted on the famous marbles which once decorated the frieze of the Parthenon and now repose in the British Museum. By all this, Peisistratus made Athena the great goddess of Athens. Athens was her city, she was its goddess, and their glory could not be separated. Civic religion and civic patriotism went together hand in hand.

The Twelve Gods

The civic religions tended to localize gods by attaching each to the cities where he or she was especially worshiped, but they could not carry this localization to its logical conclusion. No Greek city ever declared, with the exclusiveness of the Hebrews, that its patron god was the only god that existed or even the only one its citizens should worship. The Greek people had always recognized many gods, and the major outlines of their polytheistic mythology had been worked out in Mycenaean times. The great poems of Homer presented this mythology in splendid form, and thereafter Greeks felt themselves attached to the whole Olympic pantheon. In spite of the civic religion, therefore, or in addition to it, every Greek city had shrines and cults to many deities. Eventually, however, twelve gods were selected for especial reverence.

Apparently it was in Ionia during the seventh and sixth centuries that these Twelve Gods were first distinguished above all others, for in Homer and Hesiod the various deities tapered off in importance down to the very minor spirits of field and stream. First among the Twelve stood Zeus, "father of gods and men," and beside him were his sister-wife, Hera, and his brother Poseidon. The latter had once been an earth deity interested in horses, but eventually he assumed rulership of the sea. Zeus's daughter Athena had sprung fully armed from his head, while Apollo and Artemis were his twin children by Leto. Ares, a fierce warrior, and Hermes, the messenger of the gods, were likewise sons of Zeus. Hephaestus, the crippled son of Zeus and

Hera, was a skilled artisan and had Aphrodite as his faithless wife. Last of all came the two sisters of Zeus, Hestia and Demeter. Some of these gods, notably the last two, received scant attention from Homer, and others were not worshiped widely as individuals, but as a group the Twelve Gods were honored throughout Greece.

Zeus, the leader of the Twelve, was an old Nordic sky-god, worshiped under cognate names from India and Persia to Italy and Germany. From his first appearance in Greece he had shown a tendency to merge with other deities, both Nordic and Minoan, taking over their cults, their myths, and their powers. Homer and Hesiod pictured him as the most powerful of the gods and ruler over the others. He had countless sanctuaries in all parts of Greece, but he was not the tutelary deity of any city and he had no connection with any civic religion. It thus became easier for him to assume the position of god of all Greeks or of all men. He eventually came to possess nearly all the divine attributes, and it might be said that he attained universality by absorbing his rivals. In the end, Greek theologians and philosophers elevated (or degraded) him from his old position as the benign father of gods and men to the frigid dignity of an impersonal cosmic force—something like the force of gravitation perhaps. But while Zeus thus received the honor and the glory, the god who exercised the most influence in determining the higher development of Greek religion was Phoebus Apollo.

Apollo and the Delphic Oracle

The early poets and theologians did not accord to Apollo an outstanding place among the Twelve Gods, and though in many ways he was the most typically Greek of them all, his origin is obscure and controversial. Eminent scholars maintain that he came from Lycia, in southwestern Asia Minor, and thus at first was not Greek at all. Others insist that he was an old Nordic god worshipped by shepherds, whose flocks he protected and to whom he taught music and the other arts. It is not improbable that he, like Zeus and many others, was a composite deity whose attributes were drawn from many sources. Homer's Apollo was primarily an archer, "far-shooting" and "having a silver bow," whose arrows brought pestilence and sudden

death. He favored the Trojans in the great war, which perhaps may
be taken as evidence of his Asiatic origin. He developed greatly during the next few centuries, however, and eventually he came to
resemble the finest type of young Greek aristocrat, good-looking,
skilled in sports and music, an ardent lover, generous, sociable, and
high-minded—altogether a very likable sort of young fellow, "the
god of perpetual youth."

The Greeks always emphasized Apollo's purity, and he in turn
imposed a special purity upon his worshipers. In fact, this purity
was closely associated with his beauty, which the Greeks called
"radiant" (*phoibos*) and which one modern scholar has compared
to "the beauty of holiness." This personal purity gave Apollo jurisdiction over the rites of purification by which men sought to maintain
peace with the gods, and he became an expert in matters of law and
justice. Purity also gave him the divine arts of healing, and Apollo
became a physician especially skilled at curing insanity. This malady
supposedly was caused by moral stains (*miasmata*) and might be
cured by proper purifications. And finally, Apollo's gift of prophecy
gave him many oracles, the most celebrated of which was at Delphi.

Delphi lies in a little valley at the foot of Mount Parnassus in central Greece, where a round stone in the temple was supposed to
mark the exact center of the earth. At first the place was called Pytho, and from very ancient times it had been the seat of an oracle.
In these early times, Apollo had no connection with Pytho, but
presently he took it over and it was renamed Delphi. A mythological
version of his coming is preserved in the Homeric *Hymn to the Pythian Apollo,* which probably emanated from Delphi in the seventh
century. While Pytho appears four times in the *Iliad* and *Odyssey,*
there is no mention of Delphi; and Hesiod mentioned Pytho only
once, though he lived only a few miles away. Then, during the
seventh century, Delphi became famous throughout Greece, and
pilgrims began coming from all parts of the Greek world to consult
the god. The Delphic oracle became the most famous in Greece,
rivaled only by those of Zeus at Dodona in Epirus and of Ammon
(the Egyptian Amon) near Cyrene in Africa.

In the early times, apparently, the god gave his answers through the leaves of a laurel tree in the sacred enclosure. Later they came from the mouth of a priestess, called the Pythia, who sat on a tripod in the sanctuary. The details of how the oracle answered questions are not well understood, but it seems probable that an inspired priestess entered into a real or feigned trance and uttered inarticulate sounds which the priests "interpreted" and arranged in Homeric hexameters. (The theory that this trance was caused by fumes from a cavern is a late rationalization based on no good evidence.) Several years ago a number of lead tablets were found at Dodona on which were written questions that worshipers had asked the god there—or, to speak more accurately, that they had hired the priests to ask for them. These questions concerned such personal and everyday matters as recovery from illness, safe return from a journey, the paternity of an expected child, and the like. While there is no corresponding evidence from Delphi, the great majority of the questions put to Apollo undoubtedly were of the same trivial sort. When the oracle's reputation was at its height, however, rulers often sent to ask the god important questions on matters of state. The oracle spoke only on nine days in the year—the seventh of each month except during the three months of winter, when Apollo vacationed in Africa—and on these days Delphi was so thronged with visitors that two or even three priestesses were kept busy prophesying. Scores of replies allegedly given by the oracle have been preserved. While some undoubtedly are apocryphal, many are authentic.

Delphic Ethics and Politics

In addition to answering questions about mundane matters, the priests at Delphi set themselves up as religious and ethical teachers for all Greece. On the walls of their temple they inscribed a large number of ethical precepts, "Know thyself," "Nothing to excess," and the like, which expressed the spirit of sixth century Greece at its best. Delphi was also the source of the stories of the "Seven Sages of Greece," whose wisdom was expressed in similar epigrams. Countless other stories were current in Greece, each centering around an utterance by the oracle which gave the god's opinion as to who were the most pious, the most fortunate, and the wisest of men. Several of these stories appear in Herodotus, who had close connections with the priests at Delphi. The oracle also gave advice on how to worship the gods, sometimes setting new standards of justice or ordering the establishment of new cults, but more often suggesting that the best way to worship was with a pure heart. Some of these oracular utterances remind us of Gospel stories, such as the parable of the Pharisee and the publican or that of the widow's mite. The Delphic oracle thus played a distinguished role in the moral evolution of Greece.

The priests at Delphi also came to wield great political power. The policies they favored usually were conservative and enlightened, and of a broadly national character; but the priests also knew how to look after their own interests, and, it must be admitted, they were sometimes influenced by the value of the gifts given to their god. Their position at the center of Greece enabled them accumulate reliable information about conditions everywhere, which they shrewdly placed at the disposition of the god. At first the oracle encouraged the tyrants, but later it opposed tyranny, and in general it favored Sparta and the aristocracies.

Much has been written about the Delphic backing of colonization and "Delphic imperialism," and most of it is exaggerated. Colonists often consulted the oracle before setting out, and the oracle usually gave encouraging replies, but there is no reason to believe that it ever did more than encourage colonists who had already decided to go or that it gave specific directions as to where to go. If the colony failed, the colonists disappeared and the oracle's advice was forgotten or explained away; if it succeeded, the oracle's fame was spread to the corners of the Greek world. Therefore the god could always afford to encourage such enterprises.

The great causes approved by the god usually won. This success was evidence not merely of the priests' skill at picking winners but also of the oracle's influence in promoting victory. As the political power of the priests increased, ambitious persons often tried to dominate them, and several "sacred wars" were fought for the purpose—with the aggressor, of course, declaring loudly that he was defending the god's "liberty" against someone else. The first recorded sacred war came shortly after 600, and others occurred at intervals throughout Greek history. In general, however, the oracle managed to maintain its autonomy, and Delphi remained a tiny neutral state.

The Greek Mysteries

These various cults show only one side of the Greek religion in the sixth century, and that side was perhaps not the most important one. While the civic religions were no doubt an effective stimulus to patriotism, they could scarcely satisfy the religious longings of truly devout persons, and the worship of Apollo appealed especially to the upper classes. Many obscure persons had continued to worship the old Minoan gods, and these old cults took on a new popularity in the sixth century. These various Minoan cults had much in common. They all taught the doctrine of immortality, which the famous Greek cults tended to slight; they provided sacraments which assured worshipers of happiness in the next world; and they emphasized individual responsibility in religious matters. These cults were called "mystery religions." For reasons unknown to us, their followers held their ceremonies in private, admitting only properly prepared sympathizers and often requiring an oath of secrecy as to what happened—one result of which is that we still think of a "mystery" as something secret or not understood. Because of the secrecy which enshrouded them, we cannot give a full description of what the mysteries were like, but we know that their sacred ceremonies conferred powers or benefits of some sort upon the worshiper.

First of all may be mentioned the mysteries at Eleusis, an Attic town about fifteen miles from Athens. This worship dates back to Minoan times and had been preserved, quietly and obscurely, through the Mycenaean period and the Dark Ages. In the seventh and sixth centuries, it enjoyed a great revival. Before the unification of Attica, the mysteries had been under the protection of the family that ruled at Eleusis, and from this family the high priests were later chosen. The mysteries were favored by Peisistratus, who built a great temple at Eleusis, and in his day they almost attained the dignity of a state cult. Initiation at Eleusis was still sought in Roman times by such eminent persons as Cicero and Augustus, and in spite of Christianity, the mysteries continued to be celebrated regularly until Eleusis was destroyed by the Goths, A.D. 396.

Our principal source of information regarding the mysteries at Eleusis is the Homeric *Hymn to Demeter,* which originated there before 600 B.C. At considerable length, this poem tells of the abduction of Persephone by Pluto, of the wanderings of Demeter in grief at her loss, of her recovery of her daughter, and of how she founded the rites at Eleusis in memory of the event. The whole earth, which had become barren during Demeter's wanderings, again was laden with fruits and flowers when Persephone was found. The myth is the old, old story of the death and resurrection of vegetation, as typified in the dying and rising god. Those who were "initiated" into the mysteries, or went through the prescribed sacraments, were "born again," and this rebirth assured them a blessed immortality hereafter. "Happy is he among mortal men," says the *Hymn* near its close, "who has seen these mysteries; but he who remains uninitiated, and takes no part in them, never shares an equal fate in the dark Nether World."

Mysteries were celebrated twice a year at Eleusis. The "Lesser Mysteries," which consisted principally of purifications, came in the spring, and the "Greater Mysteries" lasted for several days in the fall. Only those persons might participate in the latter who had gone through the former; and further purifications and abstinences were required during the early days of the second ceremony. Then came a great procession along the "Sacred Way" from Athens to Eleusis. Next day the worshipers, who were called "mystae," assembled in the "Hall of Initiation" at Eleusis, where the ceremonies were explained in detail. Ancient writers allude vaguely to things done, things seen, and the things said there: the first probably were a

---

• Note for Plate 21. This relief, found in the ruins of the temple of Demeter at Eleusis, dates from about 450 B.C. It shows Demeter explaining the mysteries to a boy (Triptolemus) while her daughter Persephone (Kore) puts a crown on his head. Demeter is giving Triptolemus a head of grain. (*Photo, National Museum, Athens.*)

Plate 21.   Demeter and Persephone with Triptolemus

Boy Playing Lyre (Courtesy, Museum of Fine Arts, Boston)

Wrestlers (National Museum, Athens)

Plate 22

mystery play or passion play, acting out the myth of Demeter and Persephone; the second, various sacred objects on display; and the third, explanations. The *mystae* had been fasting, in memory of Demeter's fast during her search for her daughter, but "after all was said and done"—this quaint expression seems to have originated in the mysteries—they ceremoniously ate sacred food and drank a sacred drink. The ceremonies were then continued in a darkened room with the singing of hymns, the waving of torches, and the sounding of gongs; and as they reached a climax the doors of a brightly lighted room were thrown open to show statues of the two goddesses and a priest solemnly holding up an ear of wheat, the symbol of Demeter and of immortality. These ceremonies at Eleusis must have presented a very impressive spectacle (see Plate 21).

Dionysus

The mysteries of Dionysus were rather different. Though known in Mycenaean Greece (his name appears on one of the Pylos tablets), this god was probably of Minoan or Asiatic origin, and his worshipers sprang mostly from the lower classes. Homer and Hesiod barely mention him, but we have fragments of two Homeric hymns in his honor. According to the myth, he was the son of Zeus and Semele (a daughter of the king of Thebes), and he was born under marvelous circumstances. His many adventures included a journey to the east, and wherever he went he was accompanied by a troop of worshipers who introduced the cultivation of the vine. After his death, he returned from Hades with his mother, and together they ascended Olympus. He was not powerful enough, however, to force his way into the company of the Twelve Gods.

Dionysus was worshiped in a wild and unrestrained manner, especially by women called Maenads or Bacchae, who danced and shrieked on the mountains at night. These demonstrations were called *orgia*—whence our word "orgy"—and remind us of the prophets of Baal in the days of Elijah or of our own "Holy Rollers." These orgies stood in marked contrast to the solemn and stately rites with which Demeter was honored. Carried away by a divine frenzy or enthusiasm—the word "enthusiasm" means literally, "god within"

—the Maenads believed that they were possessed by the god. Most Greeks disapproved of such extreme manifestations, however, and presently the barbaric wildness of the rites was toned down. When the divine inspiration had become milder, it spread through all Greece. It was introduced into the mysteries at Eleusis and even into the worship of the eminently respectable Apollo. A tomb of Dionysus was shown at Delphi, where he presided during the three winter months when Apollo was absent and the oracle silent. Festivals known as the Greater and Lesser Dionysia were celebrated in his honor at Athens in the sixth century. Like the Eleusinian mysteries, the cult of Dionysus strengthened belief in immortality, and Dionysiac enthusiasm was taken as proof that every man has within him a spark of divinity.

Orphism

The religious movement known as Orphism developed out of these mysteries. Our first mention of the "famous Orpheus" comes from a minor poet of the later sixth century, and pictures of him on a stone carving and on vase paintings date from about that time. The Greeks believed that Orpheus was a great poet and singer, a son of one of the Muses, who had lived before the Trojan War. No less a critic than Plato himself regarded Orpheus as a poet worthy to be mentioned along with Homer and Hesiod, and countless poems circulated under his name. It was said that his sweet song had the power to move trees and stones and to tame the hearts of the most ferocious beasts. When his wife Eurydice died, Orpheus went down into Hades and by his song persuaded the gods to let her return to earth. Eventually, he was torn to pieces by the Maenads (see Plate 23d), but his head was saved and long continued to sing and prophesy. An ancient vase pictures this head speaking while a disciple busily writes down what it says.

The poems attributed to Orpheus were really the work of many different persons living at widely different times, which fact probably accounts for the legend that his head continued to speak. Most of the poems now available date from a period shortly before or after the birth of Christ. But Orphic hymns existed even in the sixth century before Christ, when a collection of them was made. For a while this collector enjoyed the patronage of Peisistratus, but later he was expelled from the city by Hipparchus for forging oracles which he attributed to another poet associated with Orpheus and the mysteries. The Orphic poems included hymns and prayers, myths to explain various rites, and mythological or philosophical accounts of the origin of the world and of man. The ideas they express show close affinity with the mysteries of Demeter and Dionysus, and the myths told how Orpheus founded mysteries which were called Orphic in his honor, or at least how he reformed them. In historic times, however, no specifically Orphic mysteries existed.

Through succeeding centuries there were people in Greece known as Orphics or followers of Orpheus. Sometimes these men wandered about leading ascetic lives, frequently as beggars, and they sold to gullible persons books of charms and poems which guaranteed future blessedness to their possessors—something like the charms from the Egyptian Book of the Dead a thousand years before. Ancient writers satirized or denounced these Orphics, and moderns have compared them to the Pardoner whom Chaucer pictured as imposing upon the ignorance of the poor and having his wallet "Bret-ful of pardoun come from Rome al hoot." Some Orphics undoubtedly deserved the contempt that Plato and others heaped upon them, but the whole movement should not be judged from such charlatans. The true Orphics were deeply religious persons, concerned with the great problems of this world and the next, and they tried to explain life in terms and ideas drawn from the mysteries. They were the first real theologians in Greece, but we must not think of these people as forming a church or a sect. There was no Orphic organization.

Orphic Theology

Orphic teachings and practices developed greatly during the thousand years of their popularity, and there were striking differences between early and late Orphism. Unfortunately, the greater part of our information comes from the early part of the Christian era and therefore represents the riper forms of Orphic theology. It is not easy to say how much of this late Orphism existed in early times, but a

certain number of ideas were intrinsic from the first. They centered
on the myth of the dismemberment of Dionysus. It was said that the
Titans—earthy giants devoid of civilization—once seized the infant
Dionysus and tore him to pieces. To hide the traces of their crime
they devoured the god's body, all except the heart, from which Zeus
created a new Dionysus. Zeus then destroyed the Titans with his
lightning, and from their ashes he made men. Mankind thus has a
dual origin and a dual nature: being descended from the earth-born
Titans, men are bound to the earth, but at the same time they inherit
a spark of divinity from Dionysus, whom the Titans had eaten just
before their destruction. This myth must have been a part of Orphism from the first, and Orphic theologians and poets made it the
basis of a broad religious philosophy. By it they explained the origin
of the earthly body and the divine soul of man. They taught the
superior merit of the latter, and they carried disparagement of the
body to such lengths that they even spoke of it as a "grave" of the
soul—helped by a play on words in Greek, where *soma* means "body"
and *sema* "grave." This belief was invoked to justify various ascetic
practices which really sprang from primeval taboos and from ancient
beliefs about purity and purifications.

The Orphics also speculated on the fate of the soul after its departure from the body, and they expanded upon the teachings of the
mysteries regarding a future life. They divided the next world
sharply into a Heaven and a Hell, with rewards for the righteous
and punishments for the wicked. Most Greek accounts of such retri-
butions had an Orphic origin. The Orphics also developed a belief
in the transmigration of souls, saying that after death a man's soul
would reappear in an animal appropriate to his character, but that
superior moral conduct—or Orphic rites—would enable it eventually to break out of this cycle of rebirths. Sometimes this superior
morality was shown by not eating beans or meat and not wearing
woolen clothes, but the better Orphics insisted upon truly admirable
standards of justice, personal holiness, and individual responsibility.
Even these large themes were not always enough to occupy the
Orphic poets, who also turned their attention to the development of
complex views on the origin of the universe.

The Orphics thus presented their followers with a complete theology, covering everything from the creation of the universe to the individual soul's eventual escape from the cycle of generation. We shall see that Plato, in spite of his criticism of Orphic charlatans, took from Orphism many of the fundamental ideas which he wove into his own philosophical system. Many centuries later, when Christianity had almost conquered the pagan world, Platonic philosophers still dared to hold up Orphism as a teaching equal or superior to that of the Gospels.

From Religion to Philosophy

Other men living in this turbulent sixth century began to cast doubt upon the value of the old myths as a guide to the nature of the world and its history. Increasing knowledge of countries beyond their own borders brought new systems of mythology to their attention, and these mythologies obviously could not all be true. Efforts were made to harmonize them by identifying various gods and heroes with each other—Amon with Zeus, for example, or Melkart with Heracles—but some Greeks were impressed when educated Orientals told them that the Homeric myths were mere fables for children. Moreover, the characters and achievements of the old gods no longer seemed very admirable or edifying to men who were accustomed to the moral standards and ideals of the new day.

The most famous of these early critics was Xenophanes of Colophon. Born about 570, Xenophanes left his home in Asia Minor when twenty-five years of age, spent many years wandering through the cities of Sicily and Italy, and finally settled at Elea where he died at an advanced age. In his poems he criticized many things, among them the widespread idea that the gods share the general character and appearance of men. He pointed out that Ethiopians had black-faced gods with flat noses while Thracians gave their gods blue eyes and blond hair; and he sardonically remarked that if lions and oxen had hands and could paint, they would doubtless picture their gods as lions or oxen. Other critics were less severe upon the old gods, whose grosser shortcomings they explained away. They invented the allegorical method of interpretation which declared that, as myths were mere fables invented to teach moral lessons, they should be judged by these underlying teachings rather than by their outward form. Allegorical interpretations of mythology remained popular throughout antiquity, and the method was taken over by early Christians to explain away troublesome passages in the Old Testament.

After the truth of the old myths had been thrown into doubt, intellectual pioneers in Ionia tried to learn the truth about the world by other methods. They bridged the gap between religion and philosophy by trying to construct a view of the universe that was based on the data of objective sense perception. The gods were not to be excluded from this universe, but they were made a part of it, not put above it; and, like men and things, they became subject to its laws. Early steps toward this conception of a naturally ordered universe may be seen even in Homer and Hesiod. Homer's gods were often quite arbitrary, but Zeus usually acted reasonably and justly, and he had the power to enforce his will. In most cases, therefore, things went in accordance with his ideas of justice and reason. Moreover, men and gods, even Zeus himself, were subject to an inexorable Fate. They might hasten or delay its workings, but in the long run everything came out as Fate decreed. Such fatalism is only one step removed from the reign of natural law.

This evolution of theological ideas closely paralleled the political development of the time in Greece. We have seen that the old aristocracy was gradually losing its arbitrary power and being reduced to a status subject to political law. The Olympian gods suffered much the same fate. Like the alleged descendants of Agamemnon and Achilles in the political order, they were brought to heel by the champions of the new intellectual order. To cushion the fall of the old gods, philosophers sometimes euphemistically said "the will of Zeus" instead of "the reign of law," but the fact remains that just as the political revolutions of the sixth century produced city-states governed by law, so the intellectual revolution produced the idea of an ordered universe operating according to eternal laws against which even the gods themselves were powerless.

Thales and the Milesian School

The leaders in this intellectual ferment were philosophers rather than natural scientists. In their speculations they used whatever scientific information they found available, but they did not add greatly to mankind's stock of scientific knowledge. Some of them even spoke disparagingly of rivals whom they accused of learning vast numbers of facts without acquiring wisdom and understanding. The aim of these early philosophers was to reduce the available information about the world to a logical system. They were simply wise men, famous as much for their sage aphorisms and their skill in practical affairs as for their knowledge of the physical world. Solon was universally accepted as one of these wise men; Pittacus, the tyrant of Mitylene, was another; and still another was Thales of Miletus.

Many stories were told to illustrate Thales' practical wisdom. It was said that he had been employed by a Lydian king to turn a river out of its course, and that he once made a fortune by cornering the olive market. He had once predicted an eclipse—perhaps in 585— a story that is not incredible, for the Babylonians had long since learned to make such predictions successfully. It was also said that he was the first to teach the Greeks geometry, after learning the subject himself in Egypt. But there was a standing joke to the effect that once while watching the stars he fell into a well beneath his feet. His speculations led him to the conclusion that all physical things must ultimately be made of one fundamental substance, and he declared that this substance was water. Homer, too, had spoken of Ocean, "from whom the gods are sprung"; but while the poet spoke in the involved terms of divine mythology, the philosopher expressed the idea as a simple and direct statement of fact. Thales was neither a poet nor a scientist nor a theologian, but a philosopher.[1]

Such speculations were continued by Anaximander, who lived at Miletus toward the middle of the sixth century. He was famous for his map of the world, on which he summarized the information gath-

---

[1] See note on Eduard Zeller, p. 353.

ered by many Ionian mariners. Because of this map he has been called the Father of Geography. He studied the relation of the earth to the heavenly bodies, and pictured the earth as a body hanging free in space at the center of the cosmos, with the sun, moon, and stars revolving around it. Like Thales, he believed that there must be an elemental matter out of which all things were made, but he could find no better way of describing it than to speak of it as "boundless." The third of the Milesian philosophers was Anaximines, best known for his statement that everything was made out of air. Our knowledge of these men is based on the remarks of later writers, for so far as we know, Thales wrote nothing, Anaximander wrote only one book of which five or six lines survive, and of Anaximines even less remains. Nevertheless, our scanty sources show that each of these philosophers attempted to explain the world by invoking natural forces rather than by attributing it to creation by man-like gods.

Heraclitus and Pythagoras

Heraclitus of Ephesus thought along somewhat different lines. He had been born to an aristocratic family shortly after the middle of the sixth century; he is said to have aided in expelling a tyrant from his city; and he deplored the subsequent expulsion of an aristocrat by the populace. His dissatisfaction with the way things were going gave a pessimistic tone to his thinking, and the ancients sometimes called him the "weeping philosopher." He was much impressed by the constant change in the world, and he summed up his philosophy in the adage, "All is change." He once remarked that a man could not step into the same river twice, for by the second time it had become a different river. Behind all this change, however, Heraclitus discerned a plan or order to the world, and he believed that the universe was arranged according to reason. The rational principle behind the cosmos he called the *logos*, (literally "word," but from it our "logic" is derived), and he thus gave philosophy a term which was later used in a wide variety of senses, even by Christian theologians. If a man fully understood this rational order, he would understand the world and could arrange his own life intelligently. Of course, everyone must act according to the laws of the universe, whether he knows them or not; but Heraclitus once remarked that the philosopher "does while awake what other men do while asleep." Heraclitus complained that too often men acted only upon their own unreasonable ideas, which resulted in constant conflict. If only they could become wise enough to recognize and follow the *logos,* or reasonable order of the universe, all would be well. The views of Heraclitus were those of an enlightened aristocrat in an age of rapid change toward democracy who was critical of much that happened yet accepted the new criticism of the old divinities. He replaced a world governed by arbitrary gods with a cosmos governed by rational law.

A few words must also be said about Pythagoras and the Pythagoreans. This strange man was born at Samos about 580 and when fifty years of age he settled at Croton, in Italy, where he died some twenty years later. He was familiar with the speculations of the Ionian philosophers, but he also was much influenced by the Orphics, and his fundamental aims were not very different from theirs. He accepted their views regarding purity, asceticism, the dual nature of man, and the transmigration of souls. His originality lay in his speculations regarding numbers and his chief interest lay in finding occult meaning for them. Nevertheless, he and his followers added considerably to ancient knowledge of arithmetic and geometry, and from their word for "lessons" (*mathemata*) our word "mathematics" is derived. Pythagoras was a man of strong and likable personality, and he imposed his views upon his pupils so successfully that among them any argument could be settled by a simple statement that *he* had taught this or that—in Latin, *ipse dixit.*

Pythagoras organized his followers at Croton into a brotherhood whose members conducted missionary work and even concerned themselves with politics in the hope of reorganizing the government along lines suggested by their studies. The brotherhoods often aroused strong opposition, and according to some accounts Pythagoras met a violent death during an armed attack upon his order in 510. Nevertheless, the brotherhoods continued active after his death, usually favoring the aristocrats against the populace, and for this reason they met continued opposition and persecution until most of them were driven from Italy. In spite of the political interests and ambitions of some Pythagoreans, others lived apart from the world in what were virtually monastic establishments, leading austere and ascetic lives and cultivating religion, mathematics, and philosophy.

Music and Poetry

Meantime, the Greeks were also learning how to express themselves in new forms of literature and in the fine arts. They had always been a musical people. Music exercised a strong influence over all aspects of their artistic life and, in their own opinion, their achievements in music equaled or surpassed those in any other field of art. Unfortunately, we know little of what Greek music was like. They had no method of recording it, and while they eventually invented a system of marks to help singers remember melodies, we have barely a dozen brief specimens of such notation, all dating from the Christian era. These fragments, and a few short theoretical discussions, are enough, however, to show that Greek music was very different from ours. Though the Greeks sang to the accompaniment of musical instruments, they never played more than one instrument at a time and their music therefore never attained the fullness of a modern symphony. They had no conception of counterpoint, and in choral singing all voices sang the same simple melody. Even their musical scale differed from ours. Modern musicologists point out that Greek music resembled that of the Orient much more than it resembled our modern music or the Gregorian music of the European Middle Ages. Undoubtedly these oriental aspects of Greek music went back to Minoan times, but in part they were due to the influence of Lydians and other Asiatics in the seventh and sixth centuries.

The chief musical instrument of the Greeks was the lyre, which had been known even in ancient Crete. The earlier lyres had only three strings, each capable of sounding only one note, but by the sixth century the number of strings had been increased to seven, which remained standard thereafter (see Plate 22). Even then, elaborate melodies were still impossible. Second in importance was a wind instrument called the *aulos*. Homer speaks of it as used by the Trojans and their allies, but not by the Greeks. Apparently, the Greeks adopted it later from the Lydians. Though sometimes incorrectly called a "flute," the *aulos* was a reed instrument resembling a double oboe in appearance and a bagpipe in sound. Its shrill and exciting music was associated with the Dionysiac orgies, just as the gentler music of the lyre was associated with Apollo.

The New Poetry

The development of Greek poetry followed this progress in music, for early poetry was written to be sung. A second powerful factor to influence the progress of poetry was the growing individualism of the new day. The Homeric bards hid themselves behind their poems so effectively that today we know nothing of their private lives and opinions. Later poets, on the other hand, did not hesitate to express their personalities. The new spirit is already visible in Hesiod.

Hesiod tells us about his father, who once lived at Cyme in Aeolic Asia Minor and who emigrated to Greece, where he settled near Mount Helicon in Boeotia. There Hesiod was born about the year 800, and there he spent his life, traveling only to nearby festivals where he competed in musical contests. He also tells us of his quarrel with his brother Perses, who had wasted the family estate. Hesiod also expressed his personal views on large and general themes. His zeal for social justice and his teachings regarding the gods suggest comparisons with the Hebrew prophet Amos, who was a generation his junior. At first glance, Hesiod's *Theogony* seems to be merely a dull list of the gods, especially the lesser ones, with their relationships and attributes, but closer study discovers in it a philosophical system which was largely Hesiod's own creation.

The new spirit was better shown by the poet Archilochus. He was born about 735 on the island of Paros in the Cyclades, and after many travels he eventually returned there, where he died about 665. Sprung from a humble family, Archilochus spent his life as a wandering mercenary soldier, and he made himself the spokesman of those who hated the aristocrats. While still at Paros he had wished to marry the daughter of a local aristocrat. When her father forbade the match, Archilochus attacked him so bitterly in his verses that, according to legend, the man and his daughter hanged themselves for shame. He was perhaps even more destructive of old aristocratic standards when he boasted that, during a battle, he had left his shield beside a bush and run away: mockingly he explained that he had thereby saved his life and he could easily buy a new shield! His writings established a new form of social criticism, and in later times the great writers of comedy, who sought the same ends as he, learned much from Archilochus.

Another new form of poetry was the elegy. Singing accompanied by the *aulos* was used to inspire troops entering battle, with the singer recounting the glorious deeds of the heroes of old. Out of such songs grew the elegy, in which the poet strove to inspire his hearers to great deeds in war or peace. Elegists in the first half of the seventh century wrote war songs during the great Cimmerian invasion, and similar songs inspired the Spartans during the Second Messenian War. Other elegies praised the Spartan social system. Early in the next century, Solon of Athens wrote elegies to arouse enthusiasm for his reforms. And toward the end of that century, Theognis, who had been banished from his home in Megara by a tyrant, composed bitter elegies on behalf of the aristocracy. His are the best-preserved of all Greek elegies and a valuable source of information on the views of the Greek aristocrats.

It was at this time, too, that the first great lyric poets appeared in Greece. Poets before this time had doubtless sung compositions less ambitious than epics while accompanying themselves on the lyre, but we have no record of their works. The first whose lyrics we possess were Alcaeus and Sappho, who lived on the island of Lesbos toward the end of the seventh century. Alcaeus belonged to the aristocratic faction and was driven into exile. Many of his poems dealt with political themes—especially a group known only through papyri discovered in Egypt in the present century—but others were drinking songs and playful discussions of everyday matters. More famous than Alcaeus was his friend Sappho, the first recorded woman among the Greek poets. She surrounded herself with a number of girls to form a school, and some of her pupils wrote verses of their own. Though she composed long narrative poems, her most important works were short lyrics expressing personal feelings and emotions. Many papyri dating from the early centuries of the Christian era contain fragments of her verse, showing how widely she was read and admired throughout antiquity.

The Greek Dance

Even less is known about Greek dancing than about Greek music, but we know that the Greeks enjoyed it and found many occasions for it. Sometimes their dances were of a wild, abandoned sort, as in the Dionysiac orgies, but usually they were more restrained and formal. The dancing was, of course, accompanied by music, usually of the *aulos*, and by singing. The Greek word *choros* ("dance") eventually took on a new meaning—still retained in English—which shows the importance of singing by the dancers.

Among the first to become famous for preparing choral dances was Alcman, a Lydian from Sardis who was taken to Sparta as a slave in the second half of the seventh century. He both arranged dances and composed the music and lyrics that the dancers sang. A generation later, a Dorian in Sicily continued the work. Meantime, at Athens, worshipers of Dionysus had developed a ritual around his altar which included dancing, music by the *aulos*, and the singing of a hymn known as the *dithyrambos* celebrating the birth of the god. A Lesbian lyrist named Arion, who lived at the court of Periander of Corinth about 625, reformed and greatly improved the dithyramb. Almost a century later an Athenian named Thespis, who enjoyed the patronage of Peisistratus, introduced further changes, adding an interlocutor to explain the dance. Out of this innovation developed the Athenian drama of the fifth century.

Early Greek Prose

In Greece, as elsewhere, poetry preceded prose, but in the sixth century prose writings began to appear. Perhaps the first important writers of prose were the great lawgivers, who, of course, had to use language exactly and accurately. Among the philosophers, Anaximander wrote in prose though his contemporary, Xenophanes, preferred to express his ideas in verse. A more strictly literary prose was first created by the fabulists. Like most primitive peoples, the early Greeks were fond of telling stories about animals, often using them to point moral lessons. Examples of such tales in verse may be found in Hesiod, but later they were written in prose. It seems probable that a man named Aesop actually lived early in the sixth century and that he wrote or collected a number of fables, but the collection which now bears his name has been much amplified since his day. Other tales and legends, and stories of a historical or quasi-historical nature, were written down and thus Greek historiography was born.

Greek historical writing had a double ancestry. One of its ancestors was the city chronicle, the other a form of geography known as the *periegesis* ("leading around") or "Mariner's Guide." The place of its birth was Ionia, and the time the sixth century. When an Ionian city achieved wealth and eminence it often discovered a new pride in its past. Stories were told of its founding; efforts were made to connect its prominent families with Homeric heroes; and great events in its history were vaguely remembered. Presently men called logographers (at first merely "prose writers," later "story tellers," and eventually "historians") began to put all these events together in chronological sequence as best they could. The task was far from easy, for many centuries had elapsed since the original events took place, written records did not exist, and there was no guide to chronology except the roughest reckoning by generations. Usually the logographers produced rather bald skeletons of history in annalistic form, but sometimes they embellished the narrative with stories that were largely or wholly fictitious. Such chronicles were of value because they preserved a few facts but more especially because they forced their authors to face the fundamental problems of historical criticism and chronology. At about the same time the first handbooks appeared for the use of mariners, describing the routes to be taken in sailing from one city to another, mentioning the cities to be passed on the way, giving information about commercial conditions in these cities, and sometimes even including résumés of their history. By fusing these two types of literature, the Ionians created history.

The first of the famous Ionian historians was Hecataeus of Miletus, who lived at the end of the sixth century and played an important role in the political life of his city. He had traveled as a merchant as far as Egypt, and perhaps to other distant places. He wrote or compiled a *periegesis* which covered the whole Mediterranean coast from Spain, past Italy, Sicily, Greece, and Macedonia to the Black Sea area, thence to Asia Minor, and south past Syria and Egypt to Libya, and he included something of the history of various places from mythological times to his own day. Hecataeus's travels gave him a wide knowledge of the world and a low opinion of Greek fables. Herodotus tells us that when Hecataeus was in Egypt he went around boasting that he was the sixteenth generation descended from a god until a priest showed him three hundred and forty-five statues of priests, each the son of the preceding, and remarked that their records showed no gods on earth during all that long time. Perhaps this humiliating experience opened Hecataeus's eyes and made him more critical thereafter—though neither he nor Herodotus seems to have doubted the truth of the priest's fantastic statement about the statues. At any rate, Hecataeus opened his history with the words, "I write what seems to me to be true, for the stories of the Greeks are many and, as I see it, ridiculous." Hesiod had said long before this that the Muses could tell plausible lies when they chose, and in spite of his opening remark, Hecataeus accepted many traditional stories that we today consider "ridiculous." Nevertheless, his skepticism has been hailed as the beginning of historical criticism.

The Art of the Greek Renaissance

It is only in the present century that critics have come to appreciate the importance of the art of the seventh and sixth centuries, for until then this art was not well known.[2] Archeologists have now brought to light thousands of Greek vases dating from the sixth century, they have laid bare the foundations of several ancient temples, and they have discovered many sixth century statues, but unfortunately no ancient Greek paintings have been found. These newly discovered examples of the art of the Greek Renaissance show how vigorous and receptive to new ideas the Greeks then were. Traces of oriental influence are everywhere to be seen; but while the Greeks learned what they could from Egypt and even from Mesopotamia,

---

[2] See the note on J. J. Winckelmann, p. 354.

they never became mere imitators. They quickly mastered oriental techniques, yet even in these early times they impressed their own character upon all their works. The general lines were then laid down along which Greek art developed during the next several centuries.

The geometric pottery of the Greek Middle Ages went out of style late in the eighth century, giving place to proto-Corinthian and later to Corinthian ware. The differences between the new and the old styles can be seen at a glance (see Plate 23). The formal lines and figures of the earlier pottery were replaced by paintings of flowers and animals and men, all of which were made as lifelike as possible. There was much experimentation, both by potters and by painters, from which many new forms emerged. The pride which Greek artists took in their work is shown by the fact that, almost as soon as writing was invented, they began signing their better pieces. Early in the sixth century still other types of pottery began to appear, with black figures against a red background, and about 525 red figures were placed against a black background. In the earlier type, the figures could be little more than silhouettes, but on the red-figured vases it was possible to add detail with thin black lines. In

---

• Note for Plate 23.   These pictures show the four principal styles of early Greek vase painting. The first vase is decorated in the "geometric style," and more particularly the "Dipȳlon style," so-called because many vases of this sort were found near the Dipȳlon Gate of Athens. Geometric decoration was popular in the ninth and eighth centuries before Christ. The second vase, in the "Corinthian style," dates from the seventh century. The oriental influences then prevalent in Greece show in the pictures of animals on this vase, which may be compared with the roughly contemporary Chaldaean lions on Plates 13 and 14. The third vase is Attic "black figured ware," so-called because the decoration is in black against a dark red background. This style of decoration was popular in the sixth century. The painting on this vase shows two hoplites fighting each other. The fourth vase is "red figured ware"; that is, the decorations are in red while the rest of the vase is colored black. Vases of this sort began to appear late in the sixth century, and in the fifth century Greek potters achieved their greatest triumphs in this style. This vase shows Maenads killing Orpheus. (Photos, Courtesy, Museum of Fine Arts, Boston.)

Plate 23.   Styles of Greek Vase Painting

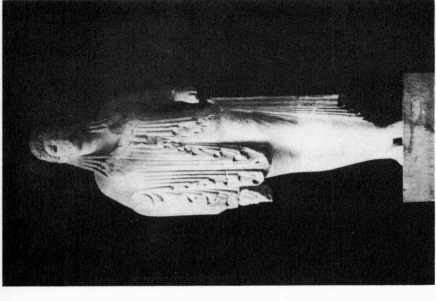

Man with Calf (Acropolis Museum, Athens)

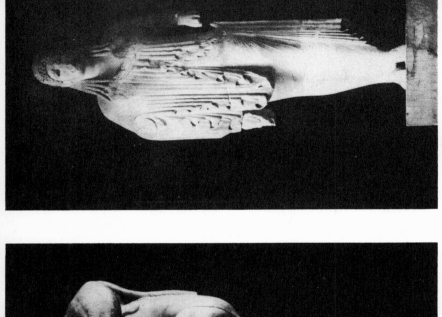

Greek Maiden (Acropolis Museum, Athens)

Plate 24.   Archaic Greek Statues (Sixth Century)

the fifth century, Greek vase painters achieved their greatest triumphs on vases of this red-figured type.

The extensive building that occurred during the age of the tyrants
encouraged rapid progress of architecture. It was at this time that
the Doric and Ionic orders received their classic forms, the simpler
Doric developing in Greece and southern Italy, the more elaborate
Ionic in Asia Minor, but both orders were fundamentally Greek.
Architects always built their temples along the lines of the old Greek
megaron, though they might add minor oriental embellishments,
such as the spiral volutes on an Ionic capital. These temples, famous
for their symmetry and restraint, are perhaps the finest achievement
of the artistic genius of the Greek people.

Lastly, it was during this period that our earliest examples of
Greek sculpture appeared (see Plate 24). It is not improbable that
wooden statues were carved in earlier times, but if so, they perished
long ago. Greece was fortunate in her marble quarries, especially
those of Attica, and her sculptors easily learned to carve stone. Early
Greek statues, like other works of the period, show unmistakable
traces of the Orient, and especially of Egypt, but before the end of
the sixth century, Greek sculptors had emancipated themselves from
foreign masters. Toward the end of the century they also learned
how to cast large statues in bronze, a medium in whose use they
later showed great skill.

Steps Toward Greek Unity

The seventh and sixth centuries brought Greeks into contact with
many foreign peoples and made them aware of their distinctiveness
from others. At the same time trade and travel brought Greeks together from different places and taught them how much they had
in common. In the colonies, persons from many parts of Greece lived
together, finding a mutual kinship among themselves, and sometimes
they returned to Greece or sent back word of what they had learned
about their fellow Greeks. It cannot be said, however, that these
circumstances produced a strong desire for the political unification
of Greece. Ancient rivalries persisted; sometimes old feuds were
carried to the colonies; and each small community in Greece con-

tinued to fear and suspect its neighbors. The unity that the Greeks recognized, and perhaps desired to foster, was cultural rather than political. It rested upon their common language, their common traditions, and their common way of life.

Language was the most obvious cultural bond of union. Though several dialects of Greek were spoken—Ionic, Attic, Aeolic, Doric, Arcadian, and others—these dialects differed so slightly among themselves that interpreters were never necessary. Greeks could always understand each other, no matter where they came from or where they met. The Homeric poems furnished a second bond of unity. They were admired by Greeks everywhere, everyone knew something about them, and they provided a common cultural background. While other literary works enjoyed less influence, singers and poets traveled throughout the Greek world, and everywhere they were greeted by enthusiastic audiences. What Herodotus tells us of the poet Arion illustrates the wide popularity of such men. Arion was a native of Lesbos who lived for many years at Corinth. He traveled as far as Tarentum and Syracuse to engage in musical competitions, and even the piratical sailors who planned to rob and murder him were eager to hear so famous a musician sing.

Greek unity was also promoted by religion. The worship of the gods of the Homeric pantheon gave Greece a sort of religious unity, and attendance at religious festivals and oracles brought people together from all parts of the country. Neighboring states would sometimes enter into a league, called an *amphictyony* (literally, "dwellers around"), to protect a shrine and maintain peace during festivals. The worship of the Delian Apollo was safeguarded by an amphictyony of which all the Ionian states and islands were members, and the Delphic amphictyony protected his oracle at Delphi. The Delphic priests used their great influence to promote better understanding among the Greeks, and the leaders of the amphictyony were fairly successful in imposing various humanitarian laws. They forbade Greeks to interfere with pilgrims seeking the oracle or even to levy high tolls upon them, and they ordered member states to keep roads to Delphi in good repair. Going farther, they made these states swear never to destroy other cities belonging to the league and not to cut off their running water, either in peace or in war. Sometimes they arbitrated disputes between member states. These amphictyonies were the first feeble efforts of the Greeks to form a federal union.

Love of athletics was a third great force helping to unify the Greek people. Both Minoans and Achaeans had been fond of sports, and in historic times famous athletic festivals were held at regular intervals. The most important were the Olympic games. A late tradition reported that the first games were held at Olympia in 776 B.C., but it now seems more probable that games of some sort were held there long before that date. Perhaps they were reformed early in the eighth century. Before long, they were attended by people from all parts of the Peloponnesus, and eventually they became the most popular festival in all Greece. The games were held every fourth year, at the time of the full moon in the month of August, and they lasted for seven days. Victors were rewarded only with laurel wreaths, but they won such high esteem from the public that the contestants trained for years and came from all parts of the Greek world. Other games were held at Delphi: at first this Pythian festival was a musical contest, but athletic events were presently added. These games, too, were held every fourth year, in the second year after the Olympic games. The Isthmian games were held at Corinth and the Nemean games in Argolis in the odd years. Athletic competitions were thus held somewhere every year and were attended by vast crowds of spectators. They were protected by a religious truce and they eventually became symbols of Hellenic unity.

"Hellenes" and "Barbarians"

When the Greeks became conscious of their cultural unity, they began using the word "Hellene" to designate all those who shared in this common culture, and they called the territories inhabited by such peoples "Hellas." This was something new. Homer knew no word for all the Greeks and none for Greece. The word "Hellene" occurs only once in the *Iliad*, "Hellas" only five times, and they always refer to an unimportant people in southern Thessaly or to their country. Historians from Thucydides to the present day have speculated upon the manner in which this small people came to give its name to the whole Greek race. Perhaps the best explanation is that offered by J. B. Bury some fifty years ago. He pointed out that the word "Hellas" occurs five times in the *Odyssey*, where it clearly refers to a small district in the northern Peloponnesus on the shores of the Gulf of Corinth. Presumably the "Hellenes" had moved south during the Dorian migrations and, as is often the case, the *Iliad* reflects Mycenaean conditions while the *Odyssey* reports those existing at the time it was composed (750 B.C.). It is also well known that many colonists migrated from the shores of the gulf to southern Italy in the eighth and seventh centuries, among whom there undoubtedly were many who were "Hellenes" in this narrow sense of the word. The Italians presently applied this name to all Greeks, and called their settlements in Italy from Tarentum to Locris "Greater Hellas." As this rather small strip certainly was not greater than the whole Greek peninsula, the comparison must have been with the tiny Hellas of the northern Peloponnesus, whence many of the settlers had come.

It was in the Italian colonies, therefore, that the name "Hellenes" first was applied indiscriminately to all Greeks. Thence the name was carried back to Greece itself, and thereafter it was used for all peoples of Greek language and culture. Archilochus, who had visited Italy, used the word in its new sense early in the seventh century, and a late writer tells us that before 586 the judges in the Olympic games were called *Hellanodikai,* or "judges of the Hellenes." The name "Greek," by which Europe still knows the Hellenes, has a very similar history. The Graii were a small tribe living in Boeotia, many of whom settled at Cumae in Italy. Here the Romans first met Hellenes and applied the name of this tribe to the whole people, whom they called *Graeci,* or "Greeks."

The second half of the story of Hellenic self-consciousness is less pleasing. When the Greeks became aware of the differences between themselves and other peoples, they quickly developed an early form of that racial arrogance which is so evident throughout the world today but from which the ancients were rather free. The Greeks began to divide the human race into two categories, "Hellenes" and "barbarians." Homer had called the Asiatic Carians *barbarophonai* ("barbarous-speaking"), by which he meant only that, as the Greeks could not understand them, their speech sounded like "bar-bar-bar." The epithet at that time carried little or no invidious connotation. A few centuries later this simple view had changed and the word "barbarian" had assumed its modern meaning: it implied that all non-Hellenes were mere savages devoid of civilization, and that any Greek was therefore infinitely superior to all foreigners. Thereafter all except a few highly educated Greeks shared this view, and the Greeks were perhaps the first people in history who deliberately thought of themselves as "super-men." In the long run this conception was one of the stronger forces making for Greek national patriotism.

Notes

Eduard Zeller

The most famous of the many histories of Greek philosophy is the monumental *Die Philosophie der Griechen in ihrer geschichtliche Entwicklung* by Eduard Zeller (1814–1908). Zeller was born in a south German village in Württemberg and studied Protestant theology at Tübingen. Here he was much influenced by Ferdinand Christian Baur (1792–1860), whose daughter he married, and here he became the lifelong friend, the defender, and eventually the biographer of David Friedrich Strauss (1808–1874), whose *Leben Jesu, kritisch bearbeitet* (1835) created a great scandal and marked an epoch in the historical study of the life of Jesus (see sketch of Strauss in Vol. II). Baur was the head and guiding genius of the "Tübingen school" which first applied modern historical criticism to the records of early Christianity. Baur's extreme positions on difficult problems are now abandoned, but his fundamental methods have been adopted by scholars of every school. Zeller later studied at Berlin, where he fell under the influence of the ideas of the philosopher Hegel, who had died but recently (1831) and whose spirit still dominated philosophical instruction at the university.

As radicals such as Strauss and Zeller could not be appointed to professorships in German universities under the reactionary governments then in power, Zeller accepted a position at Berne, in Switzerland, just as Strauss had earlier gone to Zürich. After the revolution of 1848, however, the home atmosphere cleared and Zeller was called to professorships first at Marburg, then at Heidelberg, and finally at Berlin (1872), where he remained until his retirement in 1895. For several years he edited the *Theologische Jahrbücher*, a periodical which was the mouthpiece of the Tübingen school, and he wrote copiously on theological and philosophical topics, but his reputation rests upon the *Philosophie der Griechen.*

Zeller was first drawn to Greek philosophy by his recognition of its influence upon the Fathers of the Christian Church. He published the first edition of his book in three modest volumes between 1844 and 1852, but he continued to improve and expand it until the sixth edition (1902) filled six volumes of almost a thousand pages each. It is a work of enormous learning, still indispensable to every student of Greek philosophy, though Zeller sometimes makes it seem that the old Greeks discussed only those philosophical problems that later loomed large in Hegelian idealism. So great was Zeller's authority that not until the twentieth century did historians of Greek philosophy emancipate themselves from thralldom to Hegel. Zeller's *Erinnerungen eines Neunzigjährigen* (1908) presents a pleasant picture of German university life in its great days at the middle of the last century. See also the *Gedächtnisrede* by H. Diels in the *Abhandlungen* of the Berlin Academy, reprinted in Zeller's *Kleine Schriften* (3 vols., 1910).

Johann Joachim Winckelmann

No one has exercised a deeper influence upon the modern criticism of Greek art and upon the study of Greek culture in general than J. J. Winckelmann (1717–1768). Winckelmann was born at Stendal in Brandenburg, the son of a poor cobbler, and it was with great difficulty that he acquired a university education. Though nominally a student of Lutheran theology, he spent most of his time studying the Greek classics— notably Homer, Sophocles, and the historians—and for several years he was an obscure teacher in an elementary school. His real life began in 1748 when he became librarian to a certain Count Bünau at his castle near Dresden. As Winckelmann remarked later, Dresden was then "an Athens for artists." Here he made the acquaintance of art-lovers and for the first time he saw copies of Greek statues. The enthusiasm which they aroused in him dominated the rest of his life. In 1755 he went to Rome, then possessing the world's most famous examples of Greek art, and there he remained the rest of his life. He never saw Greece, though several wealthy patrons invited him to travel there with them. In 1768 he set out to revisit Germany, got as far as Vienna, where he was received and honored by the Empress Maria Theresa, and then gave up his plan and started back to Rome. At Trieste he was murdered by a thief.

Shortly before leaving Germany, Winckelmann published a pamphlet entitled *Thoughts on the Imitation of Greek Works in Painting and Sculpture* (1755), and nine years later his *History of Ancient Art* appeared. The former was much the more influential work, and it contained all Winckelmann's fundamental ideas. To be understood, it must be studied as a criticism of the flamboyant baroque art that had long been popular in Germany and elsewhere. Critics were beginning to prefer more simple and restrained forms and to preach a "return to nature." Winckelmann said "return to Greece" instead, for he thought he detected this "primitive simplicity" in Greek art. "The most significant characteristic of the Greek masterpieces," he wrote, "is a noble simplicity and a tranquil grandeur." Modern critics cannot accept Winckelmann's views on ancient art, and they sometimes express surprise that he should have selected the tortured writhings of Laocoön as the supreme illustration of this *edle Einfalt und stille Grösse*. The Laocoön group has these merits only when contrasted with eighteenth century baroque and rococo art.

As a matter of fact, Winckelmann developed his views on Greek art long before he had seen any examples of it except a few plaster casts in a shed at Dresden, and he learned more about the Greeks from their literature than he did from their art. Classical studies had reached a very low ebb in his day, especially in Germany, where instruction was virtually limited to teaching students how to write Latin. Winckelmann seemed to link baroque art with the Latin tradition, and his enthusiasm for Greek literature and for the Greek spirit in general led him into many unfair attacks upon the Latin authors. He is responsible for much of the disparagement of Vergil that has characterized German scholarship ever since his day. On the other hand, his praise of the Greeks struck a responsive chord in the hearts of many Germans who wished to break away from the Latin tradition, which they associated with Louis XIV and French imperialism as well as with baroque art. Winckelmann exercised a strong influence upon the Homeric scholar Wolf (see above, p. 279), whose famous seminar spread Winckelmann's ideas and inspired German classical scholarship for many years. Winckelmann also touched most of the creators of the great German literature of the late eighteenth century—Lessing and Herder, Goethe, Schiller, and the rest. These writers dreamed up a cultural ideal which they believed had been realized in ancient Greece, and before long many lesser Germans had convinced themselves that, by actually achieving this ideal, the Germans had become the Greeks of the modern world. To non-Germans this conception seems strangely perverse, but from Winckelmann's day to our own it has deeply influenced most German students of antiquity. Carl Justi, *Winckelmann und seine Zeit-*

genossen (3 vols., 1866–72; 3rd ed., 1923) is the best biography; see also Goethe's famous *Winckelmann und sein Jahrhundert* (1805), "probably the most impressive monument ever dedicated to Winckelmann," and Walter Pater's essay in his *Renaissance* (1872), W. Rehm, *Griechentum und Goethezeit* (1936), and H. C. Hatfield, *Winckelmann and his German Critics* (1943).

XI The Age of the Persian Wars

THE THIRTY YEARS THAT FOLLOWED THE EXPULSION OF THE tyrant Hippias from Athens, in 510, form a troubled but fascinating period in the history of Greece. Much has been told us about the wars with Persia in 490 and 480, but our knowledge of the twenty years that preceded them is so scanty that a definitive history of the period cannot be written. Until rather recently, our information about these decades came almost wholly from Herodotus, who not only failed to understand what was happening then because he thought largely in terms of the impending war, but who also colored his narrative with the mythology and political propaganda of the victors. The publication (in 1891) of Aristotle's *Constitution of Athens* threw new light on these dark years, showing that its important developments had less to do with Persia than earlier historians had supposed. Many attempts have since been made to reconstruct the history of the two prewar decades, yet even today all that can be done with reasonable certainty is to sketch in a few outstanding events.

It was Cleisthenes, a member of the famous Alcmeonid family, who actually drove Hippias from Athens. He had been archon in 525, during the general reconciliation of factions that came early in Hippias's reign, but in 510 he and his family had been in exile for several years. Cleisthenes kept in touch with other Athenian aristocrats hostile to Hippias, encouraging them to enlist the aid of Sparta, as ever the foe of tyrannies. This aristocratic faction at

Athens was led by a certain Isagoras, who was not himself a member of an old Athenian family and whose ancestors were recent immigrants from Caria in Asia Minor. Nevertheless, he was preferred by the Athenian aristocrats and their Spartan allies to Cleisthenes and the Alcmeonidae. With the aid of these allies, Isagoras seized control of the state and replaced tyranny with a conservative aristocratic government which at once began to undo the popular reforms of the tyrants and even those of Solon himself.

When Isagoras revised the citizen lists to disfranchise many individuals who had been granted the vote by Peisistratus, Cleisthenes saw an opportunity to ingratiate himself with the populace which had supported the tyrants and now saw its gains threatened by the triumphant aristocracy. Cleisthenes and his new followers rose in revolt during Isagoras's archonship in 508. Isagoras again summoned aid from Sparta and expelled his rival, along with about seven hundred Athenian families. Within a few days, however, the Athenian populace besieged Isagoras and his Spartan allies on the Acropolis and later drove them from the city. Cleisthenes then returned and introduced a series of sweeping constitutional reforms which not only made his position secure but also assured the continued political supremacy of the social classes that supported him.

Cleisthenes' Constitutional Reforms

The first reform was a fundamental revision of the old Attic tribal system. The four Ionian tribes were replaced by ten new tribes, each named after a hero of Athenian mythology. Membership in the old tribes had been determined wholly by descent, based on the hereditary phratries and *gene*, but in the new tribes it was based on place of residence. Attica was divided into many small districts, each called a "deme," and all persons living within its boundaries were assigned to the same political unit. Once this new arrangement had been set up, however, membership in the deme became hereditary, regardless of subsequent changes of residence. Heretofore, when an Athenian had occasion to use his official name, he had given his own name followed by that of his father; under the new system he gave his personal name followed by that of his deme.

Between the tribe and the deme stood an intermediate unit, called the *trittys* or "third," three of which made up one of the new tribes. The number of demes in a trittys was not always the same, and the demes making up a *trittys* were not contiguous. In fact, care was taken to locate the demes comprising each *trittys* in different parts of Attica in order to prevent one section from dominating the whole tribe. Usually, however, the urban demes enjoyed greater prestige and power than those of the country—an arrangement which was quite acceptable to Cleisthenes and his associates. For many purposes the deme acted as a unit, for others the entire *trittys* met and acted together, and on other occasions men assembled by tribes. The real purpose of this reorganization of the tribal system was to smash the political power of the phratry and the *genos,* through which the aristocracy had formerly dominated the state. Though these ancient organizations continued to exist as religious and social institutions, they no longer played an important role in political life, and their elimination was a severe blow to the aristocracy.

A second reform enlarged the Council (*Boule*) from four hundred to five hundred members, with fifty from each of the ten tribes instead of one hundred from each of four. The representatives of each tribe were apportioned among the various demes, and they were chosen by lot. The government of Attica was then conducted by the fifty representatives of each tribe in turn, the men in office being called "presidents" (*prytaneis*). The year was divided into ten periods of thirty-five or thirty-six days,[1] each called a "prytany." During their terms of office, the *prytaneis* served as a sort of executive committee for the Assembly, or *Ekklesia,* preparing measures that were to be laid before it and settling minor matters. Undoubtedly the great majority of these actions were routine, but sometimes the *prytaneis* were called upon to make important decisions. As a man could not serve on the Council more than twice, a large number of citizens held office there in the course of the years. In fact, it has been estimated that more than a third of all the citizens of Athens

---

[1] At this time the Athenians had a lunar year of 354 days, rectified by the occasional insertion of an extra month. A more accurate calendar was devised in the next century, and the *prytany* was then lengthened to 36 or 37 days.

were members of the Council at least once in their lifetime, and that sooner or later most of those citizens would be chosen who were enough interested in public matters to attend meetings of the Assembly regularly. The Council thus gave the people of Athens an unusual political education by providing a large proportion of them with an active part in governing their city.

Cleisthenes' third great reform was the introduction of ostracism. Once each year, if the Assembly so ordered, the citizens gathered to vote against anyone whom they considered a menace to the state. If at least 6000 persons voted, the man receiving the most votes must go into exile for ten years. At the end of that time he might return, and his property would not be confiscated. The ballots on which the voter wrote the name of the man he wished to exile were broken pieces of pottery, called *ostraka,* and the process was therefore called "ostracism." Aristotle believed that ostracism was introduced primarily to prevent a return of tyranny, but so far as our information goes, no one was actually ostracised until 487, and nearly all who suffered this fate were members of the old aristocracy—including several Alcmeonids. Ostracism became a powerful weapon in the hands of democratic politicians.

Cleisthenes effected these reforms in 508 and then dropped out of history. We have no reference to later activities on his part or to his death, and we do not know the cause of his eclipse. We also know very little of the other political leaders at Athens until Miltiades and Themistocles rose to power about fifteen years later.

Later Democratic Reforms

Nevertheless, reform continued during these intervening years. The new democratic regime was strengthened in 501 when the Athenian army was reorganized on the basis of the ten tribes. Thereafter, each tribe provided the army with one *taxis,* or "regiment," drawn from its own members and commanded by a *strategos,* or "general," elected by the tribe. As an archon might not be re-elected, though the *strategos* remained in power as long as the voters wished, ambitious men preferred the army office to the archonship.

Aristotle reports that a few years later, in 487, it was ordered that the archons should again be chosen by lot from five hundred candidates previously elected by the tribes: he adds that the archons had been chosen by direct election ever since the fall of the tyranny. His remarks indicate that the tyrants had found some way of rigging the lots to obtain the election of their picked candidates, and that Isagoras substituted direct election by a restricted electorate in order to assure the choice of his aristocratic candidates. The reform of 487, re-establishing choice by lot, again gave democratic leaders a chance to become archons. Moreover, it seems quite probable that the reformers deliberately intended to reduce the power and prestige of the archons, who came only from the two upper classes of society and who were associated in the popular mind with the aristocracy. At any rate, the importance of the archons declined thereafter, and the *strategoi*, elected by the people from any class of society, took over many of the functions formerly filled by the archons. The *strategoi* soon became the actual rulers of the city, or, to speak more accurately, the first *strategos* became its real leader and ruler.

These institutions were the foundation of the Athenian democracy during its great age. They marked a continuation and perfection of the reforms inaugurated by Solon almost a century earlier, but they also owed much to the tyrants whose power, as we have seen, rested upon the support of the masses. Herodotus suggested that Cleisthenes was greatly indebted to his maternal grandfather, Cleisthenes, the tyrant of Sicyon; and Aristotle once remarked that democracy was "the last word in tyranny," or, better, "the ultimate working out of tyranny." The importance of these reforms was quickly recognized. They aroused the opposition of Sparta and the other Greek states favoring aristocracy, and their permanence was not assured until many years had passed.

Cleomenes of Sparta

Meantime Sparta was being ruled, from about 520 to about 489, by a king named Cleomenes. Herodotus gives us a most unflattering picture of this ruler, whom he accused of being a crazy drunkard. We may suspect, however, that the historian's view was warped by pro-Athenian and pro-Alcmeonid prejudices, for Cleomenes really was one of the ablest and most important Greeks of his generation. He was the last of the Spartan kings to make a strenuous effort to hold his own against the ephors and to dominate policy. Throughout his long reign he was in constant conflict with these ephors and with Demaratus, his colleague in the kingship. Regarding the details of his domestic program we know little, but we are somewhat better informed regarding his Panhellenic and foreign policies.

The Greek aristocrats were rapidly developing Panhellenic senti-ment at the end of the sixth century and Cleomenes hoped, by en-couraging them, to effect a closer unification of all Hellas. Toward the middle of the sixth century the Spartans had renounced their earlier policy of extensive conquest in the Peloponnesus and sought instead to make their gains secure by forming separate alliances with each of their neighbors. They thus came to dominate the whole Peloponnesus. Moreover, the Spartans uniformly favored the aristoc-racies against the tyrants. They do not seem to have operated outside the Peloponnesus before the days of Cleomenes, but he soon cast his glances farther afield.

Plataea, a Boeotian city-state near the frontier of Attica, appealed to him for aid against Thebes in 519. Cleomenes refused his aid and recommended that the Plataeans seek it from their neighbor Athens instead. Herodotus believed that Cleomenes' strategy was to create ill will between the Athenian tyrants and Thebes, and thus prevent them from uniting against him. At any rate, his action had that effect. When the Thebans marched against Plataea they were de-feated by the Athenians, who annexed a small patch of territory at their expense. Athens and Thebes remained hostile to each other for many years.

When Cleomenes helped drive the tyrants from Athens in 510, he doubtless hoped that he would be able to dominate the new govern-ment through Isagoras and the aristocrats; and when Isagoras was driven out in 508, Spartans and Thebans rushed to the defense of aristocracy. Had Cleomenes succeeded in restoring Isagoras to power, he might have effected some sort of a union of all Greek aristocracies under Spartan leadership—or Spartan domination—but his intervention at Athens failed because his Greek allies, notably

Corinth, were unwilling to support such schemes. This humiliation caused Cleomenes to lose face at home, and for several years thereafter his rivals dominated Spartan policy. Relations between Sparta and her allies began to follow a new pattern, and for a short time it seemed that Sparta's whole system of alliances might 'founder. About 505 or 504 the Spartans called a meeting of their friends at which new alliances were established. Presumably the assembly was called by the Spartan ephors, though from Herodotus's account we gather that it was dominated by the Corinthians.

Out of this assembly's discussions came the Peloponnesian League. It is quite probable that the League drew up and adopted a definite constitution, and it had a representative assembly to determine a common foreign policy for all its members. In later chapters we shall see that the precedent thus established was followed repeatedly during the next several centuries and that such leagues were the nearest approach to federal government ever achieved in antiquity. At the first meeting of the League, the new Spartan leaders proposed intervention at Athens in behalf of the tyrant Hippias, thus reversing Cleomenes' policy on another important point. The proposal was rejected by the League, at the insistence of the Corinthians, and for the next several years neither Sparta nor the League paid great attention to Athens.

In spite of these setbacks, Cleomenes remained one of Sparta's two kings and Sparta remained a powerful state. For a while, Demaratus and the ephors held control, but Cleomenes presently adapted himself to the new regime and regained his old supremacy, principally through a successful war against Sparta's old rival, Argos. At the battle of Sepeia (494), his armies permanently destroyed the power of Argos by killing 6000 Argives (if we may trust Herodotus) but he did not capture, or even besiege, the city of Argos itself. Upon his return home, the ephors brought Cleomenes to trial for this failure to annihilate the enemy, but victory had brought the king such prestige that he was acquitted.

To strengthen his position further, Cleomenes obtained the expulsion of his colleague Demaratus by attacking the legitimacy of his birth, claiming that he was not really the son of the former king

(491). The new king was more friendly to Cleomenes. Demaratus withdrew to Asia, where he gave valuable advice to the Persian kings when they were preparing their great invasions of Greece. Enemies continued to attack Cleomenes, however, and presently they forced him to withdraw to Thessaly, where he was living when the Persians attacked Athens in 490. Shortly afterward, he returned to Sparta, where he died under obscure circumstances. Herodotus says that he died of wounds he inflicted on himself in a fit of madness sent as punishment for various sacrileges he had committed; modern scholars suspect that this story was invented to cover up the fact that he was murdered by his political enemies. Cleomenes was the greatest of the Spartan kings; he made Sparta the strongest military power in Greece; but his great dream of uniting all Greece under his rule was impossible of fulfillment.

Darius of Persia

While these events were giving a new aspect to the political life of European Greece, the Persians were forcing a new situation upon the Aegean basin. Cyrus of Persia had defeated Croesus and conquered Lydia in 546, and soon thereafter almost the whole of western Asia Minor lay under his rule. Even Byzantium and the Thracian Chersonesus in Europe recognized Persian overlords. The Persians were not cruel taskmasters, however, and they did not destroy the economic prosperity of the Ionian cities. The upper-class Greeks in Ionia were willing to make peace with their new rulers and in return they were granted autonomy under Greek tyrants responsible to the Persian satrap at Sardis. On the other hand, the democratic factions in the Ionian cities remained restless, though it is impossible to say how much of this unrest was proof of hostility to their distant Persian rulers and how much of it was directed against their local Greek masters. However, we hear of no serious revolts in Ionia under Cyrus and Cambyses.

Cambyses died in 522, and three years of civil war distracted the Persian Empire before Darius could make himself secure upon the throne. Oroetes, the Persian satrap at Sardis, apparently took no part in the civil war, but neither did he send aid to Darius, who, of course, later interpreted this passivity as a sign of disloyalty. Oroetes' position at Sardis was so strong, however, that Darius did not dare send troops against him: he had the satrap assassinated instead. It seems probable that Oroetes had ingratiated himself with the Greek rulers in the Ionian cities. His friendship kept them from throwing off Persian rule in the critical days after Cambyses' death and assured him their loyalty when Darius thought of sending troops to punish the rebellious satrap. Oroetes apparently had dreamed of finding Greek aid and support in setting up a kingdom of his own in Asia Minor. We know nothing of the measures by which Darius reconciled the Ionians to Persian rule after the death of Oroetes, but the Persian king had no trouble in his Greek provinces for several years thereafter. Darius then turned to administrative reforms throughout the Empire, designed to prevent further revolts. These reforms occupied the rest of his life and constitute the solid basis of his glory. When he died in 486 Darius left a government which continued to function after a fashion for more than one hundred and fifty years though not one of his successors was a man of more than middling ability.

The Scythian Expedition

Darius's first aggressive war did not come until several years after he ascended the throne. The evidence does not specify an exact date, but probably it was in 513 that the Persian king first invaded Europe. With a large army he crossed the Bosporus on a bridge of boats, advanced through Thrace to the Danube, bridged and crossed that river, and entered what is now Romania. Here he fought unsuccessfully against the Scythian tribes and had to withdraw, but he left a body of troops in Thrace. The general in command occupied the whole Thracian coast of the Aegean and parts of Macedonia: we have already seen that in doing so he seized the rich silver mines of Mount Pangaeus, owned by the tyrant Hippias, and that quite inadvertently he thus contributed to the fall of tyranny at Athens.

It is not easy to explain Darius's purposes in this Scythian expedition. Herodotus, who is our sole authority for the story, says that it was in retaliation for an invasion of Persian territory by the Scyths many years before: this explanation need hardly be taken seriously. Perhaps Darius hoped to seize the gold mines of Romania, and later the silver mines of Thrace. Another theory attributes the expedition largely to domestic politics in Persia. Cyrus, the founder of the Empire, had been a great military conqueror, and his son Cambyses had annexed Egypt. A tradition was thus established that each king should add something to Persia. Darius seems to have been a man of peace, interested primarily in preventing a repetition of the revolts that had disturbed the early years of his reign. So far as we know, the Scythian expedition and the campaign against the Greeks that culminated at Marathon more than twenty years later were the only wars he fought against foreign armies, except for a few minor campaigns in defense of local frontiers. But Darius was a usurper, not the lawful heir of Cambyses. He undoubtedly had many opponents at home, even after military opposition had been crushed, and it is quite probable that critics compared him unfavorably with his predecessors who had been mighty warriors (propaganda made even Cambyses appear important) who added many provinces to the Empire. Darius, who had added nothing, was thus open to grave criticism at home, and the boastful language of the Behistun inscription, which he set up early in his reign, appears to be his reply to such criticism.

Perhaps the Scythian expedition was intended to answer the critics still more convincingly. The king himself commanded it in spectacular fashion, whereas, during the later campaign against the Greeks, which had no such political purpose, he stayed in Persia. The Scythian expedition was aimed at remote barbarians who presumably would offer no serious resistance and who would not be in a position to refute any fantastic stories of victories that the king might choose to circulate for home consumption. Whatever gold and silver mines he acquired would further confound critics at home. Darius added something about this expedition in an appendix to the Behistun inscription, but the rock is so badly defaced at this point that only a few words can now be read.

The Scythian expedition was in no way aimed at the Greeks, either in Ionia or in Europe. In fact, the Ionian Greeks helped Darius. A

Greek engineer from Samos built the bridge across the Bosporus. Ionians sailed through the Black Sea and up the Danube to a point where they built the bridge over which Darius crossed that river. Among the Greeks who accompanied Darius were Histiaeus of Miletus and Miltiades of the Chersonesus. Herodotus tell us that these two tyrants and their troops were left to guard the bridge over the Danube while Darius advanced northward, and that when Scythian envoys urged them to destroy the bridge and escape, Miltiades at first favored the project. Histiaeus, however, warned him that the defeat of Darius would be followed by democratic revolts throughout Asia Minor and the expulsion of tyrants everywhere. While the historical truth of this story is very doubtful, Histiaeus's alleged remarks were essentially sound. At any rate, the bridge across the Danube was not destroyed, although as soon as news of Darius's retreat reached the Greek cities on the Straits, the citizens of Byzantium rose in revolt and destroyed the bridge across the Bosporus. Other Greek cities quickly followed the example of these rebels. Though Darius was able to send his army back to Asia through Sestus, a Greek city ruled by Miltiades, he did not reconquer Byzantium and Chalcedon until several years later.

The Ionian Revolt

Nothing is known of Ionian history during the next ten or twelve years except that Histiaeus was presently taken to Susa, probably because Darius had found occasion to suspect his fidelity. His son-in-law, Aristagoras, was made tyrant of Miletus in his place. Aristagoras was an ambitious man who nevertheless served his Persian masters loyally until a series of events in 500 suggested to him that he might perhaps lead a successful revolt against them. In that year democrats on the Aegean island of Naxos expelled the oligarchs, who fled to Miletus and begged the tyrant's aid in regaining their former position. Aristagoras persuaded Artaphernes, the Persian satrap at Sardis, to supply troops and two hundred warships for this purpose. As the Persians had heretofore occupied none of the islands, the satrap apparently hoped to ingratiate himself with Darius by putting these islands under oligarchies subservient to Persia. Unfortunately, however, the expedition was a failure, and after besieging the citadel at Naxos for four months, the Persians withdrew in confusion.

This fiasco caused Aristagoras to revolt against the Persians. Herodotus says that he revolted in order to escape punishment by the king, but it is equally possible that the affair at Naxos had showed him the impotence of Persian armies and put ideas of rebellion in his head. Against the advice of his friends, Aristagoras threw himself into the arms of the anti-Persian faction, replaced the tyranny at Miletus with a government under elected officials, and opened negotiations with other Ionian leaders for a revival of the old Ionian League (499). Several Ionian cities expelled their tyrants and joined the insurgents. In the winter of 499–8 Aristagoras visited Cleomenes at Sparta and tried in vain to persuade him to send aid, but he had better luck at Athens, where he induced the Assembly to send twenty warships to Ionia in his support. Eretria added five vessels to this squadron.

The Ionian insurgents won important victories in 498. When the Persians advanced against Miletus, the Ionians replied with a raid upon Sardis. The rebels captured the Persian capital, thus relieving the pressure upon Miletus, but as they could not hope to hold it, they destroyed it and withdrew. This initial military victory so encouraged the Ionians that many Greek cities, from the Bosporus to Rhodes and even Cyprus, joined the rebels. On the other hand, the Athenians withdrew their ships, for reasons which are far from clear, and thereafter the Ionians got no aid from their European kinsmen. Early in 497 the Persians managed to recapture five rebel towns along the Hellespont, and Cyprus was reduced a few months later, but in this same year the Greeks badly defeated a Persian fleet off Cyprus and annihilated a Persian force in Caria that was threatening Miletus. Before the latter victory was won, however, Aristagoras and his close associates had fled in panic to Thrace, where they were promptly massacred by the natives.

The situation in Ionia changed little during the next two years, but in 494 the Persians were able to resume the offensive, for by this time the Greeks were, as usual, quarreling among themselves. A new fleet was sent from Phoenicia which defeated the Greeks near Miletus, victory being aided by the desertion of Greek ships from Samos and Lesbos in the midst of the battle. Soon afterward, Miletus was taken by a Persian army. Most of the city was destroyed, and a large part of its population was deported to Mesopotamia (494). The other rebellious cities were recaptured and punished a few months later.

After a short reign of terror the Persians relented and sought to win over their Greek subjects by favors. The tribute was assessed thereafter in a more equitable fashion; the tyrants were replaced by democracies under supervision from Sardis; and the Greek cities were allowed to set up a court for settling disputes amongst themselves instead of referring them to the Persian satrap. Ionia was thus pacified, but Darius was fated to suffer one more serious loss. He sent his general Mardonius with ships and troops to reconquer the territories in Thrace and Macedonia that had been occupied after the Scythian expedition, and that had broken away during the Ionian revolt. A storm destroyed the Persian fleet off Mount Athos, and the natives delivered attacks in which Mardonius himself was wounded. Nevertheless, the old frontiers were re-established (492).

Greek Politics on the Eve of the War

The European Greeks could not escape the repercussions of these happenings in Ionia. The attitude of Sparta toward them wavered according to whether Cleomenes or the ephors were in control, the former being aggressive and somewhat anti-Persian whereas the latter were interested principally in domestic matters. Herodotus's account of the visit of Aristagoras to Sparta early in 498 is highly fanciful, but its general purport seems to be that Cleomenes was sorely tempted to grant aid to the Ionian rebels. He could not do so, however, for the ephors then controlled Sparta. It is also noteworthy that the Delphic oracle, usually pro-Spartan, often betrayed Persian sympathies at this time.

Political conditions at Athens were even more confused. The old eupatrids, the supporters of Isagoras in 508, had long shared the vague Panhellenic sympathies of other Greek aristocrats. Cleomenes of Sparta had helped them expel Hippias and had later sent them ineffectual aid against Cleisthenes. They consequently favored Cleomenes and, while they would not have tolerated Spartan domination over Athens, they were willing to co-operate with him against tyrants, democrats, and barbarians. Their Panhellenism was reinforced, as regarded the Ionians, by a feeling of special kinship through common ancestry. By this time, moreover, many aristocrats had acquired wealthy sons-in-law (like Isagoras himself) who had commercial connections with the Ionian cities. The Athenian eupatrids therefore gave Aristagoras a warmer reception than had the Spartan ephors.

On the other hand, tyranny still had its friends in Athens, and these men usually looked to Persia for aid. In 510, Hippias had fled to Sigeum in the Troad, where his half-brother had once tyrannized, presumably under Persian supervision like the other Greek rulers in Asia. Six years later, at a meeting of the Peloponnesian League, Hippias sought aid against Athens in vain, after which he returned to Sigeum. Presently he visited Artaphernes at Sardis, filling him with ideas hostile to Athens, and then proceeded to Susa, where he ingratiated himself with Darius. Hippias returned to Greece with the Persian armies in 490, and had they been victorious they undoubtedly would have restored him as tyrant at Athens. Domestic politics and foreign policy thus became inextricably tangled at Athens, and we shall see that not every Athenian leader forgot domestic feuds even when Attica was invaded.

The Role of the Alcmeonidae

Much has been written in recent years about the role of the Alcmeonidae at this time, accusing them of trying to strengthen their political position at Athens with Persian aid. They had enjoyed close connections with pro-Persian factions in Asia Minor for almost a century, and Herodotus mentions charges that they communicated with the Persians at Marathon: he correctly denies the truth of these charges, but he indicates that many Athenians believed them. Moreover, the hostility between the Alcmeonidae and the Peisistratidae must not be exaggerated. The two great families had quarreled and made up several times in the past, and there is no very obvious reason why they should not have done so once more. We have seen that the political policies of the two families were, after all, not so different as their partisans pretended, that each curried the favor of the commercial classes as well as of the populace, and that the real enemies of both factions were the old aristocrats at Athens and Cleomenes at Sparta. It would therefore not be surprising if the Alcmeonidae flirted with the Persians from time to time, though unlike the Peisistratidae, they never committed themselves so deeply as to make retreat impossible.

Apparently the Alcmeonidae first sought Persian aid in 508, several years before Hippias began his intrigues at Sardis. Herodotus tells us that as soon as Cleisthenes returned to Athens after the fall of Isagoras, he sent a delegation to Sardis begging aid in his anticipated war with Cleomenes. Artaphernes replied that if the Athenians would "give earth and water to King Darius"—that is, if they would admit his sovereignty over them—he would conclude an alliance. The envoys accepted these hard terms but, on returning home, they fell into disgrace for their compliance. By this time Cleomenes had left Attica and the Persian alliance was no longer needed. On the basis of this narrative, historians sometimes call Cleisthenes the "first Medizer." It has even been suggested that his sudden disappearance from the political scene at Athens was caused by popular repudiation of his Persian policy. Herodotus (who was strongly pro-Alcmeonid) obviously tries to put the blame for the compliance at Sardis on the Athenian envoys, and his silence about the ultimate fate of Cleisthenes may result from a desire to shield that prominent Alcmeonid.

We know little of what happened during the next few years, not even which party or group governed Athens, but probably the Alcmeonidae and their friends were still in power. When Hippias reached Sardis, some time after 504, the Athenians sent a second delegation to urge the satrap not to listen to the tyrant, obviously wishing to have the Persians on their side; but when Artaphernes replied that if they wished to be safe, they had better take Hippias back, they rejected his advice. Herodotus marks this act as the beginning of open enmity between Athens and Persia.

Such was the situation at Athens when Aristagoras arrived in 498.

We have seen that he persuaded the Athenian Assembly to send
twenty warships to aid the Ionian rebels, but that these vessels were
withdrawn soon after the sack of Sardis. Herodotus points to these
ships as "the beginning of the woes of the Greeks and the barbarians." The historian also remarks that whereas Aristagoras was unable
to deceive Cleomenes (of whose intelligence Herodotus had no high
opinion), he easily deceived thirty thousand Athenians. "Apparently
it is easier to deceive many than one," he observed wryly. These un-
complimentary remarks doubtless reflect Alcmeonid criticism of
their aristocratic opponents who sent the ships and their explanation
of how they lost control of the Assembly.

Then came the withdrawal of the twenty Athenian warships. Our
sources give no reason for the sudden reversal of policy, but various
suggestions have been made: a realization that the war was lost
(though Ionian cities were still joining the rebels); a war nearer
home with Aegina (the existence of such a war may be doubted);
or a political overturn in Athens. The last suggestion is by far the
most plausible. A son and a nephew of Hippias were elected archons
for 497 and 496, and though the elections followed the withdrawal
of the ships, they give clear enough evidence of a general reversal
of policy after the ships had been sent to aid the Ionians. As it is
very doubtful whether the Peisistratidae had enough friends to effect
such a change unaided, we may assume that they had patched up a
new friendship with the Alcmeonidae. It was these pro-Persian political allies in Athens that stopped aid to the Ionian rebels.

Themistocles, Miltiades, Aristides

The next few years were marked by the appearance of three new
political leaders at Athens—Themistocles, Miltiades, and Aristides.
Themistocles was a man of humble origin, born about 525, who made
himself a popular leader and presently won a large following at
Athens. His followers came principally from the fickle populace that
once had followed Peisistratus. These men had been drawn to Cleisthenes by his democratic reforms, and now Themistocles won their
favor. In his day, Themistocles was accused of demagoguery and
criticized for attacking his social betters, but later generations

praised him as a champion of democracy. After several years of leadership he was driven from Athens and eventually became a pensioner of the Persian king; but in his early days he was active in
arousing sympathy for the Ionian democracies in their struggle
against Persia. He may have had a hand in sending the twenty ships.
A few years later, probably in 493, the poet Phrynichus presented a
play entitled *The Fall of Miletus* which so aroused the Athenian
people that the pro-Persian faction had him fined and secured a law
forbidding the play ever to be presented again. We know that in 476
Themistocles financed the chorus for another play by Phrynichus,
and he may have promoted the earlier production as well. At any
rate, Themistocles was archon in 493 and distinguished himself
thereafter by his vociferous opposition to Persia.

Miltiades was born about 545, a nephew of the oikist Miltiades
who had planted a colony in the Thracian Chersonesus. His family
belonged to the ancient aristocracy of Athens (see genealogical
table, p. 394), and it was said that his father had been murdered
at the order of Peisistratus. If so, the two families were reconciled
after the old tyrant's death, for another Miltiades, a cousin of the
oikist, served as archon in 524. Meantime, the elder Miltiades, dying
childless, had been succeeded by his nephew, the third and young-
est Miltiades. This young man was sent by Hippias to rule the
Chersonesus, and a few years later he accompanied Darius on the
Scythian expedition. Though he took no part in the Ionian revolt,
the Persians expelled him from the Chersonesus, presumably in conformity with their new policy of replacing tyrannies with democracies everywhere. Miltiades returned to Athens in 493, breathing fire
and slaughter against the Persians. The Alcmeonid leaders brought
him to trial on charges of having tyrannized over Athenians at
Sestus, but their power was waning and Miltiades was acquitted.
Perhaps he owed his acquittal to the influence of the archon Themistocles, for the two men were already allies in their denunciations
of Persia. It was probably at this time, too, that Miltiades began
circulating the very dubious story of how he had wished to destroy
Darius's bridge over the Danube, but had been prevented from
doing so by Histiaeus—who was now safely dead. Actually, Histiaeus

when alive had been less loyal to the Persians than Miltiades was at that time.

The third of the new leaders was Aristides, sometimes called "the Just," who was an aristocrat born about 530. He was often in bitter rivalry with Themistocles, who eventually obtained his ostracism. While he shared with Miltiades the support of the aristocracy, he differed with him on various points of domestic policy. But all three men were united in a common opposition to Persia and to the pro-Persian group at Athens.

Two important events in the next two years added greatly to the strength of the warmongers in Athens. The Thracian expedition of Mardonius that culminated in the disaster off Mount Athos was easily misrepresented as an attack aimed at Athens herself, and it convinced many Greeks that Darius had designs upon them. A year later, in 491, Darius took a much more serious step. He sent envoys to various Greek cities, demanding that they give him earth and water in token of subserviency. Several cities acceded to his demand, but both at Sparta and at Athens the envoys were murdered. Such acts could not be overlooked by Darius, as the Greeks well knew.

Meantime Cleomenes had again become supreme at Sparta, and the anti-Persian leaders in Athens complained to him about Aegina, charging her with "Medism"—that is, with giving earth and water to Darius. As Aegina had long been Athens' principal rival, an attack upon her would surely arouse popular enthusiasm in that city and help discredit the Medizing factions everywhere. In spite of the opposition of Demaratus and the Spartan ephors, Cleomenes went to Aegina, where he seized ten eminent hostages and sent them to Athens. Moreover, this quarrel enabled Cleomenes to secure the deposition of his colleague. Like Hippias before him, Demaratus withdrew to Asia, where he joined the Persian king and was given estates in the Troad that his descendants still held a century later. Cleomenes' victory was short-lived, however, for the ephors soon forced him to withdraw to Thessaly.

It thus came about that when the Persians invaded Greece in 490, Sparta was in the hands of the ephors, who had little enthusiasm for foreign wars, while in Athens the anti-Persian faction was supreme and had just elected Miltiades general. Not much help could be expected from the other Greek states: Corinth was interested chiefly in the West; Argos had been crushed by the Spartan war of 494 and a slave insurrection that followed; and Thebes, the other central Greek states, and most of the islands were Medizers.

Marathon

As soon as Darius had suppressed the Ionian revolt, he began planning to make war on Athens. His reasons for so doing are not easy to fathom. Herodotus seems to think that it was to punish the Athenians for the aid they sent to Miletus during the revolt; but as their slight aid was quickly withdrawn, it can hardly have been the whole explanation of the expedition. Since Darius was not present in person, the attempt cannot be called a second Scythian expedition, designed primarily to augment the king's popularity at home. A more probable explanation emphasizes the possibility of new revolts in Ionia and the danger that Greek aid might be more effective next time. As echoes of the anti-Persian agitation of Miltiades and Themistocles had doubtless reached him through Hippias and Demaratus, Darius may have decided that his Ionian territories would never be safe until he controlled friendly governments in European Greece. At any rate, he sent the envoys in 491 to demand earth and water: if this token were given, the local governments might be allowed to go on much as before, but as loyal vassals of Persia; if they turned against their new overlord, they would be punished for rebellion. To make such a demand upon a free people, proud of its liberty, was of course an insolent and dangerous step, no matter how essential Darius might consider it to the safety of his empire, and as we know, the Athenians and Spartans murdered Darius's envoys. This offense made war inevitable.

A year later Darius was ready to advance against Greece. A fleet and an army, including a large contingent of cavalry, were prepared under the command of two men—a Mede named Datis, and Artaphernes, son of the satrap at Sardis and a nephew of Darius himself. Ancient figures are, as usual, quite fantastic, but reasonable estimates place the size of the force between 30,000 and 40,000 men.

In the spring of 490, the armada sailed from Samos and stopped at
Naxos to destroy the city where all the trouble had begun ten years
before. It passed Delos without inflicting injury upon that sacred
island, collected hostages from various Medizing islands, and even-
tually reached Carystus at the southern tip of Euboea, just north of
Attica. The city was easily taken, and the Persians proceeded to
Eretria, a more important port whose possession was necessary if
Datis was to hold southern Euboea as a base against Athens.
Athenian efforts to aid the Eretrians were ineffectual and, after six
days of siege, Greek traitors admitted the Persians to their city.

The aged tyrant Hippias had accompanied the Persian army,
which he now guided against Athens, pointing out the route his
father Peisistratus had taken more than half a century before when
on his way from Eretria to Athens to establish himself there as
tyrant. Early in September, the Persians landed near Marathon on a
small plain along the eastern coast of Attica about twenty-six miles
from Athens. As they did not seize the passes over the mountains to
Athens, though they had ample time to do so, they must have
planned either to fight a decisive battle on this plain (which was
well adapted to cavalry action) or else to entice the Greek army
there and give traitors in Athens an opportunity to seize the de-
fenseless city.

The Athenians had taken no active measures to meet the enemy
before he reached Euboea. They then sent a professional long-
distance runner, Philippides (sometimes called Pheidippides), to
Sparta seeking aid. He covered the distance of about 140 miles in
less than forty-eight hours, but the Spartan ephors declared that,
since they were in the midst of a religious festival, troops could not
be sent until several days later. The Athenians therefore marched
out against the Persians alone. They pitched their camp in a strong
position in the hills behind Marathon, whence they could block the
two roads to Athens. Here they were joined by 1000 Plataeans, their
only allies in the campaign. The Athenian army, apparently about
ten thousand strong, was nominally commanded by the polemarch,
Callimachus, but its real commander was Miltiades, who persuaded
the polemarch and the nine other generals to follow his strategy.

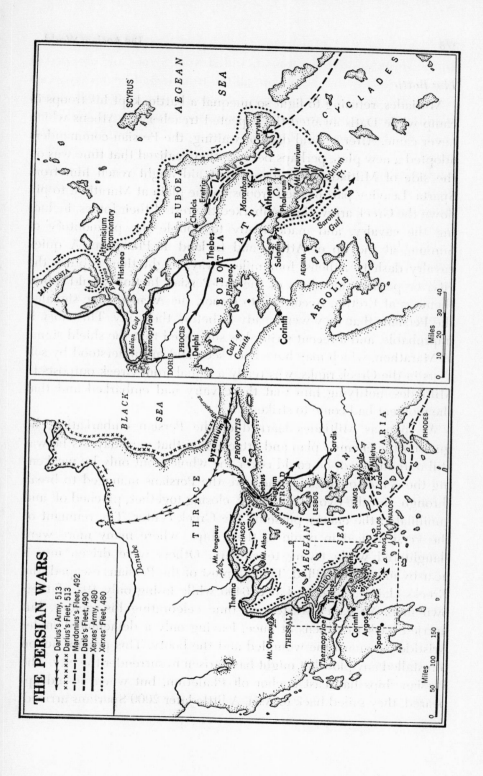

THE PERSIAN WARS

- ←—— Darius's Army, 513
- ××××× Darius's Fleet, 513
- —·—·— Mardonius's Fleet, 492
- ——————— Datis's Fleet, 490
- ————— Xerxes' Army, 480
- ·········· Xerxes' Fleet, 480

The Battle

Miltiades, refusing to fight so unequal a battle, kept his troops in camp while Datis awaited the expected treachery at Athens which never came. After several days of waiting, the Persian commanders adopted a new plan, perhaps because they realized that time was on the side of Miltiades and feared that aid might reach him from Sparta. Leaving part of their troops on the plain at Marathon to pin down the Greek army, they embarked the rest of their forces, including the cavalry, and made ready to double the promontory of Sunium, at the tip of Attica, and to land at Phalerum. A quick cavalry dash to Athens, four miles away, might then capture the city, or perhaps members of the pro-Persian faction would admit them, as at Eretria. According to rumor, the Alcmeonidae signaled the Persians that they were ready to betray their city. This story is improbable, and a recent writer has suggested that the shield signal at Marathon, which may have been seen and misunderstood by soldiers in the Greek ranks, was really a signal from Greek outposts to Miltiades, notifying him that the cavalry had embarked and that the moment had come to strike.

As soon as Miltiades learned of the Persian embarkation, he guessed the enemy's plan and attacked on that very day. As he was still outnumbered, he could cover the whole front only by weakening the center of his line, and here the Persians managed to break through. But the two Greek wings, closing together, pinched off and annihilated the enemy pursuing the Greek center. The remnant of the Persians fled in panic to their ships, where many more were slaughtered while trying to embark. Others were driven into a near-by marsh and killed. Though most of the Persians escaped, the Greeks claimed to have killed 6400 while losing only 192 of their own men. Miltiades wasted no time celebrating his victory, but hurried back to Athens at once, leaving only a detachment under Aristides to guard the wounded and the booty. This prompt action forestalled any plot that might have arisen to surrender the city. The Persian ships had cast anchor off Phalerum, but when no aid appeared, they sailed back to Asia. A little later 2000 Spartans arrived, viewed the Persian dead at Marathon, congratulated the victors, and returned home. Miltiades had won his victory and saved Athens without their aid.

The Legend

It was, of course, inevitable that a lush growth of legend should soon overshadow the true story of Marathon. Herodotus alludes to a few of these legends—a dream of Hippias, a promise of aid from the great god Pan, a mysterious giant on the battlefield helping the Greeks—and later writers show how popular imagination embellished the story. Herodotus's account of the campaign is surprisingly brief (less than three pages for the battle and barely twelve for the whole campaign, including legends, dreams, and speeches) which may indicate that after fifty years he found it difficult to gather material which he deemed reliable. The most famous of the Marathon legends tells of the courier who ran to Athens from Marathon and shouted "Nike!" (Victory!) with his last breath as he fell dead in the agora, thus inaugurating the Marathon race. Miltiades had every reason to let the city learn of his victory at the earliest possible moment, in order to prevent possible betrayal, yet we find no reference to this runner until more than six hundred years later.

Legends of another sort, arising in modern times, have given a fantastic significance to the battle. Marathon has been pictured as a victory of tiny Athens over all Persia, or of Europe over Asia. Writers have even declared that if the Greeks had lost on that fateful day, all Europe would now be Asiatic. Such a statement is nonsense. Had the Persians been victorious, they would undoubtedly have restored Hippias as tyrant in Athens, with a Persian bodyguard to hold him in office, but at the moment their ambitions soared no higher. Later, perhaps, Athens under Hippias might have served as a bridgehead for further invasions of Europe. Ten years later the Persians came again, won other victories, burned Athens, and established their bridgehead; but again they were driven out. Had the Persians won at Marathon, they would soon have been defeated somewhere else. The Greeks were too strong, too devoted to liberty, and too far away, ever to be subjugated by Persian kings.

Greece Between Two Wars

The battle of Marathon left Miltiades the most eminent man in Athens, but within a year he died in disgrace. Victory had filled his head with dreams of further triumphs; the ambition which had driven his uncle and himself to the Chersonesus remained unquenched; his hatred of Persia still burned high; and his thoughts turned to conquests in the Aegean. His prestige was so high that when, in the spring of 489, he vaguely promised his fellow citizens great wealth, they entrusted him with a fleet of seventy warships which he led against Paros. This island is one of the larger Cyclades, lying only a short distance from Naxos, whose importance for the command of the Aegean the Persians had already recognized. In theory, Miltiades proposed to punish the Parians for their Medism by levying upon them a fine of one hundred talents; in practice, this punishment would have amounted to subjugation. His plans were doomed to failure. He besieged the city for twenty-six days in vain; he returned home defeated and wounded; and there were ugly rumors afloat that his failure was caused by his sacrilegious conduct on the island. His enemies immediately brought suit against him for having "deceived the Athenian people." Although gangrene had so deeply infected his wound that he could not conduct his defense in person, his friends carried him into court and pleaded his great services to Athens. Nevertheless, in spite of his prestige, he was convicted and fined fifty talents. A few days later he died.

The attack upon Miltiades was led by Xanthippus, who had married a niece of Cleisthenes and probably was the instigator of the first suit against Miltiades in 493. The fact that the Alcmeonidae were able to convict their rival shows that they had not been deeply or openly committed to the Persian cause during the war, but their victory did not restore them to power in Athens. The elections of 489 had been held before the disaster at Paros, and Miltiades' friend, Aristides, had been chosen archon. A year later the democratic faction, of which Themistocles was a prominent and aggressive member, was returned to office and began a series of purges. The new rulers' first act was to ostracize Hipparchus, the Peisistratid archon of 496, whose conduct during the war had cost him his last friends. In the next year Megacles, nephew of Cleisthenes and now head of the Alcmeonid family, was ostracized. Aristotle calls this man a "friend of tyranny," and perhaps it was at this time that the story of the shield signal at Marathon first gained wide credence. The poet Pindar seems to refer to it in an ode composed in 486. Megacles' brother-in-law, Xanthippus, was ostracized in 485. When the chief Alcmeonidae had thus been eliminated, the democrats ostracized the aristocratic Aristides (483). Themistocles was the man actually responsible for these acts, though he then held no high office.

Themistocles and the Athenian Navy

Meantime, a second military misfortune had befallen the Athenians. The old rivalry and hostility between Athens and Aegina had broken into war a year or two after the victory at Marathon. The citizens of Aegina had demanded back the hostages Cleomenes had taken and sent to Athens in 491, and when the demand was refused, the Aeginetans took their revenge by seizing a consecrated ship carrying a number of prominent Athenians to a religious festival at Sunium. They then exchanged the prisoners for the hostages (488). As the Athenian navy was no match for that of Aegina, the Athenian democrats sought more roundabout ways of getting even with their adversary. They persuaded a disgruntled Aeginetan to stage a democratic revolution in his native island, promising prompt intervention in his behalf. The revolution failed, largely because the Athenians were late with their aid. The Aeginetans attacked the inferior Athenian fleet, won a victory, and for several years continued to ravage the coasts of Attica.

These events turned Themistocles to a policy that was destined to have the greatest importance for Greece, though in a way very different from that which he foresaw. Ever since the days of the tyrants, Athens had drawn much of her revenue from the state-owned silver mines in Mount Laurium. About 484 a new lode was discovered, richer than any yet opened, and the revenue of Athens was thereby increased by about one hundred talents annually. Jubilant politicians at once proposed to distribute this new wealth among the citizens in equal shares—it was estimated that each man's share would be about ten days' wages for unskilled labor—but Themistocles had other views as to its proper disposal. He had long favored building a navy, and even during his archonship in 493 he had begun the construction of a great harbor at Piraeus to supersede the rather unsatisfactory one at Phalerum. He now persuaded the Athenians to devote the money from Mount Laurium to building warships for the war against Aegina. Two hundred vessels were built, but before they were ready, the war with Aegina was forgotten and the Persians were again invading Greece. The ships built by Themistocles became the backbone of the navy that ultimately won the war.

Leonidas had followed his half brother Cleomenes as king of Sparta about 489. His colleague in the kingship was Leotychidas, who had succeeded Demaratus two years earlier. Neither of the new kings was disposed to quarrel with the ephors, and little is known of Spartan history during the next few years. But thanks in part to the Peloponnesian League, organized twenty years before, Sparta remained the most powerful military state in Greece.

Xerxes Invades Greece

We are not informed as to Darius's reaction to Marathon. Herodotus would have us believe that the king flew into a towering rage on hearing the news (as may well have been the case) and immediately began planning his revenge (which is doubtful). It is equally possible that he haughtily announced that, having punished the Greeks adequately for their insolence, he considered the matter closed. The prisoners from Eretria, who were settled in the neighborhood of Susa, served as ocular evidence to convince the skeptical that punishment had indeed been meted out. At any rate, Darius made no serious efforts to continue the war. The old king's health soon began to fail; his last year was disturbed by a serious revolt in Egypt; and he died in 486, after a reign of thirty-six years. He was succeeded by his son Xerxes, whose mother was a daughter of Cyrus. The new king's first task was to reduce Egypt, which took more than a year. Further confusion sprang from a revolt at Babylon. Not until 483 was Xerxes ready to turn his attention to the great project with which he hoped auspiciously to open his reign. This project was the conquest of Greece.

Persian preparations for the new war took on enormous proportions, for Xerxes planned the conquest of the whole peninsula, not just a punitive expedition against one city. The Greeks later overrated the size of the Persian army fantastically, partly in order to magnify their own victory and partly perhaps because they—like all other peoples—liked to think that their enemies relied upon mere numbers while they themselves could safely trust the superior valor and intelligence of individual soldiers. Herodotus declares that Xerxes' host contained 1,700,000 infantry and 100,000 cavalry and camel corps. To these he adds the crews of the fleet, replacements, allies picked up in Greece, and an equal number of noncombatant troops, to reach the prodigious total of 5,283,220, plus countless male and female camp followers. The best modern estimates indicate that Xerxes really had about 250,000 men—perhaps seven or eight times the force participating in the Marathon campaign.

As it was quite out of the question to transport so large an army to Greece by boat, Xerxes was forced to march around through Thrace and Thessaly and thus to invade Attica from the northwest, after which he hoped to proceed across the Isthmus of Corinth to Sparta. Two bridges were built across the Hellespont, and large supplies of food were stored along the way in Thrace and Macedonia. Xerxes also prepared a fleet of 1000 vessels according to some ancient writers, or 1207 according to Herodotus. A modern estimate allows for five squadrons of 120 triremes each, or a total of 600 warships, with enough transports and cargo vessels to make about a thousand in all. The fleet had orders to coast along the shore within hail of the army; and in order that it might avoid the promontory of Athos, where Mardonius had met disaster in 492, a huge canal was dug across the neck of the peninsula. Xerxes himself accompanied this mighty force, although actual command devolved upon his brother-in-law Mardonius.

Xerxes successfully used diplomacy to supplement military force. Again envoys were sent to Greece in 481 to demand earth and water, and many states complied; but the envoys, mindful of the reception accorded their predecessors ten years before, failed to visit Athens or Sparta. Xerxes also stirred up trouble between the Carthaginians and the Greeks of Sicily in order to prevent the latter from aiding their kinsmen in Greece. Herodotus, who followed Athenian sources, reports nothing of these efforts in the West, but Sicilian writers tell the story, presumably on the basis of authentic Sicilian records. It was more than a coincidence that, as we shall presently see, Carthage attacked the Sicilian Greeks just at the moment when Xerxes was launching his invasion of Greece.

The Hellenic League

The envoys demanding earth and water from Greece made it evident that the Persians were preparing to renew hostilities. The Spartans at once took the lead in organizing resistance. Late in 481 delegates from various Greek states met at Corinth, where they concluded peace between Athens and Aegina and made efforts to persuade the other Greek states to join an anti-Persian coalition. Envoys asking aid were sent to Argos, Syracuse, Crete, and elsewhere, but they met with little success. The Argives were still resentful because of the defeat suffered many years before at the hands of Cleomenes, and they were later accused of Medism. Gelon of Syracuse refused aid unless he were put in command of all Greek forces, a demand possibly dictated by his growing fear of Carthage. Others approached by the Greek envoys either feared or were friendly to the Persians. But Sparta and Athens, the strongest military and naval powers in Greece, united with several lesser states to stand shoulder to shoulder in resisting the impending invasion. The "Hellenic League" thus organized remained in force for twenty years. The delegates at Corinth agreed that Sparta should command both land and sea forces; but it really was Themistocles who drew up the plans for meeting the enemy and persuaded the Spartans to adopt them, using silver arguments on one occasion and more drastic measures on another.

The tremendous weight of the Persian forces gave the Greek generals a serious problem. Their first task was to select a spot where nature would help them in delaying or stopping the enemy advance.

Three such places were available—one at the Vale of Tempe in northern Thessaly near Mount Olympus, a second at Thermopylae in central Greece, and the third at the Isthmus of Corinth. Tempe was their first choice, and troops were sent there early in 480, but the generals withdrew when they found that they did not have the strength to defend the several parallel passes which the Persians might use. The whole of Thessaly then deserted to the enemy. The Spartans would have preferred to make their stand at the Isthmus of Corinth, but to avoid the sacrifice of Athens and all central Greece they reluctantly sent a small force to Thermopylae, promising vaguely to send more after a religious festival was over. The reinforcements were not sent, and apparently the Spartan commanders in the north did not expect them.

At none of these passes could the Greeks hope to do more than delay the enemy. As long as the Persian fleet was intact, it could always land troops behind their lines. Moreover, it outnumbered the Greek fleet by at least two to one, and there seemed little likelihood of a successful naval battle unless the enemy could be divided or forced to fight in an unfavorable position. If, however, the Greeks could win command of the Aegean, their own lines would be safe and they might even threaten Persian communications at the Hellespont. Should a victorious Greek fleet sail, or merely threaten to sail, in that direction, the Persian commanders might be forced to send back so many troops to defend Thrace that the Greek armies could fight the remainder on relatively equal terms. Amphibious warfare thus made its appearance, and for the first time in history a major military campaign, upon which the freedom of a great people depended, was to be determined largely by sea power. Themistocles grasped the situation perfectly and laid his plans accordingly.

Thermopylae

At Thermopylae the road led through a narrow pass between cliffs of steep hills on the one side and the waters of the Malian Gulf on the other. Here the numerical superiority of the Persians would be of little advantage. The site was equally well adapted to naval defense, for the Malian Gulf empties into the Euripus—the straits separating Euboea from the mainland. At its northern end near Artemisium, the Euripus is only a few miles wide, capable of defense by the Greek fleet; and at Chalcis, some fifty miles to the south, it narrows down to two hundred yards. The gulf and the straits were therefore relatively safe from the Persian fleet. The Spartan king Leonidas undertook to defend Thermopylae with about 7000 men, of whom only 300 were Spartans, while the major Greek fleet (268 triremes and 9 penteconters) was stationed near Artemisium. A detachment of 53 vessels was left to guard the straits at Chalcis.

Herodotus indicates that Xerxes reached Thermopylae before his fleet left Therma (the modern Salonika) and that he had to wait there four days doing nothing. During this time four of the five squadrons of his navy reached the vicinity of Artemisium and cast anchor off the Magnesian coast of the mainland north of Euboea; the fifth squadron attempted to circumnavigate the island, hoping to pen up the Greek fleet in the Euripus and land troops behind Thermopylae. At this moment, a terrific storm descended from the northeast, destroying the fifth squadron completely and dashing many other vessels against the Magnesian coast. The Greek fleet escaped serious injury by sailing around to the lee of Euboea. As soon as the storm had passed, the Greek ships returned to their stations, where they were presently reinforced by the 53 vessels no longer needed at Chalcis. On the next two days the Greek navy delivered several hit-and-run attacks upon detachments of the main Persian fleet which, because of its size, was compelled to find anchorage in several different harbors, but on the third day the Persians managed to destroy about seventy Greek vessels. This engagement is known as the Battle of Artemisium.

Meantime Xerxes had been marking time at Thermopylae, sparing his troops the losses inevitable in a frontal attack, and hoping that the Greeks would retreat or that landings behind their lines would simplify the task of destroying them. Upon learning of the loss of his fifth squadron, he decided to delay no longer. For the next two days he delivered furious assaults upon the Spartan lines, but he failed to break them. A Greek traitor then showed the Persians a difficult mountain trail which debouched on the main road a mile or so behind the Greek lines. Leonidas had stationed a force of Phocians on this trail at a point where a path led south through Doris to Phocis and the Corinthian Gulf. Shortly before dawn on the third day, the Persian force reached this point, and the Phocians retreated south into their own country. Leonidas soon learned of the Persian maneuver from deserters and from a few Phocians who scrambled down the cliffs into his camp. He hurriedly sent the bulk of his forces back to block the exit of the mountain defile while he held the pass at Thermopylae with his 300 Spartans, 700 Thespians, and 400 Thebans. It might still have been possible to save the army if only the major force had blocked the mountain trail long enough for the whole army to retreat in orderly fashion out of the pass. Instead, the main force fled, and the Persians pushed into the pass behind Leonidas. The Thebans then deserted. Only the Spartans and Thespians stood firm and fought to the death. This battle took place on the same day that the Greek fleet suffered its reverse at Artemisium (August, 480). As the fleet no longer had an army to protect, and as a successful engagement with the enemy seemed impossible at the moment, it withdrew to Attica.

The battle of Thermopylae was won by the Persians, but the heroic stand of Leonidas and his Spartans remained an unforgettable page in Greek history. A few years later the amphictyonic council set up a stone at Thermopylae upon which was engraved a famous epitaph for the fallen Spartans:

> Go, passing stranger, to the Spartans tell
> That here, obedient to their laws, we fell.

Herodotus also quotes two other inscriptions set up on the battle-field. It seems likely that these epitaphs did much to create the legend of Thermopylae and that several of Herodotus's stories of the campaign are unjustly deduced from words in these epitaphs. Like some modern epigraphers, he and his successors deduced more than the inscriptions warrant. One such deduction was that the Spartan laws alluded to in the epitaph forbade a general to retreat. As a matter of fact, a Spartan general might maneuver as he deemed best, and serious students of the campaign now agree that Leonidas fully intended to withdraw until the flight of his allies left him no choice. In any case, the Spartans appropriated to themselves all the glory for this romantic last stand, even though the seven hundred Thespians shared the fate of the three hundred Spartans. As on other occasions, a poet's flight of fancy has prevailed over the sober accounts of more accurate chroniclers.

Salamis

After their victory at Thermopylae, the Persians advanced rapidly across central Greece. Some followed the fleeing Phocians through Doris to Delphi, where they were welcomed by the priests; others proceeded to Thebes, which promptly joined them; and within ten days Xerxes crossed the border of Attica. A few Athenians fortified themselves for resistance on the Acropolis, but Themistocles persuaded the great majority to flee, some to the nearby island of Salamis, others to Aegina, and still others to Argolis. Those who remained at Athens were soon destroyed, and the Persians burned the city.

Meantime, the Spartans and their allies were frantically fortifying the Isthmus of Corinth. The allied fleet, raised by reinforcements to 310 triremes, lay in the harbor at Salamis, though the Spartan commanders were anxious to withdraw it to defend the shores of the Peloponnesus. Themistocles, on the other hand, wished to fight. When he failed to win over his allies, he threatened to withdraw all his ships, which made up more than half of the navy; and when this threat failed, he secretly notified Xerxes that the Greek fleet was about to withdraw. That night the Persians took battle stations at both ends of the channel separating Salamis from the mainland in order to prevent the Greeks from escaping, thereby dividing their own fleet just as Themistocles had hoped they would.

Next morning (September 23, 480) the Greeks sailed out of the harbor to attack the eastern half of the Persian fleet. The opposing forces were of approximately equal size, but the Persians were reckless because of their recent victories, and their commanders were no match for Themistocles. By feigning retreat, the Greeks managed to crowd the Persians into a small area where their ships could not maneuver, and a large part of the Persian fleet was destroyed. Xerxes

lost command of the Aegean. Fearful lest the victorious Greeks
might next capture the Hellespont, he ordered the remnants of his
fleet back to defend the bridges while he returned to Asia by the
land route, taking much of the army with him. Mardonius was left
with a force of about 60,000 men in Thessaly to continue the war in
the spring. Themistocles had wished to sail for the Hellespont immediately after his victory at Salamis, but he could not prevail over
the allied commanders even though he was now heroized as the
savior of Greece.

At the beginning of the war the Athenians had recalled their
various exiles, among them Aristides and Xanthippus. These two
men were elected generals for the following year when Themistocles
retired from office. Leonidas had been succeeded as king of Sparta
by his young son, and after a brief interval Pausanias was made
regent for the new king. During the winter Mardonius tried to make
peace and an alliance with the Athenians, knowing that with the aid
of their fleet he could certainly conquer the rest of Greece, and
hoping, perhaps, that the new generals would be more amenable
than Themistocles. Aristides and Xanthippus refused to listen to his
honeyed words, but lesser states in central Greece contributed to his
forces.

Early in the next summer Mardonius marched south and reoccupied Athens in June, 479, ten months after Xerxes' first entry. By
this time the Spartans, commanded by Pausanias, had a force of
about 80,000 men, two-fifths of whom were hoplites, to meet an equal
number of Persians and Medizers. The Greek army advanced into
Boeotia, and Mardonius, withdrawing again from Attica, established
his headquarters at Thebes. After several weeks of maneuvering the
two armies engaged in a decisive battle near Plataea (August, 479),
in which the Greeks were victorious and Mardonius was killed. The
remnants of the Persian army withdrew from Greece.

The Greek fleet, now commanded by Xanthippus, had been operating in the Aegean from Delos. At about the time of the battle
at Plataea the Samians asked aid in throwing off the Persian yoke.
The fleet moved to the vicinity of Mount Mycale, on the Ionian shore
opposite Samos, where it landed marines who defeated a Persian

army, burned its camp, and destroyed a fleet. Several Ionian cities thereupon rose in revolt and drove out their Persian overlords. Later in the year Xanthippus besieged and captured Sestus in the Thracian Chersonesus. No formal peace was concluded with Persia, but as the Persians made no further attempts to invade Greece, we may say that the war was over.

The War in the West

One other aspect of the conflicts deserves brief mention. As indicated above, war between Greeks and Orientals also flared up in Sicily. For several years a certain Terillus, tyrant of Himera, had been busy building an empire for himself out of the Greek cities of northern Sicily, enjoying the aid and patronage of Carthaginians stationed at the western tip of the island. In the spring of 480, Terillus was expelled from his city by the ruler of Acragas who, with his father-in-law Gelon of Syracuse, had been the tyrant's chief opponents. Terillus at once called upon the Carthaginians for aid. It is not improbable that the Carthaginians were already planning active intervention of some sort in Sicily for they had a large army ready for action. The Carthaginians landed at Panormus (now Palermo) and advanced to Himera. Here they fought a battle against the troops of Gelon, in which the latter were completely victorious.

Not long afterward, the legend arose that the battle of Himera was fought on the very day of Salamis. A curious quirk of mind made the Greeks fond of such sychronisms, which they invented freely. They later alleged that Mycale was fought on the same day as Plataea, and that the date of Himera and Salamis was also the birthday of the poet Euripides (more probably born in 484) and of the historian Hellanicus. Nevertheless, the legend contains a certain amount of poetic truth, for Himera produced the same results in the West that Salamis won in the East. Greeks were not much bothered by Orientals thereafter, either in Greece or in the West.

XII The Athenian Empire

T HE BATTLE OF MYCALE AND THE GREEK CAPTURE OF Sestus really closed the Persian wars, but at the time of these events no one could be sure of this. On the contrary, men had every reason to fear that the Persians would soon attempt a third invasion of Greece, and ordinary prudence dictated that they prepare at once for such a possibility. Moreover, hostilities did not cease immediately. Sestus was not captured until 478; Ionian cities continued to revolt; Thrace, which remained in Persian hands for several years, was the scene of further fighting. When the fighting in these areas eventually died down, the calm that followed was that of an armistice rather than of peace, and a definitive peace settlement with Persia was not concluded until thirty years later. It is not surprising, therefore, that fear of Persia dominated Greek domestic and foreign politics long after Xerxes had withdrawn his last troops from Greece. Nevertheless, the various Greek states continued to quarrel and maneuver against each other just as they had when Persian armies were on Greek soil.

Sparta suffered less than her rivals from the war. Her territories had not been invaded, and only at Plataea had she made major contributions to the war effort or suffered serious casualties. Many Spartans now planned to exploit their favorable position and establish themselves as the unquestioned masters of all Greece. A few minor rivals were punished for their alleged Medism, and an army was sent to conquer Thessaly on the same pretext. Athens could not be eliminated so easily, however, and the Spartans tried by more devious methods to keep her powerless. They proposed that her fortifications, destroyed by the Persians, should not be rebuilt, pointing out that their own city had no walls (because of its location, it needed none) and arguing that to fortify Athens would arouse the suspicion of other Greeks and make it more difficult to expel the Persians if they again occupied the city.

Had the Athenians agreed to this wily proposal, they would of course have been at the mercy of Spartan troops. On the other hand, a quarrel with Sparta, or seeming opposition to her Hellenic program, would likewise be bad for Athens. Themistocles therefore persuaded the Assembly to send him and two other envoys to confer with the Spartans. He at once hurried there himself, to make sure that the Spartans took no serious step to prevent the rebuilding of the walls, but he instructed his colleagues to follow him only at their leisure in order to delay discussions as long as possible. The entire population of Athens then went to work rebuilding the walls. When rumors of what was going on reached Sparta, Themistocles flatly denied them and suggested that the ephors send reliable agents to see for themselves. At the same time he secretly warned his fellow citizens to hold these agents until the walls were finished. Eventually his two colleagues arrived with the news that the walls were high enough to resist attack. Themistocles then threw off the mask and notified the ephors that, as the walls were now built, there was nothing for them to discuss. The Spartans were angry at his deception, but there was nothing they could do about it now, and they accepted the accomplished fact as best they could.

Meantime, naval operations were continuing against the Persians. While the Spartans had no share in the attack upon Sestus, the regent Pausanias that same year (478) assembled a Greek fleet with which he attacked the Persians in Cyprus, liberating a few Greek cities. Later he captured Byzantium, seizing enormous booty and clinching Greek control of the Bosporus. Unfortunately, however, Pausanias did not have the strength of character to make a great leader. He antagonized many Greeks by excessive boasting about his victory at Plataea; the capture of Byzantium so turned his head that he became intolerable; his insolence cost him the favor of all his troops except the Spartans; and he was accused not only of aping

Persian manners and tyranny, but even of entering into treasonable correspondence with the enemy. He was recalled to Sparta for trial, and though he was acquitted, his prestige was gone. The conduct of Spartan affairs returned to the ephors, who as usual occupied themselves mainly with local matters.

Cimon and the Delian League

An important change came over the political scene at Athens shortly after the war. Themistocles secured the completion of the walls and built a strongly fortified harbor at Piraeus. Then, about 478, he dropped mysteriously out of Athenian political life and for several years we hear nothing of him. The historian Plutarch, our sole authority for these events, explained his disappearance with the casual remark that the Athenians had had their fill of him. This was another way of saying that in the postwar years the Athenians turned away from the radical democracy of Themistocles to follow more conservative policies. Aristotle declared that during the next seventeen years the Areopagus again ruled Athens in an aristocratic spirit. The new leaders were men who accepted the reforms of Cleisthenes and Themistocles and yet found ways of leading the populace in the direction they desired. One of these aristocratic and conservative leaders was Aristides. Another was Cimon, the son of the great Miltiades.

Cimon had been born about 510, the son of the victor of Marathon and of his wife Hegesipyle, the daughter of a Thracian chieftain. Miltiades' death in 489 had left him to pay his father's fine of fifty talents, and he had raised the money by marrying his sister to one of the richest men in Athens. A few years later, Cimon married Isodice, an Alcmeonid whose grandfather, Megacles, was a brother of the reformer Cleisthenes. The union of these two great houses apparently was part of a general reconciliation of the aristocratic factions against the rising democracy led by Themistocles. Though it brought the conservatives back into power, the reconciliation was only temporary.

Cimon made his political debut under the aegis of his father's friend, Aristides, and his policies were those of Miltiades and the old Athenian aristocrats. Like many aristocrats in all parts of Greece in

those days, Cimon had a strong feeling of Hellenic solidarity. He
was a patriotic Athenian, but he favored friendly co-operation with
Sparta and a Panhellenism inspired by enmity toward Persia. He
showed his Panhellenic sympathies even by the names he gave his
three sons—Lacedaemonius, Thessalus, and Eleus. He did not share
what has been called the "ostentatious probity" of Aristides, but he

The Family of Miltiades and Cimon

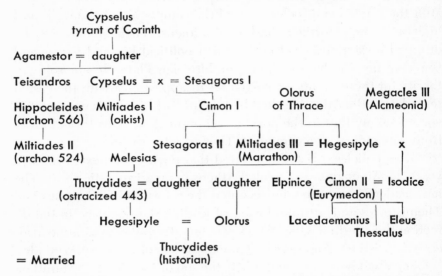

was an honest man in an age and country where not many politicians
were noted for that virtue. Cimon was the ablest general that Athens
ever produced, and for fifteen years he was her most eminent statesman.

Athens was the undisputed leader in Greek opposition to Persia.
The city's walls were now rebuilt, her new harbor at Piraeus was
fortified, her navy was the strongest in the Aegean, and the events of
recent years had taught Athens the importance of sea power. Her
people, inspired by victory, were eager to complete the war against
Persia and to drive the enemy from the whole Aegean area. Partly
for this purpose, and partly also for mere defense in case of another
Persian attack, the Athenians united the Aegean Islands and the free
cities of Ionia in an anti-Persian league.

This Delian League was founded in 477. It had a representative assembly, or "synod," which met on the island of Delos, and its funds were kept in Apollo's temple there—hence the name "Delian." The member states swore to follow a common offensive and defensive policy, and to maintain a navy, with each state contributing ships or, if it preferred, a money equivalent. Aristides was appointed to draw up a schedule showing what the contribution of each ally should be. As Athens was stronger than all her allies combined, it was inevitable that in the long run she should dominate the League, but in the early years there were no complaints that she abused her power. She guaranteed the independence and form of government of each ally, and the assessments levied by Aristides were admittedly very fair. All the high officials of the League were Athenians, however, and the League eventually became nothing more or less than an Athenian Empire, dominated and exploited by Athenian politicians.

Cimon's Victories

The League's guiding spirit almost from the first was Cimon. The Athenians elected him *strategos* (general) in 476, and he continued in that office until 462. During these years he made the League supreme in the Aegean. His first task was to drive Pausanias from Byzantium. The Spartan regent was again being accused of tyranny and treasonable correspondence with the Persians. Cimon drove him into the Troad, thus returning the Bosporus to Athenian control. In that same year, Cimon captured Eïon, a city located near the mouth of the Strymon River on the border of Macedonia, and drove the last Persians from Thrace (476). Next he conquered Scyrus, an island in the central Aegean whose inhabitants were famous as pirates (475). Here Cimon had the good fortune to discover what he declared to be the bones of the Athenian hero Theseus. He transported them to Athens, buried them with great pomp and circumstance, and erected a temple over them. He next turned to Carystus, the Euboean city where the Persians had first landed in 490 and which had been punished by Themistocles for alleged Medism after Salamis. About 473, Cimon forced Carystus to join the Delian League.

When ten years had passed and Xerxes showed no signs of planning to renew his attacks upon Greece, the allies began to grow restless and to begrudge their payments to the common fund. Dissatisfaction reached a crisis in 469 when the Naxians—once a rich and proud people who had suffered severely from civil war, siege, and Persian conquest, and who therefore found their payments especially burdensome—decided to withdraw from the League. There had been no provision against resignation when the League was founded, but the Athenians now declared that members could not withdraw. When the Naxians protested, the Athenians besieged their city and compelled them to re-enter the League. The fate of Carystus had shown that free and independent states might be forced to enter the League against their will; that of Naxos showed that free members of the League could not withdraw. The League was no longer a free union of free states.

During these years Cimon had not forgotten the Persians, and at last, about 467, he was ready to attack them in a major campaign. Assembling a fleet of two hundred triremes, he captured and forced into the League several Greek or half-Greek cities in Caria and the important city of Phaselis on the southern coast of Lycia. Proceeding eastward along the coast of Pamphylia, he met a large Persian squadron near the mouth of the Eurymedon River. The Persians retreated upstream until the pursuing Greeks forced them to turn and fight. Being unable to maneuver effectively in the cramped space, the Persian fleet was defeated and destroyed. Cimon at once landed his troops, and on that same day they defeated a Persian army. A few days later a Persian squadron of eighty triremes, coming from Cyprus with reinforcements, was likewise destroyed. This victory at Eurymedon was Cimon's crowning triumph. He annexed no territory east of Phaselis, but he made the Aegean safe from Persian intrusion.

Athenian Cleruchies

While busied with these military campaigns, Cimon was also formulating plans to make his conquests the foundation of a vast colonial empire. He began establishing colonies which differed greatly from those settled around the Black Sea and in the West two centuries before. In the old days, colonists had set up new and independent states, retaining only a vague, sentimental attachment to their mother-city. The new colonists retained Athenian citizenship, and the colony was really a part of Athens overseas. These colonists were called "cleruchs" (*klerouchoi*) because each received an allotment (*kleros*) of land when the colony was founded. The colony itself was called a "cleruchy." Cleruchies were located primarily with an eye to imperial strategy, and the cleruchs were really an armed force sent to defend the outposts of the Empire.

Experiments along such lines had been made in the days of Peisistratus with Miltiades' settlements in the Chersonesus. The fact that in 493 the younger Miltiades (III) was sued for tyrannizing over Athenians shows that the colonists at Sestus had retained Athenian citizenship. We also read of cleruchs in Euboea shortly before Marathon. Cimon greatly expanded his father's program. An elaborate project was launched about 466 when ten thousand cleruchs were sent to a place not far from Eïon, called Ennea Hodoi ("Nine Ways"). This colony was abandoned soon after native Thracians had defeated the colonists, but another attempt was made several years later (437), and the new colony, called Amphipolis, became a key point in the Athenian Empire. The unsuccessful settlement at Nine Ways aroused the apprehensions of the inhabitants of nearby Thasos, who feared that the Athenians had designs upon their markets and that they coveted a rich mine owned by Thasians on the mainland. The Thasians revolted from the League, tried in vain to get help from Sparta, were besieged for two years, and eventually were forced to pay tribute after surrendering their fleet and the mine (463). Thasos was no longer reckoned a member of the League but a subject of Athens.

The End of Pausanias and Themistocles

While Cimon and the Athenians were thus making Greece secure against the Persians, the Spartans were hard put to it to hold what they already had, for many Peloponnesians were restive under the Spartan yoke. Moreover, the Argives were recuperating from defeats suffered early in the century, and sometimes they intrigued with

Sparta's discontented subjects. The ephors found even greater trouble with Pausanias. For two or three years after his expulsion from Byzantium in 476, Pausanias had lived in the Troad, where he plotted with the Persian satrap and dreamed of becoming king of all Greece with Persian aid. Presently the ephors summoned him home to stand a second trial. He was imprisoned at Sparta, though eventually he was released without trial. He then conceived the much more dangerous plan of calling upon the helots to rise and overthrow the ephors. Unfortunately for him, the ephors learned of his schemes, and Pausanias fled to the sanctuary of a temple. The ephors ordered him bricked in and allowed him to starve (about 472 or 471).

The fate of Pausanias dragged Themistocles to ruin. The Athenian leader had been out of power for several years, and shortly before the death of Pausanias he was ostracized. He took up his residence in Argos, where he engaged in various intrigues and entered into correspondence with Pausanias. He apparently hoped that if he made enough trouble for Sparta he might return to Athens as a democratic hero. After Pausanias's death, the ephors published what purported to be evidence of Themistocles' guilt and demanded that he be brought home for trial. The aristocratic rulers at Athens were glad to oblige. Themistocles escaped by a roundabout route to Asia Minor, where he eventually became a pensioner of the Persian king. The king gave him three cities to rule, one of which was Magnesia, where he died a few years later. Themistocles was one of the most brilliant men that Greece ever produced. He saved his city in her darkest hour; yet because of his obscure birth, he never won the wholehearted confidence of his fellow citizens. Among ancient historians only Thucydides had an inkling of his true greatness, and it certainly cannot be said that Thucydides admired the man.

The ostracism of Themistocles left a certain Ephialtes the leader of Athenian democracy. At first the democrats could do nothing, for Cimon was at the height of his popularity. The long siege of Thasos gave them their first plausible opportunity to attack the popular commander. Cimon had commanded the Athenian armies at Thasos, but apparently his heart was not in the task, and when he reached home his opponents accused him of accepting bribes. Though he was acquitted, Cimon's trial was important for several reasons. It marked the advance of aggressive imperialism at Athens, it showed the declining prestige of the aristocracy, and it enabled the great Pericles to make his political debut in Athens as one of the accusers.

The controversy between the two factions at Athens was resumed with greater vigor a year later. A disastrous earthquake had recently shaken down much of Sparta, killing several thousand persons, and the helots took advantage of the attendant confusion to rise in revolt. When the Spartans found it difficult to pacify their subjects, they called upon Athens for aid (462). Ephialtes opposed aiding their ancient rival, but Cimon's Panhellenism caused him to urge the Athenians "not to let Greece go lame and not to let Athens lose her yoke-fellow." Cimon won his last victory, and was sent to Sparta with four thousand men. Before long, however, the Spartans grew suspicious of Athenian intentions and demanded that their guests withdraw. Athenian feeling was inflamed by the insult, and the democrats made the most of their opportunity. Their attacks upon Cimon were resumed, and in 461 he was ostracized. Cimon was not yet through with Athenian politics, but his ostracism put the democratic leaders into power. The triumph of Ephialtes was short-lived, however, for he was assassinated soon after his victory. Leadership in the democratic faction and in Athens then fell to his lieutenant, Pericles.

Periclean Democracy

Pericles was born shortly before 490, the son of Xanthippus, the victor at Mycale, and of his wife Agariste. It was Xanthippus who brought charges against Miltiades in 489, and probably he who sued him in 493, so Pericles was merely following in his father's footsteps when he prosecuted Miltiades' son Cimon in 461. On the other hand, Agariste was an Alcmeonid, the niece of Cleisthenes and a sister of the Megacles who was ostracized in 487. We have seen how ancient was the hostility between the Alcmeonidae and the other eupatrid families, such as those that produced Aristides and Cimon. On more than one occasion the Alcmeonidae had been allied with the tyrants, and Agariste's aunt had married Peisistratus himself. Pericles continued many of the policies ordinarily associated with the Alc-

meonidae and even with their tyrant friends. Like them, he favored
peace with Persia but had little sympathy with the aristocratic Panhellenism of Cimon. He preferred the commercial classes to the
aristocracy, and did what he could to promote their interests; he
found his chief political support among the populace; and he well

THE ALCMEONIDAE

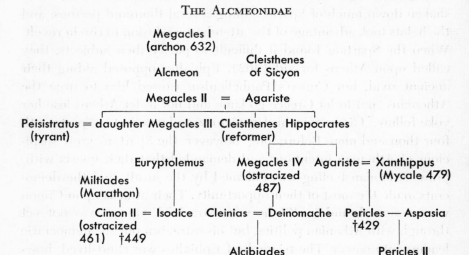

= married; —mistress; †died.

understood the earthy arts of the practical politician. The importance of this family inheritance must not be exaggerated, however,
for Pericles rose above family and factional politics to become the
greatest statesman and leader that Athens ever produced.

Pericles received an excellent education, and throughout his life
he sought the society of the leading literary men, artists, and thinkers
of the day. His high seriousness, coupled with the standing of his
family, gave him an aristocratic aloofness that contrasted strongly
with Cimon's good-natured sociability and enabled critics to ridicule
his "Olympian" detachment. His success as a statesman may have
been the result in part of his skill as a political manipulator, but to a
greater degree it is to be attributed to his fine intelligence, his large
though realistic views, and his oratorical skill. Unfortunately, we

know his speeches only through reports by the historian Thucydides, but apparently they showed the soul of the man himself—solemn, stately, enlightened, idealistic.

Pericles was elected *strategos* in 461 and, except for one setback in 444, he was re-elected to that office regularly year after year until his death in 429. During all this time he had no close rival as leader and ruler of Athens. He presided over his city in the days of her greatest glory, and the most glorious achievements of those great days were in considerable measure to be credited to him personally or to his closest associates. Historians have lauded him more highly than any other statesman in antiquity, with the possible exception of Caesar.[1] Nevertheless, he had many critics in his own day, and modern scholars have condemned many of his measures. In the end, policies which he inaugurated or encouraged brought catastrophe to Athens.

Democratic Reforms

Soon after the ostracism of Cimon, Ephialtes carried through a measure relieving the Areopagus of all its powers except those dealing with homicide. According to Aristotle, this venerable body had, during the preceding seventeen years, acquired various powers which were now transferred to the Council, to the Assembly, or to the courts. This change was highly significant. The Areopagus was composed of ex-archons who for twenty-five years had been chosen by lot from the two upper classes of society, and the court therefore symbolized these upper classes. Attacks upon it were important principally because they indicated the advance of democratic feeling after several years of aristocratic rule. A few years later Pericles opened membership in the court to *zeugitae* (members of the third class) by allowing them to be chosen archons. Members of the lowest and largest class of citizens (*thetes*) remained technically ineligible to this office, but somehow their names were occasionally drawn.

More important than the reform of the Areopagus was the introduction by Pericles of the practice of paying officials regular salaries. This practice is so universal today that we find it hard to imagine a

---

[1] See note on George Grote, p. 427.

government whose officials are not paid, or to appreciate the fundamental revolution that Pericles effected. Heretofore, high political
offices at Athens could be held only by rich men whose independent
incomes afforded them the leisure to perform their duties. Pericles
made it possible for anyone to hold office. All this, however, is only
half the story. Pericles also increased the number of officials greatly.
Among these paid citizens were six thousand jurors, five hundred
members of the Council, seven hundred magistrates in Athens and
seven hundred others sent out to govern the cleruchies, and about
twelve thousand soldiers and sailors, making a total of about twenty
thousand persons. They made up more than a third, and possibly
almost a half, of the entire citizenry. Pericles also established the
"theoric fund," from which each citizen was entitled to draw two
obols to enable him to attend the theater on the days of the three
great festivals—this amount theoretically being what he would have
earned had he been working during the performance. Before long,
citizens were also allowed to draw liberally from this fund on other
occasions as well. Thousands of persons were thus supported by the
state and other thousands drew subsidies from time to time.

The wisdom of these measures has been much debated. Ancient
writers, including Plato and Aristotle, as well as many moderns, have
criticized them severely, charging that they merely served to maintain the poorer classes in idleness and that they eventually bankrupted the state. Others praise them as a form of social insurance.
The jurors were mostly old men, it is claimed, and the payments
they received should be counted as old-age pensions; and payments
from the theoric fund are compared to modern poor relief. Aristotle,
on the other hand, regarded the payments to jurors and others as
simply a form of bribery. He pointed out that Cimon, enjoying "the
riches of a king," distributed gifts lavishly among the populace,
whereas Pericles, a rather poor man, could not rival this munifi-
cence until one of his advisers suggested that he "bribe the people
with their own money." After he had thus devised ways of charging
his expenses to the state treasury, it is said, Pericles' generosity surpassed Cimon's.

Today we cannot choose between these rival interpretations of

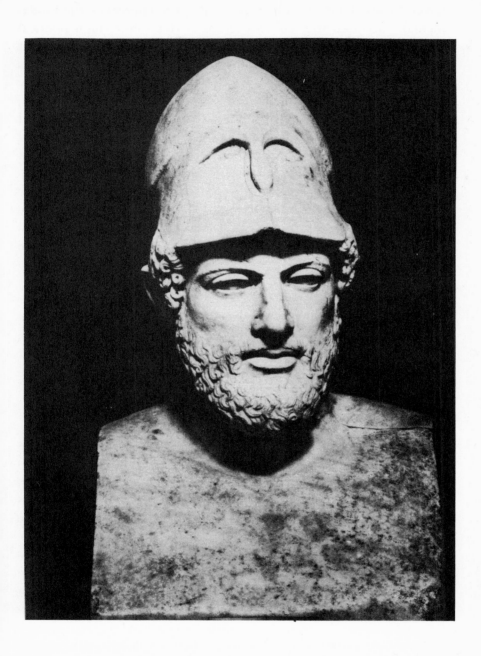

Plate 25.   Pericles *(Vatican Museum)*

Pericles on any but subjective grounds. But whether Pericles' motives were humanitarian or corrupt, he made Athenian citizenship a
valuable asset to its possessors. These fortunate persons became
eager to limit the number of those who might enjoy their lucrative
privileges. Solon and the tyrants had been quick to extend citizenship to foreigners settling in Athens, but naturalization now became
virtually impossible; and in 451 Pericles obtained the enactment of
a law providing that no one might claim citizenship unless he could
prove that both his parents were Athenians. A few years later, in 445,
the citizen rolls were carefully scrutinized and nearly five thousand
names stricken off. As we shall presently see, however, it is not improbable that this culminating step was taken by Pericles' aristocratic opponents, who hoped thus to hoist him with his own petard
—and who were momentarily successful.

Periclean Finance

These various payments placed a heavy burden on the treasury,
and when Pericles launched his enormous building program, the
load became still heavier. Difficulties were increased by the fact that
Athens had no carefully planned budget and no permanent treasury officials. Athenian citizens refused to pay direct taxes, and expenditures were often authorized by the Assembly for which no
revenue was provided. Like all states in antiquity, Athens led a hand-
to-mouth existence financially. Her revenues came principally from
state properties (the most valuable of which were the mines in
Mount Laurium), from direct taxes upon metics and freedmen, and
from a few indirect taxes, including 2 per cent import and export
duties and a small sales tax.

These sources of revenue were supplemented by a special tax
upon the rich. From ancient times it had been the custom for rich
men to court popularity by personal donations of one sort or another,
such as giving public banquets, providing the chorus for a theatrical
performance, or even paying for a trireme. In the fifth century these
public services, called "liturgies," were taken for granted, and every
year the tribes and demes designated wealthy men to provide them.
Liturgies thus virtually became a form of supertax. Underwriting a

trireme was of course expensive, but other liturgies were not so burdensome. The system was not abused by Pericles, though in the next century his successors made it the basis of a deliberate "soak-the-rich" policy in taxation.

The general economic prosperity of the Periclean age assured a liberal revenue from these sources, yet even in time of peace they were not enough to cover the huge expenditures. Pericles helped himself out of his difficulty by appropriating the treasury of the Delian League and channeling the revenue from the League's annual assessments into the city treasury. He justified this procedure by arguing that the allies made their payments for protection and that, so long as they enjoyed this protection, they had no right to demand an accounting of how their money was spent. The assessments thus became mere tribute to Athens, and it has been estimated that they made up at least half of the city's revenue. Pericles, his followers, and Athens herself were thus committed to a policy of imperial exploitation. Periclean democracy was too expensive to function unless subsidized by the tribute of a rich empire.

Limitations of Democracy at Athens

We thus reach the fundamental question, just how democratic was Athens in the days of Pericles? All citizens were entitled to a share in the government, it is true, but these citizens were a very select body. There were more metics and slaves than citizens, and Athenian women had nothing to do with politics. An American election-district with the same population as Attica would contain at least four times as many voters. Moreover, many Athenian citizens could not afford to exercise their rights. The Assembly met at Athens every ten days, more often than most men in the city could take a day off, and regular attendance was out of the question for a farmer living ten or twenty or perhaps even thirty miles away. Thucydides reports an orator who declared, undoubtedly with some exaggeration, that barely five thousand Athenians attended meetings of the Assembly. He might have added that a very considerable proportion of those actually in attendance would be citizens drawing some sort of dole from the state treasury. Pericles maintained his ascendency over these citizens partly by his idealistic praise of democracy and partly by largess from the public funds. Periclean democracy therefore had more in common with the tyranny of Peisistratus than with a modern democracy. Or, as Thucydides remarked, this government was a democracy in name, but in fact a government by the first man. Things went well, however, as long as Pericles himself was that first man. After his death, less worthy leaders took over the machine he had set up and soon brought Athens and her Empire to ruin.

The Aristocratic Opposition

We are not informed as to the activities of the aristocratic opposition during the ten years of Cimon's ostracism, but the struggle of the factions was resumed when he returned to Athens. It was at this time (451) that Pericles secured the law restricting Athenian citizenship, and apparently it was then that he added jurors to those persons drawing state pay. The result of the struggle was that Pericles retained control of domestic policies while Cimon managed foreign affairs.

After Cimon's death (449), leadership in the conservative faction passed to his brother-in-law, Thucydides the son of Melesias—who must not be confused with the historian named Thucydides. The new leader of the opposition attacked Pericles for using funds from the Delian treasury to "bedeck Athens like a harlot" with thousand-talent temples and other costly buildings. We cannot say whether Thucydides was motivated primarily by conscientious scruples in fiscal matters, or by Cimon's Panhellenic feeling coupled with a conviction that Athens could be strong only if her allies in the Delian League were happy in their alliance. Or he may simply have wanted to overtrump Pericles by insinuating that if less money were spent on buildings, more would be available for public distributions. A few years later, in 445, came the purging of the citizen lists. A large consignment of grain from Egypt became available for free distribution among the citizens, and the deletion of five thousand names from the lists meant larger shares for each of those who remained. Our evidence does not indicate who was responsible for the purge, but it seems very likely that by this neat trick the aristocrats won popular favor by passing out larger doles, and at the same time robbed Pericles of five thousand voters. In this same year, 445, Pericles was forced to sign a humiliating treaty of peace with Sparta. The aristocrats exploited the situation to the full, and in 444 Pericles failed of re-election for the first and only time in his life. The victory of the aristocrats was fleeting, however, for in the next year Pericles was again elected, and he crowned his triumph by obtaining the ostracism of Thucydides.

For several years thereafter, Pericles faced no organized opposition. The old aristocrats were far from satisfied with the way things were going, but they could do little except grumble. Not being able to argue effectively, they took up ridicule instead, filling contemporary comedies with their anti-Periclean jokes. Enemies who dared not attack Pericles directly began to attack him indirectly through his friends. One of their targets was his mistress Aspasia, a highly cultivated lady from Miletus, who was brought to trial for "impiety"; another was the sculptor Phidias, who was sent to jail for graft in connection with his famous statue of Athena; a third was the philosopher Anaxagoras, who was denounced as an "atheist" and expelled from Athens. A collection of the more serious arguments invoked at this time against Periclean democracy was published a few years after Pericles' death in a twelve-page brochure under the title *Athenian Policy*: once erroneously attributed to Xenophon (a writer of the next century), this tract is now ascribed merely to "The Old Oligarch."

Until this time the people of Athens had usually been willing to accept rulers from the aristocracy, and even democratic leaders like Pericles had sprung from the old families. Democratic agitation now encouraged men of humble origin to aspire to leadership as well as to mere office-holding. These new aspirants to power were called "demagogues" by their aristocratic opponents. We know them only through their enemies—notably the comic poet Aristophanes and the historian Thucydides—but it is clear that they were unwilling to conduct their political agitation in the traditional manner. Instead of imitating the restrained and idealistic speeches of Pericles, they made oratory a flamboyant and shameless art. A century ago, however, the English historian, George Grote, attempted to redeem their reputation by picturing them as a "parliamentary opposition" whose function it was to criticize the measures proposed by the government in power. He maintained that the charges brought against such demagogues as Cleon and Hyperbolus were often the result of the class prejudices of our informants. Grote's view is not generally accepted, but there can be little doubt that some demagogues really were very able men.

Periclean Imperialism

Greek fear of Persia virtually ceased to exist after Cimon's victory at Eurymedon (467), and with it died the Hellenic League as well as the brief friendship of Athens and Sparta. Ephialtes dissolved the League soon after coming into power, and presently he entered into alliances with Sparta's hostile neighbor, Argos, and with the Thessalians. Pericles went much further. He had inherited the anti-Spartan feeling that was traditional with the Alcmeonidae and the Athenian democracy, and he believed that Athens' natural enemy was Sparta, not Persia. He developed vast plans for safeguarding his city against this rival. His first step was an alliance with the Megarians. Lying across the northern end of the Isthmus of Corinth, Megaris separated the Peloponnesus from Thebes and central Greece. The Megarian alliance therefore reduced the likelihood of an invasion of Attica by dividing Athens' potential enemies. Moreover, this alliance provided Athens with a friendly port on the Gulf of Corinth leading to Italy and the West. Pericles built strong walls connecting the citadel at Megara with its Aegean port (Nisaea) and stationed an Athenian garrison there. Friendship quickly degenerated into domination.

Meantime, Pericles was strengthening the fortifications of Athens in a way that indicated the plans he was already maturing for making his city supreme in Greece. A stout wall was built along the northern side of the road from Athens to Piraeus and another along the eastern side of the road to Phalerum, the two walls and the sea enclosing a triangle several square miles in area. Later a third wall was built parallel to the first on the opposite side of the road. Communication between Athens and the sea was thus made secure.

Athens could never be starved out so long as her navy commanded the Aegean and ships could bring food to Piraeus. The city was a fortress from which raids might be launched against other parts of Greece while Athens itself was impregnable. The plan also provided that if Athens were attacked, the rural population of Attica was to retire within the city walls, leaving the countryside to be devastated by the enemy. Obviously, Pericles' first concern was for the commercial classes and the city dwellers who supported his democracy, not the country aristocrats and their followers who opposed it.

These measures alarmed the rest of Greece and presently led to hostilities. The Corinthians felt themselves menaced by the Athenian occupation of Megara and, according to Thucydides, this was "the principal reason why they conceived a deadly hatred for Athens." The Spartans promptly renewed their old alliance with Thebes, sending troops to Boeotia by ship across the Gulf of Corinth. After a year or two of minor skirmishing, the armies of Athens and Sparta were ready for action in the summer of 457. A battle was fought at Tanagra, in Boeotia, where the Spartan expeditionary force won a slight victory, but the victors were quite willing to return home afterward. The Athenians rallied, and a few weeks later, at Oenophyta, they defeated the Boeotians, whom they forced into an alliance with themselves. Pericles expelled the Boeotian oligarchs and set up democratic governments friendly to Athens.

The Athenians had also been besieging their ancient enemy Aegina, and toward the end of 457 the island capitulated. It was forced to join the Delian League after paying a large indemnity. A year or two later, an Athenian fleet sailed round the Peloponnesus into the Gulf of Corinth. Its commander ravaged the lands of Sicyon, forced an alliance upon Achaea (which held the western half of the southern shore of the Gulf), and settled helots who had escaped from Messenia at Naupactus on the opposite shore. Athens would then have been able to close the Gulf to Corinthian shipping at will. Going still farther afield, Pericles made alliances with two cities in western Sicily in 453. At about the same time he came to terms with Leontini, a neighbor and rival of Syracuse, and with Rhegium in Italy which guarded the Straits of Messana. Athenian settlers were sent to establish a new colony at Sybaris in southern Italy in 446, and two years later others founded near-by Thurii. By these western interests, Pericles provoked still further the hostility of the Corinthians, who had long regarded the West as their especial domain.

Military Setbacks

Meantime, fortuitous events had brought renewed hostilities with Persia. A Libyan prince had stirred up a revolt in Egypt and, after seizing part of the Nile Delta, had called upon Athens for aid in driving out the Persians (about 459). A fleet of two hundred Athenian and allied warships was sent to Egypt, and within a short time the whole Delta was in rebel hands, with the Persian governor besieged in Memphis (457). After some delay the Persian king sent a large army which defeated and destroyed most of the Athenian army (454). This was the most severe defeat that Athens had yet suffered. It prevented her from exploiting her recent victory over the Thebans at Oenophytae, and it enabled Cimon, when he returned from exile in 451, to persuade his fellow citizens to accept a five-year truce with Sparta. The price exacted by Sparta from Athens was the renunciation of the alliance with Argos which dated from 462. Argos then entered into a thirty-year alliance with Sparta. Early in 450, Cimon collected a new fleet of two hundred triremes and prepared to avenge the defeat in Egypt. The old warrior sailed to Cyprus, where he died while besieging Citium (449). After his fleet had defeated a Persian squadron, the Athenians were glad to make peace with Persia. A treaty was drawn up by which the Persians agreed to keep out of the Aegean (as they had actually done ever since Eurymedon), and in return Athens promised not to attack Persian territories.

Pericles had never desired war with Persia, and he was eager to make peace in order to devote the whole power of Athens to forwarding his program for hegemony in Greece. A year or so after the treaty with Persia, he announced plans for a congress of all Greek states to arrange for rebuilding the temples destroyed by Xerxes more than thirty years before. Fearing that such a congress might be interpreted as a recognition of Periclean leadership throughout Greece, the Spartans refused to attend and the congress never met. Perhaps Pericles never expected it to meet, and it is quite possible that the whole project, like so many beautiful proposals in international diplomacy then and now, was designed primarily for home consumption. By this time Cimon's five-year truce with Sparta was drawing to a close and Athens' various enemies were preparing to resume the war. The Boeotian oligarchs, rising in revolt, defeated the Athenians badly at Coronea (447), and the Spartans instigated an uprising against Athens in Euboea (446). While Pericles was away with the army pacifying that island, the Megarians massacred their Athenian garrison, and a Spartan army prepared to invade Attica. Pericles hurried back from Euboea, but as Athens was in no condition to undertake war against most of Greece, he signed a Thirty Years Peace with Sparta (445). He was thus left free to put down the Euboean revolt and to guard other rebellious islands in his Aegean empire. The only gains that Athens still held after fifteen years of Periclean aggression were Aegina and Naupactus.

The Subjugation of the Delian League

Pericles was willing to make these sacrifices because the uprising in Euboea showed the restlessness of the allies in the Delian League. Upon these allies were founded all his plans for assuring his own leadership in Athens and the hegemony of Athens in Greece, and, furthermore, he knew that, in view of the hostility of the rest of Greece, Athens could not survive the loss of those allies. As early as 454, Pericles had moved the treasury of the League from Delos to Athens on the pretext that the loss of the fleet in Egypt laid Delos open to Persian attack. One-sixtieth of the tribute collected thereafter went to Athena; the rest simply went to Athens. Since the League was supposedly for defense against Persia, it might seem that peace should have made possible a considerable reduction in tribute, but the actual decrease was temporary and slight. Pericles had no illusions about the changed status of the League, and he was well aware of the growing hostility of its members. At least eight thousand Athenian citizens were therefore settled as cleruchs on various Aegean Islands or the Chersonesus in 447 and 446, and after the revolt in Euboea a large cleruchy was established there.

The Athenians, too, had no illusions about what was going on. The aristocratic faction under Thucydides, son of Melesias, attacked Pericles and his measures with all the means at their disposal. At last, as we have seen, the humiliating treaty of 445 enabled them to oust him from office, and for a moment it seemed that Thucydides might lead Athens back to the old Panhellenism of Miltiades and Cimon. The new colony at Thurii may be cited as an example of this spirit: it was in no sense a cleruchy, but a Panhellenic enterprise open to citizens of all Greek states, and only two-fifths of the colonists were Athenians. This arrangement was probably made by Thucydides and his friends during their year of office (444) to appease Corinthians and others who had been frightened by Pericles' activities at nearby Sybaris in 446. Our scanty evidence seems to indicate that after the colonists had been enrolled, but before they sailed, Pericles returned to power. He decided to go ahead with the project, hoping that the new colony might even yet become an Athenian outpost. He therefore put two friends, both hostile to Thucydides, in charge of the colony and included among the colonists others —one of them being the historian Herodotus—who were to defend Athenian interests there. His hopes failed, however, and within ten years Thurii went over to the anti-Athenian party.

The ostracism of Thucydides in 443 may be taken as marking the end of the old Panhellenism at Athens and of the old Delian League. As soon as Pericles was again firmly in power, he reorganized the League as an Athenian Empire and began taking extreme measures to suppress dissatisfaction. In 443 he divided the 160-odd states composing the League into five groups to facilitate collection of the tribute. A major revolt which had meantime broken out in Samos was suppressed only after Pericles had starved the city into surrender (439). The walls of the city were torn down, its fleet was confiscated, the oligarchic rulers were deported, and a heavy indemnity was imposed. Other allies showed themselves restive during the siege, and Byzantium revolted; but the severe punishment of Samos restored an outward calm. Pericles honored the Athenians who died at Samos with an eloquent oration in which he used a famous phrase—that the loss of these fine young men made it seem that the year had lost its springtime. Nevertheless, Cimon's sister Elpinice annoyed the orator extremely by remarking to him at the close of his speech that her brother had died while fighting the enemies of Athens, not while butchering her friends and allies.

The reorganization of the League was no sooner completed than Pericles began expanding the Empire to the north and northeast. His first step was the foundation, in 437, of Amphipolis in Thrace, near the site of the old colony, Nine Ways. Amphipolis became the center of Athenian power in the North and obtained the trade and mines of that region. Even more important was Athenian expansion across the Black Sea to the Crimea. The Persian capture of the Hellespont and Bosporus in the sixth century had put an end to the commercial relations with that area which had existed in the days of Peisistratus. Pericles re-established friendly relations with the local dynasts in 437, thus assuring Athens of an inexhaustible supply of grain from the Crimea and completing a program inaugurated more than twenty years before when he built the Long Walls from Athens to the sea. The Athenian Empire seemed to stand upon infrangible foundations.

Preparations for War

We may be sure that Pericles had not forgotten the humiliation of the Thirty Years Peace, but no evidence warrants saying what he thought about it ten years later. Was he making elaborate preparations for a war of *revanche?* Had he forsaken his youthful dream of Athenian hegemony over Greece? Or had he transformed and idealized this hegemony into an intellectual and cultural, rather than a political, leadership? The historian Thucydides, who was a very keen observer living at the time, inclined to the latter view. In one passage he makes Pericles speak of Athens as "the school of Hellas"—though authorities often regard such views as Thucydidean rather than Periclean. But even if Pericles now envisioned a more ethereal leadership, it is not certain that he had completely forsaken his earlier dreams; and above all, there is no reason to suppose that his foreign enemies gave him credit for such a change of heart. The historian admitted that the rest of Greece still feared Athenian aggression.

Whether Pericles desired it or not, he knew that a resumption of hostilities was very likely and laid his plans accordingly. One indication of his preparations for war is the gradual increase of tribute, along with decreased expenditures for public works, which enabled him to store up a war fund amounting to six thousand talents. As the impending war would be fought partly against Corinthian trade in the West, Pericles began showing a renewed interest in western politics. Except for the ill-starred enterprise at Thurii, he had paid little attention to the West since 445, but about 437 he sent an Athenian admiral to cruise along the coast of northwestern Greece and conclude alliances with various Acarnanian cities. He thus alarmed his enemies and caused them to suspect that he was planning to plunge Greece into war once more.

War was brought appreciably closer by a series of events beginning in 433. The first concerned Corcyra, the modern Corfu. Although this island, lying off the coast of Epirus, had been colonized from Corinth, it had long enjoyed complete independence. The Corcyraeans, in their turn, had planted a colony at Epidamnus on the mainland, farther north. At about this time, the Epidamnians fell into trouble with native neighbors and begged aid of Corcyra, who refused it. They next appealed to Corinth, who sent troops and colonists to help. Corcyra became alarmed, demanded that the colonists return home, and, when their demand was refused, attacked Epidamnus (435). Corinth threatened to intervene, and the Corcyraeans, after various futile negotiations, appealed to Athens. Pericles concluded an alliance with them and presently sent a few ships to western waters. Late in the summer of 433, the Corinthian fleet defeated the Corcyraeans, with the Athenians standing by. The Athenian ships covered the Corcyraean retreat, and the Corinthians let the enemy escape rather than fight the Athenian ships. Corcyra's location across the route to the West enabled her to menace Corinthian trade with Sicily, and Corinth therefore regarded the Corcyraean alliance with Athens as a threat.

A second incident concerned Potidaea, a city in Chalcidice that was menaced by the new Athenian colony at nearby Amphipolis. Potidaea had once been a Corinthian colony, but in the days of Cimon she had joined the Delian League. When Athens raised their tribute for 434 from six talents to fifteen, the Potidaeans prepared to revolt, in which course they were encouraged both by the king of neighboring Macedonia and by Corinth. The revolt broke out in 432 and Corinth sent two thousand volunteers to help the Potidaeans. Other cities in the neighborhood joined the rebellion, but they were easily pacified—partly by a reduction of their tribute—and the Athenians settled down for a long siege of Potidaea and its Corinthian garrison.

At approximately this same time (432), Pericles decided to regain his former foothold at the head of the Gulf of Corinth through Megaris. To bring the Megarians into a receptive frame of mind, he passed a decree through the Assembly at Athens forbidding them to trade in any port of the Athenian Empire. This exclusion was intended primarily as a demonstration of the power Athens could exert without formally going to war, and for Megara it meant ruin. Pericles also renewed the treaties made with Leontini and Rhegium several years before, thus threatening Corinthian supremacy in the West at still another point. Matters were rapidly approaching a crisis when the Thebans decided that the time had come for them to regain Plataea, which had been allied to Athens for almost a century. In March, 431, they made an unsuccessful attempt to occupy this frontier town and all Greece was soon at war.

The Peloponnesian War: First Phase

Thucydides, the most thoughtful of the ancient historians, believed that "the truest causes of the war, but the ones most rarely mentioned in the talk of the time, were the growth of Athenian power and Spartan fear of it." In this judgment Thucydides was undoubtedly correct. The historian hastened to add, however, that the affairs of Corcyra and Potidaea did much to precipitate war at just that time. The Spartans, who dominated the Peloponnesian League, were still attached to their traditional isolationism, but the Corinthians, after their humiliation at Corcyra, were constantly urging the necessity of armed resistance if Athens were to be checked. When the Athenians besieged Potidaea, Corinthian envoys were sent to a meeting of the Peloponnesian League at Sparta with instructions to urge immediate war. They first addressed the Spartan Assembly; Athenian envoys, who happened to be in the city on other business, gave a blustering reply; and Archidamus, king of Sparta, cautiously urged further diplomatic negotiations. The Assembly voted, however, that the Athenian action at Corcyra was a violation of the Thirty Years Peace, and the League voted for war (late 432). Pericles was quite ready to take up the challenge, though his aristocratic opponents favored peace.

The diplomats spent the next several weeks seeking new allies and maneuvering to make their opponents take the first step and thus show themselves to be aggressors before gods and men. Encouraged by a Delphic promise of aid from Apollo, the Spartans made bold to demand that Athens expel Pericles, alleging that the Alcmeonidae had been tainted ever since they murdered Cylon's followers in 632.

Of course the Athenians found no difficulty in retaliating by raking up various sacrileges committed by prominent Spartans, of which they loudly reminded heaven and earth. The Corinthians and Spartans spoke of preserving the liberties of Greece in the face of Athenian aggression, and the Athenians declaimed with equal, or perhaps greater, eloquence about Spartan dictation. By the spring of 431, both parties were ready to fight, and the Boeotian attack upon Plataea was the spark that set all Greece ablaze.

The Athenian army consisted of 13,000 hoplites and 1000 cavalry, but as 3000 hoplites were at Potidaea, this force was outnumbered more than three to one by the enemy. The Peloponnesian League provided 24,000 hoplites while Boeotia had 10,000 hoplites and 1000 cavalry. The Athenian navy, on the other hand, was far superior to the enemy's. Pericles had foreseen just this situation and now he refused to fight on land, counting upon sea power and finance to win the war. He had saved up a war chest of six thousand talents, and tribute from the Empire amounted to six hundred talents annually. But while Pericles excelled at laying plans of this sort, he was not an able general in the field, and Athens had no other commander of outstanding ability. The troops of the Peloponnesian League were commanded by the Spartan king Archidamus who, after ruling for over forty years, favored diplomacy rather than war; but he was an able general who led his troops well. A much more brilliant general was Brasidas, an energetic and aggressive Spartan, popular with his soldiers, who was able to comprehend the Periclean strategy and eventually to construct a counterplan which threatened the Athenian Empire.

Archidamus reached the Athenian frontier soon after the Theban attack upon Plataea, which had meantime been occupied by a small Athenian garrison. He sent envoys to Athens with still another offer of negotiations, hoping that Athens might yield at the last moment. But Pericles persuaded the Athenians to receive no embassies while the enemy were on Attic soil, and the envoys were sent back after making the prophetic remark, "This day will bring many woes to the Greeks." Thereafter, the war proceeded as planned. The Attic farmers transferred their cattle and movable property to Euboea

and shut themselves up within the walls of Athens. Archidamus occupied and ravaged much of Attica, meeting no opposition, and
after a few weeks he withdrew. Meantime, the Athenians raided
various places in the Peloponnesus with their fleet and, doubting
the loyalty of their old enemies in Aegina, they drove out all the

THE PELOPONNESIAN WAR
431-404 B.C.

inhabitants of that island and settled an Athenian cleruchy there.
The Aeginetans were given new homes in Laconia by the Spartans.
Late in the year, the Athenians, following their usual custom, held
funeral ceremonies at which Pericles delivered his most famous oration—a magnificent tribute to the glory of Athens and the strength
of her democracy.

The second year of the war was merely a repetition of the first until a misfortune befell Athens which Pericles had not foreseen. Plague
broke out in the city where, because of crowded and unsanitary
conditions, it wrought fearful havoc. Before it had worked itself out,

almost a third of the population was dead. The aristocrats, who had always opposed the war, were enraged and embittered by Pericles' refusal to defend their estates; now the people turned against him, too. He was removed from office, brought to trial for misappropriating public funds, and fined fifty talents. There was even talk of peace negotiations, but Archidamus refused to listen. Within a short time, however, hysterical public opinion had swung to the opposite extreme again, and Pericles was re-elected general. As his two lawful sons had died of the plague, the people even passed a special decree legitimizing his son by Aspasia. Eventually Pericles, too, died of the plague (429) and leadership at Athens fell to a former tanner named Cleon.

Cleon and Brasidas

Historians have often criticized Cleon in unmeasured language, following the precedent set by his aristocratic contemporaries, Thucydides and Aristophanes. Yet Cleon was a man of high ability, and it is quite probable that he expressed the opinions of the Athenian democracy more accurately than did Pericles. Under his leadership, the war dragged on, and the longer it lasted the more terrible it became; but it is not fair to blame Cleon for everything that happened. These terrible things are inherent in war itself.

Shortly before the death of Pericles, Potidaea finally fell. It was forced to surrender by sheer starvation, the surviving citizens were expelled with only the clothes they wore, and an Athenian cleruchy was settled in their place. Pericles must bear the blame for this atrocity as well as for the comparable one at Aegina the year before. A year later the oligarchs of Mytilene decided that the time had come to throw off the Athenian yoke, and the whole island of Lesbos rose in revolt. Not until 427 were the Athenians able to reduce the city. About thirty of the ringleaders were sent to Athens for trial and execution, and Cleon persuaded the Assembly to order the execution of all male citizens, while the women and children were to be sold into slavery. The next day the Assembly met again and by a slight majority revoked this harsh order after a critic had argued that it was bad policy for Athens to be so barbarous. The lives of the Mytileneans were spared, but an Athenian cleruchy was planted on the island of Lesbos. On this occasion Cleon certainly showed himself more bloodthirsty than Pericles had been in the cases of Samos, Aegina, and Potidaea; but also, the provocation was greater. Meantime, the Athenian treasury had been depleted. The siege of Potidaea alone had cost two thousand talents, and the other campaigns had gobbled up the rest. During the siege of Mytilene it had become necessary to levy a direct property tax upon Athenian citizens—for the first time in more than a century. This new tax, perhaps, was another reason for Athenian vindictiveness. Two years later the tribute exacted from the allies was more than doubled, with the total amount collected reaching 1460 talents, or more than thrice what had been assessed by Aristides fifty years before. Still, in this measure as in so many others, Cleon was merely following and accentuating Periclean policy.

Fighting continued on many fronts. The Spartans captured Plataea, opening the road from the Peloponnesus to Boeotia. The Athenians won naval victories at the western end of the Gulf of Corinth, and twice they made demonstrations in Sicily, inflicting serious losses upon Corinthian trade. Yet neither side could win a decisive victory. In 427, the war returned to Corcyra, where the democracy favored Athens against the pro-Corinthian oligarchs. The latter managed to seize control, but an Athenian fleet soon arrived with aid for the democrats, who overthrew their masters to the accompaniment of atrocious massacres.

Two years later, in 425, the Athenians managed to land troops at Pylos, in the southwestern Peloponnesus, where they captured a considerable Spartan force. As Cleon commanded the Athenian troops in the last part of this campaign, he won a high military reputation. The Spartans retaliated a year later by the capture of Amphipolis and a thrust in the direction of Thrace. The loss of Amphipolis was a serious blow to the Athenian Empire. To us it is also important because one of the generals sent to defend the city was the historian Thucydides; as he did not arrive in time, Amphipolis was lost and Thucydides was exiled by his fellow citizens. Had it not been for this misfortune, he would probably not have had the leisure to write down his profound reflections upon the war and we would today be the poorer for it.

After the capture of Amphipolis, the Spartan commander, Brasidas, began planning an extensive invasion of Thrace. Apparently he hoped to seize the Bosporus and stop the importation of Crimean grain to Athens, a move which, had he been successful, would have quickly won the war for Sparta. In the same year the Athenians attempted to invade Boeotia, where they suffered a severe defeat at Delium. These defeats made the Athenians anxious to conclude peace, and the Spartans fell into a chastened mood. They had never been enthusiastic for the war, and early in 423 they were glad to conclude a truce for one year. Neither Brasidas nor Cleon was satisfied, however, and hostilities were resumed in 422. Realizing that Amphipolis was essential to the safety of Athens, Cleon persuaded the Assembly to put him in command of a large force to recapture the city. The two generals fought a battle in which the Spartans were victorious, though both commanders were slain—Brasidas while trying to help a friend, Cleon while running away.

These events turned men's thoughts once more to peace. Trouble was brewing for Sparta in the Peloponnesus, and Athens turned more and more to the peace party under Nicias, the wealthy aristocrat who had negotiated the truce of 423. Peace discussions lasted all winter, and at last the "Peace of Nicias" was signed at Sparta in March, 421, just ten years after hostilities had begun. Each of the belligerents promised to return all territories seized during the war and to release all prisoners. By a separate treaty signed a few days later, Sparta and Athens became allies for fifty years. These treaties were of no effect. Corinth, Megara, and Thebes felt that they had been betrayed by their ally and refused to accept the peace. The Spartan commander at Amphipolis handed the city over to the native Chalcidians, not to the Athenians as ordered, whereupon the Athenians refused to return Pylos to Sparta. Athens also refused to surrender Nisaea to Megara until Thebes returned Plataea to them. This the Thebans refused to do, since they were to get nothing in exchange. The fighting had of course settled nothing; the peace was only an armistice; and the Greek states were soon at war once more.

The Fall of the Athenian Empire

The peace brought Nicias momentary popularity, but he soon was overshadowed in Athenian politics by Alcibiades, the last and in some ways the most brilliant of the Alcmeonidae. This young man was a cousin of Pericles (see genealogical table, p. 400). His father had distinguished himself as a young man fighting against the Persians at Artemisium, but he was among those slain at Coronea in 447. Thereafter the young Alcibiades lived in the house of Pericles, where he associated freely with the most distinguished men in Athens. He had a brilliant and versatile mind, good looks, and wealth; his manners were charming, and he was encumbered by neither scruples nor morals. He felt that he personally was above the law, and he was determined to rule Athens at any cost. He was elected *strategos* in 420 as an opponent of Nicias, but the two men soon joined forces against the leader of the democratic faction, a demagogue named Hyperbolus—whom one Attic wit had called a "Cleon in hyperbole." Alarmed at the political progress made by Alcibiades, Hyperbolus had proposed that the young man be ostracized, but the alliance with Nicias caused the ostracism to fall upon Hyperbolus instead (417). Taking over leadership of the democratic faction, Alcibiades then revived the aggressive imperialism of Pericles.

The thirty-year alliance of Sparta and Argos had expired in 421, shortly after the conclusion of peace. In spite of Spartan offers, the Argives were unwilling to renew it. Having remained neutral throughout the war, they were in a strong position, and anticipated regaining their ancient hegemony in Hellas. They therefore established friendly relations with Sparta's disgruntled neighbors, and the Peloponnesian League collapsed. These maneuvers gave Alcibiades his chance. He denounced Nicias's Spartan alliance, which had marked a return to Cimon's old aristocratic friendship with that state, and he revived Pericles' democratic hostility to Sparta by making alliances with her neighbors, Argos, Mantinea, and Elis (420). Though the alliances were supposedly defensive, Alcibiades already looked forward to new wars. Athens was not yet ready to support such aggression, however, and failed to re-elect him general in 418. The Spartans seized this opportunity to smash the hostile alliance, and in a battle at Mantinea they defeated the allied armies. Argos was forced into a new alliance with Sparta, the Peloponnesian League was restored, and once more Athens was isolated in Greece. In spite of this misfortune, Alcibiades managed to regain public favor, and two years later he added Melos to the Empire. When the Melians resisted, a military force captured the island, executed all the male citizens, and enslaved the women and children. An Athenian cleruchy was then settled on Melos (416).

Alcibiades' Sicilian Expedition

Alcibiades then announced his most ambitious project. Athens had long been an ally of Segesta in Sicily when, in 416, a request came from that city for aid in a war against her neighbor Selinus. Alcibiades promptly espoused Segesta's cause, seeing it in an opportunity for great things, and he persuaded the Athenians to use this quarrel as a pretext for a general intervention in Sicilian affairs. According to Thucydides, Alcibiades later boasted that he had planned to conquer all Sicily, the Italian cities, and Carthage; with the resources of this vast empire, and with mercenaries drawn from Spain, he could conquer the Peloponnesus and thus come to rule the whole Greek world. But while dreams such as these may have floated through the leader's mind, vaguer ideas of adventure and conquest motivated the lesser Athenians (see map, p. 525).

In spite of the conservative opposition led by Nicias, a Greek fleet sailed for Sicily in June, 415. It consisted of 134 triremes and 130 other vessels, carrying 5100 hoplites and a total force of about 27,000 men; and it was commanded by three generals, Alcibiades, Nicias, and Lamachus. The expedition started under a bad omen, however, for on the night before it was to sail, somebody mutilated a number of statues of Hermes in Athens. Alcibiades was accused of having a hand in this sacrilege and of profaning the Eleusinian mysteries as well. When his request for an immediate trial was refused, he sailed with the fleet. A few weeks later, after he had reached Sicily, Thessalus the son of Cimon signed a complaint against him, and Alcibiades was ordered home. He managed to escape from the envoys sent to fetch him and made his way to Sparta, where he persuaded the government to send aid to Syracuse and to occupy and fortify a place called Decelea on the Attic frontier.

Meantime, the war in Sicily was going badly for the Athenians. Their first great objective was Syracuse, but delays in northern Sicily gave the Syracusans a chance to put their fortifications in order. Lamachus was killed in battle, leaving Nicias the only Athenian general in the field. He was neither competent nor enthusiastic, and the Syracusan defense was ably organized. Eventually Nicias's position became so bad that, late in 414, he sent to Athens for reinforcements. A second armada, consisting of 73 triremes with 5000 hoplites and many other troops, was sent to Sicily in the following spring, too late to prevent disaster. The reinforced Athenian fleet was destroyed in the harbor at Syracuse, and the army made a futile attempt to escape overland. Late in September, 413, Nicias surrendered. Out of a total force of 200 triremes and 40,000 to 45,000 men, only 7000 prisoners survived. The magnificent expedition, on which Alcibiades and the Athenians had based such soaring hopes, thus ended in a disaster which, thanks to Thucydides, has remained classic in history.

News of this crushing blow to Athens inflamed the rest of the Greek world. Sparta and her allies prepared to resume war immediately; Athens' allies planned to revolt, asking Spartan aid, which was promptly promised; and Persia revived her long-dormant ambitions against Greece. The Chians revolted in the summer of 412 and were speedily joined by Miletus and other Ionian cities. A Spartan fleet, accompanied by ships from Syracuse, appeared in the eastern Aegean and its commander presently negotiated a series of three treaties with Tissaphernes, the Persian satrap at Sardis. The Spartan commander acknowledged the Persian right to all the cities ever held by the Great King in Asia, in return for which he was promised financial subsidies and the support of the Phoenician fleet: the Spartans virtually sold Ionia to Persia. At about the same time, Alcibiades, of whom the Spartans had grown suspicious, withdrew to Sardis, where he began intriguing with Tissaphernes on his own account. He apparently was repeating Hippias's old dream of being set up as tyrant in Athens by the Persians when a sudden turn of events suggested an easier way of attaining that goal.

Revolution at Athens

The Sicilian disaster left the Athenians stunned, but with remarkable resiliency they took energetic measures to meet the new dangers confronting them. While they were building a new fleet with their last thousand talents, oligarchic politicians began plotting to overthrow the Athenian democracy. Led by a certain Antiphon, they assassinated a number of prominent democrats, and early in 411 they persuaded the terrified and desperate Athenians to accept an oligarchy. The proposed government was vaguely pictured as a return to the old system that had prevailed before Solon began tinkering with the constitution, but power actually fell to a Council of Four Hundred, nominated by the men who effected the revolution. The new government which took over in May, 411, with Antiphon and the extremists in control, quickly showed itself to be utterly incompetent. It abolished payments to jurors and other officials; it ruled by terror and murder; it tried to negotiate peace; and, above all, it alienated the enlisted men in the large army at Samos, who recalled Alcibiades and would have sailed against Athens itself, had he not prevented them.

After a rule of about four months, the Four Hundred fell to fighting among themselves. Antiphon was executed, other extremists were driven out, and a moderate leader named Theramenes set up a new government. The franchise was restored to all who could give the government financial or military aid—in practice, the three richer social classes, with the *thetes* still excluded. It had been expected that there would be about five thousand citizens. Actually there were almost twice that many. Both Thucydides and Aristotle approved of this government by the Five Thousand, the latter depicting it as a blending of the diverse merits of rule by the many and rule by the few, and the former praising it as the best government Athens ever had.

While Athens was thus in the throes of revolution, the Spartans were prosecuting the war, though not always with vigor and skill.

Subsidies from Persia enabled them to build a large fleet, to occupy strategic places in the Aegean and Ionia, and even to threaten Athens. In 410, this fleet and a Persian army besieged Cyzicus (an Athenian ally located on the southern shore of the Propontis) but they were destroyed by Theramenes acting with the co-operation of Alcibiades, who had been elected *strategos* by the troops at Samos. The victory of their new fleet, built the year before, aroused such enthusiasm at Athens that the Five Thousand were swept aside and the old democracy re-established.

The leader of the new government was a demagogue named Cleophon, an ardent imperialist who had learned politics in the school of Cleon and Hyperbolus. He at once restored payment to office-holders, adding new payments for other citizens. The Spartans were so discouraged by the loss of their fleet that they sued for peace on the basis of each side retaining what it then held. Historians, gifted with hindsight, have often remarked that Athens would have done well to accept this offer; perhaps so, but at the moment peace did not seem that desirable. Acceptance of Sparta's offer would have entailed the sacrifice by Athens of much of her empire, a proposal which Cleophon and the victorious democrats could not consider with equanimity as long as their fleet controlled the seas. The war therefore continued, with varying successes on each side, and the fame of Alcibiades rose steadily. At last, in the summer of 407, he ventured to return to Athens, after an absence of eight years. He was received with tumultuous enthusiasm, and it seemed possible that he might set himself up as tyrant. Caution suggested, however, that he should not risk this supreme throw until he had won another important victory. This second victory never came.

The Final Campaigns

The years after the battle of Cyzicus (410) were marked by the appearance of two new personalities in the struggle, the Spartan Lysander and the Persian Cyrus "the Younger." Lysander was a skillful and honest general and diplomat; Cyrus was the younger son of the Persian king, Darius II. Heretofore, negotiations between Greeks and Persians had been conducted largely by Tissaphernes,

with frequent interference by Pharnabazus, satrap of the Helles-
pontine provinces. To eliminate the rivalry of these two satraps,
Darius sent Cyrus to rule at Sardis and transferred Tissaphernes to
Caria. Cyrus soon established good relations with Lysander and
prepared the measures which brought Athens to her knees. A new
Spartan fleet was built with Persian aid and, in the fall of 407, it
defeated an Athenian squadron at Notium near Ephesus. Though
this was not a major battle, defeat prevented Alcibiades from returning to Athens in triumph; he retired instead to an estate near the
Hellespont where he lived for three years, before being executed by
the Persians in 404.

The Athenians avenged Notium at Arginusae in 406, but the
hysterical populace ordered death for the victorious commanders
for having failed to rescue the crews of their own wrecked vessels.
Among the six to be executed was Pericles, son of the great Pericles
and Aspasia, whom the Athenians had legitimized by special decree
twenty-three years before. Arginusae was the last Athenian victory.
Aid from Cyrus enabled Lysander to build still another fleet, with
which he hunted down the main Athenian navy at Aegospotami on
the Hellespont (September, 405). He surprised the fleet while its
crews were ashore hunting food. One hundred and sixty Athenian
vessels were destroyed and their crews captured, and as no resistance could be made, Lysander suffered no losses. The Athenian
admiral, Conon, was aboard one of the twenty vessels that managed
to escape, but not daring to return home, he fled to Cyprus after
sending word to Athens of what had happened.

It was night when the messengers reached Piraeus. The historian
Xenophon tells us how "a wail swept up between the walls from
Piraeus to Athens as each man told the news to another. On that
night no man slept." The Athenians knew well that the loss of their
fleet this time sealed their doom, and they anticipated the same punishment they had once inflicted upon the Melians, the Aeginetans,
and so many other vanquished Greeks. Spartan troops advanced
from Decelea, the Spartan fleet blockaded Piraeus, and, in spite of
Cleophon, Athens sued for peace. Theramenes went to Lysander to
ask for terms and was held prisoner for three months until conditions

in Athens had become desperate. During this time, Cleophon, the super-patriotic warmonger, had been executed as a draft-dodger, and starvation forced the Athenians to accept peace at any price (April, 404). They were required to destroy the Long Walls and the fortifications of Piraeus, to surrender what was left of their fleet, to give up their empire, to receive back all exiles, and to become a subordinate ally of Sparta. For twenty-seven years Athens had waged a war marked by tremendous destruction of property, progressive bitterness, cumulating atrocities, alternating hysterical jubilation or dejection, frantic gambling under Cleophon, starvation, and eventually complete collapse. In the end, Athens lost, and her defeat rang down the curtain on her imperial glory.

Note

George Grote

The most eminent of the modern panegyrists of Pericles is the English historian George Grote (1794–1871). Grote's father was a successful banker who sent his son to a famous public school (Charterhouse) but refused him a university education and put him to work in the bank at the age of sixteen. The young man fell under the influence of the radical thinkers of the day, notably Bentham and Mill, and presently began publishing essays on political and philosophical subjects. He was elected to Parliament in 1832, shortly after the passage of the famous Reform Bill, and for several years thereafter he actively promoted further democratic reform in England. He had a share in founding, and later in guiding, the University of London, which he envisaged as a school of higher education for the people, in contrast with the aristocratic universities at Oxford and Cambridge. He resigned his parliamentary seat in 1841, and withdrew from the bank, in order to write his long-planned *History of Greece*. The first volume appeared in 1846, the twelfth and last in 1856. Grote also published a three-volume work on Plato (1865), and death prevented the completion of one on Aristotle.

When Grote was a young man, the standard English history of Greece was one published between 1784 and 1810 by William Mitford, who wrote under the influence of the British fear and hatred of the French Revolution. He believed that democracy must inevitably lead to a reign of terror, and his history was a powerful and most unfair attack upon Athenian democracy. Grote criticized this history in an essay published in 1826—the youthful Macaulay had published a slashing attack upon it a year or two before—and at that early date he showed his deep sympathy with Pericles and the Athenian democracy. These sympathies Grote retained throughout his life and he developed them at length in his later writings. In fact, Grote managed to inject into his history his own enthusiasm for the radical idealism of early Victorian England. Though written in a sober and restrained style, and marked by thorough scholarship and deep thought, Grote's *History of Greece,* even more than most great histories, is a profession of faith as well as a history.

In spite of, or perhaps because of, his long though involuntary connection with the bank, Grote paid little attention to economics and finance, reserving his brilliance for political and intellectual history. His friend Gladstone once confessed that he had found Grote's treatment of Greek colonial expansion in the West (chaps. 22–27) helpful when formulating his own policy for the British Empire. The most famous chapter in the book deals with the Sophists (chap. 67), whom Grote strove to rescue from the obloquy thrust upon them by Plato's diatribes. Grote regarded these Sophists as the "educators of Greece," doing for their country what he hoped the University of London would do for England. In Pericles he found a kindred spirit, and many brilliant passages in the history celebrate that statesman's greatness and the excellence of Athenian democracy. Grote's book is now out-of-date in many ways—especially the early part, which was written long before Schliemann and Evans—and even his view of Athenian democracy requires fundamental modification, but persons who seek ideas and political insight rather than the most recently discovered facts can still read it with interest and profit. See Mrs. Grote, *The Personal Life of George Grote* (1873).

XIII Periclean Athens

HE PERSIAN WARS TRANSFERRED THE ECONOMIC AND IN-
tellectual center of the Greek world from Ionia to Athens. Wars and
rebellions had played havoc with the economic life of Ionia, and
when the Ionian cities threw off the Persian yoke in the years after
Salamis, they severed themselves from the Asiatic hinterland for
which they were the natural economic outlet. They did not regain
their former prosperity until the fourth century, when they once
more were united politically with their markets and with the sources
of their raw materials. Athens, on the other hand, made amazing economic progress in the fifth century. Elsewhere on the Greek peninsula, Thessaly and central Greece remained almost wholly agricultural, just as they had been before. The economic life of Sparta and
the Peloponnesus was not greatly altered. Corinth remained a great
commercial city, the center of trade with the West. In general, it was
a prosperous period, above all in Athens, and upon this solid economic foundation was erected the intellectual and artistic super-
structure which is the imperishable glory of Greece.

Rising prosperity made possible a rapid growth in the population
of Attica. The surplus population was born mostly in the farming
villages, yet there probably were fewer farmers in Attica at the end
of the century than before the Persian wars. Thousands of farm boys
went to Athens, where they found new occupations or were supported by the state, and other thousands emigrated to the cleruchies.
The population of Athens was also augmented by thousands of
metics, many of whom were merchants or artisans from the Ionian
cities, while others were non-Greeks from farther abroad. And

429

finally, there was a great expansion of slavery. Heretofore, there had not been many slaves in Greece, where they were used principally in domestic service, but in the fifth century thousands were brought to Athens and other Greek cities, some to do the heavy work in industry and mining, others as skilled artisans. Though Athens occasionally sold conquered Greeks into slavery, there was a feeling that one Greek should not own another, and these unfortunates were usually sent to foreign countries. The slaves in Greece were mostly Thracians and Asiatics, with a few from the western Mediterranean area.

Scholars have often tried to estimate the population of ancient Greece, usually on the basis of military levies and area, but their conclusions contain much that is mere guesswork.[1] It seems safe to say, however, that in 431 there were probably between seven and eight million Greeks in the world, slightly more than half of whom lived in Greece or the Aegean Islands, while the rest inhabited Ionia, Sicily, and the other colonial areas. The total population of Attica may have been between three and four hundred thousand, one hundred thousand or more living within the walls of Athens and Piraeus, about as many more just outside, and the rest in the villages. The total number of citizens (voters) has been estimated at forty to fifty thousand, which would indicate a total free Athenian population of at least 175,000 persons. There probably were sixty to seventy-five thousand metics in all, and it is virtually impossible to estimate the number of slaves. Some writers guess that there were as few as sixty-five thousand while others put the number as high as two hundred thousand. In this case splitting the difference is probably as safe a way as any to resolve the difficulty.

Agriculture, of course, remained the basic industry in most of Greece, and though conditions were much what they had been before the Persian wars, Attic agriculture declined steadily throughout the fifth century. Since the days of Solon, the great estates of Athenian aristocrats had been divided among many small landholders, and the resulting economic decline of the landed aristocracy had preceded their political downfall. At first the small farmers were

---

[1] See note on Karl Julius Beloch, p. 471.

better off than when they had been serfs, but after Xerxes' invasion, they never regained their former prosperity. They lacked the capital to finance reconstruction, and throughout the century energetic and intelligent farmers were drawn off the farms to Athens or the cleruchies. Those remaining in the villages were either the successful few who felt no need to move, or the ignorant and conservative many who dared not risk it. The latter were quite unable to master the difficult task of wresting an adequate living from the poor Attic soil by the primitive agricultural methods they knew. They had no manures, and their only method of preventing soil exhaustion was the wasteful "two-field system," by which half the land lay fallow each year. Heavy importation of grain kept its price from rising as rapidly as prices in general, and grain farmers suffered in consequence. If, on the other hand, a man had initiative and capital enough to set out vines and olive trees, he fared much better. Such plantings were costly, and several years must elapse before the first crop was ready, but with proper care orchards and vineyards became very profitable. Eventually, wine and olive oil were the principal agricultural products of Attica, but it was not until the fourth century that they achieved their supremacy.

Industry and Commerce at Athens

The new Athens was a commercial and industrial city. Situated on a peninsula jutting into the Aegean, she was admirably located for taking over the trade that was then slipping from Ionian hands. The fleet built by Themistocles protected Athenian shipping from pirates (an important matter in those days) and his harbor at Piraeus was the best in the Aegean area. The members of the Delian League provided excellent markets for the growing economy of Athens in the days of Cimon, but these markets were soon outgrown and commercial leaders began looking farther afield. Pericles, like his Alcmeonid ancestors for more than a hundred years, was closely associated with the commercial classes. His policies helped them at the expense of Attic agriculture. The peace with Persia, colonial expansion into the West, and the importation of large quantities of grain from abroad were aimed primarily at increasing the political power of the Athenian state, it is true, but they also enriched the Athenian merchants and the manufacturers whose goods now found still larger markets than those provided by Cimon and his friends.

Athenian industry had made great progress in the days of the tyrants, partly no doubt because of the influx of metics bringing new skills and new ideas from Ionia and elsewhere. In the fifth century, Athens became one of the most important industrial cities of Greece, especially in ceramics and shipbuilding. It would be a grave mistake, however, to think of her industry as in any way comparable to modern industry. Heavy industry did not exist, and many industries which loom large today—such as food processing and textiles—were then conducted almost entirely in the home. As men used only the simplest tools and machinery, there was no need for heavy investments of capital or large factories. The largest establishment of which we have a record was that of a shield-maker who employed one hundred and twenty persons at the height of the Peloponnesian War. Ordinarily, a factory with forty workers was considered large. Slaves were used along with free men, though not in large numbers, and only in the silver mines of Mount Laurium was their condition truly pitiable. The free workers worked about as hard as the slaves, and probably they had little more to show for it at the end of the day or year. The proprietor was an artisan himself, working beside his employees and slaves.

In earlier times artisans had sold their goods to the ultimate consumer themselves, but distribution had gradually been taken over by a specialized merchant class. In fifth century Athens these merchants were of several quite different sorts. At the bottom of the scale was the *kapelos,* or retail trader, who usually was little more than a peddler. He bought various goods, in rather small quantity, from manufacturers or from importers at the wharves, and he sold them at retail to the ultimate consumers, perhaps from a temporary booth or stand set up in the agora. The *emporos* was a wholesaler who traded overseas. He bought large consignments of goods from manufacturers and took them by ship from city to city, trading them for local products on the docks, and probably turning over his entire stock several times in the course of a trip that lasted through the summer months. At first the *emporos* would hire space in a ship owned by someone else, but if he prospered he might eventually have a ship of his own. In that case he became a *naukleros*, taking his cargoes wherever he wished and sometimes selling space on his ship to other *emporoi*. In the fifth century, Athenian ships sailed the whole eastern Mediterranean, and often broke into the West, as is proved by the archeologists who find articles of Athenian make in all these regions.

At this time, too, bankers and capitalists began to appear. The first bankers were money-changers who set up tables in the agora, where they sold Athenian coins to visiting merchants and foreign coins to prospective travelers. Before the end of the fifth century they were accepting money on deposit, lending part of it out again, and performing many of the other functions of a modern bank. Bankers and other rich men found it easy to lend money at high rates of interest. The profits made by a successful *emporos* were so great that he could afford to pay 20 or even 30 per cent interest on money borrowed for the stock of merchandise with which he left home; industrialists borrowed money to buy raw materials and slaves; and proud aristocrats, made to feel inferior by upstart traders whom they despised, borrowed money to maintain a social position which they could not afford. Persons with ready money were thus enabled to play an important part in the economic, social, and political life of Athens. They supported Cimon in the years after Salamis; they kept on good terms with Pericles; and they backed the oligarchic revolutions at the end of the century.

The commerce and prosperity of Athens were also aided by her monetary policy. As Athenian coins were the best in the world, Athenian traders could pass them everywhere. The rich supplies of silver from Mount Laurium enabled Athens to maintain an adequate supply of coins in spite of exportation and a steadily rising demand. In fact, this influx of silver had a marked inflationary effect, causing prices to rise steadily and making nearly everyone happy because each thought that he was getting rich. In general, prices rather more than doubled during the fifty years between Salamis and the outbreak of the Peloponnesian War.

Last but not least, we must not forget the high enthusiasm that inspired the Athenians after their victories over Persia. This contagious enthusiasm was a matter of prime importance in making the fifth century a period of unprecedented economic prosperity at Athens. Of course Greece, then as always, was desperately poor, if judged by modern standards, and the majority of the people of Attica lived at a level which most Americans would consider intolerable. But their standards were not our standards: most of them had enough to eat and wear and a place to sleep; they found more leisure than most of us; and they were not only satisfied, but enthusiastic, about the city where such things were possible.

Athenian Education

Economic prosperity provided a foundation for the brilliant literary and artistic achievements of the Periclean Age, but it takes more than economic prosperity to create a superior civilization. There must be persons who have something to say, and they must find an audience capable of understanding what they are saying. Rapidly changing conditions caused thoughtful Athenians to reconsider old ideals and old standards of thought and conduct. A series of remarkable thinkers and artists arose to express the spirit of the new age in brilliant fashion, and, at the same time, the new Athens provided audiences worthy of them. While it may be impossible to explain how geniuses arise, it is safe to say that these Athenian audiences were the result, in part, of the leisure now possible for so many citizens, but more especially they were the product of a new type of education developed in Athens at this time.

Whatever technical education the average Greek had received in the old days came from his family and consisted in learning a few simple skills. His general education and outlook were based ultimately on myths explaining the religious rites and ceremonies in which he took part. His political education, such as it was, came by absorbing the views of the leaders of his *genos*. In the seventh and sixth centuries, this system began to break down. The power and importance of the *genos* declined as its functions and duties fell more and more to the *polis*. More formal education therefore became necessary. In an earlier chapter, we noted the extremes to which state control of education went in Sparta, where the whole training of youthful citizens was directed toward making them good hoplites. The Athenians preferred to do things differently, and their state confined itself to ordering fathers to have their sons taught a trade and given at least a minimum of literary education.

In this new Athens the family was unable to retain its former place in the education of children. Craftsmen could still teach their sons a trade, to be sure, but that was about all. Men were away from home more than in the old days and consequently exercised less influence over their sons. The early education of children fell to the mother or, in well-to-do families, to the mother and her slaves. However, the Greek attitude toward women was such that mothers were rarely qualified to take an important part in the education of their sons. The Greek world was distinctly a man's world. Men did not marry until late—perhaps the average age was about thirty—and usually they took wives who were barely half that age. These girls had received little or no education except in household duties, and after marriage they did not go out in society and rarely left the house. Their views on larger matters were bound to be narrow and elementary, and naturally they could not impart to their sons knowledge they did not possess themselves. The need for new forms of education thus became imperative, and schools were established to fill this need.

Elementary Schools

There had been schools at Athens even in the days of Solon, and during the next hundred years they multiplied so rapidly that every free boy was able to receive at least a little schooling. There were few citizens in Periclean times who could not read and write—a situation which had not arisen before in history and did not recur until the nineteenth century. Athenian schools were private institutions. Anyone who wished might open a school, teachers were paid by the fathers of the pupils, and there were schools to fit every purse. The poor sent their sons to poverty-stricken masters who taught them something for a mere pittance, while the rich sent theirs to

fashionable establishments with excellent teachers. Boys first entered
these schools at the age of seven. Sons of the poorer classes usually
remained there for only three or four years and were afterward ap-
prenticed to learn trades. Those of the middle and upper classes
remained longer and received a training designed to make them
"gentlemen."

Even in the days of Pericles, elementary education bore a highly
aristocratic stamp, at least in those schools that served all but the
poorest citizens. Instruction covered three quite distinct fields, each
taught by different masters at different schools, and each teaching
things that a Greek gentleman was expected to know. These fields
were gymnastics, letters, and music. Perhaps the most important of
the three, in the minds of most people, was gymnastics. This training was designed, not to produce champions, but to enable boys to
hold their own in the sports which were so prominent and popular
an aspect of Greek life. The sports included not only running, wres-
tling, and jumping, but hunting and horseback riding, as well as
various games. Rarely in history has a whole people been as interested in sports and games as were the ancient Greeks.

Literary education, of course, began with learning to read and
write. At the earliest possible moment, however, this instruction was
followed by the study of Homer and other poets. Homer was so
highly revered by most people that he was taken as an authority on
almost everything, and pupils were required to commit to memory
many passages selected for their beauty or their wisdom. The moral
maxims and myths of Hesiod and other poets were also studied,
sometimes in anthologies or readers made especially for school use.
At the same time other masters were teaching their pupils to sing
and accompany themselves on the lyre, and perhaps to play the
aulos. Skill in such matters was expected of every educated Athenian, and philosophers declared that the study of music produced
a harmonious character. Moreover, the Muses presided over more
than mere song. They also lent their names to choral dancing, poetry,
drama, and other branches of what we would today consider part
of a liberal education, and the boys were introduced to all this as
"music."

Secondary Education: The Sophists

The secondary education that arose in the fifth century was of a less formal character and touched only the intellectual and financial elite. Teachers of the new sort were called "Sophists," and they undertook to complete the education of their pupils. Sometimes they taught courses in advanced subjects such as geometry, astronomy, logic, and literary criticism (though not foreign languages or literature), and sometimes they lectured on ethical, political, and philosophical subjects. They trained men in new skills such as public speaking and debating; and one Sophist announced that he taught his pupils "to think, to speak, and to act." More important than the courses of study, however, was the spirit of free inquiry inculcated by many of the Sophists. They taught their pupils to be skeptical of all accepted traditions and to analyze everything in the light of reason.

The Sophists also lectured to adults, and some of them attained great renown. They came from all parts of the Greek world, sometimes only for brief visits, and they did their share in making Athens an imperial city, intellectually as well as politically. In later times, partly as a result of Plato's invectives against them, the Sophists fell heir to an unsavory reputation as pretentious humbugs who taught their pupils to prove by specious arguments that black is white, and encouraged them to ridicule the old-fashioned foolishness of their fathers about gods and men. From this view of the Sophists come our words "sophistry" and "sophisticated." No doubt there were Sophists in Athens who deserved this censure. Others were brilliant men, inspired with the ideals of the new day and aware of its intellectual problems. The better Sophists criticized old ideals because they wished to bring their pupils to a more enlightened view of life. Many of them were excellent teachers who knew how to arouse the enthusiasm of young men for intellectual matters, and it was largely their influence that created the Athens which educated men have ever since revered.

Education cannot be limited to formal schooling, however, and Athens provided exceptional opportunities for non-scholastic education. One center of this less formal education was the agora, another was the gymnasium. Men found it more pleasant in such places than at home, and here they engaged in long, and perhaps deep, conversations. Anyone who wished could join the circle, especially if he had something to contribute to the discussion. The agora became the center of the intellectual life of Athens, as well as of its economic and political life, for here the problems of the day were publicly debated by the keenest minds of the city. Just as the Athenian citizen gained his political education by taking active part in the government of the city, so too he received a general education from listening to, and perhaps participating in, the discussions in the agora. In later times, the gymnasium tended to supplant the agora as an intellectual center. Gymnasiums were used not only for physical exercise but also as clubs where men could spend their leisure in discussion or conversation. Great philosophers sometimes delivered lectures there and, when Greeks flocked to the East in the wake of Alexander the Great, the gymnasiums they built in every city became centers for the spread of Hellenic culture. The gregariousness and open-air life of the Athenians, and even their passion for athletics, thus stimulated intellectual education. The agora and the gymnasium, even more than the schools, provided audiences and critics for the writers and artists, who composed their works not for the bookish few but for the citizen in the market place.

Periclean Art and Architecture

The Persians had destroyed a large part of Athens in 480, and the rebuilding was hurried and badly planned. Houses were scattered about higgledy-piggledy, good ones and bad ones side by side. Such haste was inevitable in a time of crisis, but men presently began to take pride in giving their city a fine appearance. Cimon contributed lavishly to parks and public works, and others devoted much thought to giving their city a more beautiful as well as a more convenient arrangement. Hippodamus of Miletus was employed by Pericles to lay out the new seaport at Piraeus with broad straight streets crossing at right angles and with artistic decorations in the squares and near public buildings.

Little is known of the architecture of private residences at this time. The great majority of the Athenians lived in houses of sun-dried brick, perhaps covered with stucco, whose two or three rooms would scarcely be considered habitable today. Even rich men usually lived in rather unpretentious houses in the city, for, being landed aristocrats, they preferred to spend their money on country estates. The builders of good town houses paid less attention to the exterior than to the interior, as is still the custom in Mediterranean lands. From the street, the property might present to the passer-by nothing but a blank wall and a gate, while within there would probably be a beautiful court surrounded by a pillared arcade with living rooms behind. The residences of the rich were surrounded by the hovels of the poor; streets were narrow and crooked, dirty and ill-smelling; and sanitary conditions in the city were appalling.

A visitor wishing to view the beauties and wonders of Athens would have planned to go first to the Acropolis. Beneath the cliffs on the southern side of this hill ran a road, called the "Street of the Tripods," leading to the old agora at its western end. The road then turned and ascended the western slope of the hill. Beside this road, almost at the top, stood a temple to Athena known as the "Wingless Victory." This tiny building is still cherished as a fine example of Ionic architecture. Built about 450, it stood intact almost until the end of the seventeenth century, when the Turks pulled it down to make room for a gun emplacement. About a hundred years ago it was restored from the debris still lying about. The visitor would next have entered the Acropolis area—the flat top of the hill—through the "Propylaea," or Entrance Gates, built at enormous expense by the architect Mnesicles under the direction of Pericles. A large flight of steps led up to the main gates, and on the side opposite the temple of the Wingless Victory was a building used as a picture gallery. On top of the hill were two famous temples: the Erechtheum to the northeast and the Parthenon to the south. The former, dedicated to the mythical hero Erechtheus, was an Ionic structure, measuring 74 by 37 feet, built during the Peloponnesian War. Along one side was the Porch of the Caryatids (Maidens), so-called because the roof was supported by pillars in the form of maidens.

The Parthenon was a large building, 230 by 100 feet and 65 feet high, which was begun in 447 and completed by 433. Built in the

Doric style by the architects Ictinus and Callicrates, and decorated by the sculptor Phidias, it has been accounted the supreme architectural achievement of Greece. Simple and harmonious, it is a true expression of the Greek genius. Within stood a statue of Athena, carved by Phidias of gold and ivory, and beside the temple towered another huge statue of the goddess with shield, spear, and helmet: the shining point of the spear was a landmark recognized by mariners many miles out at sea. Around the temple ran a bas-relief frieze, much of it the work of Phidias, depicting the great Panathenaic procession held every summer in honor of the goddess. In the fifth century after Christ the Parthenon was transformed into a Christian church, no longer dedicated to the Virgin Athena but to the Virgin Mary, and in the fifteenth century it became a mosque. Later, the Turks used it as a powder magazine, and it was blown up by the Venetians during their siege of the city in 1687. Early in the nineteenth century, Lord Elgin, the British ambassador at Constantinople, carried off many of the sculptures, which now repose in the British Museum and are known as the "Elgin marbles."

Other famous buildings were erected in Athens at this time or a little later. On a slight hill overlooking the agora was a Doric temple, sometimes called the Theseum but more probably dedicated to Hephaestus, the god of craftsmen. It is now the best preserved of the ancient monuments of Athens, and it was used throughout the Middle Ages as a church dedicated to St. George. The other public buildings near the agora are known only from ancient descriptions and from ruins uncovered in recent years. On the southern side of the Acropolis, beneath the walls built by Cimon but above the Street of the Tripods, was a temple to Dionysus, beside which was an open-air theater with tiers of wooden seats. East of the theater was the Odeum, or concert hall, built by Pericles, and west of it was a temple to Asclepius dating from the Peloponnesian War.

The fifth century was likewise a period of active building in other parts of the Greek world. Excavators at Olympia have dug up the ruins of the temple for which Phidias carved a gigantic statue of Zeus, and the rebuilding of the Ionian cities gave Greek architects ample opportunity to show their talents. In the next century the temple of Artemis in Ephesus burned (356) and was replaced by

Parthenon

Erechtheum

Plate 26

Discobolus, About 450 B.C. (Vatican Museum)

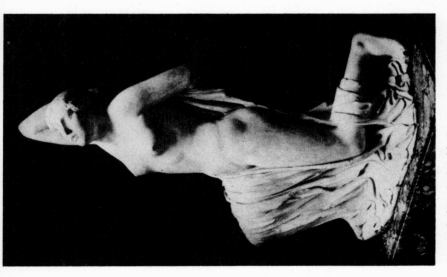

Wounded Niobid, Fifth Century (Terme Museum, Rome)

Plate 27

a magnificent structure—the temple of "Diana of the Ephesians" mentioned in the New Testament—which, together with the contemporaneous Mausoleum, or monument to Mausolus, ruler of Caria, was reckoned throughout the remainder of antiquity as one of the Seven Wonders of the World. The tyrants of the fifth and fourth centuries in the West were also great builders, and the fifth-century temple to Poseidon at Poseidonia (Paestum) in Italy is a fine example of Doric architecture.

Much of the sculpture of the classic age was closely connected with architecture, like Phidias's contributions to the Parthenon, but this period also produced many famous individual pieces as well. Greek sculpture was once known largely through copies made in Roman times, and even today the famous statues are known only at second hand. During the past century, however, archeologists have unearthed countless fragments dating from the fifth century which show the skill of the sculptors and the progress they had made over earlier times. Artists had learned to overcome the formality of "archaic" Greek statues; they copied the human body with amazing skill; and they discovered graceful and natural poses for their models. While many statues depict gods and scenes from mythology, others show athletes, sometimes in action—as Myron's "Discobolus" (Discus-thrower)—and sometimes at rest.

Not much can be said of Greek painting. Ancient critics wrote of masterpieces made at this time, but no paintings on walls or canvas have been preserved. About 450 Polygnotus of Thasos decorated the wall of an arcade near the agora with pictures of the battle of Marathon, and others of his paintings were at Delphi. At the end of the century, Zeuxis of Heraclea won renown with paintings of mythological subjects. The most famous painter of the next century was the Ionian Apelles. Our knowledge of Greek vase-painting, which reached its climax in Periclean times, is founded on hundreds of vases which may now be seen in our museums.

Poets and Dramatists

The works of the Greek poets of the fifth century have won even higher praise than those of the architects, sculptors, and painters who beautified Athens. The period of the Persian wars brought forth the poetry of Pindar. Born to an aristocratic Theban family about 522, Pindar traveled and made friends in many parts of Greece, visited Sicily about 476, and became well-to-do from the rewards of his poetry. He died in 443, at the age of seventy-nine. Pindar's reputation rests upon his *Epinician Odes* (so-called from *nike*, "victory"), written in honor of the victors in various athletic contests. He began writing when barely twenty years of age, and continued for more than half a century. The most famous of his poems come from the years during and just after the Persian wars. Pindar was a Panhellenist culturally and politically, and he was deeply ashamed of Theban Medizing during Xerxes' invasion. He admired the "violet-crowned Athens" (the phrase is his), though he more frequently praised Aegina and various Greek tyrants in Sicily; and after Athens dissolved the Hellenic League (461), he turned against her bitterly.

Pindar's odes depict the aristocratic side of Greek life in his day. They show its dignity and self-control, its love of athletics, its enthusiasm for beauty and honor, its allegiance to old ideals and beliefs, its religious sentiment, its distrust of democracy and other novelties, and its broad Panhellenism. Closely associated as he was with the priests at Delphi, Pindar considered Apollo the greatest of the gods, and he had no sympathy with the theological skepticism already appearing in Greece. He rehearsed the old myths, but he toned down the more ridiculous and scandalous escapades of the gods, or else, like a true gentleman, he passed them over in silence. In later times he was honored throughout Greece. When Alexander the Great sacked Thebes, more than a century after Pindar's death, he gave strict orders that the poet's house and descendants were to be spared. Pindar had praised Alexander's ancestor in one of the famous Odes, it is true, but it is more likely that the Macedonian conqueror was overawed by his high reputation as a poet.

More important than the poetry of Pindar was the Attic drama. We have seen how, even in the seventh century, Dionysus was honored with a choral dance called the "dithyramb." From this dance Greek tragedy developed. Our word "tragedy" is derived from the Greek word *tragoidos,* which in turn comes from *tragos* ("goat") and *oidos* ("singer"). Literally it means "goat singer." How such a word came to be associated with dramatic performances no one knows. Some authorities hold that the members of the chorus were dressed in goat skins, others plausibly suggest that originally the prize for the best song was a goat. At any rate, the practice of giving prizes every year for the best tragedies began in 534. The cost of training the choruses was paid at first by the tyrants, and after 508 by "liturgies" assessed against rich citizens, while the prize winners were selected by no less a personage than the *archon basileus* himself.

The earlier dithyrambs resembled modern oratorios and were first sung by choruses of fifty, later of fifteen, and finally of twelve voices. In the days of Peisistratus, a tragedian named Thespis modified earlier practice by appearing himself as a speaker and actor to explain the songs. His style was continued by Phrynichus, and early in the next century Aeschylus added a second actor, thus making dialogue possible. A third actor was presently added, but there were never more than three: even if a play had more characters, only three might appear on the stage at once. These actors permitted the dramatist to develop a complicated plot which was acted out, not merely sung or recited as in the dithyramb.

Dithyrambs had first been performed near the temple or altar of Dionysus, and later in any convenient open place. At Athens, they were given in the old agora until Peisistratus built an open-air theater, with tiers of wooden seats, on the southern slope of the Acropolis near the temple of Dionysus. Early in the fifth century, a new and larger theater, seating about 17,000 persons, was built on the same site. The theater here whose ruins may still be seen dates only from about 330 B.C. and was remodeled more than once by the Romans. The seats of a theater (see Plate 28) were arranged on a hillside in semicircular rows around the central "orchestra," or dancing floor (*orchesis* meaning "dance"). At the center of the orchestra stood an altar to Dionysus, and behind the orchestra was a low building, called the *skene,* in which the actors and chorus had their dressing rooms. This building also served as background during performances, and its three doors were used by actors for entrances and exits. Painted "scenery" was sometimes hung on its front wall, but Greek architects tried to arrange these out-door theaters in such a way that nature herself provided a beautiful background. Thus simply set, the action of a Greek tragedy was usually supposed to take place before a temple or palace. Until Roman times, there was no elevated stage for the actors. The chorus danced and sang in the orchestra, and here the actors recited their lines, sometimes standing close to the chorus and sometimes near the *skene*. The tragedies were performed each year on three consecutive mornings early in March, at a festival known as the Greater Dionysia.

Greek tragedies always retained the religious tone of the dithyramb. In early times the chorus had sung the myth of Dionysus, and classic tragedies dealt with themes from old mythology—or, more accurately speaking, from the heroic tales of "Homeric" times when the gods were still very close to men. The deeds of these heroes provided tragic materials aplenty. The custom of using only well-known stories of course placed serious limitations upon the dramatist. As the audience knew the plot beforehand, the author could not invent major actions. However, he could choose between various versions of the story, of which there usually were several; he could arrange, or even invent, minor episodes to develop the story dramatically; he could direct the sympathies of the audience to one character or another; he could bring out the larger problems in-

---

• Note for Plate 28.   This theater, at Epidaurus in Argolis, was built toward the middle of the fourth century before Christ and is one of the most typical and best preserved in Greece. The stone seats, cut into the side of the hill, provided places for about 15,000 spectators. The circular dancing floor, or orchestra, served as a stage for both actors and chorus. At its center stood an altar to Dionysus, called the *thymele*. Behind the orchestra may be seen the foundations of the house called the *skene*. In front of this building stood a row of columns, behind which was an arcade. The actors made their entrances and exits from the *skene,* which contained rooms used as dressing rooms and for the storage of properties. The *skene* served as background for the action of the play, which usually was thought of as occurring before a temple or other public building, but sometimes painted "scenery" was added to give a local touch. In Roman times the floor of the front part of the *skene* was elevated to form a stage, and the orchestra was given over to spectators, as in a modern theater.

Plate 28.   Theater at Epidaurus

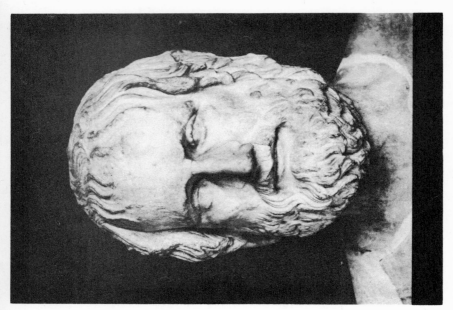

Euripides (Berlin Museum)

Sophocles (Lateran Museum, Rome)

Plate 29

volved; and he could suggest answers. Even in the fully developed tragedy, the chorus retained an important role. Its members were supposed to be quite ordinary persons watching great events, and between scenes they sang songs expressing their reflections upon them. Someone has remarked that the chorus was an "ideal audience," expressing ideas which the author wished the actual audience to take home.

The author presented three tragedies at a time, each being a unit by itself, though the three plays dealt with a single theme and might perhaps be compared to three acts in a modern tragedy. Afterward, the audience was permitted to relax during a "satyr" play—in lighter vein on a similar general theme. The thirty-three extant Greek tragedies contain only one complete trilogy (the *Oresteia* of Aeschylus) and one satyr play (the *Cyclops* by Euripides), though large fragments of another (by Sophocles) have been discovered on a papyrus.

Aeschylus

The first of the great Athenian dramatists was Aeschylus (524–456). Born at Eleusis to an Athenian eupatrid family, he fought in the battle of Marathon and ten years later he fought again at Salamis. Like Pindar, he was invited to Syracuse by Hiero; and he died during a second visit to Sicily in 456. He was buried at Gela and on his grave they inscribed an epitaph, composed by himself: "of his high prowess let the grove of Marathon speak, and the long-haired Mede who knows." It was not as a tragedian, but as a "Marathon fighter," that Aeschylus wished to be remembered.

Aeschylus wrote his first play in 500 and first won the prize in 484. He wrote about ninety plays, or more than twenty tetralogies, which indicates that he competed approximately every second year. He won first prize thirteen times, or about twice for every three times he competed. We know the titles of more than eighty plays, but only for seven has the text been preserved. The two earliest of the extant plays, *The Suppliants* and *The Persians,* are characterized by extreme simplicity of plot. More than half the lines are sung by the chorus, and the speeches, divided between two actors, are little more than declamation. The exact date of the former play is uncertain; the latter was performed in 472. *The Seven against Thebes,* produced in 467, and *Prometheus Bound,* of about the same date, show great progress in dramatic technique; and the author's art reached its culmination in the last three plays (*Agamemnon, The Choephori,* and *The Eumenides*), which formed a trilogy on the Orestes legend, produced in 458.

We have already seen the political significance of Phrynichus's play, *The Fall of Miletus,* which appeared about 493, possibly with the support of Themistocles (p. 373). Aeschylus's early tragedy, *The Suppliants* also was connected with contemporary politics. It deals with the legend of Danaus, which centers around the flight of that hero with his fifty daughters from Africa to Argos, once the home of their ancestors, when his brother Aegyptus proposed that his fifty sons marry the fifty daughters of Danaus. The play opens with the arrival of Danaus and his daughters in Argos: they beg asylum of the king, who rules over all Greece, and when fear of war with Aegyptus causes him to hesitate, they eloquently plead the rights of suppliants and kinsmen. The king consults his people, who vote to extend protection to the strangers; this decision is no sooner announced than a messenger arrives from Aegyptus ordering Danaus and his daughters to return with him. When they refuse, he withdraws with threats of dire things to come. All this of course is only the first play, or first act, of a trilogy, but we can guess that the story was completed in two plays whose titles have been preserved: *The Aegyptioi* and *The Danaïdes.* In the myth, Danaus finally permits his daughters to marry the sons of Aegyptus but he orders them to murder their husbands on the bridal night; all obey except one, who spares her bridegroom, for which she is punished but eventually forgiven. Afterward Danaus marries his daughters to the young men of Greece, thus uniting the two peoples.

It is hard to imagine an Athenian audience of the early fifth century watching these plays without at once thinking of their Ionian kinsmen, who were begging aid against cruel Orientals with whom they would not be united. It is equally difficult to imagine that Aeschylus had no political motive in selecting this theme. Obviously, he was trying to arouse enthusiasm for intervention in Ionia;

and the final marriage of the Danaïdes harmonizes with the Pan-hellenic ideals held by the old aristocracy and, in later years, by Aristides and Cimon. The trilogy presumably appeared before the battle of Marathon, for the second act did not parallel actual history. Perhaps it was produced under the inspiration of Miltiades (who was a sort of Danaus) at about the time of *The Fall of Miletus*, or perhaps it appeared in 498 when Aristagoras was making his famous visit and request for aid.[2]

Many years later, in 476, Phrynichus won first place with a play for which Themistocles provided the chorus. Scholars believe that this play was *The Phoenicians* and that it dealt with the recent war. Four years later Aeschylus produced his *Persians*. The action of this play is located at the court of Susa and centers about the report by a messenger of the battle of Salamis. Pericles provided the chorus for this play, but as he was then barely twenty years old, and Aeschylus had already won first prize many times, such collaboration was an honor to the politician rather than to the poet. It does not show that Aeschylus shared the political views later espoused by Pericles. In fact, in *The Eumenides* (458), Aeschylus praised the Areopagus in striking language sometimes taken as backhanded criticism of Ephialtes and Pericles, who had recently shorn that venerable body of most of its powers. Throughout his life, Aeschylus shared the aristocratic sympathies of the generation that fought at Marathon.

In his later plays Aeschylus concerned himself especially with religious problems. He had been born at Eleusis, the seat of the ancient mysteries, and he was much influenced by Eleusinian ideas. In fact, it is said that he was once brought to trial, though acquitted, for divulging the secrets of the mysteries in a play. Usually he expressed a rather low opinion of the Olympians, whom he rarely discussed in his plays, but he was much interested in the primitive earth-deities and in the moral ideas associated with them. Thus, in *The Persians*, he attributed the fall of Xerxes to *hybris* (pride and insolence) and warned against repeating so arrogant an enterprise. The Theban

---

[2] We know that Aeschylus was presenting a play the year that the old wooden seats in the theater collapsed, some time during the seventieth Olympiad (500–496). An imaginative person might suspect that a play on this controversial subject in 498 would cause disturbances among the spectators that might lead to such a catastrophe.

trilogy (of which we have only the third member, *The Seven against Thebes*) traced the consequences of the sin of Laius through three generations to the utter ruin of his family.[3] In the Orestes trilogy, the sin of Agamemnon in sacrificing his daughter Iphigenia leads to one dreadful crime after another until at last his insane son, Orestes, is freed from the Furies by the Areopagus, with Athena herself coming to cast the deciding vote: thus law and justice replace the blood feud and blind vengeance.

The most important of Aeschylus's plays, from the religious point of view, is *Prometheus Bound*. Prometheus was a Titan, the son of Mother Earth, a friend of man but a mortal enemy of the usurper Zeus. One of the old savior gods who suffered in behalf of mankind, he had stolen fire from heaven and given it to man. In punishment for this deed, Zeus ordered him chained to a rock and sent a vulture to devour his liver, but the part eaten each day grew again during the night. The play opens with Zeus's agents binding Prometheus to the rock. This scene must have seemed as horrible to a Greek as the crucifixion in a Passion Play is to us. Prometheus explains the cause of his sufferings to the chorus and bitterly reviles the tyranny of Zeus. Presently Io appears, she, too, a sufferer at the hands of Zeus. The things these two said to each other about the king of the gods must have caused many a timid and pious person in the audience to squirm. Even at this moment, however, Prometheus knew that eventually he would triumph over Zeus. Fragments of the second play in the trilogy (*The Loosing of Prometheus*) show that, after thirty thousand years of torment, Prometheus actually was freed by Heracles, another savior god and a descendant of Io. In the final play (*Prometheus the Fire-Bearer*), the hero continues his beneficent works, for which he eventually receives divine honors. Prometheus had been freed with the consent of Zeus, who thus abandoned his old tyrannical ways to become, like Prometheus, a benefactor to

---

[3] The basic myth related that Laius, warned by an oracle that he would be killed by his son, ordered his infant son Oedipus slain; the babe was spared, however, and brought up by a shepherd, not knowing who he was. Eventually he returned to Thebes, where he unknowingly killed his father and married his mother; years later he learned his true identity, blinded himself in remorse, and withdrew with his daughter Antigone. His two sons then slew each other, fighting for the throne.

humanity. As one critic has remarked, Aeschylus may not have anticipated the views of eighteenth-century philosophers about the perfectibility of man, but he definitely believed in the perfectibility of God.

Sophocles

The second of the great tragedians was Sophocles. Born about 496 at Colonus, a suburb of Athens, he spent practically his whole life in his native city, and there he died in 406 at the age of ninety. His father was a wealthy armor-maker who brought up his son in the best society and gave him the best education that the day afforded. In later years, Sophocles held various public offices. He was a general with Pericles during the Samian War, 441–440, and it is said that he was one of the commissioners appointed to hold things together after the Sicilian disaster in 414. Though he may have been a personal friend of Pericles (who once remarked that he was a good poet but a bad general), he had been a follower of Cimon in his youth and his sympathies drew him to the conservative opposition rather than to the Periclean democracy. Sophocles also took an active interest in religion. He had a share in introducing the worship of Asclepius after the plague of 430–29; he held a priesthood; and he is said to have received divine honors after death.

Sophocles won first prize with his first play in 467, an honor which he gained eighteen times in all. He never won less than second place, and as he is said to have written 123 plays, or thirty-one tetralogies, he must have won five more firsts than seconds. Of these plays only seven remain, all dating from his later years. The earliest extant of Sophocles' plays are *Ajax* and *Antigone,* dating from about 443, when their author was over fifty years old. *The Trachinae* and *Oedipus Rex* date from the early years of the Peloponnesian War, when he was over sixty-five, and he wrote *Electra, Philoctetes,* and *Oedipus at Colonus* when he was more than eighty.

Being a generation younger than Aeschylus, Sophocles formed his basic opinions in an atmosphere very different from that which prevailed during his predecessor's youth. He set forth the views of the Athenian upper classes in the middle of the fifth century. He learned much from the Sophists, and in his later years the long war showed its effect upon his thought. He was not so bold and vigorous a thinker as Aeschylus, and he disapproved of much that the new day brought. The *Antigone* deals with the conflict between old religious duties and the law of the new all-powerful state, with the heroine championing the former at the cost of her life. While Aeschylus preferred the old gods of the mysteries, Sophocles defended the Homeric religion of the Olympians. He does so in a calm and enlightened manner, however, making countless concessions to its critics. The old myths are purified and moralized, the old gods almost completely impersonalized. Only once does he bring a god upon the stage. But the gods take care of men and warn them of coming events through prophets, dreams, and oracles. Five of the seven extant plays of Sophocles center around the fulfillment of oracles in unexpected ways. Sophocles believed in oracles though his characters did not— to their ultimate sorrow. The gods are not the willful tyrants against whom Prometheus raged, but rather a benign Fate ruling the world: arbitrary power has given way to law in heaven.

Sophocles' conception of the gods can be seen by comparing his treatment of the Oedipus legend with that of Aeschylus in *The Seven against Thebes*. Aeschylus makes it a story of sin and punishment carried to the third generation. Sophocles' *Oedipus Rex* shows that even a good man cannot escape the inexorable laws of Fate; and in the *Colonus* Oedipus dies in a calm and dignified manner, assured that all is well, for he has neither willed nor desired the terrible things he has done: he has been throughout the helpless tool of Fate. Perhaps Sophocles was brought to these fatalistic views by long meditation on the interminable war through which he lived: wars tend to make men fatalistic. In this last play Theseus, the great king of Athens, fights successfully for right and justice, and the play closes with an assurance that, since Theseus received and defended the aged Oedipus in the days of his sorrow, his city will never fall. The play is also famous for its lyrics about the beauty of Colonus and the glory of Athens. It clearly was a war play, dating from the last terrible days of that long tragedy. Sophocles died in 406, a year before

Aegospotami, and the play was presented by his grandson five years later.

Euripides

The most modern of the Greek dramatists was Euripides. He was born to a family of middle-class landowners at Phlya, probably in 484. Though only twelve years younger than Sophocles, his social background was so different that the two men seem very far apart. Euripides was a Periclean democrat, a friend and pupil of the Sophists, and a critic of ancient beliefs and prejudices of every sort. The social significance of his tragedies has been compared to that of the plays with which Ibsen and Bernard Shaw shocked conservative people at the turn of the twentieth century.[4] Because of his critical attitude, Euripides was not popular in Athens during his lifetime. Though he wrote ninety-two plays, or twenty-three tetralogies, he won first prize only four times. Later generations, however, found him the most interesting of the dramatists. Nineteen of his plays have been preserved, as opposed to seven by each of his predecessors. He has been much admired and imitated by dramatists of many different periods, and in the present century he has received more sympathetic attention from critics than his great rivals. It has been remarked that men may admire Sophocles, but they prefer to read Euripides. The poet's unpopularity at Athens increased as the war progressed, and he became increasingly unhappy. When the king of Macedonia invited him to Pella in 408, Euripides gladly left his native city; he died abroad early in 406.

Euripides persevered in the old practice of having tragedies deal only with characters and events of heroic times, but he showed his skill in developing new aspects of the old stories and in drawing from them lessons exactly the opposite of those usually drawn. More often than not, he depicts the Homeric heroes as brutal murderers while the only admirable persons in the play are the villagers of the chorus who, with consternation and horror, watch the terrible deeds of their betters. Every play contains discussions of deep moral issues, asking

---

[4] See note on Gilbert Murray, p. 472.

what good conduct is and what is the good life. They are full of paradoxes calculated to arouse skepticism about old moral standards, and
they seek to inspire the audience with broader and more humane
sentiments. The *Medea* is a case in point. Medea was a barbarous
princess whom Jason had picked up in the course of his travels and
of whom he presently wished to be rid. Earlier Greeks had seen no
great moral issue in her story, but Euripides made her his heroine,
picturing the noble Jason simply as a contemptible cad. Medea has
feelings, character, and rights, even though she does happen to be a
woman and a barbarian. Moreover, the old gods are no better than
their worshipers. In the *Ion,* Apollo, once famous for his radiant
purity, appears as a liar, a seducer, and a poltroon; elsewhere he is
pictured as an odious hypocrite and, among other things, a cattle
rustler. Many passages seem quite blasphemous and remind us of
the nineteenth-century writers who took a special delight in pointing out moral shortcomings in the God of the Old Testament.

All this, however, shows only one side of Euripides. He may
have had only contempt for the old gods of mythology; he may have
despised the fools who believed in oracles and omens; he may have
sneered at sacrifices and ritual purifications; but he did not scorn all
religion. In *The Bacchae,* the last and one of the most interesting of
his plays, though the one most difficult to understand, he entered
sympathetically into the spirit of Bacchic inspiration and showed
how deeply religious a man he really was. He had no use for the
Olympians, with their silly and immoral antics, but he could believe
in Dionysus, who was both god and man and who thus taught what
we today call the "Divinity of Man." Euripides was an idealist who
attacked unworthy conceptions of god and morality, and who was
therefore denounced by the commonplace and humdrum people of
his day as an atheist preaching gross immorality.

Nearly all the extant plays of Euripides date from the war years,
and several are closely associated with the tragic events that were
then taking place. Being a good Periclean democrat, Euripides at first
favored the war, and in several patriotic plays, such as *The Hera-
clides* and *The Suppliants,* he speaks harshly of Sparta and Thebes

while praising Athens in terms reminiscent of Pericles' famous oration. But after the death of Pericles he and many others lost their first enthusiasm. The democracy of Cleon was not that of Pericles, and Euripides presently began to speak disparagingly of the mob. In *Hecuba* (about 426), he was for the first time bitter about the way things were going. For a brief time he believed in Alcibiades, but the affair of Melos was a terrible disillusionment. The next year (415) he presented *The Troades,* which is the story of the fall of Troy told from the point of view of the captive Trojan women. These women have noble characters, but their conquerors do not, and even Athena turns away from her beloved Greeks in disgust at their insolence. Seldom have the horrors of war and the fatuousness of military glory been pictured more powerfully.

A year or two later Euripides produced his *Electra.* Sophocles, too, wrote a tragedy on the subject at about this time. The two plays treat the subject very differently, and critics suggest that one was an answer to the other. Which came first we cannot say, nor does it greatly matter. Long ago Aeschylus had considered it the religious duty of Orestes to murder his mother Clytemnestra and her accomplice Aegisthus. Sophocles now depicted the murders as fated, though justified, but Euripides pictured them merely one more horrible crime. About 410 Euripides wrote *The Phoenissae,* in which he dealt with the old Theban legend handled by Aeschylus and Sophocles before him. He discussed neither the punishment of sin nor Fate, but simply told how the two sons of Oedipus were driven by greed and ambition to fratricidal strife; this was another thinly-veiled allegory of the war. And finally, in 408, shortly before his departure for Macedonia, Euripides wrote the *Orestes,* in which Orestes and his friend Pylades seem for a moment about to destroy everything in their mad frenzy, but are eventually reconciled with the Spartan Menalaus, who had been plotting to take over the kingdom of Orestes. The point of these plays is obvious. Euripides had come to regard the war as an insane, suicidal struggle in which all Greece was hurling herself to destruction, and the only solution to her problem that he could see was Panhellenic reconciliation and solidarity.

Greek Comedy

Attic comedy, like tragedy, sprang from the worship of Dionysus, but its history was quite different. The Greeks had long held spring celebrations to promote fertility, and in due time Dionysus took them under his protection. Bands of revelers, masquerading as birds or beasts, or strange or ludicrous men, paraded in carnival spirit. This revel, or the band of revelers, was called a *komos,* and the songs were a "comedy" (*komodia*) or "song of the comus." At first, pranks and jokes were impromptu. Later the revels were organized, the revelers were carefully trained as a chorus, and after 486 prizes were awarded annually for comedies as well as for tragedies. Toward the middle of the fifth century actors were added, as in tragedies, and a loose plot was developed. Nevertheless, comedies always retained much of the ancient Dionysiac ritual.

At the festival of the Greater Dionysia, in March, comedies were regularly presented in the afternoon, following the tragedies in the morning; others were given at the Lenaean festival in January or February. The old carnival spirit was retained, jokes were often very broad, actors and chorus indulged in much buffoonery and took great liberty in mimicking, ridiculing, or slandering well known personages, sometimes attacking them openly and by name, sometimes parodying them under masks which deceived no one. In the last years of the Peloponnesian War, these attacks upon prominent politicians became so venomous that comedians were forbidden by law to portray living statesmen. This restriction took much of the life out of comedy, though new forms were gradually developed. Critics now speak of the Old Comedy, dating from before these reforms, the Middle Comedy of the fourth century which concerned itself little with politics, and the New Comedy of the third century, which had lost the chorus and other traditional characteristics and roughly resembled a modern comedy of manners. Although the names of several writers of Old Comedy have been preserved, along with scattered lines from their plays, we have complete plays only from Aristophanes, who was perhaps the most brilliant comedian in history.

Aristophanes

Aristophanes was born a few years after 450, produced his first comedy in 427, and died about 380. He sprang from a well-to-do family of the landed aristocracy. It is said that he wrote forty-four comedies, of which eleven are still extant. The nine most famous appeared during the war while the last two show the characteristics of the inane Middle Comedy. Three plays deal directly with the war. The *Acharnians* (425) shows the felicity of an imaginary Athenian citizen who made a separate peace with Sparta; the *Peace* (421) glorifies the Peace of Niceas; and *Lysistrata* (411), produced a few weeks before the revolution of the Four Hundred, suggests that a general strike by all the women of Greece would quickly end the war, whose ravages are poignantly described. The plays are highly critical of the war, whose origins they trace to ludicrous causes. (One suggested cause, the kidnapping by Megarians of two girls from a brothel managed by Pericles' mistress, Aspasia, presumably was intended as a parody on the rape of Helen and the Trojan War.) The continuance of the war, on the other hand, is attributed to demagogues and profiteers. Their author indicates that much could be said for Sparta and Thebes; and, like Euripides, he urges peace and solidarity among all Greek states.

Aristophanes certainly hated the war, but he hated Cleon even more. His second play, the lost *Babylonians* (426), opened an attack which was continued in the *Knights*, performed in 424 shortly after Cleon had made a tremendous reputation for himself at Pylos. In this play, Cleon is supposedly supplanted by a wandering sausage-peddler, more vile and ignorant than Cleon himself, who finally reforms and shows Demos (the common people of Athens) how he has been misled by Cleon. Cleon attempted to punish Aristophanes for this impertinence and, if we are to believe the poet, "almost skinned him alive"; but in the next year another play, now lost, attacked Cleon's satellites. Again, in 422, the *Wasps* satirized the juries which obediently convicted everyone whom Cleon saw fit to accuse. The villain of the piece is named *Philocleon* ("Love-Cleon"), its hero is Bdelycleon ("Loathe-Cleon"). And in the *Peace* (421), Aristophanes declared that the blessings of the new day were possible only because of the death of the old warmonger. The performance of such plays in wartime is often taken as evidence of a remarkable open-mindedness and spirit of toleration; more probably it merely shows that the aristocratic *archon basileus,* who selected the plays, held views similar to those set forth by Aristophanes and was glad to present the plays, regardless of their possible effects upon wartime morale.

Not all Aristophanes' comedies were political. The *Birds* (415), with its utopian "Cloud-cuckoo-land," is just an amusing extravaganza, and several plays deal with intellectual and literary leaders. Being a conservative aristocrat, Aristophanes disapproved heartily of much that was being said in Athens. His very first play, the lost *Daitales* (427), showed his opinion of the new education; and the *Clouds* (423) is a famous attack upon Socrates. In this play old Strepsiades, deeply in debt, hears that Socrates can teach him how to win any lawsuit easily; he seeks out the philosopher at his "thought factory," where he finds him suspended high in a basket so as to escape all earthly influences and devote himself solely to heavenly matters! After much foolery, Socrates is found to be a corrupter of youth, and his school is burned down. Sometimes modern critics take this farce too soberly. Aristophanes has a great deal of fun at the expense of Socrates, but his jokes lack the malice and hatred of those aimed at Cleon. The only scoundrelly characters in the play are Strepsiades and his dissolute son, who seek wisdom in order to learn how to cheat people. We happen to know that Aristophanes was a personal friend of Socrates, for Plato gives him a sympathetic part in his dialogue, the *Symposium.*

Much the same may be said regarding the comic dramatist's attitude toward Euripides. He obviously was fascinated by the man, whom he quotes and parodies at length. He brings his rival dramatist on the stage in at least three comedies, and makes characters speak of him in four others. The most important of these comedies is *The Frogs,* produced in 405, about a year after Euripides' death. Dionysus opens the play with complaints about the dearth of poets and goes to Hades to bring one back. For a long time he is in doubt whether to choose Aeschylus or Euripides, but finally he selects the former because of the greater weight of his tragedies! In the course of the play there is much buffoonery, and much keen criticism of the two poets. It must be remembered that, though we today are accustomed to link the three great tragedians together, it was a high compliment to Euripides in 405 even to suggest that he might rival the great Aeschylus, especially as Euripides' unpopularity had only recently caused him to shake the dust of Athens from his feet. Aristophanes was not so profound a thinker as Sophocles and Euripides, but he was a highly intelligent man who knew Athens well. To be mocked by him was a compliment, and if the mockery came in a friendly spirit, the compliment was high indeed.

The Greek Historians

The fifth century was also the great age of Greek historical writing. The old Ionian logographers, compiling prose chronicles to connect their present with the Homeric past, had been brought face to face with the fundamental problems of chronology and historical criticism, but even Hecataeus of Miletus, writing shortly before the Persian wars, was so uncritical that he accepted much mythology as true. At the end of the fifth century, on the other hand, Thucydides wrote a history which still wins the highest praise for its sober and enlightened criticism. Within a period of less than a hundred years, Greek historians had changed mythography into "scientific" or critical history.

This "new history" was part of the general intellectual development of Periclean Athens. The growing skepticism regarding mythology, the rationalistic criticism popularized by the Sophists, and the changing attitude toward old institutions of every sort were the foundations upon which it rested. The Persian wars and the ensuing expansion of Athenian power broadened the intellectual horizon, and educated Greeks wished to know more about the peoples with whom they came in contact. The new history was created by writers who had caught the spirit of their day, who were deeply concerned with its problems, and who viewed the past through the eyes of the changing present. They rejected much of the old history, and in order to justify such rejection they invented new and better criteria for deciding what had actually happened. Critical history thus came into being.

Ionian writers continued to compile the annals of their cities, mixing fact and fiction to make their stories interesting. Doubtless they were encouraged by the fact that the Ionian cities, having recently thrown off the Persian yoke, were eager to show their true Greek colors by parading ancient origins and Homeric connections. The names of several such logographers are known to us though their works are lost. More important than they, however, was Hellanicus of Lesbos, who was born about 480. He traveled widely, lived for a while at Athens, where he apparently read publicly from his works, and died after 406. He was the author of several books on mythology and history. The works in the second group included accounts of several Greek states, an *Aegyptica,* a *Lydiaca,* a *Persica,* and a *Scythica.* The most famous of his writings is the *Atthis,* or chronicle of Athens, beginning in mythical times and coming down to 406. Though Thucydides later complained of his brevity and chronological inaccuracy in dealing with the years between 480 and 431, Hellanicus devoted great pains to establishing accurate chronology, using as guides authentic lists of priestesses, athletic victors, and magistrates. It is not unlikely that his studies were more useful to Thucydides than that historian cared to admit.

Herodotus

The logographers may have prepared the way for great historical writing, but the title "Father of History" justly belongs to Herodotus. Though he learned much from his predecessors, Herodotus was not a follower of anybody, and his history is in a sense the summary of his life. He was born about 484 at Halicarnassus, a famous port in southwestern Asia Minor, where his family belonged to the Greek aristocracy. Here his cousin, who had won a reputation as a minor epic poet, instigated an unsuccessful revolt against the Persians— perhaps in the days immediately following Cimon's victory at Eurymedon (467). When the revolt failed and the cousin was executed, his family fled to Samos, where Herodotus lived for several years. It was said that the fugitives afterward returned and drove out the Persians, and it is certain that Halicarnassus was in the Delian League before 454; but it is doubtful whether Herodotus ever lived in his native city again. As his family had lost its property during the rebellion, Herodotus undertook to redeem his fortunes by going on trading expeditions to distant lands. One of his early trips took him to the Black Sea region, another to Cyrene, another to Egypt, where he ascended the Nile as far as the First Cataract; and he traveled in Syria and Mesopotamia as far as Babylon. He also visited cities in Asia Minor and the Aegean Islands, and at last, when he was almost forty years old, he reached Athens.

The historian's stay at Athens marked an epoch in his career. His success introduced him to the intellectual leaders of the day. He was a friend of the poet Sophocles, and he became acquainted with Pericles himself. He caught the spirit of the Athens of the 440's, and he fell in love with the city. Here the former revolutionist found that liberty of which he had dreamed in his youth, and here the traveler found friends with whom he could discuss the broad ideas developed by his contacts with many peoples. Yet when colonists were sent to found Thurii in southern Italy (443), Herodotus went with them, perhaps as a special agent of Pericles. He spent the rest of his life in the West, visiting cities in Italy and Sicily, and writing his history. It is doubtful whether he ever returned to Greece, for he died at Thurii between 430 and 425.

Herodotus wrote one of the world's greatest histories. As it stands today, his work is a history of the Persian wars, with rather more than half the space devoted to background. This is not what he first planned to write. Even a casual examination shows that the book was put together from many independent narratives, which Herodotus called *logoi*, or "stories." These *logoi* had originally been lectures he delivered about the countries he had visited. He was an incomparable raconteur, and his travelogues were so successful at Athens that he repeated them many times in other Greek cities and in Italy and Sicily. They dealt with different countries—Lydia, Egypt, Scythia—and included accounts of the geography and resources of each, the people and their customs, and something of their history.

Apparently these *logoi* resembled the books which Hellanicus and others were publishing at about that time. During his stay in Greece, he collected new material which was worked up into *logoi* about the great battles of the Persian wars. After settling at Thurii, Herodotus developed larger plans. He began putting the *logoi* together in a single narrative, presumably planning something like the *Periegesis* of Hecataeus—an account of the various countries of the world, one after another, arranged in chronological order with the history of Persia from Cyrus to Xerxes as its principal guide. To these stories he then appended the *logoi* about the wars themselves.

Herodotus gives the Athenian version of the Persian wars, and his view is that of Pericles and the Alcmeonidae rather than broadly Athenian. He declares flatly that Athens saved all Greece; time and again, he points out the failures of Sparta and others; and he is on the whole less severe upon the Persians than upon the Greek rivals of Athens. He believed that the struggle between Persians and Greeks was to be regretted—just as Pericles had opposed Cimon's Asiatic campaigns. His opening pages facetiously trace the long struggle between East and West back to the Trojan War. "The Greeks attribute the war to the rape of Helen," he says in substance, "but the Persians reply that while it is indeed the work of a scoundrel to carry off another man's wife, still the husband who complains about it is a fool, for no woman could thus be carried off against her will." He speaks of the aid sent to Miletus—against the advice of the Alcmeonidae—as the beginning of the "woes of Greece." In his amazingly brief account of Marathon (which had been won by the wrong faction!), he goes out of his way to contradict the story that the Alcmeonidae helped the Persians and at the same time he emphasizes the ridiculous excuse of the Spartans for not sending aid in time. And the final sentences of the book warn against conquests in Asia, attributing the words to Cyrus though obviously aiming them at the followers of Cimon. The history did not reach final form until after the outbreak of the Peloponnesian War—it parenthetically mentions two or three events that occurred in 431 or 430—but Herodotus had made up his mind about things long before. He knew little of what happened in Greece after he left, and his history sets forth views current in Periclean Athens during the early 440's, before Pericles had been forced to sign the Thirty Years Peace.

It would be a grave mistake, however, to think of Herodotus as concerned exclusively or even primarily with politics. His chief interest was in men. He regarded the events of history, not as the result of deep and abstract causes, but as the works of men. His book is largely a collection of stories about men, individual men, all kinds of men. Herodotus has been called the "Father of Ethnology." Indeed, his accounts of foreign peoples and their customs must have had the same broadening effect upon his readers that the writings of such anthropologists as Sir James Frazer had upon the thoughtful people in England and America at the beginning of the present century. He showed his readers that things could be done in many different ways, and that the traditional Greek ways were not necessarily the best. His remarks about the gods, especially the more extravagant oriental deities, were equally calculated to disconcert unenlightened persons, for he frequently suggested that these gods were at bottom similar to the Greek gods, in spite of their different names and myths. Nevertheless, Herodotus was a great friend of the priests at Delphi and not disposed to attack religion as such. He once remarked that Cambyses must have been insane to mock the gods of Egypt. His theological views resembled those of his friend Sophocles: much mythology is foolish, of course, but the gods certainly direct human events, and oracles always come true in one way or another.

Even in antiquity Herodotus was often accused of inaccuracy. Ancient critics called him the "Father of Lies," and in the nineteenth century he was severely taken to task by many writers. Today we are less inclined to carp. Many of the things Herodotus reported were untrue, but he often reports these stories as hearsay, and sometimes he adds that he does not believe them himself. Far from being gullible, Herodotus was extraordinarily skeptical regarding his informants and took great pains to learn the truth about things. As a pioneer he inevitably fell into many errors which his admirers now dismiss as minor blemishes. They praise the breadth of his views, his wide human sympathies, his enthusiasm for freedom, the skill and artistry with which he collected and presented his facts. Herodotus is never dull. No matter what he is discussing, he can always find time for a good story; and as these stories pile up, the reader gradually discovers the unrolling of a mighty epic. Not for nothing was he the cousin of an epic poet, and an ancient critic once called him the "most Homeric" of men. Stories are the stuff of which he wove his book, but he arranged them carefully in a brilliant pattern. This perhaps is the reason why, as a recent writer has observed, Herodotus is enjoyed most by children and philosophers.

Thucydides

The other great Athenian historian, Thucydides, was born about 460 and was therefore a full generation younger than Herodotus. His father owned an estate in Thrace which included a mine in Mount Pangaeus that had been seized by Cimon in 463. Tradition reported that Thucydides was related through both parents to Cimon and to the Miltiades of Marathon fame; and in later times the historian's tomb at Athens was shown in the family plot next that of Cimon's sister Elpinice. The historian's father was probably a grandson of Miltiades through a daughter, and probably his mother was a daughter of the statesman Thucydides, son of Melesias, who had married another daughter of Miltiades. This would make the historian the grandson of the statesman Thucydides, the great-nephew of Cimon, and twice the great-grandson of Miltiades (see genealogical table, p. 394).

Thucydides received the education of an Athenian aristocrat, and later it was said that he, like Aristophanes, had once been a pupil of Antiphon, the orator and leader of the Four Hundred, concerning whom he wrote sympathetically. Though the aristocrats were out of power, Thucydides presumably had held lesser offices before 424, for in that year he was elected *strategos* and sent to save Amphipolis. His failure resulted in his banishment until after the fall of Athens in 404. Even in 431, Thucydides foresaw the importance of the impending war, and he tells us that he began at once to keep accurate records of what happened. These records underlie much of his narrative, though doubtless he used other written sources as well. Most

Thucydides (Naples Museum)

Herodotus (Courtesy of the Metropolitan Museum of Art)

Plate 30

of the history was written—or at least drastically revised—after 404. Our present text breaks off in the middle of a paragraph dealing with events in the summer of 411, and while he may have written a few more pages, he never completed the book. The date and place of his death are unknown, but he died early in the fourth century, probably before 396.

Thucydides knew the work of Herodotus well, and on the whole he admired it. Nevertheless, his own history was a very different book, inspired by very different ideas. Perhaps he learned some of these ideas from the Sophists, whose pupil he obviously was, but fundamentally his ideas were his own, developed during long years of rumination upon the war. As an exile he watched his beloved city rushing to her ruin while he was powerless to help her, and he brooded over the catastrophe that was occurring before his eyes. He had meditated too long and too deeply upon the fate of Athens to blame either gods or men. His history therefore deals very little with persons. It contains brief though brilliant character sketches of Themistocles, Pericles, Cleon, Alcibiades, and a few others; but it rarely praises or blames individuals. Thucydides sought the fundamental causes of events. He did not ignore the economic and other aspects of life, and the space devoted to speeches shows how fully he realized the importance of public opinion, yet he considered the state to be the most important factor in social life, and with it he was primarily concerned. The comings and goings of individual politicians were of little importance, for even the best of them were the victims of circumstance, and could not have acted otherwise than they did.

Thus Thucydides, like his contemporary Sophocles, came to recognize the inevitability of what was happening. The poet attributed it all to Fate; the historian preferred to invoke natural causes. He believed that what had happened once was sure to happen again under the same circumstances; and, after thinking out the story to satisfy himself, he wrote his book in order that others might calculate intelligently the consequences of their decisions. A history such as he planned to write—one that was at once sober, dispassionate, and true—would therefore be, in his famous phrase, "a possession forever." Yet he was no pure scientist, dwelling in a tower of ivory and speculating abstractly upon the course of human events. Rather he was a patriotic citizen making a supreme effort to avert a repetition of the catastrophe of 404. His candor and his dispassionate objectivity were such that he has been taken as an example and model by the better historians from that day to this. "The only way to write history," declared the distinguished German historian of antiquity, Eduard Meyer,[5] early in the present century, "is that first used by the Athenian Thucydides."

Much of the narrative of the history is of course taken up with accounts of marchings back and forth and of minor battles which are neither interesting nor important. The pages that stand out in the reader's memory, making the book "a possession forever," are those in which the author analyses events of lasting significance. One famous passage discusses the plague at Athens. Though the description of medical symptoms is so vague that modern physicians cannot diagnose the disease, the account of its social consequences is unforgettable. The story of the revolution at Corcyra is another masterpiece of social analysis, leading to universal conclusions about how revolutions occur. The picture of the progressive demoralization of Greece under the influence of war is masterly. Thucydides was one of the greatest of social scientists.

As we read his book, Thucydides gradually forces upon us his conviction that, in the final reckoning, the woes of Athens were due to Periclean imperialism. This imperialism caused other Greeks to fear and hate Athens, and thus brought about the war. It caused Athens to fear her own subjects, which led her to punish rebellions ever more ferociously, making the war more and more bitter. It divided all Greece into factions, both vertically by states and horizontally by social classes, adding the horrors of civil war to those of inter-city war. And it was civil dissension that finally brought about the fall of Athens. This hatred of Periclean imperialism perhaps came naturally to the great-nephew of Cimon; but Thucydides had long since ceased to be a party man, and he certainly was not writing a party tract.

---

[5] See note on Eduard Meyer, p. 473.

The only long excursus in the history comes early in the first book and traces the history of the Athenian Empire from the days of Aristides and Cimon to the pacification of Samos in 439. It is written in such restrained language that only a few phrases about "enslavement" and "violation of treaties" by Athens reveal the author's sympathies. In the third book, however, the whole story is told over again more succinctly by Mytilenean ambassadors to Sparta, and in their words it is not a pretty story. There can be no doubt that Thucydides shared the views of the ambassadors, for his sympathies are always on the side of Athens' subject "allies." After twenty years of meditation, his reasoned judgment upon Athenian imperialism remained that expressed by his great-aunt Elpinice in her famous reply to Pericles (p. 412).

A more serious charge brought by Thucydides against Periclean imperialism is that it changed Athens into a tyranny. He makes this statement in his own name, and he puts it into the speeches of one man after another. Pericles admits it quite frankly in his final speech defending himself for leading Athens into the war. Cleon says it brutally when demanding death or slavery for the Mytileneans. The Athenian ambassadors say it grossly when preparing the greatest atrocity of the war, the massacre of the Melians (here Thucydides manages to make their language seem even more infamous than their deeds). And Alcibiades repeats it when urging the Syracusan expedition that was to be the beginning of the end. Long before the Spartan armies entered the city, Periclean imperialism had destroyed most of what Thucydides deemed worth-while in Athens. Even the famous funeral oration which he puts into the mouth of Pericles, extolling the glory of Athens in words of unforgettable beauty, can only have served to remind postwar Athenians that fine words and democratic idealism cannot perpetuate a state that depends for its very existence upon the imperialistic exploitation of subject peoples.

Scientists and Philosophers

Speculation about nature continued through the fifth century, with Ionians still taking the leading part. Athens produced no important scientists, though most of the famous Ionians visited the city sooner or later. Thus Anaxagoras, born at Clazomenae in Ionia about 500, spent many years at Athens as the tutor and later as the intimate friend of Pericles. Eventually he was expelled from the city on charges of impiety by opponents who wished to attack his patron indirectly. Among other things, he taught that the sun is a burning mass of stone, "bigger than the Peloponnesus," that the moon reflects the light of the sun, and that on it are mountains and valleys like those on earth. He was also an able mathematician and, like his predecessors in the sixth century, he philosophized about the ultimate substance from which all things are made. He held that the universe is made up of many sorts of things but that a universal Mind, which he called "Nous," gives order and unity to all.

Oenipides of Chios was a contemporary mathematician who attempted to reform the calendar. The Greeks were still using the old calendar of twelve lunar months or 354 days, inserting a thirteenth month three times every eight years to bring this year into harmony with the solar year. Oenipides made a more exact calculation of the solar year, which he put at 365 days, eight hours, and fifty-seven minutes. His pupil Meton recalculated the year, reducing the fraction of a day to six hours and nineteen minutes—which is barely thirty minutes too long—and in 432 he proposed a nineteen-year cycle to synchronize the solar and lunar years. His reform was not accepted, however, and Athens continued to use a calendar that was neither so accurate nor so convenient as the one Egyptians had been using for over two thousand years or the one used by Central American Mayas many centuries before Columbus.

The most important of the fifth-century scientists was Democritus of Abdera, a city in Thrace. He was born about 460, traveled widely, visited Athens, and wrote books on a variety of subjects before he died in his native city at an advanced age. His reputation rested partly upon the wide extent of his knowledge, in which he has been compared to Aristotle, and partly upon the literary skill with which he presented his views, in which he has been compared to Plato. Unfortunately, only fragments of his works and digests of his theories have been preserved. His name is associated especially with his theory of atoms. He decided that all material things are made of tiny particles so small that they cannot be divided. These he called "*atoma somata*" ("atomic" bodies) from *a* meaning "not" and *tomos* from *temno*, "cut." Atoms differed in size, shape, weight, and other qualities, and were constantly moving about in space, their motions being determined solely by natural law. As atoms and space were the only things whose existence Democritus recognized, his philosophy was thoroughly materialistic. The atom he talked about had only a superficial resemblance to the one studied by modern physicists, and he can hardly be called their predecessor. A badly authenticated story, probably untrue, illustrates the difference between Democritus and the modern scientist. It is reported that he put out his eyes in order that passing sights might not disturb his speculations. It may be that the old Greek who concocted this tale intended to ridicule Democritus, in which case he unwittingly hit upon a pertinent criticism of the philosopher as a scientist. Democritus's theories were spun out of his head, and a blind man might have observed as much as he.

Greek Medicine

It is often said that the only fifth-century Greeks who approached the point of view of modern science were physicians. Most Greeks still considered disease a visitation from the world of spirits, and sought cures by religion and magic. Thus after the great plague at Athens, they introduced the cult of Asclepius, a deity honored with a temple near the theater of Dionysus. A favorite practice was "incubation," by which sick persons would sleep overnight in a temple, hoping to be cured by the god. Priests sometimes went beyond reciting charms over their patients, however, and did what they could to help the deity effect a cure. Some of them thus acquired a certain knowledge of medicine. Though superstitions continued throughout ancient times, there gradually grew up schools of physicians who held a more objective view of disease. Here again, Ionians took the lead, having learned much from Egyptians and other Orientals whose local superstitions they could disregard.

The two principal schools of Greek medicine were those of Cnidus and of Cos, and the great light of the latter was Hippocrates. Little is known of this remarkable man, who wrote books and lectured to pupils toward the end of the fifth century. His writings were later supplemented by those of lesser men, and in the third century before Christ, they all were collected and published as the "Hippocratic corpus." Much of this corpus is still available. We cannot state with certainty which of its treatises come from the pen of Hippocrates himself, but a group of them stand out by the clear views and intellectual power of their author, and these are usually ascribed to the master. Hippocrates laid great emphasis upon diagnosis, and he recorded case histories to aid his pupils in understanding this art. Modern physicians admire the scientific clarity of these clinical reports and can easily diagnose the diseases. Hippocrates believed that, while cures came only from Nature herself, the physician could help his patient by watching diet and using drugs. Though Greek sentiment did not permit the dissection of human bodies, physicians managed to acquire a knowledge of anatomy, and their treatment of dislocations and fractures was almost modern. Minor operations were performed, but of course internal surgery was out of the question until the discovery—in the nineteenth century—of anesthetics and antiseptics.

The New Philosophers

Just as Ionia had been the home of skepticism, so southern Italy was the center from which emanated new theological views and the religious philosophy of the Pythagoreans. Ionians had long been in contact with the high civilizations of the East, but the West provided less that might cause Greeks to doubt the merit of their ancestral views. Thinkers of the West therefore continued old traditions and deplored the materialistic skepticism of the Ionians.

The earliest, and in many ways the greatest, of these western philosophers was Parmenides of Elea. He was born in this Italian city a few years before 500, and he set forth his views in a long poem "On Nature," of which we have a part. Parmenides was a deeply religious man, distressed by his predecessors, Xenophanes and Heraclitus, and he learned much from the Pythagoreans. In contrast to

Ionian talk of an ever-changing material world known by sense perception, he dreamed of another "world," known only by reason, where all things are immutable and eternal. The wise man, he said, should devote his attention to this "real" world rather than to the transitory world of the Ionians. His pupil Zeno owes his reputation to a number of riddles he invented to show that motion is logically impossible and therefore does not exist in the "real" world of reason. It would be impossible, he reasoned, for the fleet-footed Achilles ever to overtake a slow-moving tortoise, for if the tortoise were once ahead it could always go a little farther while Achilles was reaching the spot where it had once been. Ancient mathematicians were baffled by Zeno's subtle dialectics.

The other great Western philosopher was Empedocles, who flourished in Sicily toward the middle of the fifth century. He was a wise and learned man, familiar with Ionian science, a good physician, and a democratic politician. He was also much interested in Orphism. He wrote a book about purifications, and he attempted to harmonize the materialism of the Ionians with the theology of Parmenides. As we shall see in a later chapter, some Athenians found consolation after the fall of their city in the religious overtones of this eternal world of philosophic thought. Plato was heavily indebted to these Western thinkers, and in the last centuries of the ancient world, when everything was going to rack and ruin, Neoplatonists revived and elaborated such ideas, which they passed along to Christianity.

Conditions in Periclean Athens were such that serious thinkers found much to consider besides the eternal verities. Just as the dramatists concerned themselves with problems of morals and ethics, so philosophers reflected upon matters which we now call the social sciences. Thucydides was the greatest of these thinkers, but many lesser men speculated upon such matters. Herodotus tells us of a discussion between three Persians about the relative merits of democracy, oligarchy, and monarchy. The words are put into the mouths of Persians, but the ideas are fundamentally Greek, and though Herodotus insists that the conversation actually took place, his story seems to be based on an essay by some Greek philosopher which he mistook for an authentic record. Many similar writings on

political science were current in Athens, and men such a Hippodamus of Miletus—a friend of Pericles—drew up what they considered
ideal constitutions for a city.

Constitutional changes, coupled with skepticism regarding the
gods, raised questions as to the ultimate sanctions of law and government. Philosophers began to say that, while many things depend
upon man-made law, others are right by nature. Some may have
argued, like the notorious Athenian ambassadors to Melos, that the
law of nature ordains that the strong shall rule, but others declared
that human law is sometimes tyrannical, and that all men have certain inalienable rights by nature. Plato reports a certain Hippias of
Elis as saying that by nature all men are fellow-citizens and brothers.
Thus arose the concept of a law of nature which later played a great
role in the development of jurisprudence. Still other philosophers
took the first steps toward establishing a system of ethics that was
divorced from religion.

Prominent among these social philosophers was Protagoras of
Abdera, another of Pericles' friends. He was a well-known Sophist
who undertook to teach men ethics. Pericles engaged him to draw
up a constitution for the colony at Thurii, and Plato made him the
subject of a famous dialogue. Two of his dicta are often quoted:
"Man is the measure of all things," and "Concerning the gods I know
not whether or not they exist, or what they are like if they do exist."
The point of the latter statement is sufficiently obvious, the second
half being the more important. The former remark may be taken as
a key to his social and political philosophy. He pointed out that men
built cities for their mutual protection, and he apparently judged
all other social and ethical institutions and ideas by their value to
men—not by their divine origin, their antiquity, or any other conventional standard. He was tried for impiety by the conservative
Four Hundred at Athens in 411, and was lost at sea soon afterward
while on his way to Sicily.

Socrates

In the hurly-burly of intellectual Athens, Socrates stood high
above his contemporaries. He was a familiar figure in the agora and

all other public places. While Aristophanes was gently ridiculing him as a Sophist, the Delphic oracle declared him the wisest of the Greeks. After the fall of Athens, when democratic politicians needed someone to blame for the city's misfortunes, they condemned Socrates on the charge that he had corrupted the youth of Athens (399). In his early days, Socrates, like other Sophists, had a school in which the scholars led ascetic lives and studied natural phenomena; but in later years, he devoted his mind especially to ethical problems. Among his associates were such men as Alcibiades, Critias, and Charmides, the first of whom deserted Athens while the other two became leaders of the "Thirty Tyrants" who ruled the city in 404. For this, too, Socrates was blamed by the democrats five years later.

It was the great joy of Socrates' life to converse with young men about problems of social and philosophical importance. By skillful questioning he would lead them through long trains of reasoning to conclusions very different from the cocksure and conventional views they had first expressed. The unorthodoxy of his opinions annoyed and sometimes enraged the conservative fathers of his youthful companions, but he won the eternal friendship of the young men themselves. He was one of the greatest teachers in history. The young man who once fell into his clutches was marked for life, and practically every Athenian of intellectual attainments in the next generation claimed—rightly in most cases—that he had once been associated with Socrates.

Notes

Karl Julius Beloch

The first serious attempt to estimate the population of the ancient world by a scholar familiar with the methods of modern statistical science was made by K. J. Beloch, *Die Bevölkerung der Griechisch-römischen Welt* (1886). This work has served as starting point for most later studies of the subject though scholars usually hold that Beloch's estimates were too low. Karl Julius Beloch (1854–1929) was the only child of a well-to-do landowner in Lower Silesia, Germany. Ill health forced him to seek a warmer climate, and from the age of seventeen he passed practically all his life in Italy. Here he took his doctorate and became a professor at the University of Rome in 1879; here he married an American wife; here he trained most of the Italians who have done important work in ancient history in the present century; and here he remained except for one year (1912–13) when he was a professor at Leipzig.

Living outside Germany, Beloch watched with a critical eye what happened there after 1870. He was much interested in politics and declared that he had always been a Republican—though in his last years he added that the Weimar Republic was not what he had dreamed of. In 1893 he returned to Germany long enough to run, and be defeated, for a seat in the Reichstag on the ticket of the ill-starred "Fortschrittspartei." Beloch's criticisms also touched German scholarship; much of his life was spent in feuds with various German scholars; and the value of his work was recognized abroad sooner than in Germany.

Beloch's early work on population was intended to be the first part of a comprehensive study of the population of Europe from ancient times to the end of the Renaissance. Much material was collected but the complete work never appeared. He also published monographs on many aspects of the history of Rome and Italy, but his reputation rests primarily upon his *Griechische Geschichte,* the first edition of which appeared in three volumes between 1893 and 1904, the second between 1911 and 1924. The new edition, largely rewritten, appeared in four double volumes, the first half-volume in each case containing the narrative history while the second consisted of monographs on various special topics. The *Griechische Geschichte* is noteworthy for its emphasis upon economic and intellectual history and for its attention to other parts of the Greek world than Athens. Beloch's highly independent mentality led him to treat modern scholarship and even the ancient sources in too cavalier a fashion, and sometimes he confidently put forward sweeping reconstructions in support of which little can be said. Nevertheless his learned book is the best German history of Greece. Beloch's autobiographical sketch in *Die Geschichtswissenschaft der Gegenwart in Selbstdarstellungen* (ed. Dr. Sigfrid Steinberg [1926], II, 1–27) is both interesting and illuminating.

Gilbert Murray

The most brilliant modern interpreter of Euripides is the British scholar Gilbert Murray. Although born in Australia, Murray was educated at Oxford, married the daughter of the ninth Earl of Carlisle, spent a few years as professor at Glasgow, and served as Regius Professor of Greek at Oxford from 1907 until his retirement in 1936. Murray was always much more than a good Greek scholar. Like his hero Euripides, he was a man of radical views on many political, social, and artistic matters, and he was known in radical literary circles. He dedicated one of his books to "My old friend, G. B. S." and critics recognize in him the model from whom

George Bernard Shaw drew the radical Euripides-quoting Greek scholar from Australia who married the granddaughter of an earl in *Major Barbara* (1905).

Murray was twice the Liberal Party's candidate for Parliament, but in ultra-conservative Oxford his defeat was a foregone conclusion. A pacifist and an internationalist, Murray was much upset by the outbreak of World War I, and he was among the first to propagandize for a League of Nations to prevent a recurrence of that tragedy. After the war he attended several meetings of the League at Geneva as a member of the British delegation, and he actively encouraged international co-operation among intellectuals.

Murray's studies of Euripides led him first to prepare the standard edition of the Greek text of the plays (1902–09). He then made several poetical translations, some of which were successfully staged in London and elsewhere, thus enabling the non-academic world to discover Euripides. Though his little volume entitled *Euripides and his Age* (1913) was intended only as a popularization to appear in the "Home University Library" (Murray was an editor of this famous series of booklets), it is a brilliant interpretation of the poet: its second chapter contains a remarkable sketch of intellectual conditions in Periclean Athens. In later years, Murray devoted himself to Aristophanes and Aeschylus. He was also the author of a stimulating *History of Ancient Greek Literature* (1897) and of works on Greek religion. In these last works, as in his account of the origins of Greek drama, Murray made much use—too much use at times —of the anthropological theories of Sir James Frazer (see p. 24) and similar writers.

Eduard Meyer

Eduard Meyer (1855–1930) was born in Hamburg, Germany, took his degree at Leipzig, and in 1902 became Professor of Ancient History at Berlin. He was both an Orientalist and a Hellenist, and his masterwork, the great *Geschichte des Altertums* (5 vols., 1884–1902) was the first successful attempt to weave into one narrative the various threads of oriental and Greek, and even Carthaginian and Roman, history from the earliest times to the eve of Alexander's conquests. This massive work had an enormous influence in creating modern conceptions about the course of ancient history. His *Forschungen zur alten Geschichte* (2 vols., 1892–99) and *Kleine Schriften* (1910; 2nd ed., 2 vols., 1924) contain valuable monographs on a number of subjects connected with the ancient world, including famous studies of its economic development and of slavery in antiquity. In the early years of the twentieth century, after the completion of his *magnum opus*, Meyer was widely hailed as the greatest living historian, and his students were to be found in every civilized country. He visited the United States in 1904 and again in 1909–10, on the second occasion as exchange professor at Harvard. In this country he was much lionized, he traveled and lectured widely, he spent his spare moments writing a history of the Mormons, and he left behind him a large crop of stories about his brusque manners.

His words on Thucydides, quoted in the text above, form the closing sentence of an essay entitled "Zur Theorie und Methodik der Geschichte," originally published in 1902 and reprinted in the *Kleine Schriften*, I, 67. At that time it was possible to say that Eduard Meyer was a worthy disciple of the great Greek master. During World War I, however, he showed himself incapable of that dispassionate objectivity which characterized Thucydides during the Peloponnesian War. He quickly disgraced himself with a scurrilous brochure entitled *England* (1915), which he followed, long before America entered the war, with a companion volume, written in similar style, about the United States. The return of peace did not restore Meyer's composure. His chagrin at Germany's defeat warped all his writing thereafter. Like practically all German classicists since Winckelmann, Meyer had identified Greece with Germany in his own mind; he now proclaimed the thesis that the decline of Greek civilization after Alexander was caused by the indemnities imposed upon her by Roman conquerors—in which he saw a foreshadowing of the United States and the Treaty of Versailles. Meyer attempted a new edition of his great *Geschichte,* but the new materials discovered during forty years were too copious to be fitted into the old pattern, and he no longer had the strength to rewrite the book from beginning to end. The opening volumes were republished in expanded but less brilliant form; those dealing with Greece were reprinted with little change. During the war Meyer published a volume entitled *Cäsars Monarchie und das Principat des Pompeius* (1918), which has been widely criticized; and the ambitious *Ursprung und Anfänge des Christentums* (3 vols., 1923–26), with which he hoped to crown his career, was even less successful. The most important volume of the latter work is the second, dealing with Judaism from about 200 B.C. to 70 A.D. The story is falsified by constant harping upon "Roms perfide Politik," and in many respects the book was out of date long before it was written. Eduard Meyer, the disciple of Thucydides and once the greatest living historian, was really a casualty of World War I.

XIV Fourth Century Greece

T HE FALL OF ATHENS IN 404 WAS FOLLOWED BY WAR'S usual aftermath of violence, social demoralization, political corruption, economic ruin, and intellectual confusion. While hostilities were still in progress, partisans on every side had talked much about security and freedom, but the overthrow of Athens failed to assure these blessings either to the victors or to the vanquished. The destruction of Athenian power merely opened the way for Spartan domination, and the lesser states remained as far as ever from that independence for which they had fought. Wars soon broke out anew between the various states once allied against Athens, and hostilities continued with only brief intermissions until all Greece was conquered by Philip of Macedon in 338. As a matter of fact, our present designation of the fighting between 431 and 404 as the "Peloponnesian War" comes largely from Thucydides, who treated these disturbances as a unit. As a matter of fact, these twenty-seven years were not much more troubled than the rest of a bloody period that lasted for almost a century. The sad political and social history of the fourth century centers around the consequences of the Peloponnesian War and bears witness to two great truths: first, that while a triviality may easily start a war, even the utter defeat of the enemy cannot really stop it; and second, that the only peace that war and victory can bring is the peace of a desert or of death.

The Spartan general Lysander, who had won the war at Aegospotami, was now the most highly respected and powerful man in Greece. Bronze statues of him were set up at Delphi beside those of the gods and the semi-divine heroes. Games were instituted in his honor and cities erected altars and sacrificed to him as to a god. But though his ability as a general and a diplomat were above question, and his personal honesty was recognized by all, Lysander's statesmanship was not equal to guiding Greece in such troubled times, and the officers with whom he had to work were even more unsatisfactory. Their narrow Spartan training had taught them no way to rule except by military force, and they could think of nothing to do but set up an elaborate military system for the domination of Greece.

The allies had captured the Aegean Islands one by one during the last years of the war, and had put new governments in them, with oligarchies replacing the democracies through which Athens had once ruled. Boards of ten native but pro-Spartan commissioners, called "decarchs," were in charge of the administration; a Spartan garrison, commanded by a "harmost," was stationed in each city; and the tribute once collected by Athens was now exacted by the new rulers. Often the harmost stood idly by and watched the decarchs drive out the democrats in fierce and brutal fashion. The new rulers also permitted those whom the Athenians had exiled from Aegina, Melos, and elsewhere to return home, and the fury of the returning exiles sometimes wrought fearful vengeance upon the Athenian cleruchs who had supplanted them. The Spartans thus substituted a new empire for the old, and its inhabitants were no better off than before.

The cities of the Greek mainland that had once sided with Athens now received vindictive decarchs and harmosts whose rule was heavier than that of Athens, and Lysander continued to maintain Spartan garrisons in the cities of his own allies. These troops, originally sent to defend the allies against Athens, remained to hold them in the Spartan alliance. And finally, the Greek cities of Ionia were handed over to the Persian Cyrus in payment for the aid he had given Sparta. It was not long, therefore, before most Greeks sadly realized that their long war for liberty had brought only a change of masters, and that usually the change was for the worse.

The Punishment of Athens

Even greater difficulties hampered the establishment of an effective government in Athens. During the summer of 404, the oligarchic and democratic factions within the city were engaged in civil war while Athens' victorious enemies were preparing their vengeance. Theban and Corinthian leaders urged that the Athenians be punished in their own style: their city should be turned into a sheep pasture and they themselves sold into slavery. To this brutal proposal the Spartans would not listen, saying that Athens' earlier services to Greece entitled her to a better fate. They therefore permitted the selection of thirty Athenian oligarchs, friendly to Sparta, to whom they entrusted the city much as lesser cities were handed over to decarchs. A harmost and a Spartan garrison were quartered in the city, and when the Athenians failed to destroy their walls as ordered, Spartan soldiers tore them down to the accompaniment of music by flute girls.

The government of these thirty oligarchs quickly degenerated into a bloody tyranny, directed by an Athenian aristocrat named Critias. The leaders of the democratic faction were executed or fled. The constitution was amended to restrict the franchise to three thousand well-to-do persons, and the Thirty received dictatorial powers. When moderate oligarchs disapproved of Critias's measures, they too were executed and their estates confiscated. About fifteen hundred Athenians were put to death during the eight months of this rule. But Critias went too far when he persuaded the Spartans to order their allies to surrender all Athenian refugees for punishment. Several of the allies, already restless under Spartan domination, refused to comply with this bloodthirsty demand.

A democrat named Thrasybulus then managed to collect seventy refugees in Boeotia and captured a small fort at Phyle just inside the Attic frontier. Recruits flocked to his standard until he commanded a force of one thousand men. Critias endeavored to drive him out, but was himself killed in battle, and Thrasybulus occupied Piraeus. Democrats in Athens then revolted against the Thirty, driving them and their partisans to Eleusis. As these democrats were not strong enough to establish their own rule in the city, a board of ten moderates took over the government. Three mutually hostile governments thus existed on Attic soil in the summer of 403.

The extreme democrats under Thrasybulus made notable progress against their adversaries until the Thirty and the Ten each called upon Sparta for aid against them. Lysander again blockaded Piraeus, and an army marched into Eleusis. Before long, however, domestic politics at Sparta led to Lysander's recall and to the substitution of the pacific king, Pausanias, who arranged a truce between the rival Athenian factions. Thrasybulus and the Ten united to set up a moderate democracy in Athens, while the Thirty were allowed to remain at Eleusis. These two groups continued fighting until the remaining leaders of the Thirty were captured and executed in 402–01. Eleusis was then reunited to Athens, and the moderate democrats took over all Attica.

The oligarchs under Critias had been interested primarily in holding power themselves and in abolishing democracy. The extreme democrats under Thrasybulus were eager to renew the war as soon as possible in the hope of regaining the Empire that had once supported them. But the moderates, both under the Ten and under the new government, pursued a policy of peace, set up a democratic government, renounced Periclean imperialism, and began to lay new foundations for the economic life of their city. For several years after 403 they ruled Athens.

Confusion at Sparta

Meantime, all had not gone well for Sparta. The growing restlessness of her allies was shown by numerous complaints against the Spartan general Lysander or his harmosts, and by the refusal of such important allies as Thebes and Argos to surrender Athenian refugees. The Spartans themselves were far from satisfied with the results of Lysander's policies, and in the summer of 403 the ephors relieved him of his command. When King Pausanias returned to Sparta after his pacification of Athens, Lysander charged him with treason. The king was acquitted, though by only one vote—which was a severe blow to the general. A few months later, Lysander was permitted to visit the Spartan outposts along the Hellespont, but he was recalled when the satrap, Pharnabazus, accused him of plundering Persian territory. Lysander withdrew to Libya as a voluntary exile, and after his departure the Spartans removed from office and executed several of his close associates.

Nevertheless, unrest continued unabated in Sparta. A dispute regarding the succession followed the death of Agis, the second Spartan king (398). Though Lysander returned from Africa and obtained the throne for Agesilaus, half brother of Agis, the new king quickly emancipated himself from the general's tutelage. Lysander then began plotting a constitutional change by which the two hereditary kings would be replaced by elected officials, hoping no doubt to gain the highest office for himself. But before reform could be attempted, a war of major proportions broke out in Greece, and Lysander was soon killed in battle (395). This new series of wars lasted for sixty years and completed the ruin of Greece.

Economic Devastation

The Peloponnesian War left Greece bankrupt. The prosperity of the Periclean age had enabled both Athenians and their rivals to store up capital which was now largely lost. When Pericles, at the beginning of the war, called the inhabitants of Attica into Athens and allowed the Spartans to ravage the countryside, he imposed a heavy sentence upon Attic agriculture: cattle were driven off and houses, orchards, and vineyards were destroyed. These losses could be replaced by years of labor, but devastation had also allowed much of the scanty soil of Attica to be washed from the hillsides to the bottom of the Aegean, and this soil was irreplaceable. The Athenians were equally destructive when fighting in hostile territory, and while central Greece and the Peloponnesus were not invaded seriously or often, they suffered severely during the wars of the next century.

During the great war, moreover, Athens built fleet after fleet at enormous expense, and the savings of a generation sank with these fleets to the bottom of the sea. The Spartan navies were built with Persian money, to be sure, but the wealth of Corinth and other commercial cities was devoured by their war efforts. The loss of shipping, the loss of empire, and the return of the Ionian cities to Persian rule were terrible blows to Athenian commerce; and the rise of a powerful Greek empire in Sicily, shortly after the Athenian disaster of 413, played havoc with Corinthian trade in the West. This economic collapse of Greece was a major cause of the hysterical political changes of the years immediately after 404.

The population of European Greece declined slowly during the century that followed 431. The direct casualties of the war were not heavy, for most of the land fighting was mere skirmishing, and the losses in a major battle rarely exceeded a few hundred. Naval defeats might entail a higher loss of life, but only on the Syracusan expedition were Athenian losses so heavy as to be noticeable in the total population. The indirect casualties of war were much greater. There was heavy loss of life among displaced persons, and the plague at Athens exacted a dreadful toll in 430 and 429. Modern writers have suggested—though without conclusive evidence—that the ravaging and subsequent neglect of the countryside led to an increase of swamps and consequently of mosquitoes and malaria. The natural vitality of the Greek people probably replaced most human losses from the war within a rather short time, but the declining productivity of Greece made it impossible to support as large a population as formerly. Lower standards of living caused a great revival of emigration, especially by mercenary soldiers, and the exposure of superfluous infants became a widespread substitute for birth control.

While the total population of Greece may have been reduced only slightly during these years, certain classes of society suffered out of all proportion to their numbers. The direct casualties of the war fell mainly upon the more substantial citizens, who served as hoplites, rather than upon the thetes at Athens or the helots at Sparta. The upper class bore almost the entire loss in the numerous civil wars that followed, and the multitudes of exiles—practically all from this class—were lost to their cities even though their lives were spared. It thus came about that while there had been eight thousand Spartan peers in 480, there were only about two thousand a century later, and barely seven hundred in 330. The number of Athenian citizens declined from more than forty thousand in 431 to barely twenty thousand a century later, though the total population of the city was somewhat larger at the later date and the admission of metics to citizenship was more common than in Periclean times. Wars and revolutions decimated the former ruling classes of Greece.

The Peloponnesian War and its aftermath also brought financial inflation to Greece. A general rise in prices resulted from wartime scarcities and lack of man power, from heavy importations of the precious metals, and from the shortsighted—though perhaps necessary—financial policies of many Greek states. Greeks of all parties confiscated temple treasuries, Cyrus sent great quantities of bullion to Sparta and her allies, raids into Asia Minor a few years later produced still more gold, and returning mercenaries added further to the stock of precious metals, thereby reducing its value and inflating prices. Bankruptcy forced many cities to debase their currency by lowering the amount of silver in coins and thus further reducing the purchasing power of money. Between 400 and 330, the prices of most commodities doubled and those of many trebled.

Reconstruction

It was against this background that men turned to the economic reconstruction of Greece. Their first task was the re-establishment of agriculture, especially in Attica, where devastation had been worst. Although small farmers, who lacked the capital necessary for reconstruction, often sold what was left of their holdings to richer men, there does not seem to have been a marked increase in the number of large estates. The new owners were, however, more intelligent and more enterprising than the old and introduced improved methods of farming. Agriculture had formerly been conducted under the two-field system, whereby a field lay fallow in alternate years to regain its fertility; now crop rotation and the three-field system enabled farmers to use each field two years out of three, though grain was raised only every third year instead of every second. At the same time, good land was planted with orchards, and the devastated and eroded fields were used as pasture for sheep and goats.

The new methods may have produced more valuable crops, but they still did not provide enough grain to feed the people. Even before the war Athens had imported much of her grain from abroad. Other Greek cities were now forced to adopt the same practice, and the price of grain trebled in fifty years. Another misfortune was that the new agriculture gave employment to fewer persons than the old. Farmers therefore migrated to the cities or became mercenary soldiers, and the depopulation of rural Greece began. It continued throughout the remainder of antiquity, and in the long run it became a major cause of the collapse of Greek civilization.

Constantly rising prices encouraged speculation in industry and commerce. Factories remained small and were operated by the owner with only a few workmen and slaves, but their number increased. Articles such as clothing and bread, once prepared at home, were now purchased outside, and the rich demanded new luxuries. There was also a marked growth of international trade. The increased imports of grain had to be balanced by exports of olive oil, wine, and manufactured goods. At first it was not easy to find markets for these goods, for the grain-raising states of the Black Sea area were beginning to manufacture for themselves, and the rise of Syracuse robbed Greeks of their Italian markets. Nevertheless, new markets presently appeared. Mercenary soldiers and other Greeks living in foreign countries, notably in Persia and Carthage, augmented the demand for Greek goods throughout the Mediterranean area. Before the middle of the fourth century, the trade of Athens had probably regained its former proportions. Greek cities along the Hellespont and in Rhodes, Cyprus, and Cyrene were more important than ever, and the Greeks of Syracuse and Massilia shared the general prosperity.

Rising Class Feeling

This inflationist prosperity of the fourth century enabled some men to accumulate enormous fortunes, and we read of a few "millionaires" who had one hundred and fifty or two hundred talents—wealth undreamed of in the days of Pericles. Only a few prospered in this magnificent fashion, of course, but there were many more who would have been considered rich in the old days. Wages, on the other hand, did not keep up with the rising cost of living. Skilled workmen continued to earn about the same real wages as before and could therefore maintain their old, pitifully low, standard of living. (The daily wage of a skilled artisan at Athens would buy slightly more than one bushel of wheat, and if he were fortunate he could work about 80 per cent of the time.) But the wages of unskilled labor did not rise as rapidly as did the cost of food and such workers were consequently worse off than before.

Thus, while the upper classes were becoming fewer and richer, the lower classes were becoming poorer and more numerous. In 431 the poorest class (*thetes*) at Athens made up about 47 per cent of the total citizenry, and early in the next century it was slightly more than half. In spite of rising prices, Athens shortly reduced by one quarter the amount of wealth required for admission into the next higher class (*zeugitae*) and many rich metics were enfranchised as members of the upper classes. Still the thetes included about 60 per cent of all citizens in 330. Thousands of slaves were imported to swell the numbers of the poor: they were even worse off than the thetes.

This division of society into the rich and the poor inevitably led to bitter class conflicts. Leaders of the populace urged programs which modern scholars have characterized as "socialistic," or even as "communistic," though what they most resembled were the various "share the wealth" schemes of American demagogues in the 1930's. There were countless revolutions in the fourth century, each entailing wholesale confiscations and the cancellation of debts, as well as massacres, banishments, and even the murder by hired assassins of leaders who had escaped to other cities. The resulting tension between rich and poor made peaceful and orderly government impossible. Aristotle, writing in the third quarter of the century, reported an oath supposedly taken by the oligarchs in certain cities: "I will be a foe of the common people and will devise whatever evil I can against them." Another contemporary asserted—presumably with some exaggeration—that the democrats took greater pleasure in robbing the rich of their property than they did in receiving it themselves, and that it was more dangerous for a man to seem rich than for him actually to be criminal.

Factional quarrels were further embittered by the Athenian practice of championing democracies everywhere while Sparta championed the oligarchies. This began as war propaganda but was continued afterward. In every city, therefore, part of the citizens preferred foreign domination to rule by the opposite faction of their fellow citizens; and considering the vindictiveness of each group when in power, it is not hard to understand such unpatriotic preferences. Class warfare had undermined civic loyalty and patriotism throughout Greece.

Conditions in Athens differed somewhat from those in other Greek states, though the general tendency was the same everywhere. The rule of the Thirty had turned almost everyone against the oligarchs, and the civil commotions accompanying their fall had given even the oligarchs a distaste for revolutionary activity. Consequently, Athens was the only important city in Greece which suffered no serious revolutions during the sixty years after 400, although class conflicts played a large part in Athenian political life. Popular demagogues attained a power and an unscrupulousness heretofore unknown. Post-war troubles had brought great suffering to the Athenian poor, and the demagogues demanded that something be done to relieve this distress. At first their demands were not unreasonable, but with the passing of time one new form of popular subsidy after another was devised and voted.

Pericles had made small payments from the "theoric fund" to enable the poor to attend theatrical performances; such payments now rose from two obols to five drachmas (or two days' pay for a skilled workman) and were distributed on an increasing number of occasions. Payment for attendance at the Assembly rose to a drachma and a half. Occasions for handouts from the treasury were multiplied until a philanthropic politician once granted each citizen fifty drachmas—three weeks' wages—out of the public funds to enable him to celebrate one minor festival properly! When the treasury could not support such vast expenditures, demagogues increased their popularity by "soak the rich" taxation. They forced taxes up to unprecedented heights and, when taxpayers adopted every possible expedient for evading taxes, they made the state more and more tyrannical in collecting them. The rich and the moderately well-to-do allowed class feeling to replace patriotism, while the poor came to regard the state as a cow waiting to be milked.

The Decline of the City-State

Other forces were equally active in undermining the Greek city-state. We have repeatedly seen that, in the ancient world generally, patriotism was intimately associated with the state religion. Deep changes now came over the popular religions of Greece. The thousands of peasants who left their farms and villages to enter mercenary armies, or to migrate to the cities, were torn from the ancestral shrines and ceremonies about which their religious life had once revolved. They could not in their mature years build up devout sentiments toward new sanctuaries, new ceremonies, and new gods; and they were not deeply moved by the strange rites of the state cult in their new homes. While some preserved a vague recollection of their old religion and its sanctions, and others turned to Orphism or to exotic religions from the Orient, the majority of these migrants could find no religion to fill an important gap in their new lives. The Sophists in the days of Pericles had led Athenian intellectuals to doubt the old gods, but such unbelief had not touched the lower classes—who, for example, were panic-stricken with fear of divine vengeance when drunken revelers disfigured the statues of Hermes in 415. In the next century, however, men of all classes fell victims to a contagious skepticism. Men who knew nothing of philosophy forsook their old religions and began to neglect their old gods. Agitators ridiculed these gods before the lowest classes of urban society, and their ideas were welcomed by the populace. The resulting decay of the old religion removed another powerful prop from the city-state.

The social changes of the fourth century also created a spirit of individualism unknown to earlier times. The peasants who left their old homes soon abandoned their old social restraints and conventions. They became *deracinés*, persons torn from their moorings, and they looked after themselves as best they could. Strong and unscrupulous persons could go far. The inflationist economic prosperity gave lucky gamblers great fortunes. Mercenary armies offered tempting oppores to adventurers. Demagoguery opened political careers and ewards to skillful manipulators of the mob. On the other hand, class consciousness and class conflicts caused the well-to-do to feel themselves apart from and better than the masses, while their wealth and education enabled them to find other pleasurable activities to replace the politics that had once engrossed their attention. Men ceased being citizens to become individuals.

Bureaucracy

Development of the arts of government, war, and finance gave new directions to the political evolution of the Greek cities. As usual, Athens offers the best illustration of these new tendencies. In military affairs, the old citizen army was being replaced by mercenary troops who were loyal to their commanders and perhaps to their employers, though not inspired by any ardent feeling of patriotism. Elected officials had little to do with the army except to pay it, and soldiers took no interest in politics so long as they were paid regularly. When class warfare flared up, the mercenaries supported the class that paid the largest bonuses. In some parts of the Greek world, especially in Sicily, the commanders of mercenaries often seized cities and governed them as tyrants.

At the same time, complicated problems of finance could no longer be solved by the general public or by demagogic leaders. The treasury fell into the hands of expert financiers with skill enough to prevent complete bankruptcy. The complexities of legislation likewise became too great for ordinary men, and a body of commissioners, called "nomothetes," virtually usurped the power of legislation. Government thus gradually evolved from a democracy to a bureaucracy. The new bureaucratic rulers of the state had no need of votes and consequently felt no sympathy with the demands of the extreme democrats. They found effective ways of checking the exuberance of demagogues, and before the middle of the century, the government of Athens had been brought to a more moderate temper. When the common people lost the power to direct the government, they also lost interest in it. The new bureaucrats reconciled the rich to their burdens and lulled the populace with occasional distributions of cash, but they also extinguished the old patriotic enthusiasm for freedom and democracy.

The economic and social developments of the fourth century thus shook the Greek *polis* to its very foundations. Though the city-state continued to exist, after a fashion, even in Roman times, its great days were over. New political systems were contrived, the more radical of which abandoned the concept of the city-state altogether. Men even began to say that the world (*kosmos*) was their city (*polis*) and coined the word "cosmopolitan." Social and intellectual individualism and cosmopolitanism pointed the Greek world toward the imperialism of Alexander and his successors. As long as the Greek people were divided into many hostile camps, their leaders could not succeed in foreign conquest, but the decline of the city-state prepared the way for a cosmopolitan world empire.

Intellectual Readjustment

The best Athenian thought was always associated with the fortunes of the city, and the fate which overwhelmed Athens in 404 entailed a fundamental intellectual readjustment. Men did not cease to study and think, to write books, and to produce works of art, but those who lived through the last tragic years of the war were marked forever, and they could not recapture the spirit of the classic age. The sciences such as medicine, astronomy, and mathematics fared about as well in the fourth century as they had in the fifth, perhaps because in both periods the important scientists were non-Athenians. But the great days of Attic tragedy and comedy were over, and the literature that flourished in the new age—oratory, history, philosophy—differed profoundly from the corresponding productions of the fifth century. Men of intellectual tastes fell into skepticism or despair, or retreated into the clouds. Many of them came to resemble the uninspired and unimpassioned bureaucrats who governed their city. Their ideas and ideals were eventually to be important for the history of the world, but in general they lacked the old intellectual courage and self-confidence. As we review their works, we feel that decline had set in. Exhaustion and defeat had taken the heart out of Athens.

A few years after 404 a second blow shook the young intellectuals of Athens almost as deeply as had the fall of their city. Democratic politicians executed Socrates. This beloved teacher had criticized democracy during the war, and his pupils included such unpopular aristocrats as Alcibiades and Critias. As soon as the democratic faction was firmly ensconced in power once more, it charged him with introducing strange gods and corrupting the youth of Athens and executed him in the summer of 399. It soon appeared, however, that Socrates dead could be just as troublesome a gadfly to politicians as the living Socrates had been. Admiring pupils took up his defense and published booklets about him, describing in detail his trial and death, and refuting the charges of his enemies. Tracts written for this purpose by Plato and by Xenophon are still extant. From that time forth the popular opinion of Socrates rose until he was hailed as the font of all wisdom. His character was so idealized that he became the great saint of paganism. In later ages, Christian theologians regretted that so noble a man could not be numbered among the saints of the Church. Nearly everyone of the next generation who set himself up as a philosopher claimed to be a pupil of Socrates, no matter how greatly he might pervert the master's teaching.

Socrates' most illustrious pupil was Plato, whose life and writings will be described below, but many another of his pupils taught philosophy in fourth-century Athens. Three such men deserve passing mention as illustrating the skepticism and mental confusion of the new day, when no one could be very sure just what was worth while in life. Euclides of Megara (died c. 370) was really a successor of the Eleatic philosophers Parmenides and Zeno, but he had studied at Athens long enough to imbibe Socrates' supreme regard for virtue: as the methods of Eleatic logic could not show what is morally good, his disciples were noted chiefly as captious quibblers. Likewise Aristippus of Cyrene (died c. 356), who had come to Athens as a young man to hear Socrates, concerned himself with the problems of ethics. He taught that pleasure is the most worth-while goal of man —though, of course, a man seeking pleasure wisely will master his passions rather than allow them to master him. On the other hand,

Antisthenes of Athens (died *c.* 365), who perhaps best embodied the spirit of Socrates, taught that self-discipline and training (*askesis,* whence our "asceticism") are the best roads to virtue. All three men agreed that virtue and knowledge are the only things in the world really worth having—the only ones which were secure in such troubled times—but they never seemed very certain just what knowledge and virtue were, or how or where they could be acquired. And we cannot help remarking that their skepticism in no way resembled the idealistic criticism of Socrates, Euripides, and their friends: it showed nothing of the intellectual courage of strong men seeking new truths; it was instead the trifling skepticism which accompanies decadence, debility, and despair.

Diogenes and the Cynics

Greek life in the fourth century found another characteristic expression in the philosophy known as Cynicism. The founder of this school of philosophy was Diogenes of Sinope, whose father had been a rich banker in Asia Minor. He reached Athens as an exile from his native city about 350, and he died, perhaps at Corinth, some thirty years later. Like the philosophers just mentioned, Diogenes insisted upon the supreme importance of virtue, but he expressed his views more forcibly and more radically than they. He professed to see no difference between men, whether they were rich or poor, freemen or slaves, wise or foolish, dirty or clean, Greek or barbarian, except in so far as one man excelled another in virtue. Moreover, he taught that civilization was the chief enemy of virtue. A philosopher, he said, must be absolutely independent of civilization and society, and even of other men, if he is to devote himself entirely to the pursuit of virtue. Life should be a training (*askesis*) in virtue, conducted along austere and ascetic lines, and Cynic homilies were filled with references to the training and struggles of an athlete and to the crown of victory.

One modern writer has called Cynicism "the philosophy of the Greek proletariat," but if we are to accept Diogenes as a proletarian leader, we must first forget all Marxian and similar ideas about the

cause and cure of poverty. Diogenes' efforts to alleviate the sufferings
of the poor and needy were limited to reminding them that riches
would undoubtedly corrupt their morals! It would be much nearer
the truth to regard Cynicism as the philosophy of the displaced persons then flocking to the Greek cities. Torn away from their old manner of life and failing to find an adequate substitute, these men
railed against the civilization of the time and turned individualists
and cosmopolitans. According to some accounts, it was Diogenes
who first called himself a "cosmopolitan," by which he meant that, as
an exile from Sinope, he had no city of his own except the cosmos.
In this, as in much else, Diogenes was highly typical of the fourth
century.

Diogenes was, among other things, a first-class showman, and
countless stories were told of how he attracted attention to himself
and his ideas. He carried a lighted lantern through the streets of
Athens at noonday, saying that he was looking for an honest man;
he slept in a barrel or in the porches of temples, wore the scantiest
clothes, and ate his food raw, in order to show that houses, clothes,
and fires are unnecessary. He made his living by begging. His disregard for social conventions and usages lead at times to utter shame-
lessness, which he justified on the ground that he was living in
harmony with nature. The very name "Cynic" was associated with
the Greek word for "dog" (*kyon*), an animal regarded as especially
shameless. The style of Diogenes' diatribes against the rich has given
the word "cynicism" its modern meaning of sneering disbelief in the
virtue of others, but we must not assume that he was flippant or a
trifler. On the contrary, he was a man in dead earnest, who spared
himself and his followers nothing in their quest for virtue. In spite
of his eccentricities, his force of character made a deep impression
upon all who knew him. He established a conception of philosophy
and of the philosopher which remained popular with the lower
classes until the end of the ancient world. In later days, many a
Christian saint accepted his austere ideal. His views and practices
were taken over by Stoics and other eminently respectable philosophers and even by the early Christians—St. Paul himself using figures of speech that had been popularized long before by Diogenes.

Spartanism and Panhellenism

Meantime, other persons, with different social backgrounds, were concerned with the same problems. Among the young aristocrats of Athens, there were many who took their city's fate deeply to heart. They were men of education and political ambition, but with the democratic faction firmly in the saddle at Athens, they could not find an outlet for their energies in political life. Some of them gave themselves up to brooding and dreaming; others dissipated what was left of the family fortunes in riotous living; but a few tried to discover what had caused the failure of Athens and hoped to lead her back along new and better paths to her former glory. Before and during the war, their social background had inclined them to be critical of Athenian democracy: now they blamed this democracy for the ruin of their city. Spartan victories, of course, encouraged the belief that Spartan institutions had a superior merit. These Athenian aristocrats now sought to save their city through the patriotic discipline which they imagined was the cause of Sparta's victories. Yet though their minds were filled with dreams of Spartan virtue, none of them seriously considered allowing Spartan politicians to dominate Athens or Greece.

Still another direction taken by the minds of thinking men at this time is illustrated by Isocrates (436–338). Born to a good Athenian family, he was for several years a pupil of the Sophists, and, if we are to believe a statement by Plato, he was once singled out by Socrates as a young man from whom something might be expected as an orator and philosopher, and perhaps even as a statesman. His weak voice made a political career impossible, however, and for a while he earned a living writing speeches for others. His aristocratic sympathies led to his exile from Athens after the fall of the Thirty, but presently he was allowed to return. About 390, he opened a school which became a force in the history of Greece. Three centuries later, Cicero remarked that more great men had issued from that school than ever came out of the Trojan horse. Isocrates was always something more than a schoolteacher. He retained his old political ambition and he was much concerned with the problems facing post-war

Athens. He became the intellectual leader of those who saw in a revival of Panhellenism the sole salvation of Greece. The political aspects of Panhellenism will be discussed in the next chapter; here we need only remark that its implications reached far beyond the political sphere, and that Isocrates and his friends set out to recreate Greece culturally as well as politically.

Fourth Century Historians

Historical writing remained a popular form of literature throughout the fourth century, and most historians considered themselves successors of Thucydides. In fact, Thucydides might be classified as a fourth-century historian himself, not only because his history was published and much of it written after 404, but also in a larger sense because he was led to write by his anxiety over the Peloponnesian War and its aftereffects. The historians of the new age were, like him, deeply concerned with the consequences of the war; and, though none of them approached him in intellectual power, they shared his belief that historical writing could help statesmen solve their problems and guide them in formulating their policies.

More than one writer in the new century attempted a formal sequel to Thucydides' history—which, it will be remembered, breaks off suddenly in the midst of events occurring in 411. The ablest of these continuators was a man whose work was quite unknown to modern scholars until 1906, when a papyrus fragment of about twenty pages was discovered at Oxyrhynchus in Egypt. As the author's name is unknown, the work is called the *Hellenica Oxyrhynchia*. Though our fragment tells the events of only about eighteen months in 396–95, the complete history probably covered the years from 411 through the first quarter of the next century. The author closely followed the manner of Thucydides, and the fullness and accuracy of his narrative, his breadth of view, and his comprehension of politics prove him a worthy disciple of the great historian. He was among the best historical writers of the century, and scholars believe that much of what he wrote was preserved by others who excerpted his history without giving credit to their source.

Xenophon

The historian Xenophon was a less intelligent writer, but he has since enjoyed a higher reputation than this unknown author. Xenophon was born to an upper-class Athenian family about 430, became a pupil and admirer of Socrates, fought in the last part of the Peloponnesian War, and found himself at loose ends in 404. Three years later, he joined a famous mercenary force of Ten Thousand Greeks (to be discussed below) that the rebellious Persian prince, Cyrus the Younger, led against his brother Artaxerxes II. Later, Xenophon accompanied Spartan armies raiding Ionia, for which he was exiled from Athens. He became the intimate friend and panegyrist of the Spartan king Agesilaus, whom he accompanied on various campaigns —including one against Athens. The king presented him with an estate at Scillus near Olympia in 387. Here he wrote his books and lived as a country squire for sixteen years, until the place was destroyed by the Eleans in 371. Xenophon spent his last years at Corinth, where he died about 354. So far as we know, he never returned to Athens, though the decree of exile against him was repealed in 369. His son returned to die fighting in the Athenian cavalry at Mantinea in 362.

Xenophon was a journalist rather than a scholarly historian, and his numerous writings include light articles on a wide variety of topics, such as hunting, horsemanship, military strategy, government, economics, education, and philosophy, as well as the histories. His *Memorabilia* are a useful supplement to Plato's account of Socrates, for they show that philosopher as seen by one of his less imaginative pupils. Xenophon's reputation as a historian rests upon two books, the *Anabasis* and the *Hellenica*. The former is an account of the ill-fated expedition against Artaxerxes and the retreat of the Ten Thousand, written in so smooth and easy a style that it remained popular throughout antiquity and has served to initiate countless generations of modern youth into the mysteries of beginning Greek. The *Hellenica,* a history of Greece from 411 to 362, was a more ambitious undertaking at which Xenophon worked, off and on, for more than thirty years. The first part of the book, covering the last years of the war and the rule of the Thirty, apparently was written before his exile, for in it he presents the story from a strongly Athenian point of view. The second part, continuing the story to 387 and containing the best chapters in the book, was probably written at Scillus; and the last rather dreary part dates from his old age.

Xenophon may have thought that he was a second Thucydides, but in reality he shared little with his model. He rarely bothered to do careful research or make inquiries, though he might easily have done so, knowing leaders as he did. He simply wrote what he remembered, giving his work the character of memoirs rather than of history. His superficial mind was incapable of the great historian's insight into causes, and he attributed events to individual personalities or, occasionally, to the gods—factors which Thucydides reduced to a minimum. His pro-Spartan bias, as well as his "great-man" theory of history, in each of which he was quite typical of the fourth century, also led him to write a laudatory biography of his friend Agesilaus, founding a type of literature which later became very popular.

The intellectual content of Xenophon's historical writings was slight, yet these writings became a force in history. The *Anabasis,* the *Hellenica,* and the *Cyropaedia* (a historical romance purporting to describe the education of the elder Cyrus), vividly convey to the reader Xenophon's belief that the Persians of his day were utterly decadent. He thus encouraged politicians to suggest a war against them long before Alexander took up the project. It was not alone the expedition of the Ten Thousand that prepared the way for Alexander: more especially it was Xenophon's brilliant and popular account of the expedition. It is also reported that Zeno, the founder of Stoicism, was converted to philosophy by hearing the *Memorabilia* read aloud. Xenophon turned out to be one of those significant historians who make history by writing it.

The other historians of this period were less important. A Sicilian Greek named Philistus wrote a large history of his island. Born about 430, he served the tyrant Dionysius I of Syracuse, who hoped to unite the island under his rule. It is quite possible that Philistus wrote the history primarily to emphasize the unity of Sicily, and the superior merit of the Greeks there, and thus to promote the tyrant's plans for uniting the island politically. In any case, Philistus performed an important service in composing a history covering many cities and several centuries by weaving together materials drawn from varied Greek and Carthaginian sources. Meantime, continued interest in Persia had led to new histories of that empire, of which the best known was one written by a certain Ctesias, a Greek, who for many years was physician to Artaxerxes II (404–358). He used little historical criticism, and his writings should properly be classified as romance rather than history, but many of his successors took him quite seriously.

Panhellenic Historians

Toward the middle of the century, the influence of Isocrates began to make itself felt in Greek historical writing. Though Isocrates wrote no formal history himself, he recognized the persuasive force of arguments drawn from history and he used them in his orations. His panegyric of Evagoras shares with Xenophon's similar work on Agesilaus the distinction of being the first of Greek biographies. Isocrates influenced later historians both in their manner of writing and in the subjects they chose. In each case, the new history marked a sad decline from the standards set by Thucydides. Like him, the new writers sought to impose their views upon their readers, but for persuasiveness they relied upon rhetoric rather than intellectual power. They did not emulate Thucydides' high impartiality, they were less scrupulous than he about accuracy, and they filled their books with preaching and invective.

The new historians shared Isocrates' desire for Panhellenic solidarity in Greece. They trailed behind the politicians in propagandizing this ideal, but their new enthusiasm inspired them to write histories of Greece rather than histories of individual cities. Their horizons were no wider than those of Thucydides, and not so wide as those of Herodotus, yet they showed a far broader view than the chroniclers of the fifth century. When Philip of Macedon assumed leadership of the Panhellenic movement, shortly after 350, they wrote histories that were little more than panegyrics upon the new leader. In their desire to replace the old city loyalty of the Greeks with national patriotism, they filled their pages with glowing reminders of the greatness of the Greek people, admitting nothing bad about any of them and constantly belittling foreigners, especially Persians. Historical writing of this sort was practiced by nationalistic historians such as von Treitschke and Froude in the nineteenth century, but it was quite beneath Herodotus and Thucydides.

The most famous of the Panhellenic historians was Theopompus. Born about 378 on the island of Chios, he was still a child when his father was sent into exile, and he probably never returned to his native island. After studying under Isocrates, he followed the profession of orator in various Greek cities. He lived for a while at the court of Philip of Macedon while Isocrates and other Panhellenists were encouraging Philip in his ambition to unite the Greeks. Theopompus's great work was an enormous history of Greece from early times to 334—the year in which Philip's son, Alexander, invaded Asia. He first wrote the *Philippic History,* covering the years from 360 to 334 in fifty-eight books and dealing principally with the Panhellenists' hero; then he prepared a prefix by abridging Herodotus and Thucydides and writing a sequel to the latter, called the *Hellenica,* which carried the story down to 394. The gap between 394 and 360 was filled by the *Hellenica* of Callisthenes, a nephew of Aristotle who set himself up as a historian and later became a sort of press agent for Alexander. Theopompus's book was largely a glorification of Philip, and two hundred years later the Greek historian Polybius justly criticized the author for having treated Greek history as a part of Philip, rather than Philip as a part of Greek history. Nevertheless, this history was much admired in antiquity, largely because of its flowery style and its platitudinous moralizing.

Meantime, the historian Ephorus was composing a work which better illustrated the significant accomplishments of fourth-century historiography. Little is known of Ephorus's life except that he was born at Cyme in Aeolic Asia Minor about 408, and that he lived to see Alexander conquer Asia. He began his great work with the Trojan War and covered the history of the various Greek states, including those of Ionia and Sicily, down to 341. He collected his materials diligently from a wide variety of earlier writers: Hecataeus, Herodotus and Thucydides, the *Hellenica Oxyrhynchia,* Hellanicus and the *Atthides,* the various *Persica,* and pamphlet literature. Ephorus was primarily a literary man—perhaps the only really important historian in antiquity, someone has remarked, who was nothing but a literary man—and he often betrays the qualities of a shears-and-paste-pot historian. He had little insight into politics, his battle pictures and other pieces of fancy writing are childish, his speeches are absurd. His choice of authorities was usually good, however, though sometimes surprising. Thus he followed Thucydides for the Peloponnesian War, but he rejected that author's account of the rise of the Athenian Empire for a more patriotic version; and to Thucydides' thoughtful and impersonal account of the origins of the war he preferred another, drawn from the pamphleteers and Aristophanes, attributing everything to the machinations of Pericles. His prejudices in favor of his native Cyme were so great that he made her the cradle of innumerable great men—even including Homer—and his general attitude toward her is shown by the gibe of Strabo (a writer of the first century B.C.) that when Ephorus could find nothing else to say about her, he gravely chronicled the fact that Cyme was then at peace. The taunt, incidentally, shows what sort of history Ephorus and Strabo thought worth recording. Nevertheless, Ephorus was the best historian of his century, and his version of early Greek history prevailed until almost the end of the ancient world.

Plato and the Academy

The fourth century also produced the two greatest philosophers of antiquity, Plato and Aristotle. The former was born in 427 to a family of the old Athenian aristocracy. Through his father, he traced his ancestry to Codrus who, according to legend, was the last and noblest of the kings of Athens. His mother connected him with more recent statesmen: one of her ancestors was a kinsman of Solon, her cousin Critias was leader of the Thirty, and her brother was a member of that notorious group. Her uncle (who became her second husband) had in his youth been involved in a murder trial of such political importance that he was prosecuted by Pericles himself and successfully defended by Thucydides the son of Melesias. Family connections thus predestined Plato to a political career, and he tells us that from early manhood he felt the call to statesmanship. But the ill repute of the Thirty after 403 made a political career impossible for him, and the execution of Socrates disgusted him with Athenian politics. As a youth, Plato was also interested in literature. He once wrote and tore up a tragedy, and he developed the literary skill which later glorified his writings. Today those who disagree most heartily with his philosophical opinions are charmed by his mode of expressing them. The third great force in his early life was Socrates, whom he probably had known from childhood. Plato was present at Socrates' trial in 399, where he offered to guarantee payment of a fine if the jury decided to impose such a punishment, but illness prevented him from attending Socrates during his last days. Plato then withdrew to Megara, where he studied with Euclides, and later he traveled, possibly in Egypt and certainly to Tarentum and Syracuse. After returning to Athens about 387, he opened a school in a house just outside the city walls near a gymnasium and park dedicated to the hero Academus. The school itself was therefore called the "Academy," and in it Plato continued to teach until he died in 347, aged eighty years.

Plato's writings reveal a deep sympathy with religion of the type expressed in the mysteries at Eleusis and with the Orphic interpretations of Eleusinian doctrines: presumably he had been reared in a family sharing such views. Aristotle tells us that "from his youth upward Plato was acquainted with the doctrines of Heraclitus," and no doubt he was equally familiar with the views of the other Ionian philosophers. During his stay at Megara, and perhaps even earlier, he studied the Eleatic philosophy, and it seems not improbable that his visit to the West was motivated by a desire to investigate Pythagorean communities there. There is no doubt that Plato was well-informed on earlier Greek thought, but above all he was influenced by Socrates.

For us, however, it is less important to know whence Plato derived his ideas than it is to know what he did with them after he had them and why he thought it worth while to do anything at all with them. No one will ever understand Plato who forgets for a moment that he was a patriotic Athenian aristocrat, that he grew up during the Peloponnesian War, and that he lived through the tragedy of 404. Of Plato's loyalty to his city we can have no doubt, and countless passages in his writings, describing her beauty and grandeur, show how deeply he had been moved by her fate. But why had Athens fallen? And what must she do to regain her former glory? These were the questions that dominated Plato's thinking throughout the remainder of his life.

Plato may have renounced his early dream of becoming an active politician, but he continued to think about social and political questions. His instruction at the Academy, like that of Isocrates at his equally famous school, was designed first of all to train statesmen. The curricula at the two schools differed as widely as they well could, for the two teachers disagreed fundamentally in their political and educational ideas, and Plato had a far richer and more complicated view of life and the world. Yet both men were concerned primarily with training pupils who could lead Athens out of the slough into which she had been dragged by the war and its aftermath.

Plato's reputation and success caused several Greek politicians to call upon him for aid, and at least half a dozen of his pupils made names for themselves by preparing constitutions or law codes for several Greek cities. The most spectacular case of this sort centered around Plato's visits to Syracuse. During his visit to that city in 387, he made the acquaintance of the tyrant, Dionysius I, and his brother-in-law Dion. Twenty years later, when the king was succeeded by his son, Dionysius II, Dion persuaded Plato to return to Syracuse to train the new ruler. Plato soon quarreled with his pupil, partly because another advisor (Philistus, the historian) proposed an immediate war to drive the last Carthaginians from Sicily whereas Plato insisted that Dionysius, who was thirty years old, begin with a stiff course in geometry. Plato returned to Greece where he stayed until 361, when he was induced to make a third visit to Syracuse. Again he was engulfed in the intrigues at court; again he lost the favor of the tyrant; and once more he withdrew. Plato made no further efforts to influence public life directly. He devoted himself thereafter to speculation and study, teaching and writing, but political science and statesmanship remained one of his principal interests. He did not forget his early ambition, but pursued it by a longer and more indirect route.

Plato's answer to the great question of why Athens fell is shown by the various hatreds that color his writings: hatred of the democracy that had misled Athens and brought her to ruin; hatred of the Sophists who had set up false ideals and whose eternal quibbling had distracted her; hatred of Homer and the other poets who had taught her lies; and hatred of the wealth and luxury that had debilitated her. Socrates had criticized all these things before Athens fell, and Plato continued his criticisms, not out of antiquarian zeal for recording the master's teachings, but because he believed that the things criticized had truly been the ruin of Athens.

Plato's program for redeeming Athens is set forth with equal clarity. Political reorganization was of course essential, and throughout his life Plato meditated upon the proper organization for a state. Revival also required that Athenians return to the ancestral virtues which they apparently had forgotten, and it was equally important that the Athenians find a new and better manner of living. Plato believed that they should return to the old religion of Greece—not to the monstrosities of the Olympians, to be sure, but to the old gods of the mysteries, purified and enlightened though still retaining intact their ancient teachings regarding virtue, the immortality of the soul, and punishment after death. Time and again he reverts to this doctrine of the immortality of the soul, putting forward virtually every rational argument ever devised in its favor. And finally, Plato took up the belief of Socrates that to act correctly one must first think correctly, and he interpreted correct thinking as mathematical and dialectical thinking.

The Dialogues

Plato expressed his ideas in dialogues which he composed for the general public with great literary skill. Piously preserved by his pupils, the dialogues are thirty-five in number, and they vary in length from brief skits to two books of about four hundred pages each. Perhaps two or three dialogues were written before the death of Socrates. Chief of these is the *Protagoras,* in which the youthfully exuberant author chuckles as Socrates reduces the great Sophist to confusion and at the same time expresses his views on democracy, education, and the teaching of virtue. A few years after 399 came the *Apology,* which purports to be the speech Socrates addressed to his jury. During the next few years Plato wrote several brilliant dialogues, in a strongly Socratic spirit, discussing beauty and the moral virtues. Thus in the *Laches* he analyzed courage; in the *Charmides,* temperance; and in the *Euthyphro,* piety. Later he dealt with immortality in the *Phaedo,* with love and beauty in the *Symposium,* and with justice in the *Republic.* All these dialogues were written before the crucial second visit to Syracuse in 367. The later dialogues dealt with more abstruse and metaphysical subjects. Though he had much to say about religion and God, sometimes in a highly mystical strain, Plato continued to think about social and political problems until he wrote the *Laws,* the last and longest of the dialogues.

Socrates appears as a major character in all these dialogues except the last. There can be no doubt that he is often made to express Plato's own views, and it was once believed that little of the historic Socrates remained in the idealized picture drawn by Plato. Recent studies have modified this opinion. Philologists have been able to arrange the dialogues approximately in their chronological order, synchronizing them with periods in Plato's life, and have traced the development of his opinions, beginning with his dependence upon Socrates and following through various stages to the end. The Socrates of the earlier dialogues appears as the historical Socrates, in the middle group he is merely a mouthpiece for Plato, and in the last dialogue he disappears completely.

The Republic

The most famous of the dialogues, the *Republic,* was composed in the 370's. It opens with a discussion of justice in the early style; a large central section pictures an ideal state; and the last part contains much about correct thinking and knowledge. It thus sets forth the three principal aspects of Plato's thought.

The model state which Plato dreamed up was an idealized *polis,* governed in the Pythagorean fashion by rulers who were also philosophers. Its citizens were divided into three classes—workers, soldiers, rulers. While individuals theoretically were assigned to their respective classes on the basis of their talents, the classification was in practice largely hereditary. Each person was trained from birth with Spartan thoroughness for his future duties. Education was not merely technical, but covered every aspect of life, with elaborate precautions to make sure that every influence touching the pupil was the one best calculated to make him function well in that state of life to which he had been assigned. Especial care was devoted to the education of future rulers. Members of this class were recruited by carefully planned eugenic matings, while owning property in common freed them from coveteousness and stimulated their public spirit. The state pictured by Plato is an aristocratic schoolmaster's Utopia, and the whole educational system reminds the modern reader of that technical and ideological indoctrination which recent totalitarian dictators have praised so volubly. We are inclined to suspect that such a state, had it ever been set up, would have been a dull and unhappy place where the poetic and idealistic Plato would have been thoroughly wretched until he was expelled by its philosopher-tyrants. That fate would have overtaken him as quickly in his own Utopia as it did in Syracuse.

Plato had little to say about how philosophers would govern the state, but he was quite sure that only they could do it well. "Until philosophers become kings," he makes Socrates remark, "or the kings and princes of this world have the spirit and power of philosophy, cities will never have rest from their evils." All actually existing states he divided into four categories in descending order of merit: first, timocracies governed by men who were respected, as in Sparta; second, oligarchies, which really were plutocracies; third, democracies, as at Athens; and last and worst of all, tyrannies such as Persia. Each form had inherent weaknesses which sooner or later would drag it to the next lower level, until at length a hopeless tyranny was reached by all.

The *Republic* was written by a man who had found much to admire in the institutions of Sparta, but we shall see that soon after Plato completed his book, Spartan hegemony in Greece was overthrown (371) and the Spartan institutions which Greek aristocrats had admired for so long were thereby discredited. A few years later came Plato's ill-starred efforts to make Dionysius II into a philosopher-king. Plato was then over sixty years of age, saddened and disillusioned. Thereafter he shut himself up more and more with his pupils in the Academy, and his writings became more abstruse. Several of his later dialogues are discussions of difficult metaphysical problems. In the *Timaeus* he tried to be scientific by having a Pythagorean philosopher describe the universe and its creation according to the tenets of his school. A deepening spirit of piety and religion runs through his writings of this period. Statesmanship was not forgotten, however, and he returned to the subject in the *Politicus*—a pessimistic discussion of the ideal king and of the faults of actually existing forms of government—and again in the last and longest of his dialogues, the *Laws*.

The Laws

The *Laws* was written by a thoroughly disillusioned old man. Though it once was customary to neglect this work, recent scholars have emphasized its importance and admired its vast learning. It gives Plato's philosophy of politics and education in their final form. Plato still believed that, in the final analysis, a state depends upon the education given its citizens, and a large part of the book is devoted to educational questions. He begins with a sharp criticism of the now discredited Spartan education, decrying it as likely to fit men only for war, and he discusses at length the devices that should be used to train citizens. All education should be under the direction of a philosopher who might be called the "minister of education," and who would also be prime minister *ex officio*. The rest of the book is concerned principally with the laws by which a state should regulate civil and criminal matters and with the machinery by which magistrates should be chosen—mundane matters that had been passed over in the *Republic*.

As in all Plato's later works, great attention is given in the *Laws* to religion and public worship. A "nocturnal council"—so-called because it would meet at night to augment its impressiveness—should be set up to watch over the interests of the state. One of its chief duties would be to root out those who deny the existence of the gods, who deny that the gods are concerned with the affairs of men, or who (worst of all) suggest that their unswerving justice may be bought off with prayers and sacrifices. Persons holding these pernicious views should first be argued with by members of the council. To aid the councilors, Plato here develops at length two arguments for the gods which have ever since been favorites with the theologians: the argument from design (the harmony of the universe implies that it was designed by a rational creator) and the argument from common consent (since all men, Greeks and barbarians, believe that there are gods, there must be some truth behind the belief, for all men could not be utterly mistaken on so important a matter). Though Plato would have preferred to use argument and persuasion to induce men to think as he wished them to, the aged and disillusioned philosopher was quite prepared to extirpate ruthlessly all those who proved recalcitrant. After all, Plato was still a nephew of Critias. He was not a bloodthirsty person, but a sad old man who had convinced himself that the salvation of mankind depended upon the universal acceptance of his opinions. Then as now, whoever is too sure about the "eternal verities" is at heart an inquisitor and a menace to society. Plato's "nocturnal council," which reminds us so strongly of the Inquisition and the Gestapo, was one of the most carefully considered plans known to history for the persecution of theological belief or lack of it. Those numerous Torquemadas and Himmlers who have wrought such fearful havoc in the world are all Platonists under the skin.

Platonic "Ideas"

A word must also be said about Platonic "ideas," though only a trained metaphysician can discuss them adequately. There were two

philosophical theories against which Plato's conservative tempera-
ment revolted strongly: the teaching of Heraclitus that all things are
in a constant flux, and that of Protagoras that man is the measure of
all things. Moreover, he attributed the weakness of Athens to the
fact that her citizens had accepted such teachings. The fate of their
city would have been far different, he believed, had the Athenians
only known that courage and beauty, truth and justice, are realities
and not mere fluctuating figments of the imagination as the Sophists
taught. To confute these Sophists, Plato developed his doctrine of
ideas.

Plato began by reviving the theories of Parmenides and the
Eleatics about a rational world which is apart from or above the
world we know by our senses. In this supersensible world, change
cannot exist. He insisted that courage and justice are quite independent of brave and just men, that there is "beauty itself" as well as mere
beautiful things, and that this courage, justice, and beauty are real,
unchanging, and eternal. Going further, Plato declared that all visible and tangible things likewise have their ideal counterparts. As
there is a material bed, so there is also the "form" or "idea" of a bed
existing only in the mind. The lumber of the material bed forms a
bed only in so far as it approximates this mental concept of a bed.
The material bed resembles the "idea" of a bed much as the picture
of a bed resembles a material one, or as a circle drawn in the sand
by a geometer resembles the perfect circle which exists only in his
mind and to which alone his theorems apply. In a famous passage
at the beginning of Book VII in the *Republic,* Plato compares men to
prisoners in a cave, chained with their backs to the entrance, who
can see only the shadows cast on the back of the cave by various
things as they pass its mouth. He then goes on to say that if the
prisoners could escape and see the real things that cast the shadows,
they would know the truth. Likewise, men should learn from philosophy that beds, circles in the sand, and the other material things that
they see with their eyes are only shadows of reality. The man who
has once come to know the pure and unchanging "ideas" of things
will never again be satisfied with less. Plato thus led his followers
into a world of pure beauty and truth, which is also the realm of God,

and from that day to this, Platonists have cherished this idealistic philosophy as their dearest possession.[1]

Aristotle

Aristotle, who became Plato's most famous pupil, critic, and rival, was born in 384 at Stagira in Chalcidice, the son of a physician attending the king of Macedon. At the age of seventeen, he went to Athens, where he was a student in the Academy until Plato's death in 347. He then withdrew from the city—perhaps because of pique at not being chosen head of the school to succeed Plato—and settled at Assus in the Troad. Here he married the daughter of Hermias, the Greek ruler of the city. Hermias was presently suspected by the Persian king of intriguing with Philip of Macedon, and later he was crucified (341). Meantime, Aristotle had left Assus for Mytilene, whence he proceeded to Philip's court at Pella. For three years (343–40), he was tutor to the king's son, the future Alexander the Great. After Philip had conquered Greece, and Alexander had succeeded him as king, Aristotle returned to Athens, where he opened a school in a gymnasium called the Lyceum (335). He was by this time recognized as the leading philosopher in Greece, and pupils flocked to him from every part of the Greek world. Since Aristotle was a foreigner, protected by Alexander and an intimate friend of the Macedonian regent in Athens, he shared the conqueror's unpopularity, and after Alexander's death he was made to suffer. Charges of impiety were trumped up against him and he withdrew to Euboea, saying that he would not permit the Athenians to sin twice against philosophy. In the following year (322) he died.

Modern editions of Aristotle's works contain forty-six treatises, of which about fifteen are usually considered spurious. A dozen others, attributed to him in antiquity, are now lost, and a long part of another (the *Constitution of Athens*) has been recovered from the sands of Egypt. These works are arranged as follows: first come six books on logic, often grouped together as the *Organon;* then twenty-six treatises (several spurious) deal with the different natural sciences, ranging from physics and astronomy through biology and

---

[1] See note on Later Platonists, p. 511.

physiology to psychology; after a few other apocryphal works, the *Metaphysics* is followed by four works on ethics (two spurious) and the *Politics;* and lastly come three works on rhetoric and poetics. Aristotle's writings thus covered virtually every field of knowledge cultivated in his day. The sequence in which his books are arranged may be the work of Aristotle himself, for it probably indicates the order in which different subjects were studied at the Lyceum. The books as they now stand are not finished works. They are full notes for lectures, put in shape by pupils after his death. As individual books sometimes contain lectures given at widely different times, they often express conflicting views, and several of the works now rejected as spurious may contain authentic cores upon which pupils later expanded.

Modern scholars have succeeded in arranging these books, or parts of books, roughly in their chronological order and in tracing the development of Aristotle's thought through three distinct phases. During his years at the Academy, he was under strong Platonic influence; at Assus, he slowly broke away from the teachings of the master and laid the foundations of his own system; and in the years at the Lyceum, he reached his full maturity. During the first period, he wrote dialogues in the Platonic manner which are now lost except for fragments; at Assus he wrote, among other things, the works on logic, the *Physics,* part of the *Metaphysics,* the *Eudemian Ethics,* and part of the *Politics;* and at Athens he wrote other parts of the *Metaphysics,* the *Nicomachean Ethics,* the rest of the *Politics,* and most of the scientific works.

Plato's Influence on Aristotle

All his life Aristotle bore the marks of Plato's teaching, yet the two men differed widely in their fundamental characteristics and points of view. Aristotle could not share Plato's deep love for Athens, which never really was his home; and he therefore was untouched by the emotional forces that determined so much of Plato's thinking. Moreover, his father was a physician, and he himself had received medical training in his youth. At the age when Plato was learning dialectics from Socrates, Aristotle was learning from his father how to observe symptoms and what steps to take in order to effect a cure. Plato was a mathematician who speculated upon the differences between ideal circles and actual circles drawn in the sand. Aristotle was a biologist who generalized on his observation that living beings act as they do for some purpose or toward some end.

Nevertheless, Plato's intellect and personality were so powerful that they impressed themselves indelibly upon the pupil's mind. Aristotle knew Plato and the Academy only in their last years, when Plato and his colleagues were discussing science after a fashion (as in the *Timaeus*), but when their best thought was devoted to religion and the doctrine of ideas. Aristotle's early dialogues preserved not only the form but also the content of the Platonic dialogues. Thus the immortality of the soul was discussed in the *Eudemus* much as in Plato's *Phaedo;* the *Gryllus* resembled the *Gorgias;* and a book *On Justice* was probably modeled on the *Republic.* Aristotle also shared Plato's religious sentiments at this time and for several years thereafter. Even in the *Eudemian Ethics,* written at Assus, there is a strain of Platonic piety which is absent in the later *Nicomachean Ethics.*

During his years at Assus, Aristotle gradually emancipated himself from the influence of Plato's personality and began to criticize the Platonic teaching. In a tract entitled *On Philosophy,* of which large fragments remain, he attacked the Platonic doctrine of ideas and suggested the outlines of his own later system. His associations with Hermias, and later with Philip and Alexander, gave him new and less bookish views on politics. At the same time his early training showed its influence by turning him to his famous scientific observations, and he began substituting a cold-blooded study of natural phenomena for Plato's warm-hearted and poetical idealism.

Aristotle's Scientific Researches

At Athens Aristotle found the facilities to continue his researches on a greater scale. He collected a large library—the first library of the sort known to Europe—and gathered around him pupils to whom he assigned special topics for investigation. These researches covered many fields—history, the social sciences, and especially the natural sciences. The priests at Delphi engaged him to compile a list of win-

Socrates *(Vatican Museum)*

Plato

Aristotle *(Terme Museum, Rome)*

Plate 31

ners in the Pythian games. He also drew up the list of tragedies and comedies that had won the annual prizes at Athens, perhaps in connection with the erection of the stone theater about 330. This list is the basis of our information about the dates of the classic dramas of the fifth century. Above all, he and his pupils collected information on the constitutional history and government of 158 cities. Aristotle himself wrote the volume on Athens, which is our invaluable *Constitution of Athens*. The first two of the above-mentioned research projects obviously required the examination of records in the official archives, but the third was compiled in the library, using published histories as sources.

Aristotle's investigations of natural phenomena were, in his own eyes, much more important than his other studies at the Lyceum. It is a great mistake, however, to picture him as engaged in scientific research along modern lines. His scientific writings were no doubt based in part on his own observations, or those of pupils working under his direction, but he and they apparently did more research in the library than in the laboratory. They wrote up what scientifically-minded Greeks of that day knew, without adding much to what was already known. Aristotle's pupils included most of the intellectual leaders of the next generation, but they failed to advance the scientific work he began—which would be quite inexplicable had he really fired them with an enthusiasm for "research." On the other hand, their unproductiveness is easily explained if he merely had them assemble, analyze, and synthesize what was already known. They presumably had about completed this task before his death. Aristotle was an encyclopedist who succeeded so well in summing up what earlier Greeks had said about scientific matters that in later times there seemed no need for copying the books of his predecessors, of which only the scantiest fragments now remain. Finally, it must be added that Aristotle's scientific writings report many things which he certainly never saw. In spite of his high critical faculties, he copied many of his predecessors' mistakes and even accepted statements that were nothing but old wives' tales.

It is one of the paradoxes of intellectual history that Aristotle's scientific writings, to which he devoted such care during his mature

years, are now largely ignored while his political, ethical, and rhe-
torical works, which are more highly esteemed today, had little to
do with his co-operative research. Except for the central part of the
Politics, they were written before the great researches began. Likewise, the books on logic, which were completed in the Assus period
and probably contained little that had not been said in the Academy,
are the basis of most modern manuals on the subject—even the illustrations of correct and fallacious reasoning being piously handed
down from one author to another.

Aristotle's Metaphysics

Modern philosophers usually direct their greatest interest to Aristotle's metaphysics. His large treatise on the subject has given its
name to that intellectual discipline, but Aristotle called the book
"First Philosophy" or "Theology." Its present name comes from the
fact that in the standard edition of his works, prepared after his
death, this treatise came "after" (*meta*) the *physica*, or books on
nature (*physis*). The name "Metaphysics" is also significant as showing that his pupils liked to believe Aristotle reached these views
through a study of natural science. As a matter of fact, his metaphysical views are largely his revision of Plato. Much of the book
was written at Assus, and the general principles expressed in it
guided, rather than resulted from, his scientific researches. The
elaborate metaphysical system which he constructed need not be
described in detail here. As a biologist, Aristotle was impressed by
the fact that living things go through long evolutions to various ends
(the egg to the chicken, the caterpillar to the butterfly) and he noted
that their parts are fitted for definite functions. From these observations, he developed a "teleological" (*telos*, "end") view of life and
the universe. All things aim at some end, he taught, and the highest
and most perfect end of all is God, toward whom all things move.
God is pure thought, himself unmoved and unmoving, yet all things
strive toward him. This striving is the ultimate cause of all motion,
and Aristotle spoke of God as the "Unmoved Mover."[2]

These two men, Plato and Aristotle, achieved the final triumphs of

---

[2] See note on Aristotelianism, p. 512.

Greek thought. Each followed a long tradition; each summed up and expressed in imposing fashion what his predecessors had said, adding his own supreme genius to theirs; and each established a school that perpetuated his teachings. These schools could add little to the thinking of their founders, however, for each of the two great thinkers had carried his speculations through to their ultimate conclusions. There was nothing more to be said until new conditions forced men to view a new world in a new light.

Notes

Later Platonists

Plato's philosophy was taught at the Academy by a succession of disciples until 529 A.D., when the Emperor Justinian closed the school and the few remaining teachers and pupils migrated to Persia. All this time, educated men had been familiar with and admired the Platonic writings, and in the third century after Christ Plotinus revived popular interest in the theological and mystical views of the later dialogues. His Neoplatonism became the philosophy of paganism in its declining days and it deeply influenced the great Church Fathers from Origen to Augustine. Apparently the early Middle Ages had direct knowledge of only one Platonic dialogue (the *Timaeus*), but Christian theology remained largely Neoplatonic until the thirteenth century, when the influence of Aristotle became predominant.

Platonic studies were revived by the Florentine humanist Marsilio Ficino (1433–99), who published a Latin translation of all the dialogues in 1482. A wide variety of philosophers and theologians have since derived their inspiration from Plato, especially after the German theologian Schleiermacher (1768–1834) rediscovered him early in the last century. A splendid English translation of the dialogues, retaining much of the literary charm of the original, was made by the Oxford scholar Benjamin Jowett (1817–93). In addition to making this translation (and one of Thucydides as well), Jowett was a leader in liberal theology and in educational reform, and he actually achieved what Plato would have liked to accomplish as a teacher: his many distinguished pupils included not only leaders in scholarship and the church but famous statesmen as well, among them two foreign secretaries and one prime minister of England.

Ulrich von Wilamowitz-Moellendorff (1848–1931) was the most brilliant student of Plato in our century, but he also was much more: he stands among the finest of German classical scholars and humanists. Belonging to a Prussian family of Junkers living east of Posen, only a few miles from the Polish frontier of that day, Wilamowitz should by family tradition have sought a career in the army or the civil service. He preferred philology, and after taking his degree, serving in a fashionable Guards Regiment during the Franco-Prussian War, and traveling in Italy and Greece, he held professorships at Greifswald and Göttingen, and after 1897 at Berlin. Here he soon established himself as a leader in intellectual circles. As a member of the Prussian Academy of Sciences, he took an important part in guiding that body's varied activities, especially its extensive program of scholarly publication, and his voice carried weight in all discussions of higher education. His numerous writings covered almost every aspect of Greek literature and thought; but in his later years he concerned himself especially with Greek religion. His brilliant personality and his broad and deep scholarship enabled him to present appealingly the best that the Greeks have to offer. He continued the great tradition of the German humanists and idealists of the days of Goethe, and admiring colleagues and pupils declared that no man ever understood the ancient Greeks so well as he. Wilamowitz published his *Erinnerungen, 1848–1914* in 1928.

Aristotelianism

After Aristotle's death, his teaching was continued and his writings were put in their present form by pupils at the Lyceum, under the direction of the botanist Theophrastus, who died about 287. Early in the third century the school went into decline, and for many years Aristotle was known only by his early Platonic writings—especially the *Protrepticus,* a dialogue written in his Academy days, and the tract *On Philosophy,* which he wrote soon after reaching Assus when he was still largely a Platonist. After the death of Theophrastus, the manuscripts of the treatises comprising the present Aristotelian corpus were taken to Assus and hidden in a cellar, where they lay forgotten until they were rediscovered early in the first century B.C. Thereafter throughout antiquity they were known to educated men. Between the second and sixth centuries after Christ, scholars composed a number of extensive commentaries on these writings. The simple logical treatises were translated into Latin by Boethius (who died 524 A.D.), but the other Aristotelian writings were unknown to western Europe during the early Middle Ages. Meantime, Arabic translations of several scientific treatises had been made (probably from Syriac translations dating from the last days of the Roman Empire) and in the twelfth century these were translated into Latin by Jews living in Spain. A little later, the *Politics* and *Ethics* were translated directly from the Greek.

At first the Church tried to suppress Aristotle, and when this effort failed, Dominican scholars were commissioned to recast his teaching in a Christian mold. This they did with great success. The great Dominican scholastics of the thirteenth century, notably Thomas Aquinas, called Aristotle "the Philosopher." In their opinion, he spoke as authoritatively with the voice of reason as the Church spoke with that of revelation. The poet Dante referred to him as "the master of them that know." Even in the thirteenth century, two English Franciscan friars, Robert Grosseteste and Roger Bacon, complained of the reverence accorded to Aristotle's writings, but their criticisms received scant attention. For centuries thereafter, his authority in scientific matters was universally acknowledged. His doctrines eventually became a strait jacket, restraining all thought in scientific fields. The attack upon Aristotle was revived late in the Renaissance period by such men as Francis Bacon and Galileo who overthrew his authority and thus laid open the way for modern science. See R. Shute, *History of the . . . Aristotelian Writings* (1888).

XV Panhellenism and Philip of Macedon

CONDITIONS BEING WHAT THEY WERE IN GREECE AFTER 404, it is not surprising that hostilities were soon resumed. Only nine years passed before the major Greek states were again at war with each other, and only five before some were at war with Persia. Three years after the fall of Athens, large armies of Greek mercenaries entered the service of Cyrus, the satrap of Ionia who had intrigued with and aided the Spartans during the last part of the Peloponnesian War. The achievements of these mercenaries were publicized far and wide by Xenophon, the Athenian historian and soldier of fortune who wrote up their expedition in his *Anabasis* and made it an episode of importance in Greek history.

After the old king of Persia, Darius II, had died in 404 and was succeeded by his elder son, Artaxerxes II, Darius's widow encouraged their younger son, Cyrus, to revolt and seize power. Cyrus had been satrap of Ionia for several years and was already on bad terms with his neighbors, Pharnabazus in Bithynia and Tissaphernes in Caria. He now seized parts of their territories (402) and began raising an army, ostensibly to defend himself against their anticipated vengeance. Because of the troubled state of Greece—the country was full of unemployed soldiers, refugees, and ruined peasants—Persian agents found it easy to enlist about thirteen thousand Greeks. These mercenaries are sometimes called the "Ten Thousand" because the force included about that number of hoplites. While Sparta gave Cyrus no aid officially, neither did she hinder his recruiting officers. The leader of the Greek mercenaries was Clearchus, one of Lysander's harmosts who had recently been removed by the ephors, and the great majority of his soldiers came from states belonging to the Peloponnesian League.

Cyrus and his army marched east from Ephesus in the spring of 401, rapidly crossed Asia Minor and Syria, and met Artaxerxes not far from Babylon. The two armies fought a pitched battle at Cunaxa, where the Greeks were victorious though Cyrus himself was slain. A few days later, Tissaphernes, who had commanded a Persian army during the battle, treacherously murdered Clearchus and the other principal Greek leaders during a parley, and Artaxerxes offered to take the entire Greek force into his own army. The mercenaries refused the king's offer, chose new leaders (among them Xenophon), and withdrew through Armenia to Trebizond on the Black Sea, whence they sailed to Thrace. Early in 399 they crossed back to western Asia Minor, thus returning to their starting point. In the course of just two years, the Greeks had marched more than four thousand miles, much of it along uncharted trails through mountainous country, and they had defeated a major Persian army.

Spartan Foreign Policy

The death of Cyrus gave a new direction to Spartan foreign policy. Asia Minor fell to Artaxerxes' satraps, who were not disposed to overlook the Greek aid given Cyrus. Moreover, many Greeks had criticized the Spartan surrender of the Ionian cities to Persia in 404, and when Tissaphernes occupied and punished these cities, traditional Greek enthusiasm for a war of liberation in Asia was easily revived. In the summer of 400, the Spartans decided upon war, and a force of five thousand men was sent to Ephesus that autumn. It was joined by the remnants of the Ten Thousand early in 399, and during the next three years it fought successfully against Pharnabazus.

The Spartans were ready for peace in 396, but when Tissaphernes would listen to no terms short of the complete evacuation of Asia, they sent a new army under the command of Agesilaus. Within two years, Agesilaus extended his raids over the western half of Asia Minor. The Persian king replaced and executed Tissaphernes, and

Agesilaus was beginning to dream of following in the steps of the Ten Thousand to Persia when conditions at home required his immediate return to Greece (spring, 394). Meantime, the Persians had prepared a large fleet at Cyprus, which they placed under the command of Conon, the Athenian admiral who had escaped from Aegospotami in 405 and entered Persian service as a mercenary. He presently induced Rhodes to revolt against Sparta (396) and in August, 394, he met and completely destroyed the Spartan fleet off Cnidus at the southwest tip of Asia Minor. Persia thereby became mistress of the Aegean. The islands and the Greek cities of Asia expelled their few remaining harmosts, and the former Athenian Empire was "liberated" from its Spartan "liberators" by a Persian fleet under an Athenian admiral. After an imperial history of barely ten years, Sparta was reduced once more to her possessions on the Greek mainland.

Dissatisfaction with Spartan domination also rose rapidly in Greece itself. The Athenians dared refuse troops to Agesilaus when he invaded Asia Minor. They watched Conon's progress with pride, and secretly provided him with ships and rowers. Envoys laden with Persian gold reached Greece from Rhodes and when they began to spread anti-Spartan propaganda, many Greek politicians were suspected of profiting from the king's largess. Thrasybulus, the restorer of Athenian democracy, then dissolved his alliance with the moderate democrats and began echoing the demands for aggressive imperial expansion that were traditional with his party. When two minor Greek states (Locris and Phocis) fell into a frontier quarrel in the spring of 395, the Thebans made bold to support the side that Sparta opposed.

Lysander was killed in the first battle of the resulting war, and Thebes was quickly joined by Athens, Corinth, Argos, and several lesser states. Athens began to rebuild her walls, aided by Persian money from Rhodes, and in the spring of 394 the Spartan ephors were so frightened that they recalled Agesilaus from Asia. Leaving about four thousand men to hold the cities he had captured, the king returned to Greece and succeeded in winning two battles over the allies, but his triumph was nullified by Conon's naval victory off

Cnidus. Early in the following year (393) Conon, entering the harbor of Piraeus with his fleet, was received with delirious joy by his fellow Athenians. His Persian sailors completed the new walls and began building a new Athenian navy. A few months later, the Corinthian democrats seized control of their city (March, 392), allied it with Argos, and thus penned up the Spartans in the Peloponnesus. Agesilaus hastily offered Persia a peace based on the surrender of all his conquests in Asia, including the Greek cities of Ionia, and demanded only a guarantee of autonomy for all European Greece. These proposals the Persian king refused to consider.

The King's Peace

Though the war in Greece continued, it became a new war for quite different purposes. The Athenians, no longer satisfied with freeing themselves from Spartan domination, began to dream of winning back the Empire they had lost twelve years before. They entrusted their armies to a soldier of fortune named Iphicrates, who had invented effective ways of using mercenary light infantry against the heavily armed hoplites. This new-model army inflicted crushing defeats upon the Spartans. The Athenians also completed a navy, with which they hoped to command the Aegean, and they reoccupied some of the Aegean Islands as well as a few of their former colonies along the Hellespont. They entered into alliances with other Aegean Islands, and opened negotiations with the Greeks at Cyprus and with Dionysius I, tyrant of Syracuse.

The prospect of a revived Athenian Empire worried both Spartans and Persians. By uniting their navies, they bottled up the Athenian fleet, and at Sparta's instigation the Greek states sent delegates to discuss peace at Sardis (387). After long delay, the Persian satrap haughtily announced the terms which his master, Artaxerxes II, was pleased to grant: the evacuation of Asia, the retention by Athens of three islands (Lemnos, Imbros, Scyros), and autonomy for all other Greek cities. The terms of this "King's Peace" of 386 were approximately the same as those offered by Agesilaus nearly six years before, but they were now handed down by the Persian king. By exploiting Greek quarrels, by filling his army with Greek mercenaries, by putting his navy under a Greek admiral, and by extensive bribery, Artaxerxes had raised Persia to the position of arbiter of Greece. His predecessors could scarcely have done more, had they won at Marathon or Salamis.

The Greek cities of Asia Minor were quickly absorbed by Persia, but they were governed in various ways. Some enjoyed almost complete autonomy (Cyme, Clazomenae, and the cities along the Hellespont) while others groaned under oligarchs and the Persian garrisons that were quartered upon them. In general, however, the Ionian cities were granted a high degree of economic liberty and profited greatly from their new status. Ephesus became the commercial outlet of central Asia Minor, a position which it retained until well into the Christian era. The prosperity of Halicarnassus enabled the ruler of Caria, Mausolus, to become one of the most magnificent persons of his day. The abundant coinage of such cities as Lampsacus, Cyzicus, and Clazomenae indicates their wealth. Prosperity lulled the desire of Greek citizens for freedom and, in spite of occasional agitation inspired from Athens or Sparta, no Greek city of Asia Minor caused the Persian government serious trouble during the next fifty years. Meantime, the wealth they poured into the Persian treasury, coupled with the notorious venality of Greek politicians of every school, enabled Artaxerxes and his successors to play an important role in the politics of European Greece.

Spartan and Theban Hegemonies

The King's Peace worked greatly to the advantage of Sparta, and allowed her to dominate Greece for several years. The treaty's provisions for autonomy required Athens, Thebes, Corinth, and other anti-Spartan states to dissolve their alliances but permitted Sparta to retain her Peloponnesian League, whose individual members enjoyed a technical autonomy. The treaty also permitted the Spartans to continue their practice of aiding oligarchic and pro-Spartan governments throughout Greece. Persons who had been exiled by the democrats were brought back to their native cities in triumph, their property was restored to them, and democrats were massacred or exiled and dispossessed—all in the name of "autonomy." The Spartans repressed democratic revolutions against their system in blood-thirsty fashion, as when they destroyed Mantinea (384) and seized the citadel at Thebes (383) with the aid of traitorous oligarchs within the city. A revolt by the cities of Chalcidice, encouraged by the Athenians, forced Sparta to wage a formal war for four years (383–379), until at last she dragged the leading Chalcidic city, Olynthus, into a subservient alliance. "To all outward appearance," wrote Xenophon after this last coup, "the foundations of Spartan power were at length well and securely laid."

Within a few months, however, the decline of Spartan hegemony had begun. Toward the end of 379 a group of seven Theban exiles returned to their native city, assassinated the oligarchic rulers who had betrayed it to Sparta, and effected a democratic revolution—all in one night. War with Sparta followed. The Thebans built up an army which became celebrated for the efficiency of its "Sacred Band," a group of three hundred picked warriors who served as spearhead in the attack, and they recovered most of the neighboring cities which had once been members of the Boeotian League. Then a Spartan general had made an unsuccessful attempt to occupy Piraeus. Some said that this attack was a private affair designed to augment the general's prestige at home, others that he had been bribed by the Thebans who foresaw that it would force Athens into the alliance. At any rate, the Spartans refused to punish their general, and Athens entered the war. In spite of numerous efforts to patch up a truce, hostilities continued for eighteen years and were brought to an end only by the exhaustion of the major contestants and their mutual destruction as military powers.

Soon after the conclusion of the King's Peace in 386, the Athenians began quiet negotiations for continued friendship with their naval allies in the recent war, and as soon as war broke out anew, they openly invited all Greek states to join them as allies. Several Aegean and Hellespontic cities united with Athens to form the Second Athenian Confederacy (377). This Confederacy was primarily a war alliance against Sparta, but it was also intended to be a permanent federation of states. It carefully preserved the autonomy of its individual members, thus respecting the terms of the King's Peace, and it prohibited the tribute and cleruchies which had enabled Athens to convert the Delian League into a tyrannical empire. All the federated states except Athens sent representatives to a Congress (*synedrion*) sitting at Athens. The decisions reached by this body were referred to the Athenian Assembly and, if approved there, became law binding the whole group. Athens thus shared power equally with her allies. After the navy had won a decisive victory over the Spartan fleet off Naxos (376), most Aegean cities entered the Confederacy.

The Spartans were now eager for peace, but a treaty of 374 was no sooner signed than broken. A Spartan army invaded Boeotia, and relations between Athens and Thebes were severely strained when the Thebans destroyed Plataea (373). A second peace conference was held in 371, at which the Persian king was represented, and a new peace treaty was drawn up. Autonomy was again proclaimed, and further articles provided for the withdrawal of all harmosts and for general disarmament; but the conference collapsed when the Thebans insisted upon signing for the whole of Boeotia if the Spartans signed for all Lacedaemonia. Hostilities were again resumed, with Athens openly in the anti-Theban group. Three weeks later the Thebans virtually annihilated the Spartan army at Leuctra in Boeotia (July 6, 371). Sparta's pretensions to leadership collapsed, and the Spartan state never recovered from this shattering defeat.

Epaminondas and the Day of Theban Glory

For nine years the Thebans tried in vain to exercise that dominion over Greece from which they had expelled the Spartans. Their sole assets were an excellent army and a commander of genius named Epaminondas, whose improvements in military tactics rendered the Spartan hoplite formations obsolete. As a general he prepared the way for Alexander the Great. Shortly after Leuctra, he forced the Spartans to remove their harmosts from all Greek cities, and this sudden withdrawal of Spartan garrisons left the whole Peloponnesus in chaotic civil war. Epaminondas invaded the peninsula to restore order toward the end of 370. He took over the Arcadian League, which was made up of several Peloponnesian states formerly subject to Sparta, and founded a new city, Megalopolis ("Big Town"), to be its capital. Located not far from the ancient Mantinea, razed by the Spartans fifteen years before, the new city soon became an important center in Greek political life. Sparta's remaining possessions were liberated, and the Messenians regained their freedom after centuries of servitude.

Three peace conferences were held during the next three years. One met at Delphi with the Persian king represented, another at Susa heard his views, and a third at Thebes discussed them. All three were failures because the Athenians would not surrender their navy, and the other Greek states would not submit to Theban hegemony. The Thebans could not dominate Greece, or even Boeotia, except by the constant use of force. An anti-Theban coalition therefore arose under the leadership of the Athenian Confederacy and the new Arcadian League. Epaminondas invaded the Peloponnesus once more and attacked his enemies near the ancient Mantinea, but when he seemed about to win the battle he received a mortal wound and the battle remained indecisive (July 4, 362). The Theban leader's death brought an end to his city's glory. That glory had been won by the greatness of one man, for whom Thebes could find no successor.

The Exhaustion of Greece

The elimination of Thebes set the aged Spartan king, Agesilaus, to dreaming of re-establishing his city's hegemony in Greece. Exhaustion from seventy years of almost uninterrupted warfare did not deter him from his lofty ambition, and he began seeking the financial means of waging a new war. Though over eighty years of age, he led a thousand Spartan hoplites to Egypt, where he hired them out as mercenaries. By treacherously changing sides in mid-campaign, he managed to save the army of his new employer and to replenish his own war chest; but on the way home the old man died (360), and his successors failed to inherit his dreams. Agesilaus was the most prominent man of his generation in Greece, an able though not a great general, who well illustrated the good and the bad sides of the Sparta of his day—its patriotism, courage, and devotion to duty no less than its narrowness, lack of statesmanship, brutality and

essential barbarism, and its utter inability to appreciate or understand those things of the spirit which made Greece great. During
his long reign, he brought great suffering to all Greece and ruin to
his own city.

No sooner had the threats of Spartan or Theban domination disappeared than rifts appeared within the Athenian Confederacy.
Even while the wars were in progress, the allies resented the growing tendency of Athens to dominate. During the late 360's the Athenians had seized new territories in the Thracian Chersonesus, Chalcidice, and Euboea, and established cleruchies in Samos and at
Sestos and Potidaea. All this made the allies feel themselves menaced
by a new Athenian imperialism. The crisis came in the spring of 357
when Rhodes, Chios, and Byzantium withdrew from the Confederacy, quickly followed by several lesser allies. A "Social War" (so-
called from the Latin word *socius,* "ally") dragged on for two years
(357–355) and ended with the complete collapse of the Confederacy.
Next Mausolus, the semi-independent satrap of Caria, established
oligarchies in Rhodes and Chios, but he died (353) before proceeding further in his dreams of empire. No Greek city could pretend
to hegemony thereafter, and at last that "autonomy" which for so
long had been a battle cry was realized. A precarious balance of
power prevailed among the Greek states, but the resulting peace
was a peace of exhaustion, not of reconciliation. The rivalries of the
city-states had brought Greece to ruin, and she offered herself as
a tempting prey to any power that saw fit to attack her.

Dionysius and the Western Greeks

While several cities were thus vainly trying to establish their hegemony in Greece, Dionysius I of Syracuse was more successful in making himself lord over the Greeks of Sicily and Italy. Syracuse had
been so weakened by her war with Athens in 413 that for a while she
lost whatever authority she had once enjoyed over the rest of Sicily.
The other Greek cities of Sicily were left free to continue their ancient
quarrels, and Carthage seized the opportunity to resume her Sicilian
conquests, which had ceased after the Greek victory at Himera in
480. The quarrel between Segesta and Selinus—which had been the

excuse for Athenian intervention in 415—was still rumbling and, after considerable Segestian begging, a Punic army invaded Sicily in 409. Within a short time, the Carthaginians captured and destroyed Selinus, after which they marched north to Himera to avenge their defeat of 480 by capturing and sacking the city. A year later they captured Acragas on the southern shore. The terror of the Greeks enabled Dionysius to establish himself as tyrant in Syracuse.

Dionysius, the son of a mule-driver, had acquired enough education to become a clerk and later a leader of mercenary troops. He distinguished himself in the defense of Acragas, and after first serving Syracuse as one of several generals, he became sole general. False reports of an attempt upon his life persuaded his fellow citizens to grant him a bodyguard, with whose aid he established a tyranny (405). He ruled Syracuse thereafter until his death in 367. Without formally abolishing the old democratic constitution of his city, he managed it as he saw fit, being re-elected general year after year. His rule was marked by bloody cruelty and sacrilegious acts which shocked the Greeks, yet he was capable of conspicuous kindness when he believed it would redound to his advantage. As was usual with Sicilian tyrants, his support came from the lower classes upon whom he conferred great benefits. He freed thousands of slaves, receiving them into citizenship, and he emancipated the agricultural serfs.

Perhaps his most important accomplishments were in advancing the art of war. He and his engineers developed siege artillery to a point hitherto unknown, probably learning much from the Carthaginians, who in turn had learned indirectly from the Assyrians. He knew how to build engines capable of throwing enormous stones 300 yards, battering-rams that could demolish city walls, catapults that shot arrows with incredible penetrating force, and siege towers on wheels, six stories high, from the top of which archers could shoot over city walls or scale walls and houses.

Dionysius's great building program, his mercenaries, and his wars kept him ever on the verge of bankruptcy and forced him to desperate expedients to maintain solvency. He taxed the rich ruinously, he debased the coinage, he even robbed temples. Sometimes he made

war a profitable enterprise by demanding enormous ransoms for
prisoners and by selling whole towns into slavery. His secret police
terrorized the upper classes who might possibly plot against him,
and suspected persons were punished with execution or with banishment and dispossession. He thus gained the reputation of being the
most bloodthirsty of all tyrants.

Dionysius Creates a Greek Empire

The Carthaginians were already besieging Gela when Dionysius
seized power at Syracuse in 405. He refused to defend the city and
ordered it to surrender after its population had been withdrawn. He
then negotiated a treaty with the enemy providing that each should
keep what he held, which meant that half the northern coast and
two-thirds of the southern coast of Sicily went to Carthage. During
the next few years, Dionysius was busy fortifying Syracuse, building
up an army of Italian mercenaries, and defending himself against
aristocratic revolts at home. When these things had been accomplished, he turned his arms against the Greek cities of eastern Sicily,
conquering some and ruthlessly destroying others. When he was
sure of no further opposition from hostile Greeks, he resumed the
war against Carthage in 398.

Dionysius invaded western Sicily and, with the aid of his siege
artillery, captured Motye at the extreme western tip of the island.
Within a year, however, the Carthaginians had sent a large force to
Sicily, where they recaptured what they had lost and besieged Syracuse itself. Unfortunately for the Carthaginians, plague presently
decimated their army and Dionysius was able to drive away the sur-
vivors. The tyrant then devoted four years to conquering the native
Sicels of the interior—heretofore neither Greeks nor Carthaginians
had penetrated far from the coast—after which he resumed the war
against Carthage. When peace was concluded (392), Carthage retained the western corner of the island but Dionysius held the rest,
both Greek and Sicel. He thus justified the title "Ruler of Sicily"
which he had assumed on seizing power.

Dionysius next cast covetous eyes on Italy across the Straits of
Messana. He crossed to the mainland in 391 and attacked Rhegium

EMPIRE OF DIONYSIUS I
OF SYRACUSE

Miles
0   25   50   75

at the tip of the "toe." Failing in this first attempt, he formed alliances with various tribes of natives and with their aid he captured several Greek cities. Rhegium was finally taken in 387, and its inhabitants were punished for their defiance by being sold into slavery. A few years later, after he had captured Croton and the whole toe of Italy, Dionysius made alliances with Thurii, Heraclea, Tarentum, and other Greek cities on the southeastern coast.

Dionysius's ambitions presently expanded to include all Italy, where there was no strong power at the moment. The Etruscans had been declining for a century, and just as Dionysius entered Italy from the south, Gallic tribes were crossing the Apennines from the Po Valley and capturing one Etruscan city after another. Shortly before he took Rhegium, the Gauls had even sacked Rome (about 390). These Gallic attacks were raids rather than invasions, and the victors soon withdrew, leaving a wasted land behind them. The time therefore seemed favorable for Dionysius's undertaking. As he planned first to obtain the Adriatic, he established several colonies on the Dalmatian and the Italian shores of that sea, among them Ancona and Hadria near the modern Venice. He then raided and ravaged the Etrurian coast, seized Elba, and sent a colony to Corsica, thus surrounding the peninsula with his fortified posts. When at the height of his power, shortly before 378, Dionysius was the most powerful man in Europe, and his empire was so vast that he seemed likely soon to rule all Italy as well as Sicily. In that year, however, war with Carthage broke out anew, and Dionysius suffered a severe defeat. Punic forces reoccupied about a third of Sicily. Ten years later Dionysius made a great effort to retrieve his losses, but he died before a victory was won (367).

Dionysius was the most amazing Greek of his generation. By his enormous energy, his unscrupulousness, his freedom from even a semblance of decency, his Machiavellism, and his military genius, he made Syracuse the largest and strongest city and himself the greatest despot in all Europe. As in the case of many dictators, he was a man of simple and abstemious tastes who made pretensions to culture. His friendship with Plato has been mentioned. Dionysius set himself up as an author in his own right, and persons who criticized his poetry were apt to be put to work in the stone quarries. His tragedies won second or third prizes occasionally at Athens, and shortly before his death he won first place with *The Ransom of Hector*. His theater at Syracuse was the first permanent stone structure of the sort in the world. Nevertheless, Dionysius was not an ardent Hellenizer and, though he claimed to be leader of the Sicilian Greeks against Carthage, he was quite willing to use barbarian mercenaries against his Greek neighbors. Greek politicians were constantly angling for his aid, but he remained unpopular with the Greek people as a whole, and he was not much interested in their affairs.

Collapse of Dionysius's Empire

Like the creations of many another dictator, Dionysius's empire did not long survive its creator. His son, Dionysius II, did not inherit his father's abilities. The government fell to the old tyrant's minister and brother-in-law, Dion, who attempted to guide the young man in the direction of greater democracy. He persuaded Plato to pay his second and third visits to Syracuse to help the young prince become a philosopher-king, but we have seen how dismally he failed and how the disillusioned Plato sadly returned to Athens.

The next twenty years were consumed by civil wars between the adherents of Dionysius, of Dion, and of various minor aspirants to tyranny. The empire in Italy was lost; the Greek and Sicel cities of Sicily fell to fighting amongst themselves; and it was said that grass grew in the agora of Syracuse. At last, in 344, the Syracusans invited a Corinthian named Timoleon to re-establish the affairs of their distracted city. The new ruler set up a moderate democracy, restored prosperity to the city, brought in many Greek immigrants, and defeated and drove back the Carthaginians to the line of 378. Timoleon then retired to private life (338) and spent the remainder of his days on an estate granted him by the city. Twenty years elapsed before new Punic invasions brought forth a new Greek dictator.

After the collapse of the Syracusan Empire, the Greeks of Italy were hard pressed by the native Italians until 334, when the citizens of Tarentum received aid from Alexander of Molossia—an uncle of Alexander the Great who ruled a people in Epirus. This Alexander united most of the Italian Greek cities under his rule and was planning an empire in Italy when he was murdered about 331. Fifty years later Pyrrhus, another Greek soldier of fortune related to Alexander the Great, revived the family dream, but he came too late. Rome had by then begun her career of expansion and conquest, and the Greeks were no longer the most powerful people in the peninsula.

The New Panhellenism

This fourth-century background of civil war and general pandemonium revived enthusiasm for the Panhellenic dreams of the old Greek aristocrats. For several centuries, the Greeks had recognized their fundamental unity against barbarians, and politicians often took such feelings into account when formulating their policies.

After the Persian wars, Cimon and his friends attempted to perpetuate the Hellenic League, and his aristocratic successors criticized Pericles severely for turning against the Greek allies. Toward the end of the Peloponnesian War, thoughtful Greeks came to regard the hostilities as a mere civil war. Thus the Sophist Gorgias, who as a Sicilian watched the conflict through neutral eyes, expressed Panhellenic ideas in an oration delivered during the Olympic games in 408. The great Athenian dramatists considered the war as an offense against the Greek people, and Thucydides put similar remarks into the mouths of leaders on both sides.

The tragic history of Greece in the postwar years reinforced the lessons of the war itself. Class conflicts tended to divide the population of Greece horizontally rather than vertically, and members of each social class had greater sympathy with the corresponding class in other Greek cities than with their rivals at home. Metics had no particular loyalty to their adopted cities though they often were conscious of Greek nationality. The disgrace of the King's Peace of 386 showed Greeks how their dissentions helped the Persians. The orator Lysias, who was an Athenian metic, spoke in favor of Panhellenism at the Olympic games in 388, and a decade later Plato devoted a long passage in the Republic to expressing the fundamental ideas of the older Panhellenism. Because of their kinship and common culture, he declared, Greeks should never enslave other Greeks; and because of their need for common defense against barbarians, they should conduct their wars with each other according to rules designed to limit devastation. While Plato conceded that each tiny state must remain autonomous, he implied that wars between them were civil wars nevertheless. Aristotle's views did not differ greatly from his master's.

The task of bringing the various Greek states to more peaceful sentiments regarding each other was not an easy one. The situation resembled that prevailing in the opening years of the twentieth century, when most people agreed that something ought to be done to reduce the likelihood of war, yet politicians and statesmen were quite unable to find a program that would calm long-standing fears and hatreds or reconcile the conflicting ambitions of traditionally hostile states. Simple exhortations to peace clearly were not enough, but no one knew just what else could be done. Military domination by one strong power had been tried and failed; leagues and confederacies were built up only to collapse; and while some people considered these alliances steps toward peace—just as Bismarck called the Triple Alliance, of evil memory, *unser Friedensliga* ("our League of Peace") and Germany's critics said much the same things of the rival Triple Entente—nevertheless, then as in 1914, such alliances actually made more wars inevitable. Greece therefore continued to tear herself to pieces. The last serious effort of intelligent Greeks to ward off catastrophe was the new Panhellenism of Isocrates.

Isocrates

We have already seen something of the school for training orators and statesmen which Isocrates opened at Athens about 390. As he belonged to an old aristocratic family, Isocates was predisposed to Panhellenic sympathies, which no doubt were intensified during the tragic postwar years. The school became a center for Panhellenic propaganda, and as its pupils came from every part of the Greek world, they later disseminated such ideas wherever they went. Isocrates also found other ways to influence the course of events. During the last half of his long life, he was the most important publicist in Greece. Sometimes he gave his writings the form of orations, which were delivered publicly by more effective speakers; sometimes he made them "open letters" addressed to prominent men; but he really addressed both letters and speeches to the general public of Greece and he had them circulated far and wide as pamphlets. They were read everywhere in Greece, especially by the upper classes, and they became a factor of incalculable importance in molding public opinion during the middle decades of the century.

The first of these orations or pamphlets, entitled the *Panegyric*, was delivered by an orator before the crowd assembled for the Olympic games in 380. In it Isocrates set forth impressively the idea, already expressed by others, that the various Greek states should cease their quarreling and unite in a war against Persia. In one or two sentences, Isocrates, following the line marked by Cimon long before, declared that Athens and Sparta should assume joint leadership in the proposed war; but he devoted his major attention to showing that Athens deserved leadership because of her experience, her ancient right, and her many services to Greece. He openly attributed the present sad state of all Greece—which he described in harrowing detail—to the policies of Sparta.

Scholars often assume that this speech was designed primarily to prepare public opinion for the Second Athenian Confederacy, set up three years later. Perhaps this was the case, for Xenophon attributes to contemporary politicians language that is strikingly similar to that of the *Panegyric.* As all Greece except Sparta was then smarting under the humiliation of the King's Peace, it was natural that democratic politicians in Athens should have taken advantage of the anti-Persian feeling to promote their plans for empire, and perhaps steal Isocrates' ideas. Moreover, it is quite clear that Isocrates did not anticipate Spartan participation in his program. When the Confederacy was actually established, however, it was far from what Isocrates had anticipated and desired. It was directed against Sparta, not against Persia, and we have seen that it dragged Greece into a new series of civil wars that lasted more than twenty years.

When the Athenian Confederacy failed to come up to Isocrates' expectations, he began seeking new ways to unite Greece as a free union of autonomous states. He no longer thought or spoke of Athenian leadership but sought an outsider to lead Greece. His sympathies were with the conservative faction at Athens—he looked back to the days of Marathon and the constitution of Cleisthenes as to a Golden Age—and he turned bitterly against the radical democrats when, under their leadership, the Second Athenian Confederacy began to tyrannize over Athens' allies. His political ideals, like those of his contemporaries such as Xenophon and Plato, tended in the direction of monarchy, and during the later 370's, he published three tracts favoring monarchical government.

Isocrates Seeks a Leader

Isocrates then began looking for a king who could unite all the Greeks, lead them against the Persians, and perpetuate the war union thus effected by treating all Greeks with equal justice. His attention was first attracted by Jason of Pherae, an adventurer who had united Thessaly under his rule and was declaiming loudly against Persia; but Jason was murdered in 370. Isocrates then addressed a letter to Dionysius I of Syracuse, inviting him to assume the role of Greek leader (368), but the Sicilian tyrant had other things to do, and he died in the next year anyhow. For some time thereafter, Isocrates said little, but several of his pupils were busy helping the Panhellenic agitation along. Some were statesmen in responsible positions and others were orators and publicists like their master.

The outbreak of the Social War in 357 again brought out the need for Greek union and, though now eighty years old, Isocrates redoubled his propagandist activities. Between 355 and 353 he published three major orations and a letter. The first oration, the *Peace*, called upon the Athenians to make peace with their rebellious allies at once and to dissolve the Confederacy. This policy was not based on defeatism, as his opponents charged, but upon a clear recognition of the facts: as his fellow citizens were again oppressing their allies, they must expect frequent revolts and a general hostility such as had caused the Peloponnesian War, and secondly, the anti-Spartan Confederacy was incompatible with peace and Panhellenism. Isocrates urged the abandonment of the Confederacy and the substitution of a free union of all Greeks. The second oration urged that the radical democracy at Athens be curbed by a return to the old system established by Cleisthenes. The third oration gave a general review and defense of the orator's whole career. The letter was written to Archidamus, king of Sparta, urging him to lead Greece against Persia.

The final stage of Isocrates' career began in 346 when, at the age of ninety, he addressed an oration (the *Philippus*) to Philip of Macedon, inviting him to assume leadership of the Panhellenic movement. Four years later, a letter was addressed to Philip, along with a brief note of encouragement to his son Alexander. Isocrates then began preparing a great work in defense of his policies and a eulogy of Athens. Illness delayed him for three years, but the *Panathenaicus* was finally published in 339. A year later, after Philip had defeated the Athenian armies at Chaeronea and united Greece, Isocrates sent

him a letter of congratulation and again urged immediate war
against Persia. The old man then died, aged ninety-eight years. Isocrates had preached Panhellenism to the Greeks for more than forty
years. The *Panegyric* of 380 was perhaps his most brilliant literary
performance, and as such it was honored by many generations of his
compatriots; but the *Philippus* of 346 best set forth his views in their
final form. The only fundamental difference between the two statements is the result of his decision that, since the Greeks could not
unite themselves, an outsider must be called in to unite them.

There can be no doubt that, in spite of his advanced age, Isocrates
wrote even his last orations himself. It is equally clear that they set
forth views already held by many persons for whom he served as
spokesman. Such persons included conservative and moderate aristocrats who opposed the social program and imperialism of the radicals, wealthy men who resented the heavy taxation imposed upon
them by the democracy for its wars and theoric payments, and the
metics and other "men without a city" of whom Athens was full, as
well as the politicians, orators, publicists, and scholars whom Isocrates had trained in his school and who now assisted him in his
propaganda. Many of these persons would undoubtedly have
thought along similar lines even had Isocrates never been born, but
there can be little doubt that his half century of propaganda was a
major factor in preparing the unification of Greece.

Furthermore, Isocrates' writings contain the germs of many ideas
ordinarily associated with Alexander the Great and the Alexandrian
age. He clearly expressed the idea that the new union of Greece
should be cemented by a war against Persia. He declared that the
economic distress of Greece might be relieved by extensive colonization and city-building in Asia. And he insisted that the Greeks were
a cultural rather than a racial group, which would enable anyone
who absorbed Greek culture to become a Greek. In the *Philippus*,
moreover, Isocrates urged Philip to seek divinity by following in the
footsteps of his divine ancestor, Heracles; he thereby prepared the
way for the deification of Alexander and his successors. Isocrates
thus set forth the ideas of a new and numerous social class that had
grown up during the fourth century. This class was rapidly replacing

the groups that had formerly dominated Greece, and already it was turning her history in new directions.

Philip of Macedon

Macedonia bordered on the Thermaic Gulf at the northwest corner of the Aegean Sea. It was separated from Thessaly on the south by Mount Olympus, from Thrace on the east by the Strymon River. Its population was composed of approximately the same racial ingredients as that of Greece, and their language was a dialect of Greek corrupted by many Illyrian (Albanian) words. In character the Macedonians were a wild and warlike people with savage tastes and pleasures. In culture they were backward, partly perhaps because of their character, partly because the old Mycenaean civilization had never penetrated far in their direction, and partly because their pastoral and simple agricultural life was not conducive to high civilization. The Greeks of the fifth and fourth centuries regarded them as barbarians. A Macedonian king (Alexander I), who had accompanied Xerxes' army into Greece in 480, aided the Greeks by warning them of the impending attack at Plataea, and when he later presented himself at the Olympic games, he obtained recognition as a Greek by claiming descent from Heracles. Thereafter, the Macedonian kings were regarded as Greeks ruling over barbarians.

The Northern campaigns of the Peloponnesian War brought Greeks and Macedonians into closer contact, and toward the end of that conflict the Macedonian king attempted to make his capital city, Pella, a center of Greek culture by bringing to it such distinguished persons as Euripides and the painter Zeuxis. Nevertheless, the Macedonian people, and even their monarchs, remained barbarians at heart. Early in the fourth century there were frequent wars with Illyrian tribesmen to the west, in the course of which more than one king lost his life. Other kings were murdered and succeeded by ambitious members of their families or courts. In the midst of such turbulence, Philip became king in 359.

Concerning the new king who thus rose to power Theopompus remarked, "Taken all in all, Europe has never yet produced another such man as Philip, son of Amyntas." Though a barbarian in his savage strength, wildness, and drunken orgies, Philip could—when he wished—show great personal charm and arouse the enthusiasm of those who worked with him. He had an appreciation of Greek culture, and his intellectual endowments were far above those of any contemporary Greek statesman. When only fifteen years old, he was sent as hostage to Thebes (367), where he remained for three years. He kept his eyes and ears open during that important period, and apparently he learned everything Epaminondas had to teach about military science and statecraft. Adopting and improving the organization and battle-line of the Theban army, Philip presently made his own army the best that the world had yet seen, and he became the successor of Epaminondas as the best general of his day. He was equally successful in diplomacy. When other methods of persuasion failed, he was always ready to use bribery and, Greek politicians being what they were, he usually got what he wanted. In fact, he once boasted that he could capture any city without fighting if only he could lead a mule laden with gold within its walls.

Philip returned from Thebes in 364 and soon thereafter he was entrusted with the government of a Macedonian province. When his elder brother was killed in battle with the Illyrians (359), leaving an infant son as heir, Philip took over the regency though he was then only twenty-three years old. Several rivals at once contested his claims, usually with the backing of some Greek politician, but within a short time all the pretenders were disposed of and he ruled supreme as Philip II.

Philip's Early Conquests

The new king at once turned his attention to military reorganization and to the expansion of his frontiers at the expense of Illyrians and Thracians. Having thus tested his new model army, he was ready in 357 for more serious adventures. He attacked Amphipolis and cynically offered the protesting Athenians to surrender it to them later if they would aid him against their ally, the Thessalian city of Pydna. Athens left Amphipolis to its fate. Philip captured the city by bribing traitors within the walls, after which he executed or exiled its pro-Athenian leaders. Pydna, too, was taken, but Philip refused to surrender Amphipolis to Athens, pointing out that she had not provided the stipulated aid. A little later Philip seized Potidaea, where the Athenians had settled a cleruchy in 361, and he forced Olynthus into an alliance with himself against Athens.

One result of these early aggressions was that by them Philip replenished his treasury from the gold mines of Mount Pangaeus. Nearby he founded the city of Philippi, whose fame was later enhanced by Brutus and St. Paul. The wars also gave Philip a seacoast and the opportunity to build a navy with which he could threaten Athenian grain ships from the Black Sea. He was not yet ready for a major war, however, and during the next several years he directed his energies to domestic reform, relieved by occasional raids into Thessaly or Thrace.

By this time Greece was again in the throes of a war known as the Sacred War (356–346). Epaminondas of Thebes had attempted to augment his power by exploiting the divine sanctions of the Delphic amphictyony (see page 350), an organization which had been moribund for upward of a century. He induced its officials to punish Sparta with a huge fine. The fine was never paid, but the judgment served to exclude Spartans from the sanctuary and gave them the unsavory reputation of being enemies of the god. After their general's death the Thebans continued this policy of co-operating with and defending Apollo, and presently they brought charges of sacrilege against the Phocians. The accused retaliated by seizing Delphi —Phocian territory surrounded the sacred precincts—and thus launched the Sacred War in 356. The Phocians seized the sacred treasury, melted down the gold and silver offerings, hammered the iron and bronze into weapons, and hired a large army of mercenaries. Several cities then espoused the Phocian cause from hatred of Thebes.

After this Sacred War had been raging for about three years, Philip decided that the time had come for him to intervene in Greek affairs. He occupied Methone, near Pydna, in 353, thereby depriving Athens of her last ally on the Theramic Gulf. But when he marched into Thessaly, the Phocian mercenaries defeated him twice and drove him back into Macedonia. He soon returned with a larger

army, expelled the Phocians from Thessaly, had himself declared
tagus (ruler) of that country, and advanced as far as Thermopylae
(352). This menace aroused the other Greek states, whose threats
caused Philip to withdraw once more to Thessaly, leaving the
Phocians supreme in central Greece. Philip loudly denounced their
sacrileges at Delphi and re-established his prestige at home by a
successful raid into Thrace.

Meantime Athens had lost her Social War (357–55), and her Second Empire had disintegrated. As the peace was a defeat for her
imperialistic democrats, government passed to the conservative
groups who wished to strengthen the city's finances—and their own
—by encouraging trade and avoiding costly military adventures.
Athens' new leader was an able financier, Eubulus, who was treas-
urer of the theoric fund from 354 to 350 and probably again from 350
to 346. Through a more efficient and honest collection of taxes, and
by working the silver mines in Mount Laurium intensively, he was
able to keep the treasury in a sound condition and still placate the
populace occasionally with theoric payments. He built docks and
made other improvements at Piraeus, provided Athens with a good
water supply, and increased the navy, but he insisted upon a pacific
foreign policy. Though he sent a small fleet to aid Methone in 353,
his aid was too slight to save the city; when the ramifications of the
Sacred War led Sparta to attack Megalopolis later in that same year,
he refused aid to that city; and when the widow of Mausolus of
Caria seized Rhodes (351), he again refused to intervene. But when
Philip advanced to Thermopylae in 352, he contributed troops to
the army that turned the Macedonian back. A year later he sent ships
and money to defend the Hellespont against Philip. Thus Eubulus
was not a "peace-at-any-price" fanatic. He was a level-headed statesman who believed in preparedness, who was ready to keep Philip
out of Greece and to protect the grain ships from the Black Sea, but
who at the same time opposed imperialism and foreign entangle-
ments.

Demosthenes and Philip

Greater than Eubulus was his antagonist Demosthenes. There has
been much controversy among scholars regarding this remarkable

Plate 32.   Demosthenes *(Vatican Museum)*

man. As to his superb oratorical ability and his high personal courage
there can be no doubt. Like other popular speakers of his day, he
was quick to attribute the conduct of his opponents to bribery, and
they replied in kind, accusing him of accepting bribes from the king
of Persia. Though this charge was never proved, Demosthenes was
convicted in his old age of embezzling twenty talents—an enormous
sum for those days. Modern debate concerns the wisdom of his policies rather than his personal honesty.[1] His cause was the one that
lost, and romantic writers have often pictured him as the last champion of Greek liberty. His skill at using the terminology of chauvin-
ism has led certain writers—among them the French politician
Clemenceau—to picture him as a patriot of purest ray serene. On
the other hand, his failure has caused lesser critics to see in him only
a "man of words" foolishly talking against a "man of deeds" like
Philip. He has even been adjudged "the man least capable of understanding his time of all that figured in antiquity as statesmen, unless
Cicero be taken into account."

There can be no doubt that Demosthenes was essentially back-
ward-looking and that he had far less comprehension of the fundamental needs of Greece in his day than did Philip and Isocrates. He
aimed principally at obtaining for his city the hegemony of Greece.
Had his desires been realized, the bloody and suicidal wars would
have continued until the Greek people and their civilization were utterly destroyed. In that event, presumably, the modern world would
know only those poor fragments of Greek culture that had penetrated
Sicily. Internecine wars had already dealt classic Greece a mortal
wound, but the virility of the Greek people was not yet destroyed,
and before Greek civilization expired, Demosthenes' opponents successfully transplanted much of it to new centers where it took on a
new life and enriched the culture of a new age. If the modern world
enjoys any inheritance from ancient Greece, it is in part because
Demosthenes failed in his lifework.

The history of Greece during the thirteen years after Philip's first
victories in the Sacred War centered around a mighty struggle between Demosthenes and Philip. We have no way of tracing the exact

[1] See note on J. G. Droysen, p. 543.

progress of Philip's ideas, for he was a deep schemer who carefully concealed his purposes and did what he could to deceive his contemporaries regarding them. It seems fairly clear that by 351 he had matured plans for the conquest and domination of Greece and for a war against Persia, but being a realist in politics, he was willing to await his opportunity and allow circumstances to guide the details of his course.

At about this time, too, Demosthenes set himself up as Eubulus's chief opponent in Athens. By birth and education, he belonged to a social and economic class that had supported Eubulus, and in his early political orations, delivered between 354 and 352, his views did not differ markedly from his rival's. He favored peace, preparedness, and a general regard for Athenian interests. Presently, however, he began urging a more active foreign policy in support of democracies everywhere. When he could not persuade the members of his own social class to follow him, he turned from them to become leader of the Athenian democracy. In 351 or shortly thereafter, he delivered a powerful oration against Philip, now known as the *First Philippic*. From that time until Philip's death in 336, Demosthenes devoted his public life to inciting his fellow citizens against the Macedonian.

Philip in Greece

Early in 349 Philip proceeded to the conquest of Chalcidice. When Olynthus appealed to Athens for aid, Demosthenes delivered three orations urging an alliance with that city. The alliance was drawn up and aid for the Olynthians prepared, but Philip created a diversion by stirring up a revolt in Euboea and before the Athenians could reduce that island, he had captured and razed Olynthus (348). There was nothing Athens could do but make peace, which she did early in 346. The treaty provided that Philip and Athens each should retain the territory they then held—Philip keeping Chalcidice and Athens retaining the Thracian Chersonesus. Philip professed himself unwilling to treat with the sacrilegious Phocians, however, and the Sacred War dragged on a little longer. Immediately upon concluding peace with Athens, Philip marched his troops through Thessaly to Thermopylae once more, vainly inviting the Athenians to join him in punishing the Phocians for their crimes against god and man. A few days later the Phocians surrendered. Their towns were dismantled, their people were scattered in villages, arrangements were drawn up whereby they would restore by annual installments the temple treasures they had stolen, and their votes in the Amphictyonic Council were transferred to Philip.

The two peace treaties of 346 left Philip the strongest man in Greece. For a moment he seemed disposed to co-operate with Athens, though it is impossible to gauge his sincerity or to say how long he would have retained these friendly sentiments had the Athenians welcomed his advances. Counsels at Athens were divided. The party of Eubulus was willing to co-operate with Philip. Its most prominent spokesman, the orator Aeschines, favored Philip and in a general way was a Panhellenist. At this time, Isocrates published his *Philippus,* urging Philip to unite Greece and lead her in a war against Persia. Demosthenes, on the other hand, accepted the peace as necessary but regarded it as only a temporary breathing spell. He soon resumed his attacks upon Philip and attempted to build up a Greek league against him. And finally, at about this time, Artaxerxes III became convinced that Philip was a menace to Persia and began subsidizing the war party at Athens. It was not proved that Demosthenes accepted his bribes, but it is certain that the orator's activities were all that the Great King could have desired. Likewise, it is by no means certain that Aeschines was bribed by Philip, as Demosthenes alleged, but his activities certainly promoted the interests of the Macedonian king. Athens had reached such a state that her two most eminent politicians, the leaders of rival parties, were both plausibly suspected of being in the pay of foreign potentates.

Philip Conquers Greece

After Philip had devoted three years to further preparation, propaganda, and unsuccessful efforts to placate Athens, he was ready to resume his military progress. In the summer of 342, he marched against the king of Thrace, defeated him, dethroned him, annexed his territories, and founded the city of Philippopolis (still an important place in Bulgaria) from which to rule them. When the cities of the Chersonesus appealed to Athens for aid, Demosthenes induced his fellow citizens to send a fleet to the Hellespont. Its admiral unlawfully attacked one of Philip's cities and thus inaugurated hostilities with Macedonia, but war was not formally declared. Demosthenes denounced Philip anew, demanding a Greek league against him, and spoke openly of begging aid from Persia. He then went to negotiate with the cities on the Bosporus and persuaded Byzantium and Perinthus to substitute Athenian for their Thracian alliances. Philip at once attacked them and invaded the Chersonesus (340). The attack was conducted with enormous siege engines of the type Dionysius had used in Sicily, but Philip's efforts were in vain and he returned sadly to his own country.

Philip was not checked for long. His agents on the Amphictyonic Council were soon preparing to accuse Athens of sacrilege and then launch a sacred war against her, but they were circumvented by Aeschines, the Athenian delegate on the Council, who brought similar charges against the Locrians of Amphissa and diverted the proposed war (339). When the disappointed Thebans refused to participate in this substitute war, and Demosthenes persuaded the Athenians to remain neutral, the Council invited Philip to intervene, and he asked for no better excuse to occupy Thermopylae. Meantime Demosthenes had persuaded the Athenians to seek an alliance with their old enemy Thebes and had been appointed head of the embassy sent to negotiate it. Again he was successful and Thebes entered the alliance. A few lesser states joined the allies, but most of the Peloponnesus remained neutral.

Philip had by this time conquered Amphissa and even Naupactus, a port on the Gulf of Corinth at the far end of Locris. Turning back toward Thebes, he met and defeated the allied forces at Chaeronea (August, 338). The two armies were of approximately equal size (about 32,000 men each), but the superior generalship of Philip quickly showed itself. The Theban Sacred Band, stationed opposite Philip's young son Alexander, stood its ground and was butchered to the last man. The Athenians and their allies fled in a panic-stricken rout, except for one thousand who were dead and two thousand taken prisoner. The military force of Greece was shattered. Demosthenes had got his war and had lost, which in the long run was perhaps just as well. In one pleasing detail, however, Demosthenes differed from many of the more vociferous war hawks of history. When war came, he took his place with the others, and at Chaeronea he fought as a hoplite in the Athenian ranks. He was among those who escaped, and Philip did not deign to punish his great adversary. Demosthenes was allowed to remain in Athens, where he again incited the citizens to war after Philip's death. While Alexander was in Asia, Demosthenes engaged in his greatest oratorical duel with Aeschines, whom he vilified outrageously. And after Alexander's death he made one more effort to arouse the Athenians against the Macedonians. At last he was driven from the city and starved himself to death in a temple.

After his victory at Chaeronea Philip quickly advanced to Thebes and punished that city severely. The Boeotian League was dissolved, oligarchic governments were set up in all its constituent cities, territory was given away, Macedonian troops were stationed in the citadel, and anti-Macedonian leaders were exiled. Athens escaped a similar fate. Inspired by Demosthenes, the city was strengthening her defenses and preparing to continue the struggle when Philip offered liberal peace terms which Athens accepted. She retained her full independence, the integrity of her territory, and her cleruchies in Lemnos, Imbros, Scyros, and Samos; she surrendered all claims to the Chersonesus, for which she received a patch of Theban territory in exchange; prisoners were returned without ransom, and Athens entered an alliance with Macedonia. In gratitude for these liberal terms, the Athenians erected a statue of Philip in the agora—but they also continued their rearmament. Philip met no serious opposition in the rest of Greece. An army was sent into the Peloponnesus, where it received the submission of all the states except Sparta. Though Sparta was not attacked for this show of independence, the map was redrawn at her expense.

The League of Corinth

When the entire peninsula was firmly in Philip's hands, he invited the Greek states to send representatives to discuss the question of

Panhellenic union. Delegates from all states except Sparta reached Corinth late in 338. Here Philip presented them with a plan of union that he had prepared, and under the circumstances there was little they could do but accept it. A treaty was drawn up establishing the League of Corinth. The various Greek states agreed to a general and eternal peace amongst themselves, and collectively they entered into an alliance with Macedonia, which was not a member of the League. The treaty guaranteed the complete independence and autonomy of each state in the League, but it forbade revolutionary activity or extreme social changes such as had disturbed Greece so frequently. There were to be no executions, banishments, or dispossessions for political reasons, nor was there to be any cancellation of debts or general emancipation of slaves. Foreign policy was to be determined by the League acting through a congress (*synedrion*) in which each state was represented proportionately to its military power. Sometimes these member states were the old city-states, but sometimes they were new groupings of several cities into "tribes" (*ethne*). The different states were to provide military forces for the punishment of members who violated the rules of the League or for other joint undertakings. These armies were to be under the command of a leader (*hegemon*) and this office went to Philip and his descendants. The old Amphictyonic Council served as a supreme court. The League of Corinth thus incorporated much of the Panhellenic idealism of the day, and it followed and perfected the pattern of such earlier unions as the Second Athenian Confederacy. It united the Greeks, it promised to end the civil and intercity wars that had distracted Greece for so long, and at the same time it carefully preserved local autonomy in domestic matters. Nevertheless, in spite of this fair exterior, the League was so arranged that Philip could dominate it at his pleasure.

A short time after the ratification of the treaty, the *synedrion* held its first meeting at Corinth (spring, 337) where Philip proposed a war against Persia. Isocrates had long been urging this war as a means of uniting the Greeks; others had discovered other advantages, public or private, that might be derived from such a war; and Philip wanted more conquests for his own aggrandizement. The proposal met no opposition, and Philip moved ten thousand Macedonian troops into Asia Minor, but war did not follow immediately. Philip decided that he would first take a new wife, a decision which precipitated a quarrel with his present wife, Olympias, and her son Alexander. Before the ensuing disturbances could be calmed, Philip was murdered by one of his courtiers. The accession of Alexander then inaugurated a new period in the history of Greece and of the Ancient World.

Note

Johann Gustav Droysen

The modern debate on the relative importance of Philip and Demosthenes was opened by J. G. Droysen, who eulogized Philip in the opening chapters of his famous book on Alexander (1833). Before this time it had been customary for historians to take Demosthenes at face value and to praise him lavishly at the expense of Philip. Droysen reversed this order, criticizing Demosthenes and taking Philip at practically face value.

Johann Gustav Droysen (1808–84) was born in Pomerania, the son of a chaplain in the Prussian army that fought against Napoleon. Though left an orphan at the age of eight, and in spite of great poverty, he managed to take a doctor's degree at Berlin in 1830. His great book appeared three years later, when he was only twenty-five years old. He became a professor at Kiel in 1840, at Jena in 1851, and at Berlin in 1859.

In his early days, Droysen was inspired with the idea of German unification under Prussian leadership. He became a leader of the Nationalists in Holstein while a professor at Kiel, and he was a member of the famous Frankfort Parliament of 1848, where he expressed liberal ideas which were unacceptable to the authorities and which cost him his professorship. His interest in contemporary politics led him to abandon ancient history and devote the greater part of his life to Prussian history. His lectures on the Wars of Liberation were published in 1846, and his great *Geschichte der preussischen Politik*, carrying the story only to 1756, appeared in twelve volumes between 1855 and 1886. He was the first of the "Prussian School" of historians (the others being Sybel and von Treitschke) and it has been said of him that "he perhaps more than any other German man of letters prepared the ground for Bismarck."

Droysen's nationalistic views are evident even in his writings on Greek history. These included the *Geschichte Alexanders des Grossen* (1833) and two volumes on the Hellenistic Age that followed Alexander (1836–43). Droysen drew a close parallel between the kings of Prussia and

Philip—it is said that he had been anticipated in this view by no less a personage than Frederick the Great—and his enthusiasm for Philip was the result of his Prussian politics. He wrote as he did because he believed that Philip and Alexander had saved and regenerated Greece just as unification under Prussia would save and regenerate Germany. Nevertheless, it is to Droysen that we must award the honor of having "discovered" the Hellenistic world—the Greek world of the period after Alexander—which had hitherto been neglected by students of antiquity. See Droysen's life by his son, G. Droysen, *Johann Gustav Droysen* (vol. I, to 1848 [1910]; no later vols.); R. Hübner, ed., *Johann Gustav Droysen, Briefwechsel* (2 vols., 1929); and F. Meinecke in *Historische Zeitschrift*, CXLI (1930), 249–87.

Epilogue

The Legacy of Greece

T HE BATTLE OF CHAERONEA MAKES AN APPROPRIATE END
for our account of ancient Greek history. It was not then that Greece
ceased to exist, nor had Greeks yet completed their contribution to
world civilization. Within a few years of this famous battle, however, conditions throughout the Near East were disturbed so vio-
lently that the old Greece quickly became a thing of the past. Philip
of Macedon was murdered in 336, less than two years after his great
victory, and was succeeded by his twenty-year-old son, Alexander,
later known as Alexander the Great. This romantic young prince
soon embarked upon the war against Persia which Isocrates had
urged and Philip had planned. In the spring of 334 he crossed to
Asia Minor, where in the next ten years he overthrew the Persian
Empire and led his victorious army through Persia and Afghanistan
to far-away India. When Alexander died at Babylon in the early
summer of 323, he ruled territories that extended from the Adriatic
to the Indus, and Greece had become a relatively unimportant part
of this huge Macedonian Empire. In ten brief years, this land of
warring city-states had become a corner of a world empire, never
having gone through a period of national unity. The program of
Isocrates and the Panhellenists had never been given a trial.

Alexander's untimely death was followed by long years of warfare
among his generals. At last three dynasties held parts of his former
empire—the Antigonids dominated Macedonia and European
Greece, the Seleucids held Asia, and the Ptolemies ruled Egypt. The
two latter dynasties took over territories formerly ruled by the Persians and inhabited almost entirely by Orientals. Alexander and his

547

successors made strenuous efforts to Hellenize their kingdoms by founding cities which they endowed with Greek political institutions and which they filled with Greek immigrants. Nevertheless, they quickly learned that Orientals must be governed in an oriental manner, as under the Persian regime. In the end, the Greek rulers learned more from the Orientals than the Orientals learned from them. Moreover, the Greeks were not so successful as the Persians in ruling subject populations. Whereas the Persians had made their empire last two hundred years, the Seleucids had lost the eastern half of their empire to a native dynasty (the Arsacids, or Parthians) within fifty years, and within a little more than a century the whole Near East was thrown into pandemonium by native revolts in Egypt, Palestine, Syria, Mesopotamia, and Asia Minor.

Behind all this confusion it is possible to trace the steady progress of that world unity of which Orientals had been talking for many centuries. The Persians plausibly claimed that their empire realized this ancient ideal politically, and Hebrew prophets, long before Alexander, had foretold a time when all men would be united in the worship of the one true God. Alexander's spectacular exploits advertised this idea of world unity among the Greeks, and his successors were rarely satisfied with ruling only a fraction of his former empire. They never ceased striving, by fair means or foul, to acquire it all. Likewise, the hapless peoples whom they governed desired world unity for many reasons, not the least of which was the belief that it alone offered hope of escape from the constant wars that were ruining them. Then as now, men longed for One World, but no one knew exactly how to achieve it. At last the Romans succeeded where the Greeks had failed. They stepped in to fill the vacuum and quell the anarchy that followed the collapse of the Greek dynasties. At the beginning of the Christian era, Augustus ruled a world more solidly united than it had ever been under Alexander or the Persians, and his successors maintained this unity for almost five hundred years. They passed on the ideal of world unity to the Middle Ages and Modern Times. The second half of ancient history therefore has greater interest and meaning for us today than does the first.

European Greece took little direct part in the mighty struggles that followed the death of Alexander. Her strength was ebbing fast. Her energetic and ambitious young men began pouring into the new cities of the Orient or entered the mercenary armies of Alexander's successors. Her trade was diverted to other channels. Class antagonisms became more bitter than ever, and bloody civil wars were frequent. The historian Polybius, who lived in the second century before Christ, pictures third-century Greece as truly to be pitied. The Greek people had not lost their physical or intellectual vigor but the world had passed them by.

The intellectual life of the new age created what is known as Hellenistic culture—as opposed to the Hellenic culture of the centuries before Alexander. This new Hellenistic culture was a blend of Greek and Oriental elements and it arose, not in Greece itself, but in the cities along the eastern shores of the Mediterranean from the Troad to Cyrene. Here Greeks and Orientals had long been living side by side, mingling their blood and their ideas. At first, in early Hellenistic times, the Greeks clearly held the upper hand, and the third century was an important period in the history of Greek philosophy and scholarship, science and art. Literary men continued or slightly modified old Greek traditions in comedy, poetry, and historical writing. As time went on, however, true Greeks became less common among the intellectual leaders of the Hellenistic world, and their places were taken by Greek-speaking Orientals. In the end, the Mohammedan conquests of the seventh century after Christ put the Orientals in control once more. In Syria and Egypt, oriental rulers held sway and oriental culture dominated; and even the Byzantine Empire was more oriental than Greek. Before its collapse, however, the Hellenistic world had drawn heavily upon the ancient cultures of the Orient and Greece, and had passed their best features on to Rome and the West.

It was Hellenistic Greek culture which the Romans knew. In the second and first centuries before Christ, educated Romans were deeply influenced by Greeks, and in general their instincts led them to admire the Greek rather than the oriental elements in the Hellenistic cultural amalgam. They were thus led back to a study of the Hellenic culture of earlier times. The early Church Fathers owed an equal debt to the late Hellenistic culture of the early centuries of the Christian era. Roman writers and Church Fathers preserved most of what the Middle Ages knew of Greek culture.

The great intellectual leaders of the Renaissance period spoke much of Greece, but they saw her largely through Roman eyes. When artists wished to imitate Greek statues, they used Roman copies as their models; architects knew Greek architecture through late Roman buildings (often the work of Syrians); and scholars studied Greek literature only after first saturating themselves in Roman literature. Seventeenth-century scholars knew Greek well, and printed great editions of the Greek classics, but knowledge of Greece declined sadly during the urbane and Rome-admiring eighteenth century.

Early in the nineteenth century a great revival of interest in all things Greek spread over Europe. The Greek language was taught widely in secondary schools, which were attended by rapidly increasing numbers of persons, and thousands of youngsters in all the countries of western Europe and the United States were drilled in the rudiments of Greek grammar. It cannot be said that all who painfully worked their way through a few pages of the *Anabasis* and the *Iliad* thereby became accomplished Greek scholars, or that they learned much of the true Greek spirit. But many imbibed something of this spirit, and others never forgot teachers who had been more successful in the great endeavor. The intellectual leaders of the nineteenth century, almost without exception, had received a classical training in youth. Artists studied Greek models—real ones this time—and poets imitated or translated Greek masters. Philosophers and theologians again studied Plato, and scholars drew lessons from the history of ancient Greece. In Germany an ideal Greece was created by a long succession of thoughtful men from Winckelmann and Goethe, through the great scholars of the mid-century, to Eduard Meyer and Wilamowitz; in England a rather different ideal was created by Byron and Shelley, Grote and Jowett, and Sir Gilbert Murray; and everywhere such classic ideals were held up for public approbation and imitation. The nineteenth was one of the truly great centuries in the history of human thought and civilization, and its debt to ancient Greece was enormous.

Today things are different. Greek has again become a dead language, known chiefly to the specialized scholars who use it as a tool in their researches. A young man seeking a liberal education no longer has the time to become proficient in the ancient languages. There is too much else now that he must know. Fortunately, however, there are other ways in which men can familiarize themselves with the great achievements of Greece and imbibe something of her spirit. It would be a sad day for humanity if all knowledge of the Greek miracle were to be lost. Those who esteem beauty in art and literature, or who seek truth in science and philosophy, or who wish to direct their lives according to the dictates of reason, and those who consider intellectual integrity their dearest possession, will always find sympathy and inspiration in the famous Greeks who long ago distinguished themselves for these very qualities. The many-sided and brilliant Greek people turned the thought of Europe and the world in new directions and, like the great history of Thucydides, their magnificent creations have become a possession forever.

Bibliography

Works of Reference

The Cambridge Ancient History, ed. J. B. Bury [and others], 12 vols., 1923–39, and 5 vols. of plates prepared by C. T. Seltman, 1927–39. A full history of the ancient world, each chapter written by a specialist, with full bibliographies and many maps. Vols. 1–6 cover the period before Alexander the Great. A much-needed new edition is in preparation, with the first two volumes completely rewritten.

Dictionnaire des antiquités grecques et romains, ed. C. V. Daremberg and E. Saglio, 5 vols., 1877–1919. Earlier volumes somewhat out of date, but many excellent articles.

Encyclopædia Britannica, 11th ed., 28 vols., 1910–11. The articles in this edition are good, and usually to be preferred to the watered-down versions in later editions.

Encyclopædia of Religion and Ethics, ed. James Hastings, 13 vols., 1908–27.

Oxford Classical Dictionary, ed. M. Cary [and others] (1949).

Paulys Real-Encyclopädie der classischen Altertumswissenschaft, ed., G. Wissowa and W. Kroll, 1894– . To be completed in about 60 volumes, of which 5 or 6 were yet to appear in 1940. Exhaustive and fundamental articles on all phases of classical antiquity.

Reallexicon des klassischen Altertums, ed. F. H. Lübker (8th ed., 1914).

Smaller Classical Dictionary, Everyman Library (1910; new ed. 1937), a handy little volume.

Historical Atlas, W. E. Shepherd (1911).

Atlas of Ancient and Classical Geography, Everyman Library (1907; new ed., 1933).

Periodicals

Articles and reviews dealing with ancient history appear regularly in a number of English-language periodicals: *American Journal of Archaeology* (includes news of current archeological expeditions), *American Journal of Philology, Classical Journal, Classical Philology, Classical*

Quarterly, Classical Review, Hesperia, Journal of the American Oriental Society, Journal of Egyptian Archaeology, Journal of Hellenic Studies, Journal of Near Eastern Studies, Journal of Roman Studies. See also many German periodicals, especially *Hermes* and *Klio,* and the French *Revue des études anciennes, Revue des études grecques, Revue des études latines,* and *Revue de l'histoire des religions.* Current publications are reported in *The Year's Work in Classical Studies,* published annually at London.

Textbook Histories of Antiquity

Breasted, J. H., *Ancient Times* (1916, 2nd ed., 1935).
Caldwell, W. E., *The Ancient World* (1937).
Glover, T. R., *The Ancient World* (1935).
Rostovtzeff, M., *A History of the Ancient World* (2 vols., 1927).
Sanford, Eva M., *The Mediterranean World in Ancient Times* (1938).
Trever, A. A., *History of Ancient Civilization* (2 vols., 1936–39).
Turner, Ralph, *The Great Cultural Traditions* (2 vols., 1941).
Van Sickle, C. E., *A Political and Cultural History of the Ancient World* (2 vols., 1947–48).

Prehistory

Hooton, E. A., *Up from the Ape* (1931).
Howells, Wm., *Mankind So Far* (1944).
MacCurdy, G. G., ed., *Early Man* (1937).
Coon, C. S., *The Races of Europe* (1939).
Ebert, Max, ed., *Reallexicon der Vorgeschichte* (15 vols., 1924–32) valuable.
MacCurdy, G. G., *Human Origins: a Manual of Prehistory* (2 vols., 1924).
Osborn, H. F., *Men of the Old Stone Age* (1915).
Childe, V. G., *The Danube in Prehistory* (1929). *The Dawn of European Civilization* (1925, 2nd ed., 1939). *Man Makes Himself* (1936).
Peake, H., *The Beginnings of Agriculture* (1928).
Peake, H., and Fleure, H. J., *The Corridors of Time* (1927–36), a series of nine small volumes, each with a separate title, which cover human history from the earliest times to about 1000 B.C.
"The Beginnings of Civilization in the Orient," Supplement to the *Journal of the American Oriental Society* (Dec. 1939).

The Ancient Orient

Childe, V. G., *New Light on the Ancient East* (1934).
Finegan, Jack, *Light from the Ancient East* (1946).

Hall, H. R., *Ancient History of the Near East* (1911; 8th ed., 1932).

Meyer, Eduard, *Geschichte des Altertums* (5 vols., 1882–1902; new ed., 1909–39), see note, p. 473.

Moret, A., *Histoire de l'Orient* (2 vols., 1936).

Propyläen Weltgeschichte, I (1931) well illustrated.

Schäfer, H., and Andrae, W., *Kunst des Alten Orients* (Propyläen Kunst-geschichte, II, 1925) lavishly illustrated.

Bilabel, Fr., *Geschichte Vorderasiens und Aegyptens vom 16.–11. Jahr-hundert v. Chr.* (1927).

Sumer and Akkad

Chiera, E., *They Wrote on Clay* (1938).

Delaporte, L., *Mesopotamia* (1923; Eng. tr., 1925).

Frankfort, H., *Archeology and the Sumerian Problem* (1932). *Kingship and the Gods* (1948).

Frankfort, H., and others, *The Intellectual Adventure of Ancient Man* (1947).

Gadd, C. J., *The History and Monuments of Ur* (1929). *Ideas of Divine Rule in the Ancient East* (1948).

Heidel, A., *The Babylonian Genesis* (1942). *The Gilgemish Epic* (1946).

Jacobsen, T., *The Sumerian King Lists* (1939).

Jastrow, M., *The Civilization of Babylonia and Assyria* (1915).

King, L. W., *A History of Sumer and Akkad* (1910). *A History of Babylon* (1915).

Langdon, S., *Tammuz and Ishtar* (1914). *The Babylonian Epic of Creation* (1923).

Lloyd, Seton, *Mesopotamia* (1936).

Meissner, B., *Babylonien und Assyrien* (2 vols., 1920–25).

Rogers, R. W., *A History of Babylonia and Assyria* (2 vols., 1900; 6th ed., 1915). *Cuneiform Parallels to the Old Testament* (1912; 2nd ed., 1926).

Smith, Sidney, *Alalakh and Chronology* (1940). *Early History of Assyria to 1000 B.C.* (1928).

Speiser, E. A., *Mesopotamian Origins* (1930).

Woolley, C. L., *The Sumerians* (1928). *Ur of the Chaldees* (1930).

Egypt

Breasted, J. H., *Ancient Records of Egypt: Historical Documents from the Earliest Times to the Persian Conquest* (5 vols., 1906–7). A collection of source materials in English translation; see note, p. 128.

Baikie, James, *A History of Egypt* (2 vols., 1929).

Breasted, J. H., *A History of Egypt* (1905). *A History of the Ancient Egyptians* (1908), abbreviated version of earlier work.

Engberg, R. M., *The Hyksos Reconsidered* (1939).

Moret, A., *The Nile and Egyptian Civilization* (1926; Eng. tr., 1928).

Petrie, W. M. F., *History of Egypt* (6 vols., 1894–1905) by a veteran archeologist but much criticized, especially its chronology.

Scharff, A., *Grundzüge der ägyptischen Vorgeschichte* (1928).

Sethe, K., *Urgeschichte und älteste Religion der Aegypter* (1930).

Steindorff, G., and Seele, Keith C., *When Egypt Ruled the East* (1942).

Winlock, H. E., *The Rise and Fall of the Middle Kingdom in Thebes* (1947).

Breasted, J. H., *Development of Religion and Thought in Ancient Egypt* (1912). *The Dawn of Conscience* (1933).

Capart, J. *Egyptian Art* (Eng. tr., 1923).

Ermann, A., *Life in Ancient Egypt* (1887; 2nd ed., 1925; Eng. tr., 1894). *Literature of the Ancient Egyptians* (1923; Eng. tr., 1927). *Die Religion der Aegypter* (1930).

Frankfort, H., *Ancient Egyptian Religion* (1948).

Glanville, S. R. K., *Daily Life in Ancient Egypt* (1930). Ed., *The Legacy of Egypt* (1942).

Kees, H., *Kulturgeschichte des Alten Orients*: *Aegypten* (1933).

Murray, Margaret, *Egyptian Sculpture* (1930).

Peet, T. E., *A Comparative Study of the Literature of Egypt, Palestine, and Babylonia* (1931).

Shorter, A. W., *An Introduction to the Egyptian Religion* (1931).

Smith, E. B., *Egyptian Architecture as Cultural Expression* (1938).

Smith, W. S., *A History of Egyptian Sculpture and Painting in the Old Kingdom* (1946). *The Art of Ancient Egypt* (1936).

Hittites and Syrians

The Amarna Letters have been edited, with German translations and excellent notes, by J. A. Knudtzon (2 vols., 1915), and with English translations and brief notes, by S. A. B. Mercer (2 vols., 1939).

Contenau, G., *La civilisation des Hittites et des Mitanniens* (1934). *La civilisation phénicienne* (1926).

Cowley, A. E., *The Hittites* (1926).

Garstang, John, *The Hittite Empire* (1929).

Götze, A., *Kulturgeschichte des Alten Orients*: *Kleinasien* (1933). *Hethiter, Churriter, und Assyrer* (1936).

Hrozny, Fr., art. "Hittites," in *Encyclopædia Britannica* (14th ed., 1929).

Macalister, R. A. S., *The Philistines* (1914).

Olmstead, A. T., *History of Palestine and Syria* (1931).

Schaeffer, C. F. A., *The Cuneiform Texts of Ras Shamra-Ugarit* (1939). *Ugaritica* (1939) in French.

Assyrians

See many of the works listed above under SUMER AND AKKAD, especially those of Jastrow, King, Meissner, and Rogers.

Luckenbill, D. D., *Ancient Records of Assyria and Babylonia* (2 vols., 1926–27), a companion volume to Breasted's collection of sources.

Olmstead, A. T., *Assyrian Historiography* (1916). *History of Assyria* (1923).

Persians

Cameron, George, *History of Early Iran* (1936).

Christensen, A., *Die Iranier* (1933).

Herzfeld, E., *Archeological History of Iran* (1935).

Huart, C., *Ancient Persia and Iranian Civilization* (1925; Eng. tr., 1927).

Olmstead, A. T., *History of the Persian Empire [Achaemenid Period]* (1948).

Rogers, R. W., *A History of Ancient Persia* (1929).

Rostovtzeff, M., *Iranians and Greeks in South Russia* (1922).

Benveniste, E., *The Persian Religion According to the Chief Greek Texts* (1929).

Jackson, A. V. W., *Zoroaster, the Prophet of Ancient Iran* (1898). *Zoroastrian Studies* (1928).

Meillet, A., *Trois conférences sur les Gâthâs de l'Avesta* (1925).

Moulton, J. H., *Early Zoroastrianism* (1913).

Nyberg, H. S., *Die Religionen des alten Iran* (1938).

Söderblom, N., *La vie future d'après le Mazdéisme* (1901).

The sacred books of Zoroastrianism are published, in English translation with introduction and notes, in seven volumes of the great collection known as *The Sacred Books of the East* (50 vols., 1879–1910).

Hebrews

Albright, W. F., *Archaeology and the Religion of Israel* (1942). *The Archaeology of Palestine and the Bible* (1933). *From the Stone Age to Christianity* (1940). *The Archaeology of Palestine* (1949).

Barton, G. A., *Archaeology and the Bible* (1915; 7th ed., 1937).

Bertholet, A., *A History of Hebrew Civilization* (1919; Eng. tr., 1926).

Bevan, E. R., and Singer, Chas., eds., *The Legacy of Israel* (1927).

Dussaud, R., *Les découvertes de Ras Shamra et l'Ancien Testament* (1937).

Kent, C. F., *A History of the Hebrew People* (2 vols., 1922–23).

Kittel, R., *Geschichte des Volkes Israel* (3 vols., new ed., 1922–29).

Lods, A., *Israel* (1930; Eng. tr., 1932). *The Prophets and the Rise of Judaism* (1935; Eng. tr., 1937).

McCown, C. C., *The Ladder of Progress in Palestine* (1943).

Meek, T. J., *Hebrew Origins* (1936).

Oesterley, W. O. E., and Robinson, T. H., *A History of Israel* (2 vols., 1932). *Hebrew Religion* (1930).

Olmstead, A. T., *History of Syria and Palestine* (1931).

Smith, G. A., *Historical Geography of the Holy Land* (1894, 25th ed., 1932). *Jerusalem* (2 vols., 1908). *The Prophets and Their Times* (1925).

Cook, S. A., *The Religion of Ancient Palestine in the Light of Archaeology* (1930).

Frazer, J. G., *Folklore in the Old Testament* (3 vols., 1918; 1-vol. ed., 1923).

Graham, W. C., *The Prophets and Israel's Culture* (1934).

Graham, W. C., and May, H. G., *Culture and Conscience* (1936).

Smith, J. M. Powis, *The Origin and History of Hebrew Law* (1931).

Smith, W. Robertson, *The Old Testament in the Jewish Church* (1881). *The Prophets of Israel* (1882). *The Religion of the Semites* (1889; 3rd ed., by S. A. Cook, 1927), see note, p. 243.

Bewer, J. A., *The Literature of the Old Testament in its Historical Development* (1922; rev. ed., 1933).

Chase, Mary Ellen, *The Bible and the Common Reader* (1944).

Moore, G. F., *The Literature of the Old Testament* (1911).

Peake, A. S., ed., *The People and the Book* (1925).

Pfeiffer, R. H., *Introduction to the Old Testament* (1941).

Willoughby, R. R., ed., *The Study of the Bible Today and Tomorrow* (1947).

Modern translations of the Old Testament: American Revised (1901), Moffatt (1924), An American Translation (1927). Useful one-volume commentaries on the Bible have been edited by A. S. Peake (1920) and Charles Gore (1929). The series entitled *International Critical Commentary* has full and scholarly commentaries on almost every book of the Bible: unfortunately, most of these volumes were written before the great archeological discoveries of the last twenty-five years. James Hastings, ed., *A Dictionary of the Bible* (5 vols., 1898–1904) is still the best.

General Histories of Greece

Botsford, G. W., and Sihler, E. G., *Hellenic Civilization* (1915), a valuable collection of source materials in English translation.

Cary, Max, *The Documentary Sources of Greek History* (1927).

Whibley, L., ed., *Companion to Classical Studies* (1905; 4th ed., 1931), essays on sciences auxiliary to the study of Greek history; a valuable work of reference.

Beloch, K. J., *Griechische Geschichte* (4 vols., 2nd ed., 1914–27), see note, p. 471.

Botsford, G. W., and Robinson, C. A., *Hellenic History* (1922; new ed. by Robinson, 1939; 3rd ed., 1948).

Bury, J. B., *History of Greece to the Death of Alexander* (1900; new ed., 1920), perhaps the best single-volume history.

Cary, Max, *The Geographic Background of Greek and Roman History* (1949).

Cavaignac, E., *Histoire de l'antiquité* (3 vols., 1913–19).

Cohen, Robert, *La Grèce et l'Hellénisation du monde antique* (1934; 2nd ed. 1939), full bibliographies.

Couch, H. N., *Classical Civilization: Greece* (1940).

Ferguson, W. S., *Greek Imperialism* (1913).

Glotz, G., *Histoire grecque* (4 vols., 1925–38).

Grote, George, *History of Greece* (12 vols., 1845–56 and reprints) see note, p. 427.

Jardé, A., *The Formation of the Greek People* (1924; Eng. tr., 1926).

Laistner, M. L. W., *Greek History* (1932).

Meyer, Eduard, *Geschichte des Altertums* (Vols. III–V, 1891–1902; new ed., 1925–39), see note, p. 473.

Tozer, H. F., *A History of Ancient Geography* (1897; new ed., 1935).

Wilcken, U., *Griechische Geschichte im Rahmen der Altertumsgeschichte* 1924; 3rd ed., 1931).

Appreciations of the Greek Genius

Agard, W. R., *What Democracy Meant to the Greeks* (1942).

Butcher, S. H., *Harvard Lectures on the Originality of Greece* (1904).

Cooper, Lane, *The Greek Genius and its Influence* (1917).

Dickinson, G. L., *The Greek View of Life* (1898).

Earp, F. R., *The Way of the Greeks* (1929).

Glover, T. R., *Democracy in the Ancient World* (1927).

Greene, W. C., *The Achievement of Greece* (1923).

Livingstone, R. W., *The Greek Genius and Its Meaning to Us* (1912).
  The Mission of Greece (1923). Ed., *The Legacy of Greece* (1922).
Stobart, J. C., *The Glory that was Greece* (1911).

Constitutions, Law, and Political Thought

Most of the general histories listed above discuss constitutional matters at
considerable length.

Barker, E., *Greek Political Theory: Plato and his Predecessors* (1918).
  Political Thought of Plato and Aristotle (1906).
Bonner, R. J., *Aspects of Athenian Democracy* (1934). *Lawyers and Liti-
  gants in Ancient Athens* (1929).
Bonner, R. J., and Smith, G., *The Administration of Justice from Homer to
  Aristotle* (2 vols., 1930–38).
Busolt, G., *Griechische Staatskunde* (2 vols., 3rd ed., 1920–26).
Calhoun, G. M., *Athenian Clubs in Politics and Litigation* (1913). *The
  Growth of Criminal Law in Ancient Greece* (1927).
Fowler, W. W., *The City State of the Greeks and Romans* (1893).
Glotz, G., *The Greek City and its Institutions* (1928; Eng. tr., 1930).
Greenidge, A. H. J., *A Handbook of Greek Constitutional History* (1902).
Halliday, W. R., *The Growth of the City State* (1923).
Myres, J. L., *The Political Ideas of the Greeks* (1927).
Vinogradoff, P., *Outlines of Historical Jurisprudence* (Vol. II, 1922).
Wilamowitz-Moellendorff, U. von, *Aristoteles und Athen* (2 vols., 1893).
Zimmern, A., *The Greek Commonwealth* (5th ed., 1931).

Economic Life

Andreades, A. M., *A History of Greek Public Finance* (Eng. tr., 1933).
Calhoun, G. M., *Business Life of Ancient Athens* (1926).
Francotte, H., *Les finances des cités grecques* (1909).
Glotz, G., *Ancient Greece at Work* (1920; Eng. tr., 1926).
Gomme, A. W., *The Population of Athens in the Fifth and Fourth Cen-
  turies* (1933).
Hasebroek, J., *Trade and Politics in Ancient Greece* (1928; Eng. tr., 1933).
Laistner, M. L. W., *Greek Economics* (1923), a collection of texts from
  Greek writers dealing with economic fact and theory.
Meyer, Ed., "Die Sklaverei im Altertum" and "Die wirtschaftliche Ent-
  wickelung des Altertums," in *Kleine Schriften* (1910).
Michell, H., *The Economics of Ancient Greece* (1940).
Ormerod, H. A., *Piracy in the Ancient World* (1924).

Pöhlmann, R. von, *Geschichte der sozialen Frage und des Sozialismus in der antiken Welt* (2 vols., 1893; 3rd ed., 1925).

Toutain, A., *The Economic Life of the Ancient World* (1928; Eng. tr., 1930).

Religion

Adam, J., *The Religious Teachers of Greece* (1908).

Cook, A. B., *Zeus* (3 vols., 1914–40).

Cornford, F. M., *Greek Religious Thought from Homer to the Age of Alexander* (1923), a collection of texts.

Farnell, L. R., *Cults of the Greek States* (5 vols., 1896–1909). *Greek Hero Cults and Immortality* (1921).

Foucart, P., *Les mystères d'Eleusis* (1914).

Guthrie, W. K. C., *Orpheus and Greek Religion* (1935).

Harrison, J. E., *Prolegomena to the Study of the Greek Religion* (1903; 3rd ed., 1922).

Kern, Otto, *Die Religion der Griechen* (3 vols., 1926–38). *Orpheus* (1920).

Linforth, I. M., *The Arts of Orpheus* (1941).

Moore, C. H., *The Religious Thought of the Greeks from Homer to the Triumph of Christianity* (1916; 2nd ed., 1925).

Murray, G., *Five Stages of Greek Religion* (1912; 2nd ed., 1925).

Nilsson, M. P., *A History of Greek Religion* (1925). *Greek Piety* (Eng. tr., 1948).

Parke, H. W., *A History of the Delphic Oracle* (1939).

Persson, A. W., *The Religion of Greece in Prehistoric Times* (1942).

Rhode, E., *Psyche* (1894; Eng. tr., 1925).

Wilamowitz-Moellendorff, U. von, *Der Glaube der Hellenen* (2 vols., 1931–32).

Zielinski, F. F., *The Religion of Ancient Greece* (Eng. tr., 1926).

Literature

Most of the Greek classics are available in English translation in the Loeb Library, with Greek and English texts on opposite pages. The translations are not always the best available; for others see F. S. Smith, *The Classics in Translation* (1930). George Howe and G. A. Harrer, *Greek Literature in Translation* (1927; rev. ed., 1948) and R. W. Livingstone, *The Pageant of Greece* (1923) have long passages translated from every field of Greek literature by masters. See also W. H. Auden, *The Portable*

Greek Reader (1948). The series known as *Our Debt to Greece and Rome* has a small volume on each important Greek writer.

General Histories of Greek Literature

Capps, E., *From Homer to Theocritus* (1901).
Croiset, A. and M., *Histoire de la littérature grecque* (5 vols., 1887 ff.; 3rd ed., 1910–28). "The best history of any literature in any language."
Geffken, J., *Griechische Literaturgeschichte* (2 vols., 1926–34).
Harvey, P., ed., *Oxford Companion to Classical Literature* (1937).
Murray, G., *A History of Ancient Greek Literature* (1897).
Schmid, Wilhelm, and Stählin, Otto, *Geschichte der griechischen Literatur* (2 vols., 1929–34). Very full.
Symonds, J. A., *Studies of the Greek Poets* (2 vols., 1877; 3rd ed., 1921).
Wright, W. C., *A Short History of Greek Literature from Homer to Julian* (1907).

Homer

Allen, T. W., *Homer: the Origins and the Transmission* (1924).
Bassett, S. E., *The Poetry of Homer* (1938).
Murray, G., *The Rise of the Greek Epic* (1907; 3rd ed., 1924).
Nilsson, M. P., *Homer and Mycenae* (1933).
Schwartz, Ed., *Die Odysee* (1924).
Scott, J. A., *The Unity of Homer* (1921).
Wilamowitz-Moellendorff, U. von, *Die Ilias und Homer* (1916). *Die Heimkehr des Odysseus* (1927).

Lyric Poetry

The Oxford Book of Greek Verse in English Translation (1938).
Bowra, C. M., *Early Greek Elegists* (1938). *Greek Lyric Poetry from Alcman to Simonides* (1936).
Sachs, Curt, *The Rise of Music in the Ancient World* (1936).

Drama

The entire Greek drama, in English translation, is published in Oates, W. J. and Eugene O'Neill, Jr., *The Complete Greek Drama* (2 vols., 1938).
Cornford, F. M., *The Origin of Attic Comedy* (1914).
Flickinger, R. C., *The Greek Theater and its Drama* (1918).
Goodell, T. D., *Athenian Tragedy: a Study in Popular Art* (1920).
Haigh, A. E., *The Attic Theater* (3rd ed., 1907).
Little, A. M., *Myth and Society in Attic Drama* (1942).

Norwood, G., *Greek Comedy* (1931). *Greek Tragedy* (1920).

Pickard-Cambridge, A. W., *Dithyramb, Tragedy, and Comedy* (1927).

Croiset, M., *Eschyle* (1928).

Murray, G., *Aeschylus, the Creator of Tragedy* (1940).

Smyth, H. W., *Aeschylean Tragedy* (1924).

Bates, W. N., *Sophocles, Poet and Dramatist* (1940).

Webster, T. B. L., *An Introduction to Sophocles* (1936).

Appleton, R. B., *Euripides the Idealist* (1927).

Bates, W. N., *Euripides: a Student of Human Affairs* (1930).

Descharmes, P., *Euripides and the Spirit of his Dramas* (1893; Eng. tr., 1906).

Murray, G., *Euripides and His Age* (1913), see note, p. 472.

Verral, A. W., *Euripides the Rationalist* (1895).

Murray, G., *Aristophanes, a Study* (1933).

History

The works of the major Greek historians are printed, in English translation, in R. B. Godolphin, *The Greek Historians* (2 vols., 1942): Herodotus, Thucydides, the major and some of the minor works of Xenophon, Aristotle, *Constitution of Athens,* Arrian, *Anabasis of Alexander,* and the Behistun Inscription.

Bury, J. B., *The Ancient Greek Historians* (1909).

Jacoby, Felix, *The Local Historians of Attica* (1948).

Pearson, L., *Early Ionian Historians* (1939). *The Local Historians of Attica* (1942).

Thompson, J. W., *A History of Historical Writing* (Vol. I, 1942).

Glover, T. R., *Herodotus* (1924).

Jacoby, F., art. "Herodotos" in Pauly-Wissowa *Real-Encyclopädie,* Supplement Vol. II.

Wells, J., *Studies in Herodotus* (1923).

Abbott, G. F., *Thucydides, a Study in Historical Reality* (1925).

Cochrane, C. N., *Thucydides and the Science of History* (1929).

Finley, J. H., *Thucydides* (1942).

Forbes, W. H., *Thucydides Book I* (1895).

Grundy, G. B., *Thucydides and the History of His Age* (1911).

Lamb, W. R. M., *Clio Enthroned, a Study in Prose Form in Thucydides* (1914).

Meyer, Ed., *Thukydides und die Entstehung der wissenschaftlichen Geschichtsschreibung* (1913).

Schwartz, Ed., *Die Geschichtswerk des Thukydides* (1919).

Barber, G. L., *The Historian Ephorus* (1935).

Education, Philosophy, Science

Dobson, J., *Ancient Education* (1932).

Freeman, K. J., *The Schools of Hellas* (1907).

Girard, P., *L'éducation athénienne au Ve et au IVe siècle avant J.-C.* (1889).

Jaeger, W., *Paideia* (3 vols., Eng. tr., 1939–44).

Marrou, H. I., *Histoire de l'éducation dans l'antiquité* (1948).

Bakewell, C. M., *A Source Book in Ancient Philosophy* (1907).

Burnet, J., *Early Greek Philosophy* (1892; 4th ed., 1930).

Gomperz, Th., *Greek Thinkers* (Eng. tr. in 4 vols., 1901–12).

McClure, M. T., *The Early Philosophers of Greece* (1935).

Zeller, Ed., *Die Philosophie der Griechen* (6 vols., 6th ed., 1902; Eng. trs. of separate vols. under various titles), see note, p. 353.

Taylor, A. E., *Socrates* (1932).

Burnet, J., *Platonism* (1928).

Grube, G. M. A., *Plato's Thought* (1935).

Ritter, C., *Platon* (2 vols., 1910–23). *The Essence of Plato's Philosophy* (1931; Eng. tr., 1933).

Shorey, Paul, *Platonism, Ancient and Modern* (1938). *What Plato Said* (1933).

Taylor, A. E., *Plato, the Man and His Work* (1908; 3rd ed., 1929).

Wilamowitz-Moellendorff, U. von, *Platon* (2 vols., 1920), see note, p. 511.

Woodbridge, F. J. E., *The Son of Apollo* (1929).

Jaeger, W., *Aristotle: Foundations of the History of His Development* (1923; Eng. tr., 1934).

Muir, G. R. G., *Aristotle* (1932).

Ross, W. D., *Aristotle* (1924).

Stocks, J. L., *Aristotelianism* (1925).

Dudley, D. R., *A History of Cynicism* (1937).

Farrington, B., *Science and Politics in the Ancient World* (1939).

Robin, L., *Greek Thought and the Origins of the Scientific Spirit* (1926; Eng. tr., 1928).

Sarton, G., *Introduction to the History of Science* (Vol. I, 1927).

Sedgwick, W. T., and Tyler, H. W., *A Short History of Science* (1917).

Heath, T. C., *A History of Greek Mathematics* (Vol. I, 1921).

Singer, C. J., *Greek Biology and Medicine* (1922).

Art

Anderson, W. J., Spiers, R. P., and Dinsmoor W. B., *The Architecture of Ancient Greece* (1927).

Buschor, Ernst, *Greek Vase-Painting* (Eng. tr., 1921).

Carpenter, Rhys, *The Esthetic Basis of Greek Art* (1921).

Casson, Stanley, *The Technique of Early Greek Sculpture* (1933).

Fowler, H. N., and Wheeler, J. R., *A Handbook of Greek Archaeology* (1909).

Gardiner, E. N., *Olympia, Its History and Remains* (1925).

Gardner, E. A., *A Handbook of Greek Sculpture* (1924).

Hinks, R. P., *Greek and Roman Portrait-Sculpture* (1935).

Pfuhl, E., *Masterpieces of Greek Drawing and Painting* (1924; Eng. tr., 1926).

Robertson, D. S., *A Handbook of Greek and Roman Architecture* (1929).

Rodenwaldt, G., *Die Kunst der Antike* (*Hellas und Rom*) (1927), a lavishly illustrated volume of the Propyläen-Kunstgeschichte.

Seltmann, C. T., *Attic Vase-Painting* (1933). *Greek Coins* (1933).

Swindler, M. H., *Ancient Painting* (1929).

Military Science

H. Delbrück, *Geschichte der Kriegskunst* (Vol. I, 1908).

Kromayer, J., and Veith, G., *Antike Schlachtfelder* (4 vols., 1903–26). *Heerwesen und Kriegführung der Griechen und Römer* (1928).

Parke, H. W., *Greek Mercenary Soldiers from the Earliest Times to the Battle of Ipsus* (1933).

Spaulding, O. L., Nickerson, H., and Wright, J. W., *Warfare* (1925).

Spaulding, O. L., *Pen and Sword in Greece and Rome* (1937).

Köster, A., *Das antike Seewesen* (1923).

Private Life

Blümner, H., *The Home Life of the Ancient Greeks* (1887; Eng. tr., 1893).

Gardiner, E. N., *Athletics of the Ancient World* (1930).

Gulick, G. B., *The Life of the Ancient Greeks* (1902).

Mahaffy, J. P., *Social Life in Greece from Homer to Menander* (1874; 7th ed., 1907).

Tucker, T. G., *Life in Ancient Athens* (1906).

Works on Briefer Periods

Minoan and Mycenaean Greece

Evans, Sir Arthur, *The Palace of Minos* (4 vols. and index, 1921–36).

Glotz, G., *The Aegean Civilization* (1923; Eng. tr., 1927).

Hawes, C. H., and H. B., *Crete, the Forerunner of Greece* (1909).

Pendlebury, J. D. S., *The Archaeology of Crete* (1939).

Burn, A. R., *Minoans, Philistines, and Greeks* (1930).

Hall, H. R., *The Civilization of Greece in the Bronze Age* (1928).

Lang, Andrew, *Homer and His Age* (1906). *The World of Homer* (1910).

Leaf, Walter, *Homer and History* (1915). *Troy, a Study in Homeric Geography* (1912).

Nilsson, M. P., *Homer and Mycenae* (1933). *The Mycenaean Origin of Greek Mythology* (1932).

Schuchardt, C., *Schliemann's Excavations* (Eng. tr., 1891).

Diller, A., *Race Mixture Among the Greeks before Alexander* (1937).

Myres, J. L., *Who were the Greeks?* (1930).

Kretschmer, P., *Einleitung in die Geschichte der griechischen Sprache* (1896).

Meillet, A., *Aperçu d'une histoire de la langue grecque* (2nd ed., 1920).

The Greek Renaissance

Bérard, J., *La colonisation grecque de l'Italie méridionale et de la Sicile* (1941).

Bilabel, F., *Die Ionische Colonisation* (1920).

Burn, A. R., *The World of Hesiod* (1936).

Carpenter, Rhys, *The Greeks in Spain* (1925).

Dixon, P., *The Iberians of Spain and Their Relations with the Aegean World* (1940).

Dunabin, T. J., *The Western Greeks* (1948).

Freeman, K. J., *The Life and Work of Solon* (1926).

Gwynn, A., "The Character of Greek Colonization," *Journal of Hellenic Studies*, XXXVIII (1918), 88–123.

Hogarth, D. G., *Ionia and the East* (1909).

Linforth, I. M., *Solon the Athenian* (1919).

Minns, E. H., *Scythians and Greeks* (1913).

Olier, F., *Le mirage spartiate* (1933).

Ramsay, W. M., *Asianic Elements in Greek Civilization* (1927).

Randall-MacIver, D., *The Etruscans* (1927). *Greek Cities in Italy and Sicily* (1931). *Villanovans and Early Etruscans* (1924).

Rostovtzeff, M., *Iranians and Greeks in South Russia* (1922).

Seltman, C. T., *Athens, Its History and Coinage Before the Persian Wars* (1924).

Ure, P. N., *The Greek Renaissance* (1921). *The Origin of Tyranny* (1922).

Woodhouse, W. J., *Solon the Liberator* (1938).

The Age of the Persian Wars

The ancient authors dealing with this period include: Herodotus; Aristotle, *Constitution of Athens;* Plutarch, *Lives* (Themistocles, Aristides); Nepos, *Lives* (Themistocles, Miltiades, Aristides); Aeschylus, *Persae.*

Berve, H., *Miltiades, Studien zur Geschichte des Mannes und seiner Zeit* (1937).

Grundy, G. B., *The Great Persian War* (1901).

Hauvette, A., *Hérodote, historien des guerres médiques* (1894).

How, W. W., and Wells, J., *Commentary on Herodotus* (1912).

Macan, R. W., *Herodotus, Books IV–VI* (1895). *Herodotus, Books VII–IX* (1908).

Wells, J., *Studies in Herodotus* (1923).

See also a series of articles on Sparta and the Peloponnesian League by J. A. O. Larsen, *Classical Philology,* XXVII (1932), 136–50; XXVIII (1933), 257–76; XXIX (1934), 1–19; and C. A. Robinson, Jr., "Athenian Politics, 510–486," *American Journal of Philology,* LXVI (1945), 243–54, with the literature there cited.

The Athenian Empire

The ancient authors dealing with this period include: Thucydides; Xenophon, *Hellenica,* Bks. I–II; Diodorus, *History,* Bks. XI–XII; Aristotle, *Constitution of Athens;* Pseudo-Xenophon [Old Oligarch], *Athenian Policy;* Plutarch, *Lives* (Aristides, Cimon, Pericles, Nicias, Alcibiades, Lysander); Nepos, *Lives* (Pausanias, Cimon); Aristophanes, *Acharnians, Knights, Wasps, Peace, Lysistrata.* G. F. Hill, *Sources for Greek History between the Persian and Peloponnesian Wars* (1897; 2nd ed., 1907), prints the available sources in Greek or Latin.

Croiset, M., *Aristophanes and the Political Parties at Athens* (1906; Eng. tr., 1909).

Forbes, W. H., *Thucydides Book I* (1895).

Gomme, A. W., *A Historical Commentary on Thucydides* (Vol. I, 1945).

Grundy, G. B., *Thucydides and the History of His Age* (1911).

Hatzfeld, J., *Alcibiade* (1940).

Henderson, B. W., *The Great War Between Athens and Sparta* (1927).

Laistner, M. L. W., *A History of the Greek World from 479 to 323 B.C.* (1936).

Mackenzie, C., *Pericles* (1937).

Murray, G., *Aristophanes and the War Party* (1919).

Wade-Gery, H. T., "Thucydides the Son of Melesias," *Journal of Hellenic Studies,* LII (1932), 205–27.

Greece in the Fourth Century

The ancient authors dealing with this period include: Xenophon, *Anabasis, Hellenica, Agesilaus;* Diodorus, Bks. XV–XVI; Plutarch, *Lives* (Lysander, Agesilaus, Artaxerxes, Pelopidas, Dion, Timoleon, Demosthenes); Nepos, *Lives* (Thrasybulus, Agesilaus, Iphicrates, Epaminondas); the *Orations* of Lysias, Isocrates, Aeschines, and Demosthenes.

Adams, C. D., *Demosthenes and his Influence* (1927).

Casson, Stanley, *Macedonia, Thrace, and Illyria* (1926).

Cloché, P., *Démosthène et la fin de la démocratie athénienne* (1937). *La politique extérieure d'Athènes de 404 à 308 av. J.-C.* (1934).

Glover, T. R., *From Pericles to Philip* (3rd ed., 1919).

Jaeger, W., *Demosthenes: the Origin and Growth of His Policy* (1938).

Marshall, F. H., *The Second Athenian Confederacy* (1905).

Mathieu, G., *Les idées politiques d'Isocrate* (1925).

Pickard-Cambridge, A. W., *Demosthenes and the Last Days of Greek Freedom* (1914).

Schaefer, A., *Demosthenes und seine Zeit* (1856; 2nd ed., 1885).

Index

Abraham, 45, 68, 93, 134, 206, 223, 233
Abydos, 102, 119
Academy, Platonic, 498, 511
Acarnania, 413
Achaeans, 149, 259–262
Achaemenes, 188, 191
Acropolis, 298; at Athens, 312–313, 439–440
Adapa (Sumerian Adam), 85, 87
Adonis (Tammuz), 80, 170
Aegean Islands, 247, 251, 252, 260, 305, 350, 375, 394–396, 411, 423, 430, 517, 519, 541
Aegina, 304, 306, 372, 374, 381, 408, 410, 417, 476
Aegospotami, 426, 475, 516
Aeolis, Aeolians, 260, 263, 285
Aeschines, 539–541
Aeschylus, 445–449, 456–457
Aesop, 346
Agamemnon, 268, 271, 273
Agesilaus, 479, 493, 515, 517, 521
Agni, 194, 270
Agora, 298–299, 313, 438
Agriculture, discovery of, 31, 41–43, 59; Egyptian, 33; Sumerian, 63; becomes capitalistic, 63, 297, 431; Greek, 282–283; 297–298, 307, 430–431, 479, 481–482
Ahmose I, 141, 143
Akhnaton, 152–159; mummy of, 154; monotheism of, 156–157; taste in art, 157–158; failure of, 158–159
Akkad, 65, 69
Alcaeus, 344
Alcibiades, 421–422, 423–424, 425, 426, 463, 465, 471
Alcman, 345
Alcmeonidae, 308–309, 312, 313, 314; in Persian Wars, 370–372, 373, 378; Pericles and, 399–400, 407, 415, 431; family tree, 400; Alcibiades, 421
Aleppo, 137, 171
Alexander of Molossia, 527

Alexander the Great, 167, 193, 199, 442, 506, 540, 543
Allegory, and interpretation of myths, 337–338
Alphabet, Phoenician, 167–169; Greek, 294
Amarna (Akhetaton), 152, 154–155, 157, 159
Amarna tablets, 87, 147, 153, 156, 206–207
Amenemhet, 109
Amenhotep I, 142
Amenhotep III, 147, 149, 150, 151, 152, 155
Amenhotep IV, see Akhnaton
Amon, 142, 143, 144, 146, 153, 156, 337
Amorites, 149, 205
Amos, 196, 234, 343
Amphictyony, 350; Delphic, 535, 539, 540, 542
Amphipolis, 397, 412, 414, 419, 462, 534
Anahita, 199
Anaxagoras, 406, 466
Anaximander, 339
Anaximines, 340
Angels, 196
Antiphon, 424, 462
Antisthenes, 489
Anu, 77, 78
Anubis, 117
Apocrypha of the Old Testament, 218, 219 n.
Apollo, 327, 334; and purity, 328; at Delphi, 328
Arabia, 26, 29, 150
Arameans, 170–171, 174, 179, 185
Arcadian League, 520–521
Archidamus, 415, 416, 418
Archilochus, 343
Archon at Athens, 307, 311, 313, 360–361
Areopagus, 307, 309, 313, 393, 401
Arginusae, 426
Argos, Argolis, 260, 300, 304; defeated

by Sparta, 363, 384, 397; alliance with
Athens, 407, 410; alliance with Thebes,
516–517
Arion, 345, 350
Aristagoras, 367–368, 371–372
Aristides, 374, 381, 389, 393, 395
Aristippus of Cyrene, 488
Aristophanes, 406, 455–457
Aristotle, 506–511, 512; cited, 357, 361,
393, 424, 483
Art, Magdalenian, 21, Plate 1; Egyptian,
123–127, 157–158, Plates 5–9, 12;
Cretan, 255–256, Plates 17–18; Myce-
naean, 265, Plates 19–20; Greek, 347–
349, 439–441, Plates 21–32
Artaxerxes II, 515, 517
Artaxerxes III, 539
Artemisium, 386
Artifacts, 13, 28
Aryans, 48, 133, 137
Asceticism, 231, 335–336, 489
Asclepius, 467
Ashurbanipal, 174, 178
Asia Minor (Anatolia), 37, 69, 94, 132,
134–135, 176, 251, 292
Aspasia, 406, 426
Assembly, Athenian (*ekklesia*), 311, 359,
403, 484, 520; Spartan, 316
Assyria, Assyrians, 162–163, 171–183,
293; militarism, 179; government, 179–
182; culture, 182–183
Assyrian plain, 35
Astarte, Ashtaroth, *see* Ishtar
Astrology, 82
Astronomy, Sumerian, 81; Egyptian,
113–114; Babylonian, 185; Greek, 339,
466, 487
Athena, 272, 325
Athenian Confederacy, Second, 519, 530,
536, 542
Athens, 248, 300, 304; tyranny at, 305–
314; imperialism, 313–314, 407–413,
464–465, 517, 519–520; democracy,
357–361, 372, 381–382, 399–407, 477–
478, 484; in Persian Wars, 368, 369–
370, 372, 376–379, 388–390; revolution of 411, 424; in Peloponnesian
War, 415–427; in fourth century, 476–
478, 516–517
Athletics, in Crete, 255; in Greece, 351,
436
Aton, 118, 153–154, 155–156, 159
Attica, 248, 260, 263–264, 269, 305–307,
429
Attis, 140

Aulos, 342
Avesta, 188, 193

Baals, 170, 229–230, 232–233, 333
Babel, Tower of, 76, Plate 4
Babylon, 71, 77, 85, 137, 149, 151, 174,
178, 185–186
Babylonia, 27, 61, 65, 89
Bacchae, 333, 334, 452, Plate 23d
Badarians, 32, 120
Bankers at Athens, 433
Behdet, 98, 117
Behistun inscription, 95, 188, 192, Plate
16
Beloch, K. J., 471
Belshazzar, 185
Berosus, 86, 88
Bethel, 207, 234
Bible, 217–219
Boeotian League, 541
Book of the Dead, 123, 335
Bosporus, 37, 395, 412
Brasidas, 416, 420
Breasted, J. H., 128
Bronze age, 60, 165; in Crete, 253; in
Greece, 259
Bronze, discovery of, 60, 131–132
Bureaucracy at Athens, 486
Bury, J. B., 352
Buto, 99
Byzantium, 285, 364, 367, 392, 395, 412,
540

Calendar, Sumerian, 76; Egyptian, 113–
114; Greek, 310, 466
Callisthenes, 496
Cambyses, 192, 364
Canaan, 166, 206–207, 233
Canaanites, 207, 223, 229, 231, 232
Canon of the Old Testament, 217
Capitalism, primitive, 46, 62
Capitalists, priests as, in Babylonia, 63–
64; kings as, in Egypt, 97
Cappadocia, 135–136, 176
Carchemish, 146, 172, 183
Caria, 251
Carthage, 287, 292, 384, 390, 422, 522–
524
Carystus, 376, 395
Cattle, domesticated, 41
Chaeronea, 531, 540
Chalcedon, 285
Chalcidice, 285, 395, 397, 420, 519, 522,
538
Chalcis, 285, 290, 300, 386
Chaldean Empire, 183–186

Chaldeans, 174

Champollion, J. F., 128

Chersonesus, Thracian, 313, 373, 397, 411, 522, 538, 540, 541

Chios, 423

Chronicles, Books of, 229

Chronology, Egyptian, 31 n., 100 n.; Babylonian, 68 n.; Assyrian, 172 n.; Hebrew methods in, 224–226

Cilicia, 176, 261, 266, 293

Cimmerians, 175, 176, 178, 285, 293

Cimon, 393–396, 398–399, 402, 409, 410, 411, 438, 530

Cities, appearance of, 59, 96

Citium, 410

City-state, Babylonian, nature of, 64; Greek, see Polis

Class conflict, 61; in Greece, 482–485

Cleisthenes, 357, 371, 530; constitutional reforms of, 358–360, 393

Cleomenes, 361–364, 368, 369

Cleon, 407, 418, 420, 425, 455, 463, 465

Cleophon, 425, 427

Cleruchies, Athenian, 397, 411, 417, 418, 422, 429, 520, 522, 535

Cnidus, 516

Cnossus, 254–255, 259, 261

Coinage, invention of, 294–295; Lydian, 294; Greek, 295

Colonization, Greek, 283–285, 290–292, 313; Phoenician, 287–288

Comedy, rise of Greek, 454

Commerce, Sumerian, 64, 69; Egyptian, 97, 107, 110; Phoenician, 166–167, 283, 288; Aramean, 170–171; Assyrian, 181–182; Cretan, 255, 257; Greek, 266, 283, 290, 296, 432–433; Etruscan, 289

Communism, primitive, 45–46

Conon, 426, 516

Copper age, 60; in Greece, 251

Corcyra, 290, 413–414, 415, 419, 464

Corinth, 290, 300, 304–305, 363, 408, 409, 414, 429

Coronea, 410

Cosmopolitanism, 487, 490

Council at Athens (boule), 311, 359, 402

Creation stories, Sumerian, 84–87; Hebrew, 86–87, 223

Crete, 34, 38; relations with eastern empires, 62, 107, 110, 130, 148, 167; Minoan culture, 250–259

Crimea, 285, 314, 412–413

Critias, 471, 477, 488, 496

Criticism, Biblical, 219–221; higher, of Old Testament, 219–222, 241–244

Croesus, 192, 293, 364

Cro-Magnon men, 19–23

Ctesias, 494

"Culture," definition of, 15; Chellean, 17; Mousterian, 17; Magdalenian, 19–22, 28; Badarian, 32; Tasian, 32; Gerzean, 33; Semainean, 33; Amratian, 33–34; Halaf, 35; Ubaid, 35; Jemdet Nasr, 36; Uruk, 36; Danubian, 38–39; Hallstatt, 263; Villanovan, 263

Cumae, 290, 292

Cuneiform writing, 72–75; decipherment of, 94–95

Cyaxares, 190, 191

Cylon, 308

Cynicism, 489–490

Cyprus, 148, 167, 176, 261, 263, 410

Cyrene, 285, 328

Cyrus, 70, 186, 190, 191–192, 215, 239

Cyrus, "the Younger," 425, 476, 481, 514–515

Cyzicus, 285, 425, 518

Damascus, 149, 167, 171, 175, 210, 214

Dance, Greek, 345

Daniel, Book of, 186, 228

Darius, 192–193; Zoroastrianism of, 197; Scythian expedition, 365–367, 373; Marathon campaign, 375–376, 382

Datis, 375, 378

David, 209–210, 221, 231

Decarch, 476

Decelea, 423

Delian League, 395, 404; subjugated by Athens, 411, 412, 431

Delium, 420

Delos, 395

Delphi, 328

Delphic oracle, 314, 328–329, 369, 388, 415, 442, 461, 471; political importance of, 330

Demagogues, 406–407, 418, 421, 425, 484, 486

Demaratus, 362–364, 374

Deme, 358

Demeter, 79, 332–333

Democracy, at Athens, 537–561; of Themistocles, 393; of Pericles, 401–405; limitations of, 404–405

Democritus, 466–467

Demos, 299

Demosthenes, 536–541

Deuteronomy, Book of, 222, 223, 236

Dialects, Greek, 260–263, 264

Diogenes, 489
Dion of Syracuse, 499, 527
Dionysius I of Syracuse, 499, 517, 522–527, 531, 540
Dionysus, 333, 336, 440, 442–443, 454, 456
Dithyramb, 345, 443
Dodona, 328–329
Dogs, 31, 41
Dorians, 251, 262–264, 281, 290, 315
Draco, 309
Droysen, J. G., 543
Durkheim, Émile, 24, 244
Dynasties (Egyptian), 31 n.; First, 100; Third, 102; Sixth, 104; Twelfth, 109, 141; Eighteenth, 141–146; Twenty-sixth, 178

Ecbatana, 190
Eclipses, 82, 339
Education, Spartan, 316–317; Athenian, 434–438; Platonic, 502
Egypt, Lower, 26, 99; Upper, 26, 100; predynastic, 31–35; first union, 98–99; Old Kingdom, 100–107; Middle Kingdom, 107–110; Empire, 141–163; conquered by Assyrians, 177; conquered by Persians, 192; rebels, 409
Eïon, 395, 397
Ekklesia, see Assembly, Athenian
Elam, Elamites, 29, 35, 36, 70, 178, 187
Elea, 290, 468
Eleusis, 79, 270, 307, 331, 334, 477–478
Elijah, 232–233, 333
Elpinice, 412, 462, 465
Empedocles, 469
Enlil, 69, 77, 81, 86
Epaminondas, 520–521, 534
Ephesus, 518
Ephialtes, 398–399, 401, 407
Ephors, 316, 363, 369, 374
Ephorus, 496–497
Epidamnus, 414
Erechtheum, 439
Eretria, 285, 290, 300, 376
Erosion, 203, 249, 479
Esarhaddon, 174, 177, 180
Ethics, Egyptian, 121; Zoroastrian, 196; Hebrew, 234–235; Homeric, 321; Greek, 321–322, 437, 451–452, 488–489; Delphic, 329–330; Platonic, 500, 505; Aristotelian, 508
Etruscans, 289, 292, 525
Eubulus, 536, 538
Euclides of Megara, 488, 498
Eupatrids, 307

Euphrates River, 26–27, 61, 146
Euripides, 451–453, 456–457
Eurymedon, 396, 407
Ewald, H., 242
Exile, Jewish, 214–215, 222, 238–239
Eye, 154, 157, 160
Ezekiel, 204, 239
Ezra, 216, 222, 240

Fayum, 109
Fertile Crescent, 26, 37
Feudalism, Egyptian, 109; Hittite, 138; Mycenaean, 268–269, 272; early Greek, 281
Fire worship, 14, 194, 196, 270
Five Thousand (at Athens), 424
Flood, Babylonian, 88–89; Hebrew, 223
Folklore, 49
Four Hundred (at Athens), 424
Frazer, Sir James G., 24, 244, 461, 473
Fustel de Coulanges, N. D., 318

Gades 167, 287
Galilee, 167, 203, 212
Gathas, 193, 199
Gauls, 525
Gaza, 166, 175, 208
Gebal (Byblus), 79, 110, 149, 166, 169
Gela, 524
Gelon, 384, 390
Genesis, Book of, 84–85, 223
Genos, 267–268, 281, 303, 309, 310, 358–359, 434
Gibraltar, 287
Gilgamesh Epic, Sumerian, 87–89, 139
Glossolalia, 83, 329
Gods, primitive, 22, 51; Sumerian, 77; dying and rising, 79, 119, 140, 332; kings as gods, 97, 99, 105, 153, 159; Egyptian, 117; Hittite, 140; early Greek, 272; Olympian, 322; Twelve Gods, 326–327, 333
Greece, geography of, 247–249
"Greeks," origin of term, 352
Grote, George, 407, 427
Gutians, 70, 89, 187
Gyges, 178, 303

Habiru, 150, 205, 230
Halaf, 35, 134
Halicarnassus, 458, 518
Halys River, 136, 293
Hammurabi, 68 n., 71, 75 n., 84, 92, 110, 134, 137, 179; Code, 90–93, 223, Plate 4
Haran, 134, 185

Harmost, 476, 477, 520
Hatshepsut, 143–145, 153
Hatti, 136, 140
Hattushash, 137, 147
Heaven, 122
Hebrews, 94, 150, 163; invade Palestine, 206–208; monarchy, 208–210
Hebron, 203
Hecataeus, 346–347, 457
Heliaea, 311
Heliopolis, 99, 118, 125
Hell, 122
Hellanicus, 458, 497
"Hellenes," and "barbarians," 351; origin of term, 352
Hellenic League, 384, 407
Hellenica Oxyrhynchia, 492
Hellespont, 37, 130, 285, 313, 412, 426, 517, 518, 536
Helots, 315, 399
Heracles, 271, 337
Heraclitus, 340–341, 468
Herodotus, 103–104, 116, 191, 198, 250–251, 303, 361, 365, 383, 458–462
Hesiod, 282, 290, 303, 321, 343
Hezekiah, 177, 214
Hieraconpolis, 99, 109
Hieroglyphic writing, 110–112; decipherment of, 128
"Hill" (Athenian party), 312
Himera, 292, 390, 523
Hipparchus, 314
Hippeis, 307, 310
Hippias, 314, 357, 363, 365, 370, 375–376
Hippias of Elis, 470
Hippocrates, 468
Hippodamus of Miletus, 438, 470
Hiram of Tyre, 166, 170, 211, 212
Histiaeus, 367, 373
Historical writing, Sumerian, 89–90; Hittite, 139; Assyrian, 182; Hebrew, 223–229; Greek, 346–347, 457–465, 492–497
Hittites, 71, 132, 149, 161, 163, 172, 253; writing, 137; monarchy, 137–139; civilization, 139–140; rediscovery of, 163–164; decipherment of writing, 164
Homer, 273–277, 321, 350, 500; Homeric theology, 272, 322; *Iliad,* 273, 275; *Odyssey*, 273–274, 275; *Hymns*, 274; Homeric question, 274–276; value as history, 276–277
Homo sapiens, 12
Hoplites, 300, 302, 308
Horus, 99, 105, 117, 118, Plate 5

Hosea, 234
Hoshea, 175, 213
Hrozny, B., 95, 164
Hurrians, 134, 137, 187
Hyksos, 110, 134, 140–141, 142, 204
Hymns, Homeric, 274, 328, 332, 333
Hyperbolus, 407, 421

Iliad, 273, 275
Illyria, 263, 533–534
Imhotep, 102, 105
Immortality, belief in, primitive, 22, 50; Sumerian, 79, 80, 88; Egyptian, 119–123; Cretan, 256; Greek, 321, 332, 336
Incubation, 467
Industry, Greek, 296–298, 302, 312; at Athens, 431–432, 482
Interest, early forms of, 63
Ionia, 260, 264, 285, 290, 323, 338–340, 364–365, 366–367, 423, 429, 465, 468, 476, 518
Ionian revolt, 367–369
Iphicrates, 517
Ipuwer, 107–108
Iran, Iranians, 133, 186, 187
Iron age, 165
Irrigation works, 33–34, 43, 63, 97, 99, 106
Isagoras, 358, 369
Isaiah, 108, 227, 235–236; Second Isaiah, 227, 239, 240
Ishtar, 78–81, 87, 170, 236, 295
Isis, 79, 119
Isocrates, 491, 495, 529–533, 537, 539, 542
Israel, 175–176, 203, 212–213

Jacob, 77, 223
Jehovah, 230
    See also Yahweh
Jehu, 212–213
Jeremiah, 227, 237–238, 240
Jericho, 206
Jeroboam, 211–212, 231
Jerusalem, 177, 184, 210, 214
Jezebel, 212–213
Jonah, 228, 241
Joseph, 206
Joshua, 206; Book of, 207, 224
Josiah, 183, 214, 223, 236, 237
Jowett, B., 511
Judah, 203, 207, 213–216
Judges (Hebrew), 208–209; Book of, 207, 224
Jupiter, 51

Karnak, 109
Kassites, 71, 94, 133, 134, 147, 172, 174, 187
Khafre, 102 n., 103–104, 124–125
Khufu, 103–104, 124
Kings, as gods (Egypt), 97; as capitalists (Sumeria), 97; as priests (Crete), 256
King's Peace, 517–518, 528
Kish, 67–68, 70

Lacedaemonia, 315
Lachish, 177, 227
Lagash, 68
Land, ownership, 46, 63, 93, 97, 281–282, 310
Languages, 47; Mediterranean, 47; Semitic, 47; Asianic, 48, 67; Persian, 48, 133; Indo-European (Nordic), 48–49, 132; Greek, 49, 132, 260, 264; Latin, 49, 132, 287; Celtic, 132; Hittite, 132, 137; Aramaic, 171
Latin, 49, 132, 287
Laurium, Mount, 307, 312, 381–382, 432, 536
Law, Sumerian, 91–93; Hittite, 139; Hebrew, 223–224; Greek, 303
League of Corinth, 541–542
Lebanon Mountains, 165, 203
Lemnos, 517, 541
Leonidas, 382, 387
Lesbos, 263, 314, 418
Leuctra, 520
Libyans, 33, 142, 162, 286
Ligurians, 286
Literature, Sumerian, 83–90; Egyptian, 115–116; Hittite, 139; Hebrew, 216 ff.; Greek, 273–277, 343–347, 441–465, 487, 492–497
Liturgy, 403–404, 443
Lugal, 65
Lugal-zaggisi, 69, 135
Luxor, 109
Lyceum, Aristotle founds, 506
Lycurgus, 315
Lydia, 178, 191, 192, 293–294, 303
Lyre, 342
Lysander, 423, 425–426, 475, 478, 479, 516

Macedonia, 247, 395, 414, 533
Maenads, 333–334
Magi, 194, 198
Magic, primitive, 21; Babylonian, 83; Egyptian, 115
Malachi, 228, 241
Malaria, 249, 480

Man, first appearance of, 8–9; Neanderthal, 11, 18, 20, 204; Neanthropic, 13, 20
Manasseh, 214, 236
Manetho, 31 n.
Mantinea, 422, 519, 521
Marathon, battle of, 192, 378; legend of, 379
Mardonius, 369, 374, 383, 389
Marduk, 77, 85, 86
Massilia, 292
Mathematics, 75–76, 112–113, 341
Matriarchate, 46
Mausolus, 518, 522, 536
Mazda, 195, 196–198
Medes, 178, 187–191
Medicine, Egyptian, 114; Greek, 467–468
Megacles, 308
Megaliths, 131
Megalopolis, 520, 536
Megara, 285, 304, 308, 312, 407, 414–415, 420
Megaron, 265
Megiddo, 145, 214
Melos, 422, 465, 476
Memphis, 98, 100, 109, 141, 184
Menes, 31 n., 100
Merodach-Baladan, 174–175
Mersin, 31
Mesopotamia, 27
Messana, Straits of, 286, 290, 408, 524
Messenia, 315, 521
Methone, 535
Methuselah, 89
Metics, 299, 429, 528
Meton, 466
Metropolis, 283
Meyer, Eduard, 114 n., 464, 473
Midas, 176, 293
Miletus, 285, 293, 305, 323, 367–369, 423
Militarism, Babylonian, 69–70; Egyptian Empire, 142–146, 150, 154; Assyrian, 179–180; Spartan, 317
Miltiades, 367, 373–374, 375, 376, 378–379, 380, 393, 397, 399, 411, 462
Minoan civilization, 255–257
Minos, 253, 256, 259
Mitanni, 134, 147, 149, 151, 152, 187
Mithra, 199, 200
Money, invention of, 294–295; Greek, 295, 303, 315; Athenian, 433
Monolatry, 233
Monotheism, Akhnaton, 156–157; Zoroaster, 196; Hebrew, 235, 237, 239, 241

Morality, Egyptian, 121–123; Greek ideas on, 270
Moses, 70, 75 n., 91, 206, 230
Mother Earth, worship of, 51, 78, 80, 118, 140, 193, 199, 229, 251, 256, 270, 272
Motye, 524
Mummification, 120
Murray, Gilbert, 472
Music, 77, 116, 127; Greek, 342, 436
Mycale, battle of, 389, 391
Mycenae, 148, 149–150, 260–261, 263
Mycenaean civilization, 264–269; religion, 269
Myron, 441
Mythology, primitive, 51; Sumerian, 77–79, 84; Egyptian, 118; Persian, 194; Hebrew, 223; Minoan, 258; Mycenaean, 269–270; Homeric, 322, 326
Mytilene, 418–419

Nabonidus, 185
Nabopolassar, 175, 184
Naram-Sin, 70
Narmer, 100
Naucratis, 293
Naupactus, 408, 410, 540
Navy, Athenian, 382, 408, 416, 419, 431, 479, 517
Naxos, 313, 367, 396
Naxus, 290
Nebuchadrezzar, 184, 237
Necho, 183
Nehemiah, 215, 216, 240
Neolithic civilization, 13, 27, 35; in Palestine, 31, 204; in Egypt, 31–35, 96; in Mesopotamia, 35–37, 59; in Europe, 37–40; in Anatolia, 135; in Elam, 187; in Crete, 251; in Greece, 251
Neolithic Revolution, 25
Nicias, 420, 421, 422–423; Peace of, 420
Nile River, 26–27, 97, 113
Nineveh, 69, 178, 179
Nippur, 67
Nofretete, 154–155, 158, 159, Plate 9
Nomarchs, 106, 109
Nomes, in Egypt, 33–34, 98–99
Nomothetes, 486
Nordics, 39, 48–49, 51, 132, 260, 286; alleged superiority of, 55
Notium, 426
Nubia, Nubians, 107, 142, 162

Odysseus, 273–274
Odyssey, 273, 275, 283, 290
Oedipus, 269

Oenipides, 466
Oenophyta, 408, 409
Oikist, 284, 303
"Old Oligarch," 406
Old Testament, 217–219; Canon, 217; Apocrypha, 218, 219 n.
Oligarchy, 478, 484, 518–519
Olives, 33, 42, 264, 297, 431, 481
Olympian gods, 272, 322, 338, 450, 452, attacked, 447, 500
Olympic games, 304, 351, 528, 529
Olynthus, 535, 538
Ombos, 98, 99, 118
Oroetes, 364–365
Orpheus, 334
Orphism, 334–337, 485, 498
Osiris, 79, 118–119, 121–122, 126
Ostracism, 360

Paleolithic age, 13; culture, 17–23
Palestine, 31, 163, 202 ff., 293
Palmyra, 171
Pangaeus, Mount, 313, 314, 365
Panhellenism, 349–351, 370, 394, 399, 405, 411, 442, 447, 491–492, 527–532, 539
Papyrus, 96, 111
Parmenides, 468, 469, 488
Parsa, 188, 190
Parsumash, 188, 190
Parthenon, 325, 439
Patesi, 64, 69, 82, 92
Patriarchate, 45
Patriotism and religion, 51, 64, 77; in Greece, 323–326, 331
Pausanias (Spartan general), 392, 395, 398
Pausanias (Spartan king), 478
Peisistratus, 312–314, 325, 331, 335, 405, 412
Peloponnesian League, 363, 370, 382, 415, 416, 518
Peloponnesian War, 415–427, 450, 452–453, 455, 460, 479–481, 528, 533
Pentateuch, 218, 219 n., 221–222, 223
Periander of Corinth, 365
Pericles, 399–415, 406, 418, 421, 431, 459, 463, 465, 479; democratic reforms, 401–405; finance, 403–404, 411, 413; war policy, 407, 413–415; imperialism, 407–413, 464
Pericles, the younger, 418, 426
Perioikoi, 315–316
Persephone, 79, 332–333
Persia, early history, 49, 133, 186–191
Persian Empire, 191–193, 215–216; wars

with Greece, 364–369, 375–379, 382–
390, 396, 409; aid to Sparta, 423, 425–
426; in fourth century, 476, 479, 516,
518
Persian Gulf, 27
Phalerum, 307, 378, 382, 407
Pharaoh, 105
Pharnabazus, 426, 478, 514–515
Phaselis, 396
Pheidon of Argos, 295, 304
Phidias, 406, 440
Philip II of Macedon, 475, 495, 506, 531,
533–543
Philippi, 535
Philippopolis, 539
Philistines, 162–163, 166, 208
Philistus, 494–495, 499
Philosophy, early Greek, 337–342, 468–
471, 488–490; Platonic, 497–506; Aris-
totelian, 506–511
Phocis, 300, 535, 539
Phoenicia, 107, 163, 165, 287–288, 293,
301
Phrygians, 162–163, 176, 178, 292–293
Phrynicus, 373, 443, 446
Pindar, 442
Piracy, 261–262, 283, 297, 301, 431
Piraeus, 382, 393, 394, 431, 438, 477,
517, 536; walls to, 407, 426–427, 517
Pithecanthropus, 9
Plague, 177, 524; at Athens, 417–418,
480
"Plain" (Athenian party), 312
Plataea, 362, 376; battle of, 389; in Pelo-
ponnesian War, 415, 419, 420, 520
Plato, 497–506; cited, 78, 335, 337, 488,
507, 528
Plow, invented, 59
Plutarch, 393
Polemarch, 307
Polis, 298–301, 318 n.; decline of, 485–
486
Poseidonia, 290, 441
Potidaea, 414, 415, 418, 522, 535
Pottery, invented, 43; Greek, 296–297,
307
Priam, 273, 276
Priests, 46–47, 50; as capitalists in Baby-
lonia, 63–64, 77; intellectual leader-
ship, 65; as bureaucrats, 65, 97
Property, private, early, 34, 35, 43
"Prophesying," 83, 234, 329
Prophets, Hebrew, 232–241; Books of
the, 218, 219 n., 227–228
Propylaea, 439
Protagoras, 470, 501

Proverbs, Book of, 116, 210, 221, 228
Psalms, Book of, 84, 157, 209, 221, 228
Psammetichus, 178, 183, 293, 305
Ptahhotep, 106
Punt, 34, 107
Pydna, 534
Pylos, 266, 419, 420
Pyramid texts, 120–122
Pyramids, 103, 113, 120, 124–125
Pythagoras, 341–342, 468

Race, defined, 52; Mediterranean, 28, 31,
32, 35, 38, 52, 135, 151; Alpine, 29,
35, 52, 251, 259; Armenoid, 29, 37,
136, 205; Dinaric, 37; Nordic, 53; and
culture, 53–54; and language, 54
Rameses II, 161, 165, 206
Rameses III, 162, 208
Ras Shamra, *see* Ugarit
Rawlinson, Sir Henry, 94–95
Re, 117–123, 126, 153
Rehoboam, 212
Religion, paleolithic, 18, 22, 23; neolithic,
50–51; Sumerian, 76–83; Egyptian,
116–123; Persian, 193–201; Canaanite,
229; Hebrew, 229–241; Cretan, 256;
Mycenaean, 269–273; Greek, 323–337,
500
Rhea, 256, 270
Rhegium, 290, 524
Rhodes, 167, 263, 368
Rome, 289, 292, 525
Russia, 39, 133

"Sacred War," 535, 538
Sacrifice, 50, 63, 194, 229, 230, 271; hu-
man, 170, 236
Sahara, 28
Salamis, 308, 309, 312, 388–389
Samaria, Samaritans, 176, 212–213, 216
Samarra, 35
Samos, 412, 424–425, 465, 541
Samuel, Books of, 224
Sanskrit, 48–49, 133
Sappho, 344
Saqqara, 103, 120
Sardis, 192, 293, 364, 368
Sargon of Agade, 69–70, 135
Sargon II, of Assyria, 174, 176, 180
Saul, 209, 232
Schliemann, H., 250, 253, 277–279, 280
Sculpture, Egyptian, 126–127, Plates 5–9;
Greek, 349
Scyros, 395, 517, 541
Second Isaiah, 227, 239, 240
Segesta, 422, 522–523

Semites, 29, 33, 37, 51, 65, 67, 70, 134, 160, 204
Sennacherib, 174, 177, 180, 236
Sepeia, 363
Septuagint, Old Testament, 217–218
Sestus, 367, 373, 390, 391, 397, 522
Set, 99, 117, 118
Seti I, 161
Shamash, 51, 75 n., 80
"Shore" (Athenian party), 312
Shuppiluliumash, 160
Sicels, 286, 524
Sicilian expedition (Athenian), 422–423
Sicily, 167, 257, 286, 290, 305, 408
Sicyon, 304–305, 408
Sidon, 166, 176, 177
Sigeum, 313
Sin, 51, 80, 185
Sinai, Mount, 51, 75 n., 91, 223
Sinai peninsula, 102, 107, 206
Sinope, 285
Slavery, primitive, 45; oriental, 91–92; in Greece, 282, 296, 297, 298, 299, 310, 430, 432, 483
Smith, W. Robertson, 243–244
"Social War," 522, 531, 536
Socrates, 456, 470–471, 488, 500
Solomon, 166, 210–211, 221
Solon, 309–311, 339, 344, 424, 430
Sophists, 437, 470, 485, 500
Sophocles, 449–451
Spain, 19, 21, 131, 167, 257, 288, 289, 292, 347
Sparta, 300, 314–318, 357–358, 361–364, 368, 374, 376, 382, 385–388, 389, 391, 397–399, 406
Spartanism, 491
Sphinx, 125
Star worship, 51, 80, 236
Stonehenge, 131
Strategos, 361, 395, 401, 418, 421, 425, 462
Sumer, Sumerians, 37, 65, 67; civilization, 71–93; legacy of, 93–94
Susa, 187
Swiss lake villages, 39, 287
Sybaris, 409, 411
Syracuse, 290, 408, 423, 480, 522–527
Syria, 27, 67, 69, 71, 107, 110, 134, 137, 145–146, 148–150, 172, 204, 293
Syro-Hittite Empire, 163, 205

Tammuz, 79, 88, 119
Tanagra, 408
Tarentum, 525, 527
Tarsus (Tarshish), 167, 211, 293

Tell, 43
Temples, 63–64; Egyptian, 125–126; Hittite, 140; no Persian, 194; at Jerusalem, 210, 215, 225, 236
Textiles, invented, 44
Thales, 339
Thasos, 397, 399
Theater, 440, 443
Thebes, Egyptian, 109, 141, 146, 159; Greek, 248, 269, 300, 362, 408, 415, 420, 519, 534, 540
Themistocles, 372–373, 375, 380–382, 384, 388, 392, 393, 398, 431
Theocracy, Sumerian, 62, 64–65, 91, 94, 97
Theology, primitive, 51; Sumerian, 77; Egyptian, 117–119; Akhnaton, 156–157; Zoroastrian, 196–197; Orphic, 335–337
Theopompus, 496, 533
Theoric fund, 402, 484, 536
Theramenes, 424, 426–427
Thermopylae, 248, 385–388, 536, 540
Theseus, 258, 269, 325, 395
Thespis, 345, 443
Thessaly, 247, 251, 260, 261, 314, 383, 385, 389, 407, 429, 535
Thetes, 282, 307–308, 311, 401, 424, 483
Thirty, the, at Athens, 477, 484, 491
Thirty Years Peace, 410, 415
Thrasybulus, 477, 516
Thucydides (historian), 462–465, 492; cited, 250–251, 256–257, 398, 405, 408, 413, 415, 419, 422, 424, 528
Thucydides, son of Melesias, 405–406, 411–412, 462
Thurii, 409, 411, 413, 459, 525
Thutmose I, 142
Thutmose III, 143, 144, 145–146, 153
Tiglath-Pileser I, 172
Tiglath-Pileser III, 174, 175
Tigris River, 26–27, 35, 61
Timoleon, 527
Tiryns, 261, 265, 267
Tissaphernes, 423, 425, 514–515
Tiy, Queen, 151, 153, 154, 159
Torah, 218, 219 n., 240
Trade, 21, 34, 59
Tragedy, rise of Greek, 442–445
Trireme, 301
Trittys, 359
Trojan War, 262, 268, 275
Troy, 37, 130, 135, 252–253, 262, 279
Tutankhamen, 158, 159–160
Tyranny, Greek, 301 ff.; supports people

against aristocracy, 302, 305; at Athens, 305–314; in Sicily, 523
Tyre, 166, 176, 184, 287

Ubaid, 35
Ugarit (Ras Shamra), 147, 148, 149,
156, 170, 229–230, 261
Umma, 69
Ur, first dynasty, 67–69; royal tombs, 68;
third dynasty, 71, 89, 90, 131, 135,
139, 229
Urartu, 172, 175
Uruk, 36, 67, 69, 70
Ussher, J., chronology of, 226 n.
Ut-naphishtim (Sumerian Noah), 88

Vedas, 133
Villages, neolithic, 43
Vine, 42, 210, 264, 297, 431, 479
Vulgate Bible, 218

Walls, Long, of Athens, 407, 413, 427
Weights and measures, 76, 294, 304, 310
Wellhausen, J., 222, 242–243
Wheat, domesticated, 42
Wilamowitz-Moellendorff, U. von, 511–
512

Winckelmann, J. J., 354
Wolf, F. A., 279–280
Women, Greek attitude to, 435
Writing, early, 34, 36; cuneiform, 72–75,
94; Egyptian, 110–113; Phoenician,
169; Cretan, 256; Greek, 266–267, 294

Xanthippus, 380, 381, 389, 399
Xenophanes of Colophon, 337, 345, 468
Xenophon, 406, 426, 493–494, 514, 515,
519, 530
Xerxes, 382–389, 396, 410

Yahweh, 221, 226, 230–241

Zagros Mountains, 26, 186
Zechariah, 215
Zeller, Eduard, 353
Zeno, 468, 488
Zerubbabel, 215
Zeugitae, 307, 310, 401, 483
Zeus, 51, 256, 258, 272, 326–327, 328,
337, 338
Zeuxis, 441
Ziggurat, 74, 76
Zoroaster, 193, 195
Zoser, 102, 120